Welcome to
Research Methods:
A Tool for Life
with *Research Navigator*™

This text is designed to integrate the content of the book with the following resources of Research Navigator™, a collection of research databases, instruction, and contemporary publications available to you online.

To gain access to Research Navigator, go to **www.researchnavigator.com** and login using the passcode you'll find on the inside front cover of your text.

Research Navigator™ includes three databases of dependable source material to get your research process started:

EBSCO's ContentSelect Academic Journal Database. EBSCO's ContentSelect Academic Journal Database contains scholarly, peer-reviewed journals. These published articles provide you with a specialized knowledge and information about your research topic. Academic journal articles adhere to strict scientific guidelines for methodology and theoretical grounding. The information obtained in these individual articles is more scientific than information you would find in a popular magazine, newspaper article, or on a Web page.

The New York Times *Search by Subject Archive*. Newspapers are considered periodicals because they are issued in regular installments (e.g., daily, weekly, or monthly), and provide contemporary information. Information in periodicals—journals, magazines, and newspapers—may be useful, or even critical, for finding up-to-date material or information to support specific aspects of your topic. Research Navigator™ gives you access to a one-year, "search by subject" archive of articles from one of the world's leading newspapers—*The New York Times*.

"Best of the Web" Link Library. Link Library, the third database included on Research Navigator™, is a collection of Web links, organized by academic subject and key terms. Searching on your key terms will provide you a list of five to seven editorially reviewed Web sites that offer educationally relevant and reliable content. The web links in Link Library are monitored and updated each week, reducing your incidence of finding "dead" links.

In addition, Research Navigator™ includes extensive online content detailing the steps in the research process including:

- Starting the Research Process
- Finding and Evaluating Sources
- Citing Sources
- Internet Research
- Using Your Library
- Starting to Write

For more information on how to use Research Navigator go to
http://www.ablongman.com/aboutrn.com

RESEARCH METHODS

A Tool for Life

BERNARD C. BEINS

Ithaca College

Boston ■ New York ■ San Francisco
Mexico City ■ Montreal ■ Toronto ■ London ■ Madrid ■ Munich ■ Paris
Hong Kong ■ Singapore ■ Tokyo ■ Cape Town ■ Sydney

Series Editor: *Kelly May*
Series Editorial Assistant: *Marlana Voerster*
Senior Marketing Manager: *Taryn Wahlquist*
Senior Editorial-Production Administrator: *Beth Houston*
Editorial-Production Service: *Walsh & Associates, Inc.*
Composition and Prepress Buyer: *Linda Cox*
Manufacturing Buyer: *JoAnne Sweeney*
Cover Administrator: *Linda Knowles*
Electronic Composition: *Omegatype Typography, Inc.*

For related titles and support materials, visit our online catalog at www.ablongman.com.

Between the time Website information is gathered and then published, it is not unusual for some sites to have closed. Also, the transcription of URLs can result in typographical errors. The publisher would appreciate notification where these errors occur so that they may be corrected in subsequent editions.

Library of Congress Cataloging-in-Publication Data

Beins, Bernard.
    Research methods : a tool for life / Bernard C. Beins.
        p. cm.
    Includes bibliographical references and indexes.
    ISBN 0-205-32771-0
        1. Psychology—Research—Methodology. I. Title.

BF76.5.B439 2003
150'.7'2—dc22

                                        2003054454

Printed in the United States of America
10   9   8   7   6   5   4   3   07   06

For Linda, Agatha, and Simon, the center of my universe.

CONTENTS

CHAPTER ONE

Psychology, Science, and Life   1

    CHAPTER OVERVIEW   1

    KEY TERMS   1

    CHAPTER PREVIEW   2

    WHY ARE RESEARCH METHODS IMPORTANT TOOLS FOR LIFE?   2
        Creating Knowledge   3

    WHY WE DO RESEARCH   4
        Description   4
        Explanation   4
        Prediction   5
        Control   6

    WHAT CONSTITUTES SCIENTIFIC KNOWLEDGE?   8
        Science Is Objective   8
        Science Is Data Driven   9
        Science Is Replicable and Verifiable   9
        Science Is Public   11

    DIFFERENT WAYS OF KNOWING   11
        The Obvious, or Intuition   12
        Authority   12
        Logic, or the A Priori Method   13
        Experience   14
        The Scientific Method   14

    THE INTERACTION OF SCIENCE AND CULTURE   16
        The Government's Role in Science   16
        Cultural Values and Science   17
        Cross-Cultural Issues and Science   18

    SCIENCE AND THE POPULAR MEDIA   18
        Psychological Terminology in Everyday Use   20
        Misinterpretations of Research in the Media   20
        Erroneous Beliefs   20
        Scientific "Breakthroughs"   22

    SCIENCE AND PSEUDOSCIENCE   22

    CHAPTER SUMMARY   25

CHAPTER TWO

Ethics in Research: Following the Golden Rule   27

CHAPTER OVERVIEW   27

KEY TERMS   27

CHAPTER PREVIEW   28

UNETHICAL RESEARCH PRACTICES—PAST AND PRESENT   29
Ethical Problems in the Early Years of the Twentieth Century   29
Is It Still Happening Today?   30

ETHICAL GUIDELINES CREATED BY THE AMERICAN
PSYCHOLOGICAL ASSOCIATION   32
Aspirational Goals and Enforceable Rules   32
Ethical Standards as They Affect You   33

LEGAL REQUIREMENTS AND ETHICS IN RESEARCH   37
Institutional Review Boards   37

THE IMPORTANCE OF SOCIAL CONTEXT IN DECIDING
ON ETHICS IN RESEARCH   40
Stanley Milgram's Research Project on Obedience   40
The Ethical Issues   40
The Social Context   42

WHAT YOU NEED TO DO IF YOUR RESEARCH INVOLVES DECEPTION   44
Some Research Requires Deception   44
The Effects of Debriefing on Research   46

ETHICS AND WEB-BASED RESEARCH   47

ETHICS AND RESEARCH WITH ANIMALS   48
Arguments and Counterarguments   49

CHAPTER SUMMARY   50

CHAPTER THREE

Planning Research: Generating a Question   51

CHAPTER OVERVIEW   51

KEY TERMS   51

CHAPTER PREVIEW   52

HOW DO RESEARCH IDEAS DEVELOP?   52
Informal and Formal Sources of Ideas   54
The Effect of Theory   56

HOW CAN YOU DEVELOP RESEARCH IDEAS?   58
Generating Research Hypotheses   59

THE VIRTUAL LABORATORY: RESEARCH ON THE INTERNET   62
Advantages to Web-Based Research   63
Potential Problems with Web-Based Research   64

The Future of the Web in Psychology   65

CHECKING ON RESEARCH: THE ROLE OF REPLICATION   66

DON'T REINVENT THE WHEEL: REVIEWING THE LITERATURE   69
What Is a Literature Review?   69
The Effect of Peer Review on the Research Literature   70

HOW TO CONDUCT A LITERATURE REVIEW   71
Electronic Databases   71
Starting Your Search   71

HOW TO READ A JOURNAL ARTICLE   75
Understanding the Format of a Research Paper   75

CHAPTER SUMMARY   79

CHAPTER FOUR

Practical Issues in Planning Your Research   81

CHAPTER OVERVIEW   81

KEY TERMS   81

CHAPTER PREVIEW   82

PRACTICAL QUESTIONS IN PLANNING RESEARCH   82

UNDERSTANDING YOUR IDEAS: CREATING VARIABLES   83
Carrying Out a Literature Search   84
Defining Your Concepts and Variables   84

CONDUCTING YOUR STUDY   89
Determining the Research Setting   90
Choosing Your Methodology   91
Selecting Research Materials and Procedures   93

CHOOSING THE PEOPLE YOU STUDY   97
The Nature of Your Participants   97
Deciding How Many Participants to Include   99

PROBABILITY SAMPLING   100
Simple Random Sampling   101
Systematic Sampling   101
Stratified Random Sampling   102
Cluster Sampling   102

NONPROBABILITY SAMPLING   103
Convenience Sampling   104
Quota Sampling   104
Purposive (Judgmental) Sampling   105
Chain-Referral Sampling   105

MAKING USEFUL MEASUREMENTS   106
Reliability and Validity   106
The SAT: Questions of Reliability and Validity   107

DIFFERING APPROACHES IN DIFFERENT AREAS OF PSYCHOLOGY   109
   Different Approaches in Different Journals   109
   Different Types of Participants in Different Journals   110
   Making Choices in Your Research Design   110
CHAPTER SUMMARY   111

CHAPTER FIVE

Conducting an Experiment: General Principles   113

CHAPTER OVERVIEW   113

KEY TERMS   113

CHAPTER PREVIEW   114

CHOOSING A METHODOLOGY: THE PRACTICALITIES OF RESEARCH   114

DETERMINING THE CAUSES OF BEHAVIOR   115
   Trying to Determine Causation in Research   116
   Requirements for Cause–Effect Relationships   116

THE LOGIC OF EXPERIMENTAL MANIPULATION   117

ETHICS IN EXPERIMENTAL, CLINICAL RESEARCH   118

EXPERIMENTAL CONTROL   119
   Lack of Control in Experimental Research:
   Extraneous Variables and Confounds   120

EXPERIMENTER EFFECTS   124

PARTICIPANT EFFECTS   124
   The Hawthorne Effect   125

**INTERACTION EFFECTS BETWEEN EXPERIMENTERS
AND PARTICIPANTS**   127

CONSIDERING VALIDITY IN CREATING EXPERIMENTS   128
   Construct Validity   128
   Convergent and Divergent Validity   131
   Internal and External Validity   132
   Statistical Conclusion Validity   136

CHAPTER SUMMARY   137

CHAPTER SIX

The Design of Simple and Complex Experiments   139

CHAPTER OVERVIEW   139

KEY TERMS   139

CHAPTER PREVIEW   140

PSYCHOLOGICAL CONCEPTS   140
    Measuring Complex Concepts   140
    Operational Definitions   141

INDEPENDENT AND DEPENDENT VARIABLES   143

TYPES OF INDEPENDENT AND DEPENDENT VARIABLES   147
    Qualitative and Quantitative Independent Variables   147
    Independent Variables Created by Different Types of Manipulations   150
    Types of Dependent Variables   151

DEFINING AND MEASURING VARIABLES   152

SINGLE AND MULTIPLE INDEPENDENT VARIABLES   153

MAIN EFFECTS   156

INTERACTIONS BETWEEN VARIABLES   157
    What Do Interactions Mean?   159
    Examining Main Effects and Interactions   159
    Patterns of Interactions   162

IDENTIFYING RESEARCH DESIGNS   166

DATA ANALYSIS   168
    Experiments with One Independent Variable   168
    Factorial Designs   169

CHAPTER SUMMARY   170

CHAPTER SEVEN

Expanding on Experimental Designs: Repeated Measures and Quasi-Experiments   171

CHAPTER OVERVIEW   171

KEY TERMS   171

CHAPTER PREVIEW   172

REPEATED MEASURES DESIGNS   173

ADVANTAGES OF REPEATED MEASURES DESIGNS   173
    Increasing Efficiency in Data Collection   173
    Increasing Validity of Data   174
    Finding Enough Participants   177
    Reducing Error in Measurement   177

LIMITATIONS TO REPEATED MEASURES DESIGNS   179
    Possible, but Unlikely, Repeated Measures Designs   179
    Subject (Participant) Variables   180
    Sequence and Order Effects   180

DATA ANALYSIS WITH REPEATED MEASURES DESIGNS   182

QUASI-EXPERIMENTAL DESIGNS   182
    Causation and Quasi-Experimental Designs   183

Combining Experimental and Quasi-Experimental Designs   184
Threats to Internal Validity   184

TYPES OF QUASI-EXPERIMENTAL DESIGNS   189
One-Group Pretest–Postest Designs   189
Static-Group Comparison Designs   190
Nonequivalent Control Group Designs   191
Interrupted Time Series Designs   193
Replicated Interrupted Time Series Designs   194

CHAPTER SUMMARY   198

CHAPTER EIGHT
Principles of Survey Research   199

CHAPTER OUTLINE   199

KEY TERMS   199

CHAPTER PREVIEW   200

SURVEYS: ANSWERING DIVERSE QUESTIONS   200
Surveys versus Junk Mail   201
Census versus Sample   201
Accuracy of Survey Results   202

ETHICS IN SURVEY RESEARCH   204

SELECTING YOUR METHODOLOGY   205

THE SURVEY INSTRUMENT   206
Question Types   206
Question Content   209

RESPONSE BIAS   214
Studying Sensitive Issues   214
Social Desirability   215
Acquiescence   217
Satisficing versus Optimizing   217
Minimizing the Occurrence of Satisficing   218

SPECIAL CONSIDERATIONS FOR INTERNET RESEARCH   219
Internet Surveys   220
Designing Surveys for the World Wide Web   223
Respondent Motivation   223
Technical Characteristics of a User's System   224
User Knowledge   225

SAMPLING ISSUES   225
Finding Hidden Populations   226

CHAPTER SUMMARY   228

CHAPTER NINE
Correlational Research   229

CHAPTER OUTLINE   229

KEY TERMS   229

CHAPTER PREVIEW   230

CORRELATIONAL STUDIES   230
Finding Relationships   230
Making Predictions   231

USING THE CORRELATIONAL APPROACH   233
Correlational Studies   233
Correlational Analysis   235
Positive and Negative Correlations   236
Strength of Association   236
Factors Affecting the Size of a Correlation Coefficient   238

TRADITIONAL CORRELATIONAL TESTS   242
The Pearson Product–Moment Correlation   242
Alternate Bivariate Correlations   243

CORRELATIONS WITH MULTIPLE VARIABLES   243
Multiple Regression   244
Factor Analysis   247
Cross-Lagged Panel Studies   249
Path Analysis   252

LIMITATIONS OF MULTIVARIATE CORRELATIONAL ANALYSIS   254
Generalizability   255
Confirmation Bias   255

CHAPTER SUMMARY   256

CHAPTER TEN
Studying Patterns in the Natural World: Observational Approaches   257

CHAPTER OUTLINE   257

KEY TERMS   257

CHAPTER PREVIEW   258

OBSERVATIONAL APPROACHES   258

SCIENTIFIC VERSUS CASUAL OBSERVATION   259

STUDYING NATURAL BEHAVIORS   260
Studying Complex Human Behavior   261
Ethology   262
Describing the Behavior of Nonhuman Animals   263

APPROACHES TO OBSERVATIONAL RESEARCH   265
Practical Steps in Observational Research   265
Structured and Unstructured Observations   267

SAMPLING ISSUES IN OBSERVATIONAL RESEARCH   268
Number of Sampling Blocks   268
Methods of Sampling Events during Observation   269
Estimating the Frequency and Duration of Behaviors   271

ETHOLOGICAL OBSERVATIONS IN CLINICAL RESEARCH   272

THE HUMAN SIDE OF OBSERVATIONAL RESEARCH   274
Ethics   275
Participant–Observer Interactions   277
Subject Reactivity   277
Observer Effects   279

DATA ANALYSIS IN OBSERVATIONAL RESEARCH   280

CHAPTER SUMMARY   280

CHAPTER ELEVEN

Research in Depth: Longitudinal and Single-Case Studies   281

CHAPTER OUTLINE   281

KEY TERMS   281

CHAPTER PREVIEW   282

LONGITUDINAL RESEARCH   282
Common Themes in Longitudinal Research   283
Cross-Sectional versus Longitudinal Research   283

VARIETIES OF LONGITUDINAL RESEARCH   285
Trend Studies   285
Cohort Studies   288
Cohort Sequential Studies   288
Panel Studies   290

ISSUES IN LONGITUDINAL DESIGNS   291
Retrospective and Prospective Studies   291
Attrition   292

DATA ANALYSIS IN LONGITUDINAL RESEARCH   295

SINGLE-SUBJECT EXPERIMENTATION   296
Experimental Analysis of Behavior   297

METHODS OF SINGLE-CASE DESIGNS   297
Withdrawal Designs   298
ABAB Designs   298
Multiple Baseline Designs   299
Single-Subject Randomized Controlled Trials   300
Strengths of Single-Participant Designs   301
Weaknesses of Single-Participant Designs   302

Misunderstandings about Single-Case Research   302

CASE STUDIES   303

CHAPTER SUMMARY   306

CHAPTER TWELVE

People Are Different: Considering Cultural and Individual Differences in Research   307

CHAPTER OUTLINE   307

KEY TERMS   308

CHAPTER PREVIEW   308

DIFFERENT CULTURAL PERSPECTIVES   308
What Is Culture?   309

DEFINING AN INDIVIDUAL'S CULTURE, ETHNICITY, AND RACE   310
Criteria for Inclusion in a Group   311
Social Issues and Cultural Research   312

CROSS-CULTURAL CONCEPTS IN PSYCHOLOGY   314
Are Psychological Constructs Universal?   314
Issues in Cross-Cultural Research   315

IS THERE A BIOLOGICAL BASIS FOR RACE?   317
The Criteria for Race   317
Current Biological Insights Regarding Race   318
Historical Error   320
Current Controversies   320

PRACTICAL ISSUES IN CULTURAL RESEARCH   320
Lack of Appropriate Training among Researchers   321

WHY THE CONCEPTS OF CULTURE AND ETHNICITY ARE ESSENTIAL IN RESEARCH   322
Differences Due to Language and Thought Processes   322
Differences in Simple and Complex Behaviors   323
Is Culture-Free Theory Really Free of Culture?   324
Similarities and Differences within the Same Culture   324

CULTURAL FACTORS IN MENTAL HEALTH RESEARCH   325
Content Validity   325
Translation Problems   326
Cross-Cultural Norms   327
Cross-Cultural Diagnoses   328

SEX AND GENDER: DO MEN AND WOMEN COME FROM DIFFERENT CULTURES?   330
Stereotypes and Gender-Related Performance   330

CHAPTER SUMMARY   332

APPENDIX A
Writing a Research Report   333

APPENDIX B
Statistics Review   352

APPENDIX C
Statistical Tables   379

APPENDIX D
Archival Research   387

References   397

Author Index   413

Subject Index   419

PREFACE

The most compelling reason I can think of for doing psychological research is that it is fun. You get to work on a question that interests you, you get to solve the puzzle of how to arrive at the best answer to your question, and you create knowledge where it didn't previously exist. When students enroll in a course on research methods in psychology, they usually don't realize how easy it is to become personally involved in conducting their own projects. This book is an attempt to lure them into the world of research by showing them that it can be meaningful to their own lives.

Throughout this book I have tried to develop examples that show what psychology has to offer. Each chapter contains at least one Controversy Box to show readers that there are vigorous debates about engaging topics. In addition to highlighting specific controversies, I have tried to give instances of research that will pique interest while illustrating methodological approaches and questions. Throughout the book, my goal has been to present research topics both rigorously and engagingly. The writing identifies the complexity of research but not in an intimidating way.

The book consists of segments on developing research ideas, on generating experiments, on using nonexperimental designs, and on understanding the social and cultural aspects of research. Most chapters can stand alone and the topics can be discussed in the order considered most reasonable for individual teachers.

The issues in the first chapters concern the interplay of science and society (Chapter 1) and scientists' ethical obligations to our constituencies (Chapter 2). Following that, students will encounter help in developing research ideas and finding out what we already know about a topic (Chapter 3). With this background, students are now exposed to practical issues of creating a research project, including defining variables, creating samples, and other critical steps in planning the project (Chapter 4).

The next set of chapters (Chapters 5, 6, and 7) focuses on the gold standard of psychological research, the experiment and its variations. Subsequently, the students will encounter survey techniques (Chapter 8), correlational approaches (Chapter 9), observational research (Chapter 10), and then designs used for in-depth research (Chapter 11). The final chapter focuses on social and cultural issues in research, a topic that has been ignored for too long in psychology and whose importance has only recently come to the fore. The appendixes include a presentation of key elements of APA-style research papers, a statistical review, the commonly used statistical tables, and the basics of archival research.

After learning the material in this book, students will have the ability to set up their own experiments. This work is more than an experimental psychology textbook, however. With the growing importance of nonexperimental techniques in psychology, I have provided the information that students will need to develop survey research, correlational studies, naturalistic observation, and archival approaches.

As students work through the book, they will encounter discussion questions that punctuate each chapter. These questions reinforce their knowledge of the content and stimulate discussion of important issues. For the instructor, I have provided suggestions for responses to the questions in the test bank; as such, there is a ready supply of subjectively scored quiz or test items and the main points from the book that relate to those questions. This will aid the teacher in scoring exams based on these questions.

Another pedagogical feature is the running glossary that briefly explains in the margins the major terms discussed in the book. Research is complex; so is the vocabulary of research. The glossary within each chapter permits the student to understand the concept immediately, without having to resort to a remote source.

In addition to providing the material in the textbook, I have also created lively classroom exercises to enhance student interest. I have implemented these activities and demonstrations in my own classes, and I have seen students respond positively to them. With each exercise in the Instructor's Manual, I have made clear the rationale for using the exercise and what I hope students will learn from it. It would not be practical (or advisable) to use all of them in one semester, but the instructor can pick and choose from among the topics.

As I have written this book, it has become eminently clear to me that this kind of project doesn't emerge fully developed like Athena from the head of Zeus. Nor can it happen in a vacuum. The potential for this book began in the mists of my memory when one of my teachers, Jim Kwiatowski, fostered the development of my critical thinking skills, Later, I received inspiration from Prof. John Jahnke in my undergraduate years at Miami University, in Oxford, Ohio. (It was John Jahnke who wryly commented that some people thought it was the wrong Miami and the wrong Oxford, with which I disagree wholeheartedly.) I also moved along my path in psychology in part due to Arthur Reber, who advised me sagaciously during my graduate years at the City University of New York.

Closer to the present, I have profited from the fastidious work of the staff at Allyn and Bacon, specifically Kelly May, Marlana Voerster, and Becky Pascal. I am also highly indebted to the many gracious authors who have granted me permission to use figures and tables from their research so that I could illustrate the complex concepts we deal with in our projects. Further, part of this book was completed when I was on sabbatical leave from Ithaca College, working as Director of Pre-College and Undergraduate Programs at the American Psychological Association. My colleagues there, including Cynthia Belar, Paul Nelson, and Martha Boenau, were wonderful resources for ideas that developed in my discussions with them. I do appreciate greatly the help of Judy Smith in the Ithaca College Psychology Department.

During the development of the book, I have benefitted from the many constructive comments of a large contingent of astute and clear-thinking colleagues who have reviewed the manuscript in its evolution. These reviewers include Patricia Alexander, Long Beach City College; Bryan Auday, Gordon College; John Broida, University of Southern Maine; Michael C. Choban, West Virginia Wesleyan College; Virginia R. Gregg, State University of New York at Oswego; Elizabeth Yost Hammer, Loyola University; Mary Kite, Ball State University; Benjamin Miller, Salem State College; Louise

C. Perry, Florida Atlantic University; Cheryl Sanders, Metropolitan State College of Denver; George E. Schreer, Manhattanville College; Beth Schwartz-Kenney, Randolph-Macon Woman's College; Janie H. Wilson, Georgia Southern University; and Lonnie Yandell, Belmont University.

Finally, I give thanks to my wife, Linda, for her psychological support (in its many senses and manifestations) during this project and to Agatha and Simon for their ability to help me keep my ideas at least partially grounded in reality.

CHAPTER ONE

PSYCHOLOGY, SCIENCE, AND LIFE

CHAPTER OVERVIEW

CHAPTER PREVIEW

WHY ARE RESEARCH METHODS IMPORTANT TOOLS FOR LIFE?
Creating Knowledge

WHY WE DO RESEARCH
Description
Explanation
Prediction
Control

WHAT CONSTITUTES SCIENTIFIC KNOWLEDGE
Science Is Objective
Science Is Data Driven
Science Is Replicable and Verifiable

CONTROVERSY: Why Do Men Rape?
Science Is Public

DIFFERENT WAYS OF KNOWING
The Obvious, or Intuition
Authority

Logic, or the A Priori Method
Experience
The Scientific Method

THE INTERACTION OF SCIENCE AND CULTURE
The Government's Role in Science
Cultural Values and Science
Cross-Cultural Issues and Science

CONTROVERSY: Should Women Serve as Jurors?

SCIENCE AND THE POPULAR MEDIA
Psychological Terminology
in Everyday Use
Misinterpretations of Research
in the Media
Erroneous Beliefs
Scientific "Breakthroughs"

SCIENCE AND PSEUDOSCIENCE

CHAPTER SUMMARY

KEY TERMS

A priori method
Authority
Control
Data driven
Description

Empirical approach
Experience
Explanation
Falsifiability
Objective

Overdetermined
Peer review
Prediction
Pseudoscience
Public

Replicable
Scientific method
Tenacity
Verifiable

CHAPTER PREVIEW

At this point in your education, you probably know a great deal about people, some interesting and important facts about psychology, but you probably know relatively little about psychological research. This book will show you how research helps you learn more about people from a psychological point of view. You can be certain of one thing: There are no simple explanations.

When you read through this chapter, you will learn that there are different ways of knowing about behavior. As a beginning psychologist, you will get a glimpse about why some types of knowledge are more useful than others. In addition, you will see that people can be resistant to changing what they believe. For instance, a lot of people believe in ESP or other paranormal phenomena, even though the scientific evidence for it just isn't there. One reason for such beliefs is that most people don't approach learning the same way that scientists do, so the evidence they accept is sometimes pretty shaky.

Finally, this chapter will introduce you to some of the cautions you should be aware of when you read about psychological research in the popular media. Journalists are not scientists and scientists are not journalists, so there is a lot of potential for miscommunication between the two.

WHY ARE RESEARCH METHODS IMPORTANT TOOLS FOR LIFE?

The great thing about psychology is that people are both interesting and complicated, and we get to learn more about them. As you learn more, you will see that there can be a big difference between what we think we know about behavior and what is actually true. If people were easy to figure out, we would have done it by now. That is why you need this course.

Your course on research begins the process of learning about how psychological knowledge emerges. This knowledge can be useful when applied to people's lives. For instance, even four years after a domestic terrorist destroyed a federal building in Oklahoma City, killing 168 people, about half the survivors were still suffering from some kind of psychiatric illness (North et al., 1999). Those most at risk refused to think about the devastation and isolated themselves socially. Other characteristics associated with the development of post-traumatic stress disorder (PTSD) are the previous existence of psychiatric problems and the degree to which the individual was directly involved or had friends or relatives who were injured; women were also at higher risk than men. We may be able to use this research to help people who survived the horror of the terrorist attacks on the World Trade Center or other traumatic events that may occur.

We don't have to rely on such extreme examples of the use of psychological research. Psychologists have suggested that some people suffer from Internet addiction (Griffiths, 1998). This is an interesting possibility, but before we come to hasty conclusions, we need to ask some important questions.

The only way to address these issues is to do research, which means that we need to create knowledge where it does not already exist. It might sound strange to think of "creating" knowledge, but that is exactly what happens in research. You end up with information that didn't exist before. This is one of the exciting parts of doing research: When you complete a study, you know something that nobody else in the world knows.

Creating Knowledge

In reading textbooks or journal articles, we might get the impression that we can carry out a research project and an explanation jumps clearly out of the results. In reality, there is always uncertainty in research. When we plan our investigations, there are many decisions to make about our procedures; when we examine our results, they are usually complicated enough that we have to puzzle through them before we are confident that we understand what we are looking at. In textbooks and journals, we only see the end product of ideas that have worked out successfully, and we do not see the twists and turns that led to those successes.

In this course, we will see that we need to use imagination, creativity, and ingenuity in developing knowledge. If we want to address the question of Internet addiction (or any other behavior), we need to understand how we can create knowledge, which is what a course in research methods is all about.

Your course in research methods will also help you prepare for a possible future in psychology. If you attend graduate school, you will see that nearly all programs in psychology require an introductory psychology course, statistics, and research methods or experimental psychology. Most programs do not specify much more than that. Your graduate school professors want you to know how psychologists think; research-based courses provide you with a glimpse of how we develop psychological knowledge. Those professors will provide courses that will help you learn the skills appropriate for your specific area of interest after you develop the basics. As a psychologist, you also need to understand the research process so you can read scientific journals and make sense of the research reports, and keep abreast of current ideas. Even if you don't choose a career as a researcher, you can still benefit from understanding research. Many jobs require knowledge of statistics and research.

In addition, every day you will be bombarded by claims that scientists have made breakthroughs in understanding various phenomena. It will be useful for you to be able to evaluate whether to believe what you hear. One of the purposes of a course in research is to help you learn how to think critically about the things people tell you. Is their research sound? Is the conclusion they draw the best one? Do they have something to gain from getting certain results? This process of questioning what people tell you is a hallmark of science, but it is also a useful tool in everyday life.

After you complete this course in research methods, you will be able to apply your new knowledge to areas outside of psychology. The research skills you pick up here will let you complete solid psychological research projects, but will also help you understand life better; similarly, when you learn about many different topics, it can help you understand psychology better.

1. Identify three ways that knowledge of research methods can prepare you for a career either in psychology or in another field.
2. What does it mean to say that scientists create knowledge?
3. Why should we be skeptical of scientific research if the experimenters will gain financially from the results of their studies?

WHY WE DO RESEARCH

People are curious, social beings. As a result, most of us are interested in what others are up to and why. By the time you read this book, you have been observing others for perhaps twenty years or more, that is, since childhood. You have probably become a sophisticated observer of others' behaviors and can predict pretty well how your friends will react if you act a certain way, at least some of the time. How did you gain this knowledge? Throughout your life, you have done things and then you observed the effect you had on others. Although you probably have not gone through life wearing the stereotypical white lab coat worn by some scientists, you have acted like a scientist when you discovered that "When I do this, they do that." One of the differences between scientific and nonscientific observation, though, is that scientists develop systematic plans and we work to reduce bias in recording observations.

As curious scientists, we generally work toward four increasingly difficult goals based on our observations: **description**, **explanation**, **prediction**, and **control of behavior**.

Description

Description—A goal of science in which behaviors are systematically and accurately characterized.

Our tendency to act and then to observe others' reactions fulfills what seems to be a basic need for us: describing the world around us. In fact, when you can **describe** events around you, you have taken the first step in scientific discovery. In research, description involves a systematic approach to observing behavior. That notion of scientific discovery may sound intimidating, but it begins very simply.

In your course on behavioral research, you will learn how, as scientists, we systematically begin to understand why people act as they do. The biggest difference between what you do in your everyday observations and what scientists do is that scientists pay attention to a lot of details that we normally think of as unimportant. Unlike most of us in everyday, casual observation, researchers develop a systematic plan for making objective observations so we can generate complete and accurate descriptions.

Explanation

Explanation—A goal of science in which a researcher achieves awareness of why behaviors occur as they do.

This leads to the second goal of science, **explanation**. When we truly understand the causes of behavior, we can explain them. This is where theory comes in. A theory helps us understand behavior in a general sense. In scientific use, a theory is a general, organizing principle. When we have enough relevant information about behavior, we can develop an explanatory framework that puts all of that information into a nice, neat package—that is, into a theory.

On the other hand, a hypothesis lets us make a prediction about a particular behavior. By testing hypotheses, we can assess how well a given theory characterizes behavior. If enough of our hypotheses support a theory, we regard it as more useful in understanding why people act in a certain way; if those hypotheses do not support the theory, we need to revise or abandon the theory. Before we conduct research, we should have an open mind about an issue, but we have to remember that one of the important elements of the scientific method is **falsifiability.** That is, we will test hypotheses to see if we can prove them wrong. If a hypothesis doesn't have the potential to be tested for its validity, it isn't useful scientifically.

> **Falsifiability**—A characteristic of science such that any principle has to be amenable to testing to see if it is true or, more specifically, if it can be shown to be false.

When we test hypotheses, we make them objective and testable. This means that we define our terms clearly so others know how exactly what we mean, and we specify how our research will assess whether a hypothesis is valid.

In everyday life, we hear people say things like, "I have a theory about why she acts as she does." When people say that, most of the time they don't mean "theory"; they may mean they have an educated guess, which is different than a theory. In scientific language, a psychologist would use the word "hypothesis."

For decades, people have used Freudian (psychodynamic) or behavioral theories to try to understand behavior. Both approaches have generated useful ideas about human behavior and have been accepted, at least in part, by the general public. You can see the impact of Freudian theory if you consider some of Freud's terms that have gained currency in everyday language, like repression, penis envy, or Freudian slips.

Many psychologists believe that many of Freud's ideas are not scientifically valid. In fact, when Freudian ideas have been subjected to experimentation, they often have not stood up well. In a perspective as complicated as psychodynamic theory, though, there is still disagreement about the scientific status of ideas such as unconscious processing of information, and some psychologists still maintain that Freudian ideas have received support from research (Westen, 1998).

Behavioral terms have also made their way into everyday language, as when people talk about positive or negative reinforcement. In the case of behaviorism, most psychologists affirm that it is a truly scientific approach. The ideas are objective and testable; in a wide variety of research programs, the utility of behavioral ideas has been well established.

In research, we use hypotheses to make predictions about behavior, and theories are useful for helping us explain why our predictions are accurate. As psychologists, we use theory to explain behavior. Our explanations differ from the ones we generate in everyday life in that scientific explanations involve well-specified statements of when behaviors will or will not occur.

Prediction

> **Prediction**—A goal of science in which a researcher can specify in advance those situations in which a particular behavior will occur.

After you describe what people are likely to do in a certain situation, the next logical step is to expand your knowledge beyond simple description. The third step is to **predict** behavior. Suppose you tell a joke. You are likely to make a prediction about how your friends will react to it. They may laugh, cry, show sympathy, or walk away in disgust. In considering whether to tell the story, you are making a prediction about their response. Every time you tell a story, you are engaging in a kind of experiment, making a prediction about the outcome. Naturally, you are sometimes wrong in your prediction because people are not easy to figure out.

Similarly, in behavioral research, we sometimes make poor predictions. When that happens, a scientist will try to figure out why the predictions were wrong and will attempt to make better ones next time. A big difference between casual and scientific predictions is that scientists generally specify in great detail what factors lead to a given outcome. For most of us in everyday life, we have a vague notion of what behaviors to expect from others and, as a result, will accept our predictions as true if somebody behaves in ways that are roughly approximate to what we expected. There is a lot of room for error.

Overdetermined—A principle stating that behaviors are often caused by more than a single cause.

In our relationships with others, we find it helpful to describe and to predict their behaviors because it gives us a sense of control; we know in advance what will happen. At the same time, most of us want to know even more. We want to know *why* people act as they do. This is a difficult process because people's behaviors arise for a lot of reasons: When there are multiple causes for behavior, we say the behavior is **overdetermined.**

Still, once we learn to predict at a basic level what behaviors will occur, we will try to move another step ahead and figure out exactly why they occur.

Control

Control—A goal of science in which a researcher can manipulate variables in order to produce specific behaviors.

The final step in the scientific study of behavior is **control.** Some people may ask whether it is right for us to try to control others' behaviors. Most psychologists would respond that we affect others' behaviors, just as they affect ours. It is not a matter of *should* we control behavior, but rather *how* does it happen. For example, parents try to raise children who show moral behavior. It would be reassuring to parents if they knew how to create such behavior in their children.

In order to exert control of behavior effectively, we need to understand why the behavior occurs as it does. To understand the elements of control, we need to have well formulated theories. At this point, we don't have a single theory of behavior that can capture the variety of human experience.

Psychologists with different theoretical orientations may use similar statements in describing behavior, but they will begin to diverge when making predictions, become even more different regarding explanation, and even more so with respect to control. Table 1.1 summarizes the four different goals of science and how psychologists have used them at various points in their research programs.

DISCUSSION QUESTIONS
1. Describe why a psychological theory can have practical implications for people's lives (e.g., in treatment of emotional and behavioral problems).
2. Describe the four basic goals of science and identify why some goals are harder to attain than others.

TABLE 1.1   Example of the goals of research and how they relate to the development of knowledge.

Description	One evening in 1964, a woman named Kitty Genovese was attacked and murdered while walking home from work at 3 a.m. in Queens, New York. Thirty-eight people saw what was happening from their apartment windows, but nobody helped; nobody even called the police.
	Two psychologists (e.g., Latané and Darley, 1970) wondered why this might happen. Their first step in understanding this phenomenon was to describe what happened. Based on descriptions of the initial event, Darley and Latané (1968) investigated some of the implications of Genovese's murder as they relate to helping behavior.
	This event was so striking, that it led to an enormous amount of research and analysis (e.g., Cunningham, 1984; Takooshian & O'Connor, 1984) and stands as a prime example of research that results from something that occurs outside the laboratory. (See Cialdini & Baumann, 1981, for a discussion of using naturally occurring events as a basis for behavioral research.)
Explanation	Once we can document and predict events, we can try to explain why behaviors occur. Psychologists have identified some of the underlying factors that may help us understand why people do not help others. As Darley and Latané (1968) have noted, when there are more people around, we are less likely to notice that somebody needs help and, even when we notice, we are less likely to offer aid. Part of this failure to act involves what has been called diffusion of responsibility; that is, when others are around, we can pass blame for our inaction to them, assuming less (or none) for ourselves.
Prediction	We can try to determine those conditions where helping behavior is likely to occur. Helping occurs as people try to avoid feeling guilty (Katsev, Edelsack, Steinmetz, Walker, & Wright, 1978), and helping diminishes if people have been relieved of guilt (Cialdini, Darby, & Vincent, 1973). In addition, if people believe that another individual is similar to them, they will help (Batson, Duncan, Ackerman, Buckley, & Birch, 1981).
	Helping behavior involves complicated dynamics, so it will be difficult to identify precisely those conditions in which helping will occur, but we have identified some variables that allow us to make generally accurate predictions.
Control	Once we are confident of our predictions, we can ultimately control behavior. Behaviors in everyday life are seldom controlled by a single variable, but we can control behavior to a degree by manipulating the relevant variables.
	Programs to help poverty-stricken people often rely on guilt or empathic pleas. Depending on the particulars of the circumstances, we may help others if our mood is positive because we tend to generalize our good mood to everything around us (Clark & Teasdale, 1985) or if our mood is negative if we think that helping will improve our mood (Manucia, Baumann, & Cialdini, 1984). Knowledge of these effects can help us control behaviors.

WHAT CONSTITUTES SCIENTIFIC KNOWLEDGE?

One of the major differences between scientific knowledge and other kinds of knowledge is that scientific work is much more systematic than casual observation. In addition, researchers abide by certain general principles in deciding what to believe. Our scientific knowledge relies on the fact that our observations are objective, data-driven, public, and potentially replicable. We will see shortly what this means, but what it all comes down to is the fact that, as scientists and as good decision-makers, we need to evaluate how well research has been done. If we decide that the investigators have done everything correctly, we should be willing to change our minds about what we believe to be true, even if we don't like the truth. As it turns out, people are so complicated that a single research study will never lead to a complete change in beliefs; the process is incremental, with a series of small steps rather than a giant leap.

Science Is Objective

Objective—Measurements that are not affected by personal bias and that are well-defined and specified are considered objective.

What does it mean for our observations to be **objective**? One implication is that we define clearly the concepts we are dealing with. This is often easier said than done. Psychologists deal with complex and abstract concepts that are not easily measured. Nonetheless, we have to develop some way to measure these concepts in clear and systematic ways. For example, suppose we want to find out whether we respond more positively to attractive people than to others.

To answer our question, we first have to define what we mean by "attractive." The definition must be objective; that is, the definition has to be consistent, clear, and understandable, even though it may not be perfect.

Researchers have taken various routes to creating objective definitions of attractiveness. Wilson (1978) simply mentioned that "a female confederate . . . appearing either attractive or unattractive asked in a neutral manner for directions to a particular building on central campus at a large Midwestern University" (p. 313). This vague statement doesn't really tell us as much as we would like to know. We don't have a clear definition of what the researchers meant by "attractiveness." Juhnke et al. (1987) varied the attire of people who seemed to be in need of help. The researchers defined attractiveness based on clothing. Unattractive people, that is, those wearing less desirable clothing, received help, even though they did not look very attractive.

On the other hand, Bull and Stevens (1980) used helpers with either good or bad teeth. In this case, attractive was defined as having good teeth, whereas unattractive was defined as having bad teeth. In this study, it didn't matter whether the researcher had good teeth or not. People were just as likely to help those with bad teeth, although they were willing to do so for a shorter length of time.

The evidence suggests that attractive people have an advantage in the job market (Marlowe, Schneider, & Nelson, 1996). Similarly, attractive people may be more likely to receive assistance when in need (Nadler, Shapira, & Ben-Itzhak, 1982), although those of us who are plain looking may not need to despair (Juhnke, Barmann, Cunningham, & Smith, 1987).

If the different research teams did not report how they created an unattractive appearance, we would have a harder time evaluating their research and repeating it exactly as they did it. It may be very important to know what manipulation the researchers used. Differences in attractiveness due to the kinds of clothes you are wearing may not lead to the same reactions as differences due to unsightly teeth.

Interestingly, Stokes and Bikman (1974) found that people may be less willing to ask help *from* attractive people than from unattractive people. In their study, they defined attractiveness on the basis of physical appearance as rated by other people. This strategy relies on a clear and consistent method of defining attractiveness. Because attractiveness can be defined in many ways, we need to tell others what we mean when we use the term, which is what we mean by objectivity.

Science Is Data Driven

Data driven—Interpretations of research that are based on objective results of a project are considered data-driven.

Our conclusions as scientists must also be **data driven.** This simply means that our conclusions must follow logically from our data. There may be several equally good interpretations from a single set of data. Regardless of which interpretation we choose, it has to be based on the data we collect.

The critical point here is that if we are to develop a more complete and accurate understanding of the world around us, scientific knowledge based on data will, in the long run, serve us better than intuition alone. Don't discount intuition entirely; quite a few scientific insights had their beginnings in intuitions that were scientifically studied and found to be true. We just can't rely on it entirely because it is not always right.

Science Is Replicable and Verifiable

Replicable—When scientists can recreate a previous research study, that study is replicable.
Verifiable—When scientists can reproduce a previous research study and generate the same results, it is verifiable.

Our scientific knowledge has to be potentially **replicable** and **verifiable.** This means that others should have the opportunity to repeat a research project to see if we get the same results each time. An approach is considered objective if others can attempt to replicate it. Maybe the researchers who are trying to repeat the study will generate the same result; maybe they will not. We do not claim that *results* are scientific; rather, we claim that the approach is scientific. Any time somebody makes a claim but will not let others verify it as true, we should be skeptical. In science, we keep no secrets from each other. The only secrets are nature's mysteries that we are trying to discover.

Sometimes even when researchers follow a completely scientific path, there can be great controversy in the conclusions about what the research is telling us. For instance, in the controversy surrounding the cause of rape, there are at least two distinctly different schools of thought. One approach invokes the ideas of evolutionary psychology. The other is more socially oriented. Both groups have data and theory to support their ideas, although both are clearly still incomplete.

In Controversy Box 1.1, you can see two very different theoretical approaches to the study of why rape occurs. The arguments are heated and each camp believes that it has useful insights into the problem.

■ ■ ■ ■ ■ ▬▬▬▬▬▬▬▬▬▬▬▬▬▬▬▬▬▬▬▬▬▬▬▬▬▬▬▬

CONTROVERSY BOX 1.1
CONTROVERSY: Why Do Men Rape?

The act of rape constitutes one of the most horrific invasions of one's person. Most rapes, as we know, are committed by men against women. Psychologists have investigated such crimes, trying to figure out why they happen. Not surprisingly, rape is a complex issue and we do not yet have a clear understanding of its dynamics.

At the same time, at least two very different views have emerged about why rape occurs. These two theoretical perspectives both deal with the same phenomenon, that is, they both describe the same behavior. The two theories begin to differ, though, in their consideration of predicting when the behavior will occur. They bear little resemblance to one another when it comes to explaining why rape occurs. Finally, they also provide contrasting pictures of how to control (i.e., prevent) rape.

One model to explain the occurrence of rape has as its basis the notion that a rapist learns his attitudes through social processes. Further, these psychologists believe that rape represents an act of power and control, not an act of sex. As such, theorists who subscribe to this notion rely on a model that rape can be prevented through adequate control of educational and learning processes.

A second model arises from evolutionary psychology, which suggests that some of our behaviors are, in part, genetically triggered. Some behavioral scientists (e.g., Thornhill and Palmer, 2000) assert that education alone is not enough to prevent rape because sexual behavior, even if it involves coercion, is part of our evolutionary, genetic sexual makeup. These theorists claim that rape is not about power and control, but rather precisely about sex. With such different views about the underlying nature of rape, we should not be surprised that the two groups argue heatedly with one another.

How can competent, knowledgeable, and intelligent scholars differ so much with one another? Both groups have objective data arising from replicable research. The answer is that any time you try to explain complex behavior patterns, you have to rely on a lot of information that might be conflicting and that is certainly incomplete. We don't know everything that we need to know.

In short, we believe things that we are predisposed to believe or that we want to believe. Scholars can legitimately differ in their interpretations, each believing in a theory that makes most sense to them. It is important to remember, though, that what is sensible to one person may be senseless to another. Nobody can generate a theory that does not rely on personal and cultural biases and predispositions.

At this point, we need to remember what theories are good for. A theory is used after we have a good idea of how to describe behaviors of interest and can make accurate predictions about them. The theory is an overall explanation that puts together as much of the information about our topic as possible.

In the present controversy about why rape occurs, some psychologists believe that a social learning model is the best explanation. Other psychologists believe that evolutionary ideas provide the best explanation. What we ultimately hope for is that we can generate enough data to help us figure out which explanation is best.

When we look at this controversy, it becomes clear that our cultural biases can influence the conclusions we draw. Many people don't want to believe the evolutionary explanation because it may be inconsistent with their personal beliefs about people and the control of their behavior.

When considering theory in this light, we can easily see why a theory is actually a very practical thing. Depending on your theory of rape, you might consider very different ways of controlling behaviors so rape does not occur. Or you might use your theory to plan therapy to help rape victims. If your theory is not the best way to understand the behavior, your ability to control the behavior will suffer.

This need to check others' research results is important in all sciences. A decade ago, a team of chemists declared that they had created a safe, unlimited source of energy through a process they called "cold fusion"; the media touted the importance of their findings. Through replication, other researchers have shown that the initial claims were wrong and that the results were based on flawed research procedures. In the end, scientific approaches to generating knowledge lead to greater confidence in our findings, regardless of whether they involve psychology, chemistry, or any other empirical discipline.

Science Is Public

Public—Scientists make their research public, typically by making presentations at conferences or by publishing their work in journal articles or books.

Peer Review—A process in which researchers submit their research for publication in a journal or presentation at a conference to other experts in the field who evaluate the research.

When we say that our research is *public,* we mean this literally. Scientists only recognize research as valid or useful when it has been scrutinized and made public. Generally, we accept research as valid if it has undergone *peer review.* For instance, when a psychologist completes research, the next step is often to write the results in journal article and submit it for publication in a research journal.

The editor of the journal will send the manuscript to experts in the field for their comments. If the editor and the reviewers agree that any major problems have been taken care of, the article will appear in the journal. Otherwise, the article will be rejected and will not appear in that journal. Among major journals in psychology, about a quarter or fewer of all manuscripts submitted are published. When the research appears in print, it is truly public.

Another approach to making our research public involves submitting a proposal to a research conference for a presentation. The process for acceptance to a conference resembles that for acceptance by a journal. In some cases, researchers may initially present their ideas at a conference, then follow up with a published article.

DISCUSSION QUESTIONS

1. Describe the four main characteristics of science. How do they differ from everyday ways of knowing and understanding?
2. Why is it important for scientists to report their research methodologies and their results in great detail?

DIFFERENT WAYS OF KNOWING

There are some things that we know to be true. For instance, consider the five following statements.

1. On a sunny day, the sky is blue.
2. When a cold virus enters our body, we wind up with a cold.
3. If a stalk of celery has fewer calories than a piece of cheese, and if that piece of cheese has fewer calories than a particular piece of cake, then if you eat the cake, you will gain more weight than if you ate the celery.

4. If a child ate a hot dog and got sick once, he or she is likely to avoid hot dogs in the future for fear of getting sick again.

5. If a person is exposed to a traumatic event, like a shooting, the person will recover better if he or she talks about it to a therapist rather than trying to ignore it.

Each of the five statements above is true, but we typically don't believe in their truth for the same underlying reason. There are different paths to factual knowledge in our lives; each item listed in the previous paragraphs embodies a different path to knowledge. We will see that not all roads to knowledge are equally useful. The nineteenth-century American philosopher Charles Sanders Peirce identified several ways of knowing, which he called *tenacity* (which I will call *intuition*), *authority*, the *a priori method* (which I will call *logic*), experience, and the *scientific approach*. Others have provided variations on this list, but these are the major points.

> **Tenacity**—A way of knowing that emphasizes what seems to be obvious or what "everybody knows is true."

The Obvious, or Intuition

Belief: When people choose partners, opposites attract. There is a widely held belief that partners in a relationship are "opposite." Sometimes, people talk about such knowledge based on tenacity; that is, we hold on to our knowledge because it is so obvious and because "everybody knows it is true."

What is wrong with such knowledge? Obviously, most of what we know to be true has to have some validity. Otherwise, life would be a daunting jumble of confusion. We know that walls are solid and that we should not try to walk through them. What could be more obvious? We count on life being predictable. In fact, our knowledge makes life reassuringly predictable.

As always, though, things are not simple. What we know is likely to be true in general, but there are things that we "know" that are actually not true. For instance, a lot of research about whether opposites actually do attract suggests that similarity is more likely to attract. That is, people favor partners who are like them.

We have to keep in mind when we try to predict and explain behaviors that even the most complicated model that we devise is simpler than real life. As a result, our predictions are not going to be perfect. There are too many contributing variables; that is, behaviors are overdetermined. So simple explanations are likely to be only partially true. One of the persistent difficulties in any type of scientific research is that our research leads to some accurate predictions but also to inaccurate predictions. We have to figure out if the inaccurate predictions result from a poor explanatory model or from the fact that simple bad luck has obscured the truth.

Getting back to the notion that we use experience to develop knowledge, we need to keep in mind that although "everybody" believes something is true or that it is so "obvious," it may not actually be true.

Authority

Belief: When a cold virus enters our body, we wind up with a cold. Another reason we believe that something is true is that an expert or an authority has said so. You may believe that the cold weather brings on colds because your parents, the first authorities in your life,

> **Authority**—A way of knowing that emphasizes reliance on experts or other people who would be expected to have valid knowledge in some domain.

told you so. Should you believe them? In many cases, parents constitute a good source of information, but they are not always right. We have a dilemma here. Who should we believe and when should we believe them? Experts have gained their reputations based on their work in some field. As such, they probably know more than we do, but that does not make them infallible.

Sometimes it is useful or even necessary for us to accept the word of authorities and experts because they are generally more right than wrong when they discuss their areas of expertise. In addition, in everyday life it may not make much difference if we believe things that are not true. When developing theories, though, our ideas will not hold water if they are based on misinformation. The trick is to remain skeptical until enough evidence accumulates to convince us that an expert is correct. This is no easy task because in many cases we do not have enough knowledge to determine whether to believe the authorities. Often the best we can do is to accept the consensus of experts in a field because their knowledge makes them likely to be correct.

Nicholson (1999/2000) provides an interesting example of potentially misguided expertise. Aztec physicians believed that the charred excrement of various birds and animals constituted useful medication (which is dubious). Before we dismiss the Aztecs as primitive and ignorant, we need to remember that a treatment we now use in estrogen-replacement therapy is derived from chemicals in the urine of pregnant horses (p. 57).

We rely on treatments that, according to medical authorities, are useful. Recently, however, surgeons have found that typical surgical procedures for osteoarthritis of the knee may not be any more useful than fake surgery (Moseley et al., 2002). Further, we have evidence that many common medicines are no more effective than placebos that, by definition, are not supposed to do anything (e.g., Moncrieff, Wessely, & Hardy, 1998; Staats, P., Hekmat, H., & Staats, A., 1998). The critical point here is that we rely on authorities to give us their best advice on what might work, knowing that they may not always be right.

Logic, or the A Priori Method

Belief: If a stalk of celery has fewer calories than a piece of cheese, and if that piece of cheese has fewer calories than a particular piece of cake, then if you ate the cake, you would gain more weight than if you ate the celery. If you ever had to solve problems using strictly logical reasoning, you may have been able to prove something is true. The statement above about calories and gaining weight relies on logic. Mathematicians use this approach with great success. Students taking geometry regularly have to derive proofs using only logic. You can sometimes determine with certainty when something is true or false. For instance, using a simple example, we know that if Line A is longer than Line B, and if Line B is longer than Line C, it has to be true that Line A is longer than Line C.

> **A Priori Method**—A way of knowing that emphasizes logical deductions.

Human behavior is not so easily understood. For instance, if you like Amy better than you like Beth, and if you like Beth better than you like Carol, it seems reasonable that you would spend more time with Amy than with Carol. Life is not so accommodating, though. You may not have the chance to spend as much time with Amy or with Beth as you would like, so you spend more time with Carol.

Another example of behavior that may not be completely logical is that animal rights activists may wear leather. This does not mean that they are insincere in their beliefs about the treatment of animals. It just indicates that trying to use strictly logical principles may not be effective in predicting human behavior.

Experience

Experience—A way of knowing that uses personal experience as the means of deciding what is true in life.

Belief: If a child ate a hot dog and got sick, he or she would likely avoid hot dogs in the future for fear of getting sick again. Everybody has probably had the experience of eating a particular food and later becoming ill, so that we associate the food with illness. This is such a powerful experience that when it happens, we develop a firm belief that we should not eat that food. Such a feeling is remarkably resistant to change; we don't eat a food, even though we might know that the food is usually safe.

We probably persist in not eating the food because our bodies have developed the strategy to avoid foods that lead to sickness. Animal pests, like rats, are very good at drawing the same conclusion about food and illness, leading to a phenomenon called "bait shyness." If we put out poisoned food, they will sample a little of it. If they get sick, they will avoid that food in the future. This is a wise decision for the animals, even if it frustrates people.

Experience can lead us to an erroneous conclusion about a certain food. Coming up with a general belief based on a single episode is not a very effective way to gain knowledge. Single episodes may not represent reality in general. We might have great confidence in our beliefs based on experience, but confidence does not equate with truth.

The Scientific Method

Scientific Method—An way of knowing that relies on data collection to generate ideas of what is likely to be true.

Empirical Approach— The method of discovery that relies on systematic observation and data collection for guidance on drawing conclusions.

Belief: If a person is exposed to a seriously traumatic event (like the Oklahoma City bombing), the person will recover better if he or she talks about it to a therapist rather than trying to ignore it. Psychologists believe that the best way to understand how people actually behave is to study behavior. The implication of the scientific approach is that we should not accept statements about people's actions based on what seems to be obvious, what authority figures have told us, or what seems logical on a personal level. Instead, we need to adopt an **empirical approach,** which means that we make observations and gather information directly. Scientists often say that they "collect data." This means exactly the same thing as "gather information."

The main advantage of this approach is that we can develop confidence regarding our factual knowledge. We could never be entirely certain that a fact is really true until we tested it in every possible situation, which is impossible. So we rely on making our best judgments with incomplete information. The scientific approach leads to confidence in our knowledge, even though what we believe to be true may change in the future when we get more complete information.

The notion that people feel better when they talk about traumatic events has not always been accepted. In fact, many people probably still believe that we should not "dwell on" traumatic events; rather we should try to forget them. In many cases, this advice results in more negative outcomes. As North et al. (1999) reported, failure to deal with trauma is a predictor of later psychiatric problems.

Yule and Canterbury (1994) discussed the treatment of post-traumatic stress disorder in children from an empirical standpoint. Based on the data they collected, they concluded that it is often better for children to talk about the trauma in a therapeutic context. The prognosis for best recovery occurs when children are allowed to explore their feelings in a safe, therapeutic setting, which is not the same as "dwelling on" the trauma.

The scientific approach to studying behavior has been instrumental in the advances we have made in the study of people. The particular methods available to us today include a wide range of techniques. Helping you understand these techniques is the goal of this book and of your research methods course.

Table 1.2 portrays the different ways of knowing and the problems associated with them. As you can see, the scientific approach is not flawless, but at this

TABLE 1.2 Examples of different bases for knowing and limitations associated with them.

	EXAMPLE OF THE WAY OF KNOWING	LIMITATIONS TO THIS WAY OF KNOWING
Tenacity or Intuition	If you don't wear a coat in the winter, you will catch a cold.	Two events might be related in time, but not because one causes another. In addition, people often ignore contradictory evidence.
Authority	Your parents tell you that if you don't wear your coat, you will get sick.	Authority figures are not always right. They may have areas in which they are usually correct, but they aren't infallible.
A Priori Method or Logic	People will not knowingly ingest poisons. People know that tobacco contains nicotine, which is a poison. Therefore, they will not smoke.	People's behaviors may show a degree of consistency, or internal logic, but that logic is not always apparent from the outside. Rather than acting on the basis of logic, people use "psycho-logic"; that is, our behavior is determined by psychological factors, not strictly logical factors.
Experience	You eat something, then get sick. You don't know it, but you were coming down with something. You avoid that food in the future because the thought of eating it turns your stomach.	The negative experience is an isolated event and may never happen again. The effect of the food is not general but your very negative experience affects your behavior.
Scientific Method	Students learn better when they spread their studying out over time, rather than simply cramming in one long session.	Scientific approaches are limited to domains where relevant ideas can be quantified and objectively observed. Further, there is always uncertainty in measurement, even though we can build up confidence in our measurements over time.

point it seems to lead to better information for understanding behavior than any of the others.

DISCUSSION QUESTIONS

1. Describe the five ways of knowing described by the philosopher Charles Sander Peirce. Give an example of each one.
2. For what types of questions would appeals to authority be better than appeals to scientific procedure?
3. Why would tenacity be a useful way of knowing in some cases, but not in others?
4. When might the scientific method be less desirable for knowing than relying on authority?

THE INTERACTION OF SCIENCE AND CULTURE

Many people undoubtedly think of science as happening in laboratories remote from the lives of real people. Nothing could be farther from the truth. Scientists live in communities and go to the same movies you do, coach their children's soccer teams, and worry about the same things that you do. Not surprisingly, culture shapes the research conducted by many scientists because our culture shapes the way we think.

For example, after the terrorist attacks in the United States, some person or persons sent anthrax spores through the mail, infecting a number of people and killing some of them. This spurred increased scientific attention to anthrax.

In addition, when there is an energy crisis, researchers in physics and chemistry are motivated to study the development, use, and conservation of energy. When environmental issues loom, those in the natural sciences may be predisposed to focus on ecological issues. With the AIDS crisis, medical researchers have often concentrated on issues related to it. Psychologists are as much a part of the community as anyone, so it should come as no surprise that our research reflects the needs and concerns of our society.

Discussion of research ideas are also affected by social attitudes. After Thornhill and Palmer (2000) proposed their evolutionary suggestions about rape in *The Sciences* (discussed in Controversy Box 1), the consequent letters to the editor took an overwhelmingly negative tone (Jennings, 2000; Müller, 2000; Steinberg, Tooney, Sutton, & Denmark, 2000; Tang-Martínez & Mechanic, 2000).

Can it be that not a single scientist, or even any reader of *The Sciences*, supports Thornhill and Palmer's ideas? It is more likely that people have refrained from writing letters in support of the evolutionary argument because they know that a great many people will take them to task for it. We can easily imagine that fear of reprisal might lead some people to avoid conducting research in the area. As such, research that might clarify the issue may never take place because nobody is willing to pursue it.

The Government's Role in Science

Societal issues often dictate scientific research, in part because of the way money is allocated for research. The federal government funds a great deal of the research that occurs in colleges and universities, where most scientific developments occur. As such, the government plays a large role in determining what kind of research takes place. How does the government decide which areas of research should have priority in funding? Ultimately, the decision-makers pay attention to issues of pressing importance to taxpayers. This view simplifies the dynamics of how federal money is allocated for research, but the ultimate point to remember is that even in the so-called pure and abstract sciences, societal demands affect the types of questions that scientists ask. If researchers do not get funding for asking one question, they will ask a different question for which they can receive financial support.

In the United States, the federal government actively directs some scientific research. For instance, the highly secretive National Security Agency employs more mathematicians than any other organization in the world (Singh, 1999). These people work on finding ways to create and break secret codes that affect political, economic, and military activities. Each mathematician who researches the use of codes does so because the government encourages it.

Further, the U.S. government has affected social research indirectly, sometimes through questionable means. Harris (1980) noted that beginning in the 1930s, the Federal Bureau of Investigation (FBI) engaged in surveillance and kept files on the American Psychological Association (APA) and the Society for the Psychological Study of Social Issues, now a division of APA. The FBI used informants who reported on colleagues. One incident that Harris cited involved an individual who informed on a colleague who had spoken out against racism at the 1969 APA convention. The result of such activities by the government, according to Harris, may have been to lead psychologists to abandon some lines of research (e.g., on racial attitudes) because they were too controversial.

Cultural Values and Science

Even when governmental interference is not an issue, there are still cultural aspects to our research. For example, some people feel strongly that a woman should remain at home raising her children rather than taking them to a daycare center. An examination of the amount of research effort devoted to the effects of childcare outside the home reveals that few behavioral scientists showed much interest in the question until the past decade or so. In fact, a search through the primary psychological database on research, PsycINFO©, reveals that the first citation with the term "childcare" in the abstract did not occur until 1927; for a long time, the use of that term was often associated with orphanages. In the early 1900s, the issue of the value of childcare was nonexistent. Work then was more likely to center around the home, and the primary caregivers, the mothers, were less likely to work outside the home. Thus, the issue of the effects of childcare centers on the development of children was irrelevant to society.

In contemporary life, women's work has moved from inside the home to outside, and there are more single parents who must have paying jobs. The increase in research on the effects of childcare centers has become important to many people, including psychologists, spurring an increase in psychological research on the topic. The issues are complex, and different researchers have generated conflicting results, so we still see considerable controversy surrounding the topic. Until the issue is resolved, this important societal concern will receive continued attention.

Because scientists are members of society, they share society's values. This means that they have the same kinds of biases we all do.

Cross-Cultural Issues and Science

Another example of the effect of culture on research involves a commonly used technique to assess attitudes and opinions. Psychologists regularly ask people to rate something on a scale of one to seven. (Technically, this is called a Likert-type scale, named after the American psychologist Rensis Likert, who pioneered this popular technique.) The use of such a scale may not be appropriate for people in cultures different than ours because it calls for a certain mindset that others don't share with us (Carr, Munro, & Bishop, 1995). People in non-Western cultures may not think it makes sense to assess a complex concept on a simple rating scale. We tend to assume that others think as we do, but such an assumption may lead to research results that lack validity. Greater numbers of psychologists are addressing these concerns and focusing more systematically on cultural issues in research (see Matsumoto, 1994; Price & Crapo, 1999).

A person's culture determines not only what behaviors are of interest, but how those behaviors are studied. Cultural perspective also influences how scientists interpret their data. An interesting example of the way that societal topics affect research occurred as Hugo Münsterberg (1914) decided to study whether women should be allowed to participate on juries. In the early 1900s, the topic was controversial. Some people thought that women wouldn't do as good a job on a jury as men did. Controversy Box 1.2 presents the issues, which were important a century ago but irrelevant now.

DISCUSSION QUESTIONS
1. How has the government affected the nature of psychological research in the United States?
2. When dealing with questions of behavior, thought, and attitude, why do researchers need to consider the effects of culture both in the way they set up their studies and the way they interpret them?

SCIENCE AND THE POPULAR MEDIA

Most people get their news about scientific research through popular media rather than from technical journals. There are some advantages to this pattern. One of them is that journalists tend to be better communicators than scientists. On the other hand, journalists are usually not trained in science. As a result, they often are not aware of the complexity of the issues that scientists investigate. So the journalists may miss important points, including the limitations of the research. The combination of science and journalism can result in an uncomfortable mix because, although the journalistic reports sound good, they may not convey accurately how the research was done, why the scientists took the approach they did, or the implications and limitations of the research.

■ ■ ■ ■ ■ ▬▬▬▬▬

CONTROVERSY BOX 1.2
CONTROVERSY: Should Women Serve as Jurors?

Psychologists are affected by the times in which they work. Their research ideas reflect the social milieu. This point is important here because the research that people view as important in one time may not carry over to another era. For instance, in the first decade of the twentieth century, Hugo Münsterberg, one of the most prominent psychologists in the United States, reported the results of investigations of the question of whether women show the appropriate mental processes that would allow them to take part in jury deliberations (Münsterberg, 1914).

He presented a group of men and a group of women a pair of displays that had different numbers of dots and asked them to vote on which display contained more dots. After a group debate of the issue, they voted again.

What does this simple procedure have to do with the way trials are conducted and whether women should serve as jurors during those trials? According to Münsterberg (1914), the psychologist studies "thoughts and emotions and feelings and deeds which move our social world. But . . . he must simplify them and bring them down to the most elementary situations, in which only the characteristic mental actions are left" (pp. 186–187). As a researcher you need to simplify complex situations so you can study each important issue individually, without being affected by complicating factors. We still do this today in psychological research; in fact, scientists in every discipline do this because reality is too complex to be studied in its fullest extent in a single study.

In Münsterberg's research, at a final vote, the percentage accuracy for the men went from guessing (52%) to reasonably accurate (78%). Women, on the other hand, began at 45 percent correct and stayed unimproved at 45 percent.

Münsterberg concluded that women were too stubborn to benefit from group discussions; they would not change their minds when confronted with evidence. He asserted that the difference in the way men and women respond to debate "makes the men fit and the women unfit for the particular task which society requires from the jurymen" (p. 198). When he published his conclusions, quite a number of people argued against them, including many women.

A few years later, another psychologist, Harold Burtt (1920) conceptually replicated Münsterberg's study. Burtt asked women and men to try to detect when people were lying to them in a laboratory study involving simulated trial witnesses. The participants then discussed the veracity of the witness and decided again. Burtt found that men and women were equally proficient in their ability to use debate to arrive at a reasonable conclusions.

Burtt's conclusion was that women were as suitable for jury work as men were. In fact, he reported that men were more willing to attribute lies to simulated witnesses who were actually telling the truth. Does this suggest that women are more appropriate for jury deliberation than men are? Because our society holds men in such high regard, the research that might answer this question might never be done.

It is interesting and important to be aware that neither Münsterberg nor Burtt ever hinted that they should ask the question of whether men should sit on juries. This is an important fact because it reveals that the social environment influences what questions are asked as well as what questions are *not* asked.

Do you believe that research projects like those of Münsterberg and Burtt could contribute answers to social questions? Should we conclude that women are unfit for jury duty? If we intend to use our research to help answer real life problems, we need to remember that no single experiment is going to answer a complex social question, but each one provides a small part of the answer. Our decisions will be better if we base them on sound research, but we also need to remember that we have to evaluate the research to see if it adequately answers the questions we are asking.

Psychological Terminology in Everyday Use

This problem is exacerbated in behavioral research because we use scientific words in describing our research, but nonscientists may use those same words very differently. For instance, as scientists, when we say that one variable correlates with another, we simply mean that there is a relationship; we do not mean that there is a causal relationship. Sometimes we can make predictions even when we do not know *why* they are accurate. One of the first lessons that researchers learn is that correlation does not mean causation. In everyday language, however, people tend to view correlations as suggesting that one factor causes another.

Another commonly used term is "negative reinforcement." Many people think that negative reinforcement is the same as punishment. In psychology, we use it differently than the general public does. The word *negative* reflects the fact that in this type of reinforcement, there is a negative situation that ends when some behavior occurs. Technically, if we use negative reinforcement, we expect some behavior to increase in frequency; if we use punishment, we expect the behavior to decline in frequency. Some examples of the inappropriate use of negative reinforcement as found on the World Wide Web appear in Table 1.3.

Misinterpretations of Research in the Media

In the popular media, it is possible for a journalist to misunderstand the concepts involved in the research. For example, a number of prominent newspapers including *The Washington Post, USA Today, The New York Times,* and *The Los Angeles Times* reported that physicians referred blacks and women only 60 percent as often as whites and men for certain heart-related treatments. Such a pattern of referrals would be entirely unacceptable if it were true. As it turns out, this 60 percent figure is simply wrong. It emerged because scientists are sometimes not very good at conveying their ideas in everyday language and because journalists can misunderstand the scientific words they are reading.

This miscommunication arose because the researchers who published their findings used a complicated statistical approach involving odds ratios. This is perfectly appropriate for publishing their results in *The New England Journal of Medicine,* which they did. Unfortunately, the *Journal* used the term "odds ratio" in a summary of the research, which journalists interpreted as "risk ratio." A risk ratio is a very different concept. Further, a university at which one of the researchers worked issued a misleading press release. The actual results of the study revealed that black women (but not black men) were only 87 percent as likely to be referred for the treatment in question than were men of both races and white women (Greenstein, 1999). It is still distressing that physicians do not treat black women the same as others in this regard, but the actual results of the research differed greatly from those reported in the media.

Erroneous Beliefs

Sometimes, people refer to research that is simply wrong. For instance, in the 2000 presidential election in the United States, the Republican party, on behalf of candidate

TABLE 1.3   Examples of the inappropriate use of the concept of negative reinforcement found on the World Wide Web.

SOURCE	STATEMENTS SHOWING INAPPROPRIATE USE
Burn the schools—Save the children http://www.cat.org.au/aprop/burn.txt	Comparisons of schools and prisons Negative reinforcement in prison—solitary confinement. Negative reinforcement in schools—suspension, detention, low grades.
http://www-psych.stir.ac.uk/documents/ 4612/learning/l2/punish.html	Skinner worried about widespread negative reinforcement in society. 1. Less effective than reinforcement—doesn't say what to do. 2. Habit-forming in punisher.
Management of Temper Tantrums http://www.jaicf.org/pedbase/temperta.htm	Negative Reinforcement: Do not respond by giving the child what they want.
http://www.healthypet.com/FAQ/ behavior-4.html	Behavior: My puppy likes to bite me when we play. How can I teach him to play without biting or scratching? Answer: You can work at solving your puppy's biting problem by doing several things simultaneously. [Y]ou provide a negative reinforcement for the objectionable behavior. You can do this by painting your skin with vinegar in the vulnerable places you know the puppy will bite.
Eden Prairie Girls Athletic Association Softball http://www.e-p.org/epgaawebsite/html/ playing_time.html	Positive reinforcement is an absolute necessity as new positions and skills are developed. Coaches must strive to avoid negative reinforcement. *Note: When a girl learns to hit the ball, the negative state of feeling bad goes away. This involves negative reinforcement. If a coach belittles a player until she learns to hit consistently, this would also constitute negative reinforcement.*

George W. Bush, aired a television commercial in which the negative word "rats" was embedded in such a way that it was on screen for too brief a period to be clearly seen. One might conclude that the Republicans were using subliminal perception to influence voters.

Most psychologists discount the notion that stimuli that we can't see will affect our behavior. One problem is that the initial reports of the effect of subliminal research were made up; the research was not actually done. Psychologists who have attempted experiments on subliminal perception have had limited success in documenting it.

The important point here is that people in general, including those in the media, are likely to lend credibility to the subliminal perception research when most psychologists minimize the potential for behavioral manipulation through stimuli that a person cannot see or hear. The media will focus on this topic because it is sensational, sexy, and scary, all of which capture public interest and improve ratings.

Scientific "Breakthroughs"

Another aspect of media coverage of scientific research involves the notion of "breakthroughs." This term suggests that an investigator completed one study and found something radically different from anything that had come before. This has unfortunate implications for the way people think about research. Too often, students beginning a research project assume that they can plan a single study that will go significantly beyond past work. The truth is that researchers virtually never complete a single study that starts a revolution. What happens is that they begin a research program that inches forward one study at a time. After sufficient, painstaking research, the scientist feels confident enough to proclaim something new and different. This proclamation is new and different for most people, but the experts in the field are probably not unduly surprised because they may have taken part in this slow progress toward new ideas.

What does all of this mean for us when we read about research in the popular media? It means that we must be cautious in accepting the details reported. Most of the time, the journalists get the major points right, but sometimes there are problems, especially when the research is complex. Further, journalists typically do not have the training to be able to evaluate possible sources of experimental error. In a number of highly visible cases, the initial glowing reports of some scientific "breakthroughs" have turned out not to be reliable; unfortunately, retractions of reports in the popular media seldom receive much prominence. The moral here is that serious scientists will read original research reports rather than relying on summaries by nonscientists.

DISCUSSION QUESTION
1. Why should we be skeptical of the reporting of scientific results in the popular media?

SCIENCE AND PSEUDOSCIENCE

Do you believe in ESP? Do you believe in extraterrestrial aliens and that they have kidnaped unwary earthlings and taken them to spaceships? Do you believe in ghosts? Surveys have revealed that a great number of Americans believe in these things. If you look at Figure 1.1, you will see the disconnect between the general public and scientists. Why do so many people lend credibility to these ideas when the majority of scientists who have studied these things have found essentially no support for them? A number of years ago the magician James Randi (whose stage name is The Amazing Randi) issued a challenge that he would award $1,000,000 to anybody who could demonstrate paranormal phenomena that he could not successfully disprove through rigorous testing. To date, nobody has been able to do so, although some people have tried.

Most scientists reject the notion that paranormal phenomena exist. The most notable reason for scientific skepticism is that, under controlled conditions, the evi-

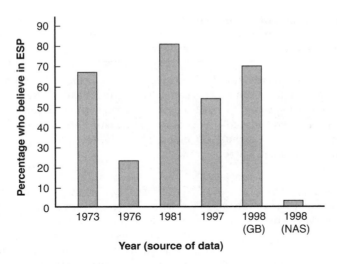

FIGURE 1.1   Percentage of respondents who claim to believe in some kind of paranormal phenomena in different studies over the years.

Sources:

[a]1973 and 1998 (GB): Radford, 1998, nonrandom samples from Great Britain

[b]1976 and 1997: Nisbet, 1998, random samples from the United States

[c]1981: Singer and Benassi, 1981, random samples from the United States

[d]1998 (NAS), sample of members of the National Academy of Sciences in the United States

dence for phenomena like ESP or mental telepathy remarkably disappear. Before we do the research, we should have an open mind about the issue, but we need to remember that one of the important elements of the scientific approach is falsifiability. If people who hold beliefs are unwilling to abandon them in the face of contrary evidence, their beliefs are not scientifically based.

Another basis for rejection of paranormal phenomena is that most of the explanations offered for such events are inconsistent with the physical laws that have so reliably produced the technological achievements that we will work with daily.

From the viewpoint of many psychologists, the term "parapsychology" is seen as unfortunate because it links our scientifically oriented discipline with **pseudoscience.** We regard a discipline as pseudoscientific when it claims that its knowledge derives from scientific research but fails to follow the basic principles of science.

Many scientists have worked to dispel pseudoscientific myths (e.g., Radner & Radner, 1982; Zusne & Jones, 1989), as have other critical thinkers, like James Randi. There are also publications that foster critical thinking about such issues, like *The Skeptical Inquirer.* This periodical exists to examine and debunk claims of paranormal phenomena. When scrutinized, these claims don't hold up well. Table 1.4 reflects some of the major characteristics of pseudoscience.

> **Pseudoscience**—A domain of inquiry that has the superficial appearance of being scientific but which does not rely on the critical scientific principles of objectivity, verifiability, empiricism, and being public.

TABLE 1.4   Characteristics of pseudoscience.

GENERAL CHARACTERISTICS	EXAMPLE
Pseudoscientists believe that there is no more to be learned; they fail to generate testable hypotheses or to conduct objective tests of theory. There tends to be no advancement of knowledge in the field, which is resistant to change. There are few tests of previous claims.	Homeopathic medicine makes claims about cures that are not based on research. The ideas never change and believers do not conduct systematic tests that would disconfirm their ideas.
Pseudoscience is based on dogma and uncritical belief; there may be hostility in the face of counterevidence or disagreement.	Creationism is accepted by some as a matter of faith. There is no attempt to subject its tenets to scientific scrutiny. In addition, when disagreements arise, believers often show antagonism toward the individual without dealing with the evidence.
There is a suppression of or distortion of unfavorable data; selective use of data, including looking only for supportive information (confirmation bias).	People who believe that psychics can foretell the future will accept just about any statement that seems correct but will ignore errors in predictions.
Many ideas are not amenable to scientific evaluation; ideas are subjective and can't be tested objectively.	There have been claims that we have an undetectable aura surrounding us. If it is undetectable, there is no way to verify its presence.
There is an acceptance of proof with data of questionable validity; the lack of evidence is taken as support that a claim *could* be true.	Some people conclude that there is evidence for the existence of UFOs on the basis of anecdotal reports in the popular media or ancient myths. There is little or no independent evaluation of ideas, but more a reliance on questionable evidence that is not questioned.
Personal anecdotes and events that cannot be tested systematically are used to provide evidence; there is often a reliance on "experts" with no real expertise.	Anybody who claims an experience about foretelling the future or who relates a supposed experience with aliens becomes an expert whose statements are not to be questioned.
Pseudoscience involves terms that sound like scientific ideas, but the terms are not clearly defined. Often the ideas violate known scientific principles.	Varieties of extrasensory perception include phenomena like *telekinesis*, which sounds scientific. In reality, it is a poorly defined (and undocumented) notion. Paranormal phenomena do not conform to known physical laws, such as the fact that for all known forms of energy, the force exerted declines over distance, which is not the case for ESP, according to its adherents.

TABLE 1.4   Continued

GENERAL CHARACTERISTICS	EXAMPLE
Pseudoscientific phenomena are "shy" or "fragile" in that they often disappear or weaken noticeably when subjected to well-designed experiments, especially with nonbelievers.	The ability to identify stimuli that are not visible is sometimes striking when two believers conduct a study; when independent scientists conduct the study, the effect is often attenuated or eliminated.
Pseudoscience involves looking for mysteries that have occurred rather than trying to generate and test explanations for the phenomena.	Sometimes people solicit incidents from people that seem unusual. For instance, mystery hunters might look for instances when a person seems to have foretold the future in a dream, ignoring the fact that if you look at enough dreams, you can find coincidental patterns that resist normal explanations.
Pseudoscientists engage in explanation by scenario. They identify a phenomenon and provide an explanation that fits the facts after they are known, but doesn't provide a means for making predictions in advance.	Some years ago, Julian Jaynes suggested that, historically, the two hemispheres in the human brain were not connected as they are now. Thus, brain activity in the right hemisphere was perceived to be the voices of gods. Unfortunately for this explanation, there is no credible evidence that it is true. In fact, given what we know about evolution, there is no realistic way that our brains could have evolved as Jaynes suggested.

In general, pseudosciences are characterized by a reliance on flimsy and questionable evidence, a resistance to change or further development of theory, a lack of ways to test the ideas, avoidance of contradictory information, and a lack of critical thought about ways to develop the theory.

DISCUSSION QUESTIONS
1. Why do most scientists reject the idea that paranormal phenomena, like ESP, exist?
2. What is it about the lack of critical thinking of pseudoscientists that leads them to accept the existence of paranormal phenomena?

CHAPTER SUMMARY

Research exerts a large impact on our lives, so we are better off as citizens when we can examine research claims that people make. Knowing how to ask critical questions is also a useful skill in many other facets of our lives.

When psychologists engage in research, we do what other scientists do: We look for ways to describe behavior accurately, to establish a basis for predicting behavior, to explain why people act as they do, and ultimately to know how to control behavior. The best way to accomplish these goals is to study behavior scientifically.

Research is considered scientific when it conforms to certain game plans. Researchers strive to make objective measurements and to define precisely what they have done in their work. This allows others to evaluate the credibility of the research and to do further work to extend knowledge. After creating a research plan, psychologists collect data and draw conclusions from the data. We hope that when scientists make a claim, they can support their arguments based on objective data, not on opinion.

Another critical component of scientific research is that it must be public. The knowledge we gain in research doesn't help us advance what we know unless researchers publicize their work, usually in the form of professional papers that appear in journals or in conference presentations attended by other scientists. Only by making clear statements about what research is all about and what discoveries the scientist has made can others verify the validity of the claims made by the investigator and attempt to reproduce those results in other research projects.

We rely on the scientific approach for the study of behavior because other ways of finding out about people's thoughts, feelings, and acts are not as reliable. Sometimes we can use intuition to understand the world around us, but too often intuition leads to poor judgments. Similarly, we can ask people who are authority figures; unfortunately, they are like the rest of us—sometimes they make mistakes. We can also use logic, but all of us know that people's behaviors often don't seem to follow any logic we can detect. Finally, all of us make judgments based on our own experience. The problem with using our own experiences is that they may not reflect general principles. These other ways of understanding the world have their place, but the systematic and scientific study of behavior provides us with the best overall picture of the human condition.

As researchers investigate human behavior, they gather information and collect data. This is often the easy part. The complex part is trying to interpret what the information means. People do research for reasons that relate to their social and cultural outlook, and they interpret their results from within their own cultural framework. Sometimes people disagree vigorously on how to interpret research in all of the scientific disciplines; this reflects that science is just another type of human activity.

After psychologists finish their research, news reporters may publicize it. We have to be careful of reports about science in the media because reporters are not always trained in science, so they may relay misinformation, or they may focus on easily understood and sensational elements of the work, which might divert attention from important aspects. One area that receives considerable attention in the press involves pseudoscientific areas like ESP that are not supported by the scientific research. Nonetheless, people still believe in paranormal phenomena, in large part because they don't consider them from the same viewpoint that scientific researchers have.

CHAPTER TWO

ETHICS IN RESEARCH: FOLLOWING THE GOLDEN RULE

CHAPTER OVERVIEW

CHAPTER PREVIEW

UNETHICAL RESEARCH PRACTICES—PAST AND PRESENT
Ethical Problems in the Early Years
of the Twentieth Century
Is It Still Happening Today?
*Ethical Problems in Psychiatric
Research*
Ethical Problems in Corporate Research

ETHICAL GUIDELINES CREATED BY THE AMERICAN PSYCHOLOGICAL ASSOCIATION
Aspirational Goals and
Enforceable Rules
Ethical Standards as They
Affect You

LEGAL REQUIREMENTS AND ETHICS IN RESEARCH
Institutional Review Boards

THE IMPORTANCE OF SOCIAL CONTEXT IN DECIDING ON ETHICS IN RESEARCH
Stanley Milgram's Research Project
on Obedience
The Ethical Issues
Criticisms of Milgram's Research
Milgram's Defense of His Research
The Social Context

CONTROVERSY: *Should Researchers Deceive Participants?*

WHAT YOU NEED TO DO IF YOUR RESEARCH INVOLVES DECEPTION
Some Research Requires Deception
The Effects of Debriefing on Research

ETHICS AND WEB-BASED RESEARCH

ETHICS AND RESEARCH WITH ANIMALS
Arguments and Counterarguments

CHAPTER SUMMARY

KEY TERMS

Active deception
Anonymity
Aspirational goals
Beneficence
Confidentiality
Cover story
Debriefing
Dehoaxing

Desensitization
Ethical standards
Fidelity
Institutional review board (IRB)
Integrity
Justice
Naturalistic observation
Nonmaleficence

Nuremberg code
Passive deception
Plagiarism
Respect for people's rights
and dignity
Responsibility
Role playing
Simulation

CHAPTER PREVIEW

Most psychological research poses little physical or psychological risk to participants. Nonetheless, because researchers in the past have conducted some notorious and some unethical projects, laws and guidelines have been developed for the protection of research participants. In addition, researchers have been known to make up data and even entire experiments and to misrepresent their data in published journal articles.

Researchers generally become very interested and excited in their programs of research. Sometimes this means that they focus very narrowly in their work and forget to consider the implications of what they are doing. In this chapter, you will see that investigators may get so caught up in their research that they may endanger the people who participate in their studies.

The American Psychological Association has developed a set of guidelines that has evolved over the past half century. Many researchers in disciplines other than psychology rely on these guidelines. We must also follow legal requirements that federal and state governments have enacted for the protection of human participants in research.

Students sometimes mistakenly believe that the APA approves or vetoes research. It would be impossible for any single organization to oversee as much research as psychologists conduct. Ethical supervision occurs under the oversight of Institutional Review Boards (IRBs) that evaluate proposed projects; this takes place in the colleges and universities where the research is carried out.

In discussing ethics in psychological research, the famous research of Stanley Milgram (1963) and Philip Zimbardo (1973) comes to mind. Milgram's research participants thought they were delivering electrical shocks to another person, often to the extent that the other person might have died. Zimbardo created a prison simulation that led participants, all of them students, to treat one another very brutally. This type of research is very rare in psychology, which is why the most illustrative examples arose over 30 years ago.

We can categorize research in two groups for our discussion. In one category, involving clinically based research, the result of ignoring ethical dictates is potentially very serious. People approach clinical psychologists because of problems that need to be resolved. If clinical research involves ethical problems, those people could be seriously harmed.

Our second category involves basic research in academic settings. Most psychological research has fairly minor risk-related implications for participants. Some psychological research can involve more than minimal risk, but most psychological research on topics like learning, motivation, social processes, and attitude change would virtually never lead to long-term, highly negative outcomes, no matter how incompetent or unethical the researcher. To decide whether a project is appropriate, we conduct a *cost-benefit analysis;* if the risk exceeds the benefit, we should not do the research; if the benefit exceeds the risk, the research may be acceptable. Before we conduct research, we need to assess the relative risk of the research compared to the benefits for two main reasons. First, it is the ethical and moral thing to do. Second, there are legal requirements that we do it. There has been an unfortunate history of abuse on the part of researchers; some of it is due to carelessness, some due to callousness, and some due to unconscionable social and governmental policies. We hope to avoid such problems in our research.

UNETHICAL RESEARCH PRACTICES—PAST AND PRESENT

Through the past century, shameful episodes of unethical research practices have occurred, in many cases leading to extreme suffering and death. The troublesome decisions made by researchers have led to the Nuremburg Code and to the various federal laws designed to protect people.

Among the most egregious examples include the investigations done by the Nazis during World War II. For example, according to Lifton (1986), the Nazi Carl Clauberg researched techniques for sterilizing women by injecting them with what was probably Formalin, which consists of formaldehyde and methanol (a kind of alcohol). Both substances are poisonous, and formaldehyde is an extreme irritant; survivors reported that the pain was excruciating.

Clauberg injected this substance into the women's cervix, with the aim of destroying the fallopian tubes that are necessary for carrying an egg to the uterus for implantation. This kind of research clearly reflects a pathological society that we want to believe could not happen anywhere else.

Ethical Problems in the Early Years of the Twentieth Century

As you will see, there have been violations in medical and psychiatric research that go beyond the bounds of good judgment and indicate a callous, sometimes horrific disregard for a person's right to be treated with dignity and fairness. The Nazis did not corner the market on horrific research. Beginning in the 1930s and continuing for the following 30 years, researchers at the Tuskegee Institute in the United States purposely withheld treatment from black patients in order to study the progress of syphilis. It is true that when the study began, knowledge of the specific course of the disease and of effective treatment was minimal, but within a short period of time, the evidence was clear that lack of treatment was devastating. Syphilis can lead to blindness, organically caused psychosis, and results in death. The negative effects on its patients were all too clear decades before the research ceased, and the research continued after treatment with penicillin was standard practice.

A recent report (Research Ethics and the Medical Profession, 1996) has documented a number of problematic studies that occurred during the 1950s and 1960s in the United States. In many cases, the guidelines that had existed regarding informed consent and voluntary participation were ignored.

As an example, researchers at the University of Cincinnati, in conjunction with the U.S. military, wanted to find out how much radiation military personnel could endure in battle and still function. When we hear about such research goals, we might agree that such knowledge would be useful. The problem lies with the means that the researchers adopted for their work. To generate a partial answer, the investigators subjected uninformed, terminally ill cancer patients to whole-body radiation to see how it affected those people (Rothman, 1994).

Further, in separate projects in the decades after World War II, researchers at the Massachusetts Institute of Technology (funded by the National Institutes of Health, The Atomic Energy Commission, and the Quaker Oats Company), and investigators at Harvard Medical School, Massachusetts General Hospital, and Boston University School of Medicine administered radioactive substances to mentally retarded children living in facilities for the developmentally disabled (ACHRE Report, n.d., available at http://tis.eh.doe.gov/ohre/roadmap/achre/chap7.html). There seems to have been no true informed consent. Parents knew that scientists involved their children in research, but not the fact that the children were ingesting radioactive food.

Such ethical breeches in medical research continued to occur into the 1960s and 1970s. For instance, pharmaceutical companies paid doctors to administer experimental drugs to patients. It is easy to see how patients would defer to their physicians' judgments; people tend to develop trust in their doctors and accept their expertise without question. As a result, there were serious limitations regarding informed consent and voluntary participation. Eventually, Congress created regulations to prevent physicians from abusing their relationships with patients.

Is It Still Happening Today?

Many of the episodes of the notorious research seem to come from the 1970s or earlier. Does this mean that we have solved the problems associated with unethical research practices? Or do ethical problems continue in research programs? Unfortunately, questionable practices still exist.

For example, dozens of experiments with human participants came to a halt at Duke University Medical Center in 1999 when the federal government discovered ethical lapses in the research. One development occurred with a participant in a NASA-sponsored study who underwent testing in a chamber designed to simulate the pressure that you would feel at 30,000 feet above sea level. The man began to lose sensation in his limbs and, after treatment, became semi-conscious. On the positive side of the ledger, as soon as this rare and unexpected problem occurred, NASA terminated the study; on the negative side, some ethicists questioned whether the project's risks had been adequately studied and whether the participant had received appropriate informed consent (Hilts & Stolberg, 1999).

In addition, the U.S. federal government's Office of Research Integrity investigates claims of scientific misconduct in research associated with federal grants. In 2001 and 2002, the office concluded that eleven researchers were guilty of misconduct related to data collection, analysis, and presentation. Although such fraud is very troublesome, the number of cases identified by the government is relatively small. Naturally, we don't know how often fraud goes undetected. The offenses included (in order of frequency of occurrence):

- Falsifying or fabricating data
- Publishing figures designed to mislead the reader
- Plagiarizing by claiming that another researcher's data were the offender's own data

- Departing from the protocol for randomizing assignment of participants to groups in ways that might affect the outcome
- Stating incorrect times of data collection in research where timing was important
- Completely fabricating three experiments published in a journal (Office of Research Integrity, n.d.)

Ethical Problems in Psychiatric Research.   In addition, in 1999 the National Institutes of Health reported a series of serious ethical violations at Mount Sinai Medical School. Researchers there stopped giving psychiatric patients their antipsychotic medications and then administered L-dopa, a precursor to the neurotransmitter dopamine, which leads to psychosis in the mentally ill.

We can seriously wonder whether these patients could really give informed consent, signifying that they understood what would happen and then consenting to it (Birnbaum & Montero, 1999). One of the momentous ethical dilemmas in such investigations is that patients may be put at risk when they participate in research that is not part of their treatment. Even when a patient's guardian is called on to make a decision, there is no guarantee that the guardian will be able to make the best decision regarding treatment of the patient.

Additional research came under federal scrutiny in 1999. The government ordered research at the Los Angeles Veterans' Administration hospitals stopped because patients had not been sufficiently protected from risks. The government order brought more than 1,000 projects to a halt (White, 1999). Clearly, we haven't halted all ethical lapses.

Ethical Problems in Corporate Research.   Decades ago Congress took action because physicians were conducting research for pharmaceutical companies, unbeknownst to their patients. The federal legislation was supposed to have put a stop to the practice. Unfortunately, history has a way of repeating itself. The *New York Times* reported that one particular physician, Peter Arcan, recommended to a patient that he (the patient) might want to join a study of a new drug to shrink enlarged prostates. Suspiciously, the patient did not have an enlarged prostate gland. The doctor insisted that the drug might prevent future problems, so the patient agreed.

In reality, the pharmaceutical company, SmithKline Beecham PLC, paid the doctor over $1,600 for each patient enrolled in the study. In addition, physicians sometimes receive highly coveted authorship on published research papers merely for recruiting enough patients. This pattern seems to have involved hundreds of thousands of patients, according to the *Times* (Eichenwald & Kolata, 1999).

Further, sometimes the drug companies employ physicians to do research in areas outside their realm of expertise. Eichenwald and Kolata reported, for example, that asthma specialists have dispensed experimental psychiatric drugs, while psychiatrists have investigated Pap smears, which are gynecological tests. There seem to be a number of physicians involved who possess little knowledge of or training in research.

Most of the research associated with such problems has been biomedical in nature. The risks associated with it may involve life and death issues. Your research in psychology is likely to have less impact. It is important to remember, though, that the behavioral research you complete also has to conform to certain ethical principles and is bound by the same laws that professional researchers must follow.

DISCUSSION QUESTIONS

1. Identify and describe two examples of unethical biomedical research that has taken place in the United States.
2. Why are ethical issues in psychiatric research so difficult to deal with?

ETHICAL GUIDELINES CREATED BY THE AMERICAN PSYCHOLOGICAL ASSOCIATION

Researchers are not exempt from some of the same lapses in good judgment that beset the rest of the population. In psychology, we are fortunate that the serious breaches of ethics are rare.

Long before the general public learned of the excesses of some researchers, the American Psychological Association had formulated a set of principles that would guide psychologists in their work. We will discuss primarily those guidelines that relate to research, although APA's guidelines pertain to all areas of psychological work, including therapy. The principles associated with ethics in providing psychotherapy are vitally important in the therapeutic realm, but are of less interest to us here. When the two worlds of therapy and research merge, psychologists must attend carefully to the ethical guidelines both for therapy and for research. This is an especially difficult area, because it is not always clear that psychiatric patients are able to make informed decisions about participating because they may be unable to understand the implications of their participation.

The first set of APA's ethical principles appeared in 1953, the most recent in 2002, and they continue to be refined. As stated in a recent version, psychologists should incorporate the rules as an integral part of their professional lives. "The development of a dynamic set of ethical standards for a psychologist's work-related conduct requires a personal commitment to a lifelong effort to act ethically" (American Psychological Association, 1992, p. 1599).

> **Aspirational Goals**— General set of ethical principles that guide psychologists in their research and other professional activities.
>
> **Ethical Standards**—A set of enforceable rules created by the American Psychological Association and by legal authorities that relate to moral values of right and wrong.

The General Principles espoused in the standards reflect "**aspirational goals** to guide psychologists toward the highest ideals of psychology" (p. 1598), whereas the **Ethical Standards** proffer enforceable rules of conduct. When psychologists violate these rules, they face possible loss of certification to work in their field of expertise. Such offenses are relatively rare and, when they occur, generally involve the areas of clinical and counseling psychology rather than research. Every year a small number of psychologists suffer such action for their violations of the ethical guidelines. Fortunately, most psychologists, like most of you, approach their work with integrity; the relatively small numbers that face censure are vastly outweighed by those whose work is creditable and valuable.

Aspirational Goals and Enforceable Rules

The six General Principles of the ethical guidelines appear in Table 2.1. As you look at them, you can see that the principles reflect the high moral character that we prize in

Beneficence and **Non-maleficence**—Acting to promote the welfare of the people a psychologists deals with (beneficence) and avoidance of harm to them (Nonmaleficence).

Fidelity and **Responsibility**—Psychologists must act professionally in ways that support the discipline of psychology and benefit their community, especially regarding the well-being of the people with whom they interact professionally.

Integrity—Psychologists should promote the honest and truthful application of the discipline in science, teaching, and practice.

Justice—Psychologists must recognize the implications of their professional activity on others and strive to make the best professional judgments they can.

Respect for People's Rights and Dignity—Psychologists must recognize the dignity and value of all people and, to the fullest extent possible, eliminate biases in dealing with people.

people around us. In part, (a) **beneficence and nonmaleficence** relates to maximizing the positive outcomes of your work and minimizing the chances of harm. Psychologists must also act with (b) **fidelity and responsibility** in dealing with others. Psychologists should also strive for (c) **integrity** in promoting themselves and their work accurately. As psychologists, we should also aspire to (d) **justice,** recognizing our biases and the limitations to our expertise as they affect others. Finally, we need to show (e) **respect for people's rights and dignity.**

We recognize that one of our goals is to promote human well-being. In addition, one of the critical aspects of such responsibility is that the public will lose faith in the work of psychologists and in the value of psychology if we don't act with the highest morals.

The enforceable ethical standards consist of ten categories related to different aspects of professional, psychological work. These standards are listed in Table 2.2. Of these categories, the one that pertains most to us here involves research.

(It probably never occurred to you, but if your professors are members of the American Psychological Association, they are ethically bound to educate and train you well. For example, the Ethical Principles of Psychologists [American Psychological Association, 2002] specify that psychology teachers make sure that syllabi are meaningful and that students be informed about grading procedures.)

As the ethical guidelines pertain to research, psychologists have certain responsibilities to provide research participants with informed consent, to minimize the use of deception in research, to report research results accurately, and to correct any errors in reporting. One further mandate is that researchers must be willing to share their data with other researchers, provided it does not violate the confidentiality promised to research participants.

There are a few areas that are of special relevance to researchers. You will have to consider them when you plan your own research because you must present a proposal to your school's IRB or to delegated representatives of that committee before you can carry out your proposed research. The committee members may approve your research as proposed, but they may require changes before you can begin. Depending on the nature of the regulations at your school, you may have to wait for a month or longer to receive permission. Your IRB will consider your research proposal based on the relevant state and federal regulations.

Ethical Standards as They Affect You

The General Principles developed by the American Psychological Association cover a wide range of psychological activities (see Table 2.1). At this point in your life, many of them will be completely irrelevant to you because you do not provide therapy for

TABLE 2.1   General ethical principles and examples of violations.

Beneficence and Nonmaleficence	A psychologist would be in dangerous territory in conducting research in which he or she has a financial interest because that interest could cloud professional judgment to the detriment of the participant and others. Further, psychologists who are aware that they are experiencing mental health problems may be acting unethically with clients if their own mental health may lead to poor judgment.
Fidelity and Responsibility	A psychologist would violate ethical principles by engaging in dual relationships with patients. One of the most notable transgressions occurs when a therapist engages in sexual relations with a person while providing therapy to that individual. Also a psychologist who knows that a colleague is engaging in unethical behavior would himself or herself be acting unethically by not taking steps to prevent further such behavior.
Integrity	Psychologists who intentionally misrepresent their research results or who falsify data are engaging in ethical misconduct because they are not striving to maximize gain to the scientific and professional community, but rather are simply trying for personal gain. In addition, psychologists who knowingly use their knowledge to mislead others, such as in courtroom testimony, are engaging in unethical conduct. In this case, they are not using their professional expertise responsibly or contributing to the welfare of society in general.
Justice	A psychologist who is not trained in the use of a test like the Minnesota Multiphasic Personality Inventory but who uses it in his or her research or with clients might be engaging in unethical behavior because the validity of test interpretations may be low.
Respect for People's Rights and Dignity	Psychologists who violate the confidentiality of their research participants act unethically. This means that if you are doing research, you may not discuss with others how a particular participant responded during a testing session. (Such a discussion could be appropriate, however, if you discuss a research session with a colleague who is also working on that project and you need to resolve a methodological problem.)

clients, engage in professional consultation, or perform psychological assessments. As a psychology student, however, you may carry out research projects, at which time the Principles will definitely apply to you.

Your research activity may not be ethically troublesome, but you need to avoid crossing the line into the realm of unethical behavior. The major points appearing in Table 2.2 do not exhaust the Principles; they merely highlight many of the points relevant to you. You should ultimately be aware of the American Psychological Association's Code of Conduct (Ethical Principles, 1992), as well as the relevant legal considerations. You should become familiar with the changes in ethical guidelines as they evolve.

TABLE 2.2   General standards of ethical behavior for psychologists.

SECTION 1—RESOLVING ETHICAL ISSUES

Psychologists need to recognize problematic ethical situations and work to resolve them on an individual level when possible. Sometimes it may be necessary to seek formal remedies to perceived unethical conduct. When there are legal issues that pose a conflict between ethical guidelines of psychologists and the law, the psychologist should work to minimize the conflict. When a conflict cannot be resolved, it may be appropriate to defer to legal authorities.

SECTION 2—BOUNDARIES OF COMPETENCE

Researchers, including you, may conduct research only within the boundaries of their competence. You need to pay attention to this, although most research you are likely to carry out will not be problematic. In certain circumstances, though, such as if you planned on using psychodiagnostic tests, you might be in a gray area because many such instruments require specialized training for adequate administration and interpretation. One potential problem is that you would expose your research participants to risk if you interpreted test results in a way that changed their behaviors for the worse.

SECTION 3—HUMAN RELATIONS

Psychologists must strive to minimize discrimination or harassment of people with whom they have a professional relationship. Exploitation of another by use of power or authority is unethical. For example, if a psychologist has power over others (e.g., a professor over a teaching or lab assistant, a resident assistant, etc.), he or she should take care not to coerce people when recruiting their participation for research. Psychologists should also avoid multiple relationships, one of the most egregious being sexual relationships with students or clients. Clients and research participants should also provide informed consent for research or therapy.

SECTION 4—PRIVACY AND CONFIDENTIALITY

You should not discuss the behavior or responses of research participants or clients with those outside your project or treatment setting if not seeking professional consultation. Your participants have a right to expect that their responses will be confidential and anonymous to the fullest extent possible.

SECTION 5—ADVERTISING AND OTHER PUBLIC STATEMENTS

Psychologists should not make fraudulent or misleading professional statements when presenting their work to the public. Nor should they misrepresent their professional expertise or credentials.

SECTION 6—RECORD KEEPING AND FEES

Psychologists must document their research and maintain their data so that they are available for legal or other reasons.

SECTION 7—TEACHING, TRAINING SUPERVISION, RESEARCH, AND PUBLISHING

Psychologists are responsible for competent education and training of students and for accurate descriptions of education and training programs. Teachers must avoid exploiting those over whom they have authority.

(continued)

TABLE 2.2   Continued

SECTION 8—RESEARCH AND PUBLICATION

Research must be approved by an IRB. Participants should give informed consent and be debriefed (dehoaxed and desensitized). In informed consent, you have to provide them with the following information:

- the nature of the research
- their right to decline to participate and to withdraw at any time without penalty
- the foreseeable consequences of their participation, such as risks, discomfort, etc.

Some research projects involving anonymous questionnaires, naturalistic observation, and some archival research do not require informed consent. If you think this applies to you, you need to check with your local IRB or its representatives. Table 2.4 provides relevant information about this.

Deception in research is acceptable only if other alternatives are not available or appropriate. Presentation of results should accurately reflect the data.

Psychologists must give appropriate credit to those involved in research but should not give credit to an individual whose work on the research was minimal.

SECTIONS 9 AND 10—ASSESSMENT AND THERAPY

Psychologists must use contemporary assessment and therapeutic techniques and the psychologists must be adequately trained to use them. This complex realm is most relevant to doctoral level psychologists who provide service to clients.

Debriefing—Informing research participants at the conclusion of a research project of the purpose of the research, including disclosure of any deception and providing an opportunity for participants to ask questions about the research.

Dehoaxing—The process of telling research participants of any deception or ruses used in a study.

Desensitization—The process of eliminating any negative aftereffects that a participant might experience after taking part in a project.

Anonymity—The practice of maintaining records so that nobody can identify which individual is associated with a certain set of data.

Among the most important practical issues you will face if you conduct research are those associated with informed consent, that is, making sure that your participants know what they are going to do and understand the nature of the research. In addition, you must provide **debriefing** in which you inform participants of any deception involved in the research, called **dehoaxing,** and you make sure that you eliminate any potential sources of negative feelings by the participants, called **desensitization.** If you think that there are likely to be any long-term consequences for your participants after they complete your research, you need to engage in compensatory followup, which means that you arrange for those problems to be remedied.

An additional requirement when you conduct research is that you must protect the **anonymity** and **confidentiality** of your research participants. It is desirable that, after a study is over, you cannot link a person's behavior in a research project with them personally. If there are no identifying characteristics in the data that allow you to know whose data you are examining, the data are anonymous. In some cases, you will not be able to separate a person's identify from the data. For example, if you are tracking people over time, you have to be able to link their current data with past data. In such a case, you need to make sure that nobody outside the research project has access to that information. When you do this, you are making sure that the data are confidential.

Confidentiality—The practice of making sure that nobody outside a research project has access to data that can be identified with a specific individual.

Plagiarism—An ethical breach in which a person claims credit for another person's idea or research.

Finally, when you develop research ideas or when you write up a report of your project, you must avoid claiming credit that belongs to others. When an investigator asserts that he or she came up with an idea, but that idea was really developed by another person, this is **plagiarism.** It is considered a very serious breach of ethics.

DISCUSSION QUESTION

1. Identify the five general principles in the American Psychological Association's ethics code regarding ethical conduct and the behaviors associated with them. Which ones would affect you as a student? How?

LEGAL REQUIREMENTS AND ETHICS IN RESEARCH

Nuremberg Code—A set of legal principles adopted by the international community after the Nazi atrocities in World War II to insure fair and ethical treatment of research participants.

Shortly after the Second World War, the international community recognized the need for laws concerning research with people. These laws are known as the **Nuremberg Code,** named for the German city where they were developed. The ten points of the Code appear in Table 2.3.

As you look at the Code, you might wonder why anybody had to enact such a code. All of the points seem to involve little but common sense. Unfortunately, the Nazi atrocities alerted people to risks to research subjects. The Nazis victimized many people in research; the Nuremberg code formalized a set of rules that could be used by researchers with integrity when they planned their studies that involve people.

Although most people would not come anywhere near the Nazi atrocities, the code is helpful because having a well-articulated set of principles to guide research might keep us from being blinded by our enthusiasm for our own research.

In addition to the internationally recognized Nuremberg Code, the U.S. government has also passed laws to protect human subjects. These procedures were initially implemented in 1966 and have evolved over time (Reynolds, 1982).

Institutional Review Boards

Institutional Review Board (IRB)—A committee that reviews research projects to make sure that the projects are in compliance with accepted ethical guidelines. An IRB is required for every institution receiving federal funding in the United States.

Changes in the regulations appear in the *Federal Register,* which reports on congressional activities of all kinds. One of the major provisions of the federal regulations mandates an **Institutional Review Board (IRB),** a committee that consists of at least five people, including a member of the community who is not a researcher. The IRB reviews research proposals for ethical problems and either approves or disapproves projects that investigators want to carry out. Although the official term for this group is the Institutional Review Board, people often refer to it as the Human Subjects Committee.

Most research must receive approval from an IRB, but there are exceptions, as listed in Table 2.4. (Federal regulations stipulate that an

TABLE 2.3   Ten points of the Nuremberg Code.

POINT	COMMENT
1. Research on humans absolutely requires informed consent.	You cannot do research on people who are not able to give voluntary, informed consent. This requires that they be sufficiently aware of their rights to be able to make a choice that is good for them. You are also not allowed to use undue influence or power you have over a person. The individual must know what risks might be involved.
2. The experiment must have the possibility of contributing to our body of knowledge.	You should not perform research that has no chance of being useful to society. This does not mean that an investigation has to produce major results, but the outcome should add to the accumulation of knowledge about human and nonhuman behavior.
3. Researchers should be informed about the topic they investigate to maximize the likelihood that the results will be useful.	Especially for biomedical research, scientists should design their research based on previous work that has been conducted using animals. In addition, the scientist must be competent enough to design a study whose results will justify the experimentation.
4. The experiment should avoid unnecessary physical and mental suffering.	Sometimes research by its nature involves discomfort of some kind (e.g., a study of sleep deprivation). Researchers should design their work to minimize the extent of the discomfort should it be necessary. Embarrassment and frustration are examples of mental suffering that might be associated with psychological research.
5. No experiment should be conducted if there is good reason to believe that death or serious injury will occur.	When an investigation involves high levels of potential risk, this restriction can be relaxed if the researchers serve as participants in this research.
6. The degree of risk must be less than the potential gain from the research.	Scientists must perform a cost-benefit analysis. If the costs exceed the potential benefits, the research is inappropriate.
7. Prior arrangements must be in place for responding to an emergency that occurs during a research project.	The investigators must make provisions for emergencies that they can reasonably foresee. Sometimes a participant may suffer harm because of an entirely unforeseen circumstance. In such a case, the researcher might not be seen as acting unethically. Points 2 and 3 relate to this—a researcher should be sufficiently well informed to know what risks are likely.
8. The investigator must have appropriate training to conduct the research.	Researchers have to know what they are doing. If a researcher fails to anticipate dangers that an expert would recognize in advance, that researcher might be judged as acting unethically. Researchers must also ensure that workers subordinate to them are qualified to carry out the tasks assigned to them.
9. Research participants must be free to terminate their involvement at any time.	When an individual has reached the point that he or she no longer feels comfortable participating in research, the person has the right to leave without penalty.
10. The experimenter must terminate a research project if he or she believes that continuing the study will lead to injury or death.	The investigator has to be aware of the dynamics of the research situation. If he or she recognizes that there is an elevated level of risk, the investigator must end the study.

TABLE 2.4 **Types of research most relevant to psychology that do not require approval by an institutional review board.**

In general, research activities in which the only involvement of human subjects will be in one or more of the four following categories are exempt from review by an IRB.

(1) Research conducted in established or commonly accepted educational settings, involving normal educational practices, such as
   (i) research on regular and special education instructional strategies, or
   (ii) research on the effectiveness of or the comparison among instructional techniques, curricula, or classroom management methods.

(2) Research involving the use of educational tests, survey procedures, interview procedures or observation of public behavior. The exemption does not hold (and IRB approval is required) if
   (i) information obtained is recorded in such a manner that human subjects can be identified, directly or through identifiers linked to the subjects; and
   (ii) any disclosure of the human subjects' responses outside the research could reasonably place the subjects at risk of criminal or civil liability or be damaging to the subjects' financial standing, employability, or reputation.

(3) Research involving the use of educational tests, survey procedures, interview procedures, or observation of public behavior is exempt as listed in paragraph (2) above; in addition, research is exempt from IRB approval if:
   (i) the human subjects are elected or appointed public officials or candidates for public office, or
   (ii) Federal statute(s) require(s) without exception that the confidentiality of the personally identifiable information will be maintained throughout the research and thereafter.

(4) Research involving the collection or study of existing, publicly available data, documents, records, pathological specimens, or diagnostic specimens; in addition, the research is exempt from IRB approval if the information is recorded by the investigator so that subjects cannot be identified, directly or through identifiers linked to the subjects.

IRB must document that research does not require formal review.) These exceptions exist because the experts who work for the government recognize that not all research carries significant risk. For example, you are allowed to conduct some survey research and simple observational research in a public area without IRB approval. The reason is that those you survey or observe do not experience greater risk because you are studying them when compared to the risks of everyday life. Survey research that probes sensitive issues may require IRB approval.

DISCUSSION QUESTIONS
1. Why is it a good idea to include nonresearchers as members of an Institutional Review Board?
2. What types of research can be exempt from Institutional Review Board (IRB) consideration, according to U.S. federal law? Do you think this research should be exempt?

THE IMPORTANCE OF SOCIAL CONTEXT
IN DECIDING ON ETHICS IN RESEARCH

Consider this: A participant volunteers to help with research. He is told that he will be in the role of the teacher, delivering electrical shocks to another person, also a volunteer, every time that person makes a mistake in a learning task. With each mistake, the strength of the shock will increase, up to a level on a panel marked "Danger: Severe Shock," followed by a mysterious higher level of shock simply labeled "XXX." The learner remarks that he has a heart condition, but the experimenter replies that it won't matter. The learner is strapped into a chair in another room and connected to the apparatus that will deliver the electrical shocks.

After the learner makes several mistakes and receives shocks, he demands to quit, but the experimenter simply says the experiment must continue. Shortly thereafter, the learner (who allegedly has a heart problem) becomes completely silent, but the researcher encourages the teacher to continue to deliver electrical shocks if the learner doesn't respond because a nonresponse is the same as a wrong answer.

Stanley Milgram's Research Project on Obedience

Suppose you were the participant. Would you continue shocking the learner? Or would you stop? If you were like the majority of people who took part in some of Stanley Milgram's (1963) experiments on conformity, you would have persisted in shocking the learner. How would you have felt afterward, knowing that you had delivered shocks to somebody with a heart condition, somebody who became utterly silent after a while, somebody you might have killed by shocking him?

(As you may already know, the victim never received shocks. Milgram employed deception to induce participants to feel personally involved in what they thought was a real set of conditions.)

Milgram (1974) described a variety of studies in his extensive research project that subjected his volunteers to this situation. Knowing what you know about the ethics of research, would you consider this ethical research? This experimentation has generated voluminous commentary. Some psychologists and ethicists believe that the studies were simply unethical (e.g., Baumrind, 1964). On the other hand, Milgram (1964) defended them as being within ethical boundaries.

The Ethical Issues

What are some of the important issues to consider here? If psychologists legitimately differ in their conclusions, it is pretty certain that we are in a gray area here. You might conclude that the research was acceptable, or you might condemn it. In the end, we need to make a judgment call using the best wisdom we can muster.

An IRB decides whether any given research project would subject people to undue risk. Formally, the IRB is supposed to weigh the costs (physical and psychological harm) against the benefits (increased knowledge and applications) of the research.

If the costs are greater than the benefits, the research should not be done; if the benefits exceed the costs, the research can be defended on ethical grounds.

Unfortunately, before researchers carry out their studies, nobody knows for sure what risks exist or what benefits will actually accrue. In advance, we are talking about possibilities, not actualities. Before a study takes place, we can guess at costs and benefits, but not until after investigators complete their work can we can identify either the risk-associated problems that arose or the actual benefits of the research.

Criticisms of Milgram's Research.   With this uncertainty in mind, we can ask whether Milgram violated the rights of his participants. Among others, Baumrind (1964) asserted that Milgram's obedience research should not have been done. She said that the "dependent attitude" (p. 421) of the participants rendered them more susceptible to the manipulations of an authority figure, that is, the experimenter. She also named several ethical problems, asserting that Milgram did not show concern for participants' well-being, that the cost (i.e., degree of psychological distress and having been lied to) exceeded the benefits of having done the research, that the participants' long-term well-being was negatively affected, and that their attitudes toward authority figures would in the future be more negative. She also noted Milgram's statement that 14 of the 40 participants showed obvious distress and that 3 suffered seizures.

Baumrind (1964) did not accept Milgram's statement that the distress was momentary and that the gain in psychological knowledge outweighed the negatives: "I do regard the emotional disturbance described by Milgram as potentially harmful because it could easily effect an alteration in the subject's self-image or ability to trust adult authorities in the future" (p. 422). She also stated that Milgram's debriefing and dehoaxing processes would not have remedied the situation.

Milgram's Defense of His Research.   Not surprisingly, Milgram (1964) responded to Baumrind's criticisms. He disagreed with her assessments, saying that he tried to predict in advance how the participants would respond and had been confident that they would not engage in the shocking behavior very long. He went to great lengths, asking psychiatrists and others to estimate how often the participants were likely to engage in blind obedience. The experts thought that participants would not administer severe shocks. Thus, at the outset, Milgram firmly believed that virtually everybody would refuse to engage in extreme behavior. As a result, he felt that the risk to his participants would be minimal. As it turned out, the estimates that the experts gave were wrong—people did administer what they thought were severe electrical shocks.

Milgram also noted that he debriefed and dehoaxed the participants, trying to ensure that they departed with no ill effects. Further, at his request, a psychiatrist interviewed 40 participants after a year. There seem to have been no problems at that time. In fact, Ring, Wallston, and Corey (1970) specifically examined participants' reactions to a Milgram-like study. These researchers reported that people may have felt distressed during participation, but the effects were short-lived. A large majority of the people responded that they were happy that they participated. Further, when Ring et al. debriefed their participants after using an approach like Milgram's, the level of tension by participants dropped relative to that of no debriefing.

Baumrind raised critically important points. According to the data we have, though, many or most of the problems she cited did not seem to materialize. Both Milgram's and Baumrind's predictions were off the mark. This is another good example of how experts can be wrong, and why we should not simply rely on authority for the "truth."

The Social Context

We might want to consider the social context in which Milgram did his work. His studies took place from 1960–1963, which was not long after the end of World War II. The Nazis carried out numerous experiments that no normal person could ever justify. In some very famous cases, the perpetrators of those acts claimed that they were merely following orders, that is, simply being obedient. Milgram, like many others, was greatly affected by the reports of these atrocities. In fact, when Milgram (1974) gave an overview of his research in his book *Obedience to Authority*, he referred directly to the Nazi crimes in the very first paragraph of the book.

The United States, where Milgram did his research, was still in the process of recovering from the war, just as citizens in many countries were. In addition, people were worried about the possibility that communists would try to conquer the world, turning people into blindly obedient automatons. War was clearly on people's minds. It was reasonable that we would try to understand how seemingly normal people could commit the wartime acts of the Nazis, or behave with blind obedience. An experimental psychologist might try to reproduce the dynamics of obedience in the laboratory to find out how and why people defer to authorities. This is precisely what Stanley Milgram did.

As members of our society, we continually decide whether behaviors are acceptable. In the early years of the century, many people felt entirely comfortable discriminating against people of color in all aspects of life. Society has changed, and the number of people who agree that such discrimination is acceptable has diminished. In a similar vein, people in the post-war years may have been very comfortable with the idea of Milgram's research because the effects of blind obedience were still fresh in people's minds. Society has changed, and the number of people who would support such research has undoubtedly diminished. The question of blind obedience is no longer as relevant as it was in the aftermath of World War II. It is unlikely that an IRB would approve such research today. But in a different era, people might consider it acceptable or even desirable. (See Controversy Box 2.1, Should Researchers Deceive Participants?)

Incidentally, Milgram's application to become a member of APA was initially questioned on the basis of the ethics of his research. Ultimately, though, the organization accorded him membership, judging that he had not violated ethical guidelines in his work.

DISCUSSION QUESTIONS

1. If you were to study obedience, how could you set it up to avoid ethical dilemmas of the kind that Milgram faced?
2. In terms of social context, discuss why Milgram's obedience research might have been approved by an IRB when he did the research, but the IRB might be much less likely to approve it now.

■ ■ ■ ■ ■ ▬▬▬▬▬▬

CONTROVERSY BOX 2.1
CONTROVERSY: Should Researchers Deceive Participants?

Do you like it when people lie to you? If you do, you are probably fairly unusual. Most people are upset when others lie to them. Over the years, psychologists have used deception in their research. Do people object to being lied to in these research settings? Or do you think that people are unconcerned?

If you were to search for published articles on ethics in psychological research, you would find that a great deal of it would relate to the use of deception. Some psychologists (e.g., Ortmann & Hertwig, 1997) have condemned the use of deception in research, calling for the outlawing of the practice, in part on purely moral grounds. In response, other psychologists have argued that moral philosophers do not agree that deception is unambiguously wrong (Korn, 1998), that the "social contract" between researchers and participants may permit behaviors that might elsewhere be considered unethical (Lawson, 1995), and that participants themselves do not condemn such an approach (Christensen, 1988).

Fisher and Fyrberg (1994) asked potential participants (i.e., college students) to evaluate research scenarios involving three types of deception, *implicit deception, technical deception,* and *role deception.* Implicit deception involves having participants complete their tasks for a purpose of which they are unaware; in this case, Fisher and Fyrberg (1994) used this type of deception to manipulate mood by means of an imagery task.

Technical deception involves misrepresentation of the use of equipment; Fisher and Fyrberg technically deprived participants by telling them that equipment had broken down when it hadn't. Finally, role deception involves misrepresenting the role of another individual in the testing session; the researchers induced participants

to believe that they had damaged another person's belongings.

The results suggested that people don't see much problem with implicit deception. Ninety percent of the students participating in Fisher and Fyrberg's study thought that the benefits of the research outweighed the costs. On the other hand, just over 70 percent of the students were comfortable with technical and role deception.

It might be informative to figure out why some research situations could lead to negative reactions. Psychologists who study embarrassment note that we feel embarrassed when we think somebody may evaluate us unfavorably (Miller, 1995). If we feel that we have been fooled in the presence of someone, we might be embarrassed because we feel that the person might think less of us. Thus, in a situation like technical deception or role deception, you might be annoyed at having been deceived. On the other hand, in implicit deception, the participants may not feel they are really interacting with another during the deception, so they don't feel uncomfortable.

If participants do not particularly mind implicit deception in a research study, does that relieve psychologists of the responsibility to consider the ethics of their actions? Not at all.

The question of using deception is complex. As Fisher and Fyrberg (1994) point out, participants are partners in research, not merely objects of study. As such, we have to balance the potential risks of psychological harm (e.g., embarrassment or anger at being deceived) with the potential benefits of research. We have to consider whether hiding the truth means that participants will not be able to make informed judgments about participation.

---

3. What arguments do opponents of deception in research (e.g., Baumrind and others) raise in their criticisms of deception?

WHAT YOU NEED TO DO IF YOUR RESEARCH INVOLVES DECEPTION

Role Playing—An approach to research in which participants act as if they were participating in a study so the investigator can avoid using potentially unethical strategies that might lead to physical or psychological harm to the participants.

Naturalistic Observation—A research technique in which the investigator studies behavior as it naturally occurs, without any manipulation of variables or intervention into the situation.

Simulation—An approach to research in which the investigator creates an environment similar to one of interest in order to study behaviors in a realistic way. This approach is also known as the simulated environment.

For decades, deception was very prevalent in social psychological research (Adair, Dushenko, & Lindsay, 1985). This means that many psychologists have accepted it as a reality of their research. As Figure 2.1 reveals, deception increased regularly from the 1940s to the 1980s, although it may have diminished recently. In spite of the criticisms leveled by opponents of deception, psychological researchers have not embraced alternate methodologies like **role playing, naturalistic observation,** or **simulation.**

When many people argue against deception, they do so because they see it as immoral. In addition, a second area of concern involves the risk for participants who are deceived. In such a case, a person cannot give informed consent about his or her willingness to participate. We cannot ignore this important notion of informed consent. It is a critical component of national and international laws. Fortunately, there is good reason to believe that keeping participants ignorant of some aspects of the research has negligible effects on them in general (e.g., Bröder, 1995).

A very different type of criticism of the use of deception is that people will develop negative attitudes or suspicion toward psychology and psychological research (Orne, 1962). There is credible evidence, however, that people regard the science and practice of psychology very positively, even after learning that a researcher had deceived them (e.g., Soliday & Stanton, 1995). Christensen (1988) even reported that research participants believed that it would be undesirable if we failed to investigate important topics that might require the use of deception.

Some Research Requires Deception

The dilemma about using deception in research is that some research projects virtually require some deception. If you want participants to act naturally, you might have to create a **cover story** that keeps them from acting in a self-conscious manner during the study. If, after careful consideration, you conclude that you need to use deception, you must keep two points in mind.

Cover Story—The story a researcher creates to disguise the actual purpose of a study when deception is considered necessary to conduct a study.

First, you should minimize the amount deception involved. You need to make sure that you do not withhold critical information that would make a difference in a person's decision about whether to participate in your research. As Fisher and Fyrberg (1994) noted, we can characterize different kinds of deception, depending on the degree to which we actually provide incorrect information to participants. In addition, some researchers distinguish between active and passive deception.

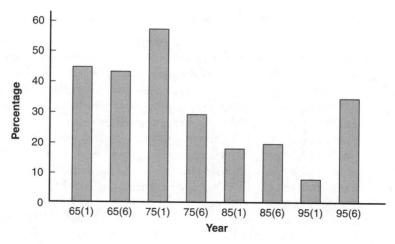

FIGURE 2.1 Percentage of studies using deception in a sample of articles from the *Journal of Personality and Social Psychology* from 1965–1995. The articles appeared in issues 1 and 6 of the journal from each year represented.

Active Deception—The process of misinforming a research participant about some aspect of a study so that the individual is not aware of the investigator's intent in the project.

Passive Deception—The failure to provide complete information to a research participant about some aspect of a study so that the individual is not aware of the investigator's intent in the project.

In **active deception**, you would actively mislead the participants by providing them with information that is not true. In **passive deception**, you would not actually tell a lie. Instead, you would withhold information that might give clues to the participants about the purpose of the study. That is, you give them incomplete information.

All research involves telling our volunteers less than we know. Participants would probably not be terribly interested in all the details of our research. At the same time, with passive deception, you intend to keep the participants in the dark, so your intent is clearly to deceive. One relevant question involves the extent to which you see an ethical difference between active and passive deception. This depends on your own point of view; psychologists differ in their beliefs in the matter.

Second, you need to debrief your participants adequately after the session ends. There are two components to debriefing. One element involves dehoaxing, which means that you tell the individuals what you did, how you deceived them, and why it was necessary. The second element involves desensitization, which means that you eliminate any potential sources of negative feelings by the participants.

We have to make sure that when we explain to participants that they were deceived, the dehoaxing does not, in and of itself, lead to discomfort. Would people feel even worse knowing that they were deceived and would there be psychological risk simply because of the debriefing itself? One problem you face is that debriefing itself might lead to problems; a participant might feel worse after learning about a deception. In rare cases, one might refrain from debriefing a participant, but this should be a last resort that has received approval from an IRB.

The Effects of Debriefing on Research

Most psychologists debrief their participants immediately after a testing session concludes. Practically, this is the easiest approach. If a researcher decides to postpone the debriefing, it takes extra effort to contact the participants. One drawback to immediate debriefing is that participants might discuss our research with others. If you deceived them in order to make sure they acted naturally, there are obvious problems if your participants talk to others who later take part in your study.

How often will participants actually discuss the research with others? According to Marans (1988), of 50 participants in a debriefing-disclosure study, 10 (20 percent) reported discussing the experiment with other, potential participants. If twenty percent of participants disclose the nature of a study to others, this could pose a serious problem to the validity of research that relies on the naïveté of participants. On the other hand, Diener, Matthews, and Smith (1972) discovered that only 11 of 440 potential participants had learned about the deceptive elements of an experiment for which fellow students had volunteered. Diener et al. concluded that leakage of information is not a serious concern.

Further, Walsh (1976) reported that when researchers asked people not to disclose any information about the research, the participants refrained from discussing the study more than when such a request was not made. These results suggest that researchers must evaluate the potential problems of immediate debriefing on a study-by-study basis. If the investigator is worried that a participant might talk about the study and forewarn other potential participants of the nature of the study, the researcher might decide to defer debriefing until the end of the project. This would solve one problem: people remain naïve about the study. At the same time, this solution itself introduces a different problem, having to contact people later, which is not always easy.

Psychologists have asked the question of whether debriefing actually serves its purpose. That is, does it remove any negative responses of the participants? Although there is controversy (see Rubin, 1985), there seem to be few noticeable effects of deception when debriefing is taken seriously. Gruder, Stumpfhauser, and Wyer (1977) studied the effects of feedback. These researchers provided participants with false feedback about poor performance after having taken an intelligence test. Gruder et al. wondered if there would be a difference in performance in a subsequent testing session depending on whether the participants learned about the false feedback in a debriefing session.

The results showed that when participants learned that the feedback was not accurate, their later performance on another test improved; there was no comparable trend among participants who were not debriefed. This suggests that false feedback about poor performance has a real effect on participants. On the other hand, debriefed participants were able to cast away the negative information more readily. There are clear implications about the beneficial effects of debriefing and potential risks if it is not done or is not done well.

DISCUSSION QUESTIONS

1. What points to researchers need to consider if they intend to use deception in their research?

2. Do you think that debriefing and dehoaxing are sufficient to overcome the ethical concerns associated with deception in research?

ETHICS AND WEB-BASED RESEARCH

A new challenge that we face as researchers involves ethical issues associated with using the internet. Neither researchers nor IRBs have much experience with this approach. Still, we are bound to protect our participants from risk, even those at remote sites.

We are in uncharted territory with web research. The community of psychological researchers has had a century to figure out how to complete in-person research; we have had over a quarter of a century to come up with legally sanctioned protections for participants. But with web research, some very tricky questions arise about how to deal with the issues of confidentiality and anonymity (especially regarding sensitive topics), informed consent, protecting participants from unforeseen negative consequences, debriefing them, and how to arrange compensatory followup if it is needed (which we may never know).

A sizeable amount of web-based research in psychology involves questionnaires. These are generally regarded as being fairly benign, so the risks associated with them are minimal. An added protection for the participants is that they can quit any time they want if they feel frustrated, overwhelmed, or otherwise uncomfortable. However, suppose a researcher wants to know about serious, private issues in a person's life. Two notable concerns appear here. First, it is absolutely required that the researcher guarantee that nobody can intercept the responses of the participant. Experts in the field of ethics will have to join experts in technology in certifying secure data transfer.

Second, merely filling out a questionnaire may trigger an emotional response; if it happens in a laboratory, the researcher can try to deal with any problems and can get help for the individual if necessary. The researcher can also arrange to contact the individual at a later point to make sure that there were no lasting problems. Nobody may ever know about the unfortunate consequences for remote people who participate online.

The research community recognizes these concerns and has begun to address them. Major, national organizations have entered the discussion. The Board of Scientific Affairs of the American Psychological Association, the American Association for the Advancement of Science, and the federal government's National Institutes of Health are trying to generate solutions to these ethical questions (Azar, 2000a).

Finally, an ethical consideration that involves researchers, not participants, has arisen. With web research, it would be both possible and easy for an unscrupulous researcher to steal the ideas of another person (i.e., commit plagiarism), conduct a similar project, then claim priority for the ideas. Unfortunately, it could be difficult to know if somebody stole another's ideas.

Internet research has become a hot topic, so it would not be surprising that two people would generate similar research projects. How could we distinguish between simultaneous discovery and chicanery (i.e., cheating)? It could be possible by examining the records of the researchers, but the issue is not easy and could besmirch the reputations of honest scholars.

DISCUSSION QUESTION
1. What ethical issues arise in considering participants' rights when they engage in research on the web?

ETHICS AND RESEARCH WITH ANIMALS

Psychologists have studied animal behavior for the past century. Much of the work has involved laboratory rats that have learned to perform tasks in different conditions, although B. F. Skinner, one of the most famous psychologists in history, worked extensively with pigeons.

Even though the study of animal behavior constituted one of the pillars of psychology, not all people have agreed on its value. Some have criticized animal research as being of limited applicability to human behavior and restricted mostly to one variant of one species, namely, the Norway rat (Beach, 1950). This is an important question: Can we learn about people by studying animals? The answer is definitely yes, although we cannot learn everything from animals.

A second group of people has condemned research with animals as being unethical. There are several aspects to their arguments. For instance, animal rights activists maintain that we do not have the right to keep animals in laboratory captivity. Some also believe that the animals are treated inhumanely. Over the past few decades, there has been growing sentiment against use of animals in research in society, although a majority of people still believe that if such research benefits humans, it is not unethical (see Plous, 1996a, for a discussion of these issues).

The use of animals in psychological research has diminished notably over the past several decades in the United States, Canada, and western Europe. According to Plous (1996a), a quarter to a third of psychology departments have either closed their animal laboratories or are giving it serious consideration. Further, there is a remarkable decrease in the number of graduate students in psychology who conduct animal research (Thomas & Blackman, 1992, cited in Plous, 1996a).

Plous has found that psychologists, as a group, show overwhelming support (over 85 percent) for naturalistic observation, which does not involve animal confinement, somewhat less support for studies involving laboratory confinement (over 60 percent), and little support for research involving pain or death (17 to 34 percent). He has also discovered that undergraduate psychology majors are highly similar to their mentors in the attitudes they hold toward the use of animals in psychological research (Plous, 1996b). He also noted that among the general public, there is significant support for research involving rats (88 percent), but less for dogs (55 percent).

If a person's own moral principles imply that it is unethical to use animals in research, then no arguments about the benefit to people will persuade that individual to accept such research. That person has the right to hold his or her moral principles and others must recognize that right. At the same time, the majority of Americans accept animal research as being beneficial, as long as the investigations might be beneficial to human welfare and do not expose the animals to unreasonable distress. We must rely on knowledge and common sense to make the best decision. If we are either to criticize or to defend research with animals, we need to know the truth of the animals' treatment at the hands of the scientists.

Arguments and Counterarguments

According to Coile and Miller (1984), some animal rights activists have made claims about the plight of animals in psychological experiments that would make most of us wonder if the research is justified. The claims include the idea that animals receive intense electrical shocks that they cannot escape until they lose the ability to even scream in pain, that they are deprived of food and water, and suffer until they die.

Coile and Miller discuss six points raised by the activists (Mobilization for Animals, 1984, cited in Coile & Miller, 1984). Coile and Miller's arguments are two decades old but are probably still reasonably valid, especially given the changes in the nature of psychological research away from the animal model. Coile and Miller examined the previous five years of psychological journal articles that commonly report the use of research animals, like *Journal of Experimental Psychology: Animal Behavior Processes* and *Journal of Comparative Psychology*. They only looked at psychological journals; other disciplines, like biology, also rely on animals to varying degrees.

The claims of some activists were simply wrong regarding psychological research. The alleged, intense electric shocks, severe food and water deprivation, smashing of bones and mutilation of limbs, and pain designed to make animals psychotic never appeared in research reported in the most prestigious psychology journals.

The fact that the claims about the research are false does not mean that the animals do not experience pain or distress in some studies. In fact, various experiments clearly involve discomfort, some of it intense. Research on learned helplessness, for example, involved such an approach.

Coile and Miller argued that there can be good reason for engaging in this type of research, particularly in the biomedical realm. For example, experimental animals have been used to investigate treatments for such maladies as cancer and AIDS in people and distemper in animals and to study ways to relieve the chronic pain that some people live with. Researchers who seek to further our understanding of depression sometimes use electrical shock as a treatment; however, as Coile and Miller pointed out, depression can lead to suicide, which is the third leading cause of death in young adults.

Miller (1985) further amplified some of the benefits of animal research for people suffering from problems like scoliosis, enuresis (bed wetting), anorexia, loss of the use of limbs due to nerve damage, chronic pain, stress, and headaches. Many people would consider it justifiable to study animals in order to ease the plight of people suffering from such problems.

As Plous (1996a, 1996b) has found, psychologists and psychology students hold quite similar attitudes about the use of animals in research. The general public also shows sympathy toward animal research; there is widespread support regarding the use of rats in biomedical research. People do not like to see animals exposed to intense suffering or distress, though. According to the findings of Coile and Miller, psychologists do not regularly expose their research animals to the kind of treatment that people find objectionable. In some ways, however, the issue may become less pressing in psychology because the use of animals in research is on the decline.

DISCUSSION QUESTIONS
1. If the majority of people consider animal research acceptable and researchers continue to study animal behavior, what steps do researchers need to take to guarantee that animals are not mistreated?
2. When people oppose the use of animal research, what arguments do they produce? How valid are these arguments? How valid are the counterarguments that researchers make?

CHAPTER SUMMARY

Scientists who study people usually show consideration for the well-being of the individuals they study. After all, scientists are just like everybody else in most respects. Unfortunately, however, there have been cases in which researchers have shown a reprehensible lack of concern about the people who participate in their studies.

Probably the most notorious violators of ethics in research are the Nazi doctors who tortured people in the name of research. Unfortunately, they are not the only ones who have violated ethical standards. For instance, American researchers studying men with syphilis for several decades beginning in the 1920s withheld treatment to see the course of the disease. The men thought they were receiving appropriate levels of treatment.

In order to protect human participants, the American Psychological Association was one of the first organizations to promulgate ethical standards in research. APA has developed a set of aspirational goals and enforceable rules that members of APA must follow. It is the responsibility of each researcher to be aware of these rules. Student researchers are just as responsible for ethical treatment of participants as professional researchers are.

Among psychologists, Stanley Milgram is undoubtedly the most famous person whose research was questioned on ethical grounds. He deceived his participants into thinking they were shocking another individual. The controversy over whether he should have conducted his projects persists. In the end, the decision about ethics involves complex issues that differ for each instance we consider.

After the Nazi atrocities, an international body created the Nuremburg Code that specifies the basic rights of human participants in research. It is an internationally recognized code. In the United States, there is federal and state legislation similarly designed to protect the welfare of participants. One of the newest areas that is receiving scrutiny is web-based research. There are questions of informed consent and invasion of privacy that have yet to be addressed and resolved.

Another aspect of research ethics that has received considerable attention in the past few decades involves the treatment of animal subjects. Some people condemn any use of laboratory animals in research, regardless of the type of projects. Other people feel that if such research will ultimately benefit people, some degree of discomfort or harm is acceptable. Medical researchers are more likely to inflict pain or distress in animals; psychological research is usually more benign and involves little, if any, discomfort for the animals. The controversial issues associated with animal rights is still an evolving field.

CHAPTER THREE

PLANNING RESEARCH: GENERATING A QUESTION

CHAPTER OVERVIEW

CHAPTER PREVIEW

HOW DO RESEARCH IDEAS DEVELOP?

Informal and Formal Sources of Ideas
The Continuum of Research Ideas
The Effect of Theory
*Reasons for Decreases
in Animal Research*
The Effect of the Cognitive Revolution

**HOW CAN YOU DEVELOP
RESEARCH IDEAS?**

Generating Research Hypotheses

**CONTROVERSY: *Does Music Make
You Smart?***

**THE VIRTUAL LABORATORY:
RESEARCH ON THE INTERNET**

Advantages to Web-Based Research
Potential Problems with Web-Based
Research
The Future of the Web in Psychology

**CHECKING ON RESEARCH: THE ROLE
OF REPLICATION**

**CONTROVERSY: *Scientists Competing
to Finish Second?***

**DON'T REINVENT THE WHEEL:
REVIEWING THE LITERATURE**

What Is a Literature Review?
*The Effect of Peer-Review on the
Research Literature*

**HOW TO CONDUCT A
LITERATURE REVIEW**

Electronic Databases
Starting Your Search

HOW TO READ A JOURNAL ARTICLE

Understanding the Format
of a Research Paper
Abstract
Introduction
Methods
Results
Discussion
References

CHAPTER SUMMARY

KEY TERMS

Abstract
Behaviorism
Conceptual replication
Construct validity
Discussion
Exact replication
Introduction

Literature review
Materials and apparatus
Methods
Participants
Peer review
Procedure
References

Replication
Replication with extension
Results
Serendipity
Type I error
Type II error
Validity

CHAPTER PREVIEW

Research questions come from a variety of sources and motivations, most of them arising from the investigator's curiosity. At the same time, our ideas develop within a social context. The questions we consider important develop because of the combination of our personalities, our histories, what society values, and other factors that may have little to do with the scientific research question per se.

Ideas arise in different ways. Sometimes, researchers notice an event that captures their interest and they decide to create research to study it. At other times, researchers have a specific question to address or a problem to solve that leads to a research project. In some cases, researchers develop research ideas to test theories. No matter how the idea develops, researchers have to figure out the best way to investigate their questions.

To generate good research, investigators should be aware of the work of other scientists. This allows the investigator to advance our knowledge and to avoid simply repeating what others have done. Such knowledge will also help a researcher generate new questions. Sources of information include scientific publications and presentations at research conferences. As your exposure to research expands, you will learn effective and efficient means of searching for prior work that relates to your own research question.

Electronic databases provide easy access to descriptions of research in psychology. By conducting a systematic literature review, psychologists can learn about the work of others, devise their own research questions, and ultimately publish research articles or make presentations at professional conferences.

New research questions are being asked using a convenient new technology: the internet. We are just beginning to explore the best ways to collect data online. The future of such research looks very promising, but a lot of methodological questions have to be resolved in this area.

HOW DO RESEARCH IDEAS DEVELOP?

If we read journal articles or listen to psychologists give presentations of their research, we get a coherent picture of what led them to do their research, how they accomplished it, and what their results mean. The final product is a nice package whose ideas flow logically; we can see how the ideas developed and how they progressed. Researchers who communicate well can weave a good story that answers questions we have. But where do the research ideas come from? Why do researchers study topics ranging from thinking and problem solving to social relationships to personality development? The answer is fairly simple: The researchers are curious and doing the research is fun. Research involves solving puzzles and getting answers, so why shouldn't it be enjoyable? Scientists like what they are doing even when they study serious and complex issues. Further, the social context of researchers' lives affect the types of questions they ask and how they ask them.

For example, people who are familiar with birth control pills know that a woman takes a pill each day for three weeks out of the month. The pills in the fourth week are placebos that allow menstruation to occur. The reason for the development of this strategy is that the developer of the first birth control pill, John Rock, was a Catholic who wanted the form of contraception to be "natural," thus acceptable to his religious authorities. As such, his plan included monthly menstruation, even though it was not necessary or maybe even desirable (Gladwell, 2002). This episode provides a good example of how a researcher's religious beliefs led to his scientific approach. It would be an interesting exercise to speculate on what might have occurred if the strictures of the Catholic church had not been part of the picture. The nature of birth control may have gone through an entirely different development.

Let's consider an example of how simply thinking about an interesting social topic can lead to research questions. For instance, consider a topic that has captured the interest of the American public: handgun control. Some people support control; some oppose it. Using surveys, researchers have investigated how often people protect themselves with their guns.

The picture is complex, which is why there is still debate on the topic. Data collected by Kleck and Gertz (1995) suggested that Americans use their guns for self-defense about 2.5 million times a year in various emergency situations. According to Harvard researcher David Hemenway (1997), the surveys imply that gun owners protected themselves against burglaries about 845,000 times in a given year. Because there weren't that many burglaries, the results suggest that "burglary victims use their guns in self-defense more than 100% of the time" (p. 6); that is, the data imply that there are more instances of self-defense during burglaries than there are actual burglaries.

How can you have more incidents of self-defense than there are situations that call for it? According to Hemenway, Kleck and Gertz's (1995) data mean that the people who returned the surveys did not report their gun use accurately. There is considerable controversy in this area and it is likely to persist. An important point to remember here is that asking questions on surveys seems like an easy way to get answers when, in truth, asking questions well requires insight into people's ways of responding as well as patient work in developing questions that lead to valid answers.

You could develop some interesting research projects here. For example, why are people's reports inaccurate? Are they lying or are their memories simply poor? People who favor handgun ownership might have convinced themselves that they have used their guns for protection; they are not lying, they just possess a very active memory system. (It is important to remember that we all have active memory systems that can distort what we remember.) Another potential research question is whether people who report such behavior define "self-defense" differently than those who have not reported the behavior.

According to Wentland and Smith (1993), people are not as accurate as you might suppose in responding to "easy" questions, such as whether they own an automobile, a home, a driver's license, or a library card. We should not be surprised that answers to "hard" questions are more problematic. It would be an interesting research project to discover the situations in which we should accept people's reports of behaviors and those situations when we should not.

In essence, any time we encounter a behavior that we do not fully understand, there is potential for a research project.

Informal and Formal Sources of Ideas

There are various ways that research ideas develop. We can characterize them on a continuum as being more or less formal. Figure 3.1 presents this continuum and the kind of question that leads to more research.

The Continuum of Research Ideas.   Sometimes a research question will arise because a psychologist observes something in everyday life and decides that he or she would like to research it. The idea does not derive from theory or from previous research, only from curiosity about some behavior that takes place. This approach represents a very informal and idiosyncratic way of generating research ideas. If it weren't for the fact that the psychologist happens to notice something worth investigating in a particular situation, the research might not take place.

One step toward the more formal or systematic end of the continuum involves solving practical problems. That is, in a particular situation, you might look around and say, "We can do this better." The next step would be to design a program to test your ideas. Psychologists who work in organizations or in industry often specialize in solving such applied problems. Their approach is not based only on personal observation and curiosity, but comes from a question that relates to the workplace. This strategy is somewhat more formal than deciding to study a behavior because it catches your eye. At the same time, it does not develop from other research or from a theory; it might be idiosyncratic to a particular time or place. The research takes place because the psychologist is in the position to solve practical problems as they arise in a particular setting.

A third point on the continuum involves researchers who evaluate the work of others or who are in the middle of a research program. Already-completed research has some loose ends, so the investigator takes the partial answers and tries to extend our knowledge. This is a more formal approach to research because the ideas that led to a particular project are embedded within a research context and help answer a question that others are also investigating.

At the most formal end of the continuum, a research idea can develop from a well-defined theory. That is, a theory predicts certain behaviors, so the psychologist tries to see whether the behaviors follow from theoretical predictions. This would represent the most formal approach because theoretical expectations may dictate the nature of the research. The questions to be answered are not the result of a single, unsystematic event, but rather unfold from a well-defined and systematic set of ideas.

FIGURE 3.1   Continuum representing the development of research ideas.

INFORMAL ←			→ FORMAL
"This is interesting. I'd like to know more about it!"	"We have a problem to solve. Let's figure out the best way to do it."	"Our earlier project answered some of our questions, but there are still some unanswered questions."	"The theory says people should act this way. Let's test the theory."

Most research ideas develop in the middle of the continuum. That is, old ideas lead to new ideas that we can test empirically.

According to Glueck and Jauch (1975), researchers in the natural and physical sciences tend to develop their projects based on a combination of their own insights and the results of previous research. Clark (cited in Glueck and Jauch, 1975) agreed that productive psychologists also tend to generate their research ideas based on earlier work. We see what others have done and we try to clear up the loose ends. As a result, any given investigation does not generally move the field a significant amount; it merely provides another piece of the mosaic. This is why science is really a partnership; we each do our part to put together a coherent explanation for some behavior.

Table 3.1 presents how researchers say they develop their ideas. Figure 3.2 illustrates the difference in importance. As you can see, investigators generate ideas on their own, from the research literature, and in conjunction with colleagues in their field at different institutions. Colleagues in their own institutions are seen as less helpful, probably because most departments have people with very different research interests.

Research ideas often arise from the personal interests of the investigators. For example, the noted psychologist Robert Sternberg of Yale University became interested in issues of intelligence because of his own experience with taking tests. Sternberg, who was elected president of the American Psychological Association and has written or

TABLE 3.1 Different sources of ideas for research in order of frequency of occurrence, as reported by active scientists. The more frequent sources appear first in the table (Glueck & Jauck, 1975).

SOURCE OF RESEARCH IDEAS	COMMENT
Researcher's own ideas	People have more interest in their own ideas, so they are more likely to invest time and resources in studying those ideas.
Research literature	Reading others' ideas can give you an idea for an extension to fill in the gaps in knowledge; it can also lead to an idea for trying to disprove a claim.
Distant colleagues	Researchers build up a network of contacts across the country or the world. Discussions with these colleagues provides stimulation to develop new ideas.
Departmental colleagues	In most science departments in colleges and universities, there may not be much overlap in specialized, professional interests among faculty in a department. It can be hard to develop joint research ideas because local colleagues very often have different interests.
Research team	In many laboratories, students carry out the research program of the director, who may develop most of the research ideas.
Local colleagues outside the department	It is rare that researchers can provide significant ideas to others outside their own area of expertise.

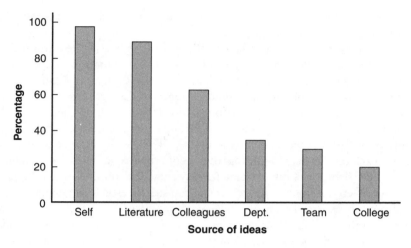

FIGURE 3.2   Percentage of the time that scientists get ideas for their research from various sources at least some of the time.

[Note: *Colleagues* refers to researchers at different institutions.]

Source: W. F. Glueck and L. R. Jauck (1975). *The Journal of Higher Education* **46**, 103–114. Copyright © 1975 by The Ohio State University Press. All rights reserved. Adapted with permission.

edited dozens of books and has authored hundreds of scientific journal articles, did not score very well on standardized intelligence tests. There is a clear discrepancy between the message given by this test scores ("he isn't very smart") and his remarkable achievements ("he is very smart"). Sternberg has spent a considerable part of his career studying the various forms intelligence can take. He currently directs a center that actively investigates intelligence and knowledge, and how we can assess them.

The Effect of Theory

The dominant theoretical perspective affects the kind of research questions that investigators ask. We can see this pattern occurring in psychology now as it relates to animal research. From the early 1900s until well into the 1960s, psychologists studied animal behavior to help understand all behavior, including that of humans. This meant creating research questions that could be asked with nonhuman subjects.

Over the past few decades, though, there has been a notable change in the way psychologists do research. For example, in Great Britain, the amount of animal research has declined precipitously. The number of doctoral dissertations by young researchers in psychology that involve animals has declined by 62 percent over the past twenty-five years (Thomas & Blackman, 1992, cited in Plous, 1996a). We haven't exhausted the entire repertoire of research questions involving animals, we have just focused our attention differently.

As we have seen in the discussion of ethics in research, many people have noted that ethical concerns lead them away from research with animals. There are other significant factors as well. Social forces are complex and major changes in the way people think reflect multiple underlying causes.

Reasons for Decreases in Animal Research.   Several reasons can help account for these changes. One reason is that there are more women earning doctorates in psychology. In general, women seem to be interested in different topics—those that don't involve animals.

A second possibility is that, as a society, we have become more sensitized to the ethical issues associated with animal research. Even though psychologists may support the use of animals in research, as we have seen in Chapter 2, these same psychologists may choose not to involve animals in their own professional work.

Another reason for the decline in animal research is that we have changed theoretical perspectives. For the first seven decades of the last century, the dominant paradigm was **behaviorism.** One of the fundamental tenets of behaviorism is that a few simple principles of learning and behavior can explain the behavior of virtually any organism of any species. Thus, it does not matter if you study people or rats; the specific behaviors may differ, but the principles of reinforcement and punishment hold true across species, according to the behaviorists. Thus, what is true for rat behavior would be true for human behavior.

> **Behaviorism**—A theoretical approach in psychology that focused on studies of observable behaviors rather than internal, mental processes.

Psychologists have expanded on this simple set of rules and have developed new ideas to explore more complex behavior and thought. Behaviorism has not been shown to be false; indeed, its principles have led to some very useful outcomes. With the new cognitive orientation, though, we have begun to ask different kinds of questions.

The Effect of the Cognitive Revolution.   What does this movement away from behaviorism and animal studies mean about the nature of the research we publish? As Figure 3.3 reveals, some striking patterns emerge. The so-called "cognitive revolution" in

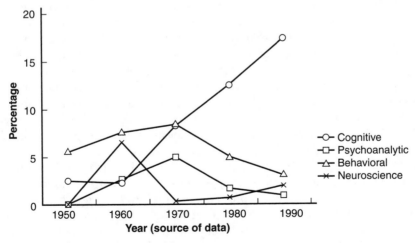

FIGURE 3.3   Percentage of articles by decade published in key psychology journals that include keywords associated with cognitive, behavioral, psychoanalytic, and neuroscience perspectives.

Source: R. W. Robins, S. D. Josling, and K. H. Craik. (1999). An empirical analysis of trends in psychology. *American Psychologist, 54,* 117–128. Copyright American Psychological Association. Reprinted with permission.

psychology is clear from the amount of research that is cognitive in nature. According to Robins, Gosling, and Craik (1999), the percentage of articles using words related to cognition have has risen dramatically since the early 1970s.

During the past three decades, the use of behavioral terms (e.g., reinforcement, punishment, discriminative stimulus) has declined. (Even though behavioral terms have decreased in use, the principles of behaviorism still account for some of the most generally useful principles of behavior.) Also, in spite of the excitement about neuroscientific approaches in psychology, researchers have seldom included terms related to it in the past half century; it falls one short step ahead of the even more scant references to psychoanalytic approaches. These trends allow us to make predictions about the future of psychological research. It is psychologically based and largely human, rather than biologically based and animal.

DISCUSSION QUESTIONS

1. Why are students more likely to use the more informal end of the research continuum for their projects than are professional researchers?
2. Why has animal research declined in psychology over the past few decades? Can you think of any circumstances in which it would start increasing?

HOW CAN YOU DEVELOP RESEARCH IDEAS?

Professional researchers have an easier time developing a research project than a beginning student researcher because professionals have more knowledge and a greater sense of the field in which they work. In addition, once a person establishes a research program, new ideas often emerge easily.

How should you begin to select a problem for yourself? The first step is to acquire as much knowledge as you can about as many different areas as you can. The greater your scope of knowledge, the more likely you will be able to bring together different ideas into a unique project. As Coile and Miller (1984) noted, research can lead in unpredictable directions; this is called **serendipity,** which refers to finding something of value when looking for something else. For example, they pointed out that ten critically important advances in cardiovascular and pulmonary medicine relied on research done for purposes unrelated to those advances. Knowledgeable researchers pulled together ideas that others might have seen as unrelated.

> **Serendipity**—The accidental discovery of something interesting or worthwhile as you search for something completely different.

McGuire (1983) has developed a set of useful techniques that you could use to generate research questions. His suggestions span the continuum from very informal to very formal. At the most personal and informal level, he suggests that you introspect about your own experiences and use your thoughts to generate research questions. At the more formal level, he proposes that you can look at research in a particular area and try to adapt some of those ideas to a new area. Table 3.2 presents a list of research possibilities that you could implement; the research questions may be relatively simple, but they can lead to productive ideas.

TABLE 3.2   Approaches to generating research ideas and some examples of ideas that could develop into research projects (McGuire, 1983).

TYPES OF PHENOMENA	AN IDEA THAT YOU COULD DEVELOP
STUDYING SPONTANEOUSLY OCCURRING EVENTS	
Intensive case studies	Study the behavior of a friend who consistently scores well on tests. Try to find out why and see if the technique works for others.
Extrapolate from similar problems already studied	Psychologists have investigated the credibility of expert witnesses. One question that remains to be answered, though, is whether jurors respond similarly to female and male expert witnesses.
STUDYING THE VALIDITY OF EVERYDAY BELIEFS AND WHEN THESE BELIEFS BREAK DOWN	
Reverse the direction of a commonsense hypothesis	Many common sayings, like "Opposites attract," suggest behavioral hypotheses. You could investigate whether opposites really do attract with a study to see if similar people are more likely to date or form friendships.
EVALUATING FORMAL IF-THEN STATEMENTS	
Use the hypothetico-deductive method of saying that "if A is true, then B should be true"	Psychologists have discovered in laboratory research that people learn better with multiple, short sessions than in single, long sessions. Conduct a survey in which you test the hypothesis that "if students study in multiple, short sessions, they should perform better in classes than students who study in single, long sessions."
USING PREVIOUS RESEARCH AS A STEPPING STONE	
Bring together areas of research that originally did not relate	Research on people with physical disabilities and research on sport and exercise psychology can come together for investigators who would like to apply knowledge on sport and exercise to a new population that has not been connected to this domain in the past (Crocker, 1993).
TESTS OF THEORY	Piagetian theory generally does not support the idea that children regress to previous levels of cognitive development; test children under difficult conditions (e.g., when they have a limited time to complete a long task) to see if they do regress.

Generating Research Hypotheses

McGuire (1983) suggested that too many people erroneously believe that generating research questions involves creativity that cannot be taught. If this were true, highly creative individuals would use their innate gift to generate research, and for the unfortunate people with less creativity, the likelihood of engaging in good research would be low. McGuire disagreed with this pessimistic view. He proposed a set of approaches to generating research questions.

Table 3.2 illustrates that it isn't always difficult to generate research ideas. One suggestion is to evaluate commonsense ideas to see when they hold true and when they don't. You may hear that "opposites attract" as a principle of human behavior. This maxim leads to testable hypotheses. Once you define what you mean by "opposites" you can find out if we tend to select people opposite to us. You may find instead that "Birds of a feather flock together." You could also combine previously unrelated topics. For instance, research on sports and physical disabilities don't usually fall together. You might be able to generate some interesting research projects by connecting them. It is important to remember that the more practice you get in developing ideas and the more knowledge you gain in a particular area, the easier it is to come up with new research projects.

You should remember that many of the ideas that you generate at first will probably have been studied already. The reason for this is that if the idea is obvious to you, it will probably be obvious to others. You may have to revise your initial plan. This can be a frustrating experience for students because you may not have enough background knowledge to be able to figure out how to proceed, so you feel that all the good ideas have been taken. This is where you can rely on professionals in the field (including your professor).

Sometimes researchers make suggestions for future projects. For instance, Goodman-Delahunty (1998) provided a set of questions of particular relevance to psychologists interested in the interface between psychology and the law.

Goodman-Delahunty reported that studies of sexual harassment typically involve college students as participants. Further, the research may not employ accurate legal definitions of sexual harassment. The mock trial transcripts are also not very complex, unlike real life. What would happen if you did a study with people from the working world? What about using more realistic scenarios? We don't know what would happen because researchers have not yet investigated these questions. Table 3.3 presents further topics for study. These examples involve psychology and the law, but you can use the same process for just about any other area of study.

You are likely to experience greater success if you pick a small research question. The temptation is often to try to revolutionize a field with a single study. This never happens. Even professional researchers investigate small questions; their advantage is that they can study many of them over a long period of time. They are not bound by a single semester, as students often are, so they can devote an extended period of time to refining their research questions, accumulating a great deal of knowledge bit by bit.

A good example of how a widely publicized research project led to subsequent investigations and correction of erroneous information took place when a research team reported that listening to Mozart had the effect of increasing one's intelligence (Rauscher, Shaw, & Ky, 1993, 1995). Other investigators repeated the research, but were unable to generate the same results. Controversy Box 3.1 shows how our knowledge in this area increased as one set of research questions led to new ones.

DISCUSSION QUESTIONS

1. Identify and describe the five classes of research ideas in McGuire's (1983) classification. Can you think of a research project you could do for each one?
2. Think of a recent event in your life that surprised you. How could you turn it into a research question?
3. Generate a research plan that brings two unrelated research topics together.

TABLE 3.3 Examples of potential research projects on gender and law that are based on existing research and legal questions.

Current Situation: Sexual harassment creates a hostile working environment, but there are differences in people's conceptualizations of what constitutes harassment. Studies of gender differences in perception of sexual harassment are complex and inconsistent (Goodman-Delahunty, 1998).

Recommandations for Related Research:
- Do results differ when we use accurate, legal definitions of sexual harassment in research, which is not always done?
- Do simple, fictitious cases result in different outcomes than rich and complex scenarios that occur in actual legal cases?
- Do convenience samples consisting of college undergraduates produce results different from studies using other people?

Current Situation: Jurors have to evaluate the credibility and the evidence presented by expert witnesses. Are female and male experts regarded the same by different participants in trials related to battered women who kill their spouses (Schuller & Cripps, 1998)?

Recommendations for Related Research:
- What happens if we vary the sex of the expert witness as well as the nature of other testimony and evidence?
- Can we identify different mannerisms and characteristics of expert witnesses that may add or detract from their credibility and that may be confused with gender effects?
- Does gender of an expert witness make a difference in more versus less serious offenses?

Current Situation: Most sexual harassment claims are made by women against men, but on occasion, men are the victims of such harassment. Those inflicting the harassment may be either female or male, although men report fewer negative reactions to these experiences (Waldo, Berdahl, & Fitzgerald, 1998).

Recommendations for Related Research:
- Given that harassment might take different forms for female and male victims, do people show parallel criteria pertaining to women and to men?
- Can we identify whether male jurors will defer to female jurors during debate, or vice versa?
- Do juries take harassment of men as seriously as they do harassment of women? Gay men versus straight men?
- Will a jury deal with the question of the severity of the harassment differently for men and women?

Current Situation: In research settings, aggressive defense attorneys seem to gain acquittal for clients more than passive attorneys do. Male attorneys are more successful than female attorneys (Hahn & Clayton, 1996).

Recommendations for Related Research:
- Do aggressive attorneys achieve the same acquittal rate with adult witnesses and child witnesses?
- Do female attorneys achieve equal success when they question female and male witnesses?
- Do female and male prosecuting attorneys have comparable success in winning convictions?

■ ■ ■ ■ ■ ▬▬▬▬▬▬▬▬▬▬

CONTROVERSY BOX 3.1
CONTROVERSY: Does Music Make You Smart?

Rauscher et al. (1993, 1995) reported that listening to Mozart's music could increase intelligence; the researchers determined that scores on a standardized test increased significantly, about 8 or 9 points. The public was enthralled. The implications were remarkable. People envisioned a populace that was suddenly smarter.

Other researchers were immediately interested. First, there were practical implications. Could we do something to make our children smarter? One plan proposed by the governor of Georgia was to give a tape of this music to each family of a newborn baby in the state. The payoff could be great, but so could the cost if the effect turned out to be imaginary.

A second reason for interest was that scientists were interested in finding out why intellectual functioning would improve. What was the actual cause? This is an interesting scientific question in its own right. Further, perhaps there were other, even more effective, means of enhancing thought processes.

Unfortunately, the first published report provided insufficient detail on the methodology, so it was difficult to replicate the study because the details were unavailable. The second report presented that information.

When details became available, Carstens, Haskins, and Hounshell (1995) found that listening to Mozart, compared to a silent period, had no effect on test performance. Then Newman, Rosenbach, Burns, Latimer, Matocha, and Vogt (1995) also reported a failure to replicate the original results. Surprisingly, they discovered that people with a preference for classical music actually showed lower test scores than others after listening to music. As the puzzle grew, Rauscher and Shaw (1998) proposed more arguments to support their original conclusions.

Subsequently, Steele, Bass, and Brooke (1999) and Steele et al. (1999) extended the methodology even further. They found no Mozart effect. Thompson, Schellenberg, and Husain (2001) then varied the types of music to which participants listened, finding that arousal levels and mood accounted for the so-called Mozart effect. Higher arousal and positive mood were associated with better test scores, not specifically having listened to Mozart.

This sequence of studies illustrates how the scientific approach, with replication, is self-correcting and leads to more complete knowledge. Although it is exciting to think that we can get smart by listening to music, it is important to know the truth—that increases in test performance are more likely to result from high levels of motivation, perhaps from positive mood, and certainly through hard work.

THE VIRTUAL LABORATORY: RESEARCH ON THE INTERNET

Some psychological research requires specialized laboratory space and equipment. Whenever we want to measure specific behaviors or responses just as they occur, we must be in the presence of the people (or animals) we measure. It is hard to imagine that a behavioral researcher could study reinforcement or punishment without having direct contact with whomever is being observed. If developmental psychologists want to see whether an infant will cross a visual cliff, parents must bring the infant to the laboratory.

However, psychologists may be able to easily accomplish research at a distance that involves judgments of opinion and attitude. For such studies, it is common to bring participants to the laboratory and administer surveys and tests to them or to mail the materials. (Unfortunately, people often do not mail them back.) With the advent of easy access to the internet, we no longer need to be in the physical presence of those who agree to participate in such research, and we don't need to go to the trouble and expense of mailing anything. The concept of the laboratory is undergoing adjustment; it can be world-wide in scope. Table 3.4 presents some examples of actual web-based research. As you can see, survey research involves attitudes and their relations to behavior. There are also experiments that involve manipulations. Creative researchers should be able to use the internet to good effect.

Advantages to Web-Based Research

We can see four clear advantages to web research. The first involves the amount of time required to test a single participant. In traditional research it takes a lot of time for a researcher to test people individually; the investigator needs to arrive at the testing site in advance in order to set up the experimental apparatus and materials. Then the researcher waits for the participant to show up. People do not always honor their commitments, though; they may forget where to go or when to show up. If the participant appears, the session runs its course for perhaps 15 minutes up to an hour. Then the researcher needs to collect all the data forms, informed consent forms, put away any equipment, and close up shop.

For some projects, it would not be unreasonable to expect the time commitment to be an hour per person. Web-based research requires the initial time to create a web

TABLE 3.4   Samples of web-based research (Azar, 2000c).

SURVEY RESEARCH

Topic: Is there a relationship between how easily a person feels disgust and whether they are likely to choose a career in medicine?
Researcher: Kathy Straub, Ph.D., Johns Hopkins University (USA).

Topic: Long-term psychological effects of war experience.
Researchers: Ian Robbins, Ph.D., and Nigel Hung, Ph.D., University of Plymouth, Devon (United Kingdom).

Topic: What attitudes, behaviors, and values predict dating relationships?
Researcher: Nancy Frye, Ph.D. Texas Tech University (USA).

Topic: How do religion and people's beliefs interact?
Researcher: William E. Snell, Jr., Ph.D., Southeast Missouri State University (USA).

EXPERIMENTAL RESEARCH

Topic: How logical is a person's thought?
Researchers: Chrisoph Klauer, Ph.D., Birgit Naumer, Ph.D., and Jochen Musch, Ph.D., Bonn University (Germany).

Topic: Judgments and decision making.
Researcher: Jonathan Baron, Ph.D., University of Pennsylvania (USA).

page, but this time commitment probably would not exceed the time required to put together the in-the-lab, paper version of the study. Over time, a web-based project could involve significantly less time per person than a laboratory-based project because there is no required laboratory setup.

A second advantage of web-based research is that the investigator does not need to be available when a participant is interested in engaging in the task. The web is open all day, every day. Data collection occurs at the convenience of the participant, not at the inconvenience of a researcher who has to set aside time from a busy schedule to be in the lab.

A third advantage of web research is that data collection is automatic and accurate. In the traditional version of research, an investigator has to transfer information from an original data sheet to some other form so data analysis can take place. When the amount of data from a single person is large, there are more opportunities for error. Even when the transfer of information is accurate, it may take a long time. When research occurs on the web, the investigator can create a means by which the data are automatically transferred to a file for data analysis. The chance for error diminishes drastically.

A fourth advantage is that we can generate a sample of participants that extends beyond college students; any interested person of any age who is living anywhere in the world can take part.

Potential Problems with Web-Based Research

As you will see throughout this book, any solution to the question of how to conduct research introduces its own problems. We want to make sure that we eliminate major difficulties and that the limitations that remain are as minimal as possible. In the case of web-based research, we eliminate the disadvantages of having to schedule participants to test in person, to code and transfer data, and so forth. At the same time, we introduce potential problems.

For example, the research can take place in the absence of the investigator, but we also lose the advantage of having a person who can help a participant who is uncertain of how to proceed, who might misunderstand directions, or who might have a question. Thus, although the investigator does not have to be present (an advantage), it is also true that the researcher *cannot* be there (a disadvantage). The question that we need to address is whether we gain or lose more through data collection in the laboratory versus on the web.

In addition, the gain in accuracy in data collection can be offset if remote participants provide poor data. If they do not take the research seriously or if they return to the web site for repeated testing, the quality of the data will suffer. Once again, because of the remote nature of the procedure, the investigator may never know about the problem. Fortunately, research on the quality of data collected on the web suggests that the quality is high (Azar, 2000b).

One aspect of the quality of our data is associated with the nature of our research participants. As psychologists, we have been willing to generalize our research results from college student populations to people in general. How wise is this? Students are different from most of the rest of the population—they are young, well-educated, intelligent, motivated, etc. Such traits make them ideal research participants, but do they act differently from other kinds of people?

We should raise the same issues regarding internet samples. People who surf the web may be quite different from people who don't. According to Krantz and Dalal (2000), the results of traditional laboratory studies with college students correspond quite closely to web-based research and the internet samples are broader than the typical college student sample. This should provide some comfort to us as researchers because the behaviors of the larger group, computer users, resemble those of college students. There are many differences between computer users and the population as a whole, but we have extended the scope of our research results with internet research.

A fourth consideration involves the ethics of internet research. As researchers, we need to act ethically, providing informed consent and debriefing, making sure that there is no immediate or long-term harm to participants, making sure that participants are of legal age, and so forth. When a participant is at a remote location, it may not be easy to guarantee ethical safeguards.

The Future of the Web in Psychology

Increasingly, psychologists are bringing research to the world at large. As we have seen, there are limitations to the kind of research that is possible, and we face new ethical concerns, but we can see the potential for increased contact with populations that we have previously ignored. The samples generated by internet research will not involve random selection, which is an ideal that psychological research seldom achieves. But internet-based studies are likely to be broader than the typical, college-student samples that most research includes. And given the ease with which we can conduct such projects, they are almost certain to increase in size and scope.

We must remember that the research results we obtain via the internet will only be as good as the methodology we develop. The same careful attention to detail is important for internet research as in any other research. Once the details of the investigation are in place, there are ways to enhance the likelihood of success in a project. Table 3.5 presents some tips for creating successful web pages for research.

Most of the serious research listed on the web is the product of professionals with extensive training. However, students are beginning to get into the act as well. For instance, students at schools that are geographically separated from one another are getting together. Students at Clarion University in western Pennsylvania and West Chester University in eastern Pennsylvania created research teams that consisted of students from both schools. They received help from students studying English at Casper College in Wyoming and from a technological specialist at Georgia Tech Research Institute when they needed it. Some of the benefits of such collaboration are that the students mimic professional researchers who collaborate at a distance, the students learn how to assemble a research project realistically, and they can benefit from the discussion of people with varied perspectives (Chamberlin, 2000).

DISCUSSION QUESTIONS

1. Even though using the internet can help diversify the nature of our research participants, why are we not likely to get a sample that is truly representative of the population?
2. What are four advantages to internet-based research? Identify a potential disadvantage that might arise in association with each advantage.

TABLE 3.5   Guidelines for creating an internet-based research project.

1. *Become familiar with related research.* You can take cues from the work others have done and avoid simply repeating research that others have already done, perhaps with a better methodology than you would have developed on your own.

2. *Keep your web page simple, but attractive.* Try not to keep your potential participants waiting as they access lengthy web pages. At the same time, you should develop an attractive, professional-looking site.

3. *Follow the regulations regarding ethics in research.* The same rules and regulations about ethics in research pertain to internet-based research. Several important points stand out; you need to check out all aspects of the approval process, however.

   ■ Virtually every academic institution has an Institutional Review Board (IRB) to evaluate the degree of potential risk associated with participation in your research. All research, whether by students or by professional researchers, requires approval by the IRB. Most schools have a specific form to complete.

   ■ You need to insure that participants understand the concept of informed consent. It will be crucial to let people know that participation is voluntary and that, by sending you their responses, they agree to let you include their responses in your analysis. You must tell them that they can terminate their participation at any time.

   ■ The law regards some people as unable to provide informed consent. That is, legally they are barred from volunteering to participate without approval of parents or guardians. For instance, people under the age of 18 may be legally unable to volunteer on their own. You should highlight this restriction.

   ■ Naturally, if there is any deception, you need to debrief your participants, but the best means of doing this is not clear at this point.

4. *Give an adequate description of your research.* It will also generate goodwill if you provide some means by which the participants can learn about the results of your research. You can gain cooperation from potential participants by educating them about the importance of your research. Tell them what questions you are addressing, how long their participation will take, and how you will protect their confidentiality. It would be ideal to keep their participation anonymous, so that nobody knows they took part.

5. *Check out your newly created web site thoroughly.* If you create a web site, you will be familiar with it, so some of the snags in using it may not be clear to you. It will help to get naïve people to test your page. In addition, you can minimize problems if you check your web page on as many different computers as possible. Not all machines display information identically; pretesting the web pages can reduce the frustrations that your participants experience and can result in data that are more valid.

6. *Find out how to disseminate information about your study.* Several web sites that list ongoing research, and various electronic discussion groups may allow you to post announcements about your research.

CHECKING ON RESEARCH: THE ROLE OF REPLICATION

Any single study cannot confirm or refute a hypothesis definitively. No matter how experienced the researchers may be, their results may be inaccurate. Their participants might have been an unusual group or the assignment of those participants to different

Validity—A property of data, concepts, or research findings whereby they are useful for measuring or understanding phenomena that they are of interest to a psychologist. Data, concepts, and research findings fall on a continuum of usefulness for a given application.

Replication—In research, the act of recreating or reproducing an earlier study to see if its results can be repeated.

Exact Replication—The act of recreating or reproducing an earlier study exactly as it was conducted initially.

Replication with Extension—The act of recreating or reproducing an earlier study with the addition of new elements to extend beyond the original work.

Conceptual Replication—The act of reproducing earlier research conceptually, not carrying it out exactly as originally done.

Type I Error—In statistics, erroneously deciding that there is a significant effect when the effect is due to measurement error.

Type II Error—In statistics, erroneously failing to decide that there is a significant effect when it is obscured by measurement error.

Construct Validity—The degree to which a measurement accurately measures the underlying concept that it supposed to be measured.

conditions may have led to nonequivalent groups. The wording of questions asked may have misled people. Or the selection of the variable to be measured might have been inappropriate. If any of these problems occurred, the **validity** of the results would suffer. Validity in this case refers to whether your results mean what you intend them to mean. When the validity is questionable, the explanations for the behavior are suspect. The reason you need to take an entire course in research methods is because these types of problems can and do occur; you have to learn to anticipate problems as well as possible to deal with them and to recognize that you cannot eliminate them all.

This may sound like a pessimistic view, but the truth is that with enough systematic research on a topic, we can identify the problems and take them into account. Ideally, researchers will **replicate** their research, which means to repeat the investigations to see if the same results emerge. Replications can take different forms. In **exact replication,** a researcher repeats an earlier investigation exactly. In **replication with extension,** the experimenter asks the same question, but adds something new. The advantage of the replication with extension is that you don't spend your time merely repeating what we think might be true and that we already know; you are advancing beyond the initial knowledge. In a **conceptual replication,** the researcher attacks the same basic question, but does it from a different approach.

Replication serves several important functions. First, replication can provide additional support for theories. Second, it can help us avoid seeing things that aren't there (**Type I errors**) and failing to see things that are there (**Type II errors**). That is, if an initial project erroneously suggested that some behavioral pattern was real, replications could confirm or deny that claim. Or if research seemed to indicate erroneously that some behaviors were likely, replications could show that to be false.

A third advantage of replication is that we can increase the **construct validity** of our concepts. This means that when we are dealing with complicated and abstract concepts, such as anxiety or depression, we develop more confidence in what they involve by making diverse measurements of the same concept.

A fourth effect of replications is to help protect against fraud. If researchers who might cheat know that their work will be put to the test, they may be less likely to engage in that fraud. If they have engaged in fraud, replications can call the earlier research into question.

Even with such clear positive aspects of replication, simple replications seldom occur; replications with extension are more prevalent, but they appear in research journals with considerably less frequency than original research reports.

We can identify several reasons as to why researchers advocate replication but do not do it. In the end, all the reasons come down to the relative payoff for the time and energy devoted to the replication. Scientists prefer to conduct original, novel research because it generates new knowledge, for which the rewards are greater. Doing a replication is like finishing second in a race. Nobody cares about the person or remembers who it was. Familiar people in the history of psychology have often worried a great deal that they would not get credit for their ideas. Outside of psychology, people are no different. Do you know who Elisha Gray was? For the answer and for a historical illustration about finishing second, see Controversy Box 3.2.

■ ■ ■ ■ ■ ■

CONTROVERSY BOX 3.2
CONTROVERSY: Scientists Competing to Finish Second

The desire to be recognized as the person who made a key discovery is and has always been prominent among scientists. As Merton (1983) pointed out, the famed nineteenth-century psychiatrist Jean Martin Charcot worked hard to claim priority for the idea of treating hysterics by isolating them from other people. Similarly, Sigmund Freud recorded on more than 150 occasions his priority in making discoveries. According to Merton, Freud even had dreams about being the first to develop his psychological ideas.

The race for priority exists in all of the sciences and is certainly not new. As Merton noted, "Almost all of those firmly placed in the pantheon of science—Newton, Descartes, Leibniz, Pascal and Huyghens, Lister, Faraday, Laplace and Davy—were caught up in passionate efforts to achieve priority and to have it publicly registered" (p. 256) In fact, according to Merton, Newton was sometimes obsessed with the question of establishing priority.

Galileo took an unusual precaution to ensure that he would be given credit for being the first to discover Saturn's rings. He created a sentence that was really an anagram; when it was unscrambled, it contained the critical information on the planet (Sobel, 2000). Unfortunately, when Galileo sent the anagram, which was in Latin, to a fellow scientist, it was unscrambled incorrectly as a message about the two moons of Mars (King, 2000).

The race for priority continued into the 1950s as scientists were rushing to discover the structure of DNA. There was a concerted effort by several different teams of scientists to be the first. More recently, scientists again fought to be the first to identify the virus associated with AIDS. The arguments by French and American scientists were especially bitter and have led to the tarnishing of reputations (Crewdson, 2002).

A historical example illustrates what happens when two people claim priority in a discovery—only one receives recognition. Everybody knows who Alexander Graham Bell (1847–1922) was—the inventor of the telephone. But who was Elisha Gray?

According to the *Encyclopedia Britannica* (1974), Elisha Gray (1835–1901) applied for a patent the same day that Bell did, but virtually nobody knows who Gray was because the courts ultimately ruled that the patent belonged to Bell.

Using an analogy, we can say that Bell first published his ideas and Gray merely replicated them. We remember Bell, but few people know about Gray. There have always been contests for priority in research discoveries because people remember the first person, but not the second. This is why researchers tend not to want to spend their time completing replications.

Actually, there is another lesson here. Sometimes priority may not go to the person who first makes a discovery, but to the person who publicizes the discovery. Bell may not really have been the inventor of the telephone. He received the credit because he received the patent on the telephone, but the truth is that Gray developed several components of Bell's first working telephone. These components did not appear anywhere in Bell's original patent application.

At the heart of this desire to be first is the recognition that the investigator gains from other renowned experts in the field. History tells us that the person who gains recognition first gets the prize, the replicator only obscurity.

The meager reward for replication dissuades most researchers from attempting them. Ross, Hall, and Heater (1998) have identified several specific reasons for the lack of published replications in nursing and occupational therapy research. The same principles hold for all behavioral research. First, they suggest, journals are reluctant to publish replications. Second, researchers may be reluctant to submit replications because they contain little that is new. Third, colleagues and professors encourage original research. Fourth, funding for replication research may be very limited. Fifth, in writing up the initial research, investigators may not provide enough detail for others who want to replicate. None of these barriers is insurmountable, but they certainly need to be overcome.

DISCUSSION QUESTIONS

1. Given the advantages of replication, why isn't it more common than it is?
2. What could be the advantage of an exact replication over a conceptual one? Why might a conceptual replication be better?
3. Why could it be more profitable for a beginning researcher to do an exact replication, while it would be more profitable for a seasoned researcher to do a conceptual replication?

DON'T REINVENT THE WHEEL: REVIEWING THE LITERATURE

All researchers recognize that replicating previous research is a good idea, but we also recognize that it is more useful to replicate with extension than simply to replicate. That is, it is important to develop and test new ideas as we verify the old ones. The implication is that it pays greater dividends if we can generate new knowledge in our research.

In order to maximize the gains in our research projects, it pays to know what researchers have already done. No matter what topic you choose for a research project, somebody has undoubtedly paved the way already. There is no doubt that they had to solve problems in developing a methodology that satisfied them. You do not need to repeat their mistakes. In fact, researchers consider it completely legitimate to borrow ideas from others, as long as we give appropriate credit to them and don't pass the ideas off as our own.

What this means is that you are allowed to borrow somebody else's methodology for your own purposes. If it worked for them, it might work for you, and it has the advantage of having been pre-tested. A journal article has generally been evaluated by experts in the field and further reviewed by the journal editor. The article will not appear in print unless these experts agree that both the methodology and the ideas are sound. You can learn a lot about what to do (and what not do to) by reading the work of respected professionals.

| Literature Review—An overview of published journal articles, books, and other professional work on a given topic. |

What Is a Literature Review?

In order to find out what has been done in an area that interests you, you should conduct a **literature review.** When we talk about literature in everyday language, we generally hear about writers like Alice Walker, F. Scott Fitzgerald, Charles Dickens, and others in the pantheon of writing. People presume that any work penned by these authors is worthwhile. On the other hand, people may minimize the importance of other writers, like the horror novelist Stephen King. The enormous success of his popular and compelling work tells us that many people enjoy it. So why is his work not "literature"? In reality, it all depends on your definition of "good writing."

Among researchers, the term "literature" refers to the body of work that is considered to be of high enough quality to appear in technical journals. Psychology has its own pantheon of writers whose words (and research) have had an impact on the field. Psychology has its own versions of Stephen King as well, whose work might be considered highly valuable by one group, but minimized by another.

At the other end of the continuum are those authors who produce temporarily popular books like romance novels. These works capture an audience, but the books (and their ideas) themselves have short lives. There is a comparable group among psychologists. Radio talk show hosts like "Dr. Laura" are popular but are not taken seriously by the psychological community. Although people may ask "Dr. Laura" for advice, she is neither a psychologist nor a psychiatrist.

The Effect of Peer Review on the Research Literature

Peer Review—A process in which scientific research and ideas are evaluated by experts in a field so that obvious errors or other problems can be spotted and corrected before a work is published or presented at a research conference.

As a researcher you need to differentiate among the various levels of writing that constitute our psychological literature. This is often a judgment call, but articles that appear in **peer-reviewed** journals have been taken seriously by experts. A peer-reviewed journal publishes articles that have undergone careful scrutiny and may have been revised by the authors several times until they have eliminated any major problems. This process is a stringent one. Among the best psychology journals, the rejection rate may be around 70 percent or more. Thus, the editor accepts only 30 percent or fewer of the articles that are submitted.

One of the reasons for such a low acceptance rate is that in psychology, our ideas are very complex and abstract. We often have to develop clever operational definitions of our concepts because we cannot observe and measure them directly. It takes considerable diligence to create and conduct a well-designed study that deals with the ideas successfully. There are many ways for ambiguities and uncertainties to creep in, so reviewers and editors frequently request an author to do additional work to take care of these problems.

In disciplines that are more descriptive, such as botany or other areas of biology, the acceptance rate for major journals is often much higher than in psychology. The ideas they work with are often straightforward and obvious, so the research is easier to design. (The tools and techniques of the natural and physical sciences may be difficult to master, but so are those in the behavioral sciences. In any case, we shouldn't confuse the concepts of a science, which are the most important elements, with the tools, which are merely tools.) The differences between psychology and other disciplines in this regard do not imply that one domain is more or less important or useful; it simply means that different areas of research make different demands on researchers.

DISCUSSION QUESTIONS
1. Why can the peer review process lead to high-quality published research? Can you think of any drawbacks?
2. What are the advantages of a literature review of research related to your own investigations?

HOW TO CONDUCT A LITERATURE REVIEW

Researchers publish an enormous amount of research each year. In fact, there are over a thousand journals that publish psychology-related articles. Most libraries will have no more than a tiny fraction of them on hand, so even if you wanted to browse through each one of them, you would not be able to.

So how do you find out what has appeared in print? The easiest way is to use an electronic database that lists psychological research. The most useful database for psychologists is PsycINFO®, which is published by the American Psychological Association. It references over 1,300 journals published in 25 languages, and in its most complete version, PsycINFO® cites articles going back to 1887.

Electronic Databases

PsycINFO® is a modern successor to *Psychological Abstracts (PA)*, which appears in a paper version. PsycINFO® is extremely easy to use compared to *PA*. The basic strategy is to select a term of interest to you and to tell PsycINFO® to search for published articles related to that term. There are strategies that you can use to maximize the likelihood of finding what you are seeking without also generating a long string of less relevant material. On the flip side, there are ways to expand the number of citations you generate so you can get a more complete picture of the research in the area.

Using PsycINFO® is easy, but you need to learn how to do it if you want to maximize the return on your time. In the following sections, you will learn about useful strategies for searching databases. Keep in mind that we will be focusing on PsycINFO®. If you use other databases, the particulars of your search may differ somewhat, but once you learn PsycINFO®, you can adapt your search strategies to other databases.

Starting Your Search

A first step in searching for information is to decide on a relevant term that matches your interest. This is an important first step because it will determine the nature of the articles listed in your output.

The number of published articles listed in PsycINFO® continues to increase because researchers keep publishing their work. Thus, any specific examples that appear here will become outdated over time. Nonetheless, you can get an idea of how to generate worthwhile search strategies.

Suppose that you are interested in finding out about psychological aspects of adopting children. You could type the word *adoption* and begin the search. In early

2001, entering the word *adoption* resulted in a list of 9,932 references. Obviously, it would be impractical to read every source, but you would not want to in any case because there are many citations that do not relate to your topic in the least. The reason that a search of *adoption* generates irrelevant references is that if you type in a word, PsycINFO® will search for the word, regardless of the way that word is used.

For example, in the search for *adoption*, 22 of the first 30 listings had nothing to do with adopting children. Table 3.6 gives the titles of the first five. Only two of them relate to adopting children. PsycINFO® does not know what meaning of the word *adoption* you intend without some help from you. If the article relates to adopting some strategy or plan, the database will include it.

TABLE 3.6   Titles of the first 5 (of 9932) articles produced by PsycINFO® for *adoption* anywhere in the citation and the use of the word *adoption* in those citations.

REFERENCE	REASON FOR INCLUSION IN A SEARCH FOR *ADOPTION*
Rosen, C. R. (2000). Integrating state and continuum models to explain processing of exercise messages and exercise initiation among sedentary collect students. *Health Psychology, 19*, 172–180.	The research explains how people tailor messages to recipients' depth of processing and intent. It discusses whether a particular approach should be *adopted* in future research.
Blalock, S., Currey, S. S., DeVellis, R. F., Giorgino, K. B., Anderson, J. J. B., Dooley, M. A., & Gold, D. T. (2000). Effects of educational materials concerning osteoporosis on women's knowledge, beliefs, and behavior. *American Journal of Health Promotion, 14*, 161–169.	The study also examined whether observed effects varied as a function of one's stage in the precaution *adoption* process. (Note: This refers to the adoption of exercise programs and dietary changes.)
Finkel, D., Pedersen, N. L. Berg, Stig, & Johansson, B. (2000). Quantitative genetic analysis of biobehavioral markers of aging in Swedish studies of adult twins. *Journal of Aging and Health, 12*, 47–68.	Replicated and extended the results of D. Finkel et al. (1995) using data from the Swedish *Adoption/*Twin Study of Aging
Stricker, G. (2000). The scientist-practitioner model: Gandhi was right again. *American Psychologist, 55*, 253–254.	Examines the *adoption* of and the ideas behind the scientist-practitioner model from the Boulder Conference.
Edwards, C. E., & Williams, C. L. (2000). Adopting change: Birth mothers in maternity homes today. *Gender and Society, 14*, 160–183.	Examined the reasons some pregnant women enter maternity homes with the plan to place their babies for *adoption*.

You can find ways to limit the search so you don't have thousands of citations, many of which are irrelevant. One of the most useful steps is to specify that the database should list citations whose *subject* is adoption. If you do not actively specify your search this way, PsycINFO® will look for the word *adoption* anywhere at all. In the current search, when the subject of the article in the search was adoption, the search led to 3,472 hits. This is a 65 percent reduction in the number of hits; most of the reduction involved work that is irrelevant to adoptions.

You can further reduce the number of irrelevant citations. Table 3.7 illustrates the steps you can take to narrow your search to be more productive. One involves using the PsycINFO® thesaurus to identify a narrower term than you are using; another pertains to setting limits on the search process, like a restricted range of years in which

TABLE 3.7   Examples of strategies to reduce the number of irrelevant citations in a PsycINFO® search.

SEARCH FOR REFERENCES TO ADOPTION	STRATEGY TO NARROW THE SEARCH	NUMBER OF REFERENCES
Adoption anywhere in the citation		9932
Adoption as the Subject of the reference	Choose "Word Appears in Subject." (You can also select "Author" if you want to name an author who has studied adoption.)	3472
Only work published since 1980	Choose "Set Other Limits" and indicate publication year of 1980 to the current year (or whatever time span you want).	2670
Only work published in the English language	Choose "Set Other Limits" and select English as the only language.	2582
Only work published in books or journals	Choose "Set Other Limits" and select material in journals, books and edited books. This eliminates hard to access material like doctoral dissertations.	1742
Only empirical studies (i.e., original research reports)	Choose "Set Other Limits" and select Publication Type = Empirical Studies.	918
Only work involving females in the adoption process	Choose "Set Other Limits" and select Population = Female.	258
Only work on adoption of children	Choose "Set Other Limits" and select Age Group = Childhood.	78

articles were published, types of studies (theoretical versus empirical), and populations (adults, children, women, men, etc.). There are quite a few ways to set limits to restrict the scope of your search.

If your search produces too few hits, there are ways of expanding it. One strategy is to insert a "wild card" in your search. For instance, in PsycINFO®, you can use an asterisk (*) to expand the search. When you enter the subject of your search as *adopt**, PsycINFO® will look for any subject beginning with *adopt*, such as *adopt, adoption*, and *adoptive*. You can also use the database's thesaurus, which tells you what terms to use when searching for a given concept. Table 3.8 gives a glimpse of the possibilities for expanding your search. By experimenting, you may be able to figure out alternate strategies for increasing the number of hits.

DISCUSSION QUESTIONS

1. Why does specifying a term as the *subject* of your search reduce the number of hits in PsycINFO® compared to simply telling PsycINFO® to search for the term?
2. Why is using a "wild card" going to expand the number of hits you get in a PsycINFO® search?
3. How can you reduce the number of irrelevant citations in a PsycINFO search?

TABLE 3.8   Strategies for expanding the number of relevant citations in PsycINFO®.

STRATEGY TO EXPAND THE SEARCH	RESULT
Use the *Suggest* option and enter "Adopt*" or "Adoption"	You get a list of terms that relate to your topic, like Adoptive, Adoptive Children, Biological Family, Interracial Adoption. You can use these as subjects for your search.
Use the *Thesaurus* option and enter "Adopt*"	You get a list of categories that PsycINFO® uses that are related to adoption.
Use the *Index* and enter "Adopt*" or "Adoption"	You get at least a dozen subject categories to search.
Example: Use the Thesaurus terms "adopted-children," "adoptees," "adoption-child," "interracial adoption," and "adoptive-parents" connected by OR (i.e., adopted-children OR adoptees OR adoption-child OR interracial-adoption OR adoptive-parents)	You get 156 citations that relate to the Thesaurus terms and that still follow the limits set in Table 3.6. Using OR tells PsycINFO® to access any citation that uses any of your terms. If you connected them with AND, PsycINFO® would only access those citations that include all those terms at the same time, which would restrict the search greatly. In fact, a single journal article is unlikely to fall into all these categories.

HOW TO READ A JOURNAL ARTICLE

When you first begin reading scientific writing, it may seem like it has been written in another language. Further, the organization of the information can seem convoluted. After you get used to the style of research reports, your task of reading journal articles will be easier. There is a reason for the organization of journal articles, and there is a skill involved in understanding scientific writing. Most likely, for your psychology courses, you will be reading articles written in a format often called *APA style*. This means that the authors have followed the guidelines set forth in the *Publication Manual of the American Psychological Association* (American Psychological Association, 2001). This style differs from others that you may have encountered, like MLA (Modern Language Association, 1995) for the humanities, or various formats for each of the scientific disciplines. APA style may seem complicated, but most of the rules are fairly easy to learn. The Publication Manual is over 400 pages long, though, so you can expect that there is a lot of detail about specific formatting and writing issues.

Understanding the Format of a Research Paper

When you pick up a research article written in APA style, you will be able to figure out very quickly where to look to find the information you seek. Writers divide their manuscripts into six sections as a rule. The actual number of sections will differ, depending on the complexity of the research report. Regardless of the exact number of sections, there are specific reasons why information appears where it does. Table 3.9 presents an overview of the different sections of a research report written in APA style and some of the questions addressed in those sections. Table 3.9 can serve as a worksheet to guide you in reading journal articles. If you write a brief answer to each of the questions in the table, you will have a pretty complete summary of the work that was done, why it was done, and what the authors think it means.

Abstract. In the **abstract,** the authors give an overview of the entire paper; this section is fairly short, usually fewer than 120 words. (Strictly speaking, the APA Publication Manual specifies that the abstract must contain no more than 960 characters and spaces.) It presents a preview of the research question and hypotheses, the methodology, the results, and the discussion. The abstract is kept short so you can get a quick glimpse into the nature of the research.

Abstract—The part of a research report that summarizes the purpose of the research, the methodology, the results of the study, and the interpretations of the research.

Introduction—The part of a research report that gives an overview of the field to be investigated and the investigator's hypotheses about the outcome of the research.

Introduction. After the abstract comes the **introduction,** which provides background information so you can understand the purpose of the research. When the research involves specific tests of hypotheses, the authors will generally present these hypotheses here. This section also gives a general preview of how the researchers have conducted their project. The purpose of the introduction is to clarify the purpose of the study and show how relevant ideas developed in previous research. You will virtually never see a journal article that does not refer to previous research on which the current article is based.

TABLE 3.9   Concepts that are clarified in the different sections of a research report.

INTRODUCTION

- What is the general topic of the research article?
- What do we know about this topic from previous research?
- What are the authors trying to demonstrate in their own research?
- What are their hypotheses?

METHODS

Participants—Who took part in the research?
- How many people (or animals) were studied?
- If there were nonhuman animals, what kind were they?
- If there were people, what were their characteristics (e.g., average and range of age, gender, race or ethnicity, were they volunteers or were they paid)?

Apparatus and Materials—What did the researchers need to carry out their study?
- What kind of stimuli, questions, etc. were used?
- How many different kinds of activities did participants complete?
- What instrumentation was used to present material to participants and to record their responses?

Procedure—What did the people actually do during the research session?
- After the participants arrived what did they do?
- What did the experimenters do as they interacted with participants?

RESULTS

- What were patterns of behaviors among participants?
- Did behaviors differ when different groups were compared?
- What type of behaviors are predictable in the different testing conditions?
- What were the results of any statistical tests?

DISCUSSION

- What do the results mean?
- What explanations can you develop for why the participants responded as they did?
- What psychological processes help you explain participants' responses?
- What questions have not been answered fully?
- How do your results relate to the research cited in the introduction?
- How do your results relate to other kinds of research?
- What new ideas emerge that you could evaluate in a subsequent experiment?

REFERENCES

- What research was cited in the research report (e.g., work published in journals or other written sources, research presentations, personal communications)?

As you read through the introduction, you will see that the first ideas are relatively broad. These ideas relate to a more general depiction of the field of interest to the researchers. As the introduction progresses, the scope of the material narrows. The authors will describe and discuss in more detail the research that relates most closely to their own project. Finally, the authors will present their own ideas. They may outline how they will clarify confusions from earlier research, correct problems, and test hypotheses. By the time you finish reading the introduction, you will have a clear picture of the logic that led from the ideas of previous researchers to those of the authors.

> **Methods**—The part of a research report that provides information about those who participated in the study, how the research was actually carried out, and the materials and apparatus used for it.

Methods.   Following the introduction is the **methods** section. This section should allow an independent researcher to reproduce the project described in the article. The methods section contains an extreme amount of detail. Very often, students regard this section as not being very important. In some ways, they are right: without it, they can understand why the researchers conducted the study and what results occurred. In another way, though, if they do not read this section, they might miss out on important details that affected the research outcome. This section is absolutely critical for those who want to replicate the original research.

> **Participants**—A subsection of the Methods Section that details the nature of the humans or nonhumans who took part in the research. Nonhuman animals are often referred to as *Subjects* whereas humans who took part are called *Participants*.
>
> **Materials and Apparatus**—A subsection of the Methods Section that details what implements and stimuli were used to carry out the study. Sometimes the materials and apparatus appear in separate subsections.
>
> **Procedure**—A subsection of the Methods Section that provides extensive detail about the actual process used to carry out the study.

Participants.   Writers subdivide the methods section into three or four sections. The first one, **participants,** characterizes those who took part in the study. It describes how many were there, what were their ages, racial and ethnic backgrounds, etc. This subsection provides the reader with enough information to understand if the nature of the participants may have influenced the outcome of the research in some way.

Materials and Apparatus.   The next subsection, **materials and apparatus,** provides details about what you would need to carry out the study. Sometimes writers will create separate subsections for the materials and apparatus if there is a need.

Procedure.   After the description of the implements of the study, the authors will describe the **procedure.** In the procedure subsection, they describe exactly what occurred during the research session. As a rule, the procedure subsection includes only what occurs during the data collection session. Based on the information in this section, an independent researcher could follow the steps that the original researchers took.

Results.   After the data collection is complete, scientists typically analyze their results with some kind of statistical test. Although choosing a statistical test seems to be a pretty straightforward task, there are actually controversies in some cases about the best approach to data analysis.

If you chose one approach, you might end up with one conclusion; if you took an alternate approach, your conclusion might be different. This issue has such great implications that the American Psychological Association created a task force that issued guidelines about research methodology and statistics. The task force wrote an important article that highlights some of the controversies associated with statistics (Wilkinson & the Task Force on Statistical Inference, 1999).

Results—The part of a research report that details the quantitative and qualitative results of an investigation, including results of statistical analyses.

The **results** section details the outcome of the study. The results reflect what happened. For example, if two groups are compared, the results section tells whether they differed and by how much. The results section also presents the results of any statistical tests that the researchers conducted. This part of a research report can be very complicated because you have to translate technical materials and terminology into comprehensible English.

One way to make sure that you understand what you are reading is to keep track of the different research questions that the investigators have asked. You can do this by making note of them when you read the introduction. Then when they present the statistics, you can try to figure out the particular question that goes along with the statistic.

You will also encounter figures and tables in the results section. The purpose of these graphic elements is to provide an overview when the results are complicated. By creating a figure or chart, the authors can combine a large amount of information into a single picture.

Discussion.   The data do not mean anything until we, as researchers, decide what they mean. When we ask a research question, our task is to take complicated data about a question that we are the first to ask and see what the data tell us. Because nobody else has done what we have, we are the ones who have to figure out what it all means. This should not come as a surprise because research is supposed to lead to knowledge that nobody else has yet developed; a successful investigation generates new information that has to be interpreted and placed in the context of earlier research.

Discussion—The part of a research report that provides an interpretation of the results, going beyond a simple description of the results and statistical tests.

This final section of text, the **discussion,** provides closure to the project. That is, the investigators tell you what their results mean. Unlike the results section, which says *what happened,* the discussion tells you *why* it happened. Another way to characterize the distinction is that the results section provides fact, whereas the discussion section provides interpretation, explanation, and speculation. The results of a study are incontrovertible; they are what they are. What may be controversial, however, is the interpretation of the results.

One interpretation of Münsterberg's research (1914) was that women were unable to profit by discussion, so they were unfit to serve on juries. You could come up with a very different, but legitimate, interpretation. You could argue that women will make up their minds and not fall victim to arguments of others that might be fallacious. You could argue that men might change their minds if there was a single strong personality on the jury, even if that individual was making a poor decision. Women might not be susceptible to this problem.

When researchers draw their conclusions, other researchers can evaluate them and develop their own research to verify or refute the initial ideas. Burtt (1920) felt that the group of men (graduate students) and women (undergraduates) in Münsterberg's study were not comparable, so he completed his own research to remove that problem and found no difference between men and women in their jury-related abilities.

If Burtt did not have enough information about Münsterberg's methodology, he would not have known that the men and women came from different populations. This attests to the importance of a complete methods section. Small details can be important details. In addition, scientific research advances when the investigative process is public, open, and accessible.

References—The part of a research report that contains complete reference information about any work cited in the research report, that is, where the work was published or presented and the source of any work that has not been published or presented.

References. In the **references** section of the research report, the authors cite any references mentioned in the paper. It is important that readers be able to go back and read relevant material rather than simply relying on what somebody else has reported. Occasionally, an author will err in a presentation or develop a conclusion from another researcher's work. By providing a complete reference section, authors allow readers to gain access to the body of literature that the authors thought was important in the development of their own ideas.

APA style dictates a specific format for virtually any kind of reference, including references from the World Wide Web. The details are quite specific. With practice, they are not hard to master.

DISCUSSION QUESTIONS

1. Why is it important to distinguish between the material presented in the results section of a journal article and that in the discussion section? That is, what different information does each provide?

2. Why is it important to include extensive detail in the methods section of a research report?

CHAPTER SUMMARY

Research ideas come from many different sources. Ultimately, it boils down to the fact that somebody has a question and wants to find an answer. Sometimes the source of a research project begins with an "I wonder what would happen if . . ." type of question. In other cases, there is a problem to be solved and an investigator will use research skills to devise an answer that can be applied to the situation. In still other cases, a theory makes a prediction that a scientist can test through research.

Regardless of the source of ideas, the scientists who investigate them take their cues from the society around them. Scientists are members of their community and share the same attitudes and values as many others in our society. Thus, social issues are important in determining what a particular researcher will think important. This consideration is true for any scientific discipline, but it is especially true in the study of human behavior.

In our current social context, the internet has become important in research. Psychologists are studying how to use the internet as a research tool. A number of important issues need to be addressed before web-based research can flourish, but scientists are working on the question.

Regardless of the topics of research or how the data are collected, we want to have confidence in the results. We want them to be meaningful. One way to ensure that scientific findings are useful is through replication, that is, repetition of the research by different investigators in different contexts. When the same results appear regularly, we can have greater confidence that our conclusions are warranted.

When you generate a research project, you can get guidance about how to conduct it by reading what others have done. This usually involves a literature review of published studies. Without such a review, you run the risk of simply repeating what others have already done. Such a replication may give you more confidence in the phenomenon you are studying, but most researchers want to include novel features in their research so they can advance the field with new knowledge. One way to increase what we know about the behaviors we study is through publication of the results in scientific journals and through presentations at research conferences.

Finally, if you conduct research, you may write it up in a formal report. You are likely to follow the style of presentation set forth in the *Publication Manual of the American Psychological Association.*

CHAPTER FOUR

PRACTICAL ISSUES IN PLANNING YOUR RESEARCH

CHAPTER OVERVIEW

CHAPTER PREVIEW

**PRACTICAL QUESTIONS
IN PLANNING RESEARCH**

**UNDERSTANDING YOUR IDEAS:
CREATING VARIABLES**
Carrying Out a Literature Search
Defining Your Concepts and Variables
  *The Importance of Culture and Context
  in Defining Variables*
  *The Diversity of Possible
  Operational Definitions*

CONDUCTING YOUR STUDY
Determining the Research Setting
Choosing Your Methodology
  Approaches to Psychological Research
Selecting Research Materials
  and Procedures
  Why Methodology Is Important

CHOOSING THE PEOPLE YOU STUDY
The Nature of Your Participants
Deciding How Many Participants
  to Include

PROBABILITY SAMPLING

Simple Random Sampling
Systematic Sampling
Stratified Random Sampling
Cluster Sampling

NONPROBABILITY SAMPLING
Convenience Sampling
Quota Sampling
Purposive (Judgmental) Sampling
Chain-Referral Sampling

MAKING USEFUL MEASUREMENTS
Reliability and Validity
The SAT: Questions of Reliability
  and Validity

***CONTROVERSY: Is the Head Start
Program Effective?***

**DIFFERING APPROACHES IN
DIFFERENT AREAS OF PSYCHOLOGY**
Different Approaches
  in Different Journals
Different Types of Participants
  in Different Journals
Making Choices in Your Research Design

CHAPTER SUMMARY

KEY TERMS

Applied research
Archival research
Basic (theoretical) research
Case study

Chain-referral sampling
Cluster sampling
Convenience sampling
Convergent validity

Correlational research
Criterion variable
Dependent variable (DV)
Experimental approach

Generalization	Population	Representative sample
Independent variable (IV)	Predictive validity	Sample
Interrater (interobserver)	Predictor variable	Simple random sampling
reliability	Probability sampling	Split-half reliability
Hypothetical construct	Purposive (judgmental)	Stratified random
Longitudinal research	sampling	sampling
Measurement error	Qualitative research	Systematic sampling
Nonsampling error	Quasi-experiment	Test-retest reliability
Observational approach	Quota sampling	Variable
Operational definition	Reliability	

CHAPTER PREVIEW

When most students are learning about research, they typically are not aware of how many decisions are made in putting a project together. You will find that when you read a journal article, you learn only what the researchers finally did, not what they tried that didn't work. The reason for this lack of information is that journal space is in short supply. There is always more to print than the journals have space for. As a result, authors omit just about everything not entirely germane to the topic they are studying. The authors report only what was successful. Another result is that as a reader, if you want to plan your own research project, you can use the information in published work, but you have to fill in a lot of details on your own.

The researchers leave out information on false starts, procedures that did not work out, and judgments that led to an unsatisfactory outcome. You can be sure that in virtually every research project ever conducted, the researchers made choices that caused them to stop and evaluate what they were doing, and to make changes to improve the research design.

Some of the tasks associated with completing a study include describing in concrete terms the concepts you are interested in, figuring out how to measure them, identifying the group of people who will participate in your study, carrying out the project itself, looking at and understanding the results, then interpreting what you've discovered. If you make poor choices or conclusions at any step along the way, your research will be less meaningful than it could otherwise be.

In each case, the choices you make will each take you in a slightly different direction than some other choice. Each of these steps will involve making quite a few decisions that, you hope, will provide you with a clear answer to your original question.

PRACTICAL QUESTIONS
IN PLANNING RESEARCH

When you read about successful research projects either in a scientific journal or in a popular magazine or when you see a report on television, the reporter makes the research sound as if it were put together perfectly and that there was only one reasonable way to have conducted it. In reality, if you were to follow a research project from beginning to end, you would see that the researchers had to make a great number of decisions about the study.

We investigate concepts that are very complex and abstract. This means that we need to simplify the complex ideas so our research doesn't become unmanageable. We also have to take ideas that don't have concrete representations and generate concrete ways to measure them. For example, sadness is an idea that can help us understand why people act as they do. But what is sadness? It is a complex set of emotions that we don't have an easy way to measure.

If we consider the goals of science, we can see that we could try to describe what it means to be sad. To do so, we have to identify what behaviors reflect sadness. If we don't describe sadness well, we can't move to the more difficult goal of predicting when it will occur. How can you predict what you can't describe? Beyond that, we will not be able to understand when it occurs, or how to control it.

In other areas of science, researchers frequently engage in descriptive research. They may count the number of plants that live in a particular type of field, or the number of animals born with deformities due to the presence of toxic substances. In this research, the concepts are fairly obvious and easy to measure. In some areas, the research may require complex tools to answer the scientists' questions, but although the tools are complex, the concepts are relatively simple. In psychology, we use tools that may be easy to develop (e.g., measuring behaviors on a scale of 1 to 10), but the concepts are complex.

Once you decide on a research question, you need to fill in the details about how you will carry out your project. This aspect of your task is not necessarily difficult, but you need to consider carefully myriad details. These details are the subject of the rest of this book. A research project can take many different paths; you have to decide how you want yours to proceed so that you arrive at the best answer to your question.

DISCUSSION QUESTIONS
1. How is psychological research methodology affected by the fact that we study complex and abstract concepts?
2. What decisions do researchers have to make in investigating complex psychological concepts?

UNDERSTANDING YOUR IDEAS: CREATING VARIABLES

If your research is going to be data-driven, you have to measure something. When you decide the topic you want to study, one of the next steps is to figure out what you will be observing. Because psychologists study complex ideas, the question of measurement sometimes poses difficulties. For instance, if you wanted to study depression, you could do so in any number of ways.

Social psychologists who study depression might investigate the extent to which a depressed person has social ties in the community. A researcher interested in family dynamics would focus on parents, siblings, and partners. Someone interested in psychological testing and assessment might try to identify tests that are most effective in identifying somebody who shows signs of depression. A neuroscientist could study the role of neurotransmitters in depression. All of these psychologists would tell you that they were studying depression, but each one would be doing it in a different way. Depending on how you approached the study of depression, you would define and measure that concept in different ways. In order to find out how to do that, your best first step would be to search the literature to see what others have already done.

You can see in Table 4.1 that investigators gather a lot of information from previously published research. The number of references cited is considerable, providing some confidence that the investigators have a firm grasp of the issues they are dealing with and that they know how the major researchers in the area have done their work. If you plan your own research projects, it is unlikely that you will have the 47 references that the typical article in *JEP: Applied* does. You are a beginning researcher without the background that professional researchers have gained in their work. It may be perfectly acceptable to include many fewer references as you develop a narrower focus in your first projects.

Carrying Out a Literature Search

Suppose you wanted to study stress levels and the effects they have on students. Investigators at UCLA found that over 30 percent of first-year college students said they frequently felt overwhelmed by what they had to do (http://www.intelihealth.com). Stress levels in college students have been rising since 1985, according to ongoing research.

This is not an easy area to investigate because the concept of importance here, stress, is not directly observable. It is an internal, psychological state. You can observe only the behaviors and reactions associated with it. To understand it, you should find out what others have already learned. You do this by conducting an initial literature search.

This strategy has several particularly important effects. First, by learning about what other researchers have discovered, you can avoid merely repeating what they have done. It is always more exciting to create a study that generates knowledge that nobody knew before you did.

A second advantage of searching through the research literature is that you find the vast range of approaches that previous researchers have used to investigate a given topic. With this knowledge, you can begin to identify the approach that might be most useful to you in answering your own question.

Third, you can see what approach others have used and how they defined their variables. This lets you see what worked for them. When planning research, there is absolutely nothing wrong with adopting the methods that others have used. If you think back on the concept that scientific knowledge is cumulative, you will recognize that researchers expect others to follow up on their work, just as they have followed up on the work of others.

Defining Your Concepts and Variables

Once you have a feel for how researchers carry out their projects, you can adapt their methods to yours. As you plan your project, you need to translate your general ideas into

TABLE 4.1 **Examples of participants included in different studies in three major psychology journals.**

JOURNAL OF EXPERIMENTAL PSYCHOLOGY: APPLIED (2000, VOL. 6, NO. 1)

Topic of Research	*Description of Participants as Given in Journal Article*
Effects of characteristics of negotiators in reaching settlements in disputes	173 undergraduates
Participants' reactions to changes in the nature of auditory displays	184 undergraduates
Effects of verbal and spatial tasks on eye movements in driving	12 adults with at least two years driving experience; 7 women, 5 men
Personal characteristics and completion of time-critical tasks	30 students
Effects of sleep loss on reasoning and eyewitness identification	93 students; 45 women, 48 men
Children's use of anatomically correct dolls in reporting genital touching in medical examinations	84 children; average age = 3 years

JOURNAL OF EXPERIMENTAL PSYCHOLOGY: GENERAL (2000, VOL. 129, NO. 1)

Topic of Research	*Description of Participants as Given in Journal Article*
Backward inhibition in cognitive processing	118 students
Memory for annoying sounds	134 undergraduates
Personality effects, frontal lobe mechanisms, and error monitoring	42 students
Differences in visuospatial and verbal memory	110 undergraduates
Remembering and classifying stimuli	104 students
Identification of visually presented stimuli	34 students; 17 women, 17 men
Vividness of imagery and memory	112 adults

JOURNAL OF APPLIED PSYCHOLOGY (2000, VOL. 85, NO. 1)

Topic of Research	*Description of Participants as Given in Journal Article*
Nature and correlates of ethnic harassment	167 students; 91 women, 76 men; approximately 80% Hispanic 90 school district employees; 81 women, 9 men; 50% Hispanic 295 graduate students; 194 women, 101 men; 48% Hispanic

(continued)

TABLE 4.1   Continued

JOURNAL OF APPLIED PSYCHOLOGY (2000, VOL. 85, NO. 1) *(continued)*

Topic of Research	Description of Participants as Given in Journal Article
Identification of departure of international participants	58 international employees; 95% men 70 workers in 40 countries; 95% men
Comparison of standardized math test results and reading accommodations	1,500 randomly sampled Kansas students
Using response times to assess guilt	72 undergraduates
The effects of reinforcement on children's mundane and fantastic claims regarding wrongdoing	120 children, ages 5–7
Influence of job familiarity and impression management on self-report and response time measurements	116 undergraduates; 87% men; 84% white 198 job applicants; 92% men, 73% white
Examination of self-reported stress among managers	841 managers; 91% men; 96% white
Evaluating social sexual conduct at work	200 workers recruited from newspaper ads; 100 women, 100 men; 76% white
Behaviors of female and male executives as they "climb the corporate ladder"	137 executives; 68 women, 69 men
Group trust and workplace conflict	380 workers; 81% men; 95% white
Comparing mechanical and computer-driven systems of creating facial composite pictures	24 undergraduates; 75% women
Openness to change in workplace reorganization	130 workers
Comparing different types of test items	1,969 freshmen; 915 women, 1,054 men (from archival data set)

Operational Definition— A working definition of a complex or abstract idea that is based on how it is measured in a research project.

Variable— An element in a research project that, when measured, can take on more than one value.

concrete terms. In considering research on stress, this involves creating an **operational definition** of stress, which is our **variable** of interest here. A variable is a something of interest to us that can take on different values.

We need operational definitions because in psychology we deal with many concepts that are hard to define in concrete terms. For instance, most people would agree that stress is a real psychological state. Unfortunately, it is completely internal, a set of feelings and responses that are hard to measure. Stress is a concept that we have created to help us understand people and their behavior. It is a **hypothetical construct** because we are hypothesizing that it is psychologically real. In just about every area of psychology, we deal with hypothetical constructs for which we need adequate measurements and operational definitions.

Hypothetical Construct—An idea or concept that is useful for understanding behavior, thought, and attitude but that is complex and not directly measurable.

Independent Variable—A variable in an experiment that is controlled and manipulated by the researcher to see what effect it has on subsequent behavior.

Dependent Variable—An outcome variable that is measured in research, specifically a variable whose value is affected by the value of an independent variable.

In experimental research, when a psychologist controls the level of the variable, we call it the **independent variable (IV).** Because the level of the IV differs from one group to the next, the IV also involves variables. Different levels of the IV may result in differences in behavior. When we measure this change, the behavior involved is called the **dependent variable (DV)** because its level can depend on the IV. The IV and the DV are both variables; the difference is that the researcher manipulates the value or level of the IV and measures any resultant change in the value of the DV.

In a general sense, a person can be experiencing a low, moderate, or high level of stress; that is, the amount of stress differs, or varies, from one person to the next or from one day to the next. Thus, we refer to stress as a variable. Establishing a person's stress level is not always easy; it may change from day to day or even from hour to hour.

If you intend to study stress, you have to figure out what observable measurements can represent this concept meaningfully. Holmes and Rahe (1967) decided they would measure stress through the amount of change a person experiences in his or her life. Think about what they had to do. They had to ask people how much change the people had experienced. This is not an easy issue. First of all, what does it mean to go through change? There are big changes and there are little changes. There are good changes and there are bad changes. What kind of change is worth mentioning? In addition, how far back should people go in their lives when they think of change? Holmes and Rahe had to answer these questions (and more) in deciding how to measure change.

They created the Social Readjustment Rating Scale (SRRS) that indicates the level of change in one's life. For instance, the death of a spouse equaled 100 change units. An outstanding personal achievement contributed 28 change units. A change in eating habits was worth 15 change units. To identify stress, they posed 43 potential episodes reflecting some kind of change in people's lives.

Miller and Rahe (1997) updated the SRRS, finding somewhat different degrees of perceived stress in current society. For reasons we don't understand, people report that the same events today invariably generate higher levels of stress than they used to. The researchers also found gender differences in ratings of the degree of stress of various events, a finding that did not occur in the original scale. Table 4.2 shows the relative amounts of stress associated with various behaviors. As you can see, change can be for the better or for the worse, but it all contributes to stress. Further, it can vary depending on the cultural context.

Subsequent research has shown that SRRS scores constitute a useful predictor of negative outcomes, like an increased likelihood of brain lesions in people with multiple sclerosis (Mohr et al., 2000) and hair loss among women (York, Nicholson, Minors, & Duncan, 1998). On the other hand, SRRS scores do not predict frequency or intensity of headaches, which are more predictable from the severity of a person's daily hassles (Fernandez & Sheffield, 1996).

The Importance of Culture and Context in Defining Variables. It is important to remember that not everybody reacts the same way to a given change; in fact, in different

TABLE 4.2   Relative amounts of stress associated with different events.

EVENT	RELATIVE STRESS (1967)	RELATIVE STRESS (1997)	PRESUMED VALENCE FOR MOST PEOPLE (POSITIVE/NEGATIVE)
Death of a spouse	100	119	Negative
Jail term	65	79	Negative
Marriage	50	50	Positive
Pregnancy	40	66	Positive
Sex difficulties	39	45	Negative
Death of a close friend	37	70	Negative
Change in work responsibilities	29	43	?
Change in schools	20	35	?
Change in recreation	19	29	?
Change in sleeping habits	16	26	?
Change in eating habits	15	27	?
Christmas	12	30	Positive

Source: Reprinted from *Journal of Psychosomatic Research*, *11*, T. H. Holmes & R. H. Rahe, The social readjustment rating scale, pp. 213–218, 1967; and *Journal of Psychosomatic Research*, *43*, M. A. Miller & R. H. Rahe, Life changes scaling for the 1990s, pp. 279–292, 1997. Copyright © 1967 and 1997, with permission from Elsevier Science.

cultures, the same amount of change leads to quite different amounts of stress. In America, the death of a spouse leads to much greater relative adjustment than it does in Japan (Ornstein & Sobel, 1987).

Subsequently, Renner and Mackin (1998) created a scale more suitable for many college students. The original SRRS included items involving dealing with in-laws, having mortgages, and other aspects of life that do not pertain to all students. So Renner and Mackin created a list of 51 events of relevance to students. These include being raped or finding that you are HIV-positive, which have the greatest impact weight of any items on the scale; difficulty with a roommate; maintaining a steady dating relationship; getting straight As; and attending a football game. This new scale has not been evaluated for validity, but it contains items that students associate with stress.

If you were studying stress and people's responses to it, you could measure stress levels through either of these scales. Change in a person's life is not exactly the same as stress, but a score on the scale would serve as a reasonable operational definition of stress. Like any operational definition, it is not perfect, but it should work within the cultural context in which it was developed. When used with people from different backgrounds, however, it may be less useful.

The Diversity of Possible Operational Definitions.   You could measure stress in many ways. If you took a physiological approach, you might measure the amount of cortisol in a person's bloodstream because this chemical is produced when an individual experiences stress. The advantage of using this particular operational definition is that you can measure the substance very accurately. The disadvantage is that such an approach would cost a lot of time and money, and it would be invasive for the person who provided the blood. Luckily, we can measure cortisol more easily with modern technology. The chemical can be measured through the simple means of getting a sample of a person's saliva.

One fact to remember here is that cortisol level does not characterize a psychological response, only a biological response. It might help you understand about biological responses to stress, but not about the psychological experience of stress.

As a researcher, it is up to you to decide how you will define your concept. There is no perfect way; there are simply multiple ways that have their own strengths and weaknesses. Depending on the question you want to ask, you choose one over another. You could use Holmes and Rahe's scale or Renner and Mackin's, or you could find out how other researchers have decided to measure stress and adapt their strategies. In the end you have to select a method that you think will work for you.

DISCUSSION QUESTIONS
1. Why do a researcher's operational definitions affect the way a study is conducted?
2. What do you gain by doing a literature search before planning your research?
3. Describe how psychologists could generate different operational definitions to study a concept like happiness.

CONDUCTING YOUR STUDY

Another important choice in creating a research project concerns whether you intend to manipulate and control the situation or whether you will simply observe what occurs naturally. In experimental research, we create an IV and actively manipulate its levels. In other research, we may not be able to manipulate variables.

Suppose you wanted to investigate the effects of stress on people. You could choose a descriptive approach in which you observe behaviors without interacting with the people you monitor. For example, you could look at behavior during stressful periods, like final exam week, compared to other less stressful times. This approach would enable you to describe stress-related behaviors that emerge during periods of differential stress.

A second method to study stress might involve administering a questionnaire that inquires about sources of stress and look at their possible effects. If you used such an approach, you would not have to worry about the ethics of increasing stress levels in already stressed students. Holmes and Rahe (1967) took the approach of developing a survey technique to study stress. They used a questionnaire to assess the amount of change in people's lives and the resultant changes in stress. These researchers found that apparently trivial events, even positive ones like going on vacation, contributed to overall stress levels that have an effect on one's health.

A third strategy is to identify existing stress levels in your research participants, then see how they respond to some manipulation. Cohen, Tyrrell, and Smith (1991) did exactly this. They used nose drops to introduce either cold viruses or an inactive saline (i.e., salt water) solution into the body and quarantined the people so they were not exposed to any other viral agents. These researchers found that people with higher levels of stress in their lives were more likely to come down with colds and, if they did, their colds were more severe.

Finally you could bring research participants to a laboratory and induce stress, but as you have learned in Chapter 2, there would be ethical questions about that strategy (just as there would be if you exposed your participants to a virus). Few researchers actively induce stress in people; if they want to control stress levels directly, they often use laboratory animals. (For an example of a study on stress and learning using animals, see Kaneto, 1997.)

The important point here is that you could study stress and its effects in a number of different ways. Each approach involves asking slightly different questions about stress and results in a slightly different portrayal of its effects. All approaches are methodologically valid and each has its own strengths and weaknesses.

When you decide how you want to conduct your study, you must consider ethical issues. When we consider research on stress, we have to pay attention to the effects it will have on research participants, both human and nonhuman, and balance those effects against the gains from doing the research. Studying the effects of stress on people's lives is certainly worthwhile. If we gain a more complete understanding of when stress reactions are likely to occur (i.e., description and prediction), why the stress builds up (i.e., explanation), and how we might avoid them (i.e., control), a lot of people will lead healthier lives. On the other hand, can we justify what we put our participants through in the research?

Determining the Research Setting

Once we decide on a research question and define our variables, we have to establish the location in which we will actually carry out the study. Some research almost by necessity requires a formal laboratory setting. If an investigation involves highly specialized equipment or a highly controlled environment, the researcher has few options other than the laboratory. For example, if you decided to study a behavior that is affected by many variables, you might want to use a laboratory to eliminate some of the variables so you can see the effect of the other variables. This approach is typical in theoretical research in which some variables have large effects that can obscure a variable that has a small effect on behavior. To study the factor that has a small effect, you need a controlled environment to offset the effects of the unwanted variables.

If the research question involves an application relating to a particular environment like a business, the investigator needs to conduct the study in a business setting. In many cases, though, the investigator can choose from a wide variety of locations, including laboratories, large classrooms, small seminar rooms, or even busy public areas.

Another decision is whether to test people one by one or in groups. If people are tested in groups rather than individually, they might perform differently on their tasks. Social psychologists have found that people perform differently when they think others are observing them. Zajonc (1965) reported that even rats and ants work differently when in groups. If you are conducting your own study, it makes a difference whether your participants are alone or in groups, but you often do not know whether their performance changes for the better, for the worse, or in ways that are irrelevant to what you are measuring.

Very often, **applied research** takes place in a natural environment where people are acting as they normally do. **Basic or theoretical research** is more likely to occur

> **Applied Research**—Research that attempts to address practical questions rather than theoretical questions.
>
> **Basic or Theoretical Research**—Research that tests or expands on theory, with no direct application intended.

in a laboratory or other controlled setting. The reason for choosing a natural environment for research is that it represents the actual question you want to answer: how do people behave in a particular situation? On the other hand, when psychologists conduct theoretical research, we often want to simplify the situation so we can identify the effect of a single variable that might get lost in a complex, real-world setting.

Choosing Your Methodology

After you have operationally defined your concepts and variables, you can establish your methodology.

Psychologists have developed many techniques to study a wide variety of behaviors. Each approach has its own strengths and weaknesses and, no matter how hard you try, you can never eliminate all the weaknesses in any single study. You simply have to make choices that maximize the amount of useful information your study provides, while minimizing the number of problems you experience.

When we actively make changes in a situation to see the effect of those alterations, we are likely to be using an experimental or quasi-experimental approach that looks at groups created specifically for comparison in a study. A quasi-experiment is like an experiment in some ways, but involves somewhat less control over some variables. If we are content to monitor events as they naturally unfold, we would adopt observational, survey, or correlational techniques.

Sometimes we are interested in an getting an extensive amount of information from our research participants. In using a detailed case study of one or a few individuals, we gain a rich and complex base of information. We can also study people repeatedly over time, using longitudinal studies.

If we are interested in a more holistic depiction of people, their attitudes, and their feelings rather than numerical information, we can use a more holistic approach known as qualitative research. Qualitative research typically does not rely on manipulating variables or measuring behavior quantitatively. Rather, a qualitative researcher observes behavior patterns and tries to interpret the behaviors without resorting to numerical analysis.

Finally, sometimes we can find out about behaviors and attitudes by studying existing records or other materials, which constitutes archival research. Ultimately, they all provide part of the picture of behavior that we can combine for fuller understanding.

Approaches to Psychological Research.   Let's take a specific example. Suppose you wanted to see if stress level is associated with learning. Given that students report high stress levels, this could be a very important question. One decision you must make pertains to whether you would manipulate a person's stress level directly or whether you would simply measure the stress level as it naturally occurs.

> **Observational Research**—Investigation that relies on studying behaviors as they naturally occur, without any intervention by the researcher.

If you decided not to actively manipulate a person's stress level for ethical or other reasons, you could make use of **observational research,** noting how people or animals behave in situations that are likely to lead to stress responses. By choosing simply to observe behaviors, psychologists engage in descriptive research. There are varied ways to conduct such studies. They all involve specifying particular behaviors and the behavioral and environmental contexts in which they occur.

Correlational Research—Investigation meant to discover whether variables covary, that is, whether there are predictable relationships among measurements of different variables.

An alternative strategy would be to measure a person's existing stress level and try to relate it to the amount of learning that takes place. This method involves **correlational research,** which is the approach that Holmes and Rahe took in their research with the SRRS. This strategy would avoid the ethical dilemma of elevating stress, but the downside is that you wouldn't know if changes in stress actually cause changes in the amount that a person learns.

Consider the situation of a student who is taking classes for which she is not prepared; she might have difficulty learning the material. When she recognized that fact, it could lead to stress. There would be a relationship between stress and learning, but the causal factor is not the stress; in this example, the stress is the result.

On the other hand, people with naturally high stress levels may not learn well because they can't concentrate well. In this case there would still be a relationship between stress and learning, with the stress being the cause of poor learning.

Experimental Research—Investigation that involves manipulation and control of an independent or treatment variable with the intent of assessing whether the independent variable causes a change in the level of a dependent variable.

Quasi-experiment—A research study set up to resemble a true experiment but that does not involve random assignment of participants to a group or manipulation and control of a true independent variable, instead relying on measuring groups based on pre-existing characteristics.

Case Study—An intensive, in-depth study of a single individual or a few individuals, usually without manipulation of any variables to see how changes affect the person's behavior.

The problem is that with a correlational design, there may be a predictable relationship between stress level and learning, but you do not know if stress affected learning, if learning affected the stress level, or if something else affected them both. If you don't actively manipulate stress levels experimentally (which could put people at risk), you can identify the connection between stress and learning, but you can't identify the causal factor.

If you actively manipulate stress to see how it affects behavior, you will be using a **experimental research.** With an experiment, you control the research situation, which is clearly an advantage. In this approach, you would randomly assign participants to groups, expose them to different treatments, then see if the people in the groups behave differently from one another. In this example, stress is the IV because, as the experimenter, you manipulate stress level to see what effect your manipulation has on some other behavior. The measured behavior that might change depending on stress level is the DV; in this example, the DV is the amount of learning that occurs.

Sometimes you might wish to compare groups to see if they differ in their learning as a result of different levels of stress, but you use existing groups, like women and men or older and younger people. Such a design would resemble an experiment but, because people come to your experiment already belonging to a certain category, and there is no real manipulation by the experimenter, it is a correlational study with a variable that only looks like an IV because it has distinct levels. We refer to it as a **quasi-experiment.**

You could also choose other approaches, such as a **case study,** in which you study a single individual's stress levels and the grades that person earns in classes. You can study the person in great depth over a long period of time. You end up with a lot of information about that person, which helps you put together a more complete picture of the behavior. Unfortunately, with such an approach, you do not know if this person's behavior is typical of other people. Case studies can be useful in formulating new research questions, but we have to consider whether it is prudent to use the behavior of a single individual as a model for people in general. Psychologists typical study groups rather than individuals, so case studies are relatively rare in the research literature.

> **Longitudinal Study**—A research project in which a group of participants is observed and measured over time, sometimes over many decades.

When we want to gather a lot of information about development over the course of the lifespan, we use **longitudinal studies.** Longitudinal research generally involves studying groups of people rather than individual people. This approach requires patience because observations can continue for months, years, and even decades. One of its advantages is that we could see the long-term effects of stress on learning; long-range changes in learning due to stress might be quite different than short-term effects.

> **Archival Research**—Investigation that relies on existing records like books or governmental statistics or other artifacts rather than on direct observation of participants.
>
> **Qualitative Research**—Investigation whose "data" do not consist of numerical information, but rather of narrative or textual information, often in natural settings.

It is even possible to study people's behaviors without ever being in contact with those people. Sometimes investigators engage in **archival research** in which they look at existing records to answer their questions. For instance, studying crime reports during periods of social unrest may provide some insights into the link between stress due to social circumstances and educational attainment.

Recently, psychologists have increased the use of **qualitative research.** This approach doesn't rely on numerical information but often uses complex description to characterize the way people respond to a situation or experience it. Analyses of behavior in qualitative studies often involve discussions of how people experience and feel about events in their lives. So a study of stress and learning with qualitative research might focus on how people react to a situation when they are trying to learn and they feel stressed.

Table 4.3 presents some of the methodologies that psychologists use to study behavior. These do not exhaust all possibilities, but they represent the major strategies in our research.

Selecting Research Materials and Procedures

The details of your research include the materials and apparatus that you use to carry out your project. For example, if you are investigating the connection between stress and learning, you need to develop materials that people will try to learn; your choice of the type of stimuli (complex or abstract ideas, classroom materials, nonsense syllables, words, pictures, foreign words, etc.) may affect your outcome. For example, researchers have known since your grandparents were children that more meaningful material is easier to remember than less meaningful information (Glaze, 1928).

In connection with stress, the choice of material to be learned could be critical. For example, Gadzella, Masten, and Stacks (1998) reported that when students were stressed, they didn't think very deeply about material to be learned. As such, if you

TABLE 4.3   Major methodologies that psychologists use to study behavior.

METHODOLOGY	MAIN CHARACTERISTICS	ADVANTAGES	DISADVANTAGES
Experiments	Variables are actively manipulated and the environment is as controlled as possible.	You can eliminate many extraneous factors that might influence behavior, so you can study those of interest. Consequently, you can draw conclusions about causes of behavior.	You may create an artificial environment, so people act in ways that differ from typical. Sometimes, there are ethical issues about manipulating variables.
Quasi-experiments (and ex post facto studies)	The design of the study resembles an experiment, but the variables are not manipulated. Instead the researcher creates categories based on pre-existing characteristics of participants, like gender.	You can eliminate some of the extraneous factors that might influence behavior (but less so than in true experiments). You can also spot predictable relationships, even if you do not know the cause of behaviors.	Because you do not control potentially important variables, you cannot affirm cause-and-effect relationships.
Correlational studies	You measure variables as they already exist, without controlling them.	You can spot predictable behavior patterns. In addition, you do not strip away complicating variables, so you can see how behavior emerges in a natural situation.	You cannot assess what variables predictably cause behaviors to occur.
Surveys, Tests, and Questionnaires	You ask for self-reported attitudes, knowledge, statements of behavior from respondents.	You can collect a significant amount of diverse information easily. In some cases, you can compare your data with established response patterns from other groups who have been studied.	You do not know how accurately or truthfully your respondents report their behaviors and attitudes. You cannot spot cause-and-effect relationships.
Case Studies	You study a single person or a few people in great depth, so you know a lot about them.	You can study people in their complexity and take their specific characteristics into account in trying to understand behavior.	You may not be able to generalize beyond the person or small group. They may not be representative of people in general.
Observational Research	You study behaviors in their natural settings without intervening (in most cases).	You can study life and behavior in its complexity.	There are so many factors that influence behavior in the natural world that you cannot be sure why people act as they do.

TABLE 4.3 Continued

METHODOLOGY	MAIN CHARACTERISTICS	ADVANTAGES	DISADVANTAGES
Longitudinal Research	You study people's behaviors over a long period of time.	You can see how behaviors change over time, particularly as an individual develops and matures.	This research may take weeks, months, or years to complete. In addition, people may change because society changes, not only because of their personal maturation.
Archival Research	You use existing records and information to help you answer your research question, even though that information was gathered for other reasons.	You can trace information historically and use multiple sources to address your research question.	The information was gathered for purposes different from yours, so the focus may be different. You also do not know how accurate the records are or what information is missing.
Qualitative Research	You study people in their natural environment and try to understand them holistically. There is reliance on descriptive rather than quantitative information.	You can gain useful insights into the complexity of people's behaviors. Very often the focus is on the meaning of text or conversation, rather than on its subcomponents.	This research often takes considerably longer than quantitative research and involves painstaking analysis of the qualitative data. Some researchers do not like the fact that numerical analysis is not critical to this approach.

wanted to see if stress affected learning, you might get a different result by using simple versus complex material. Similarly, Heuer, Spijkers, Kiesswetter, and Schmidtke (1998) found that stressors impaired the performance of more or less automatic, routine tasks, but not tasks that required more attention. Once again, your results might differ dramatically if you chose a learning task that required considerable attention.

Why Methodology Is Important.   How you decide to test your participants is critical. For instance, psychologists have studied how easy it is to learn lists of frequently occurring words versus relatively rare words. Do you think it would be easier to remember common words or uncommon words? Some creative, excellent psychological research has revealed that more common words are remembered better. Other just as creative and excellent psychological research has shown that less common words are easier to remember.

These conflicting results do not make much sense until you know about the details of the research. There are several ways to test a person's memory. One of them is to ask the person to recall as many words from a list as possible. When we do this, people tend to recall more common words better than less frequent words (Wallace, Sawyer, & Robertson, 1979).

On the other hand, we could give a test of recognition memory. In this case, we would present a large group of words and ask the individual to identify which words had occurred during the learning phase of the study. Thus, the learners do not need to search through memory; they simply have to identify the words they saw before. This methodology leads to better memory for less frequent words (Underwood & Freund, 1970).

Generations of students know about the relative ease of recognition compared to recall. "College students are aware of this fact and notoriously rely on less thorough preparation for objective (multiple choice) tests than for tests which demand recall. Recognition makes no demands upon availability of items" as Deese and Hulse (1967, p. 378) noted over thirty years ago.

When you think about it, it makes sense that a recall task favors common words, whereas recognition favors less frequently occurring words. When you try to recall information, you have to search through memory for possibilities. For instance, if you can't find your keys, you may try to locate them by asking yourself where you have been. You need to generate the possibilities yourself until you identify the correct location. If you fail to think of the correct location, you will not find your keys. It would be much easier if somebody gave you a list of places you have been; all you would have to do is to select the correct one because you know the answer is in front of you.

Regarding your memory for words, you can recall more frequent words because they are easier to generate as possibilities in the first place. You have a harder time with infrequent words because you are less likely to generate them, so you don't consider them as possibilities.

As this example shows, your research methodology is important to the development of your ideas. The conclusions you draw from your research result from the way you do your research. No matter what kind of research project you plan, if you overlook the importance of your methodology, you will not have a full understanding of the question you want to answer.

DISCUSSION QUESTIONS
1. Using learning as your example, tell how your choice of stimuli and of methodology can affect the outcome of your research. As a researcher, how could you try to overcome the limitations of each approach?
2. Identify three ways you could operationally define the concept of shyness.
3. Why is it useful to have different ways to operationally define our concepts?
4. Why do theoretical studies usually occur in the laboratory, whereas applied studies often take place in natural settings?
5. Describe what kinds of questions you could answer in a study on happiness using (a) an experiment, (b) a case study, and (c) longitudinal research.

CHOOSING THE PEOPLE YOU STUDY

Fifty years ago, psychologists studied the behaviors of rats as much as the behaviors of people. Psychologists who studied rats were often referred to as "rat runners." At the time, researchers felt that they could explain the behaviors of just about all animals, human or not, with a single set of behavioral principles. So it did not make much difference to them what kind of organisms they studied. We are in a different era now and we ask different questions, so we mostly study human behavior (Plous, 1996a).

Population—The entire set of people or data that are of interest to a researcher.

Sample—A subset of the population that is studied in a research project.

Representative Sample—A subset of the population in a research project that resembles the entire population with respect to variables being measured.

The group that we are interested in understanding constitutes our **population.** It varies in different research projects. If we are interested in stress and learning in college students, then college students constitute the population. If we are interested in how the "typical" person learns, our population consists of college students and many others. If we want to study animal behavior, then a type of animal may constitute our population.

Other than in a census, we seldom have access to the entire population and it would be too costly to observe the entire group even if we could get to them all. So we use a subset of the population, our **sample.** When the sample is similar to the population, we say we have a **representative sample.**

The decisions we make about studying people involve such questions as who we will study, how we will recruit them for our research, how many we will test, and in what conditions will be study them. We make some very practical choices. The decisions that we make depend in many cases on exactly what questions we want to ask.

The Nature of Your Participants

In general, psychologists do research with organisms that are easiest to study. Can you figure out some of the characteristics of these organisms? This question is important because it determines the type of research questions you can ask.

The typical research subject turns out to be a young, highly educated, cooperative, motivated, female, psychology student. Wouldn't you want to work with people with those characteristics? Professional researchers are like you—they want to do their work with the greatest efficiency and the least inconvenience.

Rosenthal and Rosnow (1975) investigated volunteering rates for women and men; they discovered that women tend to volunteer more than men, although the nature of the research project moderates this trend. Rosenthal and Rosnow looked at research during an era in which men were likely to outnumber women in psychology classes; the reverse is true today, so the number of female volunteers will typically outnumber the number of males by a wide margin. For very practical reasons, having access to such a population of willing volunteers (i.e., students in psychology classes) means that psychologists are going to rely on that group of people.

The good news is that when students volunteer to participate in research, they will show up and do what you tell them. The bad news is that we don't always know whether such female participants from psychology classes at a single college or university resemble the entire population. Do older people or younger people act the same way? Do men act the same way? Do less well educated people act the same way? Do people from other parts of the country act the same way?

We don't know the answers to these questions. So why do we continue to rely on this very restricted population? The answer is because they are there. It would be more time consuming and difficult to locate a more diverse group who might not want to participate in a research study anyway.

Table 4.4 presents participant characteristics typical of research in some journals and the types of research reported in those journals. As you can see, experimental work typically features students, generally undergraduates. Experimental journal articles provide very little detail about the characteristics of the participants. Traditionally, experimental psychologists assumed that we could study any population in order to understand behavior in general; they reasoned that the details of particular groups might differ, but the patterns would be valid across all of them. We now recognize that this could be a problem if we want to know about generalizing results to different populations.

TABLE 4.4   Differences in research methodologies in psychology journals.

JOURNAL	AVERAGE NUMBER OF PARTICIPANTS PER STUDY	PERCENTAGE OF DIFFERENT METHODOLOGIES	PERCENTAGE OF STUDIES IN DIFFERENT SETTINGS	PERCENTAGE OF ARTICLES USING DIFFERENT STATISTICAL TESTS	NUMBER OF REFERENCES PER ARTICLE
Journal of Applied Psychology[a]	(85 Articles; 96 Studies) Mean = 784[d]	44% Survey 23% Experimental 1% Interview 19% Archival 5% Meta-analysis 2% Theoretical	22% Workplace 20% Lab 4% Classroom 22% Other 31% N/A or unknown	27% ANOVA 49% Correlation 19% t-test 18% Chi-square 18% Other	Mean = 54 Range = 21–113
Journal of Experimental Psychology: Applied[b]	(24 Articles; 54 Studies) Mean = 39	96% Experimental 4% Theoretical	75% Laboratory 9% World Wide Web 16% Other 4% N/A	92% ANOVA 38% Correlation 33% t-test 12% Other	Mean = 47 Range: 8–124
Journal of Experimental Psychology: General[c]	(34 Articles, 26 empirical; 103 Studies) Mean = 156	76% Experimental 24% Commentary	100% Laboratory	85% ANOVA 31% Correlation 54% t-test 8% Chi-square	Mean = 59 Range = 13–121

[a]Volume 85(1–6), 2000

[b]Volume 5(4), 1999 through Volume 5(3), 2000.

[c]Volume 129(1–4), 2000

[d]One study of military personnel surveyed 29,346 participants. If this highly unusual study is removed, the mean number of participants equals 427, with a median of 236.

Investigators studying more applied questions usually give greater detail about the people they study, including age, gender, and ethnicity. This makes sense if you consider the point of much applied research, which is to identify answers to questions related to specific situations or well-defined groups.

Deciding How Many Participants to Include

After we identify our participant population, we need to decide how many people we will study. The greater the sample size, the more time and effort it will take to complete the research. At the same time, if we test small samples, we diminish the chance of finding statistically significant results and increase the relative size of error in generalizing our results to our population. Berkowitz (1992) has commented that, in social psychology, research typically relies on sample sizes that are too small. Researchers may miss potentially important and interesting findings as a result. The larger your sample, the more likely you are to spot differences that are real, even if they are small. With smaller samples, we may detect large differences, but miss the small ones.

One of the other principles that should guide you in determining how many people to include in your research project involves variability. When you measure people, they will naturally produce different scores. Some of the discrepancy results from the fact that people differ due to intelligence, motivation, energy levels, and other personal characteristics. As a result, when you test them in a research setting, differences will emerge independent of any variables you manipulate. The greater the amount of variability among your participants to begin with, the harder it will be to spot changes in behavior due to your treatment. If you separated them into groups, they would show some differences whether or not you applied the IV to one of the groups. With groups of very different types of people, you might wind up with two groups that look very different only because the people start out different.

Consider this situation: Suppose you wanted to manipulate an independent variable and create an experimental group and a control group. You could assemble your sample and assign them to two conditions. Then you would expose one group to the independent variable and leave the other group untreated. Finally, you would measure them to see if the two groups behaved differently.

If your participants were fairly similar to one another at the beginning, the effect of any manipulation you later made would be easier to spot because any differences in behavior would probably be due to your treatment. On the other hand, if the people were quite different before you manipulated your independent variable, you might not know if any differences between groups were due to initial differences or to your manipulation.

The similarity among your participants is not the only factor influencing the sample size in your research. An additional consideration involves whether you think your manipulation will have a big or a small effect. If you create two groups to compare, you might expose only one group to a treatment. The effect of your treatment might be real and consistent, but it might be small. For instance, if a teacher smiled at students in one class as they entered a classroom to take a test, it might relax them so their performance increased. The improvement would probably be fairly small, reflecting a small treatment effect. In order to be able to see a difference in scores because of a smiling teacher, you would need a large group of students.

On the other hand, if the teacher announced in advance that there would be particular questions on a test, this manipulation would have a big effect. You would not need such a large sample to see the effects of the information given to the students.

If your research manipulation is likely to have a large effect, you can get away with smaller samples, especially if your participants are relatively similar to begin with. If your manipulation has only a small effect, you will need larger samples to spot differences between groups, particularly if your participants differ from one another noticeably before the experiment begins. You cannot always know if advance how big your effect size will be, although the more you know about the research that others have done, the better your prediction will be. You also do not know how homogeneous your samples are, but if you test college students in your research, your population is likely to be more homogeneous than the population as a whole. They are similar to one another, even if they differ from the vast array of people in general. The bottom line is to test as many people as possible so even small effects show up if they exist.

DISCUSSION QUESTIONS

1. We hope to be able to generalize our research results to people other than those who actually participated in our research. For the typical psychology study, why is it hard to determine the people to whom our research will generalize?

2. Why do psychologists choose to recruit college students as participants in their research? What are the drawbacks to doing so?

PROBABILITY SAMPLING

Probability Sampling— A method used in research whereby any person in the population has a specified probability of being included in the sample.

Probability sampling is the gold standard of sampling. In its simplest definition, probability sampling means that everybody that you are interested in, your population, has an equal chance of participating in your study. Unfortunately, outside of some survey research, psychologists typically don't employ it because it would be very costly. If we were interested in how people in general behave, we would need to test people from every country, of all ages, with diverse backgrounds. For all of its desirability, researchers forego probability sampling in favor of less costly approaches, like the samples of college students that most research employs.

We know that psychology students are not typical of people in general on a lot of dimensions; they are younger, more educated, female, etc. A critical question is whether the differences are important in your research. If you are studying reaction times to the appearance of a visual stimulus on a screen, college students may be very similar to other people. On the other hand, if you want to study voting preferences, college students may be dissimilar to people not in college. In our research, we often do not know how well our sample mirrors the population of interest.

Generalization—The property of research results such that they can be seen as valid beyond the sample involved in a study to a larger population.

When the sample is similar to the population, we can be confident in **generalization** of our results from the sample to the population. We hope that if our experimental and control groups consisting of students differ by some amount, then other groups will show a similar difference. We will be satisfied most of the time if we can establish patterns of behavior, even if we can't make precise predictions.

One of the difficulties in probability sampling is purely practical. We don't have enough resources to test people who are far away; we even miss out on nearby people whose schedules are such that they don't have time to take part in our research. So we don't bring them into the lab to test them or go out into the field to track them down.

Another difficulty associated with probability sampling is that, in order to use it, we have to be able to define our population of interest. In theory, we would have to be able to list every member of the population so we could pick our participants from the list. In much of our research, it is not really clear that we could do this, even in theory.

You are most likely to encounter probability sampling in survey research like political polls. In this research, the investigators can identify their population (e.g., registered voters) pretty well and can contact a random subset of the entire population. The population is well-defined and a random sample is reasonably easy to create.

There are four general strategies for probability sampling. They result in simple random samples, systematic samples, stratified random samples, and cluster samples.

Simple Random Sampling

Simple Random Sampling—A process of sampling in research that specifies that each person in a population has the same chance of being included in a sample as every other person.

Simple random sampling (SRS) involves identifying your population precisely, then identifying some probability that each person in it will appear in your sample. (We often refer to this approach just as random sampling.) In SRS, each person has an equal chance of being selected. In professionally conducted polls, the researchers use randomly selected telephone numbers, so each household with a phone has an equal chance of being called. The result is likely to be a sample that reflects the entire population.

It is important to remember that even with a random sample, you may not have a truly representative sample; sometimes pollsters get unlucky. For instance, if the voters they get in touch with are home because they are unemployed, the sample might show certain biases because such people hold different attitudes than those who are working. But the more people you call, the less likely you are to have a sample that is quite different from the whole population when you use random sampling.

Systematic Sampling

Systematic Sampling—A process of sampling in which an apparently unbiased but nonrandom sample is created, such as by creating a list of every element in the population and selecting every nth member from the population.

If you have a list of the entire population from which you will sample, you might decide to sample every tenth, twentieth, hundredth, etc. name after selecting a random position to start. This process will generate a **systematic sample.** Some (e.g., Judd, Smith, & Kidder, 1991) have argued that such a technique deviates from randomness because if you started with the fifth name, then went to the fifteenth, twenty-fifth, etc., then the fourteenth and sixteenth names (for example) have zero probability of being chosen. The counterargument is that empirical studies have shown the results of SRS and systematic sampling to be virtually identical, particularly if your list of people is in a random order to begin with; further, in many cases systematic sampling is simply easier to do (Babbie, 1995).

Stratified Random Sampling

On occasion, you might decide that you want certain groups to be included in your sample in specific proportions. For instance, if you wanted to survey your college so that you could get responses from first-year students, sophomores, juniors, and seniors in equal proportions, you probably would not want to use SRS because you are likely to sample more first-year students because in most schools, there are more of them; the

> **Stratified Random Sampling**—A process of sampling in which groups of interest (e.g., male and female; young and old; Democratic, Republican, and Independent, etc.) are identified, then participants are selected at random from these groups.

less interested or able students have not yet dropped out, as they have with upper-level students. As a result, you could employ **stratified random sampling,** in which you identify the proportion of your total sample that will have the characteristics you want.

Theoretically, stratification can be appropriate for virtually any variable you could think of. You can stratify by age, gender, socioeconomic status, education level, political affiliation, geographical location, height, weight, etc. In practice, though, some stratification is easier than others because you may not be able to identify in advance the members of your population according to some variables (e.g., height or weight) as easily as others (e.g., sex—by using the person's first name as a guide).

Cluster Sampling

Finally, sometimes a strategy like simple random sampling will be too cumbersome to be practical, especially if you have a sampling domain whose elements you cannot list.

> **Cluster Sampling**—A process of sampling in which a number of groups (or clusters) are identified in a population, then some clusters are randomly selected for participation in a research project.

For instance, if you wanted to survey teachers' attitudes in elementary schools, you might have so many schools in an area that it would be too time consuming to engage in simple random sampling. One alternative is **cluster sampling.**

In this approach, you would randomly select some number of schools, then sample from within each school chosen. In this method, large chunks of the population will be ruled out. You should still have a random sample, though, because your selection of schools was nonsystematic, that is, nonbiased, and the subsample is also nonsytematic. So in

advance, there is no built-in bias in the sample, and you should have some confidence that your sample will represent the entire population.

In all of these probability sampling approaches, you have a good chance of ending up with samples that describe the population pretty well. As always, we should remember that we are dealing with probabilities, not certainties, so any given sample might not be useful for depicting the population. Still, this is the most certain of any strategy short of using the entire population. If you look at the results of surveys by professionals, it is clear that their techniques work very well.

DISCUSSION QUESTIONS

1. Suppose you randomly call students at your school to participate in a survey. In what circumstances could you say you have a random sample of the population of

interest to you? When wouldn't your sample be considered a random sample of the population?

2. When would stratified random sampling be preferable to simple random sampling?

3. We hope to be able to generalize our research results to people other than those who actually participated in our research. For the typical psychology study, why is it hard to determine the people to whom our research will generalize?

NONPROBABILITY SAMPLING

Most psychological research does not involve probability sampling. The implication is that we often do not know to whom our research results generalize. This means that we can say that a particular result applies to students like the ones we study, but we don't know if our results also pertain to people younger or older, less or more educated, poorer or richer, etc.

Nonsampling Error—A problem in sampling that leads to a non-representative sample because some members of the population are systematically excluded from participation.

Among the greatest problems with nonprobability samples is **nonsampling error.** This problem occurs when people who should be included in a sample are not. It results in a nonprobability sample that is not representative of the population as a whole. The end result is that a researcher doesn't know to whom the survey results apply.

To ignore nonsampling error is to jeopardize the validity of a research project's results. For instance, Wainer (1999) notes an interesting result from a historical set of data. In the mid-nineteenth century, the Swiss physician H. C. Lombard examined over eight thousand death certificates and tallied each individual's cause of death and each individual's profession. The profession generating greatest longevity was that of furriers at 70.0 years.

Surprisingly, the group with the shortest life expectancy was that of student, at 20.2 years. Has life changed so much in a century and a half? The problem, of course, is that students are typically fairly young, so if they die, their life span has been short. After they finish being students, they engage in various occupations, so they don't have the chance to die as students at age 70. This is a clear example of a nonsampling error: there is no opportunity to sample old students because they go into other categories before they die. The conclusion that being a student is dangerous clearly makes no sense, which the original researchers recognized.

The problem is less obvious in some research because you don't always know who you are surveying and who is being left out. For instance, in research on bulimia, investigators often study people referred from medical doctors. It turns out that, compared to bulimics in the community in general, bulimics referred for treatment by a doctor show a greater incidence of self-induced vomiting, greater likelihood of misusing laxatives, and a more severe eating disorder in general (Fairburn, Welch, Norman, O'Connor, & Doll, 1996). The difficulty here is with nonsampling error. Thus, conclusions about the characteristics and behavior of people suffering from bulimia will differ, depending on how a sample is drawn. If researchers rely on referrals from doctors, the sample will consist of people with more severe problems compared to a randomly drawn sample from the community.

The sampling approaches that psychologists use, particularly in laboratory studies, include convenience samples, quota samples, purposive (judgmental) samples, and respondent-driven (chain-referral) samples. Unfortunately, all of these approaches have limitations because of the people who do not participate in research.

Convenience Sampling

As you saw in Table 4.4, the journals of experimental psychology involve students almost exclusively. Fifty years ago, psychologists hoped to generalize about behavior from the activity of white rats in Skinner boxes. Rats were easy to obtain and were always there when the psychologists wanted to study them. Today, we have the same hope of generalizing from college students, who are also easy to obtain and generally pleasant to work with. As you learned before, when researchers rely on such a population because it is easy or available, we refer to **convenience sampling**.

> **Convenience Sampling**—A nonrandom (nonprobability) sampling technique that involves using whatever participants can conveniently be studied, also known as an accidental sample and a haphazard sample.

Unfortunately, in many cases, we don't really know how well our research findings generalize from our samples. At the same time, when we create experimental groups and compare them, we may not be interested in precise measurements of differences between the groups, but rather patterns of differences. For instance, Recarte and Nunes (2000) investigated how students performed in a driving task when asked to complete verbal and spatial imagery tasks. Students are probably younger, on average, than the typical driver. Do you think this would matter when we discuss the effects of verbal versus spatial thought among drivers? Students may be better or worse in their driving than older people, but will the verbal-spatial comparison differ between the two groups? When researchers conduct this type of study, they hope not.

When psychologists test theories, they may not care about the specifics of the samples they work with. In fact, in experimental journals, the researchers report very little detailed information about the participants. The philosophy is that if the theory generates certain predictions, those predictions should come true, regardless of the population tested. If the psychologists are working to develop the details of the theory, they hope the characteristics of the sample are not all that important. On the other hand, if the researchers are hoping to be able to apply their findings to a particular population, characteristics of the sample are very important.

In the end, we have to use our best judgment when deciding how important the demographics of our samples are. Sometimes, using students is just fine; sometimes, it isn't. This is where judgment and experience become important.

> **Quota Sampling**—A nonrandom (nonprobability) sampling technique in which subgroups, usually convenience samples, are identified and a specified number of individuals from each group are included in the research.

Quota Sampling

Quota sampling is analogous to stratified sampling in that, in both, the researcher attempts to achieve a certain proportion of people of certain types in the final sample. Suppose an investigator wants to know if less able students differ from better students in their political beliefs.

The researcher could recruit volunteers from a class, asking the students to indicate name, contact information, and grade point average.

Then the researcher could make sure that the proportion of students with low averages in the final sample matches the proportion of students below a certain grade point average in the population, with the proportion of good students in the final sample matching the proportion of better students in the population. In this example, the researcher would need some way to establish the relevant grade point averages, like contacting the Registrar's Office on his or her campus.

This type of quota sampling is a variation on convenience sampling. The sample is not random, so the researcher does not know to whom the results generalize.

Purposive (Judgmental) Sampling

At times, a researcher may not feel the need to have a random sample. If the investigator is interested in a particular type of person, say somebody with special expertise, the investigator may try to find as many such people as possible and study them. The result is descriptive research that may say a lot about this group of experts.

For instance, if you were interested in how engineers develop products so that consumers can use them easily, you could get in touch with people who create consumer products. Then you could find out what factors they consider in making the products they create trouble-free when consumers get them home.

> **Purposive or Judgmental Sampling**—A nonrandom (nonprobability) sampling technique in which participants are selected for a study because of some desirable characteristics, like expertise in some area.

The problem with such a sample is the same as with any other nonprobability sample—you don't know who, beyond your sample, your results relate to. At the same time, you may wind up with a general sense of the important issues associated with the group of interest. This approach is sometimes called **purposive or judgmental sampling** because it relies on the judgment of the researcher and a specific purpose for identifying participants.

Chain-Referral Sampling

Sometimes it is difficult to make contact with some populations because they might not want to be found (e.g., drug users, sex workers, illegal immigrants, etc.). They are not likely to be conveniently listed with their phone numbers. As a result, researchers have to use creative approaches to contact them. Investigators have developed several techniques to study such groups, which are sometimes called hidden populations; the broad term for these techniques is **chain-referral** methods. As a rule, these strategies are more likely to be practical for survey and interview research than for experimental studies.

> **Chain-Referral Sampling**—A nonrandom (nonprobability) sampling technique in which a research participant is selected who then identifies further participants that he or she knows, often useful for finding hidden populations.

In these approaches, the researcher may use a contact in the group of interest to provide references to others who, in turn, provide other names. Another chain-referral technique involves finding where members of the group congregate, then sampling the individuals at that location. A third approach is to use a member of the group to recruit others; there may be an advantage to this technique because a known person of the group solicits participation, not an unknown and anonymous researcher. A final approach involves finding a key informant who knows the population of interest; rather than questioning members of the population, the researcher talks with a person knowledgeable about the group.

DISCUSSION QUESTIONS

1. Why is nonsampling error more likely to occur with nonprobability sampling than with probability sampling?
2. Why are psychologists sometimes not worried about whether their samples are random?
3. Why are chain-referral methods likely to be better than probability sampling when a researcher wants to study small, hidden populations?

MAKING USEFUL MEASUREMENTS

Psychologists have spent a lot of time devising reliable and valid ways of measuring concepts that we cannot observe directly. So we may devise a test that gives good information about mental states that we cannot see. Difficulties arise when we try to measure something we can't see; we may make generally good, but imprecise, measurements. Scientists refer to this as **measurement error.**

> **Measurement Error**—An error in data collection based on poor measuring instruments or human error that leads to invalid conclusions.

Measurement error does not mean that the investigator has made a mistake. The researcher may carry out his or her tasks flawlessly. The error arises because the measurement device is imperfect and the participant may also be imperfect in providing data.

For example, if you were interested in knowing if fast readers can identify individual words more quickly than poorer readers, you could present a single word and ask a participant to press a "Yes" button if the item is a word (e.g., crow) and a "No" button if the item is a nonword (e.g., corw). You are studying word recognition skill, which is a complex, internal process. For any given trial, the respondent may respond more slowly than usual because of fatigue; this is measurement error. On another trial, the person may respond more quickly because he or she just saw the word before coming to the laboratory and it was fresh in memory. This is also measurement error.

In general, we say that measurement error occurs when something affects behavior other than the variable you are investigating. In the first example above, you would call slow responses due to fatigue measurement error because you are not studying fatigue—it has just gotten in the way. In the second example, we call the quick response due to familiarity with the word results in measurement error because the study is not focusing on word familiarity—it has just gotten in the way.

Every science faces measurement error. That is why the sciences use statistics; they help us understand the magnitude of the error that we can expect in our measurements.

Reliability and Validity

Because measurement error is a fact of life, psychologists have spent a lot of time developing the notion of **reliability.** If a measurement is reliable, then repeated measurements on the same person should result in similar outcomes each time. Reliability relates to consistency and repeatability in the results. If you completed an intelligence test, then

Reliability—A measure of the consistency or reproducibility of data collected using the same methodology on more than one occasion; across different, but related test items; or by different individuals.

Test-Retest Reliability—A measure of the consistency of data collected at different points in time.

Split-Half Reliability—A measure of the consistency of data across subgroups when the data from a test or other measuring instrument are broken down into smaller segments.

Interrater (Interobserver) Reliability—A measure of the consistency of observations of a single situation made by different people.

Predictive Validity—A measure of the degree to which one variable can be successfully used to estimate the value of a second variable, often a test score that is used to predict a future behavior.

Predictor Variable—The variable that is used as the basis for making a prediction about the measured value of some subsequent behavior.

Criterion Variable—The variable that a researcher tries to estimate based on a predictor variable.

repeated it later, you would probably get a different score each time, but they would likely be fairly similar. The similarity occurs because standardized intelligence tests are generally reliable. Just because an intelligence test is reliable, we shouldn't automatically assume that it shows validity, that is, that the test is useful. Tests can be reliable without giving us any useful information. For example, we could use your height as an estimate of your intelligence; the measurement would be reliable, but it wouldn't be valid. Similarly, standardized tests might be reliable, but we don't always know how valid they are.

When a measurement yields similar results with repeated testing, we say it shows **test-retest reliability.** There are other types of reliability as well. If questions from subcomponents of a test lead to similar results, the test may have **split-half reliability.** Another aspect of reliability involves how consistently different investigators record behaviors that they observe independently of one another. If data from two observers tend to agree, their measurements show **interrater** or **interobserver reliability.**

Reliability is not an all-or-none situation; different measuring instruments are more or less reliable. Regardless of the type of reliability in question, if measurements are to help us answer questions about behavior, they must show appropriate levels and types of reliability.

The concept of reliability differs from that of validity. Validity relates to the question of whether measurements provide information on what we really want to measure. Is the measurement really useful for what we want? In order for a measurement instrument to be valid, it must be reliable. You can get consistent (i.e., reliable) scores, but they may not give useful (i.e., valid) information. Just because scores are reliable, we don't know if they are valid.

When you prepared for your college applications, you may have taken the SAT. Colleges use this test as one of the factors in the admission process.

The SAT: Questions of Reliability and Validity

The SAT is reasonably reliable, but the question is whether it is useful in predicting how well students will perform in college. If the SAT is useful for answering this question, we say it has **predictive validity.** We have a **predictor variable,** the SAT scores, that we use to predict the **criterion variable,** which is what we are really interested in. In a general sense, SAT scores do predict how well students perform in their first year in college, but it does not provide enough information by itself to make good predictions about college performance. Admissions offices must use SAT information in conjunction with other data if they are to make the best decisions about students who have applied to their institutions.

Another type of validity relates to the actual items that appear on a measurement instrument. For instance, a classroom test that has questions that assess how well students have learned a particular body of material will show content validity. If a measurement of an abstract concept (like academic strength, for example) really seems to assess that hypothetical construct, we say that the measurement shows construct validity. Depending on what we try to measure we may be interested in different kinds of validity.

You can see the importance of validity in Controversy Box 4.1, in the consideration of the Head Start program. Depending on how researchers have measured the ef-

■ ■ ■ ■ ■

CONTROVERSY BOX 4.1
CONTROVERSY: Is the Head Start Program Effective?

Researchers have to decide how they are going to complete their study. The choices reflect the way they define their concepts. This set of choices can be of paramount importance. To examine the effect of choices, let's consider the Head Start program, a federal program that provides educational opportunities for children deemed at risk for educational difficulty because of social and cultural factors. It would be nice to know whether it is effective because, as a country, we spend millions of dollars on it each year.

One of the choices a researcher would make in studying Head Start is how to define "effective." One way is to look at later IQ scores, which are easy to measure. Or you could look at students' grades during their elementary school years, which are also easy to measure. (One of the factors that arises repeatedly in research design is how easy it is for the investigator to carry out a project. If it is too costly or difficult, the researcher will most likely simplify or abandon it.)

Evaluation of the Head Start program reveals that the children in the program might initially show gains in IQ scores, but those gains are not permanent (Barnett, 1998). If you relied solely on IQ scores, you might conclude that Head Start and programs like it are not particularly useful. Fortunately, Barnett reviewed other measures of effectiveness, like graduation rates and school achievement. On both of these measures, children who experienced early childhood education programs showed success in the long term, into adulthood.

Thus, a conclusion based on IQ scores would be that the program was ineffective; one

implication would be to discontinue the program. When you think about it, though, why are IQ scores so important? What do they tell us that is so important? Academic success and graduation lead to long-term benefits. Barnett concluded that the benefits significantly outweigh the costs of such programs.

Some studies suggest that the long-term improvements are small or nonexistent, even though most researchers have found support for the effectiveness of Head Start. When we deal with complex research, it isn't surprising to find contradictions in the research literature. Whenever we deal with complex issues, it often takes a lot of research to resolve discrepancies, especially when researchers study different samples and use different measurements in their studies. Each study that we do resolves some of the contradictions and provides another piece to the puzzle.

This example is important because it shows how important your decisions can be about your methodology. If "effective" is defined as IQ scores, the Head Start program seems ineffective. That is, the children are no better off afterward than they would have been without it. On the other hand, if you define "effective" as long-term benefit leading to becoming a productive member of society, the program clearly meets its goals. In this research, it took a decade for the beneficial effects of Head Start to become apparent. Most of us don't want our research programs to last a decade, so we generally look at short-term effects. As we see in this situation, such decisions can lead to radically different conclusions.

fectiveness of the program, they have arrived at opposite conclusions about how effective Head Start has been. The easy-to-measure variables suggested low effectiveness. Longer-term, but more important (and valid) measurements reveal that Head Start has met many of its goals. Some research has not documented long-term academic gains, but enough studies have done so. Consequently, many educators believe that Head Start has lived up to its promise.

DISCUSSION QUESTIONS
1. Why doesn't the presence of *measurement error* indicate that a researcher has necessarily made a mistake in collecting data? Explain what the term means.
2. Why would most psychologists be likely to argue that it is better to have a measurement that is valid than one that is merely reliable?

DIFFERING APPROACHES IN DIFFERENT AREAS OF PSYCHOLOGY

When psychologists plan research projects, we often use methods that others before us have developed. It is easier to use a strategy that somebody else has adopted successfully and reported in a journal article than to create your own.

The advantage of relying on the research procedures of others is that they have worked through the problems that arise in developing a new approach. In addition, the previous researchers have developed appropriate materials. As a result, we don't have to repeat the initial errors and false starts of other investigators.

Different Approaches in Different Journals

It is instructive to look at the published work of psychologists, that is, the literature of psychology, to see what decisions they have made in their work. If you look at Table 4, you will see that the articles that appear in different journals reflect different decisions by scientists as they develop their research projects. Because the American Psychological Association is the largest group of psychologists in the world, with about 150,000 members, and because APA publishes some of the most prestigious journals in psychology, you should expect that the articles in those journals reflect mainstream thinking in our field. As you can see in the table, journals have established different traditions.

Even journals with similar titles have different traditions. For example, *Journal of Experimental Psychology: Applied (JEP: Applied)* and *Journal of Applied Psychology (JAP)* are very different. Articles in *JEP: Applied* involve true experimental approaches and are more likely to take place in laboratories. On the other hand, articles in *JAP* are more likely to be correlational, to rely on survey methods, and to take place in settings outside the laboratory. As such, researchers who publish their work in *JEP: Applied* are more likely to be able to identify causes of behavior in applied fields.

In contrast, in *JAP*, the correlational articles are such that the researchers can identify patterns of behaviors that occur in natural settings, but are less likely to be able to identify causes. These two journals may publish reports describing different methodologies, but the journals reflect the common interests of the authors, namely applications of psychological knowledge in people's lives. The investigators simply make different decisions regarding how to answer their research questions.

If you examine *Journal of Experimental Psychology: General*, you will find that the authors favor experimental approaches. Although these researchers study very different topics than do authors of articles in *JEP: Applied*, they tend to use the same type of experimental approach that allows them to conclude that the level of an independent variable actually causes changes in the level of the dependent variable. Articles that appear in *JEP: General* are also much more likely to be laboratory-based.

The statistical approaches also reveal an interesting picture. Applied research often relies on correlational analysis, whereas experimental, laboratory research typically implies the use of analysis of variance (ANOVA) and t-tests. It is interesting that *JEP: Applied* resembles the other two journals in some ways but also differs at some points.

Different Types of Participants in Different Journals

Another difference in the articles across journals involves the participants. Articles in the realm of applied psychology often employ more and diverse participants. This leads to differences in our conclusions. Laboratory studies typically involve many more women than men, mostly students. Applied, workplace studies often have as many or more men than women, especially studies of managers.

Studies in the workplace are likely to be correlational rather than experimental; they are often survey studies. As a result, it is relatively inexpensive to get information from more people. As you can see in Table 4.4 (page 98), the sample sizes are much larger for *JAP* than for *JEP: General articles.*

The greater the diversity among participants, the more confidence we have when we state that our research results will extend to different people. Especially for applied psychological research, we want our results to relate (i.e., to generalize) to others. Generalizability allows us to feel confident that our findings are not specific to a single group of people. Experimental approaches typically rely on undergraduate students, usually psychology students. We need to consider whether the results of such research would be the same if the investigators relied on a different sample. We often do not know the answer to these questions.

Making Choices in Your Research Design

As a researcher, you have only so much time, energy, and money, so it is often not possible to conduct a laboratory study and a field study. Consequently, you choose one and try to get the greatest amount of information from it.

At this point, it is clear why it is important that scientific research be public. If you read about an experimental study done in a lab, you might question whether the same behaviors would occur in a more realistic setting. You could take the idea and develop a similar approach in a work setting. Most likely, the managers of the work setting are not going to let you disrupt their business with experimental manipulations, so you have to rely on correlational approaches. In the end, two projects relate to a common question, each with a different methodology.

Convergent Validity— The degree to which two measurements that attempt to measure the same hypothetical construct are consistent with one another.

We hope that both studies lead to similar conclusions. When they do, psychologists say that the research results have a type of validity called **convergent validity.** If not, we try to figure out why the two approaches lead to different conclusions, which means doing more research. Because so many variables influence human behavior, we can be assured that each research project will provide only a small piece of the puzzle and that we will need many different projects and many different methodologies in order to assemble a complete picture of the behavior.

If you use a jigsaw puzzle as an analogy to research, you might say that we have a puzzle consisting of a great number of pieces and that occasionally we find that somebody has thrown pieces from another puzzle into our box. We often don't know that the odd piece has come from another puzzle until we spend a lot of time trying to make it fit. When we become aware that the stray piece belongs to a different puzzle, we toss it out. The good news is that we become aware of another interesting puzzle to work on later.

DISCUSSION QUESTIONS

1. Describe how journals devoted to experimental and theoretical versus applied research differ in the nature of the articles they publish.
2. Why could the research methodology that investigators adopt influence the journal to which they submit their work for publication?
3. Identify the strengths of experimental applied research and of nonexperimental applied research.

CHAPTER SUMMARY

Once you decide the general nature of your research question, you have to make a lot of practical decisions about how exactly to conduct your study. These practical decisions can make a big difference both in the shape your research takes and the conclusions you draw. Researchers studying similar questions often take very different paths to their answers.

A good place to begin any project is through a literature search. By investigating how others have approached research like yours, you can avoid having to reinvent techniques that have already worked for others. If there are standard and useful ways of creating and measuring variables of interest to you, it only makes good sense for you to use them if they are appropriate. This is perfectly acceptable as long as you give credit to the researchers who developed the ideas initially. In some cases, however, you might want to create different ways of approaching the question because you might not be able to find anybody else who approached your question quite the way you would like. This is an example of the kind of practical decision you will make when setting up your project.

A different decision is to identify the group of people you will study. You will have to decide how you will contact them and how to convince them to participate. Psychologists very often solicit participation from students in beginning psychology classes who receive extra credit for their participation. It can be harder to get participants from other populations. The risk in using student samples is that you are not sure that your results generalize beyond that particular type of person.

After you construct the design of your study and decide who will participate, you need to consider how exactly to measure your hypothetical constructs. This process requires you to form operational definitions of important concepts as you use them in your work. In order for you to have confidence in your measurements, those measurements need to be both reliable and valid. Reliable measurements are repeatable. That is, if measurements are taken more than once or in different ways, the results should be the same. If your measurements are valid, you will be measuring those things that you intend to measure. In psychology, it is important to establish reliability and validity because we are often trying to assess something that is complex and abstract, something that does not lend itself to easy measurement. If our measurements are not valid, our interpretations won't be very meaningful.

Finally, it is important to remember that psychologists with different specialties will approach related questions very differently. Various areas of psychology have developed their own traditions regarding methodological approaches.

. . . . .

CHAPTER FIVE

CONDUCTING AN EXPERIMENT: GENERAL PRINCIPLES

CHAPTER OVERVIEW

CHAPTER PREVIEW

CHOOSING A METHODOLOGY: THE PRACTICALITIES OF RESEARCH

DETERMINING THE CAUSES OF BEHAVIOR
Trying to Determine Causation in Research
Requirements for Cause–Effect Relationships

THE LOGIC OF EXPERIMENTAL MANIPULATION

ETHICS IN EXPERIMENTAL, CLINICAL RESEARCH

CONTROVERSY: Withholding Treatment in Medical Research

EXPERIMENTAL CONTROL
Lack of Control in Experimental Research: Extraneous Variables and Confounds

CONTROVERSY: Do Women Fear Success?

EXPERIMENTER EFFECTS

PARTICIPANT EFFECTS
The Hawthorne Effect

INTERACTION EFFECTS BETWEEN EXPERIMENTERS AND PARTICIPANTS

CONSIDERING VALIDITY IN CREATING EXPERIMENTS
Construct Validity
Intelligence: A Controversial Concept
Convergent and Divergent Validity
Internal and External Validity
Internal Validity
External Validity
Realism in Research
Statistical Conclusion Validity

CHAPTER SUMMARY

KEY TERMS

Blind study
Causal ambiguity
Confound
Control group
Convergent validity

Covariance rule
Cover story
Demand characteristics
Divergent validity
Double blind study

Evaluation apprehension
Experiment
Experimental realism
Experimental group
Experimenter bias

Extraneous variable	Mundane realism	Statistical conclusion
Hawthorne effect	Placebo group	validity
Internal validity rule	Random assignment	Temporal precedence rule
Internal validity	Single blind study	

CHAPTER PREVIEW

If you want to study behavior, it will be interesting to be able to describe and predict behavior, but it will be more satisfying to know *why* people act they way they do. It is relatively easy to observe different kinds of behavior and, from there, to be able to predict what is going to happen. Most of us have a general sense of how people are going to act in certain circumstances (although we are fooled often enough). The real goal is to understand the causes of behavior.

In research, we choose experimental designs when we want to discover causation. Descriptive approaches can be quite useful for making predictions about behavior but they do not inform us about the reasons for those behaviors.

In the simplest experiment, the researcher creates a treatment group that will be compared to an untreated, or control, group. If the two groups start equal but end up different, we presume that the treatment made a difference. In practice, most studies employ more than two groups, but the logic is the same with such multigroup studies.

Complications arise in any research project because small details of the research situation often have effects on participants' behaviors that we don't anticipate or even recognize. Further, because an experimental session involves an interaction between people—an experimenter and a participant—social effects can contribute to changes in behavior.

Nonetheless, we try to construct our research design to have maximal reliability and internal validity. That is, we create an experimental approach that others will be able to repeat and obtain the same pattern of results; we also put together a study whose results provide meaningful answers to our questions.

CHOOSING A METHODOLOGY: THE PRACTICALITIES OF RESEARCH

In psychology, the word *experiment* has a specific meaning. It refers to a research design in which the investigator actively manipulates and controls variables. Scientists regard experimental methods of research as the gold standard against which we compare other approaches because experiments let us determine what causes behavior, leading to the ultimate scientific goal—control. In general, researchers often prefer experiments over other methods such as surveys, observational studies, or other descriptive and correlational approaches.

It is important to understand the difference between an experiment and other ways of carrying out a research project. It can be confusing sometimes because in everyday language people often refer to any data collection project as an experiment. In fact, until the middle of the 1900s, psychologists, like other scientists, referred to any research project as an experiment. Since then, however, psychologists have used the term in a specific way.

An experiment is a methodology in which a researcher controls variables systematically. As the researcher alters the level, intensity, frequency, or duration of a variable, he or she will examine any resulting change in behavior in the person or animal being studied. As such, research is experimental only when the investigator has control over the variable that might affect a behavior. By controlling and manipulating variables systematically, we can determine which variables influence behaviors that we are studying.

Given that we recognize the advantage of the experimental approach, why would we bother to consider other types of research strategies? The answer is that ethical and practical considerations dictate the approaches we use. For example, suppose we wanted to know whether the amount of sleep a pregnant woman gets affects a baby's weight at birth. It would be unethical to force a woman to get a certain number of hours of sleep each night. It would also be impossible to do. You can't force people to sleep. In addition, in the course of living a life, people don't always stick to the same schedule every day. There are too many inconsistencies in people's lives to permit strict control over sleeping schedules.

An investigator who wanted to see the relation between amount of sleep women get and their newborn babies' weights would have two basic options: to experiment with nonhuman animals or to use a nonexperimental method.

In some areas of psychology, the experimental approach predominates. In other domains, researchers choose other methods. In the end, the choice of research strategies depends on the practicalities of the project. Sometimes experiments are possible and feasible, sometimes they are possible but not realistic. Sometimes they are simply impossible. Psychologists have to use good judgment and creativity in deciding what will work best in their research.

DISCUSSION QUESTION

1. In terms of methods and conclusions, how do experiments differ from nonexperimental methods? What research question that you are interested in could be addressed experimentally? What topic are you interested in that you couldn't study experimentally?

DETERMINING THE CAUSES OF BEHAVIOR

Describing behavior is fairly easy. Predicting behavior is usually more difficult. Understanding exactly why people act as they do and controlling behavior is fiendishly difficult, especially because our ideas of causation may be affected by our favored theory or on our cultural perspective. Nonetheless, one of the ultimate goals of most sciences is to be able to exert control over events in our world.

Trying to Determine Causation in Research

Research psychologists who want to know what factors lead to a certain behavior follow a logical plan in the experiments they devise. The details of different studies vary widely, but the underlying concept is consistently very simple. In the simplest situation, we identify a factor that, when present, affects on the way a person acts (or increases the probability of a certain behavior) but that, when absent, results in the person's acting differently.

For instance, we know that depressed people have typically experienced more stressful, negative life events than nondepressed people. Positive life events may lessen depression that already exists (Dixon & Reid, 2000). This fact may be quite relevant to you because college students seem particularly prone to symptoms of depression (Affsprung, 1998).

Could we find out if positive experiences would make a difference in level of depression? We might expose depressed students to different levels of positive feedback. If those who received the most feedback showed lower levels of depression, we could conclude that more positive feedback causes lower levels of depression.

Requirements for Cause–Effect Relationships

In simple terms, if three particular conditions are met, we conclude that a variable has a causal effect. The first condition for claiming causation involves the **covariance rule.** That is, two variables need to be correlated (i.e., to vary together in predictable ways—to covary) so you can predict the level of one variable given the level of the other. In the example of depression, you can predict the degree of depression from the number of positive life events. More positive life events are associated with lower depression (Dixon & Reid, 2000).

Still, knowing that the two variables are correlated does not establish causation. As Dixon and Reid pointed out, the depression could be the causal variable, not the effect. People who were depressed might have sought out fewer positive situations.

In order to determine causation, we need to satisfy two other conditions. A second critical element is the **temporal precedence rule;** that is, the cause has to precede the effect. This makes sense based on our everyday experience. An effect occurs only after something else causes it to occur.

If covariance and temporal precedence hold, we need to meet one further criterion. We have to rule out other causal variables, satisfying the **internal validity rule.** Some unknown factor may be affecting the depression and also the number of positive life events. For instance, perhaps a person finds himself or herself socially isolated. This might cause depression; it might also cause a person to have fewer positive life events. Thus, it could be the social isolation that actually influences the degree of depression as well as the number of positive life events.

Establishing internal validity is extremely difficult. Our behaviors are overdetermined, that is, caused by multiple factors. Even in a well-

Covariance Rule—One of the criteria for assessing causation such that a causal variable must co-vary systematically with the variable it is assumed to cause.

Temporal Precedence Rule—One of the criteria for assessing causation such that the variable assumed to have a causal effect must precede the effect it is supposed to cause, that is, the cause must come before the effect.

Internal Validity Rule—One of the criteria for assessing causation such that the variable assumed to be causal must be the most plausible cause, with other competing variables ruled out as the cause.

Causal Ambiguity—The situation of uncertainty that results when a researcher cannot identify a single logical and plausible variable as being the cause of some behavior, ruling out other possible causal variables.

controlled experiment, it is not unusual for participants to be affected in ways the experimenter doesn't know. Later in the chapter, you will see how some of these extraneous variables affect our research.

In summary, the only time we are safe in determining a causal relationship between two variables is when (a) two variables covary, (b) the causal variable precedes the effect, and (c) we can rule out any other variables that could affect the two variables in question. Unless these three criteria are met, we are in a state of **causal ambiguity.**

DISCUSSION QUESTION

1. In people's everyday lives, which of the requirements for causation do you think people are likely to omit when they say that something causes another? Why do you think this?

THE LOGIC OF EXPERIMENTAL MANIPULATION

Experiment—A research project in which the investigator creates initially equivalent groups, systematically manipulates an independent variable, and compares the groups to see if the independent variable affected the subsequent behavior.

Experimental Group—The group (or groups) in an experiment that receives a treatment that might affect the behavior of the individuals in that group.

Control Group—The group in an experiment that receives either no treatment or a standard treatment with which new treatments are compared.

Placebo Group—In medical research, the comparison group in an experiment that receives what appears to be a treatment, but which actually has no effect, providing a comparison with an intervention that is being evaluated.

The logic of an **experiment** is simple, even for complex studies. Most psychological experiments involve comparison of more than two groups, but describing research with two groups involves the same logic. So we'll start with a discussion of research with two sets of people (or other animals). If you understand the idea here, you can understand the structure of any experiment.

The basic idea of our simple, hypothetical experiment is this: You start with two groups that are the same, then you do something to one group that you don't do to the other. The group that experiences the manipulation is called the **experimental group;** the group that doesn't is called the **control group.** (In medical research, this approach is called a randomized clinical trial, or RCT, and may use a control group called the **placebo group** if it receives a sham, or fake, treatment.) If the two groups behave differently afterward, whatever you did to the experimental group must have caused the change. The scheme for the simplest experimental design appears in Figure 5.1.

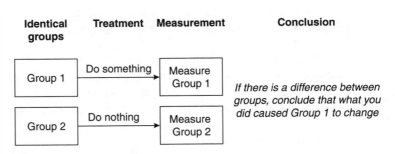

FIGURE 5.1   Logic of an experiment.

If you understand the logic of this approach, you can comprehend more complex designs. In reality, researchers seldom create a study with a single experimental group and a control group. Experimental designs usually involve multiple groups that receive different experimental manipulations; most of the time there is no control group as such. Rather, all groups receive manipulations that differ across the groups. The simple questions that would allow us to create meaningful two-group studies have often been answered; we need to create more complex designs in order to advance our knowledge. In this chapter, you will learn about the principles and the practicalities of each component of the logic presented in Figure 5.1.

ETHICS IN EXPERIMENTAL, CLINICAL RESEARCH

Let's consider for a moment the ethical issues of conducting research on people who are seeking medical or psychiatric treatment. If you were seriously ill, would you agree to participate in a research project in which one group of people received medical treatment and the other did not? In such research, the participants do not have a choice of which group they are assigned to. Would you take a risk that you were in the control or placebo group and received no actual treatment? Or the group receiving an untested treatment?

Suppose a clinician wants to assess whether a new treatment works. Is it ethical to withhold standard treatment for the sake of research? This is an important question that has no easy answer. There have been accepted medical treatments that actually did harm. In Controversy Box 5.1, you will see an example involving medical interventions and some dilemmas associated with them.

Before clinical research can begin, an IRB has to approve it. Then, at the beginning of the study, each patient must be informed about the risks associated with participating in the research, including the fact that the person might be in a placebo group or might be receiving a treatment that is not known to work as well as the standard treatment. The new treatment might work better, it might work the same, it might not work at all. Nobody knows the answer, which is why the investigator is doing the research.

In some cases, approval for research may be given only if the investigators use patients who have not responded to traditional treatment or who have exhausted all other treatments. This guarantees that only the most seriously ill patients will participate, a group whose improvement or recovery is questionable no matter what approach is taken.

On occasion, the effectiveness of a new treatment will be so superior to the standard treatment that the study will be halted in the middle, and the new treatment will be given to all participants. In such a situation, it would be unethical to continue the study because it would deprive the control group of treatment that appears to be most appropriate.

DISCUSSION QUESTION

1. In what medical circumstances do you think you would agree to be in a research study that could involve a placebo? If everybody thought as you did, what would the implications be for medical research in general?

■ ■ ■ ■ ■ ▬▬▬▬▬▬▬▬▬▬▬▬▬▬▬▬▬

CONTROVERSY BOX 5.1
CONTROVERSY: Withholding Treatment in Medical Research

One possible protocol for testing new medical treatments involves an experimental group that receives a new treatment and a placebo group that appears to be getting treatment but is not. For many maladies, people improve on their own, without any medical intervention. In the experimental/placebo design, the researchers are interested in the difference in rate of recovery or severity of symptoms between the two groups.

A critical question is whether people should be denied treatment for the sake of research that might benefit people later on, but not the patient now. Ethical guidelines prohibit sacrificing a person's health now for a future set of people. On the other hand, many current medical interventions have not been tested empirically to see if they actually work. Physicians often prescribe treatments because somebody taught them to, not because there has been research on the topic. For instance, for decades, physicians used lidocaine to prevent heart attacks even though there is evidence that it doesn't help (Olkin, 1992).

Further, many medical treatments in some specialties (up to 63 percent) have not been subjected to randomized clinical trials. (Many of these interventions are based on other kinds of evidence, though.) Still, the published research on the degree to which treatments have been empirically tested reveals that just under a quarter of them have not received scrutiny regarding their effectiveness (Imrie & Ramdy, 2000).

We have a dilemma here. If we can't use a placebo group in research, we can never perform research to establish if a treatment works. This has troublesome implications. For example, in the 1950s, premature babies were given oxygen to help them breathe. This sounds reasonable, but the oxygen caused blindness in many of the babies. For ethical reasons it would have been unthinkable to withhold oxygen or even to lower the dosage in a research study.

As it turns out, though, premature babies of poor mothers were given lower levels of treatment, including less oxygen. These infants did not suffer the blindness that babies given standard treatment did.

It is interesting that we would not consider it ethical to withhold treatment for the babies in a research project, yet society as a whole does not think it is unethical to withhold treatment for poor babies due to economic factors. Ironically, in the case of the premature babies in the 1950s, this natural experiment showed the benefit of giving less oxygen or no oxygen; for once, those on the lower end of the economic continuum benefitted.

Currently, ethical guidelines in medical research on new treatments are such that the design typically involves comparing a new approach to a standard medical treatment, so there may not be a true placebo group.

EXPERIMENTAL CONTROL

If you keep the basics of experimental research in mind, it becomes apparent why it is critical to control the research environment very carefully. The essence of good experimental research is the control that an investigator has over the situation and the people in it. When researchers create a solid experiment, they minimize the presence of factors other than the IV that affect participants' behaviors, and are able to measure a meaningful DV.

It is easy to specify on paper that you are going to manipulate a variable and measure the effect on a person's behavior. But it is safe to say that most experiments involve problems and surprises that the researcher has not anticipated. People may stop paying attention to their task, they forget instructions, they fail to show up for a lab session that requires group participation, equipment breaks down, and so on.

The problem is that surprises can arise at many different points during an experiment. For one thing, try as we might to create comparable groups, we are not always able to do so. Then when we administer the experimental treatments, initial differences that we might not know about affect the participants' behaviors.

Further, researchers may inadvertently treat people differently, leading to changes in behavior that have nothing to do with the IV. Then when we measure the DV, we can make mistakes in recording the data or we might use a DV that is not a very good measurement of what we are interested in. Finally, when we analyze the results of the research, we might use a statistical approach that is not the best one available and we might interpret it incompletely or inaccurately.

Even though life tends to throw us curve balls, there are steps we can take to maximize the likelihood that research results will be meaningful and accurate.

Lack of Control in Experimental Research: Extraneous Variables and Confounds

Extraneous Variable—A variable that is not of interest to a researcher and that may not be known by the researcher that affects the dependent variable in an experiment, erroneously making it seem that the independent variable is having an effect on the dependent variable.

Confound—A variable that is not controlled by an experimenter but that has a systematic affect on a behavior in at least one group in an experiment.

When you think of all the factors that can influence people's behaviors, you can appreciate how hard it can be to control all the variables that might influence your DV. Factors other than your intended IV that affect the dependent measure are called **extraneous variables.** They are variables that make unambiguous interpretation of your results impossible: you don't know if your results are due to the effect of an independent variable or the extraneous variable.

One particular type of extraneous variable is called a **confound.** A confounding variable systematically affects participants in a given group differently than it affects those in other groups. As a result, when groups differ at the end of a study, it may be because a confounding variable affected one group, not the independent variable. If researchers aren't aware of the confound, they may attribute differences to the IV. A confound may also obscure real differences between groups by raising or lowering the typical score in a group affected by that confound.

Thus, extraneous variables can erase the difference between two groups that should differ. Or extraneous variables can make a difference appear where none should be.

One recent example of published research provides a good example of how even experienced researchers rely on public scrutiny of their work in spotting extraneous variables. Such scrutiny lead to advances in knowledge that go beyond the original study. Quinn, Shin, Maguire, and Stone (1999) investigated whether using night lights for children under the age of two years will lead them to become nearsighted (myopic) later. Previously, scientists studying chickens noted that the birds developed visual problems if they did not experience a period of darkness each day. These researchers wondered whether nearsightedness in people might be related to the incidence of light throughout the day and night.

Figure 5.2 shows the percentage of children who became nearsighted according to whether they slept with nighttime illumination or without.

As you can see, the results are shocking. When children had slept with their rooms illuminated, the incidence of myopia was very high. The researchers knew that their findings were preliminary and, given the correlational nature of the data, not appropriate for cause–effect analysis (Quinn, Shin, Maguire, & Stone, 1999). Still, the findings were intriguing and Quinn et al. offered their results to the research community.

Subsequently, researchers have been able to identify some potential extraneous variables at work here. First, it may be that parents with myopia, which they can pass on to their children, may prefer to have night lights so they themselves can see when they enter their infant's room at night. (Stone noted that their preliminary analysis of parental vision did not reveal problems for the research.)

Second, the study was done in an eye clinic, which makes it likely that the children who were studied did not reflect children in general. Characteristics of the sample other than whether they had night lights may have affected the results.

Third, the study relied on parental memory from an average of six years before the study. Such memories are notoriously unreliable. It could be that parents with poor vision simply remember about night lights, which help them see, whereas parents with normal vision might be less attuned to such memories.

Subsequent to the publication of the Quinn et al. research, other research provided reassurance that nighttime illumination would not cause myopia (Gwiazda, Ong, Held, & Thorn, 2000; Zadnik et al., 2000).

In some studies, we may not be able to spot confounds and extraneous variables based on research reports. Fortunately, in the Quinn et al. work, because they provided enough detail about their methodology, others could continue to investigate their ideas.

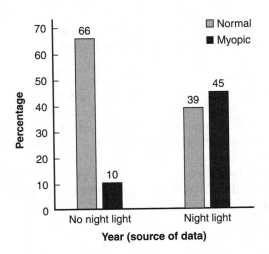

FIGURE 5.2 Incidence of myopia and normal vision according to whether a child's room is illuminated at night.

Source: G. E. Quinn, C. H. Shin, M. G. Maguire, & R. A. Stone. (1999). Myopia and ambient lighting at night. *Nature, 399,* pp. 113–114. Reprinted by permission from *Nature,* copyright 1999 Macmillan Magazines Ltd.

Problems may also arise because research is a human enterprise. If there are two groups to be compared and if a researcher acts differently toward the people (or animals) in each group, the resulting behaviors may be different because of the way the participants were treated rather than because of the IV.

Rosenthal and Fode (1966) demonstrated that visual and verbal cues by an experimenter have an effect on participant behavior. Most researchers are aware that they may have an effect on the way experimental participants act. At the same time, the cues may be so subtle that the researchers (or their assistants) don't know what changes they are causing in participant behaviors.

Consider the effect of small wording changes on behavior. Elizabeth Loftus was among the first researchers to document the effect of "leading questions," that is, wording that may lead a respondent in a particular direction. Experimenters can unknowingly use leading questions or other wording that affects the way participants behave. Loftus (1975) showed her participants a film clip of an automobile accident, then asked them one of two questions:

1. How fast was Car A going when it ran the stop sign? or
2. How fast was Car A going when it turned right?

A final question asked "Did you see a stop sign for Car A?" When participants had been asked Question 1, they were significantly more likely to respond that they had seen a stop sign. When the experimenter planted the seed of a memory, participants nourished that memory and began to believe in it. There actually was a stop sign in the film clip. Nonetheless, it was clear that the change in wording affected how people responded to later questions. There has subsequently been ample research demonstrating that false memories can be planted successfully (e.g., Mazzoni & Loftus, 1998; Loftus, 1997) and that slight changes in wording or even simply exposing a person to an idea can change later responses (Loftus, 2003). These effects are very important for you to understand because they can alter the way participants behave in an experiment, unbeknownst to the researcher.

An additional source of extraneous influences in an experiment can be the stimulus materials. When investigators change materials across different groups, subtle differences in the nature of the materials can make a notable difference in the outcome of the research.

Sometimes we are able to spot confounds and sources of error in research, but sometimes we may not recognize that research has subtle problems that may result in poor conclusions. One area of research that has been beset by a potentially very important confound involves whether women show fear of success (FOS). Psychologists have identified FOS in women with a variety of tasks. Over two decades after the initial research appeared, though, some hidden problems became apparent.

Fortunately, scientific research is done so that problems can be corrected. As a result, we have overcome one stumbling block in studying FOS. It is clear now that FOS is not a function of sex alone, as you can see in Controversy Box 5.2.

The problem with extraneous variables and confounds is that no experiment has complete control over what a participant experiences in the lab or over any of the par-

■ ■ ■ ■ ■ ▬▬▬▬▬▬▬▬▬▬▬▬▬▬▬▬▬▬▬▬▬▬

CONTROVERSY BOX 5.2
CONTROVERSY: Do Women Fear Success?

Research across the past thirty years has suggested that women fear success. A typical experimental strategy was to give participants an essay to read and then to ask them to write about it. Horner (1968, cited in Kasof, 1993) gave male participants a story in which the main character was a man; female participants read stories in which the main character was a woman. A critical sentence in the essay was "After first-term finals, John (Anne) finds himself (herself) at the top of his (her) medical school class."

Horner reported that women wrote more negative essays, which the researcher interpreted to indicate that women were more fearful of success than men were.

Subsequent to this research, investigators studied such topics as sex discrimination, sex stereotypes, and fear of success by altering experimental stimuli for women and men by changing the name of the protagonist in a story. In many instances, stimuli with female characters were rated lower than stimuli with male names.

We could debate Horner's original interpretation about women's fear of success, but there was a fundamental problem with the fear of success research that lay hidden for two decades. According to Kasof (1993), the names of the characters in the experimental stimuli were not comparable across sexes.

The tendency among researchers was to use male and female versions of a name, such as John and Joan or Christopher and Christine. Kasof reported that, in as many as 96 percent of the studies, the female names tended to be more old-fashioned, connoted lower intelligence, and were associated with being less attractive compared to male names.

As he pointed out, dependent variables in sexism studies often relate to intellectual competence (e.g., who is more competent, John or Joan). Some names are associated with lower intelligence, even though we know that how smart you are has nothing to do with what your parents named you.

In the past decade, the attractiveness of the names seems to be more nearly equal. Not surprisingly, during this period researchers have learned that fear of success has little to do with sex per se and more to do with whether a woman holds a traditional view of sex roles (Basha & Ushasree, 1999; Krishnan & Sweeney, 1998; Kumari, 1995) and careers (Hay & Bakken, 1991), and whether she is gifted (Hay & Bakken, 1991).

In addition, women who are concerned about being evaluated negatively because they are "too successful" may show higher levels of fear of success. It's not that they actually fear success; they are just sensitive to social evaluation (Exline & Lobel, 1999). Further, being a successful woman entails taking risks, and women may be less likely to engage in risky social behavior (Byrnes, Miller, & Schafer, 1999).

Sometimes, apparently small changes in the way an experiment is set up (e.g., the stimulus names) introduce extraneous variables that can be more important than the IV. Now that we are aware of the effect of stimulus names, we may be able to identify more precisely who fears success. Sometimes it can be men (Rothman, 1996).

---

ticipant's life experiences. If you set up an experiment as outlined in Figure 5.1, there are many variables other than the IV that could affect the outcome of your project. Conducting a sound study requires attention to detail and a good grasp of how researchers in the past have overcome the problems they faced.

DISCUSSION QUESTION

1. Why will an extraneous variable that systematically affects only one group in an experiment (e.g., by raising scores in the group by a consistent amount) lead to problems different from an extraneous variable that affects people in unpredictable ways?

EXPERIMENTER EFFECTS

> **Experimenter Bias—**
> The tendency of researchers to subtly and inadvertently affect the behaviors of participants in a study, obscuring the true effect (or lack thereof) of the independent variable.

One source of difficulty in research involves **experimenter bias,** the tendency for the researcher to influence a participant's behavior in a certain direction. If the experimenter thinks that one group will perform better on a task than another, the investigator may inadvertently lead the participants to act in the expected way. In this example, we will assume that the experimenter is acting with integrity, not attempting to influence the participants.

How big a problem is such behavior on the part of the researcher? It is hard to tell, although when surveyors were studied to see how often they departed from the directions they were supposed to follow in administering questionnaires, the results showed that there were notable deviations from the standardized protocol (Kiecker & Nelson, 1996).

One of the most common departures involved rephrasing or rewording a question; the interviewers reported that, on average, they had done this about 18 of the times in their last hundred sessions. (The standard deviation was 27.2 percent, indicating that some interviewers may have changed the wording around half the time.)

These data suggest that, in an attempt to be helpful or to clarify a question, the surveyors regularly rephrased questionnaire items. Given the results of research like Loftus's (1975, 1997), the changes in wording may very well have affected the survey results. We don't know how often comparable behaviors occur in experiments or how big the effects might be, but the survey results suggest that researchers deviate from their directions regularly.

Interestingly, Kiecker and Nelson (1996) reported that surveyors rarely fabricated an interview that never took place. Thus, we can infer that they were trying to be helpful. The down side is that their behaviors could have changed the way that people responded.

DISCUSSION QUESTION

1. Why should we be cautious in accepting research results if the experimenter has changed wording in the instructions for some participants?

PARTICIPANT EFFECTS

The majority of psychological research with people involves college students. Students generally have some very desirable characteristics, three of which are a high degree of education, a willingness to cooperate, and high levels of motivation. These are helpful traits most of the time. Unfortunately, in the context of an experiment, they might pose some problems.

It isn't unusual for a student who participates in a study to try to figure out what the experimenter "wants." This can be a problem because the experimenter really wants the person to act naturally.

How might we keep participants from reliably picking up on clues? One means is to use automated operations whenever possible. If the participant reads the instructions, then carries out a task on a computer, there is less risk that the experimenter will influence the person's behavior.

Cover Story—A fictitious story developed by a researcher to disguise the true purpose of a study from the participants.

Blind Study—A research design in which the investigator, the participants, or both are not aware of the treatment that a participant is receiving.

Single Blind Study—A research design in which either the investigator or the participant is not aware of the treatment a participant is receiving.

Double Blind Study—A research design in which neither the investigator nor the participant is aware of the treatment being applied.

A second strategy is to use a convincing **cover story.** This is a story about the study that either conveys the actual purpose of the study or successfully hides the true nature of the research. Some people object to deceptive cover stories, but others have argued that the nature and level of the deception is trivial. If you carry out your own research projects, you will have to decide on your own whether deception is warranted and appropriate.

Another solution is to use a **blind study.** In such an approach, the participants do not know the group to which they have been assigned, so it will be harder for participants to know what treatment they receive, so they are less likely to try to conform to expectations.

When either the participants or the researchers do not know to which group the participants are assigned, we called it a **single blind study.**

When the participants in different groups are blind, which is how single blind studies usually proceed, they don't have systematically different expectations that they might try to fulfill. When the investigators who actually conduct the study are blind to which group a person is in, it keeps a researcher from unintentionally giving clues to a participant.

When neither the investigator nor the patient knows which group the patient has been assigned to, it is called a **double blind study.**

The Hawthorne Effect

Hawthorne Effect—The tendency of participants to act differently from normal in a research study because they know they are being observed.

When people change their behavior because they know they are in a scientific study, showing higher levels of motivation, they can produce results that lack validity. The behaviors are due to the motivation rather than to the IV. This phenomenon is often referred to the **Hawthorne Effect.** This phenomenon is controversial and has been discussed at great length. It is also not particularly well described in textbooks.

The effect got its name because, in the 1920s and 1930s, researchers concluded that workers at Western Electric's Hawthorne plant near Chicago increased their output because they felt special, having been included in a research project. In reality, the studies were methodologically troublesome, including confounding variables (Adair, 1984). Further, some of the apparent improvement in weekly worker performance arose because the work week was lengthened (Bramel &

Friend, 1981), not necessarily because the workers performed more effectively. In addition, in one case, a poorly performing and disgruntled employee withdrew from one of the studies. The replacement was a very productive worker. It's no surprise that the average output went up.

Nonetheless, the term *Hawthorne effect* remains in use to describe an individual's change in behavior while trying to be helpful to the researcher.

> **Demand Characteristics**—The tendency on the part of a research participant to act differently from normal after picking up clues as to the apparent purpose of the study.

In addition to the Hawthorne effect, a commonly described participant effect involves **demand characteristics.** When participants actively try to figure out the purpose of the study and act in ways they think are helpful, they are said to be showing demand characteristics. It should come as no surprise that people are active participants in a research setting; they try to figure things out, just as they do in any other aspect of their lives.

One compelling example of a situation involving demand characteristic was provided by Orne and Scheibe (1962). These researchers told individual participants that they might experience sensory deprivation and negative psychological effects while sitting in a room. When the researchers included a "panic button," the participants tended to panic because they thought it would be an appropriate response in that situation. When there was no panic button, the participants experienced no particular adverse effects. The inference we can draw here is that when the participants concluded that a highly negative psychological condition would emerge, they complied with that expectation. When the expectation wasn't there, neither was the negative response.

> **Evaluation Apprehension**—The tendency to feel inadequate or to experience unease when one is being observed.

Another source of bias associated with participants is **evaluation apprehension.** This bias arises because people think others are going to evaluate their behaviors. As a result, the participants are on their best behavior. This is something we do all the time. Many people will litter as they walk or drive down the street, but not if they think somebody (even a stranger) is going to see them and, presumably, evaluate their littering behavior negatively.

This evaluation apprehension is not always so benign. Researchers have shown that when people begin thinking about stereotypes applied to them, their behavior changes. Thus, women may perform less well on mathematics tests because women "aren't supposed" to be good at math (Spencer, Steele, & Quinn, 1999), African Americans may perform less well on academic tests because blacks "aren't supposed" to be as strong academically as whites (Steele & Aronson, 1998), and poor people "aren't supposed" to be as proficient as rich people (Croizet & Claire, 1998). The effects of stereotyping hold true for people from different cultural backgrounds, including French (Croizet & Claire, 1998), Chinese (Lee & Ottati, 1995), and Canadian (Walsh, Hickey, & Duffy, 1999).

Surprisingly, even groups of people who are demonstrably proficient in an area can suffer from stereotype threat. Aronson et al. (1999) showed that math-proficient white males could be induced to perform more poorly than expected on a test of math skills if they were compared to a group that is expected to perform even better than they, namely, Asians.

As such, evaluation apprehension can exert notable effects on results in an experiment, making it seem that the IV has affected behavior when, in reality, a confounding variable has made the difference. This particular type of bias is likely to be more pronounced when the experimenter is examining participant (subject) variables, that is, the effects of pre-determined characteristics like sex, race, age, and so on.

Comparisons between men and women, black and white, young and old, rich and poor, and many other participant variables may result in distorted results because one group acts differently because they are "supposed to." Too many conclusions have probably been drawn about differences across groups because of effects related to evaluation apprehension in one form or another.

DISCUSSION QUESTIONS

1. Why would a single blind study be less effective in controlling for experimenter-participant communication than a double blind study?
2. Give an example from your life that has involved something like demand characteristics and evaluation apprehension. How did your behavior change?

INTERACTION EFFECTS BETWEEN EXPERIMENTERS AND PARTICIPANTS

Research projects are social affairs. This may not be obvious at first glance, but whenever you get people together, they have social interactions of various kinds. However, when you are carrying out a research project, you don't want either experimenters or participants to communicate in ways that will compromise the study.

In a research setting, behaviors that we generally take for granted as normal (and maybe even desirable) become problematic. Consider the following situation: a college student agrees to participate in an experiment and, when arriving there, finds a very attractive experimenter. Isn't it reasonable to suppose that the student will act differently than if the experimenter weren't good looking? From the student's point of view, this is a great opportunity to show intelligence, motivation, creativity, humor, etc. In other words, the research project is a social affair.

Just as the experimenter and the participant bring their own individual predispositions to the lab, they bring their own interactive, social tendencies. Research results are affected not only by experimenter bias and participant bias, but also by interactions between experimenter and participant.

Sometimes there may be friction between a participant and an experimenter, just as there might be between any two people. If a participant responds to some "natural" characteristic of the researcher, we may have a distortion of experimental results due to a biosocial effect. For instance, if the experimenter seems too young to be credible, the participant may not take research seriously. Or if the participant is overweight, the experimenter may be abrupt and not be as patient in giving directions. Other examples of factors that could induce biosocial effects could include race, ethnicity, nationality, and religion. Obviously these are not strictly biological characteristics, as the term "biosocial" implies. Nonetheless, these characteristics all pertain to what people may see as fundamental about another individual.

A different, but related, bias involves psychosocial effects. This type of bias involves psychological characteristics, like personality or mood. Researchers with different personality characteristics act differently toward participants. For instance, researchers high in the need for social approval smile more and act more friendly toward participants than those lower in this need (Rosnow & Rosenthal, 1997).

It is clear that the way an experimenter interacts with a participant can affect the outcome of a study (Rosenthal & Fode, 1966). For instance, Malmo, Boag, and Smith (1957, cited in Rosnow & Rosenthal, 1997) found that when an experimenter was having a bad day, participants' heart rates were higher compared to when the experimenter was having a good day.

DISCUSSION QUESTION

1. Identify examples of biosocial and psychosocial effects that might be important for college students at your school who participate in research.

CONSIDERING VALIDITY
IN CREATING EXPERIMENTS

As researchers, we want our work to be meaningful. That means creating research designs that relate the IV meaningfully to the DV. Another, more technical way of saying that research results are meaningful is to say that they are valid.

There are several different types of validity; some are particularly relevant in experimental research. Some types involve the nature of variables; others relate to the structure of an experiment; yet another pertains to the statistics used to analyze the data. They are summarized in Table 5.1.

Validity is not an all or none situation. Rather, a measurement may show less or more validity, and its validity may legitimately and predictably change in different situations. Further, an experiment may show high levels of some types of validity, but lower levels of different types.

Construct Validity

When investigators develop an operational definition of a variable, they work to create a measurement that shows construct validity. This means that the abstract, underlying concept is being defined, or operationalized, in a way that is useful in understanding that concept. Fortunately, we can often use measurements that others have already created.

We can measure intelligence, depression, and other psychological concepts in multiple ways. There may be no need to create a new measurement when other adequate tools are already available. So why should you try to develop something else? Most of the time there is no need unless you are breaking new ground, studying a topic that nobody before you has investigated or studying an existing topic in a new way.

We can get a glimpse of how we can apply the concept of construct validity in the measurement of depression. Depression is complex, which is why psychologists need to study it extensively in order to begin to understand it. As you will see, doing research on depression well requires paying close attention to the details.

Psychologists generally accept the construct validity of the Beck Depression Inventory (BDI) because it is useful in dealing with depressed people. According to many

TABLE 5.1   Different types of validity and how they affect our research.

Construct Validity	How well do your operational definitions and procedures capture the hypothetical constructs you want to study?
	Example: If you want to study intelligence, you can administer an IQ test. It will be reasonably high in construct validity if you are interested in educational abilities, but lower in construct validity if you are interested in problem solving in daily activities.
Convergent and Divergent (Discriminant) Validity	Are there positive correlations between your variable and variables that are supposed to be positively correlated? If several different variables that are all related give you the same information, you have convergent validity.
	Are there negative correlations between your variable and others that are supposed to be unrelated?
	Example: Research on the topic of emotional intelligence has shown that measures of emotional intelligence and personality are related. This suggests that the measures of emotional intelligence overlap with personality traits and are not being measured separately from personality (Davies, Stankov, & Roberts, 1998). There is a lack of divergent validity here. The results do not remove the possibility that emotional intelligence reflects specific skills, it only means that we haven't figured out how to measure it if it does exist.
Internal and External Validity	Is your research set up so that you can draw a firm conclusion from your data? Or are there other potential interpretations that arise because of limitations in your research design? If you have eliminated extraneous and confounding variables from your methodology, your study will have internal validity.
	Example: Mexican American students expressed preference for a Mexican American over a European American counselor. The researchers identified a social response bias, however, that led to the stated preference. When this confound was eliminated, the difference in preference disappeared (Abreu & Gabarain, 2000).
	Are your results meaningful beyond the setting and the participants involved in your research? If your findings will generalize to new people, new locations, and a different time, they show greater external validity. If your results pertain only to the context of your research project, they will have lower external validity.
	Example: In order to generalize his research results on obedience, Stanley Milgram studied nonstudents from an office building in downtown New Haven, CT. He obtained similar results as with college students, suggesting that his findings have external validity.
Statistical Conclusion Validity	Have you used the proper statistical approaches to analyzing your data? If you employ the wrong statistical model, your conclusions will be less valid. This is particularly relevant for complex approaches like complex analyses of variance, structural equation modeling, or other analyses involving multiple variables.

research findings, the BDI has useful psychometric properties, which means that it can distinguish those with depression from those without, and it can document an individual's level of depression (Dozois, Dobson, & Ahnberg, 1998). Steer, Rissmiller, Ranieri, and Beck (1994) reported that the BDI can reliably differentiate patients with mood disorders from those with other kinds of psychological problems.

The BDI also appears to be useful cross-culturally when used with Portuguese (Gorenstein, Andrade, Filho, Tung, & Artes, 1999) and with German speakers (Richter, Werner, & Bastine, 1994). It can also be useful with elderly people who are clinically depressed (Steer, Rissmiller, & Beck, 2000). Thus, we can conclude that for applications like these, the BDI's construct validity is just fine.

At the same time, the BDI may not be appropriate for all types of research on depression. Wagle, Ho, Wagle, and Berrios (2000) have provided evidence that it is not ideal for measuring depression in Alzheimer's patients, and it may perform less well than therapists' judgments in severely depressed people (Martinsen, Friis, & Hoffart, 1995). This means that the BDI is a highly valid instrument for many situations, but not for all.

In the research just mentioned, the investigators were interested in depression as an outcome or measured variable. Sometimes researchers use depression as a manipulated IV. They may induce a mildly depressed state in participants by using simple laboratory techniques, then observe the effect. An important question is whether the lab techniques used to create depression are valid.

One widely known approach was developed by Emmet Velten, who asked his participants to read positive or negative statements in order to elevate or depress their mood. By doing this, he could actively manipulate mood state and see what effect it had on a subsequent behavior of interest.

Does Velten's induced depression resemble naturally occurring depression? That is, does depression as Velten operationalized it have construct validity? Researchers have questioned the validity of the Velten mood induction procedure because there is no guarantee that reading a series of statements induces a realistic version of depression. If the result of this manipulation does not relate to depression, construct validity will be low or nonexistent.

There is reason to believe that Velten's version of depression shows adequate construct validity. For example, Bartolic, Basso, Schefft, Glauser, and Titanic-Schefft (1999) investigated whether brain activity differs depending on mood. They reasoned that positive (euphoric) and negative (dysphoric) emotional states produce different patterns of activity in the frontal lobes of the brain.

So they used Velten's mood induction procedure to change research participants' emotional states and found that the euphoric state leads to enhanced verbal performance, whereas dysphoric states lead to better figural processing. Their findings are consistent with previous studies of depression. These results suggest that experimental participants are in an emotional state that resembles depression. That is, we see evidence of reasonable levels of construct validity.

On the other hand, sometimes people who are actually depressed behave differently from those whose depression has been induced by the Velten statements (Kwiatkowski & Parkinson, 1994). Once again, when we deal with complex topics, we have to be careful that we are measuring what we think we are. Thinking about research you might do, you can often use the same operational definitions that others have used, but you also need to be aware that you can't adopt them blindly.

Intelligence: A Controversial Concept.   One very widely used operational definition is the Intelligence Quotient, or IQ score. What is intelligence? We don't really know; we can only see the results of intelligence level as people function well or poorly in various aspects of their lives. Still, if we are going to predict behavior based on a person's intelligence level, we have to come up with an operational definition of this concept; we have to measure it somehow.

Traditionally, intelligence has meant an IQ score. In everyday life, many people do not recognize any difference between the concept of intelligence and the IQ score. In truth, though, an IQ score is a pale representation of intelligence. Standardized intelligence tests are fairly good at indicating how well a person is likely to perform in school. However, they don't necessarily say much about the individual's abilities in nonscholastic domains that are major components of Gardner's (1994, 1999) theory of multiple intelligence or about some of the analytical, practical, and creative components of intelligence that are major elements of Sternberg's (1985, 1999) triarchic theory of intelligence.

This means that when we consider a complex hypothetical construct like intelligence, there are going to be different operational definitions that will be useful in different situations.

Convergent and Divergent Validity

Convergent Validity—A type of validity in which two measurements of the same construct are in agreement.

Divergent Validity—The degree to which two measurements that should be assessing different constructs lead to different values.

One way to have confidence in our findings is through **convergent validity,** which means achieving similar results with different methodologies. If two different approaches to a given question lead us to the same conclusion, our confidence in our methodology and results will increase. Similarly, we can gain confidence through **divergent validity,** which means that when two measurements that should be unrelated actually are unrelated. (Divergent validity is also called discriminant validity.)

A recently developed hypothetical construct is that of emotional intelligence (Goleman, 1996). Basically, emotional intelligence is said to relate to a person's ability to be emotionally sensitive or attuned to others. In order for this construct to be useful for psychologists, we have to be able to measure it. There should be some test that generates scores that will differentiate people with different levels of such intelligence.

A test of emotional intelligence should also be unrelated to other constructs. For instance, if IQ score and emotional intelligence were correlated, we might assume that emotional intelligence is simply part of "regular" intelligence. If we are going to consider emotional intelligence as something that exists on its own, it should not overlap with other constructs very greatly.

As of now, it is not clear whether emotional intelligence will be a useful construct in psychology in the long run. Mayer, Salovey, Caruso and Sitarenics (1999, 2001) reported their work to devise an independent measurement of it, the Multi-Factor Emotional Intelligence Scale (MEIS); they demonstrated some empirical support for it. On the other hand, Roberts, Zeidner, and Matthews (2001) claimed that the MEIS may not provide sufficient evidence for emotional intelligence as a valid construct. Further, Davies, Stankov, and Roberts (1998) reported that some attempts to measure emotional intelligence have led to low reliability.

The arguments get complicated, but some psychologists have argued that the tests of emotional intelligence do not have divergent validity because measurements that should be unrelated turn out to be related. So the different measurements are actually tapping the same underlying concept, not different constructs. If so, the current instruments designed to measure emotional intelligence have failed. This conclusion doesn't necessarily mean that emotional intelligence isn't real, just that we haven't come up with a reliable measurement of it yet.

Internal and External Validity

Internal Validity—The degree to which an experiment is designed so that a causal relationship between the independent and dependent variable is demonstrated without interference by extraneous variables.

The next types of validity we will consider are internal validity and external validity. When research shows **internal validity,** it means that you started your project with groups that were comparable with respect to the DV (or equated them using statistical procedures), eliminated confounds and extraneous variables, manipulated a variable that possessed construct validity, held everything but the IV treatments constant across your groups, and measured your participants' behaviors accurately on another variable that had construct validity.

In order to have external validity, your experiment has to be meaningful in a context outside of your laboratory with people (or animals) other than the ones who took part in your study. In other words, would your findings be replicable in another setting with different participants and at a different time?

Internal Validity.   An example of a strategy of assigning people to groups that could very easily lead to bias is as follows. Suppose you were going to test two groups of participants with ten in each group. You could assign the first ten who showed up to Group 1 and the second ten to Group 2. The first ten people might be more eager, more motivated, more energetic, more cooperative, etc. That's why they got there first. You could end up with two groups that consisted of very different types in each group. Any difference in behavior after your experimental manipulation could be due to their eagerness, motivation, energy, cooperation, etc. rather than to the manipulation. This strategy is easy but not advisable.

Random Assignment—The process in which participants in a research study are non-systematically placed in different treatment groups so those groups are equivalent at the start of an experiment.

In contrast, the chief means that scientists use to create similar groups in an experiment is to use **random assignment** of participants to groups. Random assignment means that any single individual can end up in any group in the experiment and that the individual is placed in the group on the basis of some objective and unbiased strategy. No approach to assignment guarantees that in a single experiment, the groups to be compared would have equivalent scores on the DV at the start of the study. Sometimes an experimenter is simply beset by bad luck. But, in the long run, random assignment is an effective way to create equivalent groups.

You can randomly assign participants to groups by using a random number table. Figure 5.3 illustrates how you could assign ten people to two groups on a random basis. In this case, if you took numbers from a random number table and used them to assign people to conditions, you could match the random numbers on the order in which people arrived at the lab, alphabetically, by height, by IQ score, by grade point average, or by any other means. As long as one of the lists is random, the grouping is random.

FIGURE 5.3   Example of randomization of participants to two groups.

1. Go through a random number table and write down the numbers from 1 to N (your sample size) in the order in which they occur in the table. In this example, we will move down the columns, choosing the first two digits of the column in each block of numbers. The critical numbers are shaded for this example.
2. Place your participants in order. (The actual order of listing of participants isn't critical here; any ordering will do—alphabetical, in order of arrival to the lab, etc.)
3. Pair each person with the random numbers as they occur.
4. Put each person paired with an odd number into Group 1 and each person paired with an even number into Group 2.

EXAMPLE OF RANDOM NUMBER TABLE

91477	29697	90242	59885	07839
09496	48263	55662	34601	56490
03549	90503	41995	06394	61978
19981	55031	34220	48623	53407
51444	89292	10273	90035	04758
66281	05254	35219	96901	38055
08461	61412	53378	13522	80778
36070	12377	52392	67053	49965
28751	01486	54443	01873	02586
64061	22061	10746	84070	71531

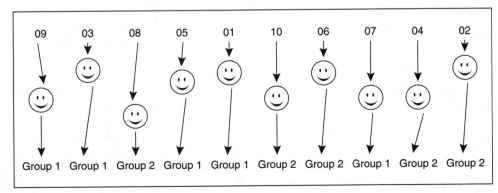

Across many experiments, this process is the most valuable in creating groups that don't differ systematically at the start. In any given experiment, you might be the victim of bad luck, so that all the smart, tall, nervous, friendly, etc. people are in one group instead of being evenly distributed across conditions. Unfortunately, there is nothing you can do about it. You have to decide on a process of randomization (random number table, drawing names out of a hat, rolling dice, etc.) then follow it and live with the results. In the long run, random grouping of participants will lead to the most valid results.

As experimental procedures get more complicated and you add groups, you will have to adjust your randomization techniques. If you plan to create three groups with 10 participants randomly assigned to each group, you need to change your assignment strategy a little. Your first step would be to identify your participants and randomly order them.

Then using the random number table in Figure 5.3, you could identify two-digit numbers starting at the upper left of the list. If you have 30 participants, you will only need to pay attention to values in the table of 01 to 30. The first number in the table is 91, which you ignore because it is greater than 30. Moving down the column, we see the next number is 09; you would put the ninth person to show up in Group 1. The next number is 03; the third person would go in Group 2. The next number between 01 and 30 is 19; so the nineteenth person would go in Group 3. You would continue until each of the 30 participants would be assigned to one of the three groups. This approach would remove systematic bias in assigning participants to groups.

Random assignment of participants to groups keeps us from introducing systematic bias into the process of creating groups. Consequently, we can have confidence that any group differences after a treatment are due to the treatment. This produces a greater level of internal validity.

The internal validity of a research project is critical to the level of confidence you have in your conclusions. The greater the internal validity, the more you can have faith that you know what factors cause an individual to act in a certain way.

External Validity.   In addition to random assignment, there is another randomization process sometimes used in research. In some research, mostly surveys, investigators make use of **random selection.** When researchers use this technique, it means that everybody in the population has a specified probability of being included in the research.

The goal of random selection is to increase the representativeness of the sample. With random selection, a scientist can have confidence that the sample used in the research is generally similar to the population as a whole. If your sample is like the population, you can conclude that the results from your sample will be similar to what would happen if you measured the entire population. When you can generalize beyond your sample, your results show **external validity.**

In terms that you should be familiar with, random assignment relates to internal validity, the degree to which an experiment is structured so that its results can be interpreted unambiguously. On the other hand, random selection relates to external validity, the degree to which the experiment pertains to those other than the participants in the study. In experimental research, it is typical to have random assignment of partic-

Random Selection (Sampling)—The process in which participants in a research study are selected so that any person in the population has the same chance of being selected as any other person, used to create representative samples.

External Validity—The property of data such that research results apply to people and situations beyond the particular sample of individuals observed in a single research setting.

ipants to groups, but not to have random selection because it is easier to use convenience samples, usually college students.

In some cases, using college students will lead to low levels of external validity. On the other hand, college students are people, and you are interested in people. In many ways, they are going to be like other older and younger people who come from the same socioeconomic and ethnic groups. As such, their behaviors during experiments might very well reflect the behaviors of others from the same background.

If you use animals in your research, you are likely to use rats, mice, or pigeons. Traditionally, psychologists who studied learning processes have used rats or pigeons; researchers studying genetics have used mice. These creatures are very different from other animals; they have been bred for laboratories and are likely to be more docile than rats that you might see in the wild. Domesticated mice, for instance, are larger than wild mice and reach sexual maturity quicker. But domesticated mice are physically weaker and have poorer vision than their wild counterparts. Mice, like all domesticated animals, show more chromosomal breakage than wild animals (Austad, 2002).

Can you generalize from white lab rats, from pigeons, or from mice to other rats, pigeons, and mice? to other animals? to people? These are not questions that are always easily answered. You have to use good judgment and expert opinion, plus a lot of caution, when you generalize across species.

When psychologists discuss generalization, we are interested in whether our research results will pertain to other organisms, other settings, and other times. Given the success that psychologists have had in applying research results to contexts outside the laboratory, we can conclude that levels of external validity are often acceptable, even if not perfect.

In any case, Mook (1983) has suggested that asking about the generalizability of research results may not really be the best question to ask. He proposed that we may want to test a set of ideas or a theory in the lab. For purposes of testing a theory, internal validity is critical, but external validity (and generalization) aren't relevant.

To illustrate his point, Mook used Harry Harlow's classic studies of young monkeys that could turn in a time of distress to either a soft and cuddly, artificial "mother" or an uncomfortable, wire "mother" from which the monkey got its milk (from a baby bottle). Drive-reduction theory would lead to the prediction that the animal would turn to the wire mother. Harlow tested this assumption and found that, in times of distress, the monkey preferred warm and cuddly.

The experimental setup was very artificial. The monkeys were probably not representative of baby monkeys in general; after all, they had been raised in a laboratory. They were certainly not like people.

The important issue here is that Harlow's results further weakened a dying theory and helped replace it with a different theory. In some ways, it doesn't matter, Mook explained, whether the results would generalize to people. The critical issue in some cases is development of ideas to test a theory.

Realism in Research.   A potential weakness of the experimental approach is that it is usually a stripped-down version of reality. In an effort to create groups that are virtually identical except for differences on one dimension, scientists try to simplify the experimental setting so that anything that will get in the way of a clear conclusion is eliminated.

Mundane Realism—The characteristic of a research setting such that it resembles the kind of situation that a participant would encounter in life.

Experimental Realism—The characteristic of a research setting such that the person participating in a study experiences the psychological state that the research is trying to induce, even if the research setting is artificial, like a laboratory.

When we use simple laboratory situations for our research, the result is often a reduction in **mundane realism.** When a situation has mundane realism, it resembles the normal environment you live in on an everyday basis. If you have ever volunteered to participate in a laboratory study, you probably saw pretty quickly that the environment was different from what you encounter normally.

The low level of mundane realism sometimes makes researchers wonder if their experimental results are applicable to normal human interaction. The simple version of reality in a laboratory can give us useful information about human behavior if the tasks of the participants have **experimental realism.** This type of realism relates to whether the participants engage in their tasks seriously.

An example of a series of studies that has little mundane realism is Stanley Milgram's obedience studies. He asked people to shock others if they made a mistake in a learning task in a laboratory. This is not something that most of us will ever do in our lives. As such, the mundane realism is fairly low. On the other hand, the research participants acted like they were very engaged in the task, showing nervousness and extreme discomfort in many cases. This behavior suggests a high level of experimental realism. When research shows good experimental realism, the research results may pertain to the real-world behaviors the researcher is investigating.

The critical element regarding realism is that we want our research participants to be in the psychological state of interest to us. The nature of the setting, whether it is a laboratory or not, may not be relevant. We are more interested in whether the person is engaged in the task in the way that will provide insights into behaviors we are studying.

Statistical Conclusion Validity

After you complete your experimental procedure, it is typical to conduct a statistical analysis of the results. In an introductory statistics course, everything seems pretty straightforward with regard to the selection of an appropriate statistical procedure.

In reality, there are times when it is not clear which test is most appropriate. As psychological methods become more complex, new statistical approaches are developed. They may be better than older ones in some cases.

Psychologists also maintain that nominally and ordinally scaled variables do not lend themselves to tests like the Student's t-test or the analysis of variance (ANOVA). They assert that you should not use the t-test or ANOVA for such variables. Statisticians have never thought that scale of measurement was a particularly critical issue.

When the noted psychologist S. S. Stevens (1946) invented the concepts of nominal, ordinal, interval, and ratio schedules, he decided that different statistical tests were appropriate for different scales of measurement. It wasn't long before others spotted the flaws in Stevens's arguments. For instance, Lord (1953) showed that in some cases, it might be entirely appropriate to use a t-test with football numbers, which are on a nominal scale. Later, Gaito (1980) further argued that Stevens had confused the numbers and the concepts that they were supposed to represent. Even Stevens (1951) recognized that his earlier proclamations could keep researchers from answering important questions appropriately. More recently, Velleman and Wilkinson (1993) have articulated arguments about cases in which scales of measurement are or are not particularly meaningful. The traditional prohibitions against using parametric tests with ordinal data often don't really have a solid theoretical or mathematical basis.

> **Statistical Conclusion Validity**—The characteristic of research results such that the conclusions drawn from the results are valid because the appropriate statistical analyses were used.

The important thing to remember is that you should give adequate consideration to your statistical tests. If you are uncertain, ask somebody who knows. Researchers do this all the time, especially when they are engaged in research techniques that are new to them. If you use the appropriate statistical test, and use it accurately, your results will have **statistical conclusion validity.**

There have been recent discussions about what constitutes adequate statistical conclusion validity in research reports. The American Psychological Association constituted a task force to deliberate the issues. The final report noted that traditional tests of statistical significance were appropriate in many cases, but that they needed to be supplemented by other statistics, like measures of effect size and confidence intervals (Wilkinson et al., 1999). The task force also recommended using the simplest statistic that will answer the question the researcher poses.

DISCUSSION QUESTIONS

1. People create informal constructs to explain behaviors. Identify a construct that people might use in everyday life and tell how they informally measure it.
2. Why is it important to be able to measure hypothetical constructs?
3. If you have to sacrifice either internal validity or external validity, which would be better to sacrifice? Why?
4. What are experimental and mundane realism? Why can a study be low in mundane realism and still be high in experimental realism? Have you ever participated in a research study? Did it have mundane realism? How did you react to the research setting?

CHAPTER SUMMARY

The single most important advantage associated with experiments is that they allow you to determine the causes of behavior. Not only can you predict the behaviors, but you can also control them.

The basic idea behind the experiment is that you start with two groups that are equivalent and apply a treatment to one of them. If differences appear after you do that, you can assume that your treatment made a difference.

If life were this simple, we would not need to pay as close attention to the details of research as we must. Characteristics of experiments, participants, and the context of the research can all affect the outcome of a research project in subtle but important ways. For instance, extraneous variables that you don't know about can affect the DV, so you mistakenly think that your IV is responsible for differences across groups. One particular type of extraneous variable is the confounding variable, which affects at least one group in systematic ways.

It is also important to remember that experiments involve social interactions among experimenters and participants. These interactions can affect the outcome of research in predictable ways, although the problem is that researchers are often not aware of these effects in their own studies.

When we are able to control for outside factors that affect the behavior of research participants, we can maximize the internal validity of our studies. Sometimes we are more concerned with internal validity, that is, the structure of the experiment itself. At other times, though, we are more concerned with external validity, the extent to which our results make sense outside the confines of our own research setting.

There are other types of validity as well, including construct validity, which relates to how well we operationally define our hypothetical constructs. We also pay attention to convergent and divergent validity, the degree to which measurements are associated with related constructs or differ from unrelated constructs. Finally, statistical conclusion validity relates to whether a researcher uses statistical tests that lead to the most meaningful conclusions possible.

CHAPTER SIX

THE DESIGN OF SIMPLE AND COMPLEX EXPERIMENTS

CHAPTER OVERVIEW

CHAPTER PREVIEW

PSYCHOLOGICAL CONCEPTS
Measuring Complex Concepts
Operational Definitions

**INDEPENDENT AND
DEPENDENT VARIABLES**

*CONTROVERSY: Should We Study
Depression Experimentally?*

**TYPES OF INDEPENDENT
AND DEPENDENT VARIABLES**
Qualitative and Quantitative
Independent Variables
Independent Variables Created by
Different Types of Manipulations
Types of Dependent Variables

**DEFINING AND
MEASURING VARIABLES**

**SINGLE AND MULTIPLE
INDEPENDENT VARIABLES**

MAIN EFFECTS

INTERACTIONS BETWEEN VARIABLES
What Do Interactions Mean?
Examining Main Effects
and Interactions
Patterns of Interactions

*CONTROVERSY: Can We
Spot Prejudice?*

IDENTIFYING RESEARCH DESIGNS

DATA ANALYSIS
Experiments with One
Independent Variable
Factorial Designs

CHAPTER SUMMARY

KEY TERMS

Analysis of variance
(ANOVA)
Ex post facto study
Factorial design
Higher order interaction
Instructional variable
Interaction effect

Main effect
Manipulated variable
Measured variable
Omnibus F-test
Planned comparison
Post hoc comparison
Qualitative variable

Quantitative variable
Quasi-experiment
Repeated measures design
Situational variable
Subject (participant)
variable
Task variable

CHAPTER PREVIEW

When you create experiments, you are trying to find the causes of behavior. In order to establish causation, you manipulate one variable to see its effect on another. Many of the concepts that psychologists deal with are complex and abstract; consequently, we are forced to create working definitions of variables that represent concepts that we cannot measure directly.

Psychologists have devised many different ways to develop independent and dependent variables. No matter how researchers define their variables, it is very important that the variables be objectively measurable. This allows others to understand how research has proceeded and how the methodology used by the investigators may have affected the outcome of the study.

Sometimes psychologists create simple studies with a single IV; most such studies in psychology have several comparison groups. In other cases, researchers manipulate more than one IV in a single experiment. The advantage of a multi-factor study is that we can get a better look at the complex interplay of variables that affect behavior. After all, in our lives, most of what we do is a result of more than a single cause.

After we finish conducting an experiment, we complete data analysis that helps us understand our results. There are several standard statistical tests that we use, but data analysis is an evolving field and new techniques and approaches are emerging.

PSYCHOLOGICAL CONCEPTS

In an experiment, a researcher manipulates and controls at least one variable. A variable is a construct whose measurement can result in different values, and it is typically contrasted with a constant, which is something that stays the same. A score on a test to measure the severity of depression would be a variable because the score can vary from one person or time to another.

Every discipline that deals with complex issues has its own set of hypothetical constructs. For instance, in physics, the concept of gravity is a hypothetical construct. We can see the effects of gravity, and knowing about it helps us function in everyday life, but we still don't really know what it is.

We measure overt behaviors, but we assume that the behaviors reflect mental and emotional processes that we can't observe. Even if we can't define exactly what cognitive or neural processes associated with depression, intelligence, motivation, or other constructs entail, our sometimes imprecise measurements have nonetheless led us to a better understanding of people.

Measuring Complex Concepts

Just about every realm of psychology deals with complex and abstract concepts. Think of the different domains that psychologists investigate. Forensic psychologists might deal with the results of a polygraph, the so-called lie detector; they don't know if a suspect is telling the truth, but can only observe the person's behaviors. Similarly, psychologists interested in intelligence can only identify behaviors that they think are related to intelligence. If developmental psychologists want to know if a child understands the world, they may see if the child shows conservation (e.g., the ability to recognize that the amount of a substance doesn't change simply because its shape does). The researchers will observe the child's response but will have to make educated guesses about cognitive processes.

What we need in our research are reasonable ways to measure complex concepts like the "truth" that the forensic psychologists seek, the "intelligence" that the cognitive psychologists want to measure, or the sophistication of thought that the developmental psychologists hope to understand.

Table 6.1 presents how psychologists measured some of these hypothetical constructs. Consider the hypothetical construct of motivation. Bell and Brady (2000) investigated the tendency of street sex workers (e.g., prostitutes) to go to health clinics depending on whether they were given motivation to do so. In this research, the investigators defined the sex workers as being motivated when they were offered monetary rewards for going to the clinic; in contrast, the researchers defined the workers as not motivated when there was no such incentive. The hypothetical construct of motivation was defined in terms of money the sex workers received.

On the other hand, Novi and Meinster (2000) defined motivation in terms of the score a participant achieved on the Thematic Apperception Test, a projective test involving ambiguous pictures that an individual tries to interpret.

In both research projects, these investigators were interested in motivation, but they defined motivation differently. These ways of measuring hypothetical constructs are not perfect, but they work to advance our knowledge. In the future we will undoubtedly have different operational definitions, but these are moving us in the right direction now.

As you see, in order to measure an abstraction, we need something with which to make a measurement. That sounds simple, but in practice, it is often quite difficult. For instance, how do you know if somebody is depressed? How do you know the extent to which the person is depressed?

To work with depression, we need a measurement that is reliable. That is, we want a measurement that will produce about the same result every time we measure the depression level of an individual (assuming that the person's level of depression hasn't changed). We need more than reliability, though. We also need a measurement that is valid, that is, a measurement that will help us make accurate predictions about a depressed person's behavior.

Operational Definitions

How would you go about measuring depression or any other hypothetical construct? You have to start with an operational definition. When we use an operational definition, we discuss an abstract concept in terms of how we measure it. For example, a clinical psychologist can't just look at an individual and know the degree of depression the person is experiencing. Some diagnostic measurement tool is necessary. The score on a test would be our operational definition. We would define a high score as reflecting greater depression and a low score as reflecting less.

TABLE 6.1   Examples of operational definitions of hypothetical constructs. Independent variables (IV) reflect manipulated variables used for creating groups to compare; dependent, or measured, variables (DV) reflect variables that are either pre-existing or are the result of manipulation of the independent variable. Some variables are not amenable for use as true IVs, such as intelligence, which can't be manipulated by the experimenter.

CONCEPT	OPERATIONAL DEFINITION AND RESEARCH TOPIC	REFERENCES
Depression	1. Score on Beck Depression Inventory (DV)—Relation between positive life events and depression 2. The mental state a person is in after reading negative or positive statements (IV)	1. Dixon & Reid (2000) 2. Velten (1968); Bartolic Basso, Schefft, Glauser, & Titanic-Schefft (1999)
Intelligence	1. Score on Kaufman Assessment Battery for Children (DV)—Cognitive Processing of Learning Disabled children 2. Score on Raven's Progressive Matrices Test (DV)—Cognitive functioning of immigrants	1. Teeter & Smith (1989) 2. Kozulin (1999)
Happiness	1. Self-report score; amount of smiling and facial muscle activity (DV)—Happiness in people with severe depression 2. Score on Depression–Happiness Scale (DV)—(a) Subjective well-being; (b) religiosity 3. Behavioral observations of happiness (DV)—Happiness in people with profound multiple disabilities 4. Mental state of a person after listening to fearful, sad, happy, and neutral nonverbal vocalizations (IV)—Neural responses to emotional vocalizations	1. Gehrick & Shapiro (2000) 2. (a) Lewis, McCollam, & Joseph (2000); (b) French & Stephen (2000) 3. Green & Reid (1999) 4. Morris, Scott, & Dolan (1999)
Motivation	1. Score on Achievement Motives Scale (DV)—Motivation in athletes 2. Score on Aesthetic Motivation Scale (DV)—Aesthetic motivation and sport preference 3. Scores on Thematic Apperception Test (DV)—Peer group influence in levels of motivation 4. Whether participants received monetary incentives (IV)—(a) Enhancing attendance at clinics for street sex workers; (b) time spent on different tasks in the workplace	1. Halvari & Kjormo (2000) 2. Wann & Wilson (1999) 3. Novi & Meinster (2000) 4. (a) Bell & Brady (2000); (b) Matthews & Dickinson (2000)

Researchers regularly use the Beck Depression Inventory (BDI) to assess levels of depression; a high test score indicates more severe depression whereas a lower score suggests a lower level. Dixon and Reid (2000) used the BDI to assess the depression levels of college students having varying numbers of positive and negative life events; Sundblom, Haikonen, Niemi-Pynttaeri, and Tigerstedt (1994) used the BDI to examine the effects of spiritual healing on chronic pain, which can lead to depression.

A simple, self-report test like the BDI is not perfect, but it provides valuable information. One important point to remember is that the score on the BDI is on a continuum and can be low or high. Although there can be a cutoff for "depressed" versus "not depressed," this criterion is arbitrary.

In a research project, using a BDI score to measure an existing level of depression is helpful. But suppose a researcher wants to manipulate an individual's mood, creating a temporary, mild state that resembles depression. The researcher could use the experimental paradigm to start with nearly identical groups, treat one of them in a certain way (like inducing depression in the participants), then measure their behaviors to see if there are any differences in behaviors across groups.

Quite a few researchers have studied the effects of depression on behavior by inducing such a version of depression. For instance, as noted in the previous chapter, Velten (1997) asked participants to read a series of statements that would either elevate or depress their mood. By doing this, he created two groups, one that was somewhat depressed, the other more positive.

You can get an idea of Velten's technique by reading Controversy Box 6.1. What ethical considerations would be important if you were to induce depression in participants in a study you carried out?

Creating depression in a research participant is something that a researcher should do only with caution. Controversy Box 6.1 deals with the question of how appropriate it is to induce depression in a research participant.

DISCUSSION QUESTIONS
1. Why do we have to rely on operational definitions to study abstract hypothetical constructs?
2. Can you study the hypothetical construct of friendliness? Devise two different ways to operationally define this concept.

INDEPENDENT AND DEPENDENT VARIABLES

The best way to begin your study of any psychological topic is to make sure you understand your concepts. Then you can come up with ways to measure them. After a while, these measurements that are critical to research are taken for granted, but they have to be developed.

Let's consider the way psychologists have measured depression in different projects associated with depression and memory. Investigators have regularly found that depressed people show poorer memory than others. As you have read, one way to

■ ■ ■ ■ ■ ▬▬▬▬▬▬▬▬▬▬▬▬▬▬▬▬▬▬▬▬▬▬▬▬▬

CONTROVERSY BOX 6.1
CONTROVERSY: Should We Study Depression Experimentally?

In an experiment, the researcher creates a situation so that every participant in a given group is in the same psychological state with respect to the concept being studied.

If a scientist wants to see whether people in a depressed state act differently from those who aren't, the researcher depresses the people in the treatment group and compares them to people who have not been depressed by the experimenter.

This raises a dilemma and a question. First, is it acceptable to depress research participants to see if they behave differently from a control group? That is, is it ethical? As you already know, the ethical guidelines for research specify that a researcher should not put research participants at risk by exposing them to physical or emotional harm. You might argue that by inducing a state of depression, you could harm participants.

Second, if it is ethical to induce depression, how could you do it realistically? When people are depressed, it is often as a result of an accumulation of negative experiences. How could a researcher operationally define depression for the purposes of an experiment?

As it turns out, researchers have effectively used different means to induce depression in research participants without endangering them. For instance, Velten (1997) asked people to read statements that would depress their mood, like

"Every now and then I feel so tired and gloomy that I'd rather just sit than do anything." Others read statements like "If your attitude is good, then things are good, and my attitude is good," which elevated their moods.

These statements had the desired effect, which was to induce different psychological states. The operational definition of depression here is the state a person is in after reading Velten's statements.

Is it fair to the participants, though? Was he exposing them to psychological or physical harm? Velten (and many other researchers using mood-changing manipulations) have asked this question and have used their expertise to anticipate the answer. Mood manipulations have weak and temporary, but consistent, effects. As a result, the researcher can induce a mood change that will not be very strong or last very long and that is easily reversed.

So it appears that we can safely and effectively induce a lowered mood. It is, fortunately, a pale copy of true depression, but we can use such changes in emotional states to study mental states related to depression. The good news is that such techniques are not harmful to participants when used carefully and can be used ethically to provide us with useful information about what happens when people are depressed.

---

assess depression is to use a score on the Beck Depression Inventory (BDI). You could define the amount of information in a person's memory simply as the number of words he or she recalls from a list of words. These two operational definitions are straightforward. However, if you want to assess a causal relationship between depression and memory, you cannot simply administer the BDI and see the relationship between the BDI score and a person's ability to recall a list of words.

In this example, the BDI score and the number of words recalled may very well covary. Depressed people may remember less than nondepressed people. But it takes more than covarying (i.e., correlation) for us to conclude causation.

The second criterion for causation is temporal precedence; that is, the cause (depression) must precede the effect (memory). If you bring participants into your laboratory and measure their BDI score and then assess their memory, you can conclude that the depression score came first. This still isn't enough to determine cause and effect.

The third criterion stipulates that you have to be able to rule out other causal variables. In this instance, perhaps if a person has a very catastrophic experience, he or she might show signs of depression and also have poorer memory because the flashbacks of the experience constantly distract them from remembering. We can't rule out such an explanation.

An optimal strategy is to use an experimental approach, inducing depression in one group and leaving a second group unaffected, then assessing their memory. If you did this, you would be investigating two variables, (a) presence or absence of depression, the IV, and (b) amount of material recalled, the DV.

> **Manipulated Variable—** A true independent variable that is manipulated by an experimenter, with assignment of participants to groups according to some system rather than on the basis of pre-existing characteristics like sex, age, etc.
>
> **Measured Variable—**A variable that is used to create groups to be compared, but assignment of participants to groups is on the basis of characteristics of the participants rather than according to a system created by the researcher.
>
> **Quasi-experiment—**A research project resembling a true experiment that involves comparison of groups that are not formed by random or systematic assignment by the investigator, but rather on the basis of participant characteristics.
>
> **Ex Post Facto Study—**A research project resembling a true experiment but using existing grouped data that did not involve random assignment of participants to conditions.

For this research involving depression, a true experimental manipulation would involve creating two groups by inducing different emotional states in them, then measuring the DV for each person. This design would make use of a true IV that is controlled by the experimenter. Sometimes we can't actively manipulate a variable. Subject (or participant) variables like age, sex, political affiliation, and so on are beyond the control of the experimenter and are not true IVs. We cannot create women and men on the spot. A person's gender comes with the person. You can measure the variable of gender; that is, you can determine if a person is a man or a woman. But you can't manipulate it.

Many researchers will treat existing depression, gender, and similar variables as true IVs for the purpose of designing research, but in reality when they study differences based on such variables, the research design is correlational, which does not permit us to conclude causation.

If a researcher manipulates the variable, like induced depression, the IV is a **manipulated variable.** On the other hand, if the value of the variable comes with the person, like gender, the IV is a **measured variable.** Manipulated variables lend themselves to cause and effect explanations; measured variables do not. Studies involving measured variables are often referred to as **quasi-experiments;** they look like experiments, but they really aren't. We'll cover quasi-experiments in detail in the next chapter.

Sometimes when researchers use existing data to create groups, like using psychiatric patients with high versus low BDI scores to create comparison groups, the approach is called an **ex post facto study.** The data may have been collected during diagnosis and not originally intended for research. It may resemble a true experiment because groups are created and compared, but it is also really correlational because variables have not actually been manipulated. Table 6.2 gives some examples of manipulated and measured variables.

TABLE 6.2 **Examples of manipulated and measured variables in true experiments and quasi-experiments.**

RESEARCH QUESTION	INDEPENDENT AND DEPENDENT VARIABLE
Measured Variables (Quasi-Experimental)	
Question: Does fitness level predict injury better than sex? (Bell et al., 2000) **Results:** Initial fitness level predicts the prevalence of injury better than the person's sex does.	**IV:** Physical fitness level at the start of army training: five levels, ranging from least fit to most fit. **DV:** Incidence of injury during training.
Question: Do dysphoric (i.e., depressed) people show better memory than euphoric people? (Murray et al., 1999) **Results:** Depressed people remembered fewer positive words than nondepressed people did.	**IV:** Depressed versus nondepressed, based on scores on the Beck Depression Inventory. **DV:** Number of positive and negative words remembered from a previously presented list.
Question: Do brain waves of women and men differ after sleep deprivation? (Armitage et al., 2001) **Results:** Women showed more dramatic increases in slow waves after sleep deprivation.	**IV:** Participant's sex **DV:** Incidence and amplitude of slow waves during sleep as measured with EEGs.
Manipulated Variables (Experimental)	
Question: Does the drug temazepam improve sleep of mountain climbers at an altitude of 17,400 ft (5,300 m)? (Dubowitz, 1998) **Results:** Temazepam improved sleep in climbers at high altitudes.	**IV:** Treatment (temazepam versus placebo). **DV:** Self-reported sleep; amount of oxygen in the blood.
Question: Does treating patients for pain before surgery affect pain and recovery after surgery? (Gottschalk et al., 1998) **Results:** Treating patients for pain before surgery begins led to less pain and quicker recovery after the surgery.	**IV:** Type of presurgical pain treatment (Epidural narcotic, local anesthesia, no presurgical pain medication). **DV:** Pain levels after surgery; activity level after surgery.
Question: Does suggestion change people's memories of the past? (Mazzoni & Loftus, 1998)' **Results:** Dream interpretations can induce people to change the way they remember their past.	**IV:** Suggestion given to participant (Dreams are indicators of prior experience versus no suggestion that dreams are indicators of prior experience). **DV:** Amount of agreement that nonevents had actually occurred.

Researchers rely on measured IVs because they have to. After all, you can't change a person's sex, age, political affiliation, etc. in your experiment. Sometimes, though, you can create a manipulated variable when you would normally expect a measured variable. As you have seen, depression, usually a measured variable, has been studied experimentally.

DISCUSSION QUESTIONS
1. How can a variable, like depression, be used either as an independent or as a dependent variable?
2. If researcher involves measured rather than manipulated variables, why is the investigation likely to involve a quasi-experiment or an ex post facto study?

TYPES OF INDEPENDENT AND DEPENDENT VARIABLES

Psychologists have shown considerable creativity in generating diverse independent variables. The need for a vast array of IVs is clear when you think of all the different areas of research in psychology.

Researchers make their decisions about their IVs based on what others have already done and on current circumstances. When you make use of ideas of other researchers, you can save yourself a lot of effort in generating new variables. If a process worked for another researcher, it might very well work for you.

Qualitative and Quantitative Independent Variables

There are different ways of considering IVs. One way is according to the type of measurement involved in measuring the IV. Another dimension of IVs is the nature of the experimental manipulation. We will consider these separately.

> **Qualitative Variable**—A variable whose different values are based on qualitative differences (e.g., female and male) rather than on numerical differences.

A **qualitative variable** involves variation on a nominal scale. That is, the change from one condition to another relies on a difference in categorization.

To understand an application of this idea, consider this situation: You hear somebody laugh, but you can't see them. What about their laughter would lead you to be more or less likely to want to meet them?

Bachorowski and Owren (2001) played recorded laughter from either a woman or a man. This represents a qualitative variable because the voices differed by the category of the laugher—female or male. The researchers were not trying to assess the difference in behavior as a result of a numerical difference in the level of the IV, but rather on the basis of sex.

In this study, the participants provided a rating of their interest in meeting the person whose recorded laughter they had heard. The results showed that, on average, participants were about equally likely to want to meet women and men after hearing them laugh.

The researchers also manipulated a second qualitative IV in the experiment. This was whether the laugh was "voiced" like a real laugh; as the investigators explained, the voiced laughs were "harmonically rich" (p. 253). The second type of laugh was "unvoiced," including "grunt-, cackle-, and snortlike sounds" (p. 253). Participants were much more interested in meeting the people who had produced the voiced laughs.

In this study, there are two IVs; both are qualitative. One IV is gender of the laugher; it has two levels, female and male. The second IV is type of laugh, voiced and unvoiced. When you report your research, it will help your audience if you identify both the IV as a general concept and also the levels or conditions.

The researchers here created qualitative IVs. The change from one group to another involves changing the quality of the stimulus, not a quantity.

> **Quantitative Variable—**
> A variable whose different values are based on numerical differences, like differences in amount, size, duration, etc.

A second type of manipulation in an experiment can relate to **quantitative variables.** Quantitative variables change along a continuum and will differ in amount, intensity, frequency, or duration. One clever experiment using a quantitative variable that tells us something interesting and important about ourselves was performed by Ross, Lepper, and Hubbard (1975). They demonstrated how we can persist in believing things that, in some sense, we know are not true.

They showed student participants pairs of fake suicide notes and told them that one was real; the participants were supposed to identify the real one. After going through 25 pairs of these notes, the researchers deceived the participants, telling them that they had either identified 24, 17, or 10 correctly. In this study, the IV was the number of correct guesses the participants were told they had made; it varied from high to medium to low. The experimenters had randomly assigned participants to one of the three groups in advance. The "24 correct" group was really no different from the "17 correct" or "10 correct" groups. This is a quantitative IV because the experimenters created three groups of participants who differed in a quantitative way—the number of correct responses they thought they had made.

The researchers then told the participants about the deception and that the feedback they were given was totally unrelated to their actual performance. The researchers then asked the participants to guess how many they really had gotten correct.

The participants ignored the fact that the feedback on their performance was completely inaccurate, persisting in their belief that their actual accuracy matched the randomly assigned condition. That is, those who had thought they identified 24 of 25 correctly still thought they were above average, whereas those who thought they had identified only 10 of 25 still felt that they were below average. As the research showed, once people believe something about themselves, they become remarkably good at ignoring evidence to the contrary.

In this study, the IV had three levels, meaning three conditions, that differed numerically. One advantage of research with quantitative variables is that you can see whether more (or less) is better. You can also find out if there is a maximum effect when your manipulation occurs on a continuum.

Some experiments lend themselves to qualitative variables, some to quantitative. You can also have a mixture of the two. Depending on the nature of your research question, you decide which approach to take. Table 6.3 presents some examples of qualitative and quantitative IVs and how they vary. As you can see in the table, researchers use qualitative variables like presence versus absence of a manipulation. For instance, Menella and Gerrish (1998) wanted to find out whether the presence or absence of alcohol in breast milk made a difference in infants' sleep.

Why would anybody add alcohol to an infants' milk to see if it would sleep differently? Some people believe that alcohol enhances sleep. It would be worthwhile to find out if there is any benefit to an infant's being exposed to alcohol; unless there are clear positive effects that outweigh any negatives, we probably don't want to give them such a drug. As summarized in the Table 6.3, the benefit of alcohol is questionable indeed.

TABLE 6.3 Examples of qualitative and quantitative independent variables and the different levels used in research projects.

RESEARCH QUESTION	INDEPENDENT AND DEPENDENT VARIABLE
Qualitative Independent Variable	
Question: Do infants sleep any differently when breast milk has alcohol in it? (Mennella & Gerrish, 1998) **Results:** Babies exposed to alcohol sleep less and showed less movement (i.e., active sleep).	**IV:** Presence or absence of alcohol in breast milk that had been expressed into a bottle. **DV:** Amount of time the babies slept; movement during sleep as recorded on a device that measured leg activity.
Question: Do bilingual people remember differently when asked questions in different languages? (Marian & Neisser, 2000) **Results:** Russian–English bilinguals displayed better memory for events experienced while speaking Russian better when quizzed in Russian; they remembered English-related events better when quizzed in English.	**IV:** Language of stimulus words (Russian versus English). **DV:** Number of events remembered when prompted with a word either in Russian or in English.
Quantitative Independent Variable	
Question: Do jurors respond differently to strong evidence versus weak evidence? (Schul & Goren, 1997) **Results:** Strong evidence led to higher judgments of guilt unless participants were instructed to ignore it. When instructed to ignore strong evidence, participants did so.	**IV:** Strength of evidence (based on witness's confidence, age of witness, and abnormality of defendant's actions). **DV:** Judgment of guilt.
Question: Does caffeine affect blood pressure and heart rate in workers? (Lane, Phillips-Bure, & Pieper, 1998) **Results:** Higher levels of caffeine intake produced higher blood pressure and heart rate in workers.	**IV:** Dose of caffeine (50 milligrams—equal to about half a cup of coffee—versus 250 milligrams—(equal to about two and a half cups of coffee). **DV:** Blood pressure and heart rate as measured by a portable monitor.
Question: Does a particular drug (methylphenidate) affect classroom performance and behavior in adolescents with ADHD? (Evans et al., 2001) **Results:** The drug caused increases in academic performance, with the largest increase arising from the smallest dosage tested.	**IV:** Dose of methylphenidate (placebo, 10 mg, 20 mg, or 30 mg). **DV:** Measurement of accuracy of classroom note taking, number of grammatical errors detected in writing, independent grading of writing assignments, on-task and disruptive behavior, and others.
Question: Do older Alzheimer's patients perform differently than other older adults in their ability to recognize when they have seen a given visual image before? (Budson, Desikan, Daffner, & Schachter, 2001) **Results:** Alzheimer's patients are less able to correctly distinguish between new pictures and pictures they have already seen than are a comparison group of older adults.	**IV:** Degree of similarity of visual images—high versus medium versus low as rated by independent participants; type of person (Alzheimer's patient versus healthy person).

(continued)

149

TABLE 6.3   Continued

RESEARCH QUESTION	INDEPENDENT AND DEPENDENT VARIABLE
Quantitative Independent Variable (continued)	
Question: Are people likely to recall syllables in a list when those syllables are repeated? (Soto-Faraco & Sebastián-Gallés, 2001)	**IV:** Whether or not syllables in a list to be learned occurred one or twice.
Results: When syllables were presented quickly and in close sequence, participants were less likely to remember both of them, showing "repetition deafness."	**DV:** Proportion of critical syllables recalled by each participant across 288 lists.

You can also see how investigators use quantitative variables in Table 6.3. Schul and Goren (1997) varied the strength of evidence in a mock trial to see how participants would evaluate evidence that was supposedly strong or weak. Sometimes results can be surprising. In the mock trial, the pretend jurors were able to discount persuasive evidence of guilt when they were told to do so.

Independent Variables Created by Different Types of Manipulations

Another dimension on which we can identify independent variables is according to how the IV is created. The IV can relate to the instructions that participants receive, the tasks they engage in, the situation, and the personal characteristics of the participant.

Task Variable—An independent variable whose different conditions involve differences in a task performed by participants.

Instructional Variable—An independent variable whose different conditions involve different instructions given by the researcher to participants.

Situational Variable—An independent variable whose different conditions involve different environments or contexts for different participants.

A **task variable** refers to an IV used to create groups that engage in somewhat different tasks. For example, in a study of the effect of expertise, Rowe and McKenna (2001) asked participants to watch a video of a tennis player and to try to anticipate which play would involve a point-winning stroke. Sometimes the participants merely watched the video whereas sometimes they engaged in a distracting task, generating a random stream of letters of the alphabet while they watched the video.

Thus, the participants engaged in two different tasks, one involving simple monitoring of the video, the other involving monitoring the video while generating letters.

An **instructional variable** is one in which the different groups of participants receive different instructions or types of information that might affect their responses. In the Ross et al. (1975) study described above involving the persistence of false beliefs, the IV was an instructional variable because the college students who took part in the study received different information depending on the group to which they were assigned. That is, they learned that they were correct on 10, 17, or 24 trials in differentiating between a genuine and a fake suicide letter.

A **situational variable** involves changing the situation or context of the experiment for different groups. For instance, researchers conducted a study to find out whether inner city residents could be educated to engage in safer sexual practices (The NIMH Multisite HIV, 1998). Participants either engaged in intensive, small group discussions of their sex lives and what they might want to change, or the participants listened to lectures and viewed a film on safe sex. All participants met twice a week for 3½ weeks.

In this experiment, the IV was situational: the participation involved different situations, the discussion versus the lecture. The outcome was that those people in the discussion groups experienced a lower incidence of sexually transmitted disease compared to the group that saw a film and listened to lectures.

> **Subject (Participant) Variable**—An independent variable that resembles a true IV but that is created on the basis of some pre-existing characteristic of the participant, as in a quasi-experiment.

A **subject variable** is used to compare people who differ on important characteristics at the beginning of a study. (Because the term *participant* has replaced the term *subject* in psychological research with people, researchers also call these variables **participant variables**). When you compare people on existing characteristics, this is not a true experimental manipulation; rather, it is quasi-experimental. Most researchers treat these subject variables as legitimate IVs, even though we know that we cannot attribute causation based on these IVs.

For example, the incidence of injuries among females in sports is higher than that for males (Bell, Mangione, Hemenway, Amoroso, & Jones, 2000). Some people have concluded that there is something about being female that predisposes women to injury or that there is something about being male that predisposes men to protection from injury. This is a good example of how a quasi-experiment could be set up: Look at men and women across some time period and monitor the number of injuries.

Recently, additional evidence has arisen that the picture regarding women's and men's injuries may be more complex than previously thought. Bell et al. studied female and male army trainees in the United States for an 8-week period. Women were two and a half times more likely to incur serious injury than the men. However, when the researchers grouped the participants according to level of fitness at the beginning of training, sex ceased to be a significant predictor of injuries. The investigators concluded that level of fitness is a better predictor of injury than sex is. The Bell and colleagues study was also quasi-experimental, but it provides a reminder that we need to be careful in assigning causation when using quasi-experimental approaches.

Similarly, researchers who have studied changes in the elderly have found a decreased sense of taste (Stevens, Cruz, Hoffman, & Patterson, 1995), but Schiffman (1997) suggested that it may be disease and medications that cause loss of taste abilities. When older adults are not on medications, she argued that their taste sensitivity doesn't decline. Age is another example of a subject variable that may speciously look like a causal variable. We are just too willing to believe that the elderly should be in a state of decline, so we attribute changes in taste sensitivity to age, ignoring other possibilities. This type of problem is always present with subject (participant) variables.

Types of Dependent Variables

Just as independent variables can come in many varieties, so can dependent variables. DVs can be categorized as either qualitative or quantitative, for instance. They can also involve measures of amount, intensity, frequency, or duration.

When DVs are qualitative, researchers investigate whether a manipulation leads to different categorical outcomes. Suppose you were on a jury that had to decide on the guilt or innocence of a defendant. Your decision would depend on the nature of the evidence regarding guilt and innocence. It would involve a categorical outcome on a nominal scale; the defendant would fall into one of two categories: guilty or not guilty.

Psychologists have investigated the variables that influence jury responses. A typical approach is to present a fictitious trial transcript that varies in content to see if the change in content affects jury decisions on guilt and innocence.

On the other hand, quantitative DVs measure on an ordinal, interval, or ratio measurement scale. If participants in jury research assigned different monetary damages in a fictitious lawsuit based on different types of testimony, such a decision would involve a quantitative DV. Investigators using quantitative DVs are often interested in amount of change or direction of change in a score.

DEFINING AND MEASURING VARIABLES

Once you identify the concepts you want to measure, you need to define them in a measurable way. For instance, suppose you want to know what effect depression has on a person's thinking and problem solving?

Several research projects have established the link between depression and poor memory. For example, Croll and Bryant (2000) found that women experiencing post-natal depression (i.e., depression after having given birth to a child) had poorer memories for events in their own lives and that it took them longer to retrieve memories compared to nondepressed women. In addition, adults over 50 years of age with unipolar major depression showed memory impairment that was unusual in a group that age (Lockwood, Alexopoulos, Kakuma, & Van Gorp, 2000).

It is not clear in advance that depression is causing the memory impairment. It could be that when people's memory begins to falter, they become depressed because of their memory difficulties. In order to experimentally explore this question of whether depression actually causes poorer memory, you have to define depression and develop some way to define thinking and problem solving. Then you have to induce depression in one group of people and not in another. Finally, you have to see whether the induced depression leads to worse cognitive processing.

Consider the research by Ellis, Thomas, and Rodriguez (1984). They induced depression in participants in one condition and did not alter the mood of people in a second group. Participants in the depressed group read a series of increasingly negative statements while the neutral participants read a series of very innocuous statements, the methodology devised by Velten (1968). In the Ellis and colleagues study, the participants with induced depression showed poorer recall of words than those in a neutral mood. (This is a good illustration of a case in which the researchers decided to use another psychologist's methodology rather than creating their own.)

In this study, the researchers operationally defined depression as the state an individual was in after reading mood-depressing statements. They measured thinking in terms of the number of critical words the participants could recall. It is important in your research to make sure that you define your variables specifically in terms of how you measure or create them. Simply talking about "depression" or "thinking" is too vague.

Others researchers have defined thinking differently. For example, Bartolic, Basso, Schefft, Glauser, & Titanic-Schefft (1998) defined thinking as the amount of brain activity, measured through electroencephalograms (EEGs), that took place when participants worked on a problem. Bartolic et al. also used Velten's methodology to induce depression in one group and to induce an elevated mood in a second group

The research by Ellis et al. (1984) and Bartolic et al. (1998) led to the same general conclusion, that depression leads to changes in cognitive processing. Previous work had established a correlation between depression and poor memory, but the Ellis and colleagues experiments helped reinforce our confidence that the depression was causing poorer memory. The results from Bartolic et al. reinforced the idea that induced depression leads to similar brain activity as naturally occurring depression does.

Both of these experiments involved one IV and one DV. Ellis et al. (1984) studied the individual's mood (either depressed or not—IV) and degree of recall (number of words recalled—DV); Bartolic et al. (1998) investigated the individual's mood (depressed or elevated mood—IV) and cognitive activity (amount of EEG activity in different parts of the brain—DV). Their independent and dependent variables are clearly defined and obviously measurable. This makes it easier to understand and interpret their work.

Because these two studies used different methodologies but produced similar results, they have a good case for claiming good convergent validity in their discussion of the effect that depression has on thinking. Convergent validity is further established by the fact that the majority of published experimental research has shown the depression-memory link.

The issue is complex, though, and some research deviates. For instance, Hertel (1998) found that depression produced no worse memory than a nondepressed emotional state when participants thought neutral thoughts, but people in the depressed state showed poorer memory when asked to focus their thoughts on themselves. Further, Kwiatkowski and Parkinson (1994) found that induced depression was associated with lower recall, but naturally occurring depression was not. The majority of research shows the depression–poor memory link, but investigators still have questions to answer.

DISCUSSION QUESTIONS
1. What is the difference between a qualitative and a quantitative independent variable?
2. Why is it hard to make causal conclusions if an independent variable involves a subject (or participant) variable? Why don't measured variables lend themselves to true experiments?
3. Intelligence is measured as a quantitative variable. How is the idea of genius similar to a qualitative variable even though it is based on a quantitative idea?

SINGLE AND MULTIPLE INDEPENDENT VARIABLES

In the last chapter, you saw the basic philosophy of the experimental approach. The discussion focused on the simplest experimental procedure, the two group design. That is a good design for an introduction to experimentation, but in reality, very few psychological experiments rely on only two groups. Most interesting questions are too complicated to be answered by comparing only two groups.

An expansion on the simplest design involves comparing multiple groups on a single IV. The advantage of this approach is that you can get a more detailed picture of behavior because you are observing them in more diverse conditions.

Sometimes these single factor designs include quantitative IVs. One example would be to see the effect of increasing dosage of a particular drug on people's or animals' behaviors. For instance, Evans et al. (2001) administered different amounts of the drug methylphenidate to students diagnosed with attention deficit hyperactive disorder (ADHD) to get an idea of the dosage that would lead to optimal performance and behavior in school.

These researchers found that a "more is better" approach is not necessarily optimal. In fact, a relatively low dose of the drug led to a very promising outcome, and improvements with higher dosages were not reliable across all students. The results of this single factor, multiple group design appear in Figure 6.1.

You can see the advantage of this research design. There are many possible dosages of the drug that could be prescribed. If Evans et al. had created a study with only two groups, it would have been impossible to get a good sense of how to use the drug most appropriately.

In other cases, investigators use IVs whose groups are qualitatively, rather than quantitatively, different. For instance, Fosse, Strickgold, and Hobson (2001) studied the incidence of hallucinatory images in varied states of waking and sleeping. These

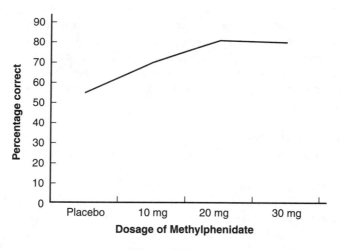

FIGURE 6.1   Results of a multiple group, single factor study. The results show the effect of a drug on performance on history worksheets among students diagnosed with ADHD. The IV here is a quantitative variable.

Source: S. W. Evans et al. (2001). Dose-response effects of methylphenidate on ecological valid measures of academic performance and classroom behavior in adolescents with ADHD. *Experimental and Clinical Psychopharmacology, 9,* 163–175. Copyright 2001 American Psychological Association. Used with permission.

researchers asked participants to report what was going through their heads at various times during the day, and when they awakened at night. The reports of these volunteers were later coded by raters who were blind to the participant's state when giving the report. The investigators then recorded the percentage of the time each person's reports included hallucinations. As you can see in Figure 6.2, there were notable differences among the various states of consciousness.

Many experiments in psychology involve more than one factor, that is, more than just a single IV. One reason for using multiple IVs is that many psychological questions are too complicated to answer with a single independent variable. Another reason is that we often gain more than twice as much information from a two-factor study than we do from a single-factor study. And, even better, we may not have to expend twice as much energy and time when we use multiple IVs in a single study.

> **Factorial Design**—A design of a research study in which the investigator manipulates more than one independent variable in a single study, with each level of one IV crossed with each level of all other IVs.

When an experiment uses multiple IVs, if each level of one variable is crossed with every level of the other variables, the approach is referred to as a **factorial design**. If there are two variables, A and B, and if A has two levels (A_1 and A_2) and B has three levels (B_1, B_2, and B_3), we would have a factorial design if A_1 is paired with each of B_1, B_2, and B_3 and A_2 is paired with each of B_1, B_2, and B_3. Table 6.4 schematically illustrates a 2×3 design.

In theory, there is no limit to the number of factors you can study in an experiment. Three IVs is not unusual, and occasionally you will see four. Realistically, though, you won't encounter more than four except in extremely rare

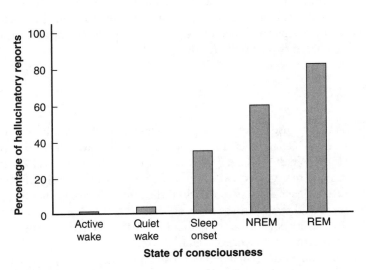

FIGURE 6.2   Example of a single-factor study with a qualitative independent variable. In this study, the researchers recorded the number of hallucinatory reports in qualitatively different mental states.

Source: R. Fosse, R. Strickgold, & J. A. Hobson. (2001). Brain-mind states: Reciprocal variation in thoughts and hallucinations. *Psychological Science, 12,* 30–36. Copyright 2001 Blackwell Publishing. Used with permission.

TABLE 6.4 **Schematic example of a factorial design involving two independent variables, A and B. Each level of an IV is paired with each level of the other IV. In this example there are six conditions because the two levels of A are paired with the three levels of B, creating a 2 × 3 design. In factorial designs, the total number of conditions is equal to the number of levels of the variables multiplied together.**

	B_1	B_2	B_3
A_1	A_1B_1	A_1B_2	A_1B_3
A_2	A_2B_1	A_2B_2	A_2B_3

instances. There are practical problems, like the number of participants a researcher would have to test, in a study with five IVs. But one of the biggest drawbacks to a study with so many factors would be trying to interpret the data.

If you had a five-factor study in which each IV had the minimum of two levels, you would have 32 separate conditions. Trying to figure out how the results in each one related to the others would be very difficult.

You can inspect different journals to see typical designs. Publications will differ, but experimentally oriented journals will probably resemble the *Journal of Experimental Psychology: General*. In one of its issues (June 2001), there were only two two-group comparisons and only a few other experiments that involved a single independent variable. The rest of the designs included two or three independent variables, the vast majority of which included two or three levels of the IV.

MAIN EFFECTS

> **Main Effect**—In a factorial design, differences among groups for a single independent variable that are significant, temporarily ignoring all other independent variables.

When we use factorial designs, we look at each IV individually. We temporarily isolate each IV and assess it as if it were the only one in the study. When we determine whether it has affected the DV, we are looking at a **main effect**. We monitor whether there is a significant main effect for each IV separately. So if the research design involves three IVs, we would test for three main effects.

Let's consider a study that links self-esteem, past experiences, and a concept called subjective distance. Ross and Wilson (2002) investigated how remote past experiences felt depending on whether those experiences were positive or negative.

Specifically, Ross and Wilson randomly assigned students to a condition in which they were supposed to recall a college course in which they either performed well or poorly. The investigators also recorded the students' level of self-esteem as measured on a self-esteem inventory (Rosenberg, 1965) and how long ago the recalled course had taken place.

Consequently, we have three IVs of interest to us here. One IV is the Grade Condition, the type of class a student recalled, Good Performance or Poor Performance. This is a true manipulated IV because students were randomly assigned to the groups.

The second IV is the students' self-esteem level, a measured variable rather than a true, manipulated IV. The third IV is how long ago the course in question had taken place, also a measured IV. Ross and Wilson included a fourth IV that isn't relevant to our discussion here.

The DV we are interested in here is the subjective distance from the class in question. That is, how far removed from them did that class seem to the participants? We all know that some memories seem recent, while other memories from the same time seem like they occurred in another lifetime. On a scale of 1 to 10, a rating of 1 reflected "feels like yesterday" and a 10 reflected "feels far away." Thus on this DV, higher scores indicated the feeling that the memory was remote.

Ross and Wilson discovered a significant main effect of time since the last class. More recent classes felt more recent. This offers no surprise. In fact, the researchers might have worried about their results if the students had consistently concluded that recent events seemed more remote than the remote events.

In addition, the investigators found a significant main effect of Grade Condition. Students who recalled classes in which they had earned poor grades tended to think of them as more remote; classes with good grades had the feel of being more recent. It's as if we keep good memories close and send bad memories to the attic. In a related study, Ross and Wilson conceptually replicated their findings with proud versus embarrassing moments. People keep proud moments close while distancing themselves from embarrassing moments.

There was no main effect of self-esteem. That is, students with high and low self-esteem were comparable in their judgments of subjective distance.

In this discussion we can see that there were two significant main effects—actual time since the class and the type of class the student recalled. One main effect was not significant—level of the student's self-esteem.

INTERACTIONS BETWEEN VARIABLES

Ross and Wilson's assessment of the main effects was interesting, but they also found some intriguing results when they examined the IVs together rather than in isolation.

Remember that courses with good grades seemed closer. This was a significant main effect. Further, self-esteem was unrelated to subjective distance. However, these patterns weren't always present.

> **Interaction Effect**—In a factorial design, differences across groups of a single independent variable that are predictable only by knowing the level of another independent variable.

Figure 6.3 illustrates the findings. High-grade courses were seen as being subjectively closer, but only for high self-esteem students. Students with low self-esteem tended to keep both successes and failures equally close, while high self-esteem students kept good memories close, shuffling less pleasant memories to a distance.

By looking at the effects of IVs together, you are examining **interactions.** In this study, Ross and Wilson found a significant interaction

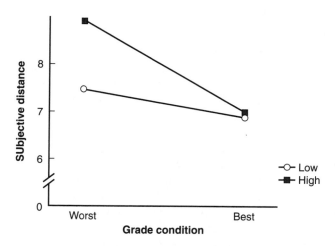

FIGURE 6.3   Subjective distance as affected by memory for a class resulting in good or poor grade and student's self-esteem. The interaction suggests that high self-esteem students distance themselves from poor performance but not from good performance, whereas low self-esteem students react to good and poor performance comparably.

Source: M. Ross & A. E. Wilson. (2002). It feels like yesterday: Self-esteem, valence of personal past experiences, and judgments of subjective distance. *Journal of Personality and Social Psychology, 32*, p. 797. Copyright American Psychological Association. Used with permission.

between grade condition and self-esteem. This means that in order to understand the effect of grade on subjective distance, you have to know whether the student showed low or high self-esteem.

Any time you need to know something about a second variable in order to understand the first variable, you have an interaction. Here we have to know about level of self-esteem in order to predict whether students keep their negative experiences subjectively close or far.

Let's summarize what you need to do with a factorial study involving two IVs. When you study two variables in a single experiment, you assess the effect of the first variable on the DV, that is, the main effect associated with the first IV. You also assess the effect of the second variable on the DV, seeing if there is a main effect of the second IV. Further, you see if the two variables, considered together, produce a combination of effects that is not predictable from either one alone, that is, the interaction effect. Some researchers recommend investigating interactions first.

Interactions can be hard to understand because they reflect a level of complexity one step up from main effects. Interactions may reflect the fact that people may engage in different thought processes or behaviors when exposed to slightly different conditions.

With interactions you have to pay attention to more than one IV at a time. In addition, you have to pay attention to each *level* of each IV because data in a single cell may be responsible for a significant interaction. Because interactions are important and because they can be difficult to grasp, we will deal with different patterns of interactions in the discussion that follows.

What Do Interactions Mean?

Interactions reflect an element of complexity in behavior when we move from simple to more complicated investigations. In interpreting them, you need to ask yourself why a change in the level of one IV leads to a different change in behavior when paired with a second IV.

In our examples of interactions here, we are going to concentrate on two-way analyses, that is, designs that involve two independent variables. Such interactions are easier to conceptualize in two dimensional graphs. If you can understand the concept of an interaction with two variables, you can understand the concept with more than two IVs, although they are harder to represent in graphs.

Some psychologists assert that, if there is a significant interaction, you should pay attention to the interaction effects first because the main effects, whether they are significant or not, might be irrelevant or they might not be particularly informative. This view has validity, but sometimes the main effects themselves can be important and interesting, even when there is an interaction.

As the number of IVs increases, the number of potential interactions to examine grows quite dramatically. If you have two IVs, there is a single interaction. If you have three IVs, there are four possible interactions. With four variables, there are six. The difficulties in interpretation often arise with the **higher order interactions,** that is, the interactions involving greater numbers of IVs. If you have a three-way interaction, it means that you need to look at every combination of three IVs combined. Gaining an understanding of what higher order interactions means can

| **Higher Order Interaction**—An interaction in a factorial design that involves the joint effects of more than two independent variables. |

very difficult. You can see the number of interactions that are possible in different designs in Table 6.5. The rare 5-variable design would require consideration of 26 potential interactions.

Examining Main Effects and Interactions

We will discuss several patterns of results that lead to interaction effects; when we graph those results, each one will look slightly different. Graphs indicate whether an interaction might exist. As you can see in Figures 6.3 and 6.4, the lines in the graph are not parallel. In fact, they cross. When lines are parallel, there is no interaction. When lines are at an angle to one another, there may be an interaction. You need a statistical test to see whether the interaction is significant.

When interactions are present, it can mean that participants are engaged in different psychological processes in the different conditions. For instance Trope and Fishbach (2000) manipulated two IVs and noted a significant interaction. The interaction reflected the fact that participants in the different groups were thinking very differently.

The investigators told participants that they would be abstaining from eating food with glucose (e.g., bread, candy, fruit, drinks with sugar) in order to take part in a study on the effects of glucose on thinking. The abstinence was supposed to last either six hours or three days. This was the first IV.

The researchers then asked one group of participants what kind of fine they would be willing to pay if they didn't actually abstain for the agreed upon time; a different group of participants estimated how much they thought participants in general (but

TABLE 6.5 The number of possible main effects and interactions in designs with 2, 3, and 4 independent variables.

NUMBER OF IVS	TWO-WAY INTERACTIONS	THREE-WAY INTERACTIONS	FOUR-WAY INTERACTIONS
2 (A, B)	1 A × B	—	—
3 (A, B, C)	3 A × B A × C B × C	1 A × B × C	
4 (A, B, C, D)	6 A × B A × C A × D B × C B × D C × D	4 A × B × C A × B × D A × C × D B × C × D	1 A × B × C × D

not themselves specifically) should pay if they didn't abstain. (This fine would supposedly cover the cost of the tests that would be scheduled, then canceled.) This was the second IV.

In reality, the participants were not gong to abstain from glucose. This was a cover story designed to get them to think realistically about the situation, that is, to establish an adequate level of experimental realism.

It probably won't surprise you to find out that participants thought the fine for participants in general ($4.18) should be higher than that for themselves specifically ($2.68). We are often more judgmental about others than we are about ourselves.

The participants didn't think that the length of supposed abstinence should make much difference regarding the fines. The difference was less than half a dollar for the six hours ($3.66) and three days ($3.20) abstinence. That is, the length of the fast was not particularly critical, according to the relatively small difference between means.

This picture is incomplete, though. When looking at a factorial design, you have to consider each component of this design (2 levels of person to be fined—self versus other—by 2 levels of abstinence—six hours versus three days). In this design, there are four conditions. We have to look at them individually. So we investigate what happened in the Fine-for-Self/6-Hour condition, the Fine-for-Self/3-Day condition, the Fine-for-Other/6-Hour condition, and the Fine-for-Other/3-Day condition. You can see each condition in their study and the proposed fines in Table 6.6. In this study, the fines across days show great differences when you consider both variables.

The results of this experiment appear in graphic form in Figure 6.4. As you can see, the pattern is complex. The participants sometimes thought they themselves should be fined less than others, as in the 3-Day condition, but sometimes the partici-

TABLE 6.6   The 2 × 2 factorial design used by Trope and Fishbach (2000) and the size of fines (in parentheses) suggested by participants in each condition.

Six Hour Abstinence	**FINE FOR SELF**	**FINE FOR OTHERS**	
	Fine for Self, 6-Hour Abstinence ($1.49)	Fine for Others, 6-Hour Abstinence ($5.82)	*$3.66*
Three Day Abstinence	Fine for Self, 3-Day Abstinence ($3.86)	Fine for Others, 3-Day Abstinence ($2.53)	*$3.20*
	$2.68	*$4.18*	

Source: Y. Trope & A. Fishbach. (2000). Counteractive self-control in overcoming temptation. *Journal of Personality and Social Psychology, 79,* 493–506. Copyright 2000 American Psychological Association. Used with permission.

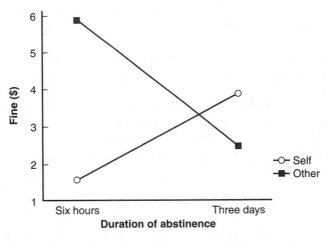

FIGURE 6.4   Illustration of an interaction in which the pattern of responses on the dependent variable for a given IV reverses, depending on the level of a second IV. In this experiment, participants proposed fines for failing to follow instructions.

Source: Y. Trope & A. Fishbach. (2000). Counteractive self-control in overcoming temptation. *Journal of Personality and Social Psychology, 79,* 493–506. Copyright 2000 American Psychological Association. Used with permission.

pants thought a heavier fine was appropriate for themselves, as in the 6-Hour condition. You can see in the figure that the pattern of proposed fines was reversed depending on who was fined and how long they were supposed to abstain from glucose.

Here is an example of the interaction effect reflecting the fact that, if somebody asks whether people give heavier fines to themselves or to others, you have to respond "It all depends." That is, it depends on whether you are talking about the short or the long duration abstinence. You can't say that there is a general pattern that applies uniformly.

If the researchers had decided to conduct two separate studies, each with only one IV, they would have arrived at a less informative conclusion. If they had paid attention only to the first IV, Self versus Others, they would have missed the reversal in the pattern of fines. Similarly, if they had only looked at the Length of Abstinence variable, they would also have missed this reversal. Only by looking at the entire combination of groups could they see this interesting pattern emerging. The advantage of using a factorial design is that you can see how the variables work independently, but you can also see their combined effects.

What is happening here? According to the researchers, when their participants assigned fines to others, they agreed that violating the rules for the long abstinence should not incur a high penalty because a three-day abstinence from glucose would be very difficult; people should not be penalized because they can't complete a very difficult task. But those same people should be penalized more severely if they don't engage in a task that most people could do with little difficulty, that is, abstain for only six hours.

Assigning fines to oneself, on the other hand, is different. Participants were harsher with themselves for the long-duration abstinence. The investigators concluded that the participants would use a heavier fine to motivate themselves to complete the three-day abstinence.

Thus, in one case, participants are showing compassion to others because those others might show typical human frailty. In contrast, the participants would be harsher on themselves in the long abstinence condition in order to enhance their own motivation; they may have been thinking that if they set up a large fine for themselves, they would be more likely to abstain from foods with glucose. The factorial design here reflects the fact that the participants are thinking one way in the Self condition and a very different way in the Other condition. When such a change in thought patterns occurs, an interaction effect may become apparent.

Patterns of Interactions

When you assess your results, in some interactions, you might look individually at each level of an IV and see how the DV changes as you move across groups on the second IV. There might be a consistent increase or decrease in scores on the second variable for both levels of the first one, but one group might change more than the other.

Consider the research by Rowe and McKenna (2001) who wanted to know if expert tennis players could anticipate a winning shot better than novices. The researchers created a video of a tennis player hitting the ball in a simulated match. The participants were supposed to identify which shot was likely to be the winning one before seeing the outcome of the shot.

Some of the participants were experts, whereas some were novices. If you look at the results in Figure 6.5a, you will see that novices are always worse at anticipating a winning shot than experts are. Another way of saying this is that experts can predict the future in ways that novices can't.

The researchers included a second variable in their study, a distracting task. If they had not included this second variable, the results would still have shown that experts were better at anticipating winning shots than novices.

(a)

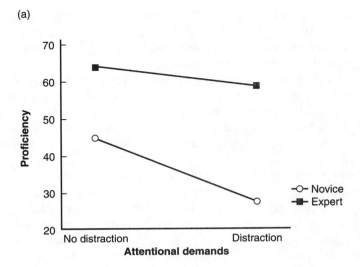

(b)

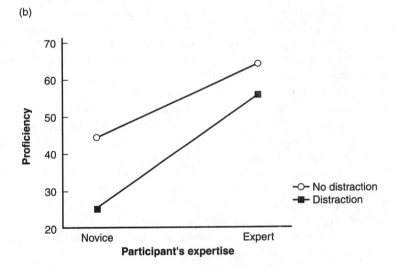

FIGURE 6.5   Two graphs of an interaction effect based on the same data. Each one highlights a slightly different aspect of the data. Figure 6.5a emphasizes the difference between novices and experts, whereas Figure 6.5b emphasizes the difference when participants engage in an additional, distracting task.

Source: R. M. Rowe & F. P. McKenna. (2001). Skilled anticipation in real-world tasks: Measurement of attentional demands in the domain of tennis. *Journal of Experimental Psychology: Applied,* 7, p. 65. Copyright 2001 American Psychological Association. Used with permission.

The effect of the second independent variable, the presence or absence of a distracting task, is apparent in Figure 6.5b. You can see that the distraction, which involved saying aloud random letters in the alphabet while watching the tennis video, led to consistently lower performance.

You can again see the "It depends" statement about interactions here. If you asked how much a distraction hampers performance, the answer is that it depends on whether you are talking about novices or about experts. One group, the novices, shows a greater decline in the presence of a distractor.

The advantage of this factorial design is that, as Figures 6.5a and 6.5b reveal, Rowe and McKenna showed that experts are better than novices all the time and distractions always lead to worse performance. But the figures also show that with distraction, the novices' performance shows more deterioration than the experts'. That is, while experts might perform less well when they are distracted, novices might fall apart completely.

This type of interaction reveals a change in performance from novices to experts, but it shows that the change is not the same when a distraction arises. You can translate these results into everyday life. If you are playing tennis or golf or basketball, or if you are driving a car, a distraction will worsen your performance; if you aren't very good to begin with, you get very bad. This is not the kind of information you would get from research if you didn't use a factorial design that was sensitive to interactions.

A final example of a different pattern of results that leads to an interaction occurs when there is no difference among most groups, but a single condition that departs from the rest. For example, in a study of prejudice against black defendants in trials, Sommers and Ellsworth (2001) created fictitious trials in which they varied the cases in several ways. For our discussion, we are interested in two specific independent variables: race of the defendant (black versus white) and type of trial (race is emphasized versus race is not emphasized in the trial summary).

The researchers asked the participants to recommend a sentence when the defendant was found guilty. As you can see in Figure 6.6, in three of four conditions, the jurors (who were white adults solicited for participation at an airport) recommended sentences of nearly equal length. The one exception involved the condition with black defendants when the trial summary did not emphasize race.

This is another instance in which a factorial design is critical. If race had been emphasized in a mock trial with the only comparison being sentences recommended for white versus black defendants, there would have been no effect of the IV because the average sentence lengths for black and for white defendants were about equal. Or if race had not been emphasized at all, it would have appeared that black defendants received harsher sentences, which is not always the case.

Do these research results reflect stereotyping by the mock jurors? Do they reflect prejudice? That is certainly an easy interpretation to make. Sometimes, though, it is hard to figure out why behaviors occur the way they do. For instance, if somebody displayed a high level of prejudice against a person of a different racial or ethnic group, would you be able to detect it? Controversy Box 6.2 illustrates research that shows that the situation may be more complex than we might think.

DISCUSSION QUESTIONS

1. In everyday life, what can you think of behaviors that might be affected by two factors? Develop an example from everyday behavior that involves an interaction.

(a)

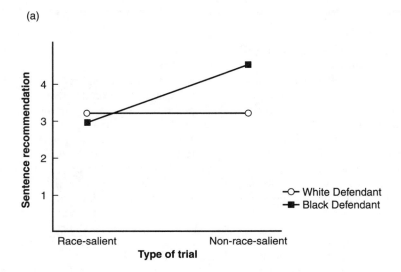

(b)

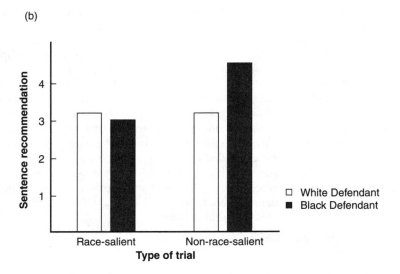

FIGURE 6.6 Interaction showing nearly equal performance for one group (white defendants), regardless of race salience, but a difference in the second condition (black defendants). The line graph and the bar graph are based on the same data.

Source: S. R. Sommers & P. C. Ellsworth. (2001). White juror bias: An investigation of prejudice against black defendants in the American courtroom. *Psychology, Public Policy, and Law,* 7, data from Table 1, p. 218. Copyright American Psychological Society. Used with permission.

2. In the Sommers and Ellsworth (2001) experiment on the effects of race on a trial verdict, explain how the interaction provided important information. Were the independent variables qualitative or quantitative? the dependent variables?

■ ■ ■ ■ ■

CONTROVERSY BOX 6.2
CONTROVERSY: Can We Spot Prejudice?

Just about everybody agrees that prejudice is undesirable. It would be hard to argue that it is desirable for people to make judgments about others without having any information about them.

Further, common sense would dictate that we could identify racially prejudiced people by observing their behavior toward another person from another group. At first glance, it doesn't even seem worthwhile to expend the energy to demonstrate that prejudiced people act in a prejudiced way.

As it turns out, though, this viewpoint is too simplistic. Sechrist and Stangor (2001) identified the prejudice level in their student participants, all of whom were white. The researchers then created a situation in which the participant would have to choose how far to sit from a black confederate. You would probably predict that high prejudiced people would sit farther from the black confederate than the low prejudiced people. In fact, this is what generally happened.

When the participants thought that others on their campus agreed with them in racial matters, low prejudiced people sat quite close to the confederate, whereas highly prejudiced people sat quite far from the confederate. That is, if they thought "everybody thinks like I do," the distance they chose to sit from the confederate strongly reflected their underlying attitude. There is no real surprise here.

An interesting complication was revealed by a significant interaction effect, however. When the high prejudice participants thought that most other students did not share their racial attitudes, they sat somewhat closer to the confederate than when they thought everybody believed as they did. That is, when participants thought they were in the minority in their racial attitudes, their seating behavior appeared less prejudiced. On the other hand, when low prejudiced participants thought most students had prejudicial racial attitudes, they sat farther from the black confederate.

The data suggest that if people are aware that others do not share their prejudices, those people will act with less prejudice. Unfortunately, if low prejudice people think that most others are racially biased, the opposite may occur.

These results give us an indication of how we might reduce undesirable behavior. If we can convince those who are racially biased that others don't share their ideas, we may be able to change behaviors for the better; perhaps attitudes will follow. The worst situation will be to allow prejudice to continue because we let others believe that everybody around them is also prejudiced. It may be difficult, but if we show no tolerance for prejudiced attitudes, we may lead others to abandon their undesirable behaviors and maybe their attitudes.

IDENTIFYING RESEARCH DESIGNS

When you create an experiment, you need to specify very clearly your IVs and your DVs. Similarly, when you read about another study, you should identify each IV and DV. If you don't have a firm idea of what you are manipulating, you will have a hard time setting up your study; if you don't understand what somebody else did, you won't be able to understand and interpret their results.

Once you establish an IV, you should determine how many treatments were involved and the nature of the IV. For example, as you discovered in Table 6.2, Murray et al. (1999) wanted to know if people in a depressed state remembered more words from a list than nondepressed people. The IV here is Psychological State, and it has two levels, dysphoric (depressed) and euphoric (nondepressed). In that experiment, Psychological State was a manipulated variable because the researchers induced either a dysphoric or a euphoric state in participants randomly assigned to one of the two groups. The DV was the number of words remembered from a list. It was the only dependent measure involved.

If Murray et al. had done nothing else, we would identify their design as a single factor, two-group design with one dependent variable. However, their experiment involved a little more complexity. They also investigated whether the participants remembered different numbers of positive and negative words. Thus, they employed a second IV, Word Type; it had two levels, positive words and negative words.

All participants were exposed to positive and to negative words during the learning phase of the study. This approach involves a **repeated measures design,** which we will cover in the next chapter. In a repeated measures design, participants are tested on all levels of at least one IV.

The design in the Murray et al. study is consequently called a 2 × 2 (which is read as "two by two") factorial design. Sometimes in journal articles, you will see such a design described as a "2 (Psychological State) × 2 (Word Type) factorial design with repeated measures on the second factor."

In a more general way of talking about a design, we would say that this experiment involved an A × B design. This tells us that there are two IVs, Variable A and Variable B. A and B are each associated with the number of conditions; in our example here, A = 2 and B = 2. So the A × B design in the Murray et al. study is a 2 × 2 design. You can easily see how many groups there are in an experiment by looking at the design. A 2 × 2 design has four conditions because, as simple arithmetic tells you, 2 times 2 equals 4.

An example of a 2 × 3 design comes from the work of Budson, Desikan, Daffner, and Schachter (2001); the design is outlined in Table 6.7. They compared Alzheimer's patients and healthy older adults on their ability to differentiate between pictures of nonsense shapes they either had or had not seen before. Some of the new shapes were very similar to the old ones, some of medium similarity, and some of low similarity.

Healthy adults were more easily fooled by new shapes that were similar to the old because they had been able to encode the previously seen shapes into memory. For the Alzheimer's patients, because their memories were generally poor, they were not fooled into thinking that they had seen a particular shape even if it was similar to ones they had actually seen because they didn't remember the similar ones to begin with.

The design was a 2 (Type of Person—Healthy versus Alzheimer's adult) × 3 (Similarity of Image—Low, medium, or high) factorial design with repeated measures on the second factor. There was a total of 6 conditions (because 2 × 3 = 6). You can see the conditions in Table 6.7.

Their dependent measure was the proportion of new images that the participants incorrectly identified as old.

Only the independent variables are specified in the design. So the Budson et al. research is a 2 × 3 design, with two IVs. Sometimes there is a tendency for students to identify the design as 2 × 3 × 1, where the 1 represents the DV. You don't include the DV when you identify the design.

> **Repeated Measures Design**—A design in which a single participant is observed and measured on more than one level of an independent variable rather than measuring different individuals on each level of the independent variable.

TABLE 6.7   **An example of a 2 (Type of Person) × 3 (Similarity of Image to Original) factorial design with repeated measures on the second factor. A 2 × 3 design implies that there are 6 different conditions (Budson, Desikan, Daffner, & Schachter, 2001).**

	LOW SIMILARITY	**MEDIUM SIMILARITY**	**HIGH SIMILARITY**
Alzheimer's Patient	Alzheimer's patient/Low Similarity	Alzheimer's patient/Medium Similarity	Alzheimer's patient/High Similarity
Healthy Elderly Person	Healthy Elderly Person/Low Similarity	Healthy Elderly Person/Medium Similarity	Healthy Elderly Person/High Similarity

DISCUSSION QUESTION

1. On a practical level, why wouldn't a researcher be likely to create an experiment with a 2 × 3 × 4 × 5 design?

DATA ANALYSIS

There are many tests available for analysis of experimental data. When data are normally distributed, there are about equal sample sizes, and the variances of the different groups are equal, we typically use a group of tests referred to as parametric tests. When the data do not meet these criteria, we use nonparametric statistics.

The parametric tests predominate by a great margin. If you look at virtually any journal dealing with experimental methods in psychology, you will see great use of the Student's *t*-test, the analysis of variance, and Pearson's correlation, all of which are parametric. The tests are useful even when there are departures from the usual criteria for their use. You can see applications of the most commonly used tests in the statistics appendix.

Experiments with One Independent Variable

Researchers have traditionally used the *Student's t*-test, more often simply called the *t*-test, for comparing two groups. This test was invented in the early 1900s by William Gossett, who performed research for the Guinness Brewery. (The Guinness Brewery did not allow its employees to publish their work, so he worked out a deal with them to publish a paper about the statistic; he used the pseudonym *Student* in his article. This is why his test is called *Student's t*.) At the time, it was the most advanced statistical technique available for experimental designs. We still use *t*-tests for such simple experiments.

When researchers use designs that call for multiple groups, the most commonly employed test is the Analysis of Variance (ANOVA), also known as the *F*-test. It was named after Ronald Fisher, who invented it. Recently, researchers have increased their use of regression analysis where they would formerly have used an ANOVA. The two approaches give the same basic information.

The advantage of the ANOVA is that it permits comparison of multiple groups in a single test. It also keeps the probability of incorrectly rejecting the null hypothesis at the level the researcher sets, which is usually .05. That is, the ANOVA lets you compare multiple groups without increasing the chance that you mistakenly conclude there is a difference between means.

If you compute an ANOVA and find that there is a significant difference between means, you don't know where the difference falls. For instance, in the research by Evans et al. (2001) with ADHD students in which there were four different dosage groups, the significant F-value didn't indicate which groups differ from one another, only that there was a difference somewhere.

> **Planned Comparison—**
> A comparison of differences across levels of an independent variable when the researcher decides during the design of the study to make the comparison rather than waiting until after preliminary data analysis.
>
> **Post Hoc Comparison—**
> A comparison of differences across levels of an independent variable when the researcher decides make the comparison after a preliminary data analysis.

When you have multiple groups, you have options for comparing them after computing an ANOVA. When you know in advance which groups you want to compare, you conduct **planned comparisons.** When you look at your results and then decide to make a comparison between two groups, you use **post hoc comparisons.** There are different statistical assumptions associated the two approaches. Without going into detail, it is enough at this point for you to know that the different statistics are designed to keep your Type I error rate from getting bigger than the .05 value you will probably use.

The philosophy underlying all of these tests is that your null hypothesis specifies that there is no difference between groups. The alternative hypothesis specifies that not all groups are equal. Supplemental tests can inform you about which groups differ if you conclude that not all are equal.

Factorial Designs

Data analysis in factorial designs typically involves the analysis of variance (ANOVA). This statistic permits the researcher to compare each IV individually and the interaction between them.

> **Analysis of Variance (Omnibus F-Test)—**A statistical analysis that permits simultaneous evaluation of differences among groups in research using multiple groups and multiple independent variables.

The first step for researchers typically involves what is called an **omnibus F-test,** commonly called **analysis of variance (ANOVA).** (There are related tests like the Multiple Analysis of Variance, MANOVA, and the Analysis of Covariance, ANCOVA, as well. They are variations on the ANOVA.) An omnibus F tells you whether the main effects are significant and whether any interactions are significant. After the omnibus F-test, researchers have several options. One is to discuss all main effects and interaction effects individually.

Researchers also use planned contrasts when analyzing their results. This can involve using t-tests to see whether individual pairs of conditions differed from one another.

Another option for data analysis is to forego analysis of main effects if there is a significant interaction effect. This is the route that Trope and Fishbach (2000) took in looking at fines participants imposed on themselves and others for not following an experimenter's directions as they agreed to do. When Trope and Fishbach discovered the significant interaction between assigning fines to Self versus Other and 6-Hour versus 3-Day Abstinence, they used only planned contrasts to compare pairs of groups and did not specifically examine the main effects. Their approach reflects the idea that, if there is a significant interaction effect, the main effects may not present a very good picture of the pattern of results. In order to understand the data, a finer analysis is needed than you can get from simply looking at the main effects.

If you decide before collecting any data to compare certain pairs of conditions, you should use planned comparisons. On the other hand, if you collect your data and conduct an ANOVA, then discover a potentially interesting comparison among groups, you should use post hoc comparisons.

You will probably be seeing greater use of confidence intervals and measures of effect size in the future. The most recent edition of the *Publication Manual of the American Psychological Association* specifies greater use of these statistics. You can refer to a statistics text for greater detail, but confidence intervals give you a sense of the range of scores that contains the true population mean from which your sample scores came, and measures of effect size inform you about whether your IV accounts for a small to a large amount of the difference across groups.

The field of statistics is constantly evolving as new and more powerful tests are developed, and as new ideas are applied to old. If you were to take a statistics or research methods course ten years from now, you would probably be introduced to a number of different procedures and concepts that are largely unknown or ignored now.

DISCUSSION QUESTION
1. Traditionally, what statistical test has been used for a single variable, two group design? Why is it not appropriate for multiple groups or multiple variables?

CHAPTER SUMMARY

In this chapter, you have seen how researchers create experiments. Psychologists recognize the importance of producing well-defined and objective definitions of the concepts we study. We have to develop concrete working definitions because many psychological topics involve very abstract ideas that are hard to study directly.

So in order to answer experimental questions, we set up one or more independent variables to see how they affect a subsequent behavior, the dependent variable. Independent variables can take many forms. The groups we study can differ quantitatively or qualitatively. Dependent variables are also quite diverse in different experiments. Most experiments involve manipulation of one to three independent variables. It is not unusual for some experiments to have multiple dependent variables as well.

The advantage of a multiple factor design is that we can see how individual independent variables affect behavior, but we can also see how these IVs interact to produce behaviors that are not predictable simply from a single independent variable. The disadvantage of factorial designs is that they can be very difficult to interpret and, when there are several IVs, may be very costly and time consuming to conduct.

After an experiment is complete, we analyze the results statistically to see if there are any significant main effects or interactions. Finally, we have to decide what the results mean as we interpret the data and relate it to behavior.

..... ■

CHAPTER SEVEN

EXPANDING ON EXPERIMENTAL DESIGNS: REPEATED MEASURES AND QUASI-EXPERIMENTS

CHAPTER OVERVIEW

CHAPTER PREVIEW

REPEATED MEASURES DESIGNS

ADVANTAGES OF REPEATED MEASURES DESIGNS
Increasing Efficiency in Data Collection
Increasing Validity of Data
Finding Enough Participants
Reducing Error in Measurement

LIMITATIONS TO REPEATED MEASURES DESIGNS
Possible, but Unlikely, Repeated
     Measures Designs
Subject (Participant) Variables
Sequence and Order Effects
     *Overcoming Sequence
     and Order Effects*

DATA ANALYSIS WITH REPEATED MEASURES DESIGNS

QUASI-EXPERIMENTAL DESIGNS
Causation and Quasi-Experimental
     Designs

Combining Experimental and Quasi-
     Experimental Designs
Threats to Internal Validity

*CONTROVERSY: Does Sex + Neuroticism
= Death?*
     Threats Associated with Participants
     Threats Associated with Measurement

**TYPES OF QUASI-EXPERIMENTAL
DESIGNS**
One-Group Pretest–Postest Designs
Static-Group Comparison Designs
Nonequivalent Control
     Group Designs
Interrupted Time Series Designs
Replicated Interrupted Time
     Series Designs

*CONTROVERSY: Can You Stop Smoking
by Watching TV?*

*CONTROVERSY: Do Laws Really Change
Our Behaviors?*

CHAPTER SUMMARY

KEY TERMS

Asymmetric transfer
Attrition (mortality) threat
Baseline

Between-groups design
Complete counterbalancing
Counterbalancing

History threat
Instrumentation
     threat

Interrupted time
  series design
Latency effect
Maturation threat
Natural pairs
Nonequivalent control
  group design
One-group pretest–posttest
  design

Order effects
Partial counterbalancing
Repeated measures
  (within-subjects) design
Replicated interrupted
  time series design
Selection threat
Sequence effects

Static-group comparison
  design
Statistical regression
  threat
Symmetric transfer
Testing threat
Transfer

CHAPTER PREVIEW

You already know the basic elements of experimental research. The ideas in this chapter will fill in some of the gaps when you need to expand on the basic issues of experimental design.

Throughout a research project you have to make many practical decisions about how you intend to carry out the project. One of the decisions includes whether you want to observe participants more than once, an approach called a repeated measures design. There are quite a few advantages to such a strategy: You are certain that participants are comparable across groups (because they are the same people being measured in different conditions), you can get a lot of information from a smaller number of participants, and you are more likely to detect small differences between groups.

Researchers frequently make use of repeated measures designs because they are very efficient and because the advantages often outweigh the disadvantages significantly. No method is without its disadvantages, though. For instance, in a repeated measures design, you have to worry that one treatment will have effects that persist, affecting later behaviors.

Another extension of the experimental design is the quasi-experiment. This approach involves comparing groups that may differ in critical ways at the outset of your study. For instance, if you compare women and men, you might conclude that they are not the same, but you cannot conclude that your treatment caused a difference. The two groups may have come into your study already differing in important ways.

This approach is really correlational. Although quasi-experiments resemble experimental designs, they lack random assignment of participants to groups. As a result, you can make meaningful and accurate descriptions and predictions, but it is hard to identify the cause of differences.

Researchers have created quite a large number of different quasi-experimental designs. As the studies get more complex, they require greater investments in time and energy, so you have to decide how to maximize your research results and to minimize your costs.

REPEATED MEASURES DESIGNS

Setting up a research project is time consuming; carrying it out may be even more so. As a result, as an experimenter you want to maximize the amount of information you get from your work.

One obvious way to increase information is by manipulating more than one independent variable in a single study, that is, by using a factorial design. Researchers do this all the time. In essence, you actually conduct two or more experiments within a single project. This approach might not save a lot of time or energy, though, because when you create a project for which you intend to test 100 participants, if you created a second independent variable, you might have to increase your sample to 200 participants. You will have saved some time and effort in planning only one study, but you will test the same number of participants as if you had carried out two separate projects.

A different way to increase the economy of your work is to set up an experiment in which you test the same individuals more than once. When you collect data from the same people more than once in the same experiment, you are using a **repeated measures design;** this approach is also called a **within-subjects design.** It is called a within-subjects design because you are trying to find out if there are any differences in the way the participants *within* a single sample behave. You can contrast it with a **between-groups design** in which you test different participants in different groups. The goal is to see if there are any differences *between* groups.

> **Repeated Measures (Within-Subjects) Design**—A research design in which the same individuals provide data in more than one group, essentially serving as their own control group.
>
> **Between-Groups Design**—A research design in which a single individual does not provide data for more than one condition or group.

ADVANTAGES OF REPEATED MEASURES DESIGNS

There are several advantages associated with repeated measures designs, some purely practical regarding carrying out your project, and others statistical. You can identify clear advantages with repeated measures designs, but you have to consider whether this approach is best for your research. In many cases, repeated measures are very helpful, but there are some situations where they will be inappropriate.

Increasing Efficiency in Data Collection

One advantage with a repeated measures design is that you might be able to increase the amount of data without a marked increase in time and effort. If your design involved three groups and you wanted to test 50 in each group, you would need a total of 150 participants. By using a repeated measures design, you could still test 50 but get the benefits of using 150.

In some studies, you may gain a great deal of extra information with repeated measures. For instance, if you wanted to know whether people could remember a list of words better with fast versus slow presentation, you could use a repeated measures design, with each participant learning the words in each presentation condition. If the experiment takes 45 minutes for one condition, it might only take 15 more minutes to add the second condition. Thus, the experiment would be 33 percent longer, but you would get 100 percent more data.

If you intend to compare performance in two groups, A and B, you could test 50 people in each group for a total of 100. Or you could test each person in both A and B, which would require only 50. You would have twice as much data with no increase in the number of people you tested. When there are small numbers of potential participants, that is, a small participant pool, it can be very helpful to test them repeatedly.

If you added a second IV and tested the same participants on each level of that variable as well, you would still need only the 50 participants, but the amount of data you collected could be much greater. Thus, you have effectively created two experiments with only a small increase the amount of time you spend testing participants.

As you can see in Table 7.1, if you had a 2 × 3 design with no repeated measures, you would need to test many more people than if you use repeated measures. In the most extreme comparison of no repeated measures on any variable versus repeated measures on both variables, you can see that you could reduce the number of people you test from 300 to 50, which can be an immense savings of your time and a notable reduction in the number of people you have to recruit.

Increasing Validity of Data

A second advantage to using repeated measures is that you may have greater confidence in the validity of your data. Psychologists have found that people may answer a given question from very dissimilar perspectives. Sometimes participants in different groups approach the same task very differently. Their behaviors may look as if the IV has made a difference when the participants' varied perspectives are causing the changes. A repeated measures approach can remedy this problem.

One clever experiment reveals how this problem could occur. Birnbaum (1999) recruited participants via the internet, asking them to serve in a "1-minute judgment study." They were asked to "judge, how large is the number 9" or ". . . the number 221." A rating of 1 reflected "very, very small," whereas a 10 reflected "very, very large."

Figure 7.1 reflects the participants' judgments. Surprisingly, the results showed that people believe that 9 is larger than 221. If you were to accept this result uncritically, you would believe that people think that a small number is bigger than a big number.

What is going on? Most likely, according to Birnbaum, people in the "Judge 9 Group" were comparing 9 to single-digit numbers or to small numbers in general; in that context, 9 is pretty large. On the other hand, the participants in the "Judge 221 Group" were comparing it to much larger numbers, so it seemed relatively small (Figure 7.2).

When you ask different people to provide ratings, you need to make sure that they are all using the same context. Thus, for this judgment task, you could provide an anchor for the participants; that is, you could say that for this judgment, 1 would be considered *very, very small* and 1,000 would be considered *very, very large*. Would this solve the problem? According to Birnbaum (1974), even when you do this, participants can rate smaller numbers as being bigger than larger ones. Participants rated 450 as larger

TABLE 7.1   Example of how repeated measures leads to greater amounts of data without increases in the number of participants for a hypothetical 2 × 3 design. In this example, the researcher wants 50 data points in each of the six cells.

Number of Participants Required for Independent (Non-repeated) Measures. Participants experience only one of the six conditions.

INDEPENDENT VARIABLE B	INDEPENDENT VARIABLE A		TOTAL NUMBER OF PARTICIPANTS
	Group A_1	Group A_2	
Group B_1	50 different people	50 different people	100 for B_1
Group B_2	50 different people	50 different people	100 for B_2
Group B_3	50 different people	50 different people	100 for B_3
Total Number of Participants	150 for Group A_1	150 for Group A_2	300 Participants

Number of Participants Required for Repeated Measures on Variable B. Participants experience B_1, B_2, and B_3, but only one of the groups for Variable A.

INDEPENDENT VARIABLE B	INDEPENDENT VARIABLE A		INDEPENDENT TOTAL NUMBER OF PARTICIPANTS
	Group A_1	Group A_2	
Group B_1	50	50	100 for B_1
Group B_2	50	50	100 for B_2
Group B_3	50	50	100 for B_3
Total Number of Participants	50 for Group A_1 because each person participates in B_1, B_2, and B_3	50 for Group A_2 because each person participates in B_1, B_2, and B_3	100 Participants (The same 100 people are in B_1, B_2, and B_3)

Number of Participants Required for Repeated Measures on Variables A and B. Every participant experiences B_1, B_2, and B_3, and also A_1 and A_2. That is, each person is in all conditions.

INDEPENDENT VARIABLE B	INDEPENDENT VARIABLE A		INDEPENDENT TOTAL NUMBER OF PARTICIPANTS
	Group A_1	Group A_2	
Group B_1	50	50	50 for B_1 because the same people are in A_1 and A_2
Group B_2	50	50	50 for B_2 because the same people are in A_1 and A_2
Group B_3	50	50	50 for B_3 because the same people are in A_1 and A_2
Total Number of Participants	50 for Group A_1 because the same people are in B_1, B_2, and B_3	50 for Group A_2 because the same people are in B_1, B_2, and B_3	50 Participants (The same 100 people are in B_1, B_2, and B_3; likewise, the same people are in A_1 and A_2)

FIGURE 7.1   The surprising results of the study in which participants rated the size of "9" and "221" on a scale of 1 (*very, very small*) to 10 (*very, very large*). The study involved independent assignment to conditions rather than repeated measures. That is, different people judged the size of 9 and of 221.

Source: M. H. Birnbaum. (1999). How to show that 9 > 221: Collect judgments in a between-subjects design. *Psychological Methods, 4*, 243–249. Copyright 1999 American Psychological Association. Used with permission.

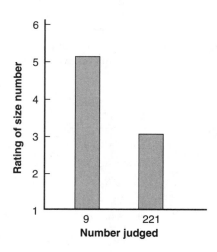

than 550 when he provided anchors. The implication of Birnbaum's findings is that for subjective judgments, like providing ratings when there are no objective guidelines for responses, it may be a good idea to include repeated measures in the research design. With repeated measures, it's the same person being measured in each condition, so changes in behavior are more likely to be due to the IV than to differing perspectives.

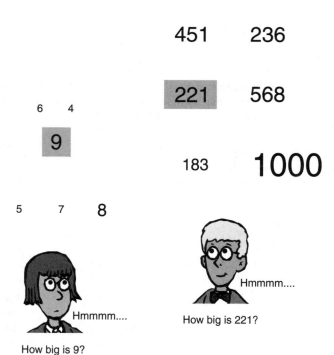

FIGURE 7.2   Relative ratings can be misleading when based on subjective criteria. A value like 9 might seem big in comparison with small numbers and 221 might seem small compared to big numbers.

Source: M. H. Birnbaum. (1999). How to show that 9 > 221: Collect judgments in a between-subjects design. *Psychological Methods, 4*, 243–249. Copyright 1999 American Psychological Association. Used with permission.

This problem of different contexts by raters occurs only for subjective judgments. It is not troublesome to use independent groups for objective measures, like grades or numbers of tasks completed in a given time, which are pretty concrete and not as subject to judgment errors.

Sometimes it makes the most sense to use repeated measures. For instance, Leirer, Yesavage, and Morrow (1991) investigated the effects of marijuana use in airline pilots over 48 hours. The researchers legally obtained marijuana and administered controlled doses to pilots who engaged in simulated flights. The investigators were interested in how long marijuana affected the pilots' performance and whether the pilots were aware of any effects of the marijuana on their behaviors.

They discovered that most of the pilots experienced residual effects of marijuana after 24 hours, but they typically were not aware of the effects. You could conduct this research without using repeated measures, but there are clear advantages in following the same individuals as the marijuana leaves their systems.

Finding Enough Participants

A third advantage of repeated measures designs is that if the group you wanted to test was rare, such as airline pilots or other highly trained experts in some field, you might not be able to find many such people. By using the repeated measures design, you can avoid the problem of running out of participants.

On the other hand, you may not have to worry about the availability of participants if they are plentiful, like students from large introductory psychology classes who look for research to fulfill a course requirement or to earn extra credit. If your testing sessions require a lot of time and effort, it may be better not to use a repeated measures design because your participants may be fatigued, bored, or otherwise worn out by the time they finish one condition. Testing them in a second condition may end up being a problem.

Most psychological research does not suffer from a lack of participants. Students in introductory psychology are often very generous in giving their time to researchers. If you were studying an unusual population, though, like twins, you might want to test them as much as you could because twins are relatively rare. You want to get the most out of the time they are willing to contribute.

Reducing Error in Measurement

Another advantage with repeated measures designs is that, in general, your groups are equivalent at the outset because they are the same people in each group. One commonly used phrase that relates to comparable groups is that we say that the participants are serving as their own control group. Further, you are simply increasing the number of data points in your analysis, which increases the power of your analysis, that is, the likelihood of rejecting the null hypothesis when you should (Vonesh, 1983).

If you have two groups of different participants, you might wind up with a difference between the means of the two groups, but if the people in each group are very different from one another to begin with, you don't know if the difference between means reflects your experimental treatment or if the difference results from the fact that the participants' scores are simply very different; one group may accidentally have some high or some low scores that lead to a meaningless difference between the two groups.

With a repeated measures design, the participants may differ greatly from one another. This may not be a problem, though, because you are comparing a single person in one condition with his or her performance in a different condition. Smart or fast or motivated people in condition A will also be smart or fast or motivated in condition B. You can compare these people in different conditions, knowing that if they have certain characteristics that should be the same in any conditions in which you might test them.

A different design related to repeated measures involves matching participants in different groups. If you were going to investigate how long it takes for people to interact with a single stranger versus a group of strangers, you might initially measure your participants regarding their levels of introversion and extroversion. Then you could match two people on introversion–extroversion, assigning one to the "single stranger" condition and the other to the "multiple stranger" conditions.

> **Natural Pairs**—A pairing of individuals, like twins, who are similar to one another in some way and are useful for comparison after being exposed to different levels of an independent variable.

In addition, researchers sometimes use **natural pairs** in a matched design. This could involve twins, siblings, or other pairs that share a variable that is important in the research. You can see how repeated measures and matching are conceptually related; the big difference is that in repeated measures, the participant is identical in all conditions whereas with matching, there is similarity across conditions, but the match is imperfect.

Matching is a less frequently used strategy in experimental, laboratory work compared to research on psychiatric or clinical issues. In a psychiatric research project, Coverdale and Turbott (2000) assessed sexual and physical abuse among psychiatric patients compared to medical patients. They matched 158 psychiatric outpatients with 158 medical outpatients; the match was based on gender, age, and ethnicity.

The benefit of matching here is that if there are differences in rates of abuse associated with gender, age, and ethnicity, the researchers could be confident that these variables were equated across the two types of outpatient participants. These researchers discovered that the two groups did not differ in the incidence of childhood abuse, whereas as adults psychiatric patients were more susceptible to both physical and sexual abuse.

Laboratory researchers often stay away from matching because matching participants well can be difficult, especially if you want to use more than one variable. Consider the situation in which you have three variables you want to match, for example, age, years of education, and family income. If you are interested in creating two groups in which the first person in Group A is matched closely with the first person in Group B, you might find that it is easy to pair people on the first variable (e.g., age). For the second variable, you lose some flexibility because you have to stick with the match on the first variable, even if the second variable isn't matched so well. By the time you get to the third variable, the match might be quite poor.

You have two basic options when you have poor matches. One is to live with the best matches possible, even if they aren't very good. The problem here is that you lose the statistical advantages of matching. The second option is to discard matched pairs that are not good and to conduct your study with the pairs that remain. The drawback here is that you may end up with a small sample size that greatly reduces the chance that you will spot small but real differences across groups.

Because of these problems, psychologists do not use matching very frequently. Further, if you match your participants, you need to make sure that the matching variable is reliably associated with your dependent variable.

DISCUSSION QUESTIONS

1. Why can repeated measures designs be more useful than nonrepeated measures designs if participants provide subjective ratings about satisfaction with the quality of the food at two different locations on your college campus?
2. Describe one group on your campus for which matching could be particularly useful in setting up a study. Do the same for repeated measures. Why would they be appropriate?
3. Why is matching on more than one variable difficult? Can you think of a study you could do on your fellow students for which matching would be helpful if you could generate good matches? Why would matching be useful in your example?

LIMITATIONS TO REPEATED MEASURES DESIGNS

Some research projects do not lend themselves to repeated measures designs and some variables make repeated measures impossible. If you conduct a study in which you compare people according to a participant variable, that is, according to an existing personal characteristic, you will not be able to use repeated measurements. If you want to compare the study habits of high and low achieving students, it would be impossible to use repeated measures because each student would fall into only one category.

Another consideration about testing the same person repeatedly is that, if you test participants over time, you have a big investment in each one. If they fail to return, you have committed time and effort that will not be repaid. This loss is less of a problem with nonrepeated designs because you don't count on extended participation by anyone.

Possible, but Unlikely, Repeated Measures Designs

Other projects could conceivably be carried out using repeated measures, but it would not be a good idea. If you are planning a study on the acquisition of study skills with a new technique compared to a control group, it is pretty clear that you wouldn't want to use repeated measures. Once the students learned a skill in the experimental group, they would no longer be naïve, so their performance in the control condition would have been influenced by the exposure to the experimental treatment.

Other research projects using repeated measures might be possible and would lead to valid results, but they would not be practical. For example, suppose you want to see whether young adults and older adults could complete a learning task with equal speed. This is a study that experimenters would not want to carry out with repeated measures because they would have to test their participants as young adults, wait for them to age for 50 or so years, and then retest them. By that time, nobody might even care about this research question or somebody else may have already answered it.

You can see an example of this situation in research by May, Hasher, and Stoltz-fus (1993). They investigated learning in people of different ages, using one set of young people and one set of old people. They could have waited for the young people to age for 50 years, but that isn't very reasonable.

The researchers had to make a compromise. Waiting for young people to get old doesn't make any sense, but there are problems with the design they chose because people growing up in different eras may simply be very different. This is particularly important in longitudinal studies (e.g., Schaie, 2000).

Age may not be the best explanatory variable. For instance, May et al. (1993) found that when young and old people engaged in a learning task during their best time of the day (which tends to be in the morning for older people but later in the day for younger people), there was remarkably little difference in performance; and Ryan, Hatfield, and Hofstetter (2002) discovered that caffeine eliminates the decline in performance from morning to afternoon. Sometimes the obvious variable is not the only variable to consider.

Subject (Participant) Variables

In addition to age, there are other subject or participant variables that you will see frequently in psychological research. You generally can't use repeated measures when you examine pre-existing characteristics, such as sex, political affiliation (e.g., Democrat versus Republican), religious affiliation (Protestant, Catholic, Jewish, Muslim, etc.), sexual behavior (homosexual, heterosexual, bisexual, or none). You can't assign people to be Democrats, Protestants, etc. They are what they are.

Another case in which repeated measure would not be desirable is when the participants' behavior in one condition is essentially independent of their behavior in another. As a general rule, if the correlation between participants' scores in two groups is less than about .25, repeated measures designs are not warranted (Vonesh, 1983).

Sequence Effects—The result of multiple or repeated measurements of individuals in different experimental conditions such that they behave differently on later measurements as a result of having undergone the earlier measurements.

Order Effects—The result of multiple or repeated measurements of individuals in different experimental conditions such that a particular behavior changes depending on which condition it follows.

Sequence and Order Effects

Another situation that limits the desirability of repeated measurements is when there may be **sequence effects** in testing, which are said to occur when different treatment sequences (e.g., A-B-C versus B-A-C) lead to different outcomes. If a particular treatment, no matter where in the sequence of treatments it occurs, affects performance in subsequent conditions, this would involve sequence effects.

There are also potential **order effects,** which are progressive effects of testing when an individual is tested repeatedly. Fatigue that sets in after repeated testing is an example of an order effect.

Sometimes sequence effects can arise when you would have little clue that they might occur. For instance, researchers have investigated whether people can actually do two things at once. (Sometimes you can.) A common strategy is to ask participants to tap their fingers on a surface while engaging in a second task, like reading. Green and Vaid

Transfer—A change in behavior in a repeated measures design that results from learning that takes place in an earlier condition.

Symmetric Transfer—A change in behavior in a repeated measures design that results from learning in an earlier condition, with the same degree of change in later behaviors, regardless of the order of conditions.

Asymmetric Transfer—A change in behavior in a repeated measures design that results from learning in an earlier condition, with differences in the amount of transfer in a later condition depending on which conditions occur first.

Latency Effect—A change in behavior in a repeated measures design that occurs when some learning takes place but is not immediately apparent, surfacing only after a delay.

Counterbalancing—In a repeated measures design, the changing of the order of conditions across individuals to avoid contamination of data because of systematic sequence, order, or transfer effects.

Complete Counterbalancing—In a repeated measures design, the use of all possible orders of experimental conditions to avoid contamination of data because of systematic sequence, order, or transfer effects.

(1986) reported that when participants engage in two such tasks at the same time, it can make a difference whether they start tapping with their right or their left hand. When participants tapped with their right hand first, their performance was worse than when they started with the left.

When early behavior effects later behavior, it is called **transfer;** there are two types of transfer, **symmetric transfer** and **asymmetric transfer.** If people are tested twice (A-B), they may simply improve after the first exposure. If the improvement in A when it occurs second equals the improvement in B when it occurs second, we have symmetric transfer. If A helps later performance on B, but B doesn't help a later performance on A, we have asymmetric transfer. Sometimes psychologists find these potential problems, such as transfer, to be interesting in themselves because they provide a clue to how people think and learn (e.g., Nygaard, Burt, & Queen, 2000).

It is also possible that participants will experience a **latency effect.** This means that a treatment does not work initially, but takes some time to develop. If a participant is tested immediately after exposure to the treatment that is actually effective, consequences of the treatment will emerge as if they resulted from the second treatment (Girden, 1992).

Most psychological research on sequence effects has involved short-term effects in the laboratory. In reality, long-term sequence effects can also occur. In market research involving grocery store retailing, Paksoy, Wilkinson, and Mason (1985) suggested that researchers provide a "rest" week in their studies so that the effects of advertising and sales in week one of a study will not affect consumers' choices in week two, when a different IV is manipulated.

Overcoming Sequence and Order Effects. When sequence effects are likely, researchers often use **counterbalancing** to avoid mistaking sequence or order effects for treatment effects. If you created a project with two conditions, A and B, you would want to test some participants in the AB order and other participants in the BA order. If you had three conditions, A, B, and C, you could order them ABC, ACB, BAC, BCA, CAB, and CBA if you wanted to use all possible orderings. This approach reflects **complete counterbalancing** because you use all possible orders.

As you add conditions, the number of orderings grows quickly and requires that you test a large number of participants. Thus, with three conditions, you have six orders; with four conditions, it grows to 24; with five, you have 120. Normally you would test multiple participants in each order; so if you had four conditions (i.e., 24 orders) and if you wanted to include three participants per order, you would need to test 72 people. In addition, you would need a multiple of 24 participants (e.g., 48, 72, 96) in your study because there are 24 orders to repeat in each block.

Partial Counterbalanc-ing—In a repeated measures design, the use of a subset of all possible orders of experimental conditions to avoid contamination of data because of systematic sequence, order, or transfer effects.

Fortunately, there is no need to use complete counterbalancing. **Partial counterbalancing** can help keep experiments manageable. Only a subset of all orders is needed.

DISCUSSION QUESTIONS

1. Why is it impossible to carry out a repeated measures study when you are studying participant, or measured, variables?
2. In what circumstances do you think a latency effect might occur in a repeated measures design?
3. What is the difference between sequence and order effects? Give an example of each.
4. Give two examples of studies that could use repeated measures but for which it would be unlikely.

DATA ANALYSIS WITH REPEATED MEASURES DESIGNS

When you create an experiment that uses repeated measures, you will be faced with choices about statistics that can become pretty complicated.

Many of the issues are beyond the scope of this book but you can see some common approaches to data analysis with repeated measures in the statistics appendix. Before you carry out a study with repeated measures, you should consult with somebody who knows the field. The last thing you want to do is to collect data that you won't be able to analyze properly. When investigators employ repeated measures designs, they often carry out data analyses that are not optimal, causing researchers either to miss differences between groups that are small, but real, or to conclude that there are differences when there aren't (Gaito, 1961; Pollatsek & Well, 1995; Reese, 1997).

A common statistical approach is to compare pretest and posttest scores with either a *t*-test or an analysis of variance (ANOVA), depending on how many groups and independent variables are involved. A closely related approach involves assessing change scores, which means subtracting a person's score at the end from the score at the beginning.

QUASI-EXPERIMENTAL DESIGNS

You have already had some exposure to quasi-experiments in the last chapter. Now you will learn about some of the specific issues associated with this approach.

In a quasi-experiment, researchers typically compare groups to see if they differ in a behavior of interest. That is, does this group of people differ from that group? Quasi-experiments can provide valuable information about group differences, but such designs are not ideal for assessing cause and effect.

The critical element here is that the researcher cannot randomly assign people to groups. Membership in the groups is based on some characteristic of the individual that is beyond the control of the investigator. The researcher can assign participants to groups based on their characteristics, but cannot actively manipulate the variable.

Questions that researchers address with quasi-experiments could include whether women and men differ in their behavior, whether young and old people are alike, whether beagles and German shepherds respond differently to children, etc. As you can imagine, there are many interesting questions that we can address with quasi-experiments. The fact that unites these examples is that participants and subjects belong in a category (female or male, young or old, beagles or German shepherds), and nothing that the researcher does is going to permit them to be placed in a different category.

What differentiates a true experiment from a quasi-experiment is that, in true experiments, the researcher randomly assigns a participant to a given group. In a quasi-experiment, the investigator has to measure the subject or participant on some dimension (are they young or old, female or male, etc.). Placement in a condition is thus based on a measurement rather than a manipulation. These independent variables are thus measured rather than manipulated variables.

Causation and Quasi-Experimental Designs

Quasi-experiments based on measured variables are really correlational in nature. Correlations do not allow you to identify causation. So if you compare female and male participants with respect to the way they act, you cannot conclude that any differences are due to sex. The problem is that from birth onward, parents (and everybody else) treat female and male babies differently. Through childhood and adolescence, and into adulthood, women and men experience the world around them in countlessly different ways.

We have different stereotypical images of women and men, including the notions that women like to shop and men like to watch sports. To the extent that these stereotypes are accurate, it is probably more prudent to attribute them to experiences that people have had, not to whether they are female or male. As such, we should not see sex as a causal variable of behavior most of the time. We can make predictions, though, reflecting a correlation. This is exactly what happens in a quasi-experiment.

It is important to remember that sex can be a causal variable. For instance, the adult height of men and women is partially a function of their sex. (Multiple factors will influence any complex development, though, so there is more to your adult height than whether you are a woman or a man.) We have to remember that even though an independent variable in a quasi-experiment might be a causal variable, we just don't have enough information to conclude that.

In order to say that *A* causes *B*, three conditions must exist: A has to precede *B*, they have to covary (i.e., *B* must occur when *A* does), and *A* must be the most plausible cause of *B* with other potential causes ruled out. In a quasi-experiment, the last condition is the source of the problem.

If you have ruled out other potential causes of a behavior, you can conclude that your measured variable was the cause. Unfortunately, in a quasi-experiment we don't know when we have excluded all of the relevant variables, so we can't be completely confident in our conclusions. In general, you should be very cautious about making causal statements with quasi-experiments, just as you should be cautious with any correlational approach.

Combining Experimental and Quasi-Experimental Designs

In some studies, we use experimental manipulations; in others, we develop quasi-experimental designs. In still other circumstances, we mix the two. The result is a design like we encountered in the discussion of factorial experiments. Each level of the quasi-experimental variable is crossed with each level of the true experimental variable.

Researchers quite commonly use a mixture of true and quasi-experiments because there are many interesting questions that can only be addressed with such a combination. For instance, it appears that highly neurotic people are more likely to associate sex with death than are less neurotic people (Goldenberg, Pyszczynski, McCoy, Greenberg, & Solomon, 1999).

If you wanted to study the effect of neuroticism on reactions to different independent variables, you would have to use a quasi-experimental design because you cannot assign people to a level of neuroticism. They bring it with them on their own. You can manipulate other variables, though, and see how those variables affect people with different levels of neuroticism.

Goldenberg et al. discovered an interesting connection between a person's level of neuroticism and the individual's tendency to connect sex and death. To do so, they developed a mixture of true and quasi-experimental variables. You can see what happened regarding this sex, death, and neuroticism study in Controversy Box 7.1.

Threats to Internal Validity

The internal validity of a research project is critical to the level of confidence you have in your conclusions. The greater the internal validity, the more you can have faith that you know what factors cause an individual to act in a certain way. We have identified certain threats to internal validity that can have important negative effects in the conclusions we draw.

The major threats to internal validity were initially elucidated by Campbell and Stanley (1966). Researchers now recognize that we have to take these potential problems very seriously. These threats are particularly troublesome when a research design uses repeated measures and nonequivalent groups. Such problems are common in applied research that takes place outside of the laboratory.

The reason that non-laboratory studies are more prone to these problems than other research is because we generally have less control over the research setting outside the lab. When we conduct theoretical or applied research in a laboratory, we can simplify the environment so that only a few easily identifiable differences exist between groups. If the groups then behave differently, we assume that a variable or a combination of variables that we manipulated had an effect.

If you create a study in a retail establishment, for instance, the company still wants to make money, so you have to work around the business that takes place. As

CONTROVERSY BOX 7.1

CONTROVERSY: Does Sex + Neuroticism = Death?

Psychologists have speculated on the link between sex and death (e.g., Becker, 1973). Although the connection may not be obvious, it surfaces at times. For instance, as Goldenberg et al. (1999) point out, one term for orgasm in French is *le petite mort* (the little death, p. 1175).

The issues that these psychologists have dealt with is that thinking about the physical act of sex reminds people of their mortality. The result, according to Terror Management Theory (TMT), is that people seek to control their fear of death by changing the way they think about sex, removing it from the realm of death. One way to do this is to adopt a new view of sex; if we can imbue it with value that extends beyond the physical, perhaps sex can be a more spiritual experience, not a death-related phenomenon.

Goldenberg et al. combined true and quasi-experimental variables to explore this question. They identified people who were high versus low in neuroticism, generating a quasi-experimental variable. The researchers then exposed these participants to questionnaires focused either on the sexual or the romantic aspects of sex, which was a true experimental manipulation. Thus, participants were either high or low in neuroticism and were primed either to the physical or to the romantic view of sex.

The researchers then gave the participants word stems (e.g., COFF__) and asked them to complete the word. The stems could be completed with death-related words (e.g., *coffin*) or non-death words (e.g., *coffee*).

Highly neurotic people were significantly more likely to complete the word stems with death-related words when they were exposed to the prime that focused on the physical aspects of sex; interestingly, these people were the least likely to generate death-related words when exposed to the romantic prime. You can see the interaction between level of neuroticism and type of prime in Figure 7.3.

In this mixture of a true and a quasi-experiment, Goldenberg et al. provide support for their hypothesis that for people who have anxi-

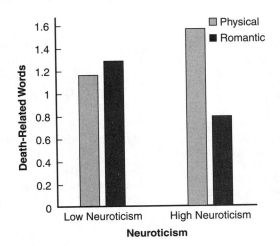

FIGURE 7.3 The relation between neuroticism and type of sex prime. According to Terror Management Theory, thoughts of sex are often linked with thoughts of death. People who are highly neurotic are more likely to think of the two together than are those with lower levels of neuroticism. That is, death-related words are more accessible to highly neurotic people after thinking of sex. The link can be broken, though, if the highly neurotic people are primed to change their thoughts of sex from physical to romantic.

Source: J. L. Goldenberg et al. (1999). Death, sex, love, and neuroticism: Why is sex such a problem? *Journal of Personality and Social Psychology*, 77, 1173–1187. Copyright American Psychological Association. Reprinted with permission.

eties toward both sex and death (i.e., highly neurotic people), thinking about the physical nature of sex makes them think of death. We need to remember that it is not necessarily the neuroticism that makes people link sex and death. Whatever has made them neurotic may have also made them link sex and death. The connection is predictable, but we don't know exactly why it occurs.

As Goldenberg et al. have shown, though, the neurotic individuals can break this link by directing their attention to the romantic rather than to the physical nature of sexual behavior.

such, you make compromises and conduct your study differently than if you could manipulate the situation to your liking.

Threats Associated with Participants. Several of the threats to internal validity pertain to the characteristics of the research sample. The first threat involves **selection.** Whenever we design a study that does not involve random assignment of participants to group, the selection threat may be a problem. This threat reflects the fact that if we compare two groups with pre-determined characteristics, they may not really be comparable. Differences other than the independent variable may cause differences in the dependent variable.

Selection Threat—A threat to the internal validity of a study such that groups to be compared differ before being exposed to different experimental treatments, so any differences after treatment could be due to the initial differences rather than to the independent variable.

For example, Bell, Mangione, Hemenway, Amoroso, and Jones (2000) noted that a lot of research has found that women suffer sports injuries at a higher rate than men. Conclusions have been drawn about the various reasons why the female body is more prone to injury. However, Bell et al. discovered that initial fitness levels among army inductees was more predictive of future injury than sex was. If so, injuries among women athletes might be reduced through increased fitness training.

You can see here one of the biggest problems associated with quasi-experiments. When you cannot assign people to groups randomly, you are never sure that you have comparable people in each condition.

A second threat to internal validity is **maturation.** People change the way they act for a lot of reasons. If you study individuals over time, they may not be the same at the end as they were at the start. Their behavior with respect to your DV might change because of the changes in the participants, not because of your IV.

Maturation Threat—A threat to the internal validity of a study due to short- or long-term changes in a participant because of psychological changes like boredom, fatigue, etc. or because of physical maturation.

Maturation is more clearly a problem if you study children over time because they mature physically and psychologically in dramatic ways. But maturation can also come into play with adults. They may not change physically in obvious ways over a short period, but they can change psychologically. In this case, maturation does not only mean maturation of the kind from infancy to older childhood to adolescence; it means any physical or psychological changes, including fatigue, boredom, having learned about the study, etc.

A third threat, **attrition** (also called **subject mortality**), can affect your results. If you test people over time, some may not return for later tests. You can't be sure that the people who drop out are like the ones that remain when it comes to your DV. For instance, if you are studying the development of skill over time, the participants who are progressing slowly may drop out, leaving you only with those people who are competent. Any conclusions you draw about your research will thus be based on a sample consisting of more proficient people.

Attrition (Mortality) Threat—A threat to the internal validity of a study when participants drop out of a study, leading to a change in the nature of the sample.

The issue is not attrition in and of itself. Rather, problems arise because of non-random attrition. That is, the participants in one group who drop out may exhibit different characteristics from those who remain, or those who drop out of one group may have different characteristics from those who drop out in a different group. In either

History Threat—A threat to the internal validity of a study that results when some event outside the research project affects participants systematically.

case, groups may look like they differ because of the IV; in reality, they may differ because of the effect of those who left the study.

A fourth threat to validity is **history.** Events during the course of a study may affect one group and not another. Even if you started with randomly assigned groups, this could happen. But if you are conducting a study with two different groups, like young people versus old people, one group may be affected by some event outside your research so their behaviors change. If you concluded that your IV is the reason for the differences across groups, you would be victimized by the history threat.

Instrumentation Threat—A threat to the internal validity of a study that results from changes in the way the dependent variable is measured, due to factors like poor calibration of mechanical equipment or changes in the way researchers record subjective observations.

Threats Associated with Measurement. A fifth threat to internal validity is **instrumentation.** This means that there is a problem in the way you measure your dependent variable over time. If you asked different questions to a group in the initial and final research sessions, your data would not be comparable because changing the questions might lead your participants to interpret them differently. Another situation in which instrumentation could be a problem would be if you used two different people to collect data at the beginning and at the end of the project; the second set of data collectors might introduce changes in the research environment, leading to changes in the way participants respond.

The instrumentation threat could also come into play if you were measuring behaviors with mechanical instruments. Sometimes these instruments need calibration or readjustment; if you don't do that, two measurements that should be the same could be different because of the machinery you are using.

Testing Threat—A threat to the internal validity of a study that results when participants' behavior changes as a function of having been tested previously.

Statistical Regression Threat—A threat to the internal validity of a study that results when participants are categorized or selected for research participation on the basis of an initial observation that involves significant measurement error that is not likely to repeat itself on later measurements, giving the false impression that change is due to a treatment when it is really due to the difference in measurement error.

A sixth threat to internal validity is **testing.** Sometimes, initial testing of your participants can sensitize them to the reasons for your research. As a result, they may act differently because they know too much about the nature of your research question, and it biases their responses.

A seventh threat to internal validity is **statistical regression.** A researcher might want to compare good and poor students who are admitted to a special program. In order to make the groups seem equivalent, the researcher might take the poorest students from the higher level group and the best students from the lower level group. This would mean that the two groups would seem equivalent to begin with.

Unfortunately, the better students who score low in their group may really be typical students who, for no systematic reason, fell at the low end of the distribution. Similarly, the poorer students at the top of their group may not be all that different from their peers; they just scored higher, also for unknown reasons.

We know that such error, on average, is zero. So, in later testing, these better students' scores are likely to be high, like those in the rest of the group from which they came. The poorer students' scores also go back where they belong, toward the low end of the scale.

This means that, even if no research were done, the average scores of the two groups would quite likely be different on the retest even if there were no independent variable at all. Such a phenomenon is very real. It is sometimes called regression to the mean.

When researchers attempt to match participants in nonequivalent groups, there is a high likelihood of statistical regression. Consequently, if you are not going to randomly assign matched pairs to the different treatment conditions, you probably should not use matching as a strategy to equate groups because statistical regression can obscure the effects of your treatment.

These threats to internal validity, which are summarized in Table 7.2, reduce our confidence in the conclusions we draw about our results. A critical assessment of a

TABLE 7.2   Major threats to the internal validity of a research project.

THREAT	DESCRIPTION
Selection	When participants are not randomly assigned to conditions, groups to be compared may differ before the experimental treatment is applied. Any difference between groups may be due to initial differences, not the treatment.
Maturation	In the short term, people become fatigued or bored, or they may learn how to perform better with practice on a task, so behaviors may differ due to changes in psychological states. In the long term, people change physically and psychologically; such changes, not the treatment, may affect behavior.
Mortality (Attrition)	When researchers monitor participants over time, some participants may leave a study. If people with certain characteristics drop out, there may be a biasing effect so that the remaining sample contains people who are very different from the original sample. Differences in behaviors may not be due to the research variables.
History	An event may occur outside the study during the course of a research project that leads to a change in behavior. If one group is differentially affected, it may appear that a treatment was responsible for the differences between groups when, in fact, it was a particular event that influenced one of the groups.
Instrumentation	If the way a researcher measures the DV varies over time due to changes in equipment or to changes in subjective judgments by the researcher, differences in measurements may have nothing to do with the research variables.
Testing	When people go through a research protocol multiple times, they may change their behaviors because they are sensitized to the testing situation itself.
Statistical regression	When people exhibit extreme scores on an initial test, one of the reasons for the extreme score may be random error. On a subsequent test, that random component of the score is no longer so prominent and the person's score regresses, that is, moves back toward the average of the group.

study's research design, attention to other researchers' methodologies, and use of a variety of different procedures can lead to a greater level of confidence.

DISCUSSION QUESTIONS

1. Why is a quasi-experiment really a correlational study?
2. Suppose you wanted to compare students in two different classes, assessing whether research methods or social psychology leads to more favorable ratings of how interesting psychology is. Why would it be important to consider selection, attrition, and history?

TYPES OF QUASI-EXPERIMENTAL DESIGNS

There are several quasi-experimental designs that psychologists regularly use. Some approaches resemble the typical experiment we have already discussed, with two or more groups being compared. Others depart from the typical model by incorporating measurements over a longer period of time than we generally see in an experiment.

Some researchers use quasi-experiments for laboratory studies, as we saw in the Goldenberg et al. (1999) study linking sex, neuroticism, and thoughts of death. But quasi-experiments are also frequently used in applied research outside the lab.

One-Group Pretest–Posttest Design—A quasi-experimental research design in which a single group is measured before a treatment is applied, then again afterward.

One-Group Pretest–Posttest Design

The simplest of the quasi-experimental designs is the **one-group pretest–posttest design.** As its name suggests, there is a single group of participants who are measured both before and after the application of a treatment. As you can see in the schematic outline below, it might be very easy to conduct this type of research.

Schematic Outline of a One-Group Pretest–Posttest Design

Single Group of Participants → Observation → Treatment → Observation

---

Commonly cited examples of this type of research include weight loss programs and test preparation courses. In theory, there would be no problem with this kind of design if we could determine that nothing of interest happens in people's lives (other than the treatment) between observations. In reality, a lot happens between the "before" and the "after." What transpires in a person's life, not the treatment, may very well affect the measurements taken at the second observation.

Although there is no selection threat to internal validity here because there is no comparison across groups, there are other likely possible threats to validity. The second observation could be affected by history, maturation, testing, and instrumentation.

Let's consider a weight loss program. If researchers wanted to know if keeping a diary made a difference in weight loss, they could weigh a group of participants, ask them to keep a diary of food (and calories) consumed over eight weeks, then weigh them again after eight weeks. If the participants weighed significantly less at the end, it would be tempting to conclude that knowing how many calories you consumed made you more aware of your eating habits, so you cut down on your intake.

Unfortunately, there could be a problem with history. If the research were done between mid-April and mid-June, the arrival of summer with its skimpy clothing might have motivated the people to lose weight; the diary may have been completely irrelevant.

This type of design is also prone to problems due to the threat of maturation. Between the start of the study and the final weigh-in, participants might become more motivated because they begin exercising and start to enjoy it.

The third threat in a one-group pretest–posttest design is testing. If an educator wanted to see if a test preparation course was effective in improving students' SAT scores, the researcher might see a gain in scores that was due to increases in familiarity with the test after taking it the first time. Sometimes the hardest part of a test is figuring out how to take it, not what the answers are.

Continuing with the SAT example, if the students took a test at the end that just happened to be a little easier, they would score higher. The threat to internal validity here is called instrumentation, which means that changes in the measurement system are problematic.

We can also easily imagine the history threat. Perhaps students became more motivated by an inspiring teacher. The validity of the conclusions about test preparation courses based on such a situation may be suspect.

It's important to remember that these threats are quite possible, but they are not absolutely certain to occur. Of course, that's the problem—we don't know if problems are present or not. If you could demonstrate that nothing other than the treatment intervened between observations that affected the second observation, you could rule out history as a threat.

Could you actually demonstrate that nothing important outside your study happened? You probably couldn't, but you might be able to make a convincing argument that history was unlikely. The same is true for the other threats to validity. They could affect your final observations, but you might be able to persuade others that they weren't likely. Thus, any differences from beginning to end could be due to your treatment. The best strategy, though, is to create a design in which these problems are minimized.

Static-Group Comparison Designs

A somewhat more useful design expands on the one-group pretest–posttest design by adding a second group. Consider this question: If an expert tennis player watched a match, would he or she be better than a novice at anticipating what was likely to be the winning shot? To answer this question, you could create two groups, experts and novices, and see if they differed. As we have seen before, experts are indeed better (Rowe & McKenna, 2001). This research tells us only that the experts were better, but it does not say why.

This type of design, called the **static-group comparison design,** can be useful, but it is far from ideal. One of the major drawbacks is that you don't know for sure if the two groups were comparable from the start.

Static-Group Comparison Design—A quasi-experimental research design in which two groups that differ on some pre-existing dimension (i.e., participants are not randomly assigned to conditions) are compared.

There is clearly a threat to the validity of this study. It is called the selection threat. The selection of participants is not randomized, so you don't know if your groups differed from the start. Consequently, you don't know how much faith to place in the conclusion that the treatment had the effect you supposed it did.

In the tennis example, those who turned out to be experts may have gravitated toward the sport because they already showed some ability to anticipate athletic moves. Their performance in the research may have been as good as it was because of abilities that preceded their expertise. That is the problem with quasi-experimental designs—you can't know about causation.

You can see the schematic outline of the static-group comparison design below. The outline shows two groups, but you could include as many different treatments as you wanted.

Schematic Outline of a Static-Group Comparison Data

Nonrandom Placement in Group 1 → Treatment → Observation

Nonrandom Placement in Group 2 → No Treatment → Observation

If the placement into groups is nonrandom, we can't be sure that the participants in the two groups would, on average, score the same on the DV in the absence of any treatment. Consequently, we can't assume that differences at the end are due to the treatment.

In the tennis example, we have even less control over the groups than in many studies. Here, the development of tennis expertise (i.e., the treatment) happened well before the researchers planned their study. There are a great many questions here. Still, the investigators' conclusions provide more information about the nature and effect of expertise. Even if their study wasn't perfect, it contributed to our psychological knowledge.

Nonequivalent Control Group Design—A quasi-experimental research design in which two groups that differ on some pre-existing dimension (i.e., participants are not randomly assigned to conditions) are measured on a pretest, exposed to a treatment, and measured on a posttest.

Nonequivalent Control Group Designs

One way to compensate for the selection threat, at least in part, would be to collect data before the treatment as well as after it. If you did this, you would be using a pretest-posttest design.

When you measure nonrandomly assigned participants on your dependent variable at the beginning of the study, apply the treatment, then measure them again, you are using a **nonequivalent control group design.** As the label suggests, your treatment and control groups may differ in important ways; that is, they are nonequivalent, even at the beginning of your study. A schematic outline of this type of design appears below.

Schematic Outline of a Nonequivalent Control Group Design

Nonrandom Placement in Group 1 → Observation → Treatment → Observation

Nonrandom Placement in Group 2 → Observation → No Treatment → Observation

---

One of the reasons that the question of equivalence is so important is because when you measure people in existing categories over time, you don't know what change they would undergo over that period, even if you didn't apply a treatment. On the other hand, when you randomly assign people to groups, you can assume that the groups start equal and, without the treatment, would follow the same course of change. You can't make those assumptions with nonequivalent group designs.

If you look at Figures 7.4 and 7.5, you can see how you could be deceived regarding your results. In Figure 7.4, the results show that participants were measured twice. It appears that the one group always scores higher than the other. However, if you had measured the participants earlier, you would have noted that the course of change of one group is markedly different from that of the other.

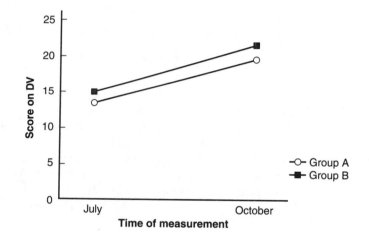

FIGURE 7.4   Illustration of possible result with a nonequivalent control group design. The inequality at the start and the different rate of change for the two groups leads to problems with interpretation of the results.

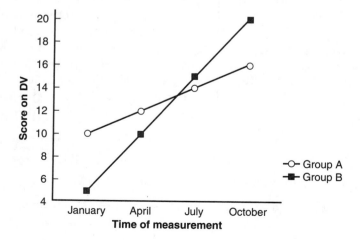

FIGURE 7.5.   Illustration of possible pattern of results in a nonequivalent control group design. The final two measurements in this figure match those in Figure 7.4. If you only measured your participants in July and October (as in Figure 7.4), you would get a very different impression than if you assessed them in January and April as well. When you do not use random assignment of participants to groups, you cannot assume that they are equal to begin with; you also cannot assume that their patterns of change are going to be the same.

If this hypothetical study had included earlier measurements, a very different pattern of results would be apparent. Group A initially had higher scores that wouldn't be seen if only the last two measurements were made.

Interrupted Time Series Designs

Interrupted Time Series Design—A quasi-experimental research design in which a group is measured at different times, with a treatment applied at some point, resulting in baseline measurements and post-treatment measurements.

In the one-group pretest–posttest design, one of the major problems is its simplicity. We measure participants only twice, but we don't know what has come before the first measurement nor what will follow the second one. We would be better off if we observed and measured the participants more than twice.

An **interrupted time series design** provides multiple measurements. It solves some of the problems of the pretest–posttest design. You can see a schematic outline of the interrupted time series design below.

Schematic Outline of an Interrupted Time Series Design*

Group or Participants → Obs → Obs → Obs → Treatment → Obs → Obs → Obs

*Obs = Observation

In this example, we see three observations before the treatment and three afterward, although you could decide to use different numbers of observations before and after the treatment. This type of design reduces the threats of maturation and testing. It is unlikely that you would be so unlucky in your research as to test your participants so that the only maturation occurs exactly when your treatment is in place. Certainly, you might be unlucky, but the possibility seems remote.

In addition, when participants become sensitized because of an initial exposure to the measurement process, they are likely to be affected right away. As a result, in the schematic example, we would probably conclude that by the time they were observed and measured three times, any sensitization would have occurred. Again, you could be very unlucky and the testing effect might take hold only after your third observation, but this possibility is also pretty remote. If you thought it might happen, you could insert more observations prior to applying the treatment. Designs like this are useful because they allow researchers to establish a **baseline** of behavior against which behaviors after the treatment can be compared.

Baseline—A series of measurements recorded before a treatment is applied to see the normal course of behavior prior to an intervention.

The threat that still exists is history. Unfortunately, the effects of history are often one-time affairs that have immediate effects. So you might be unlucky, seeing the effect of history just when your treatment goes into effect; it would be hard to spot.

An interesting application of a time series design involved a smoking cessation program. The question that the researchers investigated revolved around whether smokers could quit if they participated in a televised project (Valois, Adams, & Kammermann, 1996). They studied a program called CableQuit to see if a six-week intervention provided enough support to help smokers quit. As you can see in Controversy Box 7.2, there are reasons to be optimistic about this approach, but there is also evidence that it is not the perfect solution.

■ ■ ■ ■ ■

CONTROVERSY BOX 7.2
CONTROVERSY: Can You Stop Smoking by Watching TV?

People who smoke know how difficult it is to break the addiction. What can we do to make it easier for people to stop? One answer is to work harder to keep people from starting. Unfortunately, society clearly sends mixed messages, with its severe stance about marijuana use but a much less punitive approach to tobacco, which in the long-run can be more dangerous to people's health and to the economy (Newcomb & Bentler, 1989). It doesn't help that tobacco companies have marketed their products toward young people.

For decades, tobacco companies maintained that smoking was a choice and that people could smoke or, if they so chose, they could quit. Quitting on your own doesn't work very well, but self-help groups can be expensive both in terms of time and money. Is there an alternative that might be effective?

Valois et al. (1996) studied the effectiveness of CableQuit, a six-week program consisting of thirteen 30-minute live segments followed by 30-minute call-in periods. It was sponsored by a community cable company. The investigators speculated that maybe people could engage in self-help groups from a distance.

The researchers used an interrupted time series design. There was an initial observation, the intervention (i.e., the televised support group), and subsequent observations to see if the participants had stopped smoking. The initial observation was actually a formality because 100% of

the participants were smokers; otherwise they wouldn't have needed the program. They recruited 98 people with various public announcements; there was an initial dropout rate of 41 percent, leaving them with 58 participants. According to Valois et al., such a dropout rate is not uncommon in smoking cessation programs.

The percentage of participants who abstained at 6 weeks (right after the television programs ended), 6 months, and 1 year signaled the relative success of the program. Participants mailed questionnaires to the researchers indicating, among other things, whether they were smoking. As a check on the truthfulness of the participants' responses, they also provided saliva samples so the investigators could assess the presence of cotinine, a chemical that reliably indicates smoking. The results were slightly better than other mass media approaches, which are generally estimated at around 5 to 15 percent success rates (Flay, 1987). Unfortunately, as is generally the case, more people resumed smoking than stopped by a year. In fact, the limited success of the program was obvious within six weeks.

Those who resumed smoking by the end of one year were more depressed than those who didn't. For some people, the support they receive through the mass media may affect their resolve to throw away their cigarettes, that same mass media that initially helped get them hooked in the first place.

Replicated Interrupted Time Series Design—A quasi-experimental research design in which different groups are measured in an interrupted time series design, with a treatment being applied at a different time for each group.

Replicated Interrupted Time Series Designs

If you added a control group to an interrupted time series design, you would have a more complicated methodology, but it would be associated with fewer threats to internal validity. The **replicated interrupted time series design** provides a control group and reduces the chance that your results will be affected by history. The schematic outline appears at the top of the next page. As you can see, it is an extension to the simpler interrupted time series design.

Schematic Outline of a Replicated Interrupted Time Series Design*

Group 1 → **Obs** → **Obs** → **Obs** → **Treatment** → **Obs** → **Obs** → **Obs**

Group 2 → **Obs** → **Obs** → **Treatment** → **Obs** → **Obs** → **Obs** → **Obs**

Control Group → **Obs** → **Obs** → **Obs** → **No Treatment** → **Obs** → **Obs** → **Obs**

*Obs = Observation

There are different replicated designs. One approach is to apply the treatment at different times to the two groups. This will overcome many of our concerns about the history threat because a single historic episode is unlikely to affect the two groups at two different times. The selection threat is also reduced because we are observing the same people over time and can see a stable pattern of behaviors that is interrupted by the treatment.

A second design involves applying a treatment to one group but not to a control group. Here also the history threat is reduced. The reason we don't have to worry about it so much is that, if one occurs, it should happen to both groups, so its effects should be obvious. The selection threat is also less of a problem for the reason stated above.

This replicated interrupted time series design is not perfect, but even if the groups are not randomly assigned, the results are often amenable to a tentative causal analysis. For example, Hennigan, Del Rosario, Heath, Cook, Wharton, and Calder (1982) addressed an issue two decades ago that originated with the beginning of television broadcasting and continues today: Does television affect behavior in negative ways?

Television had appeared in a number of cities in the United States in the late 1940s, but Congress imposed a freeze that restricted expansion. Because of the freeze, television became widespread in homes in some cities while others remained out of broadcasting range. Hennigan et al. used the results of this freeze to create an interrupted time series design. They looked at larceny rates (i.e., theft that does not involve violence or force) in cities before and after 50 percent of the homes in those cities had televisions.

The researchers reasoned that if television influenced crime, cities with early television stations should have an increase in larceny while the cities without television shouldn't. On the other hand, when the freeze on new stations was lifted, the cities that then gained television stations should show an increase in larceny, but the initial cities would not.

Figure 7.6 shows the results of the study. Crime was inching upward in the absence of television, but you can see that from 1949 to 1950, when television was introduced to the early cities, there was an increase in larceny in those cities. The areas without television did not show an upsurge. When the freeze set by Congress was lifted, the later cities showed an upsurge, whereas the initial cities did not. In 1946 and in 1956, the cities had comparable crime rates, which reassures us that the cities in the two conditions were roughly equivalent with respect to the DV of crime rate. They diverged when TV became prevalent in the different cities, then became similar again after they all had easy access to television.

FIGURE 7.6   Introduction of television and incidence of larceny (cases per million population) in cities. Television became widespread by 1949 in the prefreeze cities; it was widespread in postfreeze cities around 1954. In each case, larceny increased following introduction of television. The arrows indicate the approximate time at which 50 percent of households in the two types of cities had televisions.

Source: K. M. Hennigan et al. (1982). Impact of the introduction of television on crime in the United States: Empirical findings and theoretical implications. *Journal of Personality and Social Psychology, 42,* 461–577. Copyright American Psychological Association. Adapted with permission.

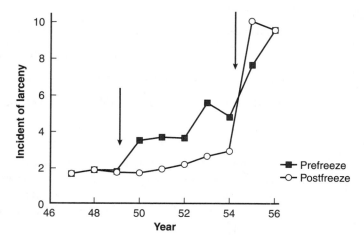

Hennigan et al. concluded that television had a causal effect on the incidence of larceny. Television programs generally depicted middle- and upper-class individuals who owned desirable possessions. The investigators suggested that perhaps viewers were frustrated because their lives were more impoverished, so they pilfered items that they couldn't afford.

Researchers frequently use time-series designs for applied research. It is typical to see these applications in studies of intervention programs, such as attempts to reduce the incidence of violence among adolescents at a runaway shelter (Nugent, Bruley, & Allen, 1998). This approach is also used in less traumatic circumstances, such as the effectiveness of psychological skills training in athletes (Brewer & Shillinglaw, 1992).

Social researchers who are interested in law and behavior can see the impact of laws on our lives. Do the laws really do what we want them to? In Controversy Box 7.3, you can see how investigators have studied very different kinds of laws and their effects using the same general approach, time-series analysis. In one study, the researchers assessed the effectiveness of a mandatory sentencing law in California (Stolzenberg & D'Alessio, 1997). In a second study, the investigators monitored the change in amounts of litter after a law was passed to reduce the trash that people leave behind in public areas (Levitt & Leventhal, 1986). Sometimes the laws work, but sometimes they don't.

DISCUSSION QUESTIONS

1. If the one group pretest–posttest design is methodologically weak, why would researchers use it?
2. Outline a one group pretest–postest design that you could carry out in your school.
3. Identify the quasi-experimental designs that can help reduce the threats of history, maturation, and testing. Why do they do so?

CONTROVERSY BOX 7.3
CONTROVERSY: Do Laws Really Change Our Behaviors?

Legislators create laws to change behaviors or to punish the people who engage in them. Laws are enacted all the time, but seldom repealed. When laws outlive their usefulness, people simply tend to ignore them. We all know of laws that are not enforced vigorously.

For example, drinking by people under 21 in the United States is illegal, but it is so widespread that we can only conclude that, as a society, we are not overly concerned with it. The public service campaigns to restrict young people's drinking might have impact on some, but the drinking is still fairly widespread.

It might be illustrative to see if laws actually change what people do. Researchers have used time-series designs to find out.

Levitt and Leventhal (1986) studied whether the New York State bottle return bill has reduced the amount of litter in New York. This bill mandated that consumers pay a five cent deposit on beer and soda bottles and cans; the deposit is refunded when they return the container. Has it made a difference? This is an important question given that over a decade, if nothing were done to reduce litter, Americans could generate a billion tons; this litter would cost taxpayers a trillion dollars to clean up over the decade.

The researchers walked along highway entrance ramps and railroad tracks, counting the number of bottles and documenting the general level of litter. They chose sites in New York before and after the bottle bill passed and in New Jersey, which had no such law.

About a year after the bill became law, the researchers found that on the highway entrances there was significantly less litter in New York than in New Jersey for cans and bottles that were returnable in New York. The amount of nonreturnable litter (i.e., general garbage and trash) did not change. The picture was a little more complex on the railroad sites, but the law seemed to be effective as well. Thus, the bottle bill seemed to have changed behaviors; consumers didn't litter cans and bottles for which they paid a deposit. Unfortunately, other kinds of litter persisted.

On the west coast of the United States, a different set of researchers (Stolzenberg & D'Alessio, 1997) studied the effect of a very different California law using a time-series design. The California state legislature passed a "Three Strikes and You're Out" law; this law mandates extended prison terms for repeat criminals. In one well-publicized example, a California man who had previously committed a felony received a mandatory prison sentence of 25 years to life after being convicted of stealing a slice of pizza from a group of children. (Fortunately, judges in California are now allowed discretion as to when they invoke this law, although the Supreme Court has ruled that people can be sentenced to lengthy prison terms for third offenses involving crimes like shoplifting.)

Stolzenberg and D'Alessio looked at the crime index for felonies and for petty theft from 1985 to 1994, when the law was passed, then monitored the crime rate for another year. California officials claimed that the law was successful; the felony crime rate was lower after the law was passed.

The researchers discovered, however, that for a year or so prior to the law, the crime rate had begun to decline. They concluded that the continued decline after the law took effect only reflected a trend that had begun well before the law was in existence.

Stolzenberg and D'Alessio suggested that if other research supports their findings, it might be a good idea to repeal such "Three Strike" laws. For one thing, they are costly; it is expensive to incarcerate people. Another reason is that there may be other programs that actually will work for no greater cost. A third reason is that we may be wasting human talent and human lives by keeping people in prison for decades. The researchers are not proposing that criminals not be punished; they are saying that everybody in society will be better off when we have a logical criminal justice system.

This type of research can provide useful information for society. Well-designed investigations can tell us if we are making progress in dealing with societal issues and, if not, how we might be able to improve the situation.

CHAPTER SUMMARY

After reading this chapter, you should recognize the benefits of repeated measures designs. Psychologists rely on this approach because of its notable advantages. When you conduct research that involves repeated measures, you can have confidence that your groups are comparable from the start because each group has the same people. Thus, any differences that emerge are likely to be due to your treatments.

In addition, repeated measures designs are efficient, allowing researchers to double or triple (or more) the data they collect with minimal increases in costs. Further, if you are studying a relatively rare population, you can benefit by collecting all the data you can with your few participants. An added benefit is that your research design is more sensitive to small differences between groups. This means that if your treatment really has an effect, even if it is a small one, you are more likely to find a significant difference.

The drawback to repeated measures designs is that exposure to a treatment may have a long-lasting effect on the participant. In later observations, the person may be tired or bored, or the individual might perform better because he or she learned how to be more effective in the experimental task. These sequence effects can obscure a real difference or make a small difference look more important than it really is. Fortunately, there are ways to overcome these problems.

Another extension to the basic experimental design is the quasi-experiment. It is set up like an experiment, with different groups that are compared to see if they show the same behaviors. Quasi-experiments differ from true experiments in that quasi-experiments do not employ random assignment of participants to groups.

The participants differ on some characteristic to begin with, and it is this difference that leads them to be assigned to different groups. The problem here is that people in each group differ from the start, so if they differ at the end, your IV may have had an effect, but differences may have resulted from something other than your IV.

Researchers have devised quasi-experimental designs to overcome many of the problems that can affect the validity of the results. As we move from simple static-group comparison designs with one group to the replicated time-series design, we can gain confidence that the various threats to internal validity are unlikely.

With the sophistication of some of the quasi-experimental designs, we can begin to form tentative, causal conclusions. We should continue to show caution about deciding that our treatment actually causes some behavior, though, because quasi-experiments are really variants on correlational designs.

CHAPTER EIGHT

PRINCIPLES OF SURVEY RESEARCH

CHAPTER OVERVIEW

CHAPTER PREVIEW

SURVEYS: ANSWERING DIVERSE QUESTIONS
  Surveys versus Junk Mail
  Census versus Sample
  Accuracy of Survey Results

CONTROVERSY: Is the U.S. Census Flawed?

ETHICS IN SURVEY RESEARCH

SELECTING YOUR METHODOLOGY

THE SURVEY INSTRUMENT
  Question Types

CONTROVERSY: Do 4 Million Adolescents Smoke?

  Question Content
    Memory Questions
    Attitude Questions

RESPONSE BIAS
  Studying Sensitive Issues

Are Telephone Surveys Appropriate for Sensitive Issues?
  Social Desirability
  Acquiescence
  Satisficing versus Optimizing
  Minimizing the Occurrence
    of Satisficing

SPECIAL CONSIDERATIONS FOR INTERNET RESEARCH
  Internet Surveys
  Designing Surveys for the World
    Wide Web
  Respondent Motivation
  Technical Characteristics
    of a User's System
  User Knowledge

SAMPLING ISSUES
  Finding Hidden Populations

CHAPTER SUMMARY

KEY TERMS

Acquiescence
Census
Chain-referral methods
Chronically accessible
  information
Closed-ended question
Hidden population
Impression management
Key informant sampling

Nondifferentiation
Open-ended question
Optimizing
Population
Respondent-driven
  sampling
Response bias
Sampling frame
Satisficing

Self-deception positivity
Self-selected samples
Snowball sampling
Social desirability bias
Survey
Targeted sampling
Telescoping
Temporary accessible
  information

CHAPTER PREVIEW

Asking questions in survey research is an important aspect of research methodology. Surveys have become a fixture in modern life, with professional pollsters examining details of our lives and social scientists uncovering trends in attitudes and patterns of behavior. Most surveys rely on samples rather than on an exhaustive questioning of the entire population, which is a census.

We have had a lot of experience with paper and pencil surveys and with telephone surveys. A new technique for data collection involves using the internet. This new means of data collection poses new problems but it also uncovers new territory to be investigated. Over time, researchers should be able to resolve the ambiguities associated with internet research.

Surveyors can choose from among different question types and content. The construction of the questions is probably the hardest part of a project because the form of a question influences responses, depending on the wording. In addition, respondents don't want to be seen in unfavorable light, so they may tailor their answers to meet what they think are the expectations of the researcher. Fortunately, there are ways to avoid the obvious pitfalls in asking questions.

Finally, survey researchers prefer probability samples, and are wary of self-selected, convenience samples that do not represent the entire population. Researchers continue to develop new sampling strategies to overcome potential problems in current strategies.

SURVEYS: ANSWERING DIVERSE QUESTIONS

Beginning half a century ago, investigators began developing the theory and techniques of survey research. Early in the 1900s, surveys took place that increased our information base on various topics, but by today's standards they were methodologically suspect. For instance, in 1936, the now defunct magazine *Literary Digest* inaccurately predicted that Franklin Roosevelt would lose the U.S. presidential election in a landslide. This may be the most famous error in the history of research. The problem was that the editors of that magazine used a sampling method that led to an unrepresentative picture of the voting population.

A little more than a decade later, a newspaper proclaimed that Thomas Dewey had defeated Harry Truman in the 1948 presidential election. The problem there was that in the forecasting, the newspaper used a sampling technique that was prone to error in depicting the population as a whole.

Today's researchers can also make mistakes, as they did in the 2000 presidential election when they declared that Al Gore won the State of Florida. In spite of this recent major mistake, current survey techniques provide very useful information most of the time. After all, in the 2000 presidential election, the pollsters called 49 of the 50 states correctly.

The implication here is that using samples to understand populations can lead to mistakes because we are using incomplete information, but if researchers use proper techniques, the number of misjudgments and the magnitude of error are small.

Survey—A research method in which an investigator asks questions of a respondent.

Surveys are one of the most widely used forms of research. When a company considers developing a new product, it hires survey marketing researchers to find out whether the product could compete in the marketplace. When politicians want to know what the voters think, surveys are the best way to find out. When social researchers want to know about behaviors and attitudes, they often design surveys.

We see so many questionnaires in all facets of our lives that we often do not realize how difficult it is to create a valid survey instrument. Over the past half century, researchers have spent considerable energy trying to find out what works best and what pitfalls to avoid. The difficulty of producing good surveys is one reason why people are so willing to use questionnaires that either they or others have already used successfully.

Surveys versus Junk Mail

Just as survey researchers want you to complete their questionnaires, retailers who send out junk mail disguised as scientific surveys want to capture your attention. And just as researchers have evaluated different strategies to increase response rates, marketers have also addressed that issue (Headden, 1997). It turns out that many of the same tactics that work for scientific surveys lead to greater responsiveness by consumers.

Researchers and junk mailers both try get your attention. Their goals differ, however. Researchers want information, junk mailers want your money. By considering the content and purposes of surveys, you may be able to spot those associated with research and those with money-making intent. As you can see in Table 8.1, research surveys tend to be personally directed and involve fewer gimmicks.

Census versus Sample

When researchers conduct survey research, they must decide whether to contact everybody in the population of interest or to sample a subset. Probably the most famous

TABLE 8.1   **Characteristics differentiating survey research and junk mail that simulates survey designs.**

RESEARCHERS	JUNK MAILERS
Letters addressed to a specific person.	Letters addressed to a specific person after an individual responds to an initial, less personal mailing.
Real signatures at the end of the letter.	Fake handwritten notes and fake signatures
Monetary incentives.	Gifts like decorative stamps or offers of free gifts.
Sincere statements of appreciation.	Appeals to fear, greed, guilt, and exclusivity; association with high-status individuals or organizations.
Distinctive envelopes and surveys.	Envelopes that appear to be from the government.

Census—Data collection that includes every member of a population of interest.

example of the former in the United States is the **census.** The constitution of the United States mandates a decennial census, that is, a complete counting of everybody living in the country every ten years. The basic purpose of the census is to inform the Congress about how many people live in each state so there can be proportional representation in the House of Representatives. There are also other uses for the results, like figuring out where the population is growing so adequate highways can be built or where to build hospitals to meet the needs of an aging populace.

Although everybody agrees that the census is necessary, we must face the fact that it is very costly. The 2000 census had a price tag of about $7 billion, or about $25 to count each person. Mailing a census form to every household in the country alone is an enormous expense; when people don't reply, a personal followup takes place, which is also expensive. We also know that many people are missed in the census, particularly people who have no fixed address, people from countries where they may have had an appropriate fear of the government, and others. In addition, some people are counted twice, like those who own multiple homes. The process of counting every resident is not easy, cheap, or perfectly accurate.

The census has never been completely accurate, beginning with the first one in 1790. Even with our increasing technical sophistication, the accuracy of the census is probably worse than it used to be. As you can see in Controversy Box 8.1, there are scientific ways to reduce the error, but they face political obstacles.

One difference between the Census Bureau and most other researchers is that most researchers are content to survey a portion of the population, that is, a sample, rather than take a census. A relatively small percentage of the population is needed to get a fairly accurate picture of the group you want to describe.

Accuracy of Survey Results

On a national level, there are about 100 million potential voters in the United States. It would make no sense to try to ask each of them about their views; it would take too long and cost too much money. If you wanted to characterize 100 million possible voters with reasonable accuracy, how many would you have to sample? Typically, political polls sample about 1000 people; ranging from 700 or 800 to perhaps 1500. These numbers reflect about .001 percent of the voting population.

How accurate are these polls? After every election, the vote count provides a test. In the 2000 U.S. presidential election, the predictions in the final pre-election polls differed from the actual vote by an average of only about 1.1 percent (High accuracy found, 2001). The polls are not error-free, but they are pretty impressive.

When you sample a subset of the population, you can count on getting some differences between what your sample is like and what the population is like. If you have a small sample, a few unusual people can distort your results; if you have a large sample, those same unusual people don't make much of a difference.

This means that you can get a pretty good picture of your population by sampling a relatively small number of people. As you increase your sample size, the accuracy of your information grows, but for a population as large as 100 million voters, once you reach a sample size of about 1,000, your accuracy doesn't grow very much for

■ ■ ■ ■ ■ ■

CONTROVERSY BOX 8.1
CONTROVERSY: Is the U.S. Census Flawed?

It would be natural to think that if the government used a census to count everybody in the country, we would know how many people reside in our land. In truth, the census never achieves the ideal of counting everybody. In fact, in the first set of mail returns for the 2000 census, about 2 out of every 5 households failed to return the form, in spite of the fact that it is required by law. Consequently, the Census Bureau dispatched over half a million workers to follow up the nonresponses.

The incomplete count is nothing new. According to Anderson and Fienberg (2000), none of the 22 census counts done since the inception of the United States has actually found everybody, even with the current $7 billion price tag.

One of the most contentious debates about the 2000 census was whether the Bureau would be able to use statistical sampling to estimate the number of people who had not responded. According to every panel of statisticians commissioned by the National Research Council, statistical sampling would at least partially remedy the undercounts, even if some error remained in the count. Some statisticians did not favor statistical sampling, but they were in the minority.

As a group, Republicans opposed correcting the undercount with statistical sampling, whereas the Democrats favored it. The Supreme Court ruled that the sample data could not be used for apportionment of seats to the House of Representatives, but could be used for all other purposes.

The undercount is greater for minority populations, so areas with larger numbers of minorities appear to have smaller populations than they actually do. The result of the Supreme Court's decision will be to reduce congressional representation of those areas.

Political considerations are nothing new in the census. In 1920, Congressional Republicans refused to recognize the results because potential changes in reapportionment would not favor them. As a result, they continued to use results of the 1910 census, even though it did not accurately represent the country. Finally, in 1929, Republican President Herbert Hoover resolved the impasse as he pressured members of his party to pass a census bill for the 1930 count. By doing this, Hoover averted a constitutional crisis.

What all this means is that simply counting people in this country involves error. The statistical, scientifically based methods designed to eliminate some of the error are affected by social and political considerations. Once again, we see that scientific research is affected by the same factors as every other aspect of our lives.

> **Population**—A set consisting of every person or data point that would be of interest to a researcher.

each new person you sample. As a result, it doesn't pay to increase your sample size above a certain point if you are not going to increase the sample greatly.

If the **population** from which you want to sample is relatively small, you might need a larger proportion in order to end up with accurate results, but the actual number will not be all that large.

DISCUSSION QUESTIONS

1. If political polls are generally accurate, why do you think that many people don't believe them?
2. Why is it often unnecessary to conduct a census to find out about an entire population? Give an example of a population for which it would be practical to do a census.
3. What characteristics differentiate research surveys and junk mail surveys?

ETHICS IN SURVEY RESEARCH

All research carries the requirement of ethical behavior on the part of the investigator. With regard to survey research, we have to pay attention to two critical, related considerations—anonymity and confidentiality.

It is standard practice to completely guarantee both the anonymity and confidentiality of responses. This means that nobody who is not part of the research will have access to information about whether an individual participates or what his or her responses might have been.

If a researcher is tracking whether people have responded and wants to send a reminder to those who have not completed a survey, some kind of identification is necessary. In the rare event that an investigator needs to keep identification information over a long period of time, the data cannot be anonymous. There is nothing wrong with such procedures in and of themselves, although at the end of the project, the researcher should destroy any information that could link a respondent with participation in the study.

When researchers cannot guarantee anonymity, they can at least assure respondents that participation will be kept confidential. Confidentiality means that nobody will be able to connect a given person with participation in a study. This is typically assured by reporting the data only in aggregate, that is, in a summarized form so that nobody can tell who responded in one way or another. For surveys that ask sensitive questions, you must provide such assurances because your respondents will either decline to respond or will not tell the whole truth.

Ironically, if you make a big point of assuring confidentiality and anonymity, it may arouse suspicions in those you survey (Singer, Von Thurn, & Miller, 1995).

In a situation involving mundane questions, it might be more reasonable to play down the confidentiality and anonymity aspects because they may distract a participant from the real purpose of the study. If you are going to ask sensitive questions about topics like sexual abuse, sexual behavior, drug or alcohol use, cheating, or behaviors that are otherwise disapproved of, you should make sure that the person knows about confidentiality and anonymity.

A further ethical constraint is that your respondents must know that they do not have to participate in your research and that they can terminate their responses at any time, without any penalty. This constitutes voluntary participation. If you stand over their shoulder or are even in their presence, you may be influencing a person's behavior; your respondent may feel compelled to enter answers because you are watching. You may be acting unethically and unprofessionally. You may also pay a price in the data. People may not respond honestly.

You can see in Table 8.2 the professional code of the Council for Marketing and Opinion Research. This code provides good guidance about ethical behavior in survey research. Naturally, you would want to follow APA's ethics code and state and federal laws as well.

DISCUSSION QUESTIONS
1. Which of the Council for Marketing Opinion Research guidelines are violated with junk mail surveys? Why would it be a good idea for researchers to educate the public about the differences between scientific surveys and junk surveys?

TABLE 8.2　The ethics code promulgated by the Council for Marketing and Opinion Research.

WHAT ARE YOUR RIGHTS IF YOU ARE SURVEYED?

Your participation in a legitimate marketing or public opinion research survey is very important to us, and we value the information you provide. Therefore, our relationship will be one of respect and consideration, based on the following practices:

- Your privacy and the privacy of your answers will be respected and maintained.
- Your name, address, phone number, personal information, or individual responses won't be disclosed to anyone outside the research industry without your permission.
- You will always be told the name of the person contacting you, the research company's name, and the nature of the survey.
- You will not be sold anything, or asked for money, under the guise of research.
- You will be contacted at reasonable times, but if the time is inconvenient, you may ask to be recontacted at a more convenient time.
- Your decision to participate in a study, answer specific questions, or discontinue your participation will be respected without question.
- You will be informed in advance if an interview is to be recorded and of the intended use of the recording.
- You are assured that the highest standards of professional conduct will be upheld in the collection and reporting of information you provide.

---

2. What issues would you have to consider when dealing with issues of anonymity and confidentiality if you survey fellow students?

SELECTING YOUR METHODOLOGY

Most research projects begin with a general question that needs an answer. After that, practical issues arise. In the case of surveys, the critical issues include identifying the

> **Sampling Frame**—A subset of a population from which a sample is actually selected.

sampling frame. The sampling frame is the entire list of elements from which the sample is drawn. In psychological research, we seldom have a list of all possible respondents; in fact, we usually do not even have any way to detail the population of interest to us. Nonetheless, any survey research that we conduct should begin with an identification of the source of our respondents that will lead to our actual sample.

We decide the specific means of constituting a sample. This step is critical if we are interested in drawing conclusions that generalize beyond our sampling frame. Researchers who conduct surveys prefer to use probability samples. There are several different methods of constructing a probability sample. If the process is done properly, researchers can be confident that the sample is likely to represent the entire population. With poorly created samples, the results will reflect the sample, but not necessarily any other group of people. Other important issues that researchers face in survey research involve how they are going to make contact with potential respondents.

Researchers also spend considerable time developing the questions. Creating survey questions seems as if it should be easy but is probably the most difficult part of survey research and requires the greatest creativity and insight.

Throughout the entire process of survey research, the investigators must make a series of very practical decisions so that at the end they can have confidence in the conclusions they draw. The discoveries in such research are only as good as the practical decisions the researchers make.

DISCUSSION QUESTIONS
1. Why is your sampling frame important with respect to your ability to generalize your results beyond your sample?
2. If you conducted a survey on your campus about sexual behavior, to whom do you think your results would generalize? Why?

THE SURVEY INSTRUMENT

Your question type has to meet your needs, the way you word your questions should not distort the responses, and the format of your instrument has to promote people's willingness to complete the task. If you meet these criteria, the quality of your data can be high.

One practical example of the difficulty in answering even a simple question involves the determination of how many adolescents in the United States smoke. A generally accepted answer based on survey research is about 4 million, but this number can be deceiving because the definition of "smoking" makes a big difference in the number that you accept as valid. Controversy Box 8.2 illustrates this problem.

Question Types

In terms of question and response structure, there are two main types of survey items:

Open-ended Question— In survey research, a question that respondents answer using their own words, unconstrained by choices provided by the researcher.

Closed-ended Question—In survey research, a question that contains a set of answers that a respondent chooses.

open-ended questions, which allow respondents to generate an answer without limitations regarding length or content, and **closed-ended questions,** which require respondents to select from a set of answers already provided. Each type has its own advantages and disadvantages. Table 8.3 shows how a researcher might develop different types of questions to investigate a topic.

If you attempted to answer an open-ended question about drinking alcohol, as illustrated in Table 8.3, you could discuss many different aspects of drinking behavior. You would determine what you thought was important and what was irrelevant, then respond accordingly. The advantage of such questions is that they provide a rich body of information. The disadvantage is that they can be harder to categorize, sort, and summarize because the responses can go in any direction the participant wants to take them. If the sample size is large, researchers may have problems inter-

■ ■ ■ ■ ■ ▬▬▬▬▬▬▬▬▬▬▬▬▬▬

CONTROVERSY BOX 8.2

CONTROVERSY: Do 4 Million Adolescents Smoke?

The U.S. government regularly conducts surveys on health-related matters. The National Household Survey on Drug Abuse specifically investigates the use of various legal and illegal drugs. Based on the results of such surveys, various prominent people (e.g., then-President Bill Clinton, the Secretary of Health and Human Services, and the Surgeon General) have publicly stated that 4 million adolescents (aged 12–17) smoke (Kovar, 2000).

This figure may be alarming and, if true, signals potentially serious health issues. In order to figure out what to do about such apparently prevalent smoking behavior, we need to understand what the data really signify. What constitutes an "adolescent"? What do we mean when we say that a person is a "smoker"?

An adolescent is somebody from age 12 to 17. This span covers a large range of development, though. A 12-year-old is very different from a 17-year-old on many behavioral, physical, and psychological dimensions. As it turns out, very few 12-year-olds smoke, so to believe that 12-year-olds are being lured into smoking is not accurate. Most of the smoking occurs toward the top of the age range.

When it came to defining a smoker in the survey, anybody who had had even one puff within the past 30 days was considered a smoker. One puff on one day is very different from a pack-a-day smoker.

About 25 percent of the adolescent smokers were heavy smokers. The survey defined "heavy"

as indicating that the person smoked 10 cigarettes a day or more for over 20 days in the past month.

Of the middle group of smokers (41 percent of adolescents), most used 1 to 5 cigarettes on the days when they smoked, and they smoked relatively infrequently.

The results also revealed that 31 percent of the "smokers" had less than one cigarette when they did smoke. Smoking less than a cigarette in many cases meant sharing a single cigarette with friends in a social situation.

What do these data tell us? The sad news is that the heavy smokers are probably already addicted in adolescence; many report smoking more than they really want to. The better news is that about 2 in 5 of these teen smokers have had less than half a pack of cigarettes in their entire lifetime and are unlikely to become addicted. The data also reveal that smoking is pretty rare among the youngest adolescents.

The survey results can provide useful information about smoking and health policies, but the simple claim that 4 million adolescents smoke hides the truth that few of the younger adolescents smoke and that a large percentage of this group experimented irregularly. Unfortunately, by age 17, addiction has occurred in more adolescents than we would like. Knowing the complete picture, which means understanding the definitions used in the survey, will allow us to generate public health policies that do what we want them to do.

preting the collection of very diverse responses. In addition, the respondent might fail to mention some elements of a response that the researcher was very interested in.

On the other hand, researchers can use closed-ended questions. These items do not permit free responding. There is a set of responses from which to choose, such as yes–no or strongly agree/somewhat agree/somewhat disagree/strongly disagree. The information provided by such questions is not as rich as with open-ended questions, but

TABLE 8.3   Examples of questions in open- versus closed-ended formats that relate to the same general topic, alcohol consumption.

OPEN-ENDED QUESTION:

Describe the situations in which you consume alcoholic beverages and what you drink. (Note: You would only ask this question after you have established that the individual does consume alcohol.)

CLOSED-ENDED QUESTIONS:

1. **On how many days per week do you consume alcohol?**
   ☐ None
   ☐ 1–2 times per week
   ☐ 3–4 times per week
   ☐ 5 or more times per week

2. **When you drink alcoholic beverages, what do you drink most frequently?**
   ☐ I do not drink alcoholic beverages
   ☐ Beer
   ☐ Wine
   ☐ Liquor (Gin, Vodka, Scotch, Bourbon)

3. **Which of the following statements describes the most likely situation when you drink alcoholic beverages?**
   ☐ I do not drink alcoholic beverages
   ☐ I am alone
   ☐ I am with one other person
   ☐ I am in a small group (2 to 5 people)
   ☐ I am in a larger group (6 or more people)

4. **Do you think it is easier, no different, or harder for teenagers to obtain alcohol compared to ten years ago?**
   ☐ Easier
   ☐ No Different
   ☐ Harder

5. **The minimum legal age for drinking alcoholic beverages in the United is 21 years. Do you agree with the statement, "The minimum legal age for drinking should remain at 21 years"?**
   ☐ Strongly Agree
   ☐ Agree
   ☐ Disagree
   ☐ Strongly Disagree
   ☐ No Opinion

they are much easier to score and summarize. Further, with closed-ended questions, the investigator can make sure that the respondent has the chance to answer questions of critical importance to the research project. For example, if the investigator wants to know whether teenagers drink alone or with others, the closed-ended question may provide that information from every respondent. Few people may address that issue in the open-ended question.

Although research has shown that both types of question format lead to answers of comparable validity, since the 1940s, researchers have preferred closed-ended questions because such a format lends itself to easier scoring.

However, recent evaluation of closed-ended questions has revealed some of their limitations. For instance, if people can choose from among answers prepared by the surveyor or can generate their own, they will often pick one of the surveyor's responses, even if they can provide their own, better answer (Krosnick, 1999). One reason is that people generally don't want to work any harder than they have to; it is easier to select a response that somebody else provides than to work to find your own. This phenomenon of selecting the first acceptable answer, even if it is not the best, is called satisficing.

Question Content

The structure and wording of survey items pose challenges for people who create surveys. Slightly different wording can lead to very different responses; consequently, researchers may end up with conclusions that vary considerably from those that they would have made with slightly different survey questions.

A key difference among questions involves what the researcher is trying to measure. In general, we can divide the purpose of the questions into three domains: measures of memory and behavior, measures of attitude and opinion, and demographics.

Memory Questions.   Most of the time in our lives, when we converse with people, we assume that they are telling us the truth. This is usually a reasonable assumption. The same is probably true regarding answers on a questionnaire. At the same time, we all know that we don't always tell the whole truth, and sometimes we lie outright. This pattern is also true for responses to surveys. When you engage in such a project, it will require you to consider the social, emotional, and cognitive aspects of the questions and answers.

People may not be lying when they misreport their behaviors. They may not know the answer to a question, but they give it their best guess (maybe a bad one), trying to be helpful. When you want people to tell you how often they have engaged in mundane behaviors that don't stand out in memory, they are prone to significant error (Rockwood, Sangster, & Dillman, 1997). For example, for many students, it would be difficult to answer precisely the question, "How often in the past two months have you eaten pizza?" The episodes individually do not stand out in memory because they are so normal. Thus, it may be difficult to come up with an accurate response.

Sometimes researchers ask respondents to answer questions that require the person to remember something. For instance, Kleck and Gertz (1995) wanted to know the extent to which people report having protected themselves with handguns against burglars. Their analysis revealed 2.5 million instances of such protection, implying that handguns in such situations exert a positive effect. Hemenway (1997) argued that the problem with Kleck and Gertz's data is that more people claim to have protected themselves with guns during burglaries than were actually burglarized.

Hemenway argued that whenever you ask a sample to remember relatively rare events of any kind, a small increase in false positives (i.e., saying something happened when it did not) leads to an inappropriately large estimate when you generalize to the population.

Hemenway's point about the reporting of rare events was reinforced by further research. Cook and Ludwig (1998) noted that reports of defensive gun use (DGU) in studies with relatively small samples suggest greater rates of DGU than are likely to be true. Considering less controversial topics, Wentland and Smith (1993) noted that people have trouble with remembering if they have a library card.

We can identify four particularly troublesome problems associated with memory questions. First, people use different strategies to recall events from the recent past and distant past in some cases. When Winkielman, Knäuper, and Schwarz (1998) inquired of people how often they have been angry either in the last week versus in the last year, the respondents interpreted the meaning of the question differently. In the "last week" group, participants decided that the surveyor wanted a report of minor irritations, whereas the "last year" group focused on major irritations.

> **Telescoping**—A phenomenon of memory in which events that occurred in the distant past are remembered as having occurred more recently than they actually did.

A second source of problems is that, when a question involves a time span (e.g., "How many times in the last year have you . . ."), people may engage in a memory phenomenon called **telescoping.** When you look through a telescope, distant objects do not seem as far away as they really are; similarly, when people try to remember events from the past, things that happened a long time ago tend to be remembered as having happened more recently than they actually did.

A third difficulty is that the nature of previous questions affects the responses to later ones. People want to appear consistent in their responses, so they may use previous answers to help them form responses to new questions. If their initial responses are inaccurate, later ones may distort the truth. Todorov (2000) discovered that people reported different levels of vision problems in a health survey depending on what questions had been asked just before a critical question.

A fourth concern involves the nature of alternatives presented in a closed-ended question. Schwarz (1999) and others have reported that the scale of alternatives can make a big difference in a person's response. For instance, if individuals are asked how often they engage in a given behavior on a daily basis, the scaling of the response alternatives can lead to very different answers.

Schwarz, Hippler, Deutsch, and Strack (1985) asked people how much daily television they watched. Respondents saw one of two scales for their response. One set of options provided response options in half-hour increments starting at zero (0 to .5, .5 to 1, 1.5 to 2, 2 to 2.5, and 2.5 or more); this was the low frequency condition. A different set of respondents saw options that began at 2.5 hours; that is, the lowest response category was 2.5 to 3 hours. This was the high frequency condition. Over a third of those who answered using the high frequency scale replied that they watched television more than two and a half hours a day. Less than half that number using the low frequency scale reported such television watching.

Why would there be such a discrepancy? For the high frequency television watching scale, respondents are likely to conclude that the surveyor is asking a reasonable question and that numbers in the middle of the scale are typical. Accordingly, if they think they watch a "normal" amount of television, their answers will gravitate toward the numbers that are in the middle of this scale, which are relatively high.

People responding to the low frequency scale expressed a belief that the typical person watched 2.7 hours of television a day, whereas those responding on the high frequency scale suggested that the typical person watched 3.2 hours. Clearly, the participants were using the scale for information about what is "typical."

Obviously, the problem with this type of question is that, as a researcher, your confidence in your answers decreases. Do the respondents watch a lot of television or not? Unfortunately, the wording of a question can leave you with considerable uncertainty. Sometimes you should simply ask a direct question to get the best answer. On the other hand, a direct question may tax a person's memory too greatly. You should rely on pretesting your questions, on your best judgment, and on the strategies that successful researchers before you have employed.

Table 8.4 provides some guidelines about asking questions when you want people to recall something. You will notice that some of the points seem to contradict one another. For example, one element says to ask for specific information and another says

TABLE 8.4 Elements for constructing survey questions involving respondents' memory.

GUIDELINE	COMMENT
Do not ask for details of mundane activities that are beyond a person's ability to remember (e.g., "How many people are usually in the library when you study there?").	Some people are better at remembering details than others are; asking for too much recall of detail may lead some groups to produce low-quality data based on faulty estimates.
If possible when you ask people how frequently they have engaged in a behavior, request the respondent to provide as specific a number as possible.	If you give respondents a series of alternatives to choose from, the scale you use will influence the answer to this question and possibly to others.
If you need to ask about specific periods of time, make sure that the respondent can accurately gauge behaviors in the time frame you specify.	People are better at the recent past than the distant past. Further, respondents are more accurate for behaviors they engage in on a regular schedule.
Avoid questions that have vague quantifiers (e.g., "rarely" or "sometimes"); instead, use more specific quantifiers (e.g., "twice a week").	Vague quantifiers like "frequently" differ depending on the person and on the event being judged. For example, "frequent headaches" means something different than "frequent brushing of teeth."
Avoid questions that require overspecific quantifiers (e.g., "How many times have you eaten at a restaurant in the past year?"); instead give ranges (e.g., "0–1 times," "2–3 times," etc.).	When people engage in commonplace activities on an irregular basis, precise estimates are little more than guesses.
Do not ask questions using words that might distract the respondent (e.g., offensive or inflammatory words).	Respondents may use negative or emotionally charged words as a cue to how often they should report a behavior, trying to avoid a negative evaluation of such behavior.

not to. When you are preparing survey questions, you need to make decisions about each question in the context in which it is asked. Sometimes you will want to ask specific questions, sometimes you will not.

Understanding the people you query and the behaviors you want to assess is critical to developing a useful survey. Pilot testing can help you decide if you have made good decisions. One noted expert once reported generating 41 different versions of a question before he arrived at one he considered "passable" (Payne, 1951, cited in Dillman, 2000).

Attitude Questions.   People have attitudes on many different issues and they are often willing to share them. But asking about attitudes is difficult. There are seven major concerns that researchers have to ponder.

One prime concern with questions about attitudes, just as with memory questions, is the wording of the item. For example, emotionally laden terms can result in answers that are more likely to be responses to the wording than to the meaning of the question. For instance, a question that refers to sexual material as "hard-core pornography" is likely to elicit negative responses because of the attitude to the words, even if those words do not describe that sexual material very well.

Professional researchers are likely to be sensitive to the biasing factor of the words they use, but sometimes the effects are subtle. Rasinski (1989) pointed out that people voiced less support for "welfare" for the poor than they did for "assistance to the poor."

Chronically Accessible Information—Memories that are available for retrieval at any time.

Temporarily Accessible Information—Memories that are available for retrieval only when cued by exposure to information that cues those memories.

A second variable that can affect responses is the order of the questions. The attitudes that people report are highly context-dependent. That is, they feel one way when thinking about certain things, but they feel another way when thinking about other things. Memories and feelings about a topic that always surface when a respondent addresses some topic are **chronically accessible.** This means that respondents call some information to mind very readily; this information will affect their responses. Other memories and feelings might be **temporarily accessible.** This information also affects responses, but only if it has been recently brought into awareness, as by an earlier question on the survey.

Such accessibility may explain why, in nationwide polls, people generally claim that their own school systems are doing a good job, but that the nation's schools as a whole are not doing well (http://www.Gallup.com/poll/releases/pr010823.asp). When events in educational settings are especially troubling, news reports highlight the problem. So people compare their own schools with the negative reports and conclude that their own system is just fine. It makes you wonder: If just about everybody reports that their own schools are doing a good job, where are the problematic schools?

A third feature that guides participants' responses is their perceptions of the purpose of the interview or questionnaire. In one study, participants completed a questionnaire that had printed on the top "Institute for Social Research" whereas others saw "Institute for Personality Research." The responses of the two groups differed, with the first group concentrating on social variables in their answers and the second group concentrating on personality issues (Norenzayan & Schwarz, 1999).

A fourth possible variable influencing the expression of attitudes is the sensitivity of the issue being investigated. People may be reluctant to admit to drunken driving, illegal drug use, some sexual behaviors, etc. There are two likely sources of invalidity for analysis of responses to these items. One source is nonresponse. That is, people simply ignore the question. The problem is that if too many people fail to answer the item, you may have problems with the representativeness of the answers you actually get. A second likely source of invalidity is simple lying.

A fifth factor that may come into play in personal interviews is the nature of the person doing the questioning. Finkel, Guterbok, and Borg (1991) discovered that white respondents were more likely to express support for a black candidate when an interviewer was black rather than white. A surprising element here is that the interview was over the telephone. You can imagine that a face-to-face interview could lead to an even greater response bias.

In considering a sixth possible source of problems with the quality of data, it is important to distinguish between attitudes and opinions that people already have, as opposed to attitudes that they create when a researcher asks them a question. Some people might not actually have an opinion on some topic until the surveyor asks them about it. They then construct one. Sometimes people even report attitudes on fictional topics.

Why would somebody state an attitude about a fictional topic? People might want to look thoughtful and would feel foolish about saying they don't know about a topic that they think they should. Another reason for making up an opinion is that respondents assume that the surveyor is asking a reasonable question, so they draw from their knowledge of apparently related topics and give an answer that would be consistent with their attitudes in general (Schwarz, 1999).

Researchers have discovered that when people have pre-existing attitudes, their response times to a question are shorter than when the respondent is creating an attitude to report (Powell & Fazio, 1984). Thus if researchers are worried about differentiating between existing and newly created attitudes, keeping track of response times might be a useful strategy.

A seventh concern about obtaining high-quality data with attitudinal questions is that people may hold a positive or a negative attitude about some topic, but it is not always clear how deeply they hold that attitude. Thus, a lot of people may favor gun control laws, but they might not hold that conviction deeply enough to write a letter to their political representatives. There may be fewer people who oppose such laws, but they may be more committed to act on their beliefs. These seven concerns are summarized in Table 8.5.

DISCUSSION QUESTIONS

1. Why do researchers prefer closed-ended questions on surveys? When do you think open-ended questions might be better?
2. What kinds of events in your own life would probably be associated with memory problems if you were surveyed about them? What kinds would be easy? Why?
3. How could you go about finding if responses to attitude questions were deeply held, newly formed, or just made up? What problems could be associated with your solutions?
4. When you ask people how often they have engaged in a given activity, what potential problems do you need to consider in how you word your question?

TABLE 8.5   Seven major concerns about surveys that investigate respondents' attitudes.

CONCERN	REASON FOR CONCERN
Wording of the question	Wording that predisposes a respondent to answer in a particular way (e.g., an item that is emotionally loaded) does not give valid information about an attitude because the person is responding on the basis of wording.
Order of the question	Early questions may prime a respondent to think about issues in a given way or may bring information into memory so that it affects responses to a later question.
Perceived purpose of the survey	Respondents may interpret the meaning of questions differently, depending on what they believe is the underlying purpose of the survey.
Sensitivity of the issue being investigated	People may alter their responses or simply lie when asked about issues that might be embarrassing or otherwise make the respondent uncomfortable. Respondents may also omit answers to such questions.
The nature of the surveyor	People may respond more frankly to a researcher who is similar to them, particularly when the survey involves sensitive issues.
Presence or absence of pre-existing attitudes about a topic	Sometimes people are not aware of the issues being surveyed, so they don't have attitudes about them. They may make up their attitudes on the spot, sometimes on the basis of previous questions and their responses to them.
The intensity with which a respondent holds an attitude	We can identify the extent of agreement with an issue, but we don't know the depth of feeling or commitment associated with that issue.

RESPONSE BIAS

Response Bias—A tendency for a respondent to answer in predictable ways, independent of the question content, such as always agreeing with a statement or always providing high or low ratings on a Likert scale.

Surveyors have long known that people may hesitate to tell you the truth when they fear a negative reaction to their answers. This should come as no surprise; as social beings, we all consider how much to reveal to another person, whether we are talking to a friend or to a stranger. As long as people think that they are going to be evaluated, they will tailor their responses in a survey.

Sometimes respondents show certain patterns in their answers, regardless of the content of the question. One person may be likely to agree with questions most of the time; another person might be likely to disagree most of the time. When people engage in such patterns of behavior, they are showing **response bias.**

Studying Sensitive Issues

Sometimes the best way to get information from people is simply to ask them. Surprisingly, many people are willing to give researchers reports of intimate details of their lives.

In fact, some people are willing to do it on national television. However, professional researchers are more interested in good data than in good television drama. As a result, researchers have developed varied techniques designed to result in meaningful results.

One approach is simply to guarantee anonymity to respondents. In many cases, this promise will suffice; naturally, it relies on trust between the researcher and the respondent. Dillman (2000) illustrated an effective method that allows a researcher to know whether an individual has returned a mail questionnaire while maintaining anonymity. He has sent postcards to the potential respondents that they complete and return separately from the questionnaire itself.

Thus, the researcher knows if somebody has returned the questionnaire, but there is no way to identify which survey is associated with any single individual. The advantage to this approach is that it allows the surveyor to contact people who have not returned the postcards, reminding them to complete the survey.

Are Telephone Surveys Appropriate for Sensitive Issues?   Researchers are appropriately concerned that telephone interviews may not generate high-quality data. However, studies show that telephone surveys can be highly effective when done properly. Johnson, Fendrich, Shaligram, Garcy, and Gillespie (2000) found that when respondents think that an interviewer is different from them, they are less forthcoming in reporting drug use in a telephone survey. A respondent talking to somebody of the same relative age, gender, race, and educational level may be more likely to report sensitive behaviors than when the interviewer is seen as different.

In a comparison of telephone and other survey techniques, McAuliffe, Geller, LaBrie, Paletz, and Fournier (1998) reported that researchers can get very high-quality data with telephone surveys, even when the topic involves an issue like substance abuse. After studying advantages and disadvantages of telephone compared to other survey types, they suggested that telephone surveys can be as useful as any other mode.

Social Desirability

Social Desirability Bias—The tendency of respondents to answer questions in ways that generate a positive impression of themselves.

Impression Management—A form of social desirability bias in which respondents actively deceive a researcher in order to generate a positive impression of themselves in the researcher's eyes.

Self-Deception Positivity—A form of social desirability bias in which respondents provide generally honest, but overly optimistic, information about themselves that generates a positive impression of them.

In an attempt to look good (or to avoid looking bad), people do not always tell the truth. Researchers have written extensively about this problem, referred to as **social desirability bias.** It can take two forms. One is **impression management,** which involves active deception by respondents to keep the researcher from forming a negative impression of the them. A second component of social desirability bias is **self-deception positivity,** which occurs when people do not consciously give inappropriate responses but, rather, give a generally honest but overly positive self-report. Both types of response bias pose problems for the researcher, even though the bias occurs for different reasons.

One domain that has received considerable attention regarding social desirability bias is self-concept and its relation to sex differences. The stereotypical belief is that women are more likely to excel in verbal and artistic areas, whereas men are more proficient in math and physical domains. In some research, female and male students report such differences in expertise on questionnaires even when performance is comparable across groups. The gender differences in beliefs seemed to occur because of impression management, the intentional form of social desirability bias, suggesting that differences in self-concept across sexes may occur because of a desire to report conformity to the stereotype (Vispoel & Forte Fast, 2000).

Researchers have found socially desirable responses to be problematic in a number of different domains, including marketing (King & Bruner, 2000), self-concept (Vispoel & Forte Fast, 2000), sexual behavior (Meston, Heiman, Trapnell, & Paulhus, 1998), mathematics ability (Zettle & Houghton, 1998), attendance at religious service (Presser & Stinson, 1998), and personality reports (Francis & Jackson, 1998).

How can you deal with social desirability bias? Enlightening respondents about the existence of such response biases can help (Hong & Chiu, 1991). Another strategy is to create forced choice questions so that respondents must select from among a number of equally attractive or unattractive choices (Ray, 1990).

Another approach to reducing social desirability bias is to give both sides of an attitude in the question stem. This technique may keep the respondent from concluding that the surveyor is giving his or her own opinion in a question, leading the respondent to acquiesce. Table 8.6 gives an example of how to present both sides of an issue in the question.

Finally, some researchers (e.g., Krosnick, 1999) believe that social desirability may not occur to the extent that other researchers claim. For instance, when people complete

TABLE 8.6   Representing both sides of an issue in a potential survey question and how to reduce the likelihood of response bias to it.

Poor Item: **To what extent to you agree that the Statistics course should be eliminated as a required course for a Psychology major?**

____ Strongly agree
____ Somewhat agree
____ Somewhat disagree
____ Strongly disagree

Problem: Only one side of the issue (i.e., eliminating Statistics) is represented. A respondent might think that the interviewer is stating his or her own opinion and might consequently give an "agree" reply, acquiescing with the interviewer.

Better Item: **Do you think that the Statistics course should be eliminated as part of the Psychology major or do you think that the Statistics course should be kept as part of the Psychology major?**

____ Eliminate the Statistics course
____ Keep the Statistics course
____ No Opinion

Note: The "No Opinion" option should be at the end rather than between the other two options so that the respondent does not confuse it with a neutral response.

surveys on voting behavior, the percentage of respondents who report voting in the most recent election exceeds the proportion of the population that actually did. Researchers have interpreted this discrepancy to reflect social desirability bias by participants.

Newer research, however, suggests two alternate interpretations. First, people who vote are more likely to respond to surveys than those who don't vote. So the discrepancy in percentages who say they voted and who actually did may reflect a bias in the survey sample, not social desirability bias. A second interpretation is that people with a habit of voting and who did not vote in the most recent election may think (erroneously), "I always vote, so I must have voted in the most recent election." This type of response indicates a memory problem, not a social desirability bias. As a result, the individual's other answers may be valid responses, not attempts to look good.

Acquiescence

When somebody asks you, "How are you?" your tendency is probably to respond that you are just fine, thanks. In general conversation, our tendency is to provide responses that are in line with others' expectations. As a rule, when people ask, "How are you?" they are really only extending a greeting. Most of the time, they don't expect (or even want) a litany of your woes.

Acquiescence—In survey research, the tendency to agree with the assertion of a question, regardless of its content.

A related dynamic can occur with surveys. Sometimes it is just easier to respond "yes" or to agree with a question. So that's what respondents may do, engaging in **acquiescence,** the tendency to agree with the assertion of a question, regardless of what it is. When the same question appears in two forms on a survey (e.g., "I enjoy socializing" and "I don't enjoy socializing"), respondents often agree with both, even though the people are directly contradicting themselves (Krosnick, 1999).

Krosnick (1999) described several explanations for people's tendency to acquiesce. One reason has to do with personality characteristics. Some people's personalities simply predispose them to want to agree with an assertion. Another explanation is that respondents often view surveyors as having higher status, so they feel compelled to agree with an assertion that the surveyor presents because we are "supposed to" agree with our superiors. Acquiescence can also be explained through the concept of satisficing, which we encounter below.

Satisficing versus Optimizing

Satisficing—The tendency of respondents to be satisfied with the first acceptable response to a question or on a task, even if it is not the best response.

Suppose you are taking a test and you encounter a difficult question. You might spend a few moments trying to conjure up the answer and as soon as you identify a possibility, you go for that answer without considering other possibilities. If you have ever done this, you have engaged in **satisficing,** which means that you adopted the first acceptable answer, even if it wasn't the best answer.

This tactic occurs regularly when people answer survey questions. Respondents don't have the same commitment to a project that the researchers do. So when respondents have to work hard to come up with a response, they often decide to reply with the first thing that sounds plausible to them or with an easy answer. Obviously, what works for the respondent can be a problem for the researcher.

Optimizing—The tendency of respondents to search for the best response to a question.

According to Krosnick (1999), satisficing is likely to occur for any of three general reasons: (a) high task difficulty, (b) lower respondent ability, and (c) low respondent motivation. **Optimizing** is the complement to satisficing. When a respondent optimizes, the person works to generate the best possible answer.

Why would a survey question pose difficulties? Understanding a question and responding to it is actually a complex process. First, respondents must work to understand the point of the question. Although this seems to be pretty straightforward, people answer the same question in various ways depending on what they think the researcher is looking for.

Second, respondents have to search through memory to find relevant information. We know that the context in which a question is asked affects a person's response. Regarding surveys, it may be hard for somebody to remember events being probed in the context of the research setting because those events are neither chronically nor temporarily accessible.

A third task required of a respondent for generating good answers to survey questions is organizing everything that has been recalled.

Finally, in order to generate a high-quality response to a question, a person must choose from among the alternatives presented on a questionnaire. When people listen to an interviewer give a series of alternatives, there can be a tendency to select the later alternatives because they are easier to remember. When a questionnaire is on paper, there is a tendency for a respondent to pay more attention to the first alternatives (Krosnick, 1999).

If a person's cognitive processes fail at any step in this chain of events, a respondent will provide lower-quality information.

Given the complexity of understanding a question and producing a response, it will be no surprise to learn that respondents engage in satisficing. They simply don't want to work any harder than they have to.

A related factor that leads to satisficing relates to the participant's level of ability. Researchers have discovered that respondents with lower ability levels tend to satisfice because they are unable to generate high-quality responses. So they go with the first reasonable reply that they encounter.

Further, after the participant has answered a few questions, the motivation to respond may decrease. You may have participated in a psychology experiment either as a requirement for a course or for extra credit. Many students in such situations are in a hurry to complete this activity, so they are often less motivated to spend time on a response or to think deeply about a question. Many people have the same experience, engaging in satisficing as a result.

Minimizing the Occurrence of Satisficing

There will probably always be tension between the desires of the respondent and the needs of the researcher. If you conduct survey research, you will want to encourage people to optimize. How can you do this?

One way to minimize the possibility of satisficing is to create survey questions that are easily understood. In addition, when you ask people to remember events, it may help to ask several related questions so the information is more accessible. People may generate more accurate responses when the surveyor encourages them to remember events related to or close in time to the critical event, rendering obscure memories temporarily accessible.

Another path to reducing the incidence of satisficing is for the researcher to consider using ranking a group of items rather than rating them individually because if a respondent has to rank different options, the person has to consider them all. Asking respondents to use a rating scale may lead them to identify a point on the scale and generally to respond with that value (e.g., giving a rating of 3 on a scale of 1 to 5) on virtually every item. This way of responding is called **nondifferentiation** because people fail to provide different responses across questions.

> **Nondifferentiation**—The tendency of respondents to give the same answer to questions, regardless of content.

Another way to reduce the probability of satisficing is to avoid giving respondents a "No Opinion" option. That is, if you want participants to think about their responses and give high-quality answers, you should not allow them to say "No Opinion."

Finally, if you can keep your respondents motivated, such as by establishing a positive atmosphere and by making sure they know that their answers are important, you may be able to decrease satisficing.

DISCUSSION QUESTIONS

1. Why might it be easier to eliminate problems of impression management than social desirability?
2. Why do you think people are likely to engage in acquiescence, even if it leads to contradictory responses on different questions?
3. How could you maximize the likelihood of getting good answers to sensitive questions when surveying fellow students?
4. Why do difficult questions lead to satisficing? How can you reduce the chance that it will occur?
5. How could your test-taking behavior in classes involve satisficing? Have you ever done it? Why?

SPECIAL CONSIDERATIONS FOR INTERNET RESEARCH

Survey research using the internet poses special problems. It is a new methodology, requiring us to think about new issues. Just as researchers had to identify critical aspects of telephone surveys forty years ago, now we have to figure out how to collect data most effectively on the internet.

Ethical issues provide a good starting point for the discussion of internet surveys. We should follow the ethical guidelines that professionals have developed, such as those of the American Association of Opinion Research and of the American Psychological Association. But we have to consider the issues a little differently here.

Some people believe that internet surveys have the potential for greater invasion of privacy than other modes of data collection. They contend that sending unwanted surveys via email invades the personal space of recipients; when people pay for their email access according to length of time they spend online, such unwanted surveys also have a real monetary cost to the potential respondent. Another type of privacy that internet surveys can violate is called informational privacy, which relates to information about an individual that is sent on the World Wide Web. It could be used for sending additional email to the unsuspecting person. Many respondents share this fear and claim to have lied on surveys (Cho & LaRose, 1999).

There is also the ethical (and legal) question of sending a research instrument to a minor via the World Wide Web. One of the prime conditions of research is that it be voluntary and that the person be informed about the nature of the research. Legally, minors cannot volunteer on their own. Further, children may not realize the implications about the information they provide, so their consent would not be truly informed.

Regarding adult participation, sometimes people read personal email at their work, which might violate company policies. Sending an email or internet survey to a person who gets it at work might be ethically questionable, even though it is the recipient who has decided to violate company rules. In addition, organizations may intercept some email messages or may even store anything a person sends. Thus, the content of the response may endanger the person both physically (e.g., loss of the job) and psychologically (e.g., embarrassment because of some responses to survey questions).

Internet Surveys

In an earlier era, researchers developed survey techniques for personal interviews and for mailed questionnaires, then for the telephone. We are now in the process of developing guidelines for the use of the internet. Just as changes in seemingly small details can make a big difference in the traditional survey formats, such small details may also lead to critical differences in internet-based surveys.

Some aspects of internet surveying mirror those in traditional formats. For instance, changing fonts and text size, including a lot of bold and italic type, and lack of contrast between the text and the background reduce the usability of paper surveys; the pattern will likely hold true for internet surveys. Similarly, obtaining nonrandom samples in traditional formats is problematic; it also is likely to be problematic for internet approaches.

It will be relatively easy to identify those aspects of internet surveys that lead to high response rates and high-quality data. However, it will be more difficult to come up with the methods to guarantee the validity of the data. Currently, a major issue is that not everybody has regular access to a computer, and many who do have such access do not regularly search for sites that offer questionnaires. Those people who respond are an unknown population that may or may not be like the population in general, so questions about generalizability remain.

It would be nice to know exactly who is likely to complete online surveys. We do have a partial picture, thanks to ongoing research by internet professionals. Table 8.7 gives a series of snapshots of who is using the Web. The picture is still incomplete but

TABLE 8.7 Some characteristics of internet users (Media Metrix, http://us.mediametrix.com/press/releases, 2001).

POPULATION CHARACTERISTIC	PATTERN
Women	Surpassed male users in the first quarter of 2000
Women 55 and older	Increase of 109% over the past year
Teenage girls	Increase of 126% over the past year
Women 18–24	Slight decrease in use over the past year
Households with income under $25,000	Under 10% of users, but growing; most frequent class of sites includes career and auction sites
Households with income over $25,000	Most frequent use includes hobby-leisure, auto, sport, and travel sites
Adults over age 35	Greater use of multimedia players than those under age 35
Teens	Less than half the time spent online compared to adults per month (303 minutes versus 728 minutes)
Republicans and Democrats	Republicans represent about 37% of web users, Democrats 28%

you can see that the demographic characteristics of internet users do not mirror those of the general population in the United States. People with incomes under $25,000 represent about one third of all households, but they constitute less than one tenth of the internet traffic; at the other end of the continuum, web users with over $100,000 income constitute about one tenth of the population, but they represent twice that proportion of those who are online.

Not only do we have to consider who is online, but we also have to pay attention to how much time they spend on the Web. Teens spend less time on the Web than adults, contrary to popular stereotypes. Reversing another popular stereotype, adults aged 35 and above showed greater use of multimedia music applications than those under 18.

People also use the internet more at work than at home. This has implications for assessing the results of online surveys. People who have access to the internet at work have jobs with different characteristics of those who cannot go online at work; they are likely to be indoors, have white-collar jobs, and have higher incomes. In addition, according to the General Social Survey, which involves face-to-face interviews, when people claim an affiliation to either the Democratic or the Republican party, 57 percent ally themselves with the Democrats and 43 with the Republicans (General Social Survey, http://www.icpsr.umich.edu/GSS). Of internet users who identify with a political party, the percentages are reversed, with 57 percent saying they are Republicans.

These patterns suggest that not only is the population of internet users different from the general population, people are using the internet in ways that differ from popular conceptions. The implications of these facts suggest that online surveys will attract different populations depending on the type of web pages with which they are associated (Media Metrix, http://us.mediametrix.com/press/releases; retrieved March 6, 2001).

One of the major problems concerning the representativeness of online surveys is that we are never sure exactly what population such surveys pertain to because there is no exhaustive specification of the population (Schillewaert, Langerak, & Duhamel, 1998). In fact, the international nature of the internet means that researchers have even less knowledge about the population of potential respondents than in other survey modes.

If you decide to conduct a survey online, you want to maximize the return on your work. What is the best way to get people to respond to a survey? This is not a question that has an easy answer.

One study of internet surveys led to response rates of 0.18 percent when notices of the survey appeared in a print magazine, requiring readers to switch to a computer to complete the survey. When a person was able to use a hyperlink to access a survey, the response rate was somewhat higher, 0.68 percent, but still extremely low. When a posting appeared in newsgroups, the response rate was estimated to be 1.68 percent. Finally, when respondents were emailed individually three times, the return rate was 31 percent, which is a respectable figure. You can see the magnitude of the difference in Figure 8.1. Not surprisingly, persistence and a personal approach provide the best results.

An added advantage to the email technique is that responses arrive very quickly, much more so than the other approaches. Further, the quality of the data (i.e., how complete the responses were) seems to be comparable, regardless of the means of notifying respondents (Schillewaert, Langerak, & Duhamel, 1998).

Online surveys aren't noticeably worse than other approaches and they have some practical advantages. It's not unreasonable to expect their frequency to increase as researchers become familiar with the characteristics of successful internet surveys and the approaches that work best.

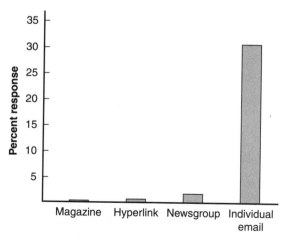

FIGURE 8.1 Response rates to online surveys for various means of contacting potential respondents (Schillewaert, Langerak, & Duhamel, 1998).

Designing Surveys for the World Wide Web

When you create a survey to be mailed to somebody, you know what it looks like. When the person receives it in the mail, the survey looks the same as it did when you mailed it. The same is not always true of internet surveys.

There are several different elements that you have to consider regarding Web surveys and email surveys. If you fail to pay attention to them, the negative consequences will affect your results. The issues that merit consideration include respondent motivation, the technical characteristics of a user's system, and visual characteristics of the survey instrument.

Respondent Motivation

It doesn't help a researcher if a potential respondent receives but ignores a survey. Over the past few decades, the response rate for surveys in general has decreased, and email surveys have lower response rates than mail and telephone surveys (Cho & LaRose, 1999).

You can try to motivate people to comply by using incentives. However, the motivating factors that work in mail surveys may not translate to the computer. Researchers have not yet determined the functional equivalents of mail incentives, which include money in mail surveys (Martinez-Ebers, 1999) and in face-to-face surveys (Willimack, Schuman, Pennell, & Lepkowski, 1995), and even tea bags (which don't work; Gendall, Hoek, & Brennan, M., 1998).

Another potential problem is that there are so many polls on the Web that it is unlikely that any single researcher's survey will stand out. Scientific investigators tend to be cautious in their approaches, which includes creating credible-looking, but not flashy, survey instruments. Such questionnaires have a hard time competing with the more glittering marketing or entertainment surveys.

For instance, the web site by Mister Poll (http://www.misterpoll.com) presents entertainment polls on a variety of topics. Fortunately, the owner of the site does include a disclaimer about what the results mean: "Mister Poll is interested in what you think about anything and everything. He maintains a directory of the most interesting and topical polls created by his staff and independent pollsters for your general entertainment. None of these polls are "scientific," but do represent the collective opinion of everyone who participates." It is hard for serious researchers to compete with such entertainment. An example of some questions from an environmentally oriented poll on that web site appears in Table 8.8.

The environmental poll may be fun to complete and submit, but it would be risky to draw any conclusions from it about people's feelings on the environment. For instance, how many people would seriously claim that they do not care about the environment? In addition, the misspellings in the table (which came from the survey itself), reduce its credibility. As mentioned before, this kind of poll is fun and entertaining, but it is not scientifically valid. Other, more serious polls appear on the such sites as the Cable News Network (CNN) web site. They too are clearly marked as being nonscientific, reflecting only those who choose to participate. Would you prefer to complete

TABLE 8.8 Example of an entertainment poll as the questions appeared on the Mister Poll web site (http://www.misterpoll.com).

QUESTION	COMMENT
Are you for the Enviroment?* ☐ Yes ☐ No ☐ Yes, but I'm not a radical	How many people do you know that would claim that they are against the environment? In addition, the question suggests that if you claim to be for the environment, you are likely to be a radical.
Do you support the work of the EPA and the GDC? ☐ Yes ☐ No ☐ Yes, but only the EPA ☐ Yes, but only the GDC	Do you know what "GDC" stands for? If not, can you say whether you support it?
What activities do you enjoy?* ☐ Computer ☐ Television ☐ Sports ☐ Cooking ☐ Fine Arts ☐ Hiking and camping ☐ Traveling ☐ Reading	What does this question have to do with the environment? When irrelevant questions appear on a survey, the credibility of the survey may diminish. This is the kind of item that appears on a marketing instrument, not in scientific research.
Which of these settings is the most beatiful to you?* ☐ The Television Screen ☐ The Veiw from you porch* ☐ The gradeur of Nature* ☐ Watching smog rise from a stack	This humorous item can clearly be seen as meant for entertainment. Would it change your opinion about the rest of the survey?

*Note: These questions (including misspellings) came directly from the Mister Poll web site and are used for illustrative purposes only.

a one-question survey on a serious topic, a longer entertainment survey, or a still-longer serious scientific survey? This is an important question for researchers.

Technical Characteristics of a User's System

Different computers translate computer code in somewhat different ways. Thus, a survey created for a PC may look different on a Mac. Further, the size of a monitor and the properties that control the appearance of a display differ from one computer to another. The nature of the web browser also affects the way a questionnaire appears on the screen. If you are using color or contrast to communicate with a potential respondent, you have to make sure that the information does not get lost because somebody's display looks different from yours. In addition, some software works properly with some web browsers, but may not work well with others.

Another important facet involving internet surveys is how quickly a potential respondent's system receives input from the internet. If somebody is using a relatively slow modem to connect to the internet, a survey instrument might take too long to download, frustrating the individual, perhaps leading to the decision not to complete it. The use of audio and video components in the survey may further limit people's ability to participate.

Another feature of a system that might affect responses is whether the computer is set up to accept the "cookies" that might be necessary for participation. Some surveyors will insert a cookie to keep a respondent from replying more than once. If the computer won't accept cookies, the person cannot respond.

User Knowledge

Although many people, including most students, are at least somewhat comfortable using computers, not everybody is. Thus, a relatively new user may not know how to access a different web page or a different part of the same web page by using an active link. If you use a filter question and instruct the respondent that "If your answer is NO, go to Question 10," you could set your survey up to go to Question 10 by clicking on the phrase "go to Question 10." If the user doesn't know to click on the link, he or she may become confused.

Similarly, when respondents record their replies by using a "Submit" button, they have to know to use the mouse to click on it. They also have to know that they should submit their responses only once. If they attempt to submit their answers and nothing happens because their system is slow, they may think they've done something wrong and will try to do it again, causing them to submit their responses multiple times.

DISCUSSION QUESTIONS
1. What issues related to invasion of privacy do researchers need to consider with respect to internet surveys?
2. Do you personally think that internet surveys are really likely to involve serious invasions of privacy? Have you had any experience with surveys on the internet?
3. Given the types of people who use the internet, for what kinds of research topics would current users give representative samples?

SAMPLING ISSUES

Most psychological research involves students, groups of people who are easily available, which is why this approach involves what is called a convenience sample.

However, there are also drawbacks with this approach. If you are interested in claiming that your research results are typical of people, you have to make sure that the people you study are typical of people in general.

Self-Selected Samples—In survey research, a nonrandom, biased sampling technique in which people choose to participate in the research rather than being selected by the investigator.

Popular surveys rely on **self-selected samples.** These are groups of people who volunteer to participate without having been contacted by the researchers. They may see a notice on the internet, for example, and decide it would be interesting to participate. Or they may be willing to call a 900-number, which costs them money, in order to express their opinion. Or they may respond to a talk show host. The types of people who engage in this responding are different from the population as a whole. In fact, professional researchers regard such polls as entirely nonscientific, therefore useless in telling us what the population thinks about a topic. Some investigators refer to such polls by the derogatory acronym SLOP (i.e., *Se*L*f*-*S*elected *O*pinion *P*oll; Horvitz, Koshland, Rubin, Gollin, Sawyer, & Tanur, 1995).

Finding Hidden Populations

In survey research, some groups of people are difficult to study because they don't want to be found. For instance, people who engage in illegal or embarrassing activities are often reluctant to admit it publicly. Such groups are referred to as **hidden populations.** Two characteristics typify hidden populations: first, it is impossible to establish who constitutes the population and, second, there are strong privacy issues associated with the groups (Heckathorn, 1997).

Hidden Population—Population of interest that is hard to study because the people in the group are engaged in activities that may be embarrassing or illegal (e.g., drug users), so they do not want to be recognized as members of that population.

Chain-referral Methods—A set of sampling techniques that relies on people who know about a population or are members of a that population to gain access to information about the group.

Snowball Sampling—A chain-referral sampling technique in which one person from a population of interest identifies another person from that population to a researcher who contacts that second person, then that new individual refers yet another person, for as many stages as desired by the researcher.

If we want to find out about such groups, we can't use probability samples because probability samples require that we be able to identify the entire pool of possible respondents. So researchers have to make compromises in collecting data. Researchers studying hidden populations have turned to a class of techniques called **chain-referral methods.**

One chain-referral method for contacting respondents involves **snowball sampling,** which relies on the fact that an individual from a hidden population is likely to know others from that group. The volunteer identifies a certain number of people that the researcher will contact; the researcher will then ask each of these second-stage individuals to provide the names of yet others. The process continues through as many stages as the researchers determine desirable.

Kaplan, Korf, and Sterk (1987) studied heroin use among addicts in the Netherlands. They identified a single user and asked for names of others who fit their target categories, either prostitutes or foreigners. These referrals then identified others, and so on. Kaplan et al. found it easier to find subsequent groups of prostitutes than foreigners, reflecting the fact that some populations are more hidden than others.

Snowball samples often contain more cooperative volunteers who have a large social network and are not considered random samples. They are a variation on convenience samples, so it is not always clear to whom the researchers can generalize their findings.

Key Informant Sampling—A sampling technique that relies on getting information from people who know about a population of interest rather than from members of that population themselves.

Targeted Sampling—A sampling technique that relies on finding locations that attract members of the population of interest and getting information from these people at such locations.

Respondent-Driven Sampling—A sampling technique in which a researcher uses a member of the population of interest to actively recruit others, often with some incentive like money for engaging in this recruiting.

A second approach to contacting respondents from hidden populations is to use **key informant sampling.** This technique relies on information from knowledgeable individuals rather than from members of the target population itself.

For example, a researcher might contact social workers to get information about patterns of sexual behavior in the population the social workers serves. Key informant sampling may reduce the respondent's reluctance to report unusual behaviors, but it may introduce the biases of that individual and is based on the limited number of people the social worker sees.

A third approach is **targeted sampling.** With this technique, researchers work in advance to identify their population as well as possible, then to find out the different places that attract the widest range of people from that population. The results will only be as good as the researcher's knowledge of where to find members of the target population.

Recently, Heckathorn (1997) has developed a new approach called **respondent-driven sampling.** In this approach, researchers use two types of incentives to attract participants. Primary incentives are offered to individuals; one such incentive may be money. The difference between this technique and other chain-referral methods involves the presence of secondary reward for getting others to join. When a participant identifies a potential candidate for the research, that participant uses peer pressure and social approval to induce a new person to join the project. That is, the researcher doesn't actively recruit the next person; that task is performed by the first participant.

The result is that people participate not only for material reward but also because of a personal relationship. According to Heckathorn, the fact that people volunteer because of their acquaintances rather than being sought out directly is important. Some hidden populations are subject to legal prosecution, so it would be undesirable for members of the population to reveal the names of others. In respondent-driven sampling, people self-identify. This means that if they worry about engaging in illegal behavior, they do not need to come forth. Heckathorn has demonstrated that samples based on respondent-driven sampling seem to be diverse and unbiased.

Your choice of which chain-referral methods to use depends on the practical issues involved in your particular study. If the population is very closed, you may need to use respondent-driven samples, as Heckathorn did with the heroin users he studied. On the other hand, if the population is only somewhat hidden, snowball sampling might be adequate. For example, Frank and Snijders (1994) were able to use snowball sampling in their study of heroin use in the Netherlands because heroin use is more open there.

DISCUSSION QUESTIONS

1. Why do self-selected samples lead to results that aren't generalizable to the population? Have you ever decided to participate or not to participate in sensitive survey research? What influenced (or would influence) your decision?

2. Identify the chain-referral methods and how they work. Do you think the results of these will lead to results that are generalizable to the population of interest to a researcher?

3. What kinds of hidden populations can you think of in your school? How could you go about surveying them? Could you do it successfully?

CHAPTER SUMMARY

Professional surveyors and pollsters have developed techniques that allow researchers to use small samples to make accurate predictions and descriptions of a larger population. As a result, the more economic practice of sampling typically means that researchers don't need a census.

The most common technique in scientific survey research is the telephone survey. For most questions, people who are available by phone adequately represent the entire population. Researchers who use probability sampling can generate a good picture of the population with a relatively small set of responses.

With half a century of research and practice on surveys, we have discovered the most effective ways of getting information by phone, by mail, and in person. The newest approach that social researchers have adopted involves data collection on the internet. There are still questions about the nature of the samples generated in such research and about how best to create surveys for the respondent, but investigators see great potential in using the internet for data collection.

Researchers also have to painstakingly create survey questions that lead to valid responses. This is often the most difficult part of conducting good survey research. Whether you are asking for attitudes or for people to remember past behaviors, subtle differences in the way questions are worded and presented can make a notable difference in the responses that a person makes.

Sometimes different respondents interpret the same question in different ways. They may also show response biases that will either make them look better or make it easier for them to complete a questionnaire without really thinking about the issues at hand. Researchers must work hard to overcome these tendencies on the part of respondents.

Finally, some populations don't want to be found, like those involved in criminal activity or other undesirable or embarrassing behaviors. Investigators have developed techniques designed to make contact with these hidden populations. The samples may not be probability samples, but they often provide useful information.

■ ■ ■ ■ ■

CHAPTER NINE

CORRELATIONAL RESEARCH

CHAPTER OUTLINE

CHAPTER PREVIEW

CORRELATIONAL STUDIES
Finding Relationships
Making Predictions

**USING THE CORRELATIONAL
APPROACH**
Correlational Studies

*CONTROVERSY: Does Media Violence
Promote Violent Behavior?*
Correlational Analysis
Positive and Negative Correlations
Strength of Association
Factors Affecting the Size of a
Correlation Coefficient
Nonlinearity
Restrictions in Range
Heterogeneous Subgroups

TRADITIONAL CORRELATIONAL TESTS
The Pearson Product–Moment
Correlation
Alternate Bivariate Correlations

**CORRELATIONS WITH
MULTIPLE VARIABLES**
Multiple Regression
Factor Analysis
Cross-Lagged Panel Studies

*CONTROVERSY: Mental Health
of College Students*
Path Analysis

**LIMITATIONS OF MULTIVARIATE
CORRELATIONAL ANALYSIS**
Generalizability
Confirmation Bias

CHAPTER SUMMARY

KEY TERMS

Bivariate correlation
Confirmatory factor
analysis
Correlational analysis
Correlational measure
Correlational study
Criterion variable
Cross-lagged
panel study
Directionality problem
Exploratory factor analysis

Factor analysis
Heterogeneous subgroup
problem
Linear relationship
Multiple regression
Negative (indirect)
correlation
Nonlinear relationship
Panel study
Path analysis
Path coefficients

Pearson product–moment
correlation
Positive (direct) correlation
Prediction study
Predictor variable
Restricted range problem
Scatter diagram
Structural equation
modeling
Test of association
Third variable problem

CHAPTER PREVIEW

Psychologists use correlational studies to investigate the relationships among variables when there is a lot of complexity in the behavior and when experimental approaches are not feasible. Correlational studies permit us to find relationships and to make accurate predictions about behavior.

There are different correlational approaches. The simplest involves bivariate relationships between two variables. Researchers typically employ the standard, well-known Pearson product–moment correlation in such circumstances, although we also use several other correlational tests associated with it.

When we want to see how variables interconnect, we rely on more complex approaches. Multivariate tests, which involve at least three variables, allow us to see a more complex picture of behavior. Some of the newer multivariate correlational approaches actually move us in the direction of making tentative statements about causation.

These varied approaches are useful, but we must use them appropriately for arriving at helpful descriptions of behavior. Many of the multivariate models of behavior are quite complex, so it is important to know how to use them and to be able to identify their limitations.

In this chapter, you will encounter the critical aspects of different correlational approaches so you can understand how we employ them in research.

CORRELATIONAL STUDIES

Psychologists, like most scientists, search for causes. We want to know why people act as they do, although this can be an elusive goal. In some cases, we are not able to identify

> **Correlational Study—**
> An approach to research that involves measuring different variables to see whether there is a predictable relationship among the variables.

what variables affect behavior directly, but we can find patterns and relationships that make behavior predictable. **Correlational studies** tell us which variables and behaviors are related. In a correlational study, we take what nature gives us and see how things interconnect.

Thus, if we are interested in complex behaviors that emerge as a result of multiple causal agents or if we are interested in variables that would be impractical or unethical to manipulate directly, we do the next best thing. We stand on the sidelines, watch how things occur, and see if we can connect them.

Finding Relationships

Many students don't like to take classes that meet early in the morning. Many professors only like to meet early in the morning. This unfortunate mix of preferences suggests that either students or professors will not be working at their best times.

Is there any reason to believe that students' peak performance is related to their preferred times? Guthrie, Ash, and Bendapudi (1995) have verified that there is a relationship between students' tendencies toward *morningness* and their overall semester grade point average (GPA). This is an example of correlational research in a relationship study, a project that aims to determine whether two variables are related to one another.

In the Guthrie et al. study, we can see that there is a relationship between morningness and class performance. The correlation is based on students' preferences for morning activities and their performance in classes. When students are not morning people, they tend to earn lower grades in classes that begin at 8:00 or 8:30 a.m. The overall relationship between students' morningness scores and their GPAs is not very strong but it is reliable.

Let's briefly go over this concept. We can make predictions about students' grades based on multiple variables: the amount of time they study, the percentage of time they go to class, the amount of time required for family activities, how many hours a week they work, who they study with, how much partying they do, how much time they spend in extracurricular activities, how much they learned in high school, and on and on indefinitely. These variables might be associated with better or worse grades. Hypothetically, if we knew about all possible sources associated with grades, we could identify the relation each one had with grades. Each variable would provide some amount of information. Ultimately, we could predict grades perfectly, accounting for 100 percent of the difference among students.

In the Guthrie et al. (1995) study, morningness accounted for between one and two percent of the difference in grades between students. This was a statistically reliable finding, although it was pretty small. For the most part, student grades are likely to be more predictable based on variables like grade point average, motivation levels, and amount of student preparation for tests.

How did Guthrie et al. discover this relationship? They conducted a relationship study in which they looked at the associations among variables like GPA, when students tended to study, etc. They assessed morningness by means of a simple 13-item scale devised by Smith, Reilly, and Midkiff (1989). Then they computed the correlation coefficients among variables.

This kind of relationship study is useful for preliminary investigations in which a researcher does not yet know if variables are related to one another. There are two important points to remember when considering relationship studies. The first is that your variables have to have construct validity. That is, they have to relate meaningfully to what you are measuring. In the case of the morningness study, you would need to have a good measure of morningness. Guthrie et al. used a scale validated by other researchers.

The second thing to remember is that if you compute correlation coefficients on a lot of different variables, you will get some significant relationships that are meaningless. Five percent of the time, variables with no relationship will appear significant. So if you are going to compute multiple correlations, you should remember that some of them will be significant when they don't mean anything.

In general, it is not a wise idea to compute correlations just to compute them; you should look for associations between variables when you expect there to be a relation, not just throw variables together and see what happens. You might end up wasting time in a followup study if you rely on correlations that appear accidentally in your study.

Making Predictions

When you find relationships between variables, sometimes you can go a step further and make predictions regarding the variables and behaviors of interest to you. Colleges

Prediction Study—A correlational study in which the goal is to predict the value of one variable given the level of another variable, with the predictor variable often occurring before the criterion variable rather than simultaneously.

Criterion Variable—In a prediction study, the variable that an investigator is trying to predict.

Predictor Variable—In a prediction study, the variable that an investigator is using to predict another variable.

and universities do this each year when they decide which students to accept. A project designed to predict some outcome variable in correlational research is called a **prediction study.**

Many variables may help predict student success in college. They include SAT scores, high school grades, high school activities, letters of recommendation, and many more. Colleges try to use such factors to predict which students will succeed.

In prediction studies, the outcome that interests us is the **criterion variable,** which we want to predict. The variable that we use to make the prediction is called the **predictor variable.** As such, SAT scores are one of the predictor variables that colleges use, while first-year GPA is the criterion variable.

SAT scores are moderately correlated to first-year GPA. About 16 percent of the difference from one person to the next is predictable on the basis of GPA. This is not too bad when you consider all the factors related to student achievement in college.

The remaining 84 percent of the difference across students is due to unknown factors. Thus, when applicants complain that others with lower SAT scores have been admitted to a college and that they haven't, it is appropriate to keep in perspective that variables other than SAT scores predict more of the variability among students than the standardized test does.

Further, grades are not the only way to measure achievement; growth in ability to engage in critical thinking and to synthesize and communicate complex information, tendencies to engage in civic activities that strengthen the community, awareness of the implications of scientific and political issues in our lives, and so on are also critical components of education that are not always reflected in grades.

If making such predictions were easy, admissions officers would have little difficulty deciding which students to admit. And the outcome would be that each student who enrolled would succeed, whereas each student who did not gain admission would not have succeeded. This is far from the truth. SAT scores may be one predictor of future performance, but an imperfect and incomplete predictor.

If meteorologists can't predict the weather any better than a few days in advance, why should we expect that we could predict human behavior years in advance?

Once researchers who are interested in a particular topic have gained some sense of the variables that are correlated, it is possible to generate predictions about behaviors.

DISCUSSION QUESTIONS

1. What is the difference between a relationship study and a prediction study? Which one is likely to be more preliminary? Why?
2. What behaviors in your life might be related to morningness? How would you go about testing to see if the relationship is as you believe?
3. Although we can't assess causation with correlational studies, why is a predictor variable more likely to be a cause than a criterion variable, if a causal relationship exists?
4. Using scientific arguments, explain why we should not rely on SAT scores alone in making decisions about college admissions.

USING THE CORRELATIONAL APPROACH

It is important to distinguish between correlational studies and correlational analyses. A correlational study relies on making measurements without controlling or trying to manipulate variables. The purpose is to identify connections among variables.

> **Correlational Analysis—** A statistical approach used in research that uses any of a variety of correlational tests, regardless of whether the research is a correlational study or not.

On the other hand, **correlational analysis** is an approach to extracting information from a data set; it doesn't necessarily tell you anything about whether the study is experimental or correlational in design. You need to know what kind of information correlational studies and analyses provide, which is not always the same.

Correlational Studies

A correlational study involves the investigation of factors that might be connected to one another. For instance, two variables that are related are the amount of time you study for a test and your grade on that test. A researcher studying the two might be able to guess your test score reasonably well given knowledge of how long you studied. Still, the relationship is associative, not necessarily causal. Students who are very interested in a class may study a long time and may earn a high score on a test. It might ultimately be their interest in the material that leads to better scores, not simply their study time.

> **Third Variable Problem—**In correlational studies, the problem in assessing cause and effect due to the fact that when two variables are correlated, an outside (or third) variable is responsible for any causation.
>
> **Directionality Problem—**In correlational studies, the problem in assessing cause and effect when two variables are correlated when a researcher does not know which of two variables has a causal effect on the other.

When you perform a correlational study, you can logically conclude that variables are associated, but not that one causes another. Keep in mind that there may really be a causal connection; the problem is that correlational studies don't give you enough information to let you know. Thus, studying a long time may be a causal variable regarding your ultimate test score; in fact, it seems reasonable to conclude so. At the same time, we don't know for sure because there may be a third variable that is really the cause; psychologists refer to this as the **third variable problem.** In this example, the third variable might be your interest in the material. It might lead you to study more and to pay more attention in class, so you score well on tests.

Another problem with assessing causation with correlational data is that you don't know which way the causation proceeds. This problem is one of **directionality.** Logically, in a correlational analysis A could cause B or B could cause A. Consider the morningness scale (Guthrie et al., 1995). It could be that students do well in early classes because they are morning people, as indicated on their responses to the scale.

On the other hand, they might conclude that they are morning people because they do well in early classes. The problem is that with correlational analyses, you can use your best logic to rule out third variables and to identify the correct direction of causation, but you could be wrong.

It is important not to fall for an apparent cause–effect relationship that is not valid. One area of research that has been prone to criticism that causal relationships are not real is whether watching violence on television leads to violent behavior.

Often researchers record how much media violence children encounter and then look at the incidence of violence, aggression, or other antisocial behavior. You could argue that people prone to violence like to watch violence on television. So their personal disposition causes them to enjoy violent images in the media. There is a real possibility of a problem with directionality.

In Controversy Box 9.1, you will see the current scientific status of the argument. A great many media researchers have concluded that there is a causal relationship here: media violence leads to violent behavior.

■ ■ ■ ■ ■ ▬▬▬▬▬▬▬▬▬▬▬▬▬▬▬▬▬▬▬▬▬▬▬▬▬▬▬▬▬▬▬▬▬▬▬▬▬▬▬

CONTROVERSY BOX 9.1
CONTROVERSY: Does Media Violence Promote Violent Behavior?

A persistent societal question is the effect of media violence on behavior. Do people who see violence enacted on television, in the movies, or in video games become violent and aggressive in their own lives?

Over the past decades, investigators have developed partial answers to this question. The introduction of television, with its violence, was associated with an increase in burglaries in the 1950s in a large number of cities in the United States (Hennigan, Del Rosario, Heath, Cook, Wharton, & Calder, 1982). Exposure to realistic crime programs among adolescents in the United States can be associated with risk taking, including vandalism and trespassing (Kremar & Greene, 2000). In India, attitudes toward violence changed after exposure to violent television programming (Varma, 1999).

The problem with such studies is that they don't really inform us about the causes of violent behavior. The research is usually correlational. You can argue that with correlational studies, you can't tell if media violence causes aggressiveness or if the aggressiveness leads to a desire to watch violent programming. With respect to specific types of violence (i.e., homicides), other variables like divorce rates and other social factors (Jensen, 2001) may be better predictors than media violence.

This question of causation is fundamental to psychologists who study complex behavior. How do we handle the dilemma of relying on correlational data when we want to determine causa-

tion? Experiments that involve exposing participants to violence may be unethical because the research could endanger the volunteers.

Researchers use different types of studies to paint a complete picture of the situation. Substantial correlational research has revealed a clear link between media violence and actual violence. In addition, experiments have consistently demonstrated a causal link between exposure to violence and self-reports of aggression and hostility (e.g., Scharrer, 2001), even though this research doesn't deal with actual violence.

The picture is not perfect, but we can draw conclusions based on the best evidence available. The overall analysis of correlational and experimental research affirms that the causal link between media violence and aggressiveness is nearly as strong as the link between smoking and cancer, and stronger than the connection between condom use (or non-use) and AIDS transmission, exposure to lead and lower IQ scores, and homework and academic achievement. The connection is apparent both in correlational and in experimental research (Anderson & Bushman, 2001; Bushman & Anderson, 2001).

Interestingly, over the last quarter century, as the science has become clearer, the news media have ignored the research. News outlets are less likely to report the strength of the connection between media violence and actual violence than before (Bushman & Anderson, 2001).

Correlational Analysis

Correlational analyses are not the same as correlational studies. A correlational analysis uses correlations as a statistical approach, but if the research design is experimental, we can draw causal conclusions. This is easy to grasp by considering a hypothetical two-group study. If we create two groups, randomly assign participants to them to generate equivalent groups, and apply a treatment to only one of the two groups, we have a basic experiment. If the two groups differ at the end, we assume the treatment made the difference.

The normal approach to data analysis with such a design is to compute a *t*-test, which lets us know if two groups differ reliably. However, we could legitimately compute a correlation coefficient. It would tell us exactly what the *t*-test does. If you look at Table 9.1, you can see how comparable the two tests are.

It is important to remember that the research design, not the statistical test, determines the type of conclusion you can draw. If you employ a correlational study,

TABLE 9.1   Illustration of how correlational and experimental analyses lead to the same conclusions.

Suppose you have two groups with 10 participants in each. Let's label them simply Group 1 and Group 2. If you compute a *t*-test for independent groups, you get: $t(18) = -3.55, p = .002$

Group 1	6	8	7	5	6	9	7	4	8	9
Group 2	5	6	3	7	2	3	1	5	4	5

You can rearrange the data, as follows, showing each score next to its appropriate group:

6	8	7	5	6	9	7	4	8	9	5	6	3	7	2	3	1	5	4	5
1	1	1	1	1	1	1	1	1	1	2	2	2	2	2	2	2	2	2	2

Now we can compute the familiar Pearson product–moment correlation coefficient on the two variables, Group and Score. (When one variable is ordinal, interval, or ratio, and the second variable is dichotomous [i.e., it can take one of two values], the Pearson *r* is called a point-biserial correlation.) When we do this, we get: $r(18) = -.642, p = .002$. The next step in a correlational analysis is to see if the correlation is significant, for which we use a *t*-test with the following formula:

$$t = \frac{r\sqrt{N-2}}{\sqrt{1-r^2}}$$

$$t = \frac{(-.642)(4.243)}{.767} = -3.55$$

If you notice, the value of *t* here is the same as when you completed your *t*-test. The analyses from the correlational and experimental approaches provide the same information.

doing a statistical test does not allow you to assess causation; similarly, if you use an experimental approach, doing a correlational analysis does not keep you from drawing causal conclusions.

Positive and Negative Correlations

Correlations can be either positive (direct) or negative (indirect) or nonexistent. Perfect positive correlations have a value of +1.00; perfect negative correlations, –1.00. Sometimes correlations are so close to zero that we conclude that two variables have no bearing on one another. For instance, Lang and Heckhausen (2001) discovered that life satisfaction and age are not correlated. The value of their correlation coefficient was .05. This value is so close to zero that, among their participants who ranged in age from 20 to around 70, knowing their age doesn't help you predict how satisfied they are with their lives. (This may surprise students who are 20, but it won't surprise students who are 40 or older.)

How would you go about assessing life satisfaction? Lang and Heckhausen simply asked their participants three questions. The researchers combined the participants' scores on the three questions. The three questions are:

- How satisfied are you with your current life?
- How satisfied are you with the meaning and purpose in your current life?
- How do you evaluate your life in general?

The respondents replied with a number from 1 (*very unpleasant*) to 7 (*very pleasant*). Participants with high scores presumably had more positive feelings about their lives than people with low scores. But as noted above, a nonsignificant correlation implies that knowing somebody's age would not lead to accurate estimates of life satisfaction, nor would knowing the degree of life satisfaction give you any information about the person's age.

A **positive or direct correlation** implies that when the value of one of the two variables being correlated gets larger, so does the other. According to another analysis by Lang and Heckhausen (2001), perceived control over life is positively correlated with life satisfaction. This means that, in general, the more control people felt in their lives, the more satisfied they were.

A **negative or indirect correlation** arises when the value of one of the two variables being correlated gets larger, the value of the other variable gets smaller. Lang and Heckhausen observed a negative correlation between the number of negative events in people's lives (like losing something or having a small accident) and their perception of control. When people experience many negative events, they are likely to feel lower levels of control.

> **Positive (Direct) Correlation**—A relation between two variables such that when the value of one variable increases, so does the value of the second variable, and when the value of one variable decreases, so does the value of the second.
>
> **Negative (Indirect) Correlation**—A relation between variables such that when the value of one variable increases, the value of the second variable decreases.

Strength of Association

The strength of the association between variables is reflected in the absolute value of the correlation coefficient. Consequently, coefficients of –.50 and +.50 reflect equally strong correlations. Further, a correlation of −.80 reveals a stronger association than does a correlation of +.50 because the absolute value of this negative correlation is .80, which is larger than .50.

You can change a negative correlation into a positive correlation simply by changing the scale on which you measure one of the variables. Returning to the example of the relation between amount of time you spend studying for a test and your score on the test, we would expect a positive correlation. You could create a negative correlation by changing one variable to the number wrong on the test instead of the number right. The absolute value of the correlation coefficients would be the same, but the sign would change. You would have the same predictability associated with each one. In Figure 9.1, you can see graphically what happens.

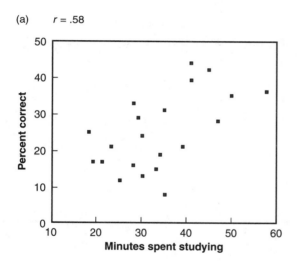

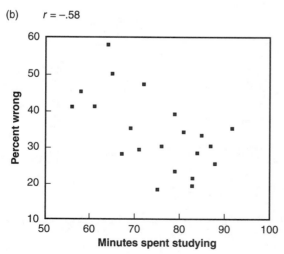

FIGURE 9.1 Hypothetical example illustrating how a single data set can lead to a negative or to a positive correlation, depending on how the variable is defined. Figure (a) shows that more studying is associated with a higher number correct. Figure (b) shows that more studying is associated with fewer errors. Both correlations are legitimate and provide the same information. The only change is in the way information is labeled on the Y-axis. In both cases, the strength of the correlation is the same.

> **Scatter Diagram**—A graphical representation showing the relationship between two quantitative variables, with one variable represented on the horizontal (X) axis and the other on the vertical (Y) axis.

If you create a **scatter diagram** to represent the relation between two variables, as the correlation coefficient approaches 1.0 or to −1.0, the points in the graph appear to form a straight line. As the correlation heads toward zero, the pattern becomes rounder until, when r = 0, the display of data points is nearly circular, reflecting poor predictability. These relationships are demonstrated in Figure 9.2. When r is close to 1.0 or −1.0, the value of Y is clearly predictable from the value of X.

Factors Affecting the Size of a Correlation Coefficient

We use correlation coefficients to see if two variables are associated. Sometimes the correlational tests we typically use can lead us to believe that variables are unrelated.

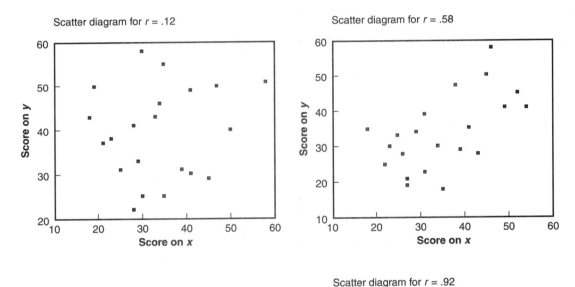

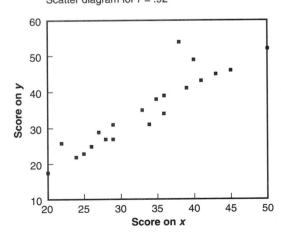

FIGURE 9.2   Scatter diagrams for different values of the Pearson product–moment correlation coefficient. Notice that with higher correlations, the scores tend to resemble a straight line where Y values rise predictably with X values. When the correlation decreases, the scores tend to become more scattershot and Y scores no longer change as predictably with X values. As the correlation coefficient approaches zero, meaningful predictability vanishes.

One problem is that our sample might turn out not to represent the entire population. When that happens, we are pretty much out of luck. We may have collected data flawlessly, but if the sample is not representative, there is nothing we can do about it and we may never know about it. All we see is a lack of a relationship without knowing why.

> **Linear Relationship**—A relationship between two variables that can be represented graphically as a straight line, with the increase in value of one unit on the first variable being systematically associated with a constant increase or decrease on the second variable.

However, there are other, more predictable reasons why two variables are correlated in reality, but a statistical analysis doesn't reveal it.

Nonlinearity.   There are patterns in the data that may obscure real relationships. The typical correlations we use work best when the data show a **linear relationship,** that is, when a particular amount of change in the value of X is associated with a stable amount of change in the value of Y, no matter where on the X axis the change occurs. Figure 9.3a shows a

(a)

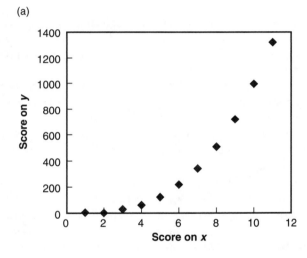

(b)

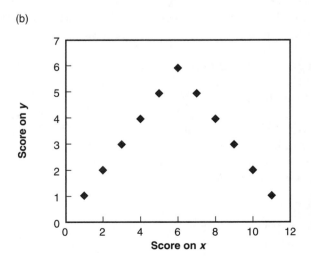

FIGURE 9.3   Examples of nonlinear relationships that obscure the strength of the association between two variables. In (a) we have a perfect nonlinear relationship, but the Pearson correlation coefficient is less than 1.0 ($r = .92$). A change in X from 1 to 4 is associated with a change in Y of 63, whereas the same size change on X from 8 to 11 is associated with a change of 819. This reflects one of many types of nonlinear relationships; you can see how the line curves. In (b) the relationship is again perfectly predictable, but the Pearson r is 0 because the Pearson r is maximally useful for linear relationships.

Nonlinear Relationship—A relationship between two variables that can be represented graphically as a curved line, reflecting the fact that a change in value of one unit on the first variable is associated with different amounts of change on the second variable, depending on the value of the first.

simple example of how the same change in X is associated with a different amount of change in Y, depending on the values of X. In Figure 9.3a, for lower values of X, a change of one unit on X is related to a small change in Y; for higher values of X, the same change is associated with large changes in Y. This pattern of change reflects a **nonlinear relationship.**

If you collect data that are nonlinear, the frequently used Pearson *r* may still result in a significant correlation, but it will suggest a less predictable relationship than actually exists. You may have a stronger association between your variables that you think. Sometimes a nonlinear correlation will give the impression that the two variables are not at all related, as in Figure 9.3b.

If you are working with variables that do not relate in a linear fashion, you should select different types of correlation coefficients created specifically for nonlinear patterns.

Restrictions in Range.   Sometimes there may be a legitimate relationship between two variables, but you may compute a lower correlation coefficient in your sample than you would have if you had access to the entire population. The problem may be with a **restricted range.**

Restricted Range Problem—In a correlational analysis, the failure to spot a real relationship between variables because the range of cores on at least one of the variables obscures that relationship.

Take a look at Figure 9.4, which represents a hypothetical population. You can see a clear, but imperfect, relation between X and Y. A problem can arise if you sample from the middle range of scores and neglect extreme scores. For instance, if you plotted the association between SAT scores and school grades for the entire population, you would see a clear pattern.

If you sampled from your fellow students, though, you would probably not find many with extremely low SAT scores (because they haven't been admitted to your school) or with extremely high SAT scores (because they are rare and may go to other schools). So you are stuck with the middle group of people, which is most of us.

The population pattern shows a trend, but the sample inside the circle shows what would happen with a restricted range of SAT scores. One of the problems is that if you wind up with a small correlation coefficient, you can't tell whether there is no relation between variables or whether you have a restricted range problem.

Heterogeneous Subgroup Problem—In a correlational analysis, the appearance of a positive correlation in an overall data set and a negative correlation in subgroups or vice versa.

Heterogeneous Subgroups.   A third problem that affects the size of the correlation coefficient is the presence of distinct subgroups within your sample that differ from one another; the problem is one of **heterogeneous subgroups.** Consider the hypothetical situation where you want to find out if the anxiety among elementary school children changes as reading proficiency increases. Suppose that, as reading skills improve, children do become more comfortable and less anxious. But suppose also that, as children get older, their anxiety levels start out higher early in the school year, then decrease.

You might end up with the pattern shown in Figure 9.5. When all the data are combined, the overall pattern seems to indicate a positive correlation, whereas each individual group shows a negative correlation. This pattern of results is likely to be fairly

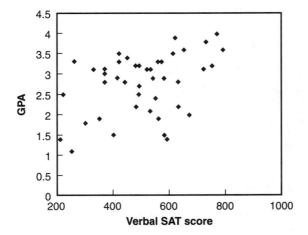

(b)

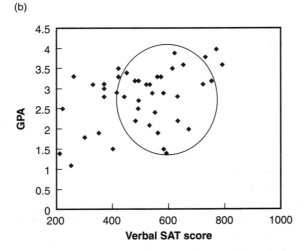

FIGURE 9.4 Fictitious example of the relation between SAT scores and GPA and how the correlation coefficient is affected by a restricted range. This scatter diagram in (a) depicts a correlation with $r = .45$ for this population. If there is a restricted range of SAT scores, which would not be uncommon at many schools, the trend toward higher GPAs as SAT scores are larger tends to disappear. The correlation coefficient for (b) is .29, which would not be significant.

rare, but when it occurs, your correlation coefficient will be lower than it should, because there is more predictability in the data than your statistics reveal.

DISCUSSION QUESTIONS

1. What distinguishes correlational studies from correlational analysis? Why is it important to recognize this distinction?

2. Identify two variables that in everyday life are likely to be positively correlated. Identify two variables that are probably negatively correlated. If you were to study them in a research project, how could you measure them?

3. Why do correlation values of +.70 and −.70 give you the same amount of information about the association between two variables?

4. If you were studying the relationship between income and attitudes in a project you created, why might you realistically face a problem with restriction of range?

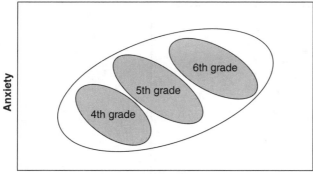

FIGURE 9.5   Example of the effect of homogeneous subgroups on the correlation coefficient. Each subgroup in the fictitious example shows less anxiety as the school year progresses, which could lead to negative correlations within each grade, while the overall correlation would be positive.

TRADITIONAL CORRELATIONAL TESTS

The first correlation coefficients were invented about a century ago; we now call them **bivariate correlations.** They involved two (bi-) variables. Typically, when you read about correlations, they are likely to involve the Pearson product–moment correlation, also called Pearson's r or more simply, just r, which was the first bivariate correlation.

Since Karl Pearson invented the correlation coefficient, there have been important extensions to it. Sometimes you read about the Spearman correlation for ranked scores, the phi (ϕ) coefficient, or the point–biserial correlation. These are alternative applications to Pearson's original correlation. You can compute these three statistics using the formula for Pearson's r. The main differences between Pearson's r and the others might come in applications that are beyond our considerations (Howell, 1992).

Generally, when we talk about finding relations among variables, if the data are dichotomous (i.e., they can take only two values, like 0 or 1 or female and male), we talk about **tests of association.** When the data fall on a continuum, we refer to tests of **correlational measures.** This semantic difference gives us information about the nature of our data, but the underlying mathematics are often identical.

The Pearson Product–Moment Correlation

The **Pearson product–moment correlation,** as noted, is the original bivariate correlation. We call it the Pearson r when we have two variables that are on an interval or ratio scale of measurement.

Bivariate Correlation—A correlational analysis relating only two variables.

Test of Association—In a correlational analysis, a statistical test that assesses whether dichotomous categorical (i.e., qualitative) variables are related.

Correlational Measure—In correlational analysis, a statistical test that assesses whether numerical (i.e., quantitative) variables are related.

Pearson Product–Moment Correlation—A bivariate, correlational measure that indicates the degree to which two quantitative variables are related.

The Pearson r is useful for assessing the degree to which scores on two different variables show a linear relation. For example, there is a linear relation between frequency of parents spanking their children and children's antisocial behavior; more spanking is associated with higher rates of antisocial behavior (Straus, Sugarman, & Giles-Sims, 1997).

Alternate Bivariate Correlations

Sometimes researchers choose different versions of the correlation coefficient. Other widely used bivariate correlations are the Spearman correlation for ranked data, the point–biserial correlation for relating a dichotomous and a continuous variable, and the phi coefficient, a measure of association for two dichotomous variables.

These tests are all variations on the Pearson product–moment correlation, for which you can use the Pearson formula. There are other formulas that researchers sometimes use, but they are merely algebraic manipulations of the standard formula.

The formula typically used for the Spearman correlation will result in the same numerical value as the Pearson formula. The Pearson formula is actually more generally useful because scores with tied ranks make the Spearman formula inaccurate, whereas the Pearson formula is still applicable.

CORRELATIONS WITH MULTIPLE VARIABLES

As a first step in finding out how variables relate to one another, the bivariate correlations we've encountered are quite helpful. At some point, though, we are likely to decide that behavior is too simple to be handled by two variables. So we begin to assemble the puzzle of behavior using many pieces (i.e., variables) and we move from the bivariate, or **zero order correlations,** to **higher order correlations** that relate multiple variables simultaneously.

Zero Order Correlation—A correlational analysis involving two variables.

Higher Order Correlation—A correlational analysis involving more than two variables.

Fortunately, we have quite a number of useful statistical tools to help us begin to fathom the interrelationships among sets of variables. Many of these tools have been around for decades, but it hasn't been until computers have eased the tedium of calculation that psychologists have adopted them.

Previous generations of psychologists (and psychology students) had to wade through hand calculations that may have taken hours for a single test. Then the general rule was to repeat the calculations to see if you arrived at the same answer. If you ended up with two different values after computing the same statistic, you had to go through the process again. The detail and complexity of the computations was such that computational errors regularly crept in. So there is no surprise that researchers were reluctant to use these statistical approaches.

Multivariate Statistics—Statistical approaches that can accommodate simultaneous analysis of multiple variables.

Today, **multivariate statistics** are a common tool in correlational research. The critical component in using them is no longer accuracy in computation because computerized statistical packages have eliminated that problem. Now we have to worry about using these statistics appropriately and interpreting them meaningfully.

Structural Equation Modeling—A correlational technique that can be used to make tentative statements of causation based on nonexperimental data.

One general approach involving more than two variables is multiple regression, which is a pretty direct expansion of the use of correlation and regression in bivariate analysis. Another important class of techniques is **structural equation modeling** (SEM). This approach involves developing models of linear relationships among variables. One interesting aspect of SEM is that researchers can use some varieties of SEM to generate tentative causal statements, even when the research is correlational. In this chapter, the models we will consider include multiple regression, factor analysis, cross-lagged panel correlations, and path analysis.

Multiple Regression

Multiple Regression—A correlational technique that employs more than one predictor variable to estimate the value of a criterion variable.

One statistical approach that has been around for quite a long time because its computations are relatively straightforward is **multiple regression.** If you can remember back to your high school algebra class, you may recall the formula for a straight line, Y = a + bX, where *a* is the Y-intercept and *b* is the slope. That simple formula lets you plot a straight line on a graph such that for every increase of 1 unit on X, you get a particular increase on the Y variable. So if *b* = 2, every increase in X leads to an increase of 2 on Y.

You can see an example in Figure 9.6. If you bought 5 lottery tickets at $1.00 each, the cost is predictable.

In multiple regression, we use the concept of predicting Y from X, but it gets more complicated than buying lottery tickets. Most behaviors are not as perfectly predictable as the cost of lottery tickets.

In multiple regression, we use more than one predictor variable to estimate the outcome. You can compute multiple regression by hand, but it will take a while and won't be much fun. Fortunately, most statistical packages will do it for you.

FIGURE 9.6 Simple example to illustrate Y = a + bX, with the Y-intercept = 0 and the slope (b) changing from 1 to 2. When b increases, the slope of the line does, too. This means that when b increases, every change in X means a big change in Y.

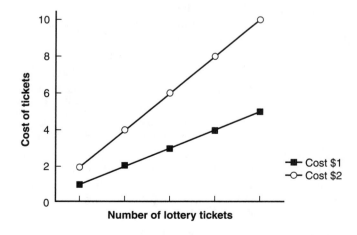

Your equation for two predictor variables would be as follows:

$$Y = a + b_1X_1 + b_2X_2,$$

which tells you that the Y score you are trying to predict, the criterion variable, will be a function of the score on the first predictor variable, X_1, and the slope associated with it, b_1, plus the score on the second predictor variable, X_2, times the slope, b_2. The formula may look intimidating, but the logic is the same as for the simple, one-variable equation: given the value of your X variables, you can generate a prediction of Y.

As an example of how psychologists use multiple regression, let's consider the psychological construct of resilience. Resilience is generally considered to be the presence of effective functioning in adverse situations. Todd and Worrell (2000) used multiple regression to identify the conditions associated with psychological resilience in low-income, African American women.

There is a demonstrable association between poverty and mental health. Poorer people are more likely to be beset by psychological and adjustment problems. Nonetheless, many poor people show resilience, demonstrating effective functioning in stressful circumstances. What differentiates these people from those who aren't resilient?

Todd and Worrell speculated that a number of different factors could be important. The factors appear in Table 9.2 and include whether people have a social support

TABLE 9.2   Predictor and criterion variables used to study resilience among African American women and the way they were defined by the researchers.

PREDICTOR VARIABLES	DEFINITION
Number of Social Supports	The number of different supportive functions performed by others
Number of Social Problems	The number of different types of problems caused by others
Number of Supporting Others	The number of people available to provide support, excluding participants' children
Number of Problematic Others	The number of different people who cause problems
Frequency of Downward Social Comparisons	The degree to which the participants compared themselves to those who were either better off or worse off (on a 5-point scale of "not at all" to "most of the time")
Consequences of Downward Social Comparisons	How well the participants said they fared in social comparisons of others (on a 5-point scale of "much worse" to "much better")
General Self-Efficacy	Score on the 17-item Self-Efficacy Scale (Sherer, Maddux, Mercandante, Prentice-Dunn, Jacobs, & Rogers, 1982)

CRITERION VARIABLE	
Total Resilience	Total of Self-Acceptance, Autonomy, Purpose in Life, and Personal Growth subscales of the *Scales of Psychological Well-Being* (Ryff, 1989)

system in place, whether there are problematic people in their lives, and so on. In advance, it wasn't clear which of them might be reliably associated with resilience, so the investigators examined them all. They determined a Total Resilience score by summing the scores on four subscales of the *Scales of Psychological Well-Being* (Ryff, 1989). They also interviewed the participants in order to rate them on the possible predictor variables.

As you can see in the table, all of their factors seem logical. Most people would probably say that your ability to cope with adversity is going to be related to the amount of support you have, the different types of support available, the number and type of problems, and so on. The reason for conducting this research was to find out if the variables really are associated with resilience.

Using multiple regression, Todd and Worrell found that the Number of Problematic Others (NPO) and the degree to which the women socially compared (SC) themselves to others who were worse off, predicted resilience.

Surprisingly, these two variables predicted resilience better than the amount of social support a person has. This is not to say that social support is irrelevant to coping; what the results suggested is that the best predictors were how many people in the participants' lives were troublesome (most frequently friends and their children's father) and the degree to which they thought they were better off than others. These two variables accounted for almost half of the variance in resilience.

This means that, even though differences in the ability to "bounce back" could be associated with countless factors, half of the difference among participants' psychological resilience was predictable from two variables. By knowing their scores on these two variables, you can get a pretty good idea of how well the participants will cope with the adversity in their lives.

The two important predictor variables fit in the regression equation as shown below. In much research, the investigators often do not worry about the Y-intercept because they are typically more interested in generating the best values for the slopes and then seeing how much variability the variables account for. The standardized regression equation with the variables of Number of Problematic Others (NPO) and Consequences of Downward Social Comparison (SC) was:

Resilience = (−.30)NPO + (.35)SC

This equation tells you that as the number of problematic friends increases, resilience is going to go down; the negative correlation (−.30) tells you this. At the same time, if they compare themselves more favorably to others (and the rating on the 5-point scale goes up), so does their resilience; the positive correlation (.35) tells you this. So this equation tells you that the participants who were most resilient had fewer troublesome acquaintances and relatives and felt that they were better off than others.

Multiple regression has some important constraints. Specifically, it is unsuitable for long-term, multiple repeated observations. In addition, it can only take a single dependent variable. A third limitation is that we can use it only when we have actually measured a given variable. If we group several related variables together to create a new, combined variable, we can't use multiple regression.

Keep in mind that these approaches are correlational. Using the resilience research as an example, convincing people that others are worse off may not cause the greater resilience. Higher levels of resilience may be the cause of favorable downward comparison, not the effect. We are simply looking at successful predictions here.

Factor Analysis

Any complex behavior is going to be associated with a large number of variables. Another way of saying this is that many predictor variables are going to relate to a criterion variable. It would be helpful if we could find a way to take a set of predictor variables that are associated with one another and lump them together, then to take a second set of different predictor variables that are associated and, in turn, lump them together. We could repeat this until we have taken a large number of variables categorized so all the variables in a given group tend to go together, but are not associated with variables in other groups.

Factor Analysis—A type of structural equation modeling in which multiple variables that are related are combined to produce a single variable that is useful for predicting a criterion variable.

Exploratory Factor Analysis—A type of factor analysis designed to explore potential relationships among variables before such relationships have been established in earlier research.

Confirmatory Factor Analysis—A type of factor analysis designed to test the reliability of relationships among variables that have already been empirically or theoretically derived.

This is exactly what happens when researchers use **factor analysis,** an application of structural equation modeling: investigators take a large set of variables and examine which of them seem to be related. In factor analysis, we assemble measured variables and group them into themes; these themes provide the basis for new, latent variables that are not directly observed, but rather are inferred.

There are two varieties of factor analysis. **Exploratory factor analysis** is used when researchers are in the preliminary stages of research on a topic. It may not be clear how variables hang together, so there may be more of a scattershot approach in which they try to puzzle out the important variables. On the other hand, **confirmatory factor analysis** is used to assess whether predictions made by a model are valid. It is a more highly constrained approach. Confirmatory factor analysis is often used to see whether tests, surveys, and inventories are valid in identifying common themes or factors.

As an example of how researchers use factor analysis, let's consider a study of racism, a problem in virtually any country with diverse populations. In the United States, psychologists have identified various measures of racism. One instrument, the Color-Blind Racial Attitudes Scale (CoBRAS), consists of 26 items dealing with beliefs associated with race, particularly regarding the existence of institutionalized racism and the sameness of the races (Neville, Lilly, Duran, Lee, & Browne, 2000).

Participants read each item and rated it on a 5-point scale from 1 (*not at all appropriate or clear*) to 5 (*very appropriate or clear*). Using factor analysis, the researchers determined the correlations among items and found that 20 of the items clustered into three groups. Each group represented a single underlying idea, or factor. The questions on the CoBRAS that relate to one another appear in Table 9.3.

The investigators looked at the first factor and concluded that it reflected Racial Privilege, relating to the fact that people with light skin are generally treated better than people with dark skin. The second factor was Institutional Discrimination, relating to discrimination in the structure of organizations. They called the third factor Blatant Racial Issues because the items pertained to the lack of awareness of pervasive racial discrimination.

TABLE 9.3   Questions on the Color-Blind Racial Attitudes Scale (CoBRAS) that relate to one another and constitute ech of three factors associated with racial attitudes. Participants rated them on a 5-point scale of 1 (*Not at all appropriate or clear*) to 5 (*Very appropriate or clear*). The researchers used factor analysis to find out which questions on the CoBRAS related most closely to one another. For half the questions, a score of 5 reflected less awareness of racial problems; for the other half, marked with an asterisk (*), a score of 5 reflected greater awareness. (Neville, H. A., Lilly, R. L., Duran, G., Lee, R. M., & Browne, L. (2000). Construction and initial validation of the Color-Blind Racial Attitudes Scale (CoBRAS). *Journal of Counseling Psychology, 47,* 59–70, p. 62.)

FACTOR 1 RACIAL PRIVILEGE	FACTOR 2 INSTITUTIONAL DISCRIMINATION	FACTOR 3 BLATANT RACIAL ISSUES
*White people in the U.S. have certain advantages because of the color of their skin.	Social policies, such as affirmative action, discriminate unfairly against white people.	Racial problems in the U.S. are rare, isolated situations.
*Race is very important in determining who is successful and who is not.	White people in the U.S. are discriminated against because of the color of their skin.	Talking about racial issues causes unnecessary tension.
*Race plays an important role in who gets sent to prison.	English should be the only official language in the U.S.	*Racism is a major problem in the U.S.
*Race plays a major role in the type of social services (such as type of health care or day care) that people receive in the U.S.	*Due to racial discrimination, programs such as affirmative action are necessary to help create equality.	*It is important for public schools to teach about the history and contributions of racial and ethnic minorities.
*Racial and ethnic minorities do not have the same opportunities as white people in the U.S.	Racial and ethnic minorities in the U.S. have certain advantages because of the color of their skin.	*It is important for political leaders to talk about racism to help work through or solve society's problems.
Everyone who works hard, no matter what race they are, has an equal chance to become rich.	It is important that people begin to think of themselves as American and not African American, Mexican American, or Italian American.	Racism may have been a problem in the past; it is not an important problem today.
*White people are more to blame for racial discrimination than racial and ethnic minorities.	Immigrants should try to fit into the culture and values of the U.S.	

If you look at the factors, you can see the common themes in the questions. Based on factor analysis, Neville et al. were able to reduce their inventory from a set of 26 unrelated items to three factors or common themes. It is much easier to understand and work with 3 items than 26.

When you consider factor analysis, you need to remember that your conclusions will only be as good as the hypothetical constructs that you are dealing with. Sometimes a data set will come up with factors that don't make sense; a number of variables may be correlated, but there may not be any sensible psychological connection between them. It is important to avoid developing a common factor that doesn't make any sense.

So let's consider the factor of Racial Privilege. Is there such a thing? Are some people treated differently because their skin is very light or very dark, independently of what these people are actually doing? People of color often report that they are more likely to be stopped by police when driving or walking through white neighborhoods in the middle of the night or watched suspiciously in stores. Both are examples of the dimension of Racial Privilege (or lack of it).

To the extent that some people can engage in normal behaviors without scrutiny whereas others doing the same things are monitored carefully and that skin color makes the difference, we are talking about a useful construct. If such a construct really exists, we should be able to make predictions about attitudes and behaviors based on it. The factor analysis of the CoBRAS reveals that a set of questions relates to this construct. Additional research should let us know how people's scores on this factor relate to their behaviors and attitudes.

In general, with factor analysis, you compute a set of correlation coefficients and see the extent to which some go together. Items on a survey (like the CoBRAS) associated with one another may be telling you about a single theme. As a researcher, you have to figure out what that theme is. Factor analysis gives you patterns of data, for which you determine the meaning.

Researchers have used factor analysis to study an issue that can be very important for college students: their mental health. As you will see in Controversy Box 9.2, college students generally show good mental health, even though suicidal thoughts occur to many high school and college-aged people (Gutierrez, Osman, Kopper, Barrios, & Bagge, 2000). With factor analysis, psychologists have looked at the emergence of suicidal ideation and identified why students may or may not seek help when such thoughts occur.

Cross-Lagged Panel Studies

Panel Study—A research design in which the same group of participants is measured at different points in time.

Cross-Lagged Panel Study—A research design in which the same group of participants is measured on multiple variables on different occasions, resulting in the possibility of identifying tentative causal relationships among the variables.

A **panel study** involves the observation and measurement of the same individuals over time. In longitudinal research designs, the measurement may occur across years or even decades, as in Lewis Terman's continuing study of gifted people through their lives, which began in 1921 and still continues (Holahan & Sears, 1995).

We can gain considerable information from longitudinal studies. Typically, though, they are not experimental, so once again, we can identify patterns, but we don't know the causes.

A variation on panel studies is the **cross-lagged panel study.** One important aspect of this approach is that it can lead to preliminary conclusions of causation. This type of study allows us to eliminate the problem of directionality, that is, not knowing which of two variables is the cause and which is the effect. The directionality problem is eliminated because each variable is measured across time, so we can see possible effects on a different variable later on.

■ ■ ■ ■ ■

CONTROVERSY BOX 9.2
CONTROVERSY: Mental Health of College Students

College students generally show good mental health. The suicide rates of college students, for example, are consistently lower than those of the general population of the same age. Still, there are high rates of suicidal ideation among young people, with 30 to 40 percent of high school and college students seriously thinking about it (Gutierrez, Osman, Kopper, Barrios, & Bagge, 2000).

Colleges and universities have to deal with the tragedy of suicides; one consideration is exactly how to work with students who may have suicidal thoughts. In the past, institutions have sometimes taken the action of sending the students home for help.

Recently, though, schools have tried to take a more proactive role, working to prevent the situation from deteriorating to the point of tragedy. We can use the information that psychologists have provided. Often their research involves complex, correlational analyses because life and death are very complex matters. There aren't going to be simple answers because the problem isn't simple.

Gutierrez et al. worked to develop the simplest model possible to predict suicidal ideation. Using factor analysis, they identified two factors associated with risk assessment among students. One factor was associated with negative themes, like repulsion by life, hopelessness, low survival and coping beliefs, and negative self-evaluation. Higher levels on these dimensions were associated with greater thought of suicide.

A second factor was associated with less suicide risk. This factor included such protective variables as fear of social disapproval, fear of suicide, and a sense of responsibility to one's family.

Based on these results, a therapist or counselor might be able to spot potential problems before they get out of hand. But this strategy relies on students seeking help in the first place. Fortunately, psychologists have also identified variables correlated with student attitudes toward seeking psychological help.

Komiya, Good, and Sherrod (2000) used multiple regression to identify important variables associated with seeking help, which include gender, the stigma associated with seeking help, emotional openness, and severity of symptoms. Women were more likely to seek help; part of this tendency is that women are often more emotionally open. As symptoms grow more severe, students are more likely to see a therapist or counselor. Finally, students are more likely to get help if there is less stigma associated with therapy.

The findings by Komiya et al. reflect correlations, so it isn't clear what is actually causing people to seek or not to seek help, but these results can suggest options for increasing student use of counseling centers. Perhaps, if we increase the visibility of psychotherapeutic success and convince people that treatment for emotional problems is as important as seeking treatment for the flu or for other medical problems, we can get students to find the help they need. Psychological research can be an important component in identifying ways to maximize student use of mental health resources.

An example of psychological research with a cross-lagged panel design involves the relation between physical and mental health. For instance, we know that physical pain can affect depression and also that depression can affect feelings of pain (Brown, 1990; Keefe, Wilkins, Cook, Crisson, & Muhlbaier, 1986). By using a cross-lagged panel study, we can figure out the relevant connections between mental and physical variables.

Hays, Marshall, Wang, and Sherbourne (1994) surveyed 2,546 adults who suffered from hypertension, diabetes, heart disease, or depression (or some combination); participants completed questionnaires three times over four years. The participants provided information on their physical functioning, limitations in their activities due to physical problems and to emotional problems, social functioning, pain, energy level, emotional well-being, and general health.

Based on measured variables from a 36-item questionnaire, Hays et al. created latent variables of physical and mental health. You can see the model they developed in Figure 9.7. The data revealed that physical health affected mental health among the variables they studied, but not very strongly. There is no evidence that psychological effects had any effect on the physical ailments included in their study. Note that their conclusions hold only for the particular variables they studied. For other variables, the links between physical and mental variables will be different. As Cacioppo, Gernston, Sheridan, and McClintock (2000) have pointed out, there are some very systematic effects of social influences on cardiovascular function, on genetic expression, and on disease.

The strength of the cross-lagged panel study is that by using it, you can see how two variables are related across time. If an earlier and a later measurement are associated, it may be that the earlier one has a causal effect on the later one. Although the directionality problem may be solved with cross-lagged panel studies, the third variable problem is not. To reduce the threat from a third variable, we can use partial correlations, which remove the effects due to other known variables. The problem is that there may be other third variables that we haven't included in the research.

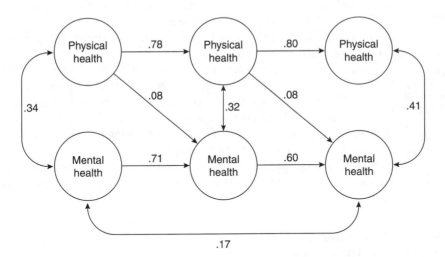

FIGURE 9.7 Illustration of the results of the cross-lagged panel study on the relationship between physical and mental health. The researchers discovered that physical health and mental health each had a causal influence on physical health of the participants. Mental health did not exert such effects on physical health. In this model, lines with a single arrow reflect directionality, that is causal effects. Double arrows reflect nondirectionality, that is correlational effects. The parameter estimates reflect the strength of the association between variables. The effects of physical health were reliable, but not particularly strong.

Source: R. D. Hays et al. (1994). Four-year cross-lagged associations between physical and mental health in the medical outcomes study. *Journal of Consulting and Clinical Psychology, 62,* 441–449. Copyright American Psychological Association. Used with permission.

Path Analysis

> **Path Analysis**—A type of structural equation modeling in which an investigator creates a hypothetical causal model among variables (i.e., a theory), then examines the correlations among those variables to see if the correlations match theoretical predictions.

Path analysis is a variation of structural equation modeling that researchers use to identify causal relationships among three or more variables. There are typically three steps involved in path analysis. First, researchers develop a model to link the constructs of interest. Second, the investigators determine variables to represent those constructs. Third, they examine the correlations between each pair of constructs in the theory.

Figure 9.8 shows the basic format of a simple, two-variable path analysis. Each variable is measured at Time 1 and at Time 2. Researchers represent correlational connections with lines having two arrows; the lines with one arrow reflect causal links. Dashed lines represent relationships that researchers test but that turn out to be unimportant to the model.

After developing the model, researchers figure out how to measure the constructs. Remember that hypothetical constructs are not directly observable, so you have to come up with an indirect way to represent them. For example, if you want to assess the effects of student knowledge on another variable, you could use test scores or grade point average to represent knowledge. These measurements reflect level of knowledge (we hope), but aren't the same as knowledge. The ultimate conclusions will only be as good as the operational definitions of the constructs.

> **Path Coefficients**—In path analysis, the correlational coefficients representing the strength of relationships among variables, with larger coefficients indicating stronger relationships.

The final step is the statistical analysis, which results in a set of **path coefficients.** These numbers are related to the correlation coefficients you already know; they give evidence of the strength of the association between your constructs. Larger coefficients signal stronger relationships.

At this point, you may be asking yourself why we need such complicated statistics to explore the causes of behavior. Behavior is seldom so simple as to be caused by a single variable. And even when one particular variable leads to some outcome, something may have influenced that variable to begin with. Path analysis can help sort out the sequence of causal events.

For example, Bergman, Langhout, Palmieri, Cortina, and Fitzgerald (2002) investigated some of the antecedents and consequences of reporting sexual harassment

FIGURE 9.8   Example of path analysis model involving two waves of data collection. In the model, lines that have two arrows represent non-causal, bidirectional associations. For causal, unidirectional associations, the direction of causation is indicated by the direction of the arrow. Researchers create a potential model, then use the data to see which relationships are potentially causal and which are not. A_1 and B_1 represent measurement at time 1; A_2 and B_2 represent measurement at time 2. A dashed line is often used to represent a path that turned out to be nonsignificant.

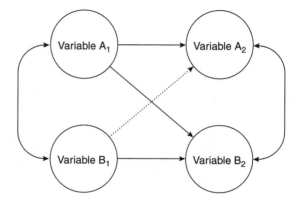

in the workplace. They cited research showing that the outcome of reporting the harassment negatively affected the worker's psychological and health status.

The researchers reasoned that certain factors are likely to influence the extent to which a worker feels that an organization responds satisfactorily to reports of harassment. Some of the variables that could affect the employee's satisfaction with the process of handling reports include the institutional climate regarding tolerance for sexual harassment, the frequency with which a single worker is harassed, the extent to which the worker can expect retaliation for reporting it, the organization's remedies, and the extent to which the organization minimizes such events.

Bergman et al. obtained questionnaire data from 5,757 military personnel for 21 variables, including those listed above. They hoped to identify the consequences of reporting sexual harassment.

With 21 variables, the results were quite complex, but a number of patterns emerged. For instance, the degree to which a victim was encouraged not to pursue a complaint and the occurrence of subsequent retaliation were associated with lower levels of satisfaction about the process of reporting harassment. The extent to which remedies for harassment were in place was positively associated with satisfaction about the reporting process.

Their model appears in Figure 9.9. The relationships here aren't terribly surprising, but the value of this research is that it shows the variables that may have caused certain responses and the strength of the association between the variables.

The frequency of harassment is positively correlated with whether the worker has suffered retribution for reporting incidents, with knowledge of remedies, and with the extent to which an organization wants to minimize complaints. Retaliation for reporting

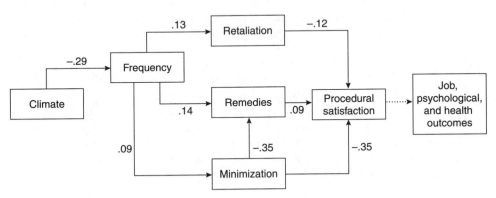

FIGURE 9.9 Example of path analysis that traces the antecedents and consequences of reporting sexual harassment in the workplace. This figure represents only a subset of the data collected by the investigators. The solid lines reflect the association between directly measured variables. The dashed line reflects the fact that the researchers used multiple measurements of job, psychological, and health outcomes; the investigators reported those separately. When variables are not connected by a line, there is no direct association between those variables.

Source: M. E. Bergman et al. (2002). The (un)reasonableness of reporting: Antecedents and consequences of reporting sexual harassment. *Journal of Applied Psychology, 87,* 230–242. Copyright American Psychological Association. Adapted with permission.

harassment and the minimizing of complaints were negatively correlated with satisfaction with the process. Knowledge of remedies for a problem were positively correlated with satisfaction with an organization's procedures to help the victim. This satisfaction, in turn, affects various measures of psychological and health outcomes.

Sometimes the results offer surprises. In this research, less action was taken against the perpetrators when the victim was of high rank than if the victim was of low rank. This outcome doesn't seem to make much sense at first. That is, why wouldn't an organization take action when a high-status person was victimized? The researchers concluded that high-ranking employees are likely to be harassed by even higher ranking people. People at the top of organizations tend to be immune from discipline.

A strength of path analysis is that, in addition to spotting relationships among variables, it can reveal that some factors that "should" be related are not. For example, Ullman, Karabotsos, and Koss (1999) studied the link between alcohol and sexual aggression. They surveyed men who had sexually assaulted women. The researchers concluded that being drunk did not cause the attacks. The predisposition to engage in such behavior was the real reason for the aggression. The attackers only used being drunk as an excuse.

These researchers followed the three steps of path analysis in creating and testing their model. First, they identified a model with a number of possible variables associated with one another and with the outcome variables. Prior research generally provides relevant variables (e.g., Fitzgerald, Swan, & Magley, 1997; Ullman & Knight, 1991).

The investigators then operationalized their variables and used an appropriate methodology to collect data to test their model. In the proposed model, they included potential causal paths that turned out to be invalid. So after their data analysis, they eliminated these paths as part of the model.

Finally, the researchers used their data to discover the most appropriate model for the data they had collected. They used statistical analysis as the basis for their conclusions. As always, the numerical analyses provide statistical facts, but it takes additional work and insight to determine what the numbers really reveal to us about human behavior.

DISCUSSION QUESTIONS

1. How can measuring multiple variables on several different occasions over time let us draw tentative conclusions about causation?
2. In everyday life, we characterize people's personalities all the time. For a personality trait (e.g., happy, which is like a latent variable), identify how you would use multiple constructs when you describe people you know.
3. Why is the choice of variables to study in path analysis critical to decisions that researchers make?

LIMITATIONS OF MULTIVARIATE CORRELATIONAL ANALYSIS

Most tools can be used for many purposes. However, it is important recognize when they should and should not be applied. This is true for the designs we have considered in this chapter.

As computers allow us to use ever more complex statistics, we should have a firm grasp of how best to use them. It can be too easy to use our statistics inappropriately and to draw invalid conclusions because we don't really understand what we are asking the computer to do for us. Further, because of the complexity of the statistics, it is too easy to misunderstand the output we get from our data. McCallum and Austin (2000) have identified some of the problematic issues in using structural equation modeling that involves multiple regression, factor analysis, cross-lagged panel correlations, and path analysis.

Generalizability

The problem of generality in structural equation modeling (SEM) is such that we first need to concern ourselves with the representativeness of our samples. There is more to generalizability, though, than the people who participate in our research. A second concern is whether our measures will generalize. There are many ways to study the topics discussed in this chapter. We can measure resilience, mental health, feelings of well-being, life satisfaction, racism, and all the other variables we have encountered in many ways.

This issue is important in SEM. The models that we develop from a single study are based on specific measurements. Those measurements might be excellent for our purposes, but there are other approaches that might be just as good. It is an empirical question as to whether those other measures would lead to the same conclusions. Once again, the issue of replication is critical.

A third aspect of generalizability to consider involves the effects of time on our measurements. For instance, in their study of physical and mental health, Hays et al. (1994) studied their participants over four years. We don't know if their model would be valid for noticeably shorter or longer time spans.

Some researchers have found that time between measurements is an important consideration. For example, Sher, Wood, Wood, and Raskin (1996) studied alcohol use among college students. These researchers looked at alcohol use and what students expected to gain from drinking (e.g., "drinking makes me feel less shy").

The investigators found that across one year, the students' past drinking pattern predicted the gain they expected from drinking. That is, the students' drinking patterns predicted their expectations about the benefits of drinking. Over three years, however, a reversal occurred: students' expectations predicted their drinking pattern. This is a good example of how our research conclusions may be dependent on the time frame of measurements.

If we want our research to have maximum generalizability, we need to make sure that we consider the people we study, the time over which we study them, and the specific ways we measure them.

Confirmation Bias

One of the strengths of structural equation modeling is that the approach allows us to create models that link important variables to the behaviors that we are interested in. The goal of investigators is to find models that fit the data.

One potential problem in the use of SEM, however, is confirmation bias. As McCallum and Austin (2000) have pointed out, a model that results from the data we collect is only one possible model. They noted that all models are, to some degree, incomplete; the most we can hope for is a reasonably good fit between our data and the unknown reality. This is true because human behavior is much more complicated than even the most complex models we have developed. Thus, no matter how good the match between the data and the model, there are generally other models that provide just about as a good a fit with the data. If you read journal articles featuring path analysis or factor analysis, you may see different models that researchers have proposed for the same analysis.

Researchers are sometimes led toward particular conclusions because of their preconceptions, just as all people are. This tendency may cause them to ignore perfectly good models that, in the long run, may be better than the one they choose.

Most of us show a confirmation bias in our lives, looking to support our beliefs rather than refuting them. The same can happen in the development of models. McCallum and Austin (2000) encourage researchers to take a more active role in considering alternate models, although too often, published research tends to confine itself to testing a single model.

DISCUSSION QUESTION
1. Give an example of a construct that you could measure in different ways. How does the fact that there are multiple ways to measure a construct relate to generalizability?

CHAPTER SUMMARY

We have seen how psychologists use correlational approaches to study complex behavioral patterns. Experimental approaches are useful and often preferred, but correlational studies may actually provide a better means of understanding complex aspects of behavior.

By using correlational approaches, we can see how different behaviors interrelate and we can often apply this knowledge to predicting behavior. When we recognize the power (and limitations) of the approaches, we can begin to understand the complex interconnections among variables that simplified experimental settings do not.

Researchers use correlational approaches to spot associations among variables and to make predictions about behavior. The reason that we cannot use such analyses to be certain about causation is that there may be other variables influencing the ones we are investigating and that if there is a causal relationship, we don't always know which variable is the cause and which is the effect.

The first correlation coefficient was invented about a century ago. Afterward, different correlational statistics flourished and newer approaches have emerged. Some of them permit us to develop complex models of behavior and even to get a hint of causal connections that are not logically possible based on the initial correlational tests.

These relatively new approaches include multiple regression and factor analysis, which serve the same purpose as simple, bivariate regression, to make better predictions about behavior based on more information, that is, based on more variables. Cross-lagged panel studies and studies using path analysis allow us to make tentative statements about causality within a correlational framework.

When used appropriately, these techniques provide us with power tools for understanding and predicting behavior.

■ ■ ■ ■ ■

CHAPTER TEN

STUDYING PATTERNS IN THE NATURAL WORLD: OBSERVATIONAL APPROACHES

CHAPTER OUTLINE

CHAPTER PREVIEW

OBSERVATIONAL APPROACHES

SCIENTIFIC VERSUS
CASUAL OBSERVATION

STUDYING NATURAL BEHAVIORS
Studying Complex Human Behavior
Ethology

CONTROVERSY: *Do Captive Animals
Behave Abnormally?*
Describing the Behavior
of Nonhuman Animals

CONTROVERSY: *Can Animals Rape?*

APPROACHES TO OBSERVATIONAL
RESEARCH
Practical Steps in
Observational Research
Structured and Unstructured
Observations

SAMPLING ISSUES IN
OBSERVATIONAL RESEARCH
Number of Sampling Blocks
Methods of Sampling Events
during Observation
Estimating the Frequency and Duration
of Behaviors

ETHOLOGICAL OBSERVATIONS
IN CLINICAL RESEARCH

THE HUMAN SIDE OF
OBSERVATIONAL RESEARCH
Ethics

CONTROVERSY: *Is Public Sex
Really Private?*
Participant–Observer Interactions
Subject Reactivity
Observer Effects

DATA ANALYSIS IN
OBSERVATIONAL RESEARCH

CHAPTER SUMMARY

KEY TERMS

Anthropomorphism
Behavior checklist
Cluster sampling
of behaviors
Continuous real-time
measurement
Ethologist
Evolutionary psychology

Interobserver (interrater)
reliability
Naturalistic observation
Observational research
Observer bias
Observer drift
One/zero sampling

Particularistic research
Subject reactivity
Systematic observation
Theromorphism
Time-interval sampling
Time-point sampling
Universalistic research

CHAPTER PREVIEW

One of the most pronounced differences between the way scientists study the world and the way that most people observe their world involves the degree to which the observations are systematic and focused. Most of the time, people (including scientists who are "off duty") manage to ignore most of the things that go on around them. If something catches our eye or attracts some interest, we pay attention to it. Otherwise, we ignore it.

In scientific research, we observe certain behaviors or events with meticulous care, trying not to miss occurrences that are critical to our research topic. Depending on the research, a scientist will pay attention to one set of behaviors and ignore others.

In this chapter, you will see how scientists set up the strategies of their research and collect data in the natural world. The approaches discussed here rely on phenomena that exist whether or not a researcher studies it. For example, a soccer game will take place whether a scientist decides to investigate the degree to which players are prone to break the rules under certain conditions. Given that the activity to be observed will take place, it is the observer's responsibility to identify which behaviors to attend to and to define them appropriately.

In addition, researchers have to consider issues of sampling. With observational studies, the question of sampling refers to when, where, and how to select the events to be recorded, not only whom to study. There are several strategies that researchers use in setting up their procedures. Very often there is a tradeoff between what is practical and what is ideal. Observational techniques may require extensive time commitments that involve resources in excess of what the researcher can devote to the project. Thus, compromises have to be made that will make the research possible without affecting too greatly the validity of the data.

Another important element in planning observational research is that of ethics. Is it appropriate to observe people without getting their consent or debriefing them? There are some circumstances where these ethical issues pose no problems, but in other conditions, there are notable ethical considerations.

Observational approaches have a distinct set of advantages and disadvantages, just like any other scientific method. Researchers still have to pay attention to issues of reliability and validity because when the researchers interpret the data to find out what they mean, the conclusions are meaningless if the data are not reliable and valid. There are also some very practical questions that investigators have to address in setting up their research.

OBSERVATIONAL APPROACHES

Researchers can search for patterns of behavior and relationships among behaviors by directly recording how human and nonhuman animals behave in their natural environments. This approach is called **observational research.** Scientists who make use of observational approaches do not typically create experimental situations to study; in many cases, they try their best to remain completely unnoticed by those they study. Observa-

Observational Research—A methodology in which investigators are trained to record human or nonhuman behavior exactly as it occurs, attempting to avoid interpretation or subjective evaluation.

tional researchers try to record behaviors as accurately as they can, noting the context in which those behaviors occur. Observational research seems as if it would be easy to conduct, but there are many pitfalls to avoid.

In this chapter, we will cover various aspects of observational research. Psychologists do not use them as extensively as some other behavioral scientists like sociologists and anthropologists. Nonetheless, these methods can provide a wealth of information about human behavior and attitudes. As with any approach in any science, observational approaches are not perfect, but when used properly, they can help fill in the gaps in our knowledge of behavior.

SCIENTIFIC VERSUS CASUAL OBSERVATION

In everyday life, we observe behavior and make predictions all the time. For instance, if you are driving your car on the highway, you monitor the way others are driving, an-

Systematic Observation—A form of observational research in which an investigator records behavior as it naturally occurs, attempting to note every behavior exactly as it emerges, often in a laboratory as an initial stage of research and prior to the development of hypotheses.

ticipating what they are likely to do. Such casual observation is very important. But it differs from scientific observation. In the latter, we pay methodical attention to behaviors because they are important for a research question that we are asking. That is, we engage in **systematic observation.** This means that we make note of behavior exactly how and when it occurs, without trying to interpret them. Systematic observation generally takes place in the preliminary stages or research, before the investigators develop hypotheses.

It is impossible to record accurately every behavior a person or group engages in, so observational researchers limit themselves to certain behaviors that are important in the current research project. Even if a researcher videotaped an event, coding behaviors is not always perfect.

Think of the behavior of referees in soccer (or any other sporting event, for that matter). In a very real sense, they are acting like scientists who are engaged in systematic observation. While on the field, they watch for certain patterns of behavior on the part of the players; in this example, the officials focus on behaviors that relate to the rules of the game. Referees do not take detailed notes as scientists do, but the referees keep track of important behaviors just as scientists do.

On the other hand, parents are likely to observe their own children in great detail, ignoring other occurrences on the field. Parents are notorious for showing low levels of objectivity: Any contact with their children should be called fouls, whereas their children seldom violate the rules.

Sports officials are supposed to maintain objectivity, just as scientists are. The events that occur are what they are; neither scientists nor referees are supposed to inject their own values or desires into their work. Sometimes, scientists and referees do bring their own biases into their work. After all, they are human like the rest of us. The unfortunate outcome is either poor science or poor sport. The advantage in science is that other researchers may try to replicate the findings; therefore, invalid scientific findings can ultimately be corrected.

DISCUSSION QUESTION

1. Why is focused observation necessary for scientific observation but not necessarily for casual observation?

STUDYING NATURAL BEHAVIORS

When behavioral researchers study people, they are generally interested in finding out how people act in normal circumstances. As such, laboratory studies very often involve behaviors that we would consider normal or natural. These could include whether people will conform to the behavior of others, whether some types of materials are easier to learn than others, or whether young children will cooperate with other children during play.

Nobody would consider this collection of behaviors unnatural. Nonetheless, when researchers discuss natural behaviors, they don't mean behaviors that we consider normal. The term *natural behavior* in research refers to behaviors that psychologists, sociologists, anthropologists, and others study in a natural setting as opposed to in a laboratory. By the same token, scientists call such research **naturalistic observation.** In many cases, those being observed are unaware that a researcher is recording behaviors.

> **Naturalistic Observation**—A form of observational research involving the recording of behavior as it naturally occurs, without any attempt at intervention, often without the knowledge of those being observed.
>
> **Particularistic Research**—Investigation taking place at a specific time and place that focuses on a single question and that is not oriented toward general questions.
>
> **Universalistic Research**—Investigation whose goal is to address a general question that extends beyond the specific time and place where the research itself occurs.

You need to remember that studying natural behavior is not inherently better or worse than studying "artificial" behaviors. (An artificial behavior is a real behavior because somebody is doing it. It is just occurring in an unusual, laboratory setting.) The approach you choose depends on your goals.

For investigators who have a specific, practical goal in their research, like solving a problem of communication among co-workers, the naturalistic approach might work best. Researchers refer to this type of research as **particularistic** because it addresses a particular or specific question that might be limited to a single setting.

Just because the research is naturalistic, we can't assume that it provides us with a high degree of external validity. If you conduct an observational study on your campus of whether men hold doors open for women more than vice versa, the results may or may not apply to any other campus, to older populations, to people in other parts of the country, etc. You have a particular result in a natural setting, but you don't know if the same thing would happen with other people elsewhere.

When the investigators are more interested in addressing general principles, like the conditions that lead people to engage in helping behavior, it is easier to test hypotheses in a controlled environment. We refer to the research goal here as **universalistic,** meaning that we don't intend to limit our conclusions to what happens in the simple laboratory setting. Rather it will have more general, theoretical implications.

Observational techniques constitute a small, but important, domain in psychology. You are likely to encounter it in three particular types of research, involving the study of children, psychiatric populations, and nonhumans. In many cases, observational research is not experimental; that is, researchers don't generally manipulate anything in the environment. Rather, they observe an organism as it behaves in a particular environment.

Studying Complex Human Behavior

People are complex; so are our behaviors. When psychologists use laboratory studies to investigate behaviors, the research generally involves relatively simple observations and measurements. For instance, how long does it take to solve a problem, how much money would a mock jury award a plaintiff in a trial, how long will an animal persist in a nonrewarded behavior, or can people be primed to conform to a group's views? Each of these topics may involve complex behavior, but the measurements that researchers make are pretty simple: number of seconds to solve the problem, a dollar amount given to a plaintiff, number of nonreinforced bar presses, and the percentage of the time a person agrees with a group.

The value of laboratory studies is that they can remove many of the effects of factors that are not of interest to the researcher. What remains is a simplified version of reality that allows complex behavior to be broken into individual elements.

Observational research, on the other hand, involves behavior in its complexity. One disadvantage is that the researcher cannot always tell what causes the behavior to occur because so many things are happening at the same time; the advantage is that the researcher can determine realistically what behaviors occur in a given situation because they indeed naturally happened.

For example, Snowden and Christian (1999) wanted to find out how parents of gifted students fostered their children's development. The researchers asked the parents to complete a questionnaire, then followed up with a visit to their home for purposes of an interview and naturalistic observation. During the observation and interview, the researchers discovered (among other things) that the parents were affectionate, allowed the children freedom of self-expression, and provided materials for creativity.

An important component of the research was finding out how the parents and children really interacted. The only way to do this is to observe directly. As you already know, a household with children is a busy, complex environment, with a lot happening that is out of control of the researchers. Consequently, the investigators could identify what factors in the household might be involved in fostering the children's intellectual growth, but it is impossible to say which specific factors or combination of factors are critical.

Naturalistic observation has also been used to understand preschool children with possible developmental or psychiatric problems. Schools provide a natural environment for observation.

Increasing numbers of children are enrolled in preschools because parents have jobs that prevent them from caring for their children during daytime hours. Thus, with children in the preschools and parents who may not have a lot of time to take the children to a psychologist or psychiatrist, it can make sense for the professional to observe the child in the preschool itself. Further, this setting is a more natural environment than a clinic or office, so the assessment and evaluation can be based on more valid observations. Finally, the preschool setting may be the cause, in part, of problems that develop.

When these reasons are combined with the fact that it is easier to discuss the problems with teachers on site, we can see that naturalistic observation may be an effective means to document difficulties among preschoolers (Kaplan, 1999).

Ethology

Most of our discussion of observational research will involve studies of human behavior. It is important to remember, though, that there are various traditions in studying natural behavior in nonhuman animals. For instance, **ethologists,** scientists who investigate broad or general patterns of behavior of organisms in a natural environment, very often try to take note of a wide range of behaviors. Typically, ethologists study nonhumans, although their techniques are appropriate for the study of human behavior as well.

> **Ethologist**—A researcher who studies behavior, usually of animals, in their natural environment.

There are several good reasons for studying animal behavior. Sometimes researchers observe animals simply because of curiosity. Jane Goodall, for example, cited curiosity as the basis of her life's work studying chimpanzees. At the same time, there are other reasons for studying animals, such as learning about the interconnections of animals and their environments, learning how to maintain the environment, protecting endangered species by understanding their needs and behaviors, developing controls for pests (like wild rats), and identifying strategies for promoting the welfare of animals in captivity.

As you saw in Chapter 2, there are ethical arguments concerning research with animals that need consideration prior to beginning an investigation. Researchers who think that animal research is appropriate are legally and ethically required to keep ethical considerations in mind in planning their work with captive animals.

In Controversy Box 10.1, you will see the importance of understanding what constitutes natural behavior and what doesn't. When animals are captive, it isn't clear that their behaviors are really normal, although we don't always know what normal means. If we choose to study animals in laboratories, as behavioral psychologists tend to do, we may be observing behaviors that an animal might seldom display in the wild.

There are many people who believe that keeping animals in captivity is desirable. These include people who raise livestock for food and dairy products. In Controversy Box 10.1, you can discover what issues are important.

Ethological studies of people can be very instructive as well. For instance, Troisi (1999) pointed out that although schizophrenia shows poorer prognosis for recovery than most psychiatric disorders, there are wide individual differences in recovery. Troisi speculated that there may be a way, using ethological approaches, to identify early in treatment those patients who are less or more likely to recover normal behavior. Based on the ethological data, Troisi, Pasini, Bersani, Di Mauro, and Ciani (1991) reported that schizophrenic patients who made less eye contact with an interviewer and who closed their eyes more had poorer prognoses than other patients. Not only is this type of research useful in predicting treatment outcomes, but it can also shed light on particular behaviors, like disturbed social behavior.

One type of ethological research program involves the degree to which people feel that somebody has invaded their "personal space." Naturally, this topic shows consider-

CONTROVERSY BOX 10.1
CONTROVERSY: Do Captive Animals Behave Abnormally?

A number of people have spoken out against keeping animals in zoos or on farms because it is an artificial environment. They maintain that the animals live abnormal lives and engage in abnormal behaviors. Do we really know if their behaviors are abnormal, though? In order to answer the question, we need to establish what it means for behavior to be normal. One way that we might try to establish normality is through research. If we take appropriate steps, we might be able to identify those situations when animals engage in unwanted, abnormal behavior, then change the conditions that led to such behavior.

If you have ever been in a school cafeteria, you might have witnessed a food fight, with youngsters flinging food across the room. It turns out that cows sometimes engage in food flinging with their muzzles (although they don't throw it at their neighbors). Is this behavior normal? Is it undesirable? According to Sambraus (1998), research has revealed that food flinging in cows is strongly correlated to the rate at which the cow blinks. Further, blinking is associated with excitement. Thus, food flinging may reflect the cow's arousal. It might be possible to identify the source of the excitement and to minimize it. In studying the animals, it is important to recognize that some species of cows fling food more than others. Only systematic research will reveal if this reflects an undesirable state of affairs.

Another bovine behavior that merits research is how often a bull has sex each day. This may seem like a farfetched topic, but it has important economic implications for breeding. In a herd of 50 cows, perhaps half a dozen will be in heat on a given day. In order to maximize pregnancies, it helps to know how often males can successfully mate each day. Some species of bulls would be perfectly happy with 6 cows in heat each day, others would be overworked. To maximize breeding success, it will be important for farmers to understand the behavior of the animals. Only research will give the answers we need.

Sometimes the research is useful for the animals' welfare. Pigs have been known to engage in cannibalism due to crowding, the presence of parasites, too little water, too much noise. The common effect of these problems is to excite the animals, which can result in cannibalism. Research has shown that simply providing straw bedding for the pigs will prevent the cannibalism.

If we are going to raise animals for food, for pleasure and companionship, and for clothing, it is important to find out what to do to enhance their welfare as they develop. Studying the animals in their environments can help identify good and poor conditions for them.

able complexity. When somebody stands inches away from us, we might feel completely comfortable or we might feel a great deal of anxiety. It depends on factors like who the person is, characteristics of the situation, the other person's sex, our own nationality, and many moderators. In fact, distance alone does not determine the degree to which somebody has entered our personal space; variables like eye contact can affect our comfort.

Describing the Behavior of Nonhuman Animals

Depending on what kind of animal a researcher investigates, we see different terminology in descriptions and interpretations of the results. When an investigator studies nonhuman animals, explanations of how the animals act in the presence of others might invoke the idea of territoriality. For instance, birds that alight on railings or power lines tend to maintain a "comfortable" distance between themselves and their neighbors. When the distance between two birds becomes small, they begin to peck at one another, gradually separating to an acceptable distance (Dixon, 1998). Imagine two children in a car who are taking a long trip. They show the same "pecking" behavior with one another.

When the investigator studies people in this kind of situation, results are likely to be characterized in terms of an individual's personal space or comfort zone. Researchers tend to describe the *behavior* of animals, but to discuss the *motives and thoughts* of people.

Even though researchers are studying the same underlying phenomenon, they often use different terms that reflect the history and traditions of the field. When research involves nonhuman animals, we tend to avoid developing explanations that make use of internal, mental processes. Thus, many investigators who study animal behavior may give a description of how an animal responds to the presence of another, but you will seldom see a statement that the animal is "uncomfortable." Discomfort is a human feeling that we can describe because we have language; we can't tell if an animal is experiencing the same emotion that we would in a similar situation.

Part of the reason for this tendency is that psychologists began studying animal behavior in great depth when behavioral theory dominated. Behaviorists were loathe to invoke mental concepts for human or nonhuman behavior. Behaviorists studied behavior, not thought processes that were unobservable and therefore not thought to be scientific.

Another reason for a cautious approach in describing animal behavior is that, prior to the behaviorists, scientists would too freely attribute human emotions to nonhuman animals. Such attribution is called **anthropomorphism.** If you were to say that your dog runs to you when you get home because it likes you, you would be anthropomorphizing. That is, you would be attributing a human emotion to a nonhuman animal. Researchers often prefer **theromorphism,** which focuses more on the animal's perceptions and behaviors than on the way a human would respond.

Anthropomorphism— The attribution of human characteristic to non-human animals, such as an animal being called lonely.

Theromorphism—The attempt to understand the behavior of nonhuman animals by speculating about the behavior within the context of the animal's perspectives.

Evolutionary Psychology—A relatively recent branch of psychology whose focus is human behavior from the perspective of its evolutionary development.

The distinction between anthropomorphism and theromorphism is an interesting one because it can dramatically affect the way we view behaviors. In Controversy Box 10.2, Estep and Bruce (1981) discuss whether nonhuman animals engage in rape in the same sense that humans do. It is clear that the terms used to discuss an issue can be very important.

Ethological approaches can be useful in comparing behaviors across species. In fact, ethologists have a long tradition of such comparative research. Currently, the domain of **evolutionary psychology** attempts to provide an overriding theoretical approach to explaining the behaviors of people with an evolutionary focus. This approach may also be useful in understanding the interrelatedness of behaviors of different species.

Although virtually all scientists recognize the explanatory power of the theory of evolution in biological sciences, the field of evolutionary psychology is still a controversial area; we do not know how useful it will ultimately be in explaining human behavior. At the same time, that is what science is all about. Hypotheses are generated and tested. If the results of research support the hypothesis

■ ■ ■ ■ ■

CONTROVERSY BOX 10.2
CONTROVERSY: Can Animals Rape?

Rape is a vicious offense against another person. It is associated with contempt for the victim, a desire for power, or other inappropriate emotions. Can animals engage in rape? At times, researchers have used this term to describe animal behavior.

Does it make sense to call it rape when a male animal forces himself sexually on a female? Estep and Bruce (1981) argued that we should not use such anthropomorphic terms when describing animal behavior. In describing human forms of rape, we can gain insight into causes and into the motivations of the perpetrator. We can't do that with animals.

Further, in some animals, resistance to sexual intercourse is a normal part of the species behavior. Cox and LeBoeuf (1977) pointed out that female elephant seals normally resist the advances of the male, even when they are willing to mate. Thus, does it make sense to say that elephant seal bulls rape the cows? To do so would be to engage in inappropriate anthropomorphism.

Another reason for taking care in our terminology, according to Estep and Bruce, is that the term *rape* as a human assault carries with it notable emotional and ethical implications. Is it reasonable to talk about animal behavior using human standards? In humans, rape results in severe psychological and, often, physical trauma; it is an egregious break with societal ethics. Our feelings about resistance against mating are probably not the same as those in other species, for whom evolution may have led to such resistance as a natural and normal part of the continuation of the species.

and the theory, we increase our confidence in the explanatory power of the theory, at least until a better set of explanations comes along.

DISCUSSION QUESTION
1. What could be the advantages of studying animals in their natural environments compared to in a laboratory? What are the disadvantages?
2. Give an example of how people anthropomorphize regarding animals, using the human perspective to interpret nonhuman behavior. Draw an analogy to interpreting behaviors of people in different cultures.

APPROACHES TO OBSERVATIONAL RESEARCH

As with any research project, observational investigators have to make some very practical decisions. These decisions are important because they can affect the outcome and conclusions of the research. Some decisions revolve around how to collect observational data. Some techniques require that the observer record behaviors simply and descriptively. Other approaches lead to categorization and summarizing of behaviors that occur.

Practical Steps in Observational Research

Observational strategies differ from laboratory approaches in a number of ways. One commonality is that you have to make decisions about exactly how you want to carry out your study. Some decisions are similar to those in laboratory studies, but there are some unique determinations as well.

First, you need to find out what others have already done that relates to your project. Replication is useful, but you don't really want to devote a lot of time and energy to research that only repeats what others have done. You want to extend your research beyond what others have found. Thus, a literature review will begin the process.

Second, you should develop and employ specific methods that experts in the area will recognize as valid. This means you should develop ways to measure the hypothetical constructs of interest to you. If published research has provided you with tools, make use of them. For instance, Troisi's (1999) Ethological Coding System for Interviews (ECSI) could give you the means for documenting behaviors when people talk. The ECSI was developed for Troisi's work with psychiatric populations, but you could adapt it to your own nonpsychiatric population. The concepts are identified, and the behaviors are well defined. You can save time and maximize the validity of your observations by using an existing methodology.

Third, you must determine the details of your observations. You have to identify the settings in which you will observe behaviors. This will involve the location or locations where you will collect data, the times of day and days of the week you will do it, and the duration of data collection.

Sometimes these decisions may be nearly fixed. For instance, if you are going to set up a videotape recorder and complex instrumentation, you may have to determine which location you want to use and stay there. Similarly, if you are going to monitor behaviors in places where you have limited access, you will be constrained by the realities of the situation.

A fourth step is to determine your sampling strategy. In most psychological research, sampling is largely concerned with the participants who provide the data. In observational studies, you also have to consider what events you are going to code and what your strategy will be during observation.

Continuous Real-Time Measurement—The measurement of the duration of behaviors as they occur.

Time-Point Sampling—The measurement of the occurrence of a behavior by selecting specific points in time and recording whether the behavior is occurring at that instant.

Time-Interval Sampling—The measurement of behavior by noting whether it has occurred within a specified time interval or intervals.

For instance, with respect to temporal aspects of collecting data, you may engage in continuous real-time measurement, time-point sampling, or time-interval sampling. **Continuous real-time measurement** involves monitoring how long behaviors of interest last. Each time the observed person engages in the behavior being studied, the researcher records how long the behavior persists over the course of the recording session. On the other hand, in **time-point sampling,** observers determine points in time when they look to see whether a behavior is or is not occurring. In **time-interval sampling,** the observer notes whether or not a behavior has occurred within a predetermined interval. Neither of the time sampling approaches is appropriate in situations for monitoring infrequent behaviors or when you want to know an exact count of how frequently a behavior appears. We will go over some of the implications of the various approaches shortly.

The fifth step is to train the observers so that data collection is reliable. Because observational research often takes place in the field, there are going to be a lot of distractions; it will help for observers to know exactly what they are supposed to pay attention to. Further, the observers must follow a strict protocol in observing, judging, and recording relevant behaviors. If all the observers are not doing the same thing, validity will suffer. Consistency among observers is important so we know that each person is using the same set of rules in the same way. If researchers don't define the behaviors of interest well, we can't be confident that the observers are paying attention to the same behaviors.

By following these steps, you will be able to create a study that will result in high-quality data. The effect will be that you will have more useful information about behavior in natural settings.

Structured and Unstructured Observations

When you observe behavior as it naturally unfolds, you have to make decisions about what to record. If you are using the traditional approach of watching and recording in a notebook, it will be impossible in most situations to identify every behavior your subject engages in. There will be large and small movements, changes in facial expressions, vocalizations, and so on. They are so numerous and varied that you won't be able to keep track of them all accurately.

In the past couple of decades, researchers have made increasing use of videotaping to capture behaviors. This allows the investigator to view the behaviors as many times as necessary to provide a complete description of what is happening. Even this approach will not solve all observational problems because the camera angle emphasizes some behaviors but misses others. Thus, there is still going to be ambiguity in observation with videos of behavior.

As an example, you only need to watch replays of a major college or professional football game. All too often, even with the multiple camera angles they employ, it isn't entirely clear what happened in a play. There is also room for subjectivity and interpretation. Two people who cheer for different teams will see the same tape and interpret it quite differently.

The advantages of videotaping, though, are that it can reduce the ambiguity of observation and it preserves a record of the behavior more or less permanently. (Video tapes may have a life of perhaps ten years before they deteriorate so as to be unusable.)

Some researchers prefer to make relatively unstructured observations. Such observations entail as complete a description as possible of relevant behaviors that occur. The observer does not categorize or interpret the activity, but only records what happens simply and descriptively.

Ethologists often refrain from developing initial categories of behaviors to record, focusing instead on descriptions of behaviors of interest. The point is to find out what is happening, not necessarily to test hypotheses or confirm prior expectations.

On the other hand, other researchers may decide to focus on specific behaviors from the start. In this situation, behaviors are identified prior to the observational period. These behaviors are categorized and precisely defined so the investigator can keep an accurate and reliable record of behaviors that occur.

DISCUSSION QUESTIONS

1. Identify the five steps that you need to consider in setting up an observational study.
2. What are the advantages of using video recording for observational research? Why are there still going to be uncertainties in what you see or observe?
3. Why might a researcher decide to use unstructured observations early in a research program but change to structured observations later?

SAMPLING ISSUES IN OBSERVATIONAL RESEARCH

In observational research, the question of sampling can be quite complex. In observational studies, the investigator needs to worry about samples of people, of behaviors, and of times during which behaviors are sampled.

Most research does not use random sampling either of people or of behaviors. That is, we decide what materials the participants will see and we collect convenience samples of college students or white laboratory rats, then we observe behaviors that are convenient for one reason or another (e.g., others used them in their research). For example, Jenni (1976) and Jenni and Jenni (1976) studied differences in the way female and male students carry their books on campus. This behavior is one of many behaviors that the investigators could have investigated. Rarely do reports of experimental research involve serious consideration of the representativeness either of participants or of behaviors.

We have to make practical decisions about how to do our research. This is as true for observational research as for any other kind.

Number of Sampling Blocks

Moore (1998) provided a good example of how much data is needed to represent behavior accurately, at least in the observation of problem students in school. He observed three students continuously through the day on 20 different days, collecting data in 8-minute blocks. He monitored several target behaviors: on/off task, isolating self, verbal refusal, daydreaming, inappropriate verbalization, noncompliance, disruptive behavior, and aggression.

He then investigated what the results would have been like with smaller amounts of sampling. Using the data he had collected, he took randomly selected groups of 4, 8, 12, 16, 20, and 30 blocks from the population of 48 8-minute blocks and compared the subsamples to the entire set of 48 blocks. This process simulated a large number of studies with 4, 8, etc. observation periods.

When he used 4 or 8 observations, he found notable discrepancies between the samples and the criterion. Keep in mind that a researcher who used eight 8-minute blocks would devote over an hour's worth of time to the task. Moore studied three students with four independent observers during actual observations. If a researcher observed three children, the time commitment would be over three hours. Multiply this by the number of different observers used. In Moore's study, the observation time rises to over 12 hours.

What happens with twelve 8-minute blocks? Such a study would involve over four and a half hours of data collection per observer on three students. This is a lot of time and energy to expend if the data are questionable. According to Moore, the quality of the data even at twelve observation periods is still suspicious. Figure 10.1 shows the degree of difference between the smaller samples and the criterion value based on forty-eight 8-minute blocks. The dependent measure is the number of times that the students engaged in group activity.

As you can see in the figure, the deviations are striking. If this study had been done with only four 8-minute observation periods, then, according to the data collected by the investigators, the researchers would, on average, be wrong in their estimate of group activity by 50 percent.

How long do researchers actually observe behavior in their studies? According to the data by Odom and Ogawa (1992), researchers collected data over a wide range of periods, but sometimes as little as six minutes. The implication of such a small observation period is that we may not be able to place much faith in the data generated. Moore (1998) pointed out that if researchers are interested in studying changes in behavior over time, small numbers of sampling blocks may provide inaccurate baseline data and followup data. The result would be an undesirably low level of both reliability and of validity.

Methods of Sampling Events during Observation

The goal of making observations is to understand behavior beyond the time of data collection. As such, the events sampled during observation are only a subset of a person's or animal's behaviors. We hope that our sample of observed behaviors is representative of the larger population. One way to increase the likelihood that the behaviors we sample are representative of the population is to use random sampling of behaviors. In the case of observational research, the population is the entire set of behaviors of interest. Random sampling of behaviors is as important as random sampling of people.

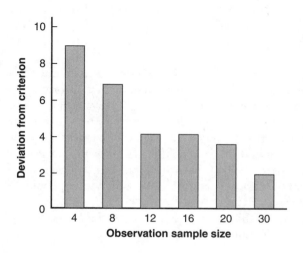

FIGURE 10.1 The degree to which samples showed deviations from the number of instances of actual group activity. The estimates of group activity deviated from a valid criterion of about 17, with greater error associated with fewer observations sampled. With only four observation periods, the estimate of the amount of group activity was off by about 50 percent; with 30 observations, the error fell to about 13 percent. The greater the number of 8-minute blocks sampled, the more accurate the estimate of activity.

Source: S. R. Moore. (1998). Effects of sample size on the representativeness of observational data used in evaluation. *Education and Treatment of Children, 21,* 209–226. Adapted with permission from *Education and Treatment of Children.*

One implication of random sampling of behaviors is that the researchers need to be able to monitor them at any time, in any place, and under any conditions (Peregrine, Drews, North, & Slupe, 1993). This is an unlikely combination. Researchers have personal lives and don't want to be in the field all the time; those who are observed are unwilling to let researchers invade their privacy.

In order to see the implications of various random and nonrandom sampling techniques on research results, Peregrine et al. (1993) monitored touching behavior of children in a child development center on a college campus. They videotaped 32 hours of interaction, recorded the action taking place, and counted the number of touches and their duration. The investigators watched the videotaped behaviors as many times as they needed to code all the variables. (They coded more information than described here.)

Every time they rewound and reviewed the tape, it increased their time commitment. If they had to watch each event twice, they would have needed 64 hours of viewing time to code the data, plus the time to stop and rewind the tape and to enter the data. Two coders watched all the tapes so they could estimate their reliability in coding. In the end, they divided the tape into 32 hours of 3-second intervals, generating over 38,000 time intervals, each one with several pieces of data.

Once this gigantic task was completed, the investigators sampled from among the 3-second intervals, simulating what would happen with different observational techniques.

As expected, when the researchers randomly sampled 10 percent of the data, the results were very similar to the data from the entire population. This means that if the investigators randomly sampled 3,800 3-second periods, they would capture the same basic information as they had when they used all the data. Systematic sampling of 10 percent also worked well. For this, they sampled every tenth time interval.

They concluded that if they were interested in touching behavior within a child development center, they could sample 3,800 random 3-second intervals and end up with a representative sample. It would not be representative of touching behavior in different settings, though.

Peregrine et al. also looked at what would happen if they restricted their observations to a single type of activity, like playing with blocks. The result was that their estimates of touching behavior were higher than had actually occurred through the entire set of 3-second intervals. As they pointed out, playing with blocks involves reaching for them, which might result in greater accidental or cooperative touching than other behaviors.

The implication here is that if researchers select some activity and monitor behavior only during that activity, they might end up with a distorted picture of what happens in general; their results might pertain only to the particular event they sampled. Suppose, for example, that instead of choosing to observe while the children were playing with blocks, they observed during a reading period. Their conclusions would also lack generalizability. The point is that you have to sample across a variety of behaviors if you want to make general statements about what people do in a variety of situations.

Cluster Sampling of Behaviors—In naturalistic observation, the recording of behaviors in specified, extended time periods, a method that can lead to biased estimates of how often particular behaviors occur over the long run.

They also employed a third sampling technique, **cluster sampling of behaviors.** In cluster sampling, researchers pick a start time and watch for some predetermined time period. So instead of 3-second intervals, the researchers investigated what would happen if they observed behavior during fewer, but longer, time intervals.

They found out that cluster sampling is a poor way to collect data. The results from of 15–30- and 60-minute clusters was unlike that from the entire population of 3-second intervals. In fact, Peregrine et al. discovered that in order to generate valid data, they needed to sample 57 percent of the entire 32 hours. This is more than a fivefold increase over the 10 percent needed for random sampling. The researchers noted that the effect of using long clusters is to increase the variability of the measurements, so it is possible that estimates of the occurrence of a given behavior will be either very high or very low.

We can see that random sampling is the most efficient way to collect valid data. The drawback is that sometimes it is difficult to do. Cluster sampling, for example, has its advantages: you can spend a few long periods of observation and be finished. Making observations in more, smaller intervals is likely to be more tedious. The tradeoff is time and energy versus quality of the data. As such, you have to decide on the best compromise for your own research.

Estimating the Frequency and Duration of Behaviors

When you observe behavior naturalistically, you could be overwhelmed with choices about what behaviors to study and how to study them. Research by Zinner, Hindahl, and Schwebbe (1997) shows what is sometimes involved. These investigators conducted a study in which they generated a population of observed behaviors in a group of hamadryas baboons (*Papio hamadryas*). The researchers recorded frequency and duration of locomotion (moving about), grooming, approaches to another baboon, and threats.

The researchers engaged in an enormous initial data collection task. Their database consisted of 324 videos of 45 minutes of continuously videotaped activity in several different settings. They counted how often the target behaviors occurred and for how long.

One/Zero Sampling—In naturalistic observation, the recording of whether a behavior occurs (earning a score of one) or not (earning a score of zero), a technique that tends to overestimate the amount of time a behavior is exhibited but underestimates the frequency of its occurrence.

One technique they investigated was **one/zero sampling,** which is used with time sampling. It involves recording whether a target behavior occurs at all in an interval. If it appears, the interval gets a score of 1; otherwise, the score for that interval is 0. Zinner et al. reported that one/zero sampling tends to overestimate the amount of time an animal engages in a behavior and underestimates how frequently it occurs. Still, they noted that one/zero sampling can be an effective strategy for short intervals; its reliability decreases as the sampling interval increases.

They also reported difficulty with cluster sampling. The main problem is that with longer intervals of observation, events within a period may affect one another and not carry over to nonobserved periods.

DISCUSSION QUESTIONS

1. Research has revealed that small numbers of time samples of behavior do not provide a good indication of how often behaviors really occur. Why do you think researchers continue to use small numbers of samples?

2. For what types of behaviors would one/zero measurements be useful as opposed to real time measurement or time-interval sampling?
3. Even though cluster sampling is not as efficient as random sampling, why do you think researchers would prefer it?

ETHOLOGICAL OBSERVATIONS IN CLINICAL RESEARCH

Ethological research tends not to involve real-life applications, although some interesting research by Troisi (1999) reveals how this approach can be used to study human behavior. He recorded behaviors of schizophrenics during an interview using structured observations. He employed the Ethological Coding System for Interviews (ECSI), a 37-item list of definitions of behavior for analyzing the data after interviews. Table 10.1 shows some of the behaviors and how they were defined. You can see that the definitions vary in detail. The definition of a laugh allowed him to differentiate among different facial expressions, like grins, smiles, and so forth.

Could you differentiate in recording a smile versus a grin? Although in everyday life we can do it, it is not easy to come up with a formal definition of each one that will fit all people and that will result in reliable and valid coding. Troisi, Spalletta, and Pasini (1998) concluded on the basis of ethological coding that schizophrenics tend to show less friendliness and less gesturing than a control group. They also pointed out that some schizophrenics had ethological profiles that were essentially the same as those of people in the control group, which is typical of research on schizophrenia. Interestingly, this type of behavior coding could have practical implications for people prior to the onset of schizophrnia. Troisi et al.'s (1998) results are consistent with earlier research findings that preschizophrenic children showed some of the same abnormal patterns of facial expression that occur after schizophrenic symptoms appear (Walker, Grimes, Davis, & Smith, 1993).

Psychiatric researchers typically do not employ ethological methods. Instead, they use randomized clinical trials (RCTs) and rating scales to study their patients. This approach typically involves creating two or more groups that received different treatments and perhaps a placebo; the investigator usually records changes in behavior or degree of improvement in people exposed to different treatments. The RCTs and rating scales are simply more efficient, taking perhaps ten percent of the time that ethological approaches would require (Troisi & Moles, 1999). Investigators have to balance the extra time and money that ethological approaches require against the added information that is gained. As Troisi and Moles demonstrated, though, ethological approaches provide information that RCTs and clinical rating scales do not.

For instance, gender differences among depressed patients are clear with the ethological approach. Troisi and Moles (1999) found that their depressed female participants showed greater hostility as reflected in the ethological profiles. This leads to the hypothesis that women would be less likely to respond to antidepressant medications than men are. In fact, research has revealed this to be true (e.g., Overall, Hollister, Johnson, & Pennington, 1966). This type of research is important because we

TABLE 10.1   Examples of definitions from the Ethological Coding System for Interviews (ECSI). Specific definitions are critical in allowing observers to record and code data reliably and accurately, especially when there are behaviors that can be closely related to one another, like a laugh and a grin. The ECSI has 37 defined behaviors that measure affiliation, submission, prosocial behavior, flight, assertion, displacement, and relaxation.

BEHAVIOR	DEFINITION
Facial Expressions	
Smile	The lip corners are drawn back and up.
Laugh	The mouth corners are drawn up and out, remaining pointed, the lips parting to reveal some of the upper and lower teeth.
Twist mouth	The lips are closed, pushed forward, and twisted to one side.
Head Movements	
Look at	Looking at the interviewer.
Look away	Looking away from the interviewer.
Head to side	The head is tilted to one side.
Bob	A sharp upwards movement of the head, rather like an inverted nod.
Thrust	A sharp forward movement of the head towards the interviewer.
Other Movements	
Shrug	The shoulders are raised and dropped again.
Wrinkle	A wrinkling of the skin on the bridge of the nose.
Groom	The fingers are passed through the hair in a combing movement.
Yawn	The mouth opens widely, roundly, and fairly slowly, closing more swiftly. Mouth movement is accompanied by a deep breath and often closing of the eyes and lowering of the brows.

Source: Reprinted from A. Troisi. (1999). Ethological research in clinical psychiatry: The study of nonverbal behavior during interviews. *Neuroscience and Biobehavioral Reviews, 23,* 905–913. Copyright 1999, with permission from Elsevier Science.

know that hostile people are less likely to respond to psychotropic medication than are others.

Further support for the use of ethological methods is shown by the fact that depressed patients had higher levels of assertion during psychiatric interviews than controls did. In addition, women showed greater levels of assertion than men, particularly when depressed women and men were compared. The pattern appears in Figure 10.2.

Troisi and Moles (1999) suggested that interpersonal factors underlie women's depressions more so than men's and that it is important for therapists to be aware of this fact if therapy is to be successful. Ethological studies will reveal such patterns, they argued. RCTs and simpler clinical rating scales will not.

(a)

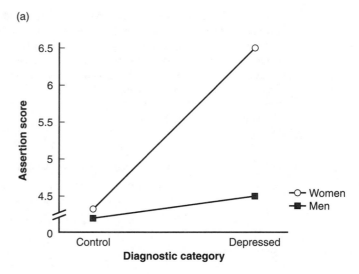

FIGURE 10.2 Differences in level of assertion (a) and submission (b) by depressed men and women compared to controls. The data were collected using an ethological approach that allows coding of behaviors that are not easily obtained with rating scales. This type of information can be important because patients with interpersonally based depression, which will have a large component related to assertion and submission, are less likely to respond to medical intervention than are others.

Source: Reprinted from *Journal of Psychiatric Research, 33,* A. Troisi & A. Moles, Gender differences in depression: An ethological study of nonverbal behavior during interviews, pp. 243–350, copyright 1999, with permission from Elsevier Science.

(b)

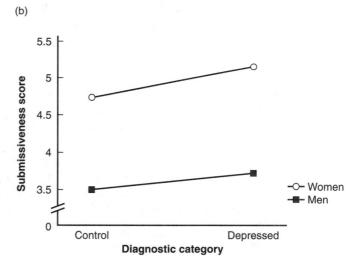

THE HUMAN SIDE OF OBSERVATIONAL RESEARCH

As with any method, there are details that we have to consider when planning observational studies. The issues include the setting in which we will observe the behaviors, the means of recording behavior, and how long we will observe and how we sample the events. We have already covered these topics. There are other issues we have to consider that deal with the interactive and human side of research. These involve the ethics of observing behavior, the investigators' relationships with those being observed, and how personal and social issues affect both the researcher and the subject.

Ethics

Any time you study people, you need to be aware of the impact you are going to have on them. In a controlled, laboratory study you are sure that participants know what is going on because you provide them with sufficient information in advance to decide if they want to participate, then you debrief them at the end. At the conclusion of an experimental session, you can be confident that they know as much as they should know and that you have answered all of their questions.

Observational studies are somewhat different. The people being monitored do not necessarily know that they are the subjects of study. In most cases, they neither give informed consent nor receive a debriefing. In fact, they may lead their entire lives without knowledge that they were studied. It is important to have a serious discussion regarding the ethics of observing them without their knowledge.

In the abstract, the ethical issues of observational research are very clear and straightforward. In general, researchers (and the federal officials who issue governmental guidelines) agree that there is absolutely no problem in observing public behavior when the researcher doesn't manipulate any variables or intervene in the situation.

So if you are going to observe people's behaviors as they walk down the street or in any public setting, you don't need their permission and you don't need to concern yourself with informed consent or debriefing. If you intend to manipulate any variables or intervene in the situation, though, the situation changes. At this point, you are not merely an observer of public behavior. You are a researcher who is changing the course of people's behavior, even if in an apparently trivial way. As such, you should seek approval from your Institutional Review Board (IRB).

Another important issue is defining what constitutes *public* behavior. A common-sense rule can sometimes be all we need. For example, we would probably get no disagreement if we concluded that any behavior in a public park, on a public beach, or at a sporting event is public behavior. It doesn't seem reasonable to believe that people in such a setting believe that nobody would observe them. We would also be likely to get little argument if we were to maintain that when people engage in sexual behavior in their homes, they can expect to be left unobserved.

The problem, of course, is that life doesn't involve only clear-cut cases. Ambiguity is all too predictable in our lives. One notorious example of research that has generated serious controversy involved an investigator who studied men who engaged in sexual activity (which you could consider private behavior) in a men's restroom in a public park (which might make it public, at least to men). Humphreys (1972) studied the behavior of men who engaged in anonymous sex in a generally public area. What is the ethical status of such research?

You might not want to conduct such research yourself, but that is not the issue here. Our personal sensibilities differ, so what one person thinks is unsavory, another might not object to. The critical issue is whether research like that of Humphreys is within ethical boundaries. Such a proposal would probably not be approved by any IRB now; at the time the research took place, in the late 1960s, IRB approval was not mandated; in fact, there were no IRBs at all.

Controversy Box 10.3 presents some of the issues associated with the ethics of this research. You could legitimately argue that the research might have been on the borderline but does not violate ethical principles; in fact some have done so (e.g., Reynolds, 1982). On the other hand, you could legitimately argue that this research is beyond the gray area and should never have been conducted. The important point is to realize that any decision about research needs to come from serious discussion of the important issues, not simply whether we like it or not.

■ ■ ■ ■ ■

CONTROVERSY BOX 10.3
CONTROVERSY: Is Public Sex Really Private?

Normally, we think of sexual behavior as being an intimate and private affair. This feature makes sex difficult to study, especially when the sexual activity is relatively unusual. In spite of this limitation, one particular researcher (Humphreys, 1975) managed such research. It was a highly controversial study of sexual behavior that generated a great deal of debate regarding its ethics.

Humphreys wanted to find out how men who engaged in anonymous homosexual behavior differed from men who were not known to have done so. He went to a certain restroom in a public park where men would go to engage in anonymous homosexual sex. His role was to act as a lookout in case the police or rowdy teenagers approached. While acting as the lookout, he recorded the nature of the sexual activity.

After they had finished, he noted their license plate numbers, then went to the police and, using a cover story, obtained their names and addresses through the license plates. Eighteen months later, he went to their homes to interview them, surveying them regarding other topics.

Is this research ethical? Should he have been watching them engage in sexual activity? You could argue that he invaded their privacy, he lied to the police, he helped them engage in illegal activities. If he had ever had to turn his records over to the police and the men's names became public, they might have been put at risk for psychological

harm (embarrassment and ostracism) or physical harm (legal prosecution). The research took place in the 1960s, when people were imprisoned for such behavior. You could probably come up with other ethical questions.

Consider this, though. You could argue that he wasn't deceiving them because he agreed to act as a lookout, and he did. (He actually got arrested a couple of times while doing it.) You could also maintain that he didn't invade their privacy. After all, they were engaging in behavior with a total stranger that they would never again see and were doing it in a public facility in front of a lookout. For them, you could argue that the behavior was private only to the extent that they need protection from people who might bother (or arrest) them.

What about the possible physical or psychological risk? Humphreys took great pains to keep his records out of the hands of others. He rented a safe deposit box in another state that would have been inaccessible to police in just about any foreseeable case. In reality, there was little chance of harm befalling the men due to his research.

Finally, what did he find? Humphreys discovered that the men who engaged in this behavior did not differ in any systematic ways from men who were not known to have done it. That is, there was remarkably little difference between "them" and "us."

In discussing controversies like this, you should remember that most psychological research is completely within the boundaries of ethical guidelines. Sometimes extreme cases can illustrate the issues that we have to deal with, but these extreme cases are just that—extreme. They don't resemble the kind of research that the overwhelming majority of scientists engage in. The point to consider here is that we ultimately want to treat people with respect. By discussing cases that are potentially troublesome, we can get a sense of how our own research should proceed.

Participant–Observer Interactions

An ethical issue that is closely allied to practical issues is the extent to which an observer interacts with those being watched. In the classical observational study, researchers are removed from the subjects of their study.

A quarter of a century ago, a researcher used a non-interactive approach to see how students carried their books (Jenni, 1976). (This was before the era in which students used backpacks, and the only people who used them were hikers). She observed 2,626 people in the United States, Canada, and Central America and found that girls and women carried books with their arms wrapped around the books and held near their chest; boys and men held the books on their hips. She attributed the differences to psychological, social, and biological factors. This might be an interesting study to conduct now. Have the psychological and social factors changed since the original study?

The investigator had no need to interact with a student; she merely noted how the students carried their books. The situation involved public areas and public behaviors; there would be no particular ethical issues with this research. But sometimes we can't get the type of information we want by using simple, remote observation. It can be helpful to be part of a group in order to see how it functions. This raises ethical questions. If you joined a group in order to study them, you would be creating relationships with the group members.

We could argue that you are deceiving them. Further, we could argue that you are invading their privacy. You might be putting them at risk of psychological harm if they discover your true purposes after they form a close friendship with you. Is it ethical to establish such a relationship with people simply to be able to study them?

We can depict observational research according to whether the investigator interacts with the group and whether the subjects know whether they are being observed. Table 10.2 indicates some of the ethical issues associated with the different approaches.

Subject Reactivity

Subject Reactivity—The tendency people being observed to act differently than normal as a result of their awareness of being monitored.

When we are aware that others are watching us, we often act differently than when we are confident of being unobserved. When people know that a researcher is investigating them, the problem of **subject reactivity** arises. With subject reactivity, people act in unusual ways, so the researcher may not be getting a realistic depiction of the way behavior unfolds. Unfortunately, researchers may not know whether behavior is natural or not.

TABLE 10.2   Relationship between observer and participant in observational research. There are different ethical considerations associated with each approach.

	RESEARCHER INTERACTS WITH PEOPLE BEING OBSERVED	RESEARCHER DOES NOT INTERACT WITH PEOPLE BEING OBSERVED
PEOPLE KNOW THEY ARE BEING OBSERVED	Ethical considerations are minimal as long as those being observed are aware of the nature of the research.	Ethical considerations may be minimal if behavior is public. If behaviors are normally considered private, however, there may be ethical issues associated with this research, depending on whether those being observed consent to such observation.
PEOPLE DON'T KNOW THEY ARE BEING OBSERVED	The researcher might be invading the privacy of the group, deceiving them, and putting them at psychological risk if they discover that a friendship has been based on such deception. The researcher may need to seek IRB approval before undertaking this research.	Ethical considerations may be minimal if behavior is public. Because people don't know they are being observed, they may engage in private behaviors, raising potential ethical issues.

Psychologists who study behavior in laboratories are aware that participants can purposefully change their behaviors, but in the lab, we can control the environment so as to minimize the effects of reactivity. Because observational research does not involve manipulation or intervention most of the time, we can't control reactivity as well. This is why investigators like to keep subjects unaware that they are being observed.

When people know that researchers are monitoring their behaviors, it sometimes does not affect their activities. For example, Jacob, Tennenbaum, Seilhamer, Bargiel, and Sharon (1994) monitored two types of families, distressed and nondistressed. In the distressed families, the father was diagnosed either as alcoholic or as depressed; in the nondistressed families, there were no major psychiatric problems among the parents.

The researchers arranged the methodology so that the families did not always know whether their behaviors were being tape recorded. They discovered little reactivity in either type of family. That is, people in distressed families, who might have tried to be "on their best behavior" when being recorded, did not change the nature of their interaction when they were aware of being recorded, compared to the situations when they did not know. Similarly, there was no change among the nondistressed families.

Why would the families not change their behaviors, given that we know that reactivity is a potentially major problem in observational studies? According to Jacob et al., there are three possible reasons.

First, families have developed routine ways of interaction; it may be hard for them to reliably change the dynamics of their interactions. Second, because families are routinely very busy, they may not have the luxury of trying to figure out how to change their behaviors during monitoring. Third, there may be little motivation for them to change their behaviors. After all, the families have limited interaction with the researchers and no deep, personal relationships with them. So there is little reason for the family to invest energy in changing their behaviors for a group of strangers.

We can't count on such natural behavior, though. As Pepler and Craig (1995) have pointed out, when children move into adolescence, aggressive behaviors may change when the children know they are being observed. Pepler and Craig videotaped and audio-taped children on a playground. The video was remote, but the children wore wireless microphones. The younger children seemed to act naturally during the monitoring. The oldest children in the study acted more self-consciously and were reluctant to participate. If they changed their behaviors, we could expect lower levels of validity in the observations. If they simply declined to participate, we could expect lower levels of external validity because the research would involve a nonrepresentative sample of children.

Observer Effects

There are two noteworthy observer effects that can occur in naturalistic observation. When people have to monitor behavior and make decisions about it, there is ample opportunity for the individual to selectively observe or remember some behaviors and to ignore others. This may not represent a lack of integrity by the researcher, just an unwitting human tendency. Still, it is a real research dilemma.

One problem involves **observer bias.** Just like the rest of us, observers have their own points of view that can affect the way they observe and record information. We all know that any given behavior could be interpreted in very different ways. As objective as observers try to be, we know that people are going to insert their predispositions into everything they do. One way to reduce the effects of observer bias is to create a **behavior checklist** with objective definitions of behaviors to be coded. When Troisi (1999) observed the behaviors of schizophrenics, he used a checklist that would enhance the reliability of measurements. Some of the behaviors he studied are shown in Table 1. With explicit definitions on such a checklist, researchers have little latitude for letting their predispositions interfere with the data collection.

The second problems is **observer drift,** in which the coding scheme used by an observer changes over time. This is similar to the threat to validity called instrumentation that you encountered with regard to quasi-experimental designs. Basically, the criteria used by the observer change from the beginning to the end of data collection.

One of the ways that we try to avoid a lowering of the reliability of our observations is to use multiple observers. We assess the reliability of their measurements to see if they are doing the same thing in their coding by assessing **interobserver reliability** (also called interrater reliability), the extent to which they agree in their coding. Unfortunately, at times two (or more) observers may begin to code in the same idiosyncratic way. They unknowingly change their way of looking at things so that they are engaged the same inappropriate coding patterns. If we compared two observers whose coding strategies had

Observer Bias—The tendency on the part of observers to bring their biases and predispositions to the recording of data, a process that may be unintentional.

Behavior Checklist—A list of behaviors to be recorded in naturalistic observation.

Observer Drift—The tendency on the part of an observer to change criteria for recording behaviors over time.

Interobserver (Interrater) Reliability—The degree to which two or more observers agree in their coding and scoring of behaviors they are observing and recording.

drifted, we would find that, although they tended to agree with each other, their data would not be consistent with that of other observers.

We can minimize the effects of observer drift by taking these steps:

- Using objective criteria
- Systematic training of observers
- Retraining observers
- Looking at interobserver reliability
- Changing pairs of observers so the same people don't always collect data together

DATA ANALYSIS IN OBSERVATIONAL RESEARCH

Data analysis in observational research spans the range from simple descriptions of behavior to complex statistical analysis. In a naturalistic observation study of children on a playground at school, Pepler and Craig (1995) relied on simple Pearson product–moment correlations, whereas in an ethological comparison of differences in schizophrenics and controls, Troisi et al. (1998) conducted analyses of variance.

You can find about as many different statistical approaches in observational studies as you will in any other form of research. Because there is no control of variables, though, you have to remember that the research is correlational. Even though researchers use t-tests and ANOVAs, they can't identify causation. In observational studies, as in every other approach, the statistical treatment will depend on the specific question being asked, the method of collecting data, and the nature of the data.

CHAPTER SUMMARY

Observational research provides us with interesting ways to understand behavior. In the most basic form, a researcher simply monitors and records the behaviors of interest. It is a good way to study human and nonhuman activity as it naturally unfolds. Although observational studies are conceptually fairly simple, they actually require attention to a considerable number of details. In order to guarantee reliability and validity, researchers have to develop very specific definitions of variables and to define precisely those conditions in which the behaviors will be observed.

Depending on the nature of the research, observations can be structured or unstructured. Structured observations entail paying attention only to a very restricted set of behaviors; unstructured observations are wider in scope. The investigators need to decide who they will observe, for how long, whether they want to count the number of behaviors or the duration of those behaviors (or both), and the time and location of observation. All of these factors can play critical roles in the results of the research.

Most observational studies are field studies because laboratory environments are generally too simple to capture complex behaviors and complex interaction. So when researchers begin their planning, they need to consider the ethical issues associated with observing people who may not know they are under scrutiny. The problems don't disappear if you tell people they are being observed because the subjects of your study may begin to act differently when they know you are watching. We need to take great care so that personal characteristics of the subjects and the observers don't produce misleading results.

CHAPTER ELEVEN

RESEARCH IN DEPTH: LONGITUDINAL AND SINGLE-CASE STUDIES

CHAPTER OUTLINE

CHAPTER PREVIEW

LONGITUDINAL RESEARCH
Common Themes in
Longitudinal Research
Cross-Sectional versus
Longitudinal Research

VARIETIES OF LONGITUDINAL RESEARCH
Trend Studies

CONTROVERSY: How Many Students Think of Suicide as a "Way Out"?
Cohort Studies
Cohort Sequential Studies
Panel Studies

ISSUES IN LONGITUDINAL DESIGNS
Retrospective and Prospective Studies
Attrition

DATA ANALYSIS IN LONGITUDINAL RESEARCH

SINGLE-SUBJECT EXPERIMENTATION
Experimental Analysis of Behavior

METHODS OF SINGLE-CASE DESIGNS
Withdrawal Designs
ABAB Designs
Multiple Baseline Designs
Single-Subject Randomized
Controlled Trials
Strengths of Single-Participant
Designs
Weaknesses of Single-Participant
Designs
Misunderstandings about Single-Case
Research

CASE STUDIES

CONTROVERSY: Do You Taste Pointed Chickens or See Colored Numbers?

CHAPTER SUMMARY

KEY TERMS

ABA design
ABAB design
Case study
Cohort effects
Cohort sequential
design
Cohort study

Cross-sectional
research
Gerontologist
Grounded theory
Longitudinal research
Multiple baseline
design

N of 1 randomized
clinical trial
Panel study
Prospective study
Retrospective study
Trend studies
Withdrawal design

CHAPTER PREVIEW

In this chapter we will cover some techniques that deal with different types of research questions than we have encountered previously. The approaches here are typically employed by researchers with questions that involve in-depth study of people.

Each of these domains has developed its own traditions that sometimes differ from the ones we have already covered. This research may also answer different types of questions. All of these specialized designs have strengths and weaknesses. Both of them have added to our understanding of behavior.

Psychologists who study development across time make use of longitudinal research. In this field, we have to deal with change over a long period, sometimes years and decades. As a result, there are special considerations to ponder. When our studies are temporally compact and can be created and completed within a matter of weeks, we think differently from when our studies will not be over for a very long time.

A second specialized research design involves single-participant research. In applied fields, particularly in psychotherapeutic settings, and in theoretical work, we may be interested in studying a single individual in depth. We can do so in a quantitative way, with N of 1 randomized clinical trials and experimental analysis of behavior that often entails animal research. We can also use the relatively rare case study approach that tends to be more qualitative.

LONGITUDINAL RESEARCH

If you observe people long enough, you will see that they change in predictable ways. Sometimes the changes take place fairly quickly. Infants one year old are very different than they were even a month or two before. College students become much more sophisticated thinkers between the start of their college careers and their graduation. More mature adults show consistent developmental changes as they progress from being the "young-old," the "old," and finally, the "old-old."

Psychologists have developed techniques to study people at different stages in their lives. One such approach is called **longitudinal research.** In psychology, longitudinal research refers to the study of individuals over time, using repeated measurements. It is similar in many ways to the other methods you know about, but there are also some elements that are unique because such projects can extend over long periods.

Longitudinal Research—A design in which an investigator studies the same people or the same population (but different individuals) over time, sometimes across decades.

Gerontologist—A researcher who studies people in old age and the aging process.

Within psychology, developmental psychologists make greatest use of longitudinal research. A developmental psychologist, or developmentalist, is interested in the nature and causes of change. Developmentalists may specialize in a particular part of the lifespan, including infant years, adolescence, early adulthood, or old age. Just as psychologists who study children may limit their focus to infancy, the toddler period, or some other pre-adolescent time, psychologists specializing in the elderly (who may be called **gerontologists**) sometimes focus on one of the specific categories of old age.

Common Themes in Longitudinal Research

When researchers study change over either a short or a long time span, they investigate the psychological and physiological causes of development. We can conveniently categorize the sources of difference among people into three general groups. First, some researchers may focus on genetic differences that underlie behavior. Scientists recognize that genetic factors can affect behaviors that psychologists study, but the extent to which genes control behavior is overwhelmed by other factors. Genetic factors may explain up to 25% of the variability in cognitive ability across different people, but much less for personality characteristics (Schaie, 2000). These figures suggest that the vast majority of individual differences arise from causes other than genetics.

A second potential cause for individual differences is environmental. Thus, a person's education, family structure, socialization, and access to good nutrition and health care will have an effect on behavior and attitudes. Not surprisingly, these situational factors are important for the emergence of most of the variability in behavior. Another environmental (i.e., social) aspect of change involves cohort effects that begin to exert pronounced consequences beginning with school years, but less so during infancy and toddlerhood.

Research on environmental causes of change is complex because it is virtually impossible to identify all of the individual factors that affect even the simplest of behaviors. Further, almost all longitudinal research is descriptive, not experimental. That is, the investigators do not manipulate independent variables in a controlled setting. Rather, they follow the course of a person's life over some time span and try to isolate important causes of behavior. This correlational approach allows us to spot relationships among variables, but not causes.

A third domain involves the interaction between genetics and environment. The reason for complexity here is that we still have a very incomplete knowledge base related to how genes and the environment interact for different people. For some behaviors, we will probably ultimately conclude that a complete understanding requires knowledge both of genetic and of environmental factors, particularly for some psychological disorders.

Many of the underlying research concerns are similar, regardless of time of life studied. We have to pay attention to the sample and whether it represents the population we are interested in. We also have to minimize the threats to internal and external validity. In this section, you will see how psychologists plan longitudinal research so that it is maximally informative.

Cross-Sectional versus Longitudinal Research

When we discuss contemporary research, it is easy to assume that psychologists have always used the methods we now use. In reality, research strategies have to be invented. Normally, we persist in using the approach with which we are most comfortable. It is likely to be the approach that our peers and contemporaries use. That is why so many research reports describe similar methods.

On the other hand, when we become aware of the limitations of the dominant strategies, we work to overcome them. It isn't always clear how to fix the problems. It takes a lot of thought and testing to determine how to replace a current method with a valid new approach. When somebody develops a new strategy, it might be "obvious" that it is appropriate, but until we create a new blueprint, it really isn't all that obvious.

Psychologists who study developmental processes have developed increasingly useful strategies. Initially, the approach to developmental questions, particularly for studying aging, did not include longitudinal research. Instead researchers used **cross-sectional research** (Schaie, 2000). From the beginning of the 1900s and for the subsequent several decades, if investigators wanted to know how younger and older adults differed in their intellectual functioning, they would locate two samples, one younger and one older, and assess differences in their abilities.

> **Cross-Sectional Re-search**—A design in which an investigator studies groups differing on some characteristic (e.g., age) at the same time, in contrast to a longitudinal approach that studies the same individuals over time.

Although cross-sectional studies dominated, not all psychologists used them exclusively. Lewis Terman's longitudinal study of gifted people from childhood into old age is a case in point. The research began in the 1920s, when cross-sectional studies were the norm. (The vast majority of experimental research still employs cross-sectional research.)

Although a cross-sectional plan seemed like a reasonable approach for the first three decades of the twentieth century, after a while some cracks appeared in the foundation. For instance, researchers discovered that they could not replicate the well-documented decline in cognitive functioning across the lifespan that early cross-sectional studies reported (Jones & Conrad, 1933). Gradually through 1930s, longitudinal studies became more common.

Researchers began to realize that in a nonequivalent groups design that investigates groups of people who grew up in different eras, the participants differed in more than just age. They experienced life from a different viewpoint, and may have had different opportunities for education and health care. Any of these factors (or countless others) could affect mental abilities; age might be important but it might also be irrelevant.

> **Cohort Effects**—Differences across age groups having to do with characteristics of the era in which a person grew up rather than to age effects specifically.

Differences between groups that result from participants having had quite different life experiences are called **cohort effects.** A cohort is a population whose members have some specific characteristic in common, like a birth cohort, a group of people born about the same time. A cohort doesn't have to rely on age; studying psychology majors as compared to other majors will also involve different cohorts.

Once researchers accepted the notion of studying the same people over time, investigators often used two-point studies, with researchers observing their participants twice. Such studies were useful, but they were not perfect. One of the problems with two-point studies is statistical regression, sometimes called regression to the mean. It refers to the fact that when people are measured and show extreme scores, they often have less extreme scores the next time. In many cases, extreme scores include a large amount of measurement error. That error is unlikely to repeat itself in subsequent measurements. So when changes in scores occur, the result might be meaningless in a developmental sense.

Further, some variables that researchers measure show different results in cross-sectional and longitudinal studies, with longitudinal studies sometimes failing to replicate cross-sectional studies and sometimes showing greater differences (Schaie, 1992).

The methodological innovation that has allowed greater understanding of the developmental process is the longitudinal approach. Once psychologists recognized the realities of cohort effects, they began to study the same individuals across time. This strategy removes some of the difficulties associated with cross-sectional research.

DISCUSSION QUESTIONS

1. Of the four sources of differences that psychologists have identified, which are likely to be important in student learning? Why?
2. In your own life, there may be different cohort effects than age. Give an example of a study you might conduct with your fellow students that could involve cohort effects.

VARIETIES OF LONGITUDINAL RESEARCH

Researchers generally categorize longitudinal research according to the way participants are selected for a study. In some longitudinal research, the measurements at each time interval involve the same people. In other designs, the measurements include different people across time. Psychological research is more likely to include the same people in each observation frame. Other research may sample from a population without concerns as to whether the same individuals are included. Such studies often involve large, perhaps national, samples.

Another way to categorize psychological studies may involve direct observation of behaviors or questionnaires and frequently involve panel studies, which are described below. Sociologists and medical researchers are often more likely to make use of trend and cohort studies, which are often much larger in scope than those done by psychologists who have direct contact with participants.

Trend Studies

When investigators assess a general population across time, they sometimes sample randomly at each data-collection point. Depending on the nature of the study, this approach can result in a completely different sample each time. This total replacement of participants is characteristic of **trend studies.**

Trend Studies—A variety of longitudinal research in which an investigator samples randomly from a generally defined population over time, with different individuals constituting each sample.

The National Assessment of Educational Progress (NAEP) project is an example of a trend study. Since 1971, students at grades 4, 8, and 12 have been tested in a variety of subject areas, such as reading, mathematics, and science. The results are often called the "nation's report card."

In Figure 11.1, you can see how twelfth-grade high school students have progressed in their reading since 1971. In spite of complaints about how students cannot read as well as they used to, it is pretty clear that, if any trend is apparent, students have shown improvement over the past 30 years. If you look at the scores of the high school girls, their average performance rose dramatically in 1984 and has continued to inch upward since then. Boys, on the other hand, peaked in 1988 and declined somewhat, although their scores are higher than those of boys in 1971.

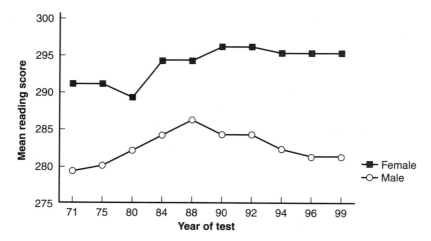

FIGURE 11.1   Reading scores by gender on the National Assessment of Educational Progress (NAEP) test for students 17 years of age since 1971. The assessment uses a random sample of students at each data collection point so there is little or no overlap among participants. This is an example of a trend study.

At each NAEP testing, there will be a different set of students because when the test is administered every two or three years, the students in the twelfth grade will have changed. The samples used in NAEP can be considered to involve different cohorts in one sense because the actual participants differ each time, but they involve the same cohort in the sense that they sample twelfth graders each time. (The unfortunate student who is in the twelfth grade for three years and is selected to participate in two tests is rare and unlikely to be sampled more than once.)

Another type of trend study might include some of the same participants. If we were interested in the extent to which eighth-grade teachers include novels in their reading assignments, we could sample from that population of teachers periodically. Some teachers might appear in both samples. As long as the sample is large, though, the instances of such overlap will be minimal. In any case, if the sampling is random, we will likely generate a representative sample each time, regardless of the degree of overlap among participants.

Trend studies typically involve applied research. They may be associated with long-term changes associated with critical societal issues. For instance, contemporary students often claim high levels of stress. Will pressures on students lead to thoughts of suicide? The state of Vermont has researched this topic. Vermont public officials have commissioned trend studies of various aspects of the lives of adolescents. The surveys assess the degree to which the students have used alcohol and other drugs, engaged in sexual behavior, and thought of suicide, along with many other issues.

In Controversy Box 11.1, you can read about the prevalence of suicidal thoughts and attempts in Vermont. The problem of suicide among young people, including college students, isn't something that we can ignore.

CONTROVERSY BOX 11.1
CONTROVERSY: How Many Students Think of Suicide as a "Way Out"?

Late adolescence and young adulthood seem like precarious times for youth in the United States. One manifestation of the problem is suicides on college campuses. Such tragedies are in the news all too frequently. As of a few years ago, Penn State suffered an average of two student suicides a year, according to its online student newspaper, *The Digital Collegian* (July 24, 1997).

In other well publicized news, three Massachusetts students (at MIT, Harvard, and the University of Massachusetts at Amherst) died during a single week in 1998 amid suspicion that the deaths were suicides, according to a story in the *Christian Science Monitor* (April 7, 1998). MIT and Harvard lead the nation in student suicides, as noted in the University of Illinois's *Daily Illini* (February 14, 2001). When these deaths occur, college administrators and faculty ponder what they can do to keep students from feeling the despair that leads them to take their lives.

Any suicide is a calamity for the friends and family of the victim, but we don't know whether suicide rates are going up or down, or staying the same. Colleges only began keeping track of suicides in 1990. Ironically, given the media attention when suicides occur on campuses, the suicide rate among students is half the rate of others the same age. Over the past decades, suicides among the young have increased dramatically, though.

We can figure the suicide rate among students, but how many students actually think about suicide? Fortunately, researchers in Vermont, in an attempt to anticipate and prevent problems in the state, have collected data from middle- and high-school students over time that may shed light on the question. This trend study sampled from the state's population of high school students in 1993, 1995, and 1997.

The percentage of students who have had suicidal ideation (i.e., thoughts of suicide) in the twelve months prior to the survey was alarmingly high, as shown in Figure 11.2. As many as a quarter of the students in middle and high school have

thought about suicide. Luckily, many fewer make plans or attempt suicide. The results of this trend study suggest that we cannot ignore the problems of the young. In fact, David Satcher, former Surgeon General of the United States, has declared that suicide is a public health crisis. College officials have begun to pay significant attention to ways of preventing student deaths.

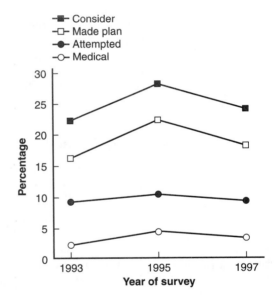

FIGURE 11.2 Incidence of suicide ideation and attempts among students in Vermont. Thoughts of suicide occurred to up to 25 percent of students, while decreasing numbers actually made a plan, attempted suicide, and required medical attention after an attempt. (*Consider* = Considered committing suicide; *Made Plan* = Actually make a plan to commit suicide; *Attempted* = Carried out a suicide attempt; *Medical* = Carried out an attempt that required medical intervention)

Cohort Studies

> **Cohort Study**—A variety of longitudinal research in which an investigator samples randomly from a population selected because of a specific characteristic, often age.

When researchers study a specific, well-defined population over time but sample different people at each data collection point, they are using a **cohort study.** (Trend studies examine more general populations.)

One of the most well known cohort studies is the Nurses Health Study, which began in 1976. It involves about 122,000 nurses from the original cohort, followed by a new generation of nurses in 1989. (This research design is known in the medical field as an observational epidemiology study.) The project began in order to study the long-term effects of using oral contraceptives. Every two years, cohort members receive a survey with questions about health-related topics. At the request of the participants, the investigators began adding questions on a variety of topics, like smoking, nutrition, and quality of life issues. The researchers even collected toenail clippings so they could identify minerals in food that the participants ate.

Psychologists do not use trend studies or cohort studies very extensively. These approaches are more within the province of medical research. Psychologists can benefit from the data, though. It is not unusual for researchers to make their large data sets available to others. Thus, when there is a large database that extends across years or decades, psychologists can identify questions of interest and see how respondents have answered. For instance, the Nurses Health Study includes quality of life information that might help us answer behavioral and attitudinal questions.

Cohort Sequential Studies

If you wanted to compare younger and older people, you could use a cross-sectional design wherein you select samples of such individuals and investigate differences that might exist between them. The problem in interpretation, as mentioned before, is that the people have different life experiences because of the times in which they grew up. You may not be able to attribute differences to age alone.

> **Cohort Sequential Design**—A variety of longitudinal research in which an investigator repeatedly measures a cohort group (e.g., people 60 years of age) over time, adding a new cohort (e.g., new 60-year-olds) in each wave in order to differentiate between cohort effects and age effects.

One solution to this problem is the **cohort sequential design.** In this approach, you study people of a given age, for example, 60 years old, then study them at some later point, like when they are 67. During the second test, you could also investigate a new group of 60-year-olds.

This gives you the opportunity to test 60-year-olds from slightly different eras to see if there is something special about being 60. You can also see how people change over time. The cohort sequential design mixes the cross-sectional approach with the longitudinal.

A classic example of this research began in the 1950s by Warner Schaie. He selected a group of elderly people and tested them every seven years. At the second testing phase, he assessed the original group but also included a new group of people that he tested every seven years. This second group was as old when tested as the first group was at its initial testing. Then, at the third testing phase, he included a new group that was as old as his first group at their initial testing. So he started with a group of 60-year-olds. Seven years later, he tested these people who were now 67 and began assessment of a new group of 60-year-olds. After another seven years, he brought in a new group of 60-year-olds to compare with the second group, now aged 67, and the first group, now aged 74.

Over four decades, he tested different groups at the same age in their lives but who grew up in different times. He was able to spot changes in their behavior as they aged and was also able to look for differences that might be attributable to cohort effects. Figure 11.3 shows some of Schaie's (2000) results on inductive reasoning tasks. (In general, inductive reasoning tasks require a person to consider individual facts and to draw some kind of conclusion from them.)

As you can see, people performed very differently depending on when they were born. Earlier birth dates were associated with poorer performance for the same age. When people born in 1896 were tested at age 60, their performance was clearly lower than the cohorts from all other birth years. In fact, you can see that with each successive cohort, performance at age 60 was higher than that of the previous cohort.

Thus, there is nothing special about the absolute test scores at age 60 (or at any other age); it is more reasonable to believe that having been born later led to different experiences, perhaps involving education, nutrition, health care, etc. that would be important in development and maintenance of their skill in inductive reasoning.

The strength of the cohort sequential design is that it can help you spot changes due to age as well as to differences in the environment in which people develop.

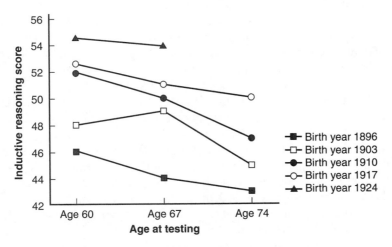

FIGURE 11.3   Inductive reasoning scores for adults born at 7-year intervals from 1896 through 1924. Notice that the more recent cohorts show greater performance in inductive reasoning at any given age.

Source: Schaie, K. W. (2000). The impact of longitudinal studies on understanding development from young adulthood to old age. *International Journal of Behavioral Development, 24,* 257–266, p. 263. Reprinted with permission of The International Society for the Study of Behavioural Development.

Panel Studies

Panel Study—A variety of longitudinal research in which an investigator studies the same individuals over time.

Another general category of longitudinal studies is the **panel study.** In this design, the same participants are followed throughout the course of the study. The most famous study of people throughout their lifespan was initiated by Lewis Terman in the 1920s. When he began, he didn't suspect that it would become a lifelong enterprise for him. At his death in 1956, the research was still going strong. In fact, his successors have kept it alive through its seventh decade.

Terman was born in Indiana in 1877 but moved to Los Angeles after contracting tuberculosis. (Ironically, the relocation was for the clean air that he could expect in Los Angeles at that time.) While teaching there, he identified 1,528 children with IQ scores over 135 and compared them to a comparable group of unselected children, a typical cross-sectional approach. Many writers have detailed the research (e.g., Holahan & Sears, 1995) but, in essence, the gifted children and adolescents matured into adults who tended to be happy, healthy, successful, and productive through the seven decades of the project.

A more typical example of a longitudinal study involved a project that investigated the effects of bullying on young teenagers. This project lasted through one school year and into a second (Bond, Carlin, Thomas, Rubin, & Patton, 2001). Investigators have documented that being bullied is strongly associated with depression (Hawker & Boulton, 2000). Unfortunately, the cross-sectional studies comparing depression in bullied and non-bullied groups do not allow assessment of causality because these nonequivalent control groups designs are correlational. One remedy is to engage in a prospective study in which individuals are monitored over a period of time; this approach contrasts with retrospective studies in which people must recall events from the past.

Bond and colleagues (2001) examined bullying among high-school students in Australia in three waves, that is, at three data collection points. They administered questionnaires to 2,680 students, twice in grade 8 and once in grade 9. The investigators found that recurrent victimization like being teased or excluded, having rumors spread about them, and being physically threatened predicted depression for girls, but not for boys.

One tentative conclusion was that being bullied might cause depression. The researchers noted that previous depression did not predict being bullied; that is, depressed students were not singled out for bullying because they appeared fragile or vulnerable. Students with no sign of depression who were bullied subsequently showed depression, so bullying might be a causal agent. However, as with most longitudinal research, this project was correlational. Longitudinal studies that involve manipulated independent variables are relatively rare in psychology.

DISCUSSION QUESTIONS

1. Why are sampling issues an important consideration in trend studies?
2. What is the difference between a cohort study and a cohort sequential study? Give an example of a cohort sequential study you could conduct on your fellow students.

ISSUES IN LONGITUDINAL DESIGNS

Longitudinal designs have provided us with a wealth of information about the ways we develop over time. They can be adapted for use with populations ranging from neonates and infants to the very old. If you are patient enough, you can monitor changes over months, years, and even decades.

As with any design, though, we have to recognize the weaknesses as well as the strengths of this approach. Researchers have discovered effective uses of long-term studies, but we have also looked at those situations where the information from longitudinal research may have lower validity than we would like.

Retrospective and Prospective Studies

When we want to see how people change over time, it is generally easier to ask them about critical events at a single point in time, relying on their memories for past events.

> **Retrospective Study—** An approach to studying change over time that relies on people's memories and recollections of the past.

This happens in a **retrospective study.** It is certainly more convenient for the researcher. Unfortunately, it is also prone to distortions from memory lapses. There is ample evidence, particularly from survey researchers, that our memories are predictably faulty over time. An additional consideration regarding retrospective research is that it cannot involve experimental manipulation of variables, so it is always quasi-experimental or ex post facto. Consequently, it is not possible to identify causal relationships among variables with confidence.

We have trouble with mundane information. For instance, Wentland and Smith (1993) found that a significant percentage of people have a hard time remembering if they have a library card. As an example of faulty memories for major events, Cannell, Fisher, and Bakker (1965, cited in Judd, Smith, & Kidder, 1991) demonstrated that people erred in determining how many times they have been hospitalized in the past year.

We are also likely to reconstruct details of the past, in effect creating memories that fit the overall structure of what we are trying to recall. We don't do this intentionally, but it happens just the same. In longitudinal research, we shouldn't expect people to show high levels of mnemonic accuracy for remote events, even for significant events. This is particularly true when we want to know about children's behaviors. Asking their parents does not lead to greater accuracy.

> **Prospective Study—An** approach to studying change over time that identifies research participants at the beginning of the project who are followed throughout the course of the research.

The alternative to a retrospective study is a **prospective study.** In this approach, researchers identify the participants they want to observe and follow them forward in time. Sometimes this is relatively easy, as in Bond et al.'s (2001) study of bullying behavior. They identified their population, created a sample, and questioned them while the events of interest were likely to be fresh in memory.

Other prospective studies rely on some event whose impact the researchers want to assess. Researchers sometimes initiate research when something of interest happens in society. For instance, Hurricane Andrew hit Florida in 1992, causing massive damage and suffering. A team of psychologists used that event to study the course of posttraumatic stress in children.

La Greca, Silverman, Vernberg, and Prinstein (1996) studied 442 elementary school children after the hurricane. The investigators administered the Posttraumatic Stress Disorder Reaction Index for Children (RI), the Hurricane-Related Traumatic Experiences (HURTE) measure, the Social Support Scale for Children (SSSC), the Kidcope survey, and the Life Event Schedule (LES). Measurements were obtained three, seven, and ten months after the hurricane. They found that 12 percent of the children experienced severe to very severe levels of posttraumatic stress disorder (PTSD) at ten months.

You can see that it would be nearly impossible to obtain valid data with a retrospective study of the effects of the hurricane. You can't go back in time to administer the RI (or any of the other scales). It is also unreasonable to think that the children could reconstruct their reactions from seven or ten months previously. In order to know how feelings and emotions change over time, the only viable approach is prospective.

As in the latter example, the decision to use a prospective or a retrospective design is sometimes not under the control of the researcher. Prospective research is possible when the investigators identify a question and have a group that they can follow into the future. Retrospective research is called for when the answer to a research question lies, at least in part, in what has already happened.

Attrition

The single largest methodological concern in longitudinal studies is the fact that some people will stop participating. In and of itself, the loss of data reduces the amount of information that you have for drawing conclusions, but if your sample is sufficiently large to begin with, the loss of a small amount of data may not be problematic. The study of bullying by Bond et al. (2001) began with 2,680 students, but by the end of their data collection, only 2,365 remained. Still, that is a significant sample; the loss of over 300 participants is notable but may not affect the power of statistical analysis.

The biggest issue associated with this loss of participants, known as attrition, is that you don't always know whether those who disappear differ from those who remain. (If this phenomenon sounds familiar, it is because you encountered it in the context of experimental research, where it is sometimes called subject or participant mortality.) Bond et al. (2001) reported that the attrition rate in their bullying study was higher for boys than for girls. They also noted in their results that boys showed a lower incidence of depression associated with bullying in boys. Could it be that a significant proportion of the boys who left the study experienced depression from bullying?

Further, attrition was greater for students with non-intact (e.g., single parent) families. Is it possible, or even likely, that students in such circumstances are more susceptible to depression? Without being able to ask them, we don't know. Thus, the conclusion by the researchers that boys experience less depression may have been biased to reflect the remaining participants, who could very well differ from those who departed.

Sometimes it is hard to anticipate whether attrition will affect outcomes. Hayslip, McCoy-Roberts, and Pavur (1998–99) conducted a three-year study of how well adults cope after the death of a loved one. They reported, first of all, that attrition at six months was associated with an active decision to leave the study whereas at three years, the researchers had simply lost track of the individuals, some of whom might have participated if found.

The investigators also discovered that attrition did not seem to affect the nature of the results of their research on the effects of the death of a spouse. The results and conclusions would have been pretty much the same whether or not those who left had been included.

On the other hand, Hayslip et al. (1998–99) noted that those who had suffered a nonconjugal loss (i.e., somebody other than a husband or wife) and who dropped out were younger, less active in their coping, were in better health, and were less lonely at the beginning of the study. The researchers pointed out poorer psychological recovery after the death of a spouse or other loved one is associated with younger age, poorer health, and more loneliness. Given that nonconjugal dropouts were younger, they might be expected to show poorer outcomes. Their attrition might affect conclusions greatly because those remaining in the sample were the types of people you would expect to do well. Thus, typical outcomes would appear rosier because of those who had left.

Dropouts were also in better health and less lonely, factors associated with better psychological outcomes. If your study experienced attrition by those who are healthy and not lonely, you would lose people who typically recover well. As a result, your sample would look bleak, not because people can't recover from bereavement, but because the people who agree to be studied are likely to have worse outcomes than those who leave.

Hayslip et al. (1998–99) concluded that we need to be very sensitive to the nature of those who leave longitudinal projects. There is a realistic chance that dropouts lead to biased results, therefore less valid conclusions. Given the potential importance of attrition, it is common for researchers to report the degree of attrition in their reports. This information can help readers gain a sense of how confident they should be in the results. The reality of longitudinal research is that you can count on losing people. An important question is whether those who leave a study differ in relevant ways from those who remain.

When LaGreca and her colleagues (1996) studied students over 10 months who suffered through Hurricane Andrew, they recorded the dropouts, documented the reasons for the attrition, and formally compared participants and non-participants. Figure 11.4 displays the percentage of the initial 568 students in the Hurricane Andrew study who departed and the general reason for having done so. As you can see, over 8 percent had departed by seven months and a total of about 22 percent by ten months. These attrition figures are not unusual for such research.

Fortunately, La Greca et al. discovered that those who dropped out did not differ from those who remained in terms of grade, gender, ethnicity, or initial symptoms of PTSD. It is likely that the students who participated throughout the study were representative of the entire set of 568 who began the project.

We have found ways to reduce the attrition rates, although they are not without cost. The tactics involve a commitment of time and expense on the researcher's part.

Wutzke, Conigrave, Kogler, Saunders, and Hall (2000) studied a group of 554 people who engaged in heavy drinking in Australia. The project extended for ten years, a period of time that generally leads to notable attrition among highly educated and cooperative participants, and extremely high levels among people with substance abuse problems. At the end of their ten years, Wutzke et al. randomly sampled and reviewed

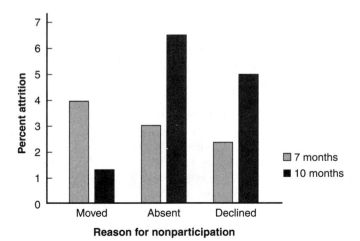

FIGURE 11.4   Reason for nonparticipation in the Hurricane
Andrew study of posttraumatic stress disorder (PTSD). The
researchers documented the reasons for nonparticipation and
compared those who left the study with those who remained. Of
the initial 568 elementary school students, just over 22 percent
dropped out of the study for reasons that were sometimes clear
(e.g., they had moved) or vague (e.g., they simply declined). Those
who participated did not differ from those who dropped out.

Source: A. M. LaGreca, et al. (1996). Symptoms of posttraumatic stress in
children after Hurricane Andrew: A prospective study. *Journal of Counseling and Clinical Psychology, 64,* 712–723. Copyright American Psychological
Association. Adapted with permission.

20 percent (n = 109) of the records to see how well contact had been maintained. Surprisingly, 72.5 percent of the 109 people had been successfully located for the study;
over 78 percent of the total group of 554 had been located.

The researchers had prepared well and worked diligently throughout the study to
keep in touch with the participants. They enhanced their success by taking a number of
steps as they initiated their project and as they conducted it. Table 11.1 presents their
strategies to avoid losing track of people and maintaining the participants' motivation to
continue in the project. Some of these steps are very relevant for studies of a large and
heterogeneous population. Researchers face different concerns when dealing with longitudinal research with children, although the same general principles will apply.

Finally, when you are studying older people, an additional reason for attrition is
likely, namely, the death of the participant. In the 80-year study begun by Terman in
1921, there has been considerable attrition, as you might expect. However, in the 35th
year of the study (1955), over 88 percent of the women and over 87 percent of the men
remained in the project.

When Terman died in 1956, the attrition rate increased, possibly because the
participants had felt a very strong personal connection with him. Between 1955 and 1960,

TABLE 11.1 Steps taken by researchers to decrease attrition of participants in a longitudinal study involving heavy drinkers (Wutzke et al., 2000).

PREPARATION

- Ensuring that dates of birth and middle names were collected (to make later tracing easier)
- Identifying a contact person who lived at a different address
- Maintaining contact throughout the project with such mailings as birthday cards or regular newsletters

PERSISTENCE

- Beginning a trace of the person as soon as contact is lost
- Making multiple phone calls to set up appointments for interviews
- Showing willingness to conduct interviews at times and locations convenient for the respondent
- Providing incentives to offset the inconvenience of participation

the number who actively declined to participate exceeded the total attrition since 1921 (Holahan & Sears, 1995). Since 1972, attrition has been more likely due to death than to a choice to drop out. Remarkably, only 8 percent of the women and 6 percent of the men have been "lost," the researchers term for loss of contact because they can't find the person.

It is ironic that the exceedingly low attrition in the Terman study is fairly unimportant in some ways. The sample he chose in 1921 wasn't representative either of the population generally or of gifted children specifically. As a result, we don't know exactly to whom we can generalize the results of the research.

DISCUSSION QUESTIONS
1. Provide an example of a study you might do that would involve a prospective design. Provide an example of a study you might do that would involve a retrospective design. What are the advantages and disadvantages of each?
2. Why would the reasons for attrition rates be different for children and for adults?

DATA ANALYSIS IN LONGITUDINAL RESEARCH

Because measurements in longitudinal research are not fundamentally different than those in other types of research, we see the same statistical approaches in long term projects that we do in cross-sectional studies. You can review the common techniques for data analysis in the Statistics Appendix.

Most longitudinal research is correlational, so data analyses reflect that fact. Research that involves multiple variables of interest typically involves correlation or regression analysis. Such tests give us critical information about what variables are associated with one another and what variables are useful in predicting outcomes.

For instance, Hayslip et al. (1998–99) used a sophisticated correlational approach called discriminant analysis to combine the effects of variables such as health, adjustment, loneliness, and distress (as measured by different tests) so they could examine how people cope with the death of a loved one. La Greca et al. (1996) used simple regression analysis to find the associations posttraumatic stress symptoms and other variables that included exposure to a hurricane, the amount of loss or disruption, demographics, and social support afterward.

Sometimes researchers use tests related to the analysis of variance (ANOVA) in longitudinal research. Such use typically occurs when the design involves nonequivalent control group designs. For example, Bosworth and Schaie (1999) used the database associated with Schaie's Seattle Longitudinal Study to compare the cognitive functioning of two groups of older adults. In this project, running since 1956, researchers have tested old adults every seven years. Thus, there are records of various aspects of intellectual functioning for decades. The researchers compared performance over the years of a group of people who had died versus a comparable group of survivors. Bosworth and Schaie (1999) looked at changes in performance over time for the two groups, finding that the deceased group had shown declines on some measures years prior to their death. To spot differences between groups, Bosworth and Schaie employed repeated measures analysis of covariance (ANCOVA), a variation of the ANOVA that removes the effects of variables that may correlate with the DV.

Hoekstra-Weebers, Jaspers, Kamps, and Klip (2001) studied the psychological adaptation among parents of children with cancer over one year. They used a simple repeated measures ANOVA to see if they could identify factors associated with the way parents cope with their children's cancer. Needless to say, the results were complex and predictions about parental coping were difficult. Still, the researchers identified variables that might affect parental outcomes.

In short, you can expect to see just about any type of statistical approach in longitudinal research that you see in other varieties of research. An important reminder about interpreting the results of the statistical tests is that, even if we use tests like an ANOVA, we can't make conclusions about causation if we haven't manipulated an independent variable. In longitudinal studies, we have to remember that the data are usually correlational, so we can't make causal statements.

SINGLE-SUBJECT EXPERIMENTATION

In the past century, psychologists have developed the tradition of conducting studies with groups of participants, ignoring the behavior of single individuals. As a discipline, psychology was not always oriented toward this approach. In the early years of psychology, researchers often studied a single person intensively.

Experimentalists and clinicians shared this methodology. Freud used single-participant studies in his clinical work, as did John Watson (e.g., Little Albert) in his research on learning. Then in the early decades of the twentieth century, experimental psychologists gravitated toward the study of groups. Single-subject experimental research did not return until the middle of the century. When it was resurrected, researchers often conducted long-term studies of single subjects, often rats and pigeons. The research reports were largely devoid of statistical analysis; visual displays of data replaced statistics. The behaviorists who resurrected single-subject research believed that enough data over many experimental trials would reveal important patterns of behavior, so statistical treatment wasn't necessary. Today, single-subject studies with people tend to involve those with psychological problems.

Experimental Analysis of Behavior

The experimental analysis of behavior reflects a unique tradition in research. It arose from the behaviorist tradition and had significant focus on the study of reinforcement contingencies. Because one of the major tenets of behaviorism was that we can discover general principles and laws of behavior, researchers believed that studies with large numbers of subjects were not only unnecessary, but also undesirable. By using many subjects and averaging the data on their performance, the behaviorists thought that we would lose sight of individual details.

Consequently, the tradition of using one or a few subjects emerged. Psychologists who engage in the experimental analysis of behavior often still rely on single subjects or perhaps small groups and may rely on visual presentation of results rather than on complex statistical analysis. These researchers are not immune to psychological culture, though, so even these psychologists have altered their traditions somewhat, using statistical analysis to help them understand their research results.

Within the realm of experimental analysis of behavior, two distinct paths have developed. Some experimenters rely on studies of animal behavior; their work is largely theoretical. When researchers use experimental analysis of behavior, their projects sometimes focus on theory, but sometimes the projects involve applications. Their investigations often involve people in clinical settings and tend to be less theoretical, although clearly based on behavioral theory. The experimental analysis of behavior is likely to be highly objective and quantitative.

DISCUSSION QUESTION
1. What research project could you design that would probably be better with a single-case design rather than a group design?

METHODS OF SINGLE-CASE DESIGNS

Studies with single individuals, whether human or nonhuman, do not differ in concept from many of the other approaches we have already covered. The biggest difference involves the number of people or animals tested, not necessarily the methodology. In fact, this difference in the number of participants is not necessary; single-case research can involve multiple cases. The researchers are likely to report on them individually, though. Case studies can involve controlled observations, like experiments. They can also rely on questionnaires and naturalistic observation.

Another difference between single-case analyses and group analyses is that single-case research involves continuous monitoring of behavior over time. In this sense it resembles time-series or longitudinal designs more than the typical cross-sectional design.

If you read reports about the experimental analysis of behavior or about clinical interventions with a single client, you will see a clear resemblance to time series designs. Single-case research shares a number of properties with time-series designs, the chief difference being the number of participants.

Withdrawal Designs

Single-case research can take many different forms. The general process involves assessing the behavior or behaviors of interest to monitor the baseline rate of the behaviors. Then a treatment begins. After that, different designs lead to different steps.

One design, the **withdrawal design,** entails a baseline phase, a treatment phase, then a return to a baseline phase. It is represented as an **ABA design** because researchers refer to the baseline period with the letter *A* and the treatment with the letter *B*. If treatment is effective, a simple withdrawal design should document that there is movement toward the desired outcome during the treatment phase. In medical or psychiatric research that assesses whether a drug stabilizes a person's condition, a return of the symptoms to the original level when the treatment is withdrawn may be entirely predictable, even desirable for assessing the effectiveness of a treatment. This design is most useful when researchers expect that after a treatment is removed, the original pattern of behavior will recur. In such a case, the ABA design permits the researchers to identify cause and effect relationships.

Withdrawal Design—A research method in which an investigator observes a baseline of behavior, applies a treatment, and assesses any behavioral change, then removes or withdraws the treatment to see the degree to which the behavior reverts to baseline levels.

ABA Design—A type of withdrawal design in which a treatment is applied only once, then withdrawn.

A return to baseline in such a medical study would indicate that the medication is working as it should. If the condition did not return to baseline levels when the medication was removed, the investigator might not be sure that the medication made a difference. Some alternate explanation might be better.

In much psychological research, it isn't clear what will happen in the second baseline phase. After a behavioral treatment phase ends, we hope that the desired behavior change is going to persist. So in the second baseline phase, we hope there isn't a return to the first level. Consequently, an ABA design and its variations may not be useful for studying the effects of psychological therapy.

ABAB Designs

In order to strengthen the internal validity of single-case research, investigators sometimes withdraw a treatment to see if a person's condition worsens, then they introduce a second baseline phase, followed by a re-introduction of the treatment, creating an **ABAB design.** If the individual's behavior changes predictably every time the treatment is applied and removed, it shows that the treatment is having the desired effect. Naturally, this design only makes sense if the researcher expects behavior to revert to an original state after the treatment ends.

ABAB Design—A type of withdrawal design that uses a baseline period followed by application of a treatment, the withdrawal of the treatment (as in an ABA design), and re-application of the treatment.

The basic ABAB design has many variations. Sometimes researchers want to assess different treatments, so after baseline phases, they introduce different treatments. If there are two different treatments, we represent the design as AB_1AB_2.

We can see how this type of single-case design works in a study of head injury patients. Hall, MacDonald, and Young (1992) assessed motor responses and eye movements of five individuals with serious head injury, four resulting from automobile accidents and one from a fall. In the baseline phase, the researchers monitored the behaviors of interest, then applied either directed multisensory stimulation or nondirected stimulation. This means that they exposed the patients to auditory, visual, tactile, and smell/taste stimuli and requested certain behaviors, like eye movements, from them. Directed multisensory stimulation (SDS) involved tailoring the nature of the stimuli to the individual. The researchers stimulated the patient with things that were personally meaningful for the individual. Non-directed stimulation (NDS) entailed stimulation that did not have personal relevance for the patient.

The researchers' version of the ABAB design was a single day of baseline recording, followed by alternating SDS, baseline, and NDS on a weekly basis for four to six weeks. The investigators discovered that simply providing stimulation was not particularly effective in increasing the person's awareness of the environment compared to providing stimuli that were relevant to that particular person.

Multiple Baseline Designs

Sometimes clinicians are interested in changing several behaviors of a client or in changing a behavior across different settings. These psychologists can work on such changes one at a time. For instance, for the first phase, the psychologist and the client work on one behavior. When the client's behavior reaches the desired state, they will work on a second behavior, continuing until they have worked with all relevant behaviors.

> **Multiple Baseline Design**—A research design that studies multiple behaviors that may change across baseline, treatment, and withdrawal phases.

Changing successive behaviors or the same behavior in different settings is part of the **multiple baseline design.** These designs follow the same logic as the withdrawal and ABAB designs. The investigator monitors baseline levels of the behavior of interest, then applies the treatment.

As an example of how this design is applied, let's consider the study of a woman who had been in an automobile accident and who was experiencing post-traumatic stress disorder (PTSD) as a result (Kellett & Beall, 1997). She was having recurrent nightmares; the therapist used psychodynamic-interpersonal psychotherapy to try to eliminate the dreams.

The investigators used an AB design, that is, baseline observation of nightmares followed by psychotherapy and monitoring of the nightmares. It was a multiple baseline design because the therapist was looking at multiple target variables: frequency of the nightmares, intensity of the nightmares, extent of fear and of upset, and how long it took the client to recover from the nightmare (as measured by the number of book chapters she read before returning to sleep).

The baseline period extended for 14 days, with the treatment phase covering the next 49 days and a followup at 6 months. The number of nightmares and the degree of fear both immediately diminished, only to increase temporarily three weeks into the treatment; then the nightmares and the fear again decreased. At six weeks, her distress and her nightmares again took an upswing before declining further. At 6 months, the symptoms of distress were minimal.

This type of change is not unusual in applied research with people who have severe, complex problems. There is improvement followed by relapse, then greater improvement. Sometimes idealized graphs show consistent improvement with the application of a treatment. In an ideal world, a client's progress would be continuous, but life doesn't always unfold this way.

The strength of the multiple baseline design is that as the clinician works with multiple behaviors, the effect of the therapy can be noted in each one independently. If the treatment is working, each application should change the new behavior being studied. As the therapeutic treatment is applied to different behaviors, it would be remarkably coincidental for the same hidden, third variable to be present each time. So a parsimonious conclusion would be that the treatment is responsible for the change.

The same logic applies to changing a given behavior in different environments. If you were looking at a behavior in one setting, you couldn't be certain that the treatment was effective because the third-variable problem is possible. If therapy is effective as the client and psychologist work in different environments, the third variable explanation about what is effecting the change becomes less plausible.

Single-Subject Randomized Controlled Trials

N of 1 Randomized Clinical Trial—A research design involving the study of a single person over multiple trials, with trials involving application of the treatment and trials with no application of the treatment occurring in random order.

In medical or psychiatric research, large scale studies may not be feasible. When an investigator wants to assess treatment with a single person, one option is the **N of 1 Randomized Clinical Trial (RCT).** In this approach, the researcher studies the effect of treatment on a single individual by exposing the individual to a treatment and a placebo in random order over time (e.g., ABBABAABBAB). Both the clinician and the patient are blind as to the treatment at any given time. Because neither the clinician nor the patient is aware of whether a treatment or a placebo phase is underway, there won't be any experimenter effects of demand characteristics. Any changes in the patient are likely to be due to the effectiveness of the treatment rather than to some extraneous variable.

This approach makes sense only when several criteria are met. First, the patient's problem must be chronic but relatively stable. If the symptoms are too variable or time-limited, it is difficult to attribute any changes to the treatment. Second, the treatment (usually a drug in this kind of study) should have a rapid effect and also a rapid cessation of effect. This criterion is important because the researcher doesn't want to have carryover effects that can interfere with conclusions about the effectiveness of the different approaches. Finally, there needs to be a clear and objective outcome that can be measured reliably (Cook, 1996).

An example of this approach is illustrated in the case of a 55-year-old man who sustained brain injury in a motorcycle accident. After six months, his psychometric performance included above-average IQ scores, excellent memory, and good motor performance. Unfortunately, he complained of difficulty with concentration.

The researchers used an N of 1 RCT to see if different medications could help with this problem with a pre-selected, random order of each of two drugs (Bleiberg, Garmoe, Cederquist, Reeves, & Lux, 1993). They prescribed the drugs lorazepam (treatment days 1 and 4) and dextroamphetamine sulfate (treatment days 3 and 5) and also used a placebo (treatment day 2) in a double-blind procedure. In addition, there was a day between treatments to eliminate carryover effects from the drugs.

The results revealed that dextroamphetamine led to higher levels of performance and greater stability as well. When the patient took lorazepam or the placebo, performance deteriorated relative to the dextroamphetamine; in addition, with lorazepam and the placebo, the patient showed greater variability, that is, inconsistency, in his performance on mental tasks.

Given that one person may respond to a given medication but another one won't, research on individual patients is highly desirable. Different medical regimens produce different effects, just as psychotherapeutic approaches may vary in effectiveness across people. The N of 1 RCT design can help tailor treatment for individuals in ways that group, cross-sectional designs cannot.

Strengths of Single-Participant Designs

Just like any other method of research, single-case studies help fill in the gap in our knowledge of behavior. These approaches have some notable strengths. First, one of the most pronounced advantages is the amount of detail reported about a person. Entire books can be (and have been) written about exceptional people.

These designs are time and labor intensive; you can easily see why an investigator might limit the research to a single person. The amount of detail to sort through would be overwhelming if the researcher studied many people. The researcher would also have a harder time sorting out the relevant detail from the irrelevant if multiple people were involved.

Second, case studies and single-case experiments are also useful when we want to investigate rare phenomena. Researchers may not be able to locate a large group of individuals if the phenomena of interest seldom occur.

A third strength of single-case studies relates to creating and evaluating research hypotheses. We can use the results of single-participant studies to generate hypotheses that can be tested with larger numbers of people. Single-case studies can also test hypotheses based on existing theory.

A further advantage of single-case studies is that they provide help in developing and assessing therapeutic or intervention techniques. The causes of psychological difficulties in clients and patients may be unique to each person. As a result, using large numbers of research participants may actually obscure the effectiveness of a therapeutic technique that might be helpful for a particular person.

Whenever we want to know about behaviors that are particular to a single person, single-case designs can be highly beneficial. In addition to the realm of clinical psychology, single-case research can be important in areas like sports psychology (Hrycaiko & Martin, 1999). In clinical psychology, the aim is to improve a person's psychological state; in sports psychology, the goal is to enhance performance. In both cases, there are likely to be individual characteristics that are critical to change; group research would probably not be optimal in either field.

Weaknesses of Single-Participant Designs

Probably the biggest limitation of single-subject studies involves the question of external validity. In one sense, they have a high degree of external validity; case studies typically do not use controlled, laboratory manipulations as experiments do. There is generally nothing artificial about them. Thus, the studies tell us about a person in his or her natural environment.

Another component of external validity is relevant here, though. We cannot be sure that conclusions based on a single person will generalize to anybody else. In fact, because this research often involves rare phenomena, it is not clear that there are many others to whom we would be able to generalize. The results might pertain to only one person.

In addition to questions of external validity, we are also faced with potential problems with internal validity. Causal conclusions about the person's behaviors are risky if there is no controlled manipulation of variables in the research.

Misunderstandings about Single-Case Research

Single-case research is fairly rare in psychological and psychiatric research. There are several possible reasons.

First, the tradition in psychology is cross-sectional research involving comparisons between groups. Most training in graduate programs therefore focuses on research with groups rather than with individuals. For many researchers, single-case studies don't look like normal, psychological research, and the psychologists may not be well versed in the details of single-case approaches.

Second, researchers may confuse the relative subjectivity of some case-study approaches and the relative objectivity of single-subject experiments that are highly controlled. Most psychologists and other researchers have little training in qualitative approaches. A qualitative study can provide a lot of information about behavior, but it is likely to be different information from that produced in a quantitative study. In other words, psychologists like research involving numbers and quantitative analysis.

Third, some researchers believe that the levels of internal and external validity are low in single-participant research. There is some truth to this claim, but the same can be said for cross-sectional designs. Most behavioral research involves convenience samples, so concerns about generalizability (i.e., external validity) exist for all types of data collection. Further, given that much experimentation occurs in laboratories, the question of external validity arises again. The issue of internal validity may be notable in case studies, but is less relevant for N of 1 RCT studies. Experiments with a single case may have levels of internal validity that are as high as in cross-sectional research.

Fourth, some researchers claim that the data analysis in single-case research is too subjective. It is true that there will be some subjectivity when an investigator works with subjective phenomena, like emotional states. But this is no different than with cross-sectional research. For researchers interested in the experimental analysis of behavior, they may avoid statistical analyses, but when the data are objective and when objective criteria for drawing conclusions are set ahead of time, data analysis is simply different, not necessarily less valid.

DISCUSSION QUESTIONS
1. Why would an ABA design not be appropriate for behavioral (as opposed to drug) treatment for depression?
2. Why would the flu not be a good malady for studying in a N of 1 Randomized Clinical Trial methodology? Why would a group design be better?

CASE STUDIES

> **Case Study**—A research design involving the in-depth study of one or a few people, historically with no manipulation of variables, although such manipulations can occur in contemporary designs.

Case studies are investigations that focus on a single individual (occasionally a few people) in great detail. Historically, case studies did not include controlled observations, and took place in the context of psychotherapy (Kazdin, 1998). In contemporary applications, though, investigators make use of interventions and control (e.g., Cytowic, 1993; Mills, Boteler, & Oliver, 1999).

This approach to research is often seen as having more problems than other techniques. Questions of causation, generalizability, and interpretation biases are among the most notable concerns.

In case studies, it is hard to see what factors lead to certain behaviors and which are merely correlated with those behaviors. In essence, there is the problem of too many rival hypotheses and no way to see which ones are best. A second caution about case studies concerns whether we can generalize from a particular patient or client to others.

An additional concern about single-case research in general is interpretive. That is, what does the information mean? It is possible for researchers to ignore viable explanations for behaviors because those explanations do not fit with their theoretical position. This is not an attempt to deceive. Rather, it is a natural inclination on our part to accept information that supports what we believe and to ignore information that doesn't. The problem is exacerbated by the fact that studies of a single person often rely on clinical judgment and subjectivity that another person may not be able to replicate objectively.

Because of these problems, case studies are fairly rare in the research literature. At the same time, it is easy to see why clinicians use this approach. People with ailments that are interesting (in the research sense) are likely to be rare, at least when they first appear. As a case in point, AIDS was initially a puzzle to the medical community; young, healthy people were contracting unusual, fatal diseases for no apparent reason. Initial research could only involve case studies because there were so few instances.

When the numbers began to grow, preliminary studies showed patterns. Initially, physicians thought that the disease was limited to gay men, which accounts for its initial label, Gay Related Immune Disease (GRID). Without continued research with larger numbers of people, it would have been impossible to understand the nature of what was ultimately renamed AIDS. But the initial case studies provided critical clues to the disease.

Within psychology, case studies can give us a lot of compelling information about individual people. The clinical researcher can then try to understand an individual's behavior by fitting a large number of puzzle pieces together. For example, how would you react if somebody told you that he knew that the food being cooked for dinner wasn't done yet because "there aren't enough points on the chicken?" Is this the utterance of a delusional person? What do "points" have to do with how well done a chicken is? You can see how an interesting case study shed light on the perceptions of the man for whom flavors had shapes (Cytowic, 1993), shapes that were as real to him as the flavor of chicken is to us.

Researchers have estimated that as few as one person in about 100,000 has such experiences, known as synesthesia (Cytowic, 1997), although some have produced higher estimates of one person in 2,000 (Baron-Cohen, Burt, Smith-Laittan, Harrison, & Bolton, 1996). Obviously, if you wanted to study synesthesia, you would have a hard time finding a group to study. Case studies make the most sense. In Controversy Box 11.2, you can see how Cytowic used a case study to investigate a synesthete he met.

Case studies can take very different forms. They can be used to identify characteristics, feelings, emotions, and behaviors of people that occur as part of their normal lives. This type of research is often very different from case studies in psychotherapy. In the latter, there is a clear goal toward which the client and therapist are working.

We can see an example of the attempt to capture experience and feeling in a case study that investigated women's changes in identity during their first pregnancy (Smith, 1997). The investigator used interviews, diaries, and retrospective accounts, then created a case study to which the women responded. The researcher then wrote a final case study report. Smith generally relied on qualitative data in this research. One advantage of this phenomenological, experiential approach is that he was able to see how the women felt and how they reacted on a personal level.

He discovered that the four women in his case studies engaged in reconstruction of their memories during pregnancy. He suggested that women generate a series of different stories at various points during pregnancy. The result is that there is a more positive memory of pregnancy than one might expect based on the actual course of the pregnancy.

These results gave us some interesting information about how we remember events. In addition, the research told us something about emotions and feelings during and after pregnancy.

Grounded Theory—An approach to theory development in which an investigator makes systematic observation free of prior hypotheses, generates facts, then uses those facts for development of the theory.

This qualitative approach makes use of **grounded theory,** an approach in which we start with hypotheses that help us construct meaningful descriptions of what people do and feel as we observe them. Thus, the theories are grounded in information or data that researchers have provided. Proponents of grounded theory believe that theories are assembled based on the information available, but that there is no single best version of reality.

By combining various types of rich and complex data in a case study, we try to understand psychological experiences that would be unavailable if we used cross-sectional psychological research methods.

CONTROVERSY BOX 11.2
CONTROVERSY BOX: Do You Taste Pointed Chickens or See Colored Numbers?

When somebody scratches their fingernails on a blackboard, the sound can send shudders down our spines, even though we have not been touched. This effect is an analogue to that of people who experience synesthesia, or the mixing of different sensory modalities. This mixing is so bizarre from our perspectives that descriptions sound like they are coming from delusional people.

Should we believe people who claim that the sound of a pager causes them to see "blinding red jaggers" or that the poison strychnine and angel food cake have the same "pink smell" (Cytowic, 1993, p. 48). Or that the number 257 induces "a swirl that consists of yellowish orange as the dominant color, green as the next most dominant, and lastly there is a small amount of pink" (Mills, Boteler, & Oliver, 1999, p. 183)?

Synesthesia can take many different forms. In the case of the man Cytowic studied, flavors had shapes. The most famous synesthete in the psychological literature experienced shapes and colors when he heard words; for him, a particular tone looked like fireworks tinged with a pink-red hue, an unpleasant taste, and was rough enough to hurt your hand (Luria, 1968).

In another documented case, the synesthete converted visually presented numbers to colors, but also experienced synesthesia to spoken numbers, music, voices, emotions, smells, and foods (Mills, Boteler, & Oliver, 1999). When she saw a written number, she perceived different colors in front of her eyes. For example, a 1 was white, 2 was yellowish orange, 5 was kelly green, 7 was pink. Each of the single digits had its own, consistent color. Multiple-digit numbers combined colors, with the color associated with the first digit predominating.

Synesthetes respond to the world in ways that are very consistent for them, even if they are strange to us. This is an ideal situation for a case study. Cytowic (1993) met a synesthete, Michael, and spent an extended period studying his perceptions. Cytowic became aware of how special this person was when the synesthete didn't want to serve the chicken he was cooking yet because it was round, without enough points. He also reported being able to smell a tree that nobody else could, and it wasn't because their noses were stuffed. He was able to smell the tree because his brain processed its visual components and sent information to the part of his brain that dealt with smell.

Over the course of two years, Cytowic exposed Michael to different manipulations to see how he reacted. During the development of the case study, the researcher found that quinine, a bitter liquid, felt like polished wood, whereas another liquid had "the springy consistency of a mushroom, almost round, . . . but I feel bumps and can stick my fingers into little holes in the surface" (Cytowic, 1993, p. 64).

The functioning of the brain is complex in synesthesia, as it is for everything else, but Cytowic used the results of his study with Michael to discover some important elements of the phenomenon. He presented various liquids to see what shapes and colors they generated. He also investigated the effects of amphetamines and alcohol on synesthesia; amphetamines blocked synesthesia whereas alcohol enhanced it. Cytowic also injected radioactive gas to identify the parts of the brain involved in synesthesia; he found that during synesthesia, there was minimal blood flow to Michael's cortex. At the same time, blood flow to the emotional center of the brain, the limbic system, increased greatly.

Cytowic provided an extended case study of the experiences of the synesthete and wound up with a description not only of Michael's feelings and perceptions but also of patterns of brain activity. Such research is only possible in case-study form.

DISCUSSION QUESTION
1. Why is subjectivity a problem in case studies? Why would a Freudian theorist's case study report differ from that of a behavioral psychologist?

CHAPTER SUMMARY

Psychologists have created specialized approaches to research to answer questions about behavior when traditional experiments may not suffice. Developmental psychologists use longitudinal approaches to study how people change over time. Some longitudinal research in psychology has continued for over 80 years. With research like this, the investigators have to contend with considerably different issues than they do in typical, short-term cross-sectional experiments. Psychologists have developed a variety of methods to maximize the validity of the information obtained in these long-range projects.

Longitudinal projects often involve studying the same people over time. For example, Terman's 80-year study, which is still in progress, followed a set of people identified in childhood as gifted throughout their lives. Sometimes, researchers investigate groups whose members change over time. The National Assessment of Educational Progress studies twelfth graders across time, so there is a new group of students for each phase of the research. Other research follows the same people over time, but also brings new people into the study at regular intervals.

Sometimes researchers study the same individual over time, concentrating on one person (or a few) rather than on a group. Like longitudinal studies, single-case studies involve observing the same person over time, with multiple repeated measures. Depending on the specific research question, investigators might introduce a treatment, then withdraw it, sometimes multiple times. Psychologists are often not well trained in the use of single case designs, one of the reasons that this approach is relatively rare in psychology.

■ ■ ■ ■ ■

PEOPLE ARE DIFFERENT: CONSIDERING CULTURAL AND INDIVIDUAL DIFFERENCES IN RESEARCH

CHAPTER OUTLINE

CHAPTER PREVIEW

DIFFERENT CULTURAL PERSPECTIVES
What Is Culture?
Culture
Race and Ethnicity

DEFINING AN INDIVIDUAL'S CULTURE, ETHNICITY, AND RACE
Criteria for Inclusion
in a Group
Social Issues and
Cultural Research

CROSS-CULTURAL CONCEPTS IN PSYCHOLOGY
Are Psychological
Constructs Universal?
Issues in Cross-Cultural Research

CONTROVERSY: Does Culture Make a Difference in Neurological Diagnosis?

IS THERE A BIOLOGICAL BASIS FOR RACE?
The Criteria for Race
Current Biological Insights
Regarding Race

CONTROVERSY: Are There Really Different Races?
Historical Error
Current Controversies

PRACTICAL ISSUES IN CULTURAL RESEARCH
Lack of Appropriate Training
among Researchers

WHY THE CONCEPTS OF CULTURE AND ETHNICITY ARE ESSENTIAL IN RESEARCH
Differences Due to Language
and Thought Processes
Differences in Simple and
Complex Behaviors
Is Culture-Free Theory Really
Free of Culture?
Similarities and Differences
within the Same Culture

CULTURAL FACTORS IN MENTAL HEALTH RESEARCH
Content Validity
Translation Problems
Cross-Cultural Norms
Cross-Cultural Diagnoses

SEX AND GENDER: DO MEN AND WOMEN COME FROM DIFFERENT CULTURES?
Stereotypes and Gender-Related
Performance

CONTROVERSY: Are Men Better than Women at Mathematics?

CHAPTER SUMMARY

KEY TERMS

Absolutism

Back translation

Content validity

Culture

Emic

Ethnicity

Etic

Interpretation paradox

One-drop rule

(hypodescent)

Race

Relativism

Univeralism

CHAPTER PREVIEW

Most psychologists would agree that our attitudes and beliefs affect the way we make judgments. When we draw a conclusion about somebody's behavior, our judgments may reflect us as much as the people we observe. That is, we see others in a particular way because of who we are. If we share the same culture as those we study, we may be able to gain insights into why they act as they do. On the other hand, when we observe behaviors of those in other cultures, we may not understand what motivates them.

Understanding the effects of culture on behavior requires detailed knowledge of the person being observed as well as that person's culture, which is not easy. The issues we have to consider are complex. For instance, how do culture, ethnicity, and race affect behavior? The answer is certainly complex. Even though most people firmly believe that there are several easily definable races of people, many scientists have come to the conclusion that the concept of race is a social construction, not a biological fact. According to a great number of anthropologists, sociologists, psychologists, biologists, and geneticists, race is not a particularly useful biological concept. Yet many people believe that it exists.

Even though a concept like race may be scientifically invalid, we can still identify behaviors associated with culture or ethnicity, although we need to take care in the ways we classify people. Research participants are often assigned to categories in simplistic and contradictory ways from one study to another. Fortunately, more researchers are coming to the realization that we need to have good cross-cultural knowledge if we are going to understand people.

Finally, studying differences between women and men poses problems in research. Sometimes, investigators find ways to reinforce pre-existing beliefs by failing to acknowledge what might be considered cultural differences between the sexes. The researchers may believe in myths that are not true, so their research may be flawed.

Throughout this chapter, your beliefs will be challenged, and you will have to deal with controversies that, ultimately, may make you view people differently and change the way you think about studying them.

DIFFERENT CULTURAL PERSPECTIVES

It would be a mistake to assume that all people think as we do. As a result, we should be cautious in interpreting why people act as they do when these people come from a culture that is different from ours.

For example, Stiles, Gibbons, and Schnellman (1990) asked Mexican and American adolescents to characterize members of the opposite sex. Mexican adolescents relied on stereotypes and talked about internal characteristics. American adolescents were more likely to use physical and sexual descriptors. In addition, the girls who participated in the study tended to make different drawings, depending on their culture. Mexican girls depicted men helping them more than American girls did. If we wanted to study attitudes of Mexican and of American adolescents, we might have a hard time comparing their responses because they would be using different worldviews to generate their responses.

Cohen and Gunz (2002) have documented that people born in Western and Eastern countries have quite different memories of events in their lives. Those from Asia tended to remember events in the first person (e.g., "I did this") when the memories did not involve their being at the center of attention; when they were the center of attention, their memories were in the third person (e.g., "he did this"). People born in the Western world showed memories that were just the opposite, with the center of attention being associated with the first person. The researchers concluded that the differential perspectives on the world actually dictated the way information is processed and the form of subsequent memory.

If the investigators are correct, we can expect people from different cultures to think about things very differently, so if we give them the same task to complete, they may be engaged in quite different mental processes. As such, comparisons about performance may be difficult.

What Is Culture?

Sometimes we think that we understand a concept, but when we try to express our ideas in words, it is very difficult. Culture is one such concept. We all know people who act differently than we do because of cultural differences. If somebody asked you to identify differences between your culture and that of another person, you would probably discuss differences in religious beliefs, eating habits, clothing, etc. This is typically what we mean by "culture" (Matsumoto, 1994). At the same time, we have only identified some of the signs associated with cultural differences; we haven't defined culture itself.

Throughout this chapter it will become apparent that our concepts of culture, ethnicity, and race are quite vague and subjective. Unfortunately, the research literature is at times just as confusing. Different investigators use the same term but define it differently.

Culture.   We can identify two distinct components of **culture.** Physical culture relates to objects like tools and buildings. Subjective culture, which is of interest to psychologists, refers to such things as familial patterns, language habits, attire, and a wide range of other characteristics that pass from one generation to the next (Betancourt & Lôpez, 1993; Matsumoto, 1994).

> **Culture**—The customs, behaviors, attitudes, and values (Psychological Culture) and the objects and implements (Physical Culture) that can be used to identify and characterize a population.

Other psychologists have defined culture somewhat differently from Matsumoto (1994), involving the notion that culture is not something "out there," but rather that it is a cognitive response a person makes on the basis of his or her interactions with others (Segall, Lonner, & Berry, 1998). For example, it seems unlikely that Americans are overtly conscious of being Americans on a daily basis; this categorization makes sense only when they want to make some contrast. In their communities, they are simply who they are. Similarly, think about Mexican citizens. People living in Mexico City feel no need to identify themselves as Mexicans or as Hispanics because on a daily basis, it is not a relevant consideration. On the other hand, when people live in a country different from that of their birth, they would likely describe themselves according to place of birth because that information might be relevant to understanding their behavior and because it draws a contrast between them and others.

Race and Ethnicity.   Race and ethnicity are also difficult concepts. When discussing **race,** researchers (and people in general) often think of biological characteristics. People who make distinctions this way hope to use an objective, biological means to categorize people.

On the other hand, **ethnicity** is often thought of as a more subjective concept. A person's ethnicity is associated with affiliation. That is, to what group do people think they belong or what group has affected the way an individual thinks and acts?

It doesn't help researchers that the concept of ethnicity itself is somewhat unclear. For instance, Phinney (1996) noted that "ethnicity is most often thought of as culture.... To understand the psychological implications of ethnicity, it is essential to identify the specific cultural characteristics associated with an ethnic group and with the outcomes of interest such as educational achievement or mental health" (p. 920). She pointed out that the cultural characteristics (e.g., attitudes and behaviors) are often used to explain ethnic differences.

> **Race**—A controversial concept with very limited construct validity about classification of people based on real or imagined biological traits, most often centering on skin color.
>
> **Ethnicity**—A concept related to a person's identification with a particular group of people, often based on ancestry, country of origin, or religion.

Matsumoto (1993) depicted ethnicity differently, suggesting that ethnicity "is defined most often by biological determinants; culture, however, must be defined by sociopsychological factors.... Defined in this way, the parameters of culture are 'soft,' and perhaps more difficult to distinguish, than the parameters of ethnicity, which are set in biology and morphological differences" (p. 120).

As Betancourt and Lôpez (1993) stated, in research, people often use culture interchangeably with race, ethnicity, and nationality. On surveys, people often must indicate race by selecting categories that really encompass ethnicity or nationality, not race. Latinos, for instance, can be White, Black, Asian, American Indian, or any combination thereof.

DISCUSSION QUESTIONS
1. Give an example of a difference between your own culture and some other culture that you know about with respect to subjective culture.
2. The concepts of race, culture, and ethnicity are not well defined, even in research. What other concepts that may be more readily defined can you think of that might do a better job of predicting people's attitudes and behaviors?

DEFINING AN INDIVIDUAL'S CULTURE, ETHNICITY, AND RACE

Scientific designations should be based on valid, objective, and stable scientific criteria. The categories researchers use often reflect social and political conditions. For example, in record keeping, the Census Bureau is not trying to be scientific; it is trying to describe the population of the United States. Still, scientific research relies on Census Bureau categories. Berreby (2000) has pointed out that the utility of racial classifications depends in part on how well people define the categories they use.

Further, Rodriguez (2000) pointed out that the concept of race or ethnicity may not help us understand behavior because an individual may fall into different categories, depending on who is doing the assessment. For instance, when the U.S. government collects data on an individual, the Bureau of the Census does not regard Hispanics as constituting a race, whereas federal agencies that deal with civic rights issues do have a separate racial category for Hispanics. Suppose you wanted to carry out a research project to see if people in different racial categories achieve different educational levels. Would your data include a racial category for Hispanics? With governmental categories, you could argue either way, if you consider that the government has sanctioned both approaches.

Another concern in categorizing research participants is that a researcher may use terms that are clear in the context of an investigation but that might be unclear to others. For instance, Selten et al. (2001) examined psychotic disorders among Turkish, Moroccan, and Hindustani people who had migrated to The Netherlands. But Bhui and Bhugra (2001) pointed out that the terms Turkish and Moroccan reflect place of birth, whereas Hindustani refers to religion. Such a mixture of categories can cause confusion in cross-cultural comparisons. Suppose a Turk was a Hindu. Into what category would he or she fall?

Further, the degree to which a person identifies with a given ethnic group often changes over the course of the person's life. As a result, studying the effect of ethnicity is very difficult: It is hard to define ethnicity precisely and an individual's commitment to a given ethnic group will vary according to the present circumstances. Further, asking people to place themselves into categories will often lead to different results, depending on what categories are available.

Criteria for Inclusion in a Group

The criteria for inclusion in a group change over time. For instance, over the years the United States census has classified people into ethnic groups on the basis of what language they spoke, then their last name, then their place of origin, and now, through self-identification.

In some cases, people classify themselves differently depending on what is at stake. Phinney (1996) cited research in which 259 university students self-identified as American Indian or Alaska Native. Only 52 could provide confirmation that they belonged in those categories. If tuition aid depends on ethnic status, people might classify themselves differently. Research often relies on data resulting from these self-classifications.

In addition, as Phinney (1996) pointed out, when we try to categorize people according to ethnicity, the labels we create are not particularly useful when people come from mixed backgrounds. Beyond that, Phinney noted that "a common practice is to interpret empirical results or clinical observations in terms of cultural characteristics that are assumed to exist but that are not directly assessed" (p. 921). That is, researchers make assumptions about behaviors of the groups they are studying, but the researchers often do not check to make sure that their assumptions are valid. According to Phinney, when investigators have taken the time to look at supposedly relevant cultural characteristics, the results have often shown that researchers' assumptions are misguided.

As an example of a difficulty in categorization, consider the Chinese, a group that has recently been studied extensively in cross-cultural psychology. Chang (2000) noted that the Chinese are not easy to characterize because being Chinese can mean an enormous number of things. For one thing, there is no single "race" because of the genetic and anthropological variability among the Chinese, who can count over 50 ethnic minorities encompassed under the overarching term "Chinese." In addition, the diversity in language is so great that you could find two languages labeled "Chinese" that are as different from one another as German is from French. Another consideration is that people from urban and rural areas can have very different cultures, as can people who are either literate or illiterate.

Researchers studying Chinese people living outside China sometimes use the family name as an indicator of being Chinese. This is a problematic strategy. Chang pointed out that the name Lee can be Chinese and has been used to signify Chinese ethnicity even though Lee is also a Korean and a Vietnamese name. Lee can also be a Western name—there is no evidence that the Confederate General Robert E. Lee was Chinese. Further, the most common Chinese surname, Chang, is also a Korean name.

Sometimes, researchers are even broader in their categorization schemes. Cohen and Gunz (2002), in studying the difference between Eastern and Western thought, simply included a participant in the Eastern category if he or she had been born in Asia. The range of ethnicity in such a strategy is vast. Participants in the Asian group were probably as different from one another as they were from the participants who grew up in North America. In other research, Kim, Atkinson, and Yang (1999) put into one category Asian Indians, Cambodians, Filipinos, Hmong, Japanese, Koreans, and others. This represents a stereotype that all people from Eastern cultures share significant attitudes and behaviors and that they all differ from people in the West.

To add to the confusion, Kim, Atkinson, and Yang (1999) have suggested that as people from Asian countries become acculturated to the United States, their behaviors change more quickly than their attitudes, which may not change even across generations. So in one sense, they are attitudinally still members of an ethnic group but behaviorally they are not. When we describe people within some arbitrarily determined category, we may be talking about very different types of people as though they were the same, and we may incorrectly decide that a single person is more consistently ethnic than he or she really is.

Social Issues and Cultural Research

The way we categorize people has implications for the way we think of social issues. As you can see in Figure 12.1, the National Center for Educational Statistics reported that high school dropout rates for Hispanics are very high (Kaufman, Kwon, Klein, & Chapman, 2000). What should we conclude from the fact that Hispanics are nearly 7

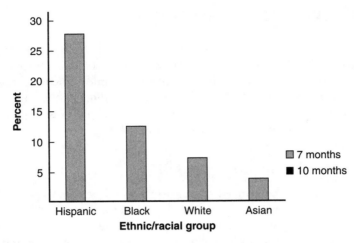

FIGURE 12.1 High school dropout rates according to ethnicity/race in the United States (Kaufman, Kwon, Klein, & Chapman, 2000).

times as likely to drop out of high school than Americans of Asian descent? This question is too simplistic because dropout rates for Hispanics drop by two thirds for families who have been in the United States for two generations or more. As such, ethnic categories are less important than degree of acculturation.

Rather than concentrating on ethnicity, it might make more sense to talk about other variables, like the number of years people have lived in a given culture, socioeconomic status, fluency in English, nature of one's peers, and so forth (Watkins, Mortazavi, & Trofimova, 2000).

Yee, Fairchild, Weizmann, and Wyatt (1993) summarized the problems nicely: They noted that psychologists themselves use common stereotypes and rely on self-identification. The use of stereotypes suffers from four notable problems: It (a) neglects important differences among people in the same group, (b) assumes with no proof that behaviors that differ across groups are based on racial or cultural differences, (c) inappropriately depicts race and other variables as being related, and (d) relies on ideas for which there is no scientific consensus.

DISCUSSION QUESTIONS

1. What problems can arise when investigators doing cultural research use data collected by the government to study people in different racial and cultural categories? Why is it important for researchers to consider the idea that people within any given group are really very heterogeneous?

2. Why is it reasonable to suppose that degree of acculturation is a better predictor of behavior than ethnic background? Give some examples of behaviors and attitudes associated with degree of acculturation.

CROSS-CULTURAL CONCEPTS IN PSYCHOLOGY

Historically, psychologists have not concerned themselves with cultural differences. From the first decades of the 1900s and into the 1960s, most psychologists were behaviorists who thought that organisms were similarly affected by reinforcement contingencies—how often they were rewarded or punished. As a result, it didn't make much difference to psychologists whether they studied rats, pigeons, or people from any background. The causes of behavior were seen as the same universally.

Are Psychological Constructs Universal?

Early cross-cultural researchers imposed their own cultural viewpoints on the behaviors of the people they studied, which meant that they failed to understand the subtleties of other cultures. Such an approach could probably be forgiven because the researchers were opening up a new field of study and knew much less than they thought they did or needed to know for complete understanding of the people they researched. Still, after a while, it became clear that things were not as simple as people had hoped.

One of the distinctions that resulted from critical analysis of the research was between an etic and an emic. An **etic** refers to findings that result from studies across cultures and that may hold true cross-culturally. Thus, many people might regard the taboo against incest or cannibalism as an etic. On the other hand, an **emic** refers to a finding that is particular to a single culture that is being studied and understood in local terms. Although these two terms are gaining wider recognition in psychology, they are still controversial because the distinction between etic and emic perspectives are not always clear (Lonner, 1999).

> **Etic**—A research finding that appears to be universally true across cultures.
> **Emic**—A research finding that is valid only within a given culture.

In the study of different cultures, Berry, Poortinga, Segall, and Dasen (1992, cited in Segall et al., 1998) identified three orientations in cross-cultural psychology, absolutism, relativism, and universalism.

The first orientation, **absolutism** assumes that behavioral phenomena are basically the same, regardless of cultures. In this view, depression will be depression; it does not differ from one locale to another. Should we believe this? Price and Crapo (1999) illustrate the difficulty with accepting the concept of depression as a single, unvarying construct across cultures. For example, the Hopi do not have a single category that corresponds to the Western view of depression; they have five different categories. For them depression as most of us view it would be too broad a label to be therapeutically useful. Further, the hopelessness of major depression would be accepted by some Buddhists as simply being "a good Buddhist" (p. 126). In a Buddhist culture, it would make no sense to describe symptoms of depression (as we know them) as a pathological condition because Buddhists believe that hopelessness is part of the world and that salvation arises, in part, in recognition of this hopelessness.

> **Absolutism**—In discussions of cultural research, the concept that maintains that behavioral phenomena can be viewed from the same perspective, regardless of the culture in which they appear.
> **Relativism**—In discussions of cultural research, the concept that maintains that behavioral phenomena can be understood only within the context of the culture in which they occur.

A second orientation is **relativism.** A relativistic approach stands in contrast to absolutism in that relativists make no attempts to relate psychological constructs across cultures. A researcher with this orientation would undertake only emic research, believing that the phenomena of any culture stands independently from those in any other. According to Segall et al. (1998), few psychologists favor either the extreme of absolutism or of relativism. Most fall between these two poles.

> **Universalism**—A moderating view in cultural research that maintains that behavioral phenomena may be based on invariant psychological processes but that each culture will induce different manifestations of those underlying processes.

The final orientation is **universalism.** This approach strikes a balance between absolutism and relativism, accepting the idea that there may be universal psychological processes, but that they manifest differently, depending on the particular culture. For example, Segall, Campbell, and Herskovits (1966) found that susceptibility to perceptual illusions was widespread and suggested universal, underlying cognitive processes. At the same time, reactions differed depending on a person's life experience.

According to the absolutist viewpoint, if perceptual illusions are caused by universal sensory processes, we should all experience illusions the same way. But that usually doesn't happen. According to the relativist viewpoint, there could be little or no similarity in perceptions across cultures because perception in this orientation arises only from experience. That, too, doesn't seem very common. According to the universalist perspective, the same internal processes take place but lead to different interpretations because of experience. The truth is likely to fall somewhere between the extreme viewpoints.

Although scientists hope for psychological constructs that are valid across cultures, careful examination of behaviors so far leads us to be careful to avoid falling prey to our own cultural biases. In Controversy Box 12.1, we see that something as objective as medical diagnosis is susceptible to cultural influences. The case study provided by Klawans (2000) provides an illustration of cultural problems in diagnosing brain damage. The patient and the physician came from different backgrounds and had radically different points of view, which could pose challenges for adequate diagnosis and treatment.

Issues in Cross-Cultural Research

When researchers pursue cross-cultural research, they can fall prey to certain problems in interpreting their data. Van de Vijver and Leung (2000) have identified four major concerns in research on people from different cultural groups.

- First, although some behavioral differences across cultures reflect important cross-cultural differences in thought and behavior, some differences in behavior are quite superficial and do not relate to important, underlying psychological processes.
- Second, sometimes psychological tests legitimately generate different patterns of scores across cultures. There is often a tendency to treat them as artifacts of measurement error, that is, to see the test as deficient rather than as identifying true differences between groups. In other words, when we indeed find cultural differences, it might be tempting to ignore them rather than share unpopular results.
- Third, researchers are prone to overgeneralization from their results. That is, differences due to small sample biases or poor measurement instruments may lead researchers to make more of their data than they should.

- Fourth, differences across groups may reflect lack of equivalence across samples. The differences could occur because the samples contain different types of people who differ in critical ways, not because the cultures differ.

■ ■ ■ ■ ■ ▬▬▬▬▬▬▬▬▬▬▬▬

CONTROVERSY BOX 12.1
CONTROVERSY: Does Culture Make a Difference in Neurological Diagnosis?

Diagnosing a medical or psychiatric condition resembles the formal research process quite closely. Physicians initially ask enough questions to allow them to form hypotheses about a problem. They then make observations and draw conclusions. If they still don't have enough information to identify the source of a patient's problems, they generate more hypotheses and ask more questions. Finally, the physician comes to a conclusion and treats the patient. In many cases, the ultimate diagnoses are correct, but sometimes they are wrong. This is exactly what happens in research. With luck, we are right most of the time, but research and diagnosing are complicated enough that sometimes we are wrong.

The neurologist Harold Klawans (2000) described a case from the 1970s in which a patient with neurological problems was initially misdiagnosed because of cultural factors. The patient, who had suffered repeated blackouts due to carbon monoxide poisoning in the workplace, was brought to a Chicago hospital.

As part of the diagnostic process, an attending neurologist asked the patient who the mayor of Chicago was. He responded correctly, but was unable to identify any other, previous mayors, asking if there ever had been any other mayors. He was also unable to name the current president or any previous presidents. The patient did not know that President John Kennedy had been assassinated, and had no knowledge of the Vietnam war, which was a very controversial aspect of American culture at the time. This patient was an American who had lived through all of these events, so it was very strange for him not to know such fundamental cultural knowledge.

The neurologist finally asked the patient to identify which of four objects was different

from the others: hammer, wood, chisel, wrench. The patient replied that none of them was different; they were all the same. At that point, the doctor concluded that the patient had suffered severe brain damage.

As Klawans discovered through further questioning, though, the patient's memory for some things (like baseball) going back forty years was very acute. The trouble with the initial diagnosis was that the first doctor had not taken culture into account. The patient, who had grown up in Mississippi in the 1930s, had gone to school for two years and had never learned to read. As a result, the patient's memories rested on what he had experienced directly. He didn't watch the news on television, so it is no surprise that he didn't know about the president, about Vietnam, about politics. None of these things had ever entered his world.

Klawans stated that people who don't read don't classify objects the way that literate people do. The task of categorizing the hammer, wood, chisel, and wrench is a foreign concept to them. It is only relevant to those of us who use written words to designate objects. The ability to read brings a set of skills that we take for granted, like classifying, but that ability is very closely bound to literacy.

If the patient hadn't experienced it himself, he didn't have a memory for an event. Imagine for yourself how much you would know about world events if you didn't read about them or see them on the news. His concept of the world was very different from that of the first doctor. In the end, it was clear that the patient's mental faculties were as sharp as anyone else's. Had Klawans not been attuned to this cultural difference, the patient might have been diagnosed with severe brain damage.

Interpretation Paradox—In cultural research, the fact that large differences between groups are easy to spot but hard to understand because there are so many factors that could be responsible, whereas small differences are harder to spot but easier to explain.

These difficulties imply what van de Vijver and Leung (2000) call the **interpretation paradox** of cross-cultural research. Large differences between very diverse cultures are easy to obtain but hard to interpret because the reasons for the differences may be caused by any of a number of multiple factors. On the other hand, small differences between people of similar cultures may be hard to spot, but when observed, are easy to interpret because the groups being assessed share many features, so the reasons for differences stand out and are easy to identify.

DISCUSSION QUESTIONS

1. Can you think of a behavior that would correspond to an emic (i.e., relevant only within a given culture)? to an etic (i.e., holding true across cultures) if you considered students with different majors as representing different cultures?
2. Describe how a psychologist would discuss the concept of happiness from absolutist, relativist, and universalist points of view.

IS THERE A BIOLOGICAL BASIS FOR RACE?

One-Drop Rule (Hypodescent)—One means by which a person is racially categorized as a member of a low status group such that if he or she has "one drop" of blood from a given group (i.e., any ancestor, no matter how remote, from that group), the individual is automatically classified as being from that group, used specifically with people of African descent who live in the United States.

Psychologists in the United States have studied one particular ethnic group to a great extent, blacks or African Americans. Very often, the research does not appear to center around culture or ethnicity. Rather, investigators cast their studies in terms of race.

You probably imagine a person's race as something that is clearly defined; many people do. The problem lies in the process we use to classify a person. In the United States, we have had a tradition of calling a person "Black" or African American if the person has any African ancestry, no matter how remote or how little. This pattern is known colloquially as the **one-drop rule,** also known as **hypodescent.** A person is black if he or she has "one drop of black blood." In Brazil, a person with any Caucasoid features is regarded as "White" (Zuckerman, 1990). The validity of such racial categorization is suspect if a person's race changes simply because he or she enters a different country.

The Criteria for Race

Race is clearly a strange concept scientifically. Why does a single ancestor determine race when there are so many ancestors who are ignored? And why does a single Black ancestor make a person Black, when a single White ancestor does not make a person white? The concept of race in scientific research is troublesome; race-determining characteristics fall on a continuum, but people create all-or-none categories. Whenever you have a continuum, but you try to make discrete categories, you have to make a decision as to where to put the cutoff for inclusion into different categories. Such decisions are arbitrary, and another person could make a different decision that has as much validity (or lack thereof) as yours.

The use of the concept of race, even among the educated, has sometimes been very loose. For instance, *The Mother's Encyclopedia* (1942) discussed rheumatic fever, asserting that "some races who live in New York are especially prone to it, particularly Italians and Jewish people" (p. 1028). Further, in the United States, there used to be a greater belief in the nature of the continuum regarding Black and White, even if there was no real scientific basis for it. Historically, an individual with one Black grandparent was classified as a quadroon; a person with one Black great-grandparent was listed as an octoroon. These "races" were considered as real as any others.

A great many scientists have concurred that race is a social construction, not a natural phenomenon. Anthropologists and some biologists seem to have caught on to this idea some time ago, but some social and behavioral scientists have been slower to adopt this conclusion.

The problem with race as a construct that might help us understand behavior is that individual differences within races overwhelm the biological differences between races. In other words, if you look at the variability between any two people in the same culture, they show much more variability in genetic makeup than do two "average" people with ancestors on different continents.

At the phenotypical level, race is often defined in terms of features like skin color, but also hair type, eye color, and facial features. These turn out to be unreliable markers for race; in fact, they are not correlated with one another, meaning that just because a person shows one "racial" characteristic, it doesn't mean that he or she will show the others (Zuckerman, 1990). In addition, there are people in the so-called Negroid groups who are lighter in skin color than others in the so-called Caucasoid groups.

As you will see in Controversy Box 12.2, scientists have identified a number of different problems associated with the use of racial categories in scientific research. There will undoubtedly be continued debate about the topic of race because of its importance as a social concept.

Current Biological Insights Regarding Race

Scientists working on the Human Genome Project, which is an attempt to identify the genetic makeup of human beings, has brought attention to this issue. According to Harold Freeman of North General Hospital in Manhattan, the percentage of genes that reflect differences in external appearances associated with race is about 0.01 percent (Angier, 2000).

Since the emergence of humans in present form, there have been about 7,000 generations. This is not a sufficiently large number to lead to clear differentiation of one group from another, according to geneticists. Further, there has always been mixing of genes of various groups when they come in contact with one another, intermarry, and reproduce. Biological variables may differentiate groups in a general way, but these variables are not, in and of themselves, markers for race because a person from any group could show them. "For instance, Afro-Americans are at a higher risk [for essential hypertension] than Anglo-Americans. From our perspective, what is of scientific interest is not the race of these individuals, but the relationship between the identified biological factors . . . and hypertension" (Betancourt & López, 1993, p. 631). The biological factors contribute causally to the hypertension; race is a correlational variable.

Still, some psychologists argue that real racial differences exist. They cite the notion that brain sizes, on average, are largest in Asians, middle-sized in Whites, and

CONTROVERSY BOX 12.2
CONTROVERSY: Are There Really Different Races?

How many races are there? Many people in the United States would list White, Black, Hispanic, Native American, and Asian, believing that these categories are valid, discrete groupings. That is, you are White or you are not; you are Black or you are not; etc. Everybody falls into one and only one category.

The truth is not so simple. In reality, there do not seem to be biologically based markers that separate people conveniently and reliably. For example, skin color, which many people use to define inclusion in a racial category, is inconsistent. There are Black people who are lighter than White people. Similarly, people of Asian descent span many different skin colors. The same is true for Native Americans and Hispanics. Skin lightness or darkness may be the most obvious trait that people rely on, but any characteristic you select has the same weaknesses.

People are very hard to classify precisely and objectively. One reason is that the differences among people are usually on a continuum. One person has more or less of this or that trait. When you have such continua, any point on the continuum that you use to create categories is going to be arbitrary; another person can justify using a different point.

Once scientists decided that racial differences were interesting, there were always problems defining race. In the 1920s, scientists agreed that there were three European races; in the 1930s, they changed it to ten European races. At the same time, there was a single African-based racial category. Africa is a big continent (over 11 million square miles); Europe is a small continent (about 4 million square miles). Not surprisingly, Africans show much greater genetic diversity than Europeans do. Why then was there only one African race? The categorization process was based on socially derived beliefs, not scientific measurement.

In addition, if you look at a map, it is not clear where Europe ends and Asia begins. The boundary is arbitrary. Further, if you look at a map, you will see that the line that divides Asia and Africa is also arbitrary. So is the distinction between Asian and African people. By the same token, why should we have any faith that the distinction between Europeans and Asians is real? It is too easy to form stereotypes and consider them to be objective, reliable, and valid. But assigning people to different racial categories based on an arbitrary boundary is questionable. In some ways, it would be similar to identifying people from Ohio and Michigan as being from different races based on an arbitrary politically drawn line.

In terms of psychological research, we see again and again that behaviors and characteristics attributed to race generally have their causes in social or environmental factors. When researchers account for these factors, the effect of "race" generally diminishes or vanishes.

If a fine analysis eliminates effects of "race" on behavior in most of situations that have been studied, a critical thinker might conclude that the remaining differences could well be due to factors that researchers have not yet identified.

Nobody has yet identified scientifically reliable and valid definitions of race based on biology or genetics. As Yee et al. (1994) and others have pointed out, even in scientific research, depictions of race are generally made from a layperson's point of view, with no real scientific backing. Finally, it seems reasonable to believe that when one argument after another falls, it becomes more parsimonious to believe that racial factors per se are irrelevant and that social and economic factors create differences between groups.

smallest in Blacks, a pattern that reflects trends in IQ scores. That is, the claim is that IQ score and brain size are positively correlated. At the same time, Peters (1993) noted that in studies of brain size and IQ, measurement error as small as one millimeter could account for the observed difference across races.

Historical Error

Unfortunately, from the beginning, research that investigated brain size and intelligence suffered from fatal flaws (Gould, 1996). In the 1840s, Samuel George Morton found that Whites had the largest brains, Indians were in the middle, and Blacks were on the bottom. As it turns out, his sample of skulls was egregiously poor. He specifically included a large number of Peruvian Inca skulls; these people were small of stature. He had very few Iroquois Indians, whose skulls were large. As a result, the mean skull size of Indians was artificially low.

Morton also decided to eliminate some Caucasian skulls, of Hindus who were small, thereby raising the average of Caucasians. There is no evidence that Morton thought he was doing anything inappropriate, because he kept meticulous records that others could investigate. If he had tried to cheat, he would not have kept such good records or made them public. He assumed that white Europeans had greater intelligence than others; the use of skull and brain size was simply meant to quantify what "everybody knew to be true." So he had little reason to doubt his methodology or his conclusions.

Current Controversies

Modern psychologists (e.g., Cernovsky, 2000) have countered the argument about brain size and intelligence with the fact that mean brain size of groups living near the equator is less than that of groups nearer the poles, so that brain size is correlated with geography of one's ancestors and not much else. Besides, women's brains are smaller than men's, even after body size is taken into consideration. There is no evidence that women are less intelligent than men.

Another problem arises when we equate a score on a standardized test with intelligence. An IQ score is just that, a test score. It relates to behaviors that the test makers regard as important, like how well you do in school. It is true that your grades in school will correlate pretty well with your IQ score, but much of that may be due to the fact that IQ scores are based, to a degree, on tasks that are valued in educational settings. Thus, it is no surprise that people who score low on intelligence tests do not do well in school.

Flynn (1999) has refuted a number of arguments that relate IQ and race, concluding that environmental differences explain differences in scores on IQ tests and that genetic (i.e., racial) interpretations, when investigated empirically, lead to conclusions that simply do not make sense. The controversy will undoubtedly persist for a long time because the issues remain socially controversial and complex and the arguments multifaceted.

DISCUSSION QUESTIONS
1. Could historical mistakes concerning the relationship between race and the measurement of IQ recur today? How?
2. What difficulties arise in using the concept of genetic differences as the source of supposed racial differences?
3. How have society's ideas affected how we have defined race?

PRACTICAL ISSUES IN CULTURAL RESEARCH

Sue (1999) has pointed out some of the major issues in carrying out cross-cultural research. One of them is that many researchers may have difficulty finding participants from different cultural groups. Just like students who have little time for anything other than home life, school work, and extracurricular activities, researchers have limited amounts of time.

The result is that when they plan their own research, they make use of student participants because of availability; it doesn't hurt that the students are also willing, bright, and motivated. The people who volunteer for research are different from people in general and in many colleges may not show much cultural diversity. The truth is that it would take a considerable amount of time, money, and energy to find the diverse samples that are desirable. Given the practical considerations, researchers generally feel that they have to live with the samples they can access, even if it limits how well their results apply to different groups.

Lack of Appropriate Training among Researchers

In addition to having access to fairly homogeneous samples, researchers may simply not have the knowledge or training needed to conduct high quality, cross-cultural research. Fortunately, the Council of National Psychological Associations for the Advancement of Ethnic Minority Interests has developed guidelines published by the American Psychological Association for research with ethnic minority communities (Council of National Associations, 2000). Some of their major points appear in Table 12.1.

TABLE 12.1   Important considerations regarding research with people of ethnic groups (Council of National Psychological Associations, 1999).

Personal Characteristics	Develop awareness of the culture of the group you study
	Become aware of the effects of the culture and oppression and discrimination
	Recognize multiple linguistic and communication styles
	Recognize the heterogeneity that exists within any simple ethnic label
	Identify the degree to which an individual is acculturated
Research Considerations	Recognize cultural assumptions and biases in creating methods and materials
	Make sure all measurement instruments make sense from the cultural viewpoint of the group you study
	Use measurement instruments that are appropriately normed and that have established reliability and validity
	Determine if the research is culturally relevant to the group you study
	Establish appropriate comparison (control) groups
	Use adequately translated materials to maximize effectiveness of communication
	Conduct a cost/benefit analysis to make sure the research is worth doing
Outcomes	Interpret results within the appropriate cultural context
	Consider alternate explanations
	Remember that difference does not mean deviance
	Request help from community members in interpreting your research results
	Increase mainstream outlets for minority research
	Recognize the existence of confounding variables like educational level and socioeconomic status

These considerations are important in any research project. They just happen to be particularly relevant to research with ethnic minorities. If you keep these points in mind, any research with any population will be better.

DISCUSSION QUESTION
1. Why is it useful to include people from cultural groups you are studying when you plan your study and when you interpret your results?

WHY THE CONCEPTS OF CULTURE AND ETHNICITY ARE ESSENTIAL IN RESEARCH

After the long discussion about the controversial concepts of race and ethnicity, you may wonder why we should consider it in our research. The reason is that various groups of people differ from one another in many ways. These groups just don't differ in the simplistic ways we normally think. We need to identify what differences occur across groups, as well as what differences occur within groups. We also need to identify factors that cause those differences because group affiliation alone may not be the only, or the most important, reason.

Differences Due to Language and Thought Processes

One research project that revealed the importance of culture on psychological processes involved asking people to rate the intensity of emotions on the faces of people in photographs. Matsumoto and Assar (1992) showed a series of photos of people displaying the so-called universal emotions of anger, fear, happiness, sadness, or surprise. Research participants rated the apparent emotion displayed in each picture. Participants were students in India who were bilingual in English and in Hindi.

The most interesting manipulation here was that in one testing session, the research took place entirely in English; in another session, everything was in Hindi. The results showed that the students recognized emotions more accurately when they used English than Hindi. According to Matsumoto and Assar, people who speak English come from cultures in which people are used to talking openly about emotions. This cultural effect may lead English speakers to greater recognition and accurate judgment of emotions. Further support for the importance of language in thought came from research by Marian and Neisser (2000), who demonstrated that bilingual people have easier access to memories when they try to recall those memories using the language they would have used when they initially experienced the event.

Language involves more than different word use. In fact, Ball, Giles, and Hewstone (1984) suggested that in order to learn a second language, you must also learn the culture of that language. You won't understand the language completely unless you know its context. Matsumoto and Assar's results on emotions suggest that culture may affect the way people think about or express their ideas. If you were conducting research that involved only speakers of English (which is true for the vast majority of psychological research), your conclusions about how people respond to the world around them will be very limited.

Language may also influence thought in other ways. Hedden, Park, Nisbett, Ji, Jing, and Jiao (2002) noted that Chinese speakers have an advantage over English speakers in some numerical tasks because the Chinese words representing numbers are shorter, thus easier to remember. They found no such advantage on a visuo-spatial task involving completing visual patterns. Thus, language may affect not only what you think but also how you think. Cross-cultural research needs to take such differences into account.

Differences in Simple and Complex Behaviors

Even simple responses may differ as a function of culture. When Chinese and American students indicated how often they engaged in certain behaviors, the Chinese participants may have had better memories than American students did because, as members of a collectivist society, the Chinese are expected to monitor their own behaviors closely (Ji, Schwarz, & Nisbett, 2000). The Americans, on the other hand, did not seem to have as reliable a memory for their behaviors and had to estimate them. Thus, even a simple memory task may lead to fundamentally different ways of responding, depending on your culture.

Not surprisingly, differences in behaviors also occur in more complex situations. For instance, people in China seem to have a different approach to problem solving than people in the Western world. Peng and Nisbett (1999) studied Chinese students and American students in several experiments to see how they responded to contradictory statements in decision making. Chinese students were generally more comfortable accepting two contradictory statements as involving partial truths; American students were more likely to look for a single, logical truth.

These differences reflect fundamentally different views of the world. If you look at the psychological literature in problem solving, you find that there is remarkably little non-Western thought. In problem solving, the emphasis in most research is on logic and rationality that arrives at a single, logically coherent response. Before we claim that such approaches are a good general characterization of problem solving, we should remember that perhaps a billion people (or more) in this world would disagree with our representation of thought and decision making.

It is important to remember that the modes of thought favored in the East and in the West are both useful and valid, but both are incomplete. As Peng and Nisbett pointed out, the world is complex and contradictory. Thus, we may have to accommodate our thoughts to accept potential contradictions and incomplete knowledge. At the same time, a non-dialectical or Western approach is useful for identifying when a particular argument is better supported by data and for generating useful counterarguments to rebut a possibly flawed argument.

If we want to generate a complete description of the way people think and solve problems, we cannot ignore the fact that our approach to problem solving reflects ways that we are comfortable with, but they are not the only ways that are valid. Knowing about culture helps us know about thought. Ignoring the effects of culture will mean that we have incomplete knowledge about thought and behavior.

Is Culture-Free Theory Really Free of Culture?

The importance of understanding cultural effects on behavior emerges when we look at the studies of how babies attach themselves to parents. Rothbaum, Weisz, Pott, Kiyake, and Morelli (2000) described the general tenets of attachment theory and assessed whether the theory is more culturally relevant in the Western hemisphere than elsewhere. This is an important discussion because many psychologists view attachment theory as evolutionarily based, thus free of cultural biases.

Three of the important tenets of attachment are as follows: First, there is a connection between maternal sensitivity and security of attachment. Second, secure children are more socially and emotionally competent than insecure children. Third, infants who show higher levels of adaptation are more likely to explore when they feel secure. These notions seem pretty straightforward. The research on attachment has typically involved middle-class American children. If attachment were strictly a part of evolutionary development, this would not be a problem. However, cultural differences may be important

As Rothbaum et al. (2000) note, when parents or teachers identify potentially problematic behavior, the Japanese may identify one set of behaviors as appropriate and a different set as troublesome. The Americans could reverse the pattern. Rothbaum et al. maintain that in order to understand the nature of children's attachment, we have to understand the culture because attachment theory is not as culture-free as psychologists have traditionally believed.

These researchers may raise valid points, but not all psychologists agree. For instance, Chao (2001) suggested that Rothbaum didn't define the term *culture* adequately, equating it with nations. Van Ijzendoorn and Sagi (2001) and Chao also argued that there is too much variability within Japanese and within American cultures for easy generalizations about Japanese people and American people. The disagreements aren't reconciled easily because of the difficulties associated with cultural research.

Similarities and Differences within the Same Culture

People who grow up in the same culture share attitudes, values, and behaviors, but such people are not merely clones of one another. Part of the problem is that people in a group may show similarities on one dimension but not on another. Matsumoto (1993) investigated differences in emotion among Americans of various ethnic groups.

He asked his research participants to identify the emotion displayed in facial photographs and rate its intensity. They also indicated how appropriate a display of the emotion was. He discovered that some differences existed among Asian Americans, Blacks, Hispanics, and Whites, but the differences were inconsistent. Sometimes the different groups rated emotions in the pictures the same, but sometimes not. For example, Americans of Asian ancestry looked at a given picture and saw less anger than an American of African ancestry. But the Asian Americans saw an equal amount of sadness as African Americans. In addition, African Americans saw more intense emotions generally in pictures of White people than did Asian, Hispanic, or White Americans.

This pattern of findings suggests that if we are studying emotions, we could sometimes treat all Americans as more or less similar (e.g., for happiness and sadness), but not all the time (e.g., for fear). Simple research like this can reflect the complexity of cross-cultural studies.

DISCUSSION QUESTIONS

1. How can culture affect our memories and our perspectives on emotion?
2. Why would the results of a problem-solving study differ if the researcher recruited Chinese versus American participants? For what kinds of problems would the Chinese show an advantage? the Americans?
3. Use Matsumoto's (1993) research on facial expressions to argue that different groups sometimes show similarities, but sometimes they don't.

CULTURAL FACTORS IN MENTAL HEALTH RESEARCH

Psychologists continue to make progress in mental health research, documenting the effectiveness of various therapies for different problems and identifying variables associated with normal and abnormal behavior. As we have recognized the diversified culture in the United States, we have begun to pay attention to the different needs of people of varying backgrounds, although we still know much less than we need to know.

One type of research that clinical psychologists conduct involves assessing the validity of psychological tests across cultural boundaries. If we cannot translate tests into different languages to convey the same ideas as they do in English, we cannot be confident that test results signify the same psychological processes. A poorly translated test will not assess the same thing in both languages. Problems also occur when clinicians try to use a test with minority or immigrant populations when that test is created for and standardized on a White population born in the United States and raised to speak English. In either case, the scores might mean different things.

Content Validity

Content Validity—The degree to which the material contained in a test relates to the concept being assessed.

The process of ensuring that psychological tests serve diverse populations is difficult (Rogler, 1999). Diagnostic and research instruments need to make sense from the viewpoint of those who use them; that is, the tests must show, among other things, **content validity.** The questions should, in expert judgment, relate to what the test assesses. When psychologists create tests, they have to decide what questions to ask. This is where their expert judgment comes in. The problem is that potential patients or clients may not share the same culture as the psychologist, so the patient or client may be answering a different question than the clinician is asking.

Rogler (1999) illustrated this point through a particular question on the Diagnostic Interview Schedule (DIS), which he noted is the most influential test in psychiatric epidemiology. The question asks, "Do you often worry a lot about having clean clothes?" This question might be useful in identifying whether people are overly distressed about unreasonable things. The problem with this question is that it assumes that the person answering it has access to running water. If you have all the water you need, then worrying about clean clothes might be a sign of psychological distress. On the other hand, if you do not have access to running water, laundry facilities, and so forth, such a worry becomes a reasonable preoccupation.

As it turns out, many Plains Indians in the United States do not have access to running water. As such, to respond that they do not worry about clean clothes would probably be more indicative of a problem than if they replied that they do worry. From this point of view, we can see that what might be an appropriate question on the DIS for many of us would be entirely inappropriate for others of us.

Translation Problems

If questions pose difficulties within the same language, imagine what problems arise if we try to translate the test into a different language for use by people whose cultural outlook does not match ours. Rogler (1999) provided another example from the DIS to illustrate the dilemma of creating a faithful translation of a test item into a different language.

He identified the question that reads, "I felt I could not shake off the blues even with help from my family or friends." In trying to translate this apparently simple and straightforward item into Spanish, he encountered great difficulty. In translation, an individual tries to stay as close to the original wording as possible, but there were no suitable Spanish equivalents. One problem here is that in English, "the blues" has a particular meaning that does not survive in a translation to the Spanish word *azul*, the color blue. Rogler also noted that in the United States, we often think that it would be possible, by force of will, to "shake off" an unwanted mood. Is this concept shared by Spanish speakers? If so, what Spanish verb would be appropriate? He wondered whether the word *sacudir* would be a good translation. It means to shake off vigorously like a dog shakes water off its body. He decided that *sacudir* would not be appropriate.

Back Translation—In cross-cultural research, the process by which comparable testing instruments are developed, by translating from an original language to a second language, then back to the first to ensure that the original version and the translation back into that language produce comparable meanings.

After considerable contemplation, he translated the item by rewording the original English sentence to read "I could not get over feeling sad even with help from my family or friends." He then found it easier to prepare a Spanish version. Normally, a translator tries not to deviate from the original form of an item, but in this case, there was probably no alternative if the translation was to be meaningful. Table 12.2 provides other examples that Rogler generated to illustrate the cultural biases of the DIS.

One useful technique for ensuring comparability of items across languages is **back translation** (Banville, Desrosiers, & Genet-Volet, 2000). In this process, an item is translated from one language to a second. Then a blind translator converts it back to the first language. For example, an item might start in English, be translated into Spanish, then back again into English. If the original version in the first language is equivalent in

TABLE 12.2 Examples reflecting a strong effect of culture that may cause problems across cultures (Rogler, 1999).

EXAMPLE	REASON FOR THE PROBLEM
In assessing dissociation, the Dissociative Experience Scale asks about the following: "Some people have the experience of driving a car and suddenly realizing that they don't remember what has happened during all or part of the trip."	The question assumes that the person taking the test takes long car trips. This kind of factual assumption is a problem because people living in the inner city rarely, if ever, drive in places that do not have heavy traffic. As such, an answer to the question will not provide useful information.
Translation of the Clinical Analysis Questionnaire into Spanish.	Thirty-six percent of test items contained grammatical errors and involved direct translation of colloquialisms that made no sense in Spanish. With these translation problems, we could conclude that the questions in the different languages did not have the same meaning.
How does schizophrenia affect decision-making among married couples in San Juan, Puerto Rico?	Among the people studied, decision making was not a critical aspect of familial interactions, as it is in the United States. In Puerto Rico, the corresponding dimension was how "men's work" and "women's work" was divided. Knowing about decision making would not help in understanding problems or devising treatments.
Description of symptoms of bipolar disorder in the Amish.	The typical examples that clinicians look for include buying sprees, sexual promiscuity, and reckless driving, which are not applicable to the Amish. Instead, relevant symptoms involve behaviors like excessive use of public telephones, treating livestock too roughly, or giving gifts during the wrong season of the year.

meaning to the version that has been translated out of, then back into, English, the item is likely to capture the same concepts in both languages.

Cross-Cultural Norms

Relatively few distress inventories have received scrutiny on a cross-cultural basis; none have involved norms with college students (Cepeda-Benito & Gleaves, 2000). Ironically, although college students form the typical research participant in psychology, the clinical literature seems to underrepresent them.

When researchers have investigated cross-cultural equivalence of inventories, they have revealed a complex picture. For instance, the complete version of the Center for Epidemiologic Studies–Depression scale seems valid for Americans of African, European, and Mexican descent (Aneschensel, Clark, & Frerichs, 1983), although the short version produces differences between Americans of African and European descent (Tran, 1997, cited in Cepeda-Benito & Gleaves, 2000).

In one study, Cepeda-Benito and Gleaves (2000) investigated the generalizability of the Hopkins Symptom Checklist-21 (HSCL-21) across Blacks, Hispanics, and Whites. This test is a short, 21-item version of a longer, 57-item inventory designed to measure distress. The HSCL-21 shows validity across a wide array of cultural groups, including Italian, Vietnamese, Latino, and European Americans. Cepeda-Benito and Gleaves investigated whether college students of differing backgrounds responded uniquely to it.

They discovered that the HSCL-21 would be an appropriate test of Black, Hispanic, and White college students. Given that other research revealed good construct validity of the inventory, one might have a degree of confidence that a clinician might use this test appropriately with students of many ethnic groups.

Cepeda-Benito and Gleaves (2000) were appropriately cautious in stating that their participants may not be representative of other ethnic college populations. Also, it is true that not every American ethnic group was represented in the research, but its generality across the three disparate groups tested provided cautious optimism. Unfortunately, the number of psychological tests that have been normed for varied groups is still uncomfortably small.

Cross-Cultural Diagnoses

One consequence of the lack of information on the validity of psychological tests for minority populations is that the tests might lead to diagnoses that are based more on ethnicity than on problematic behavior. As Iwamasa, Larrabee, and Merritt (2000) have shown, people may be predisposed to classify individuals of different ethnic groups in predetermined ways.

Iwamasa et al. (2000) identified the criteria for personality disorders listed in the Diagnostic and Statistical Manual (DSM; American Psychiatric Association, 1987). In clinical work, mental health workers observe an individual and make note of behaviors that occur. If a person shows a certain, well-specified group of behaviors, he or she may be diagnosed with a particular personality disorder as a result. In Iwamasa et al.'s study, the researchers asked their participants to sort these diagnostic criteria in three different ways: according to their presence in men versus women, by ethnicity, and by self (i.e., is this characteristic of you?). Some of the statements that the participants rated appear in Table 12.3. The participants did not know that they were dealing with clinical diagnostic criteria. Rather, they simply identified their stereotypes of the "normal" behaviors of people of different types.

The results suggest that strong cultural effects could occur in diagnosing personality disorders. The college students' beliefs about normal characteristics of Blacks are the same as the criteria used by psychologists and psychiatrists to diagnose antisocial and paranoid personality disorders. Similarly, the students' depiction of the typical behavior of Asian Americans reflects what clinicians look for in people who are schizoid. According to the research results, people of European descent showed a wide range of behaviors associated with different pathologies.

These results suggested that when people think of the behavior of Blacks, Whites, Asian Americans, and Native Americans, those behaviors are the same ones used by

TABLE 12.3 Examples of descriptions from DSM-III-R that participants rated as typical in men versus women, in different ethnic groups, and of the participants themselves.

EXAMPLES OF DESCRIPTION	PERSONALITY DISORDER WITH WHICH THE DESCRIPTION IS ASSOCIATED	GROUP IN WHICH THE "SYMPTOMS" ARE CONSIDERED TYPICAL
Has no regard for the truth Has never sustained a totally monogamous relationship for more than one year	Antisocial	African American
Is easily hurt by criticism or disapproval Fears being embarrassed by blushing, crying, or showing signs of anxiety in front of other people	Avoidant	European American
Inappropriate, intense anger or lack of control of anger, e.g., frequent displays of temper, constant anger, recurrent physical fights Chronic feelings of emptiness or boredom	Borderline	European American
Feels devastated or helpless when close relationships end Allows others to make most of his or her important decisions, e.g., where to live, what job to take	Dependent	European American
Is overly concerned with physical attractiveness Is uncomfortable in situations in which he or she is not the center of attention	Histrionic	European American
Reacts to criticism with feelings of rage, shame, or humiliation (even if not expressed) Believes that his or her problems are unique and can be understood only by other special people	Narcissistic	European American
Perfectionism that interferes with task completion, e.g., inability to complete a project because own overly strict standards are not met Inability to discard worn-out or worthless objects even when they have no sentimental value	Obsessive-Compulsive	European American
Expects, without sufficient basis, to be exploited or harmed by others Bears grudges or is unforgiving of insults or slights	Paranoid	African American
Neither desires nor enjoys close relationships, including being part of a family Is indifferent to the praise and criticism of others	Schizoid	Asian American
Odd or eccentric behavior or appearance Inappropriate or constricted affect, e.g., silly, aloof, rarely reciprocates gestures or facial expressions, such as smiles or nods	Schizotypal	Native American

Source: Adapted with permission from G. Y. Iwamasa et al. (2000). Are personality disorder criteria ethnically based? A card-sort analysis. *Cultural Diversity and Ethnic Minority Psychology, 6,* 284–296.

mental health practitioners to diagnose psychological disorders. The problem is not with Americans of various heritages. The problem is with people's biases and assumptions. If a psychiatrist or clinical psychologist used implicit stereotypes in dealing with different types of patients or clients, it could lead to differential diagnoses for what might be normal behavior.

Iwamasa et al. studied undergraduate volunteers, not clinicians. In addition, the undergraduates did not assign the diagnostic criteria in the same way that clinicians do. Would the results generalize to clinical psychologists and psychiatrists? Given that mental health workers are members of society, with the same biases, we might suspect so, although we don't know. Only when research takes place in a clinical setting will we know how cultural biases affect the ways that practitioners diagnose people. Until this research is conducted, we need to be skeptical that the best decisions are being made.

DISCUSSION QUESTIONS
1. How does culture affect diagnosis of psychological or psychiatric problems? What effect do biases and assumptions have?
2. Why would it be a problem for diagnosing psychological problems if a clinician simply translated questions on a psychological test on the spot? What could you do if a client or patient was not fluent enough to answer the questions in English?

SEX AND GENDER: DO MEN AND WOMEN COME FROM DIFFERENT CULTURES?

Much has been made of the behavioral differences between men and women. Is it really true that *Men Are from Mars and Women Are from Venus* (Gray, 1992)?

If we regard culture the way that Matsumoto (1994) defined it, as "the set of attitudes, values, beliefs, and behaviors, shared by a group of people, communicated from one generation to the next via language or some other means of communication" (p. 4), we might very well argue that men and women are culturally different in some important ways. In addition, people stereotype men and women differently, just as people stereotype Whites and Blacks differently.

Iwamasa et al.'s (2000) research on the perception of stereotypically female or male behaviors also shed light on the fact that people have certain expectations about behaviors across the sexes. The investigators found that normal but stereotypically female behavior was associated with certain disorders (e.g., avoidant personality, paranoia) and normal but stereotpyically male behavior with others (antisocial personality, schizoid personality).

In the realm of everyday behavior, people often make a big issue of the differences between women and men in math test scores, which are small when they exist at all. Although we don't understand all the factors associated with any differences, there are enough ambiguities that we should be skeptical of biological explanations. Some important issues about gender differences appear in Controversy Box 12.3.

Stereotypes and Gender-Related Performance

Could stereotypes of women negatively affect their performance in the same way that stereotypes affect the performance of African Americans and Asian Americans (Cheryan

■ ■ ■ ■ ■ ▬▬▬▬▬▬▬▬▬▬▬▬

CONTROVERSY BOX 12.3

CONTROVERSY: Are Men Better than Women at Mathematics?

It is a very widely held belief that women have better verbal abilities than men. Conversely, many people believe that men show better mathematical abilities than women do. In fact, among the general public, you don't hear much argument about it. Just take a look at high school math courses: Boys like them and are more likely to enroll in them. On the other hand, girls like poetry and literature and are more willing to enroll in them. Given that most people will gravitate toward things they do better in, doesn't this say something about the relative abilities of boys and girls in math and English?

The patterns of enrollment in math and in English definitely give us important information, but not necessarily the information we think. Maybe ability doesn't have as much to do with enrollment and success in classes as other factors like encouragement and discouragement. Consider the fact that, at one point, talking Barbie dolls complained how hard mathematics is. Is there a message here? Perhaps years of emphasizing that girls don't like math but boys do, and that boys don't like English but girls do takes its toll.

As Caplan and Caplan (1999) have noted, the popular media have reported about male superiority in mathematics. Should we believe these accounts of sex differences in mathematical abilities?

Two decades ago, Benbow and Stanley (1980, 1983) claimed that hormonal differences in math performance may have been responsible for the differences between men and women. As Caplan and Caplan pointed out, however, nobody bothered to measure hormonal levels of the men or women in the research. Thus, the argument that hormones affect performance goes something like this: Men have higher testosterone levels than women. The men scored higher than the women. Thus, higher testosterone levels lead to higher

math scores. Logically, you cannot use two true, but unrelated, statements to prove an argument. There doesn't seem to be any reliable evidence that testosterone levels bear any relationship to math ability.

According to Caplan and Caplan, people are predisposed to believe in male superiority in math. As such, they are likely to accept plausible sounding arguments ("the difference is hormonal") even though those arguments are not based on research. When people are predisposed to believe in this difference between the sexes, they tend to ignore potentially potent factors like parents' and teachers' expectations, and responses to society's stereotypes.

We also have to take into consideration the dynamics of the testing situation. As Inzlicht and Ben-Zeev (2000) have shown, the context in which women take tests can influence their performance. Women doing math in the presence of men didn't perform as well as when they were in a single-sex environment. Another point to remember is that research has consistently documented female strengths in quantitative courses (e.g., Schram, 1996). Before we accept facile explanations based on questionable theory, we should rely on well-documented information and explanations that research has provided.

Finally, how do we explain the fact that recent research has revealed that the gap in women's and men's scores is narrowing. Are women becoming more masculine? Are men becoming more feminine? Are men's and women's hormonal levels changing? These are generally unlikely explanations. Greater emphasis on female success in math courses, increased encouragement to take math courses, higher motivation levels, and the nature of the testing situation are probably better explanations.

& Bodenhausen, 2000; Steele & Aronson, 1995)? According to Inzlicht and Ben-Zeev (2000), when women attempt to solve difficult math problems in the presence of men, they are less successful than when they are in the presence of other women only.

These researchers suggest that, in the presence of men, women act out the stereotype of poorer female performance in mathematics, just as members of minority groups fulfill stereotypes.

Moving back to the question of possible cultural differences between men and women, it seems that some psychologists might be comfortable with the idea. Women see themselves as different from men in some respects; men see themselves as different from women in some respects. Knowing what you do about our culture, do you think that these perceived differences revolve around attitudes, beliefs, and behaviors that are passed from one generation to another? If so, they fit generally accepted definitions of cultural differences.

DISCUSSION QUESTIONS

1. In what aspects of life could you argue that men and women come from different cultures? In what aspects could you argue that they come from the same culture?
2. What stereotypes can you think of that are associated with people of a culture other than yours? How could these stereotypes play out in these people's lives. What stereotypes might Europeans have of people from the United States that would cause Americans to act differently?
3. Is there any evidence to suggest that stereotypes have an effect on the people who are the victims of those stereotypes? How could you investigate ways to reduce the effects of stereotype threat?

CHAPTER SUMMARY

In order to understand why people act as they do, we need to understand the cultural context in which those behaviors occur. The effects of culture, race, and ethnicity all surface in our behaviors. The problem that researchers face in considering these contextual questions is that the terms people use every day and even in scientific research are often quite vague. One researcher may refer to ethnicity in describing a behavior whereas a different researcher may refer to culture in describing the same thing. Because of the problems with definitions, the conclusions that people draw about causes of behavior are sometimes suspect.

One persistent controversy in this area involves the questionable concept of race. There are quite a number of supposed racial categories. The problem is that these categories aren't scientifically defensible. The recent work in genetics indicates that genes are not going to be a useful way of defining races. Still, some scientists maintain that racial categories are useful in their research, even if they cannot define the concept very well.

Because of the complexities of culture, race, and ethnicity, scientific researchers have to work hard to understand the relationship between these constructs and people's behaviors. Research across cultures can be difficult because cultural factors may cause people to understand even simple situations differently. Judgments made by two people from the same cultural background may differ greatly; judgments across cultural boundaries may be nearly impossible to understand without research into those factors. Within the United States, differences between men and women have provided a good deal of controversy, with many questions yet unanswered.

WRITING A RESEARCH REPORT

Most research reports in psychology appearing in journals have a standard format, which is specified in the *Publication Manual of the American Psychological Association* (5th ed.). The use of a consistent style makes it easier for readers to locate critical information. In addition, once writers learn the basics of APA style, it can be easier to write up a report because it is clear where to put various kinds of information.

In general, APA-style papers have the following components in this order

- Title Page
- Abstract
- Introduction
- Methods
- Results
- Discussion
- References
- Tables
- Figure Captions
- Figures

Occasionally there are deviations from this listing. For instance, if a manuscript reports on two or more studies, the author might combine the Results and Discussion section for each study rather than creating two sections. Then there might be a General Discussion after the final study. Once you learn the basic format and after you read a large number of published journal articles, it is often fairly easy to decide how to modify a manuscript if you need to. Following APA style isn't difficult, but you have to pay attention to a lot of small details. The hardest part of formatting is keeping track of those details.

As with any writing you do, it is important to communicate well. The former editor of the journal *Teaching of Psychology*, Charles Brewer, has commented that writers should strive for "clarity, conciseness, and felicity of expression." This means that you should be clear in making your points; you should use economy in your writing, keeping it as short as you can while still getting your message across; and you should write so that your readers don't have to fight their way through a tangled thicket of words to get your point.

Each section of your report will answer certain questions for your reader. For instance, if readers want to know the topic of your research, they know to look in the Introduction. If they are asking what you found when you analyzed your data, they know to look in the results section. If they would like to use your ideas and conduct their own research, they know to look in the methodology section to find out how you carried out your study.

This appendix is designed to help you learn appropriate formatting so your reader knows where to find information. It will also be somewhat useful in giving you guidance on writing style. When it comes to the content, you will have to develop that on your own. Remember that this guide to APA style only highlights the material in the *Publication Manual of the American Psychological Association.* The information here will be useful for creating a basic APA-formatted manuscript. There are many other details in the publication manual itself.

FORMATTING YOUR MANUSCRIPT

There are a few general considerations involved in formatting an APA-style manuscript. To begin with, you should set your margins at one inch on the top, bottom, and sides. Then leave them that way. In addition, everything in the manuscript should be double spaced. Set your word processor's line spacing at double spaced. Then leave it that way. (If you are using complex equations, you might need triple spacing, but that is about the only exception to double spacing.)

Another aspect of APA style is that every page should be numbered in the upper right-hand corner, next to the page header. The best way to display the header and to paginate appropriately is with your word processor's function for creating a page header. By using the header function, you guarantee that this information appears where it needs to on every page. If you type in the header and the page number manually, every time you add or eliminate material in your manuscript, the header and page number will wind up in the wrong place.

When you are typing your manuscript, you will create several different sections (e.g., introduction, methods, results, discussion). Do not begin a new section on a new page. As a rule, just continue to type, using normal double spacing between lines. There are some exceptions to this; they are explained below.

In addition, you have to create headings for each section. There are different levels of headings, depending on the complexity of your manuscript. For most single-study manuscripts, you will use two different types of headings.

When you finish typing the main body of the manuscript and the references, you then add any tables that you want to include. The tables do not appear on the pages with the normal text. They are put at the end, right after the references. Each table goes on a separate page. Following the tables is a page that has the figure captions. All of the figure captions go on the same page, followed by the figures themselves. Graphs, charts, and pictures are all classified as figures. When you prepare them, you put only the figure on a sheet, not the caption.

The general points in this section appear in Figure A.1. Remember that this is a primer on APA style. There are other guidelines that are relevant to more complex

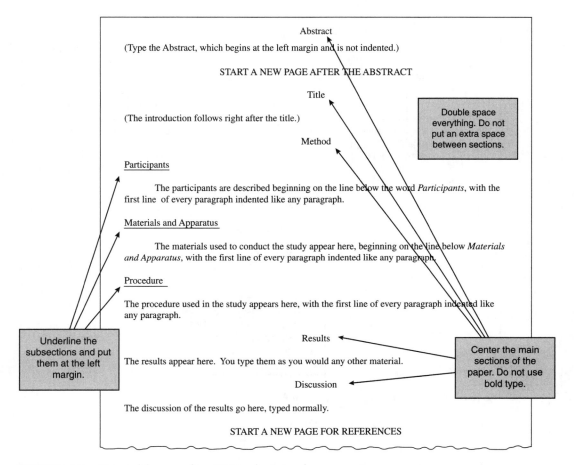

FIGURE A.1 General format of an APA-style research report.

manuscripts than you are likely to produce. You can refer to the *Publication Manual* for those details. You can also learn from reading and referring to journal articles that have been published.

TITLE PAGE

The title page is pretty simple to construct, but it is important to include all the information that is required. You can see the general format in Figure A.2. There are three main components of the title page: the short title, the running head, and the title and author information.

Short Title

The short title consists of the first two or three words of the paper's title, followed by the page number. The short title helps others keep your manuscript together and in the

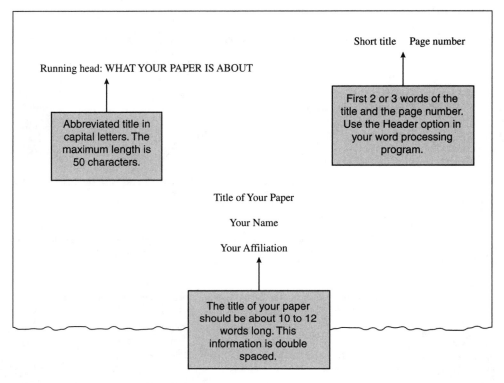

FIGURE A.2   Format of a title page in APA style.

right order if the pages become separated. If the title of your paper is "Study habits of college students over four years," the short title would be *Study habits of.* (You should not italicize it. The examples in this appendix appear in italics so you can see them, but you rarely use italics in a research report.)

The short title appears on every page of the manuscript, so it is best to use your Header/Footer capability on your word processor to create it. In this way, your computer will make sure that the pages are numbered correctly and that the short title is in place, even if you revise your paper, adding or eliminating material.

Running Head

The running head is like an abbreviated title. It should explain the general nature of your project. It is limited to a maximum of 50 characters (i.e., letters and spaces). If your full title is "Study habits of college students over four years," an abbreviated title for the running head could be *STUDENT STUDY HABITS.* (It should be in capital letters.)

Title and Author Information

The title of the paper should clue the reader into the nature of your project. The recommended length is 10 to 12 words. Your name and your affiliation, which will be your school (unless your instructor tells you otherwise for a class paper), appear just below the title of the paper. They let the reader know who you are and where you come from.

ABSTRACT

The abstract is a brief description of the purpose of the project, what methods the author used to address the issues of interest, the results of data collection, and the conclusions and interpretations the author drew. This section gives the reader a general sense of the paper so he or she can decide whether to read the entire paper.

The abstract is typed on its own page, immediately after the title page. It appears as a block. That is, the first line is not indented. According to APA style, the abstract should be no longer than 960 characters and spaces. In practice, this means that it should be no longer than about 120 words.

INTRODUCTION

The introduction section begins with the title of the article you are writing. The word *Introduction* does not appear. So type the title, then begin the introduction itself. As with the rest of your manuscript, use double spacing, with no extra space between the title and the beginning of the introduction. This section addresses several questions that prepare the reader for the ideas discussed throughout the manuscript:

- What is the general topic of the research article?
- What do we know about this topic from previous research?
- What are you trying to demonstrate in your research?
- What are your hypotheses?

The introduction sets the stage for the development of all ideas that follow. When you write the introduction, you explain what we already know about the topic addressed in the paper. You describe previous research and talk about the ideas others have developed. Then you present your own ideas, the ones that your research focuses on. There should be a logical connection between the issues you raise about previous research and the project you are introducing. That is, how does the previous work help lead to your ideas?

You are likely to make your first mention of the work of previous researchers in the introduction. There is a general format for referring to that work. When you cite a published journal article, you typically use the authors' last names and indicate the year of publication or presentation of their work. As you see in Figure A.3, you might mention names in the text per se or in parentheses. The APA *Publication Manual* describes the conventions in detail for citing authors. The highlights are in Figure A.3.

The first time you mention a reference, list the last names of the authors, but cite all of them. Put the year of publication in parentheses.

If you wanted to discuss whether people equate sex and death, you could refer to the research by Goldenberg, Pyszczynski, McCoy, Greenberg, and Solomon (1999). They provided evidence about the sex-death link. Or you could cite the research questioning the effectiveness of the so-called "three strikes" laws that mandate lengthy prison sentences (Stolzenberg & D'Alessio, 1997)

If your first citation of a work appears in parentheses, give the last names of all authors, using an ampersand (&) instead of the word *and* prior to the last author's name. The year of publication goes last, following a comma after the last author.

The second time you refer to work done by three or more authors, cite only the first author. So when mentioning the work linking sex and death by Goldenberg et al. (1999), you use the first author's last name and the Latin abbreviation *et al.*, which stands for *and others* (but you do not use italics). The year goes in parentheses. If you refer to work by two authors, you cite them both any time you mention them, such as the work on prison sentences (Stolzenberg & D'Alessio, 1997). If you mention work done by six authors or more, like the work by Hennigan et al. (1982), you include only the first author's name, even the first time you cite it.

If a work has six or more authors, list only the first author's last name, followed by the designation et al., with a period after al. You do this even the first time you mention it.

FIGURE A.3   Reference formats for citing work in a manuscript in APA style.

METHOD

This section of the manuscript contains several subparts. Each one is pretty much self-contained. The purpose of the method section is to let the reader know how you actually carried out your project. There should be enough detail so another person could read your words and reproduce your study in nearly identical form.

You should present only those details that would be relevant to the purpose and outcome of the study. It isn't always clear what to include, but you have to make your best judgment. For instance, the size, shape, and location of the room in which you conducted your study would not normally be very important. But if the room turned out to be very crowded, it might have affected your results. Or if there was a lot of noisy traffic outside the room, the participants' behaviors might have been affected. You have to decide which details are important and which can be left out.

The different segments of the method section describe who took part, what materials and implements were important in carrying out the study, and the procedure used to complete the research.

Participants

In this subsection, you tell the reader who participated in the study, how many people (or rats, mice, pigeons, etc.) were involved and the demographics of your sample (e.g., age, ethnicity, educational level, etc. as appropriate). The information that gives your reader appropriate information about your participants include the following:

- How many humans or nonhumans were studied?
- If there were nonhuman animals, what kind were they?
- If there were people, what were their characteristics (e.g., average and range of age, gender, race or ethnicity, were they volunteers or were they paid, etc.)?

Apparatus and Materials

The basic issues in this subsection involve what you needed to carry out your study. Sometimes you have used machines, computers, or other instrumentation. Much psychological research also requires materials that participants read, learn, memorize, and so on. When you have created your own apparatus, you should describe it in great detail. If you used commercially available apparatus, you can simply mention the type of apparatus (with make and model), the company that provided it, and any other relevant details that would be useful for somebody who might want to replicate your study or simply to understand your approach. Important information about materials and apparatus include:

- How many and what kind of stimuli, questions, etc. were used?
- What instrumentation, if any, was used to present material to participants and to record their responses?

Procedure

This subsection addresses the issue of what the participants actually did during the research session. The details here should give a complete account of what your participants did from the time the study began until the debriefing was done. You do not need to give details about what you did prior to the session or afterward; if this information is important for some reason, it is probably more appropriate to connect with the apparatus and materials. The important elements of the procedure are as follows:

- After the participants arrived, what did they do?
- What did the experimenters do as they interacted with participants?

RESULTS

In this section, you give a description of your results, accompanied by appropriate quantitative information (e.g., means and standard deviations, statistical analyses). It is often difficult for a reader to understand your results if you simply list all of them without describing them. A long series of means, for instance, can be hard for a reader to comprehend without some narrative to accompany them. The critical questions in the results section include the following:

- What were patterns of behaviors among participants?
- Did behaviors differ when groups were compared?
- What type of behaviors are predictable in the different testing conditions?
- Were there predictable relationships among variables?
- What were the results of any statistical tests?

Your results section can also include tables and figures. Sometimes a table or a figure can present important information much more simply than you can describe it in words. When that is the case, make good use of tables and figures. At the same time, try to avoid using tables and figures that do not contain enough useful information. You probably don't want to use a graph, for example, if you have only two data points to compare.

In detailing your results, make sure that you give enough of a verbal description so the reader has a good idea of what you found. If you only present numerical information, the reader may have difficulty understanding which results were most important and how they related to one another. When you supplement your writing with tables and figures, you can often get your point across very effectively. Tables allow you to present exact values for your data, whereas figures (which may require the reader to estimate numerical values) allow the reader to get an overall picture of the pattern of results.

Tables

Tables can present data very effectively and efficiently. They are relatively easy to create with the Tables function in your word processing program. Figure A.4 outlines some of the main considerations in the use of a table. Figure A.5 shows how an actual table might appear on a page.

At times, tables can get quite complex, especially when there are many groups being compared or when researchers use complex statistical analyses. The basic format is pretty simple, though. The table consists of a label that gives enough information to the readers so they don't have to refer back to the text to comprehend the contents of the table. The table also contains data, often organized by conditions or groups. Sometimes, mean values appear in the margins of the tables, the so-called marginal means. In some cases, tables may not contain numbers, but involve only words and text. This type of table follows the same general principles as numeric tables.

Figures

Graphs and charts used to be difficult to construct when an author had to draw them by hand. Currently, however, data analysis software and spreadsheets permit easy con-

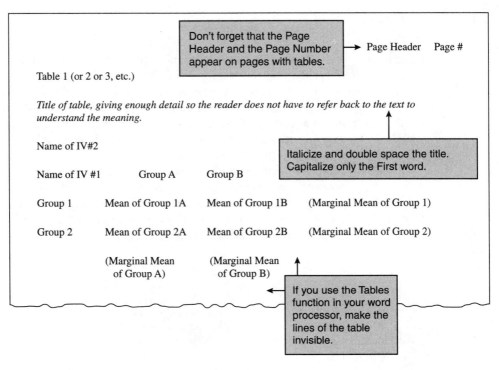

FIGURE A.4 Format of a results table in APA style.

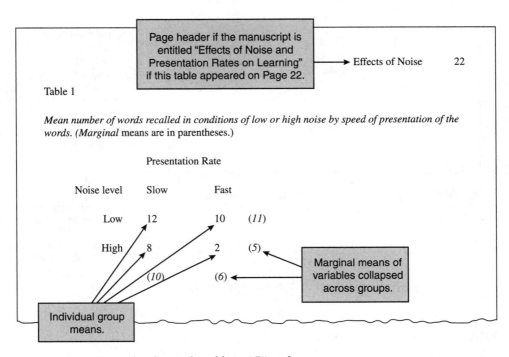

FIGURE A.5 Example of a results table in APA style.

struction of graphs. It is important to remember that when you use graphic presentations, you should make sure that they convey the information you want in a manner that is easy for the reader to comprehend. As noted before, graphs should not contain too little information because they would be a waste of space in a journal. On the other hand, graphs should not be too cluttered. It takes some practice in creating effective visual presentations; you can learn how to construct them by looking at published figures to see which ones are effective and which are not.

The main types of figures used in research articles are line graphs, bar graphs, and scatter diagrams. Line graphs show the relation between two quantitative variables. Bar graphs are often used to represent relations among categorical variables. Scatter diagrams usually reflect correlational analyses. Figures A.6 and A.7 provide examples of line graphs that look slightly different, but that convey the same information.

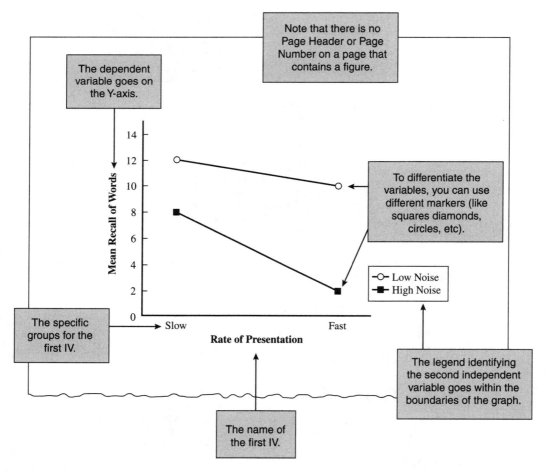

FIGURE A.6   Example of a line graph in APA style.

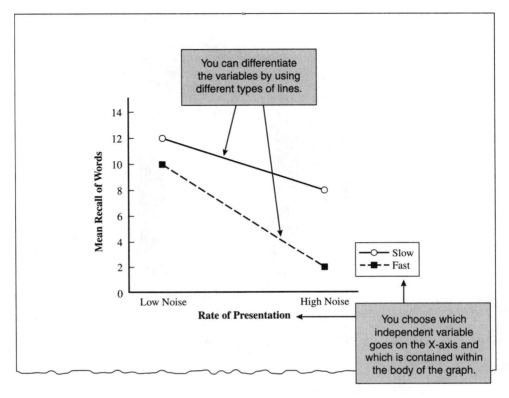

FIGURE A.7   Example of a line graph in APA style.

The two graphs show that the depiction can look different depending on which independent variable you put on the X-axis and which variable you place in the graph.

You can represent your data in bar graphs. Typically, bar graphs represent categorical data, but the example in Figure A.8 is based on the same continuous data we've been working with in these examples. You can see that the visual representation of the bar graph shows the same pattern that you saw in Figure A.6.

If you have completed a correlational analysis, you might want to present a scatter diagram that reveals the relation between two variables. The basic format of this type of figure is the same as for line graphs and bar graphs. The type of information in a scatter diagram is different in an important way, though. Unlike line and bar graphs, which present data at the level of groups, a scatter diagram includes data points from each individual on two variables being measured.

In a scatter diagram, if the overall pattern of data is circular, there is little correspondence between the measurements on the two variables. If all points in the scatter diagram were to fall on a single line, there would be a perfect correspondence between measurements on the two variables. In psychological research, because of the complexity of people's behaviors, the relationships are far from perfect and scatter diagrams tend to be more cigar-shaped.

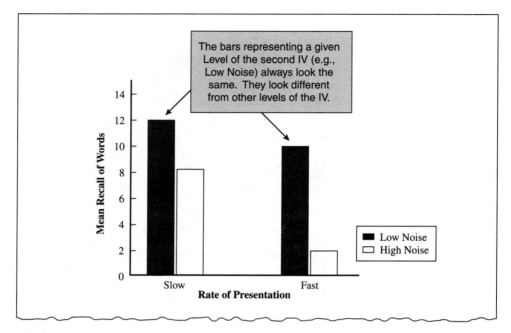

FIGURE A.8   Example of a bar graph in APA style.

Statistical Results

The statistics that you are most likely to use in your research report are the analysis of variance, the Student's *t*-test, the Pearson product-moment correlation, and the chi-square test. When you type your research results, you need to follow specific guidelines about including necessary information. Figure A.9 gives the formatting for these tests.

DISCUSSION

After you tell the reader what has happened, you need to spend some time explaining why it happened. The results section is simply a description of the results, without much explanation. By contrast, the discussion offers you the opportunity to explain why your results occurred as they did and why they are important to the psychological community.

When you discuss your findings, it is important to relate them to the ideas you presented in your introduction section. The introduction set the stage for the research, so your reader will expect you to show why those ideas are important to your ideas. This is the section of the manuscript that allows you to draw inferences about important psychological processes that are taking place among your participants. It is perfectly appropriate for you to speculate on the meaning of your data. If others disagree, they can always do their own research to provide support for their ideas. When you speculate, you should give the logic behind your arguments. Otherwise, you are only

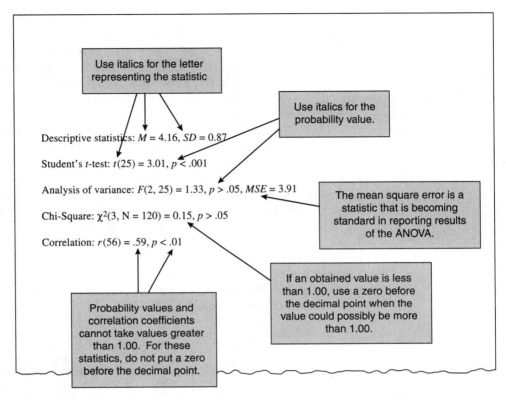

FIGURE A.9   Format for presenting statistical results in APA style.

giving an opinion, not logical speculation. The discussion section addresses the following questions:

- What do the results mean?
- What explanations can you develop for why the participants responded as they did?
- What psychological processes help you explain participants' responses?
- What questions have not been answered fully?
- How do your results relate to the research cited in the introduction?
- How do your results relate to other kinds of research?
- What new ideas emerged that you could evaluate in a subsequent experiment?

REFERENCES

The reference section includes the full citation for any work that you referred to in your writing. This section is only for works cited in your paper; it is not a general bibliography related to your topic. The rule is that if something was referred to in the manuscript, it belongs here; if a work was not alluded to in your writing, it does not appear here.

The reference section is actually fairly easy to create because you know exactly what the section must contain. The only difficulty is making sure that you use the correct format in the citation. You may be familiar with styles other than APA's, like MLA (from the Modern Language Association) or the Chicago style. They are considerably different from APA style. Fortunately, in your manuscripts, you are likely to use only a few of the many types of sources available, so it is easy to become familiar with the rules for citing references. Examples appear in Figures A.9, A.10, and A.11.

The most common sources are journal articles, books and book chapters, presentations at conferences, and electronic resources. Examples of reference formants in APA style are shown in Table A.1. You can see how to format them in Figures A.10, A.11, A.12, and A.13. Each of these can come in several different varieties, so you will have to make sure that you are following the APA guidelines exactly. For details on the less common types of references, you can consult the *Publication Manual of the American Psychological Association*. There are also numerous web sites that provide help. The technical information about the citations tells the reader:

- What research was cited in the report (e.g., work published in journals or other written sources, research presentations, personal communications)?
- Where was the information made public?

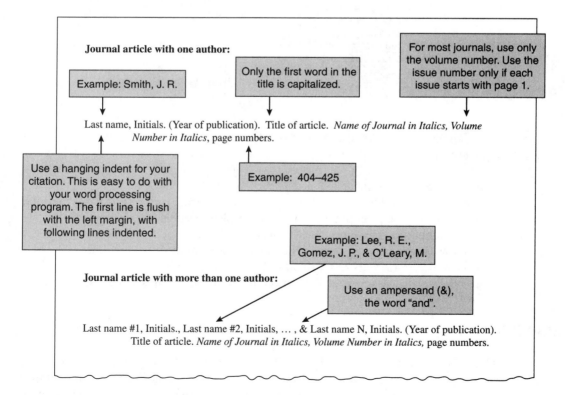

FIGURE A.10   Format for journal article references in APA style.

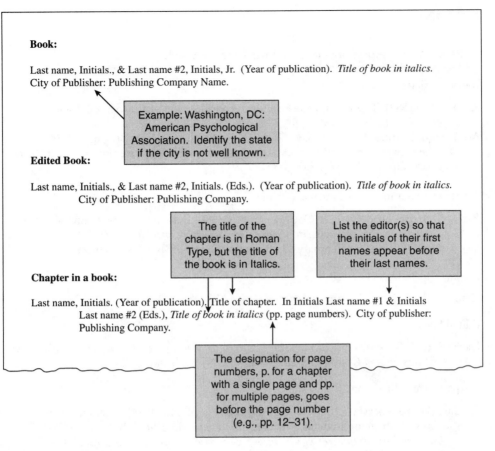

Book:

Last name, Initials., & Last name #2, Initials, Jr. (Year of publication). *Title of book in italics.*
City of Publisher: Publishing Company Name.

> Example: Washington, DC:
> American Psychological
> Association. Identify the state
> if the city is not well known.

Edited Book:

Last name, Initials., & Last name #2, Initials. (Eds.). (Year of publication). *Title of book in italics.*
City of Publisher: Publishing Company.

> The title of the
> chapter is in Roman
> Type, but the title of
> the book is in Italics.

> List the editor(s) so that
> the initials of their first
> names appear before
> their last names.

Chapter in a book:

Last name, Initials. (Year of publication). Title of chapter. In Initials Last name #1 & Initials
Last name #2 (Eds.), *Title of book in italics* (pp. page numbers). City of publisher:
Publishing Company.

> The designation for page
> numbers, p. for a chapter
> with a single page and pp.
> for multiple pages, goes
> before the page number
> (e.g., pp. 12–31).

FIGURE A.11   Format for book references in APA style.

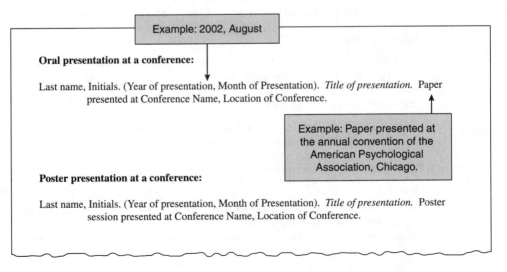

> Example: 2002, August

Oral presentation at a conference:

Last name, Initials. (Year of presentation, Month of Presentation). *Title of presentation.* Paper
presented at Conference Name, Location of Conference.

> Example: Paper presented at
> the annual convention of the
> American Psychological
> Association, Chicago.

Poster presentation at a conference:

Last name, Initials. (Year of presentation, Month of Presentation). *Title of presentation.* Poster
session presented at Conference Name, Location of Conference.

FIGURE A.12   Format for oral and poster presentation references in APA style.

TABLE A.1   Examples of reference formats in APA style.

Journal articles:

Adair, J. G. (1984). The Hawthorne effect: A reconsideration of the methodological artifact. *Journal of Applied Psychology, 69,* 334–345.
Aronson, J., Lustina, M. J., Good, C., Keough, K., Steele, C. M., & Brown, J. (1999). When white men can't do math: Necessary and sufficient factors in stereotype threat. *Journal of Experimental Social Psychology, 35,* 29–46.

Article from a print journal accessed online:

Berns, S. B., Jacobson, N. S., & Gottman, J. M. (1999). Demand-withdraw interactions in couples with a violent husband. *Journal of Consulting and Clinical Psychology, 67,* 666–674. Retrieved February 13, 2003, from PsycARTICLES database.

Book:

Cytowic, R. E. (1993). *The man who tasted shapes.* New York: G. P. Putnam & Son.

Edited book:

Davis, S. F., & Buskist, W. (Eds.) (2002). *The teaching of psychology: Essays in honor of Wilbert J. McKeachie and Charles L. Brewer.* Mahwah, NJ: Erlbaum.

Chapter in an edited book:

Gardner, H., Krechevsky, M., Sternberg, R. J., & Okagaki, L. (1994). Intelligence in context: Enhancing students' practical intelligence for school. In K. McGilly (Ed.), *Classroom Lessons: Integrating Cognitive Theory and Classroom Practice* (pp. 105–127). Cambridge: MIT Press.
Ball, P., Giles, H., & Hewstone, M. (1984). Second language acquisition: The intergroup theory with catastrophic dimensions. In H. Tajfel (Ed.), *The social dimension* (Vol. 2, pp. 668–694). Cambridge, UK: Cambridge University Press.

Online document:

Lloyd, M. A. (2001, January 20). *Marky Lloyd's Careers in Psychology Page.* Retrieved February 13, 2003, from http://www.psywww.com/careers/index.htm

Oral presentation at a conference:

Loftus, E. F. (2003, January). *Illusions of memory.* Presented at the National Institute on the Teaching of Psychology. St. Petersburg Beach, FL.

Poster presentation at a conference:

Wimer, D. J., & Beins, B. C. (2000, August). *Is this joke funny? Only if we say it is.* Poster session presented at the annual convention of the American Psychological Association. Washington, DC.

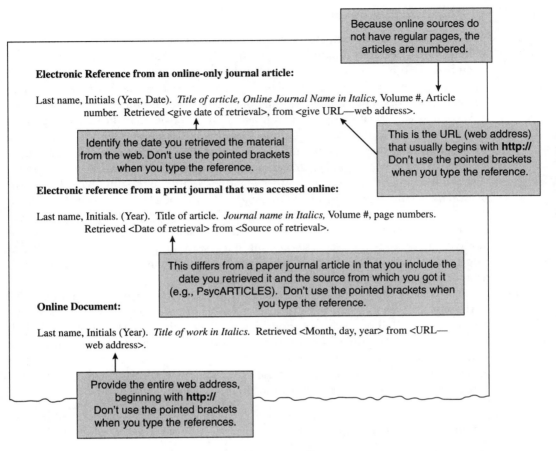

FIGURE A.13 Format for electronic references in APA style.

WRITING STYLE

As the *Publication Manual of the American Psychological Association* points out, scientific writing is different from fiction or other creative writing. Scientific writing benefits from clear and direct communication, whereas creative writing benefits from the creation of ambiguity, abrupt changes in perspective, and other literary devices. When you write a research report, you should concentrate on making your point clearly, avoiding prose that doesn't contribute to the logic of your arguments.

This section presents some common problems in writing that you should note. Much of your writing to this point has probably been more literary than scientific, so you might have to unlearn some habits that you have developed.

Precision of Expression

When you write, avoid using more words than you need and avoid words that are more technical than necessary. Sometimes communication is better when you use a technical term because it has a specific meaning that the term transmits very efficiently. On the other hand, when you use complex wording to describe a simple situation, the reader can get confused. Using impressive terminology may not help you get your point across.

Just as you should avoid being too technical, you have to make sure that you are not too informal in your language. If an experiment has some methodological flaws, for example, and the results might be confounded, you should not make vague statements like *The methodological flaws skewed the results* because the word *skew* could mean just about anything. You would want to be more specific, suggesting that *The methodological flaws led to higher mean scores in Groups A and B*, or something equally explanatory. Or if your participants engaged in a behavior in some circumstances, you should specify how often the behavior occurred; ill-defined statements like *most of the time* do not communicate as precisely as you want in a research report. Writing is a skill that you need to develop. Keep in mind that if you fail to communicate, the problem is with you most of the time, not with your reader.

Another grammatical feature that leads to problems is the use of passive voice verbs (e.g., *they were asked to move* instead of *I asked them to move*). For one thing, such verbs make for dull prose. Another problem is that passive voice verbs lead to lack of clarity. That is, to say that *The participants were given the materials* means that you are not telling your reader who did the giving. When you use passive voice verbs, the actor is often hidden. In some cases, it is important to know who completed the action. In virtually all cases, active voice verbs make your prose more lively.

Avoiding Biased Language

When you describe or refer to people in your writing, it is important to use language that gets your point across but also shows sensitivity to the individuals and groups to which you refer. For example, sexist language can be problematic. If you make a statement that *The pioneers, their wives, and their children who settled the western states experienced hardships we cannot even imagine*, you are showing bias in your language. The implication is that the men were the pioneers, whereas the women and children were not.

Another type of bias that we see less than we used to regarding the sexes is the use of the word *man* to refer to people in general. The convention of using *man* to refer to people also led to the use of male pronouns (i.e., *his*, *him*) when the meaning supposedly included women. This change has led to the use of plural pronouns in referring to a single person (e.g., *A student can be rude when they use their cell phone in class*). Although this has gained acceptance in speech, it is not appropriate in formal writing because if you use a pronoun to refer to *a student*, the pronoun must be singular. One solution is to use plural nouns (e.g., *students*) so the use of plural pronouns is grammatically consistent. The use of *he or she*, *his or her* or other double pronouns can also solve the problem if you use a singular noun.

A further issue regarding pronouns involves the use of first person pronouns (e.g., *I* or *we*). Many students have learned to avoid using the personal pronoun *I*. Teachers have said to use passive voice verbs or to use *we* in their writing when they mean only a single person, that is, themselves. According to APA style, it is appropriate to use *I* when referring to yourself (although not in the Abstract section). This makes it clear that you are talking about yourself, a single person, rather than a group. Using *I* also avoids the use of passive voice verbs, which you should keep to an absolute minimum.

Another issue involves sensitivity to diverse groups, particularly with respect to the labeling of those groups. It is impossible to state a set of unchanging rules because the terms we use to denote people in various groups change. It may not be possible to satisfy everybody in every group, but you should be aware of the terms that any particular time are appropriate for describing them. Incidentally, if you use the words *Black* and *White* as racial or ethnic terms, these words should be capitalized.

Recently, authorities on writing have concluded that it is not appropriate to refer to people as though a single characteristic defined them completely. For example, in discussing people with handicaps, you should avoid calling them *the handicapped* because such a term implies that the handicap is perhaps their most significant characteristic. Noting that they are either *handicapped people* or *people with handicaps* highlights the fact that they are, first and foremost, people. Similarly, referring to *depressives* hides the fact that people with depression show other important characteristics that are unrelated to depression. People are more complex than a single attribute.

For a task as difficult as writing well, these few rules will not suffice by themselves. But they provide a good start. For best results, you should consult with good writers, refer to writing manuals, read well-written reports, and revise your own work extensively. If you combine these approaches with diligence in creating your own prose, your ability to communicate your ideas will develop nicely.

STATISTICS REVIEW

In this appendix, you can review basics of how psychologists use statistics. The most common approaches include the *t*-test, analysis of variance and its related tests, and correlational tests. If you are interested in exploring different approaches or the theory that underlies statistical usage, you should consult a statistics textbook.

As psychologists use them, statistics are merely a tool to help us understand our data. Sometimes there are theoretical complexities regarding statistics that are difficult to understand; sometimes there are controversies. The critical point is that for us, although statistics are only a tool, you need to understand the basics of how to use that tool.

You should develop your statistical plan during the design of your research. There are few things as frustrating as finding out after completing a lengthy study that your design is not amenable to statistical analysis. You have results but you can't analyze them; as a result, you won't have as good a grasp of the question you are investigating as you would like.

You may discover that, after you design your research, you have to make changes because your initial design does not lend itself to easy analysis. Perhaps your design doesn't lend itself to any analysis that an experienced researcher would have confidence in. What it comes down to is that you have to know what kinds of questions your methodology permits and what statistical tests will help you answer them.

THE USE OF STATISTICS

A century ago, psychologists used descriptive statistics like correlations, means, and standard deviations. An advanced test was the *z*-test, which let investigators understand probability analysis. The statistical tests that we take for granted had yet to be invented.

At the end of the nineteenth century, Karl Pearson invented the correlation coefficient as we know it after Francis Galton proposed the initial concept. In the first decade of the twentieth century, William F. Gossett invented the *t*-test. By the 1930s,

Ronald Fisher (1932, 1935) devised the analysis of variance; the F value of the analysis of variance stands for Fisher.

Fisher is responsible for the use of the null hypothesis testing that dominates psychology today. He argued that a null hypothesis of equality between means could never be proven, but it could be disproven. So he argued that we should set up a test to see if the null hypothesis is universally true; if the difference across groups was large enough, we could use that fact as a demonstration that the null hypothesis of no difference was false. The only option left is to accept the idea that the groups were not universally equal.

Fisher showed us how we can demonstrate, through manipulation of variables, that we can reliably show that scores in different groups vary. Differences were said to be significant, which doesn't necessarily mean important. It just means that we can expect them to occur reliably. Significant as used by statisticians doesn't mean the same thing as significant in everyday language.

With the advent of these ideas, the way was paved for refinement of statistical approaches. By the middle of the twentieth century, the statistics most commonly used today were becoming increasingly well known.

When computers made complex data analysis feasible, the highly complex statistical designs of today became practical. Theoretical and applied statisticians continue to work on new approaches, most of which have their theoretical basis in the initial work of Fisher and Pearson.

Common Statistics

As you read research reports, you will see that certain statistics appear repeatedly. These include the ANOVA, *t*-tests, correlations, and regressions. This set constitutes most of the tests known as *parametric statistics*. When you use these tests, you generally want to have equal sample sizes, equal variances, and normally distributed scores.

With equal samples sizes and variances and with normally distributed scores, the answers we arrive at will be statistically sound. Our decisions about whether to reject the null hypothesis will be relatively free of Type I and Type II errors. The tests are robust, though, in that they can withstand some notable departures from these assumptions. For instance, as long as the number of data points in any cell is not more than about twice as large as the smallest, the use of these tests will lead to decent conclusions. Similarly, as long as the ratio of the largest variance to the smallest is not more than about four or five, we can have confidence in our conclusions. If the distribution of scores is not normal, the tests can still be remarkably useful (Howell, 1992).

Problems arise, though, if we begin to violate all of the requirements. If our sample sizes and our variances grow more different, the decisions we make based on our data become less reliable. Even though the tests can withstand departures from equal sample sizes and variances and from normality, we should be aware that we can't ignore departures entirely. Sometimes we will need to select different tests that do not have these requirements.

Contemporary Statistics

For several decades, some psychologists have criticized the use of tests of the null hypothesis (e.g., Falk, 1986; Falk & Greenberg, 1995; Wilcox, 1998), although you can still find cogent arguments in its favor (Frick, 1996).

Recently, the American Psychological Association created a task force to investigate the use of statistics and to provide guidance for researchers. The task force concluded that null hypothesis testing was appropriate for answering some questions, but that the standard parametric statistics should be supplemented with other information.

An important point raised by the task force is that we should rely on the simplest statistical test that will allow us to answer our questions. Complex analyses might needlessly obscure the concepts we are dealing with. That being said, we need to realize that there is sometimes a need for very complex statistical analyses because the psychological questions we ask are often complex.

SCALES OF MEASUREMENT

The highly respected psychophysicist S. S. Stevens (1951) argued that the numerical information provided by the data we collect depends on the type of measurements we make. Some data are relatively crude, providing information about categories in which observations fall. Other data are more mathematically sophisticated, permitting more complex algebraic manipulation.

As such, he reasoned, some data are appropriate for a given psychological test, but other data are not. His arguments have had significant impact on the way psychologists analyze data, even though there are compelling reasons to believe that Stevens overstated his case greatly (Lord, 1953; Gaito, 1980; Velleman & Wilkinson, 1993). Nonetheless, controversies and misunderstandings about the issues Stevens raised still persist.

Nominal Scales

Stevens labeled four different scales of measurement. At the simplest level, *nominal scales* involve simple categorization. People are generally recognized to come in two sexes, female and male (although there is some argument on that count, too; Fausto-Sterling, 1993). When we categorize people or things, we are engaging in the simplest form of measurement. As we conclude that one person is female and another is male, we are measuring them on a nominal scale.

Usually we talk about measurement in the context of "real" numbers, not categories, but assigning people to categories involves a simple variety of measurement. There isn't much arithmetic we can do with these numbers other than counting. We can tally the number of people who fall into categories of interest. With nominal data, though, we can differentiate among the categories themselves only descriptively.

Although we can tally different numbers of observations in each category, as when we say that there are more female psychology majors than male psychology majors, we can't compare any two measurements (e.g., one male, one female) and say that they differ quantitatively, that is, numerically. We can only say that the observations differ, but we can't give an amount by which they differ because these measurements are don't fall on a number line.

Ordinal Scales

When our measurements do fall on a number line, we are dealing more quantitatively, not only descriptively and categorically. When we are able to compare two measurements and have the ability to decide that they differ (e.g., perhaps one is larger than the other), but we can't say how large the difference is, we are dealing with an *ordinal scale*.

In this case, we have some quantitative information, but only enough to say that one measurement falls above or below another on the number line. An absolute measure of the difference isn't possible on an ordinal scale. A typical example of measurements on an ordinal scale are ranks. Somebody who ranks first is ahead of somebody who ranks second; the second place person is, in turn, ahead of the third ranked person. But we don't know by how much they differ. First and second could be very close, with third very far away. On the other hand, first might be well ahead of second and third, who are close.

Interval and Ratio Scales

As we have seen, sometimes we use data that permit us to identify two people or things as being the same or different, which involves a nominal scale. These data may also allow us to identify which of two measurements is larger (or smaller) when they do differ; this involves an ordinal scale.

In many cases, we can go beyond ranking and assess an amount of difference between two measurements. When we are using such measurements and when the measurement system has an absolute zero (i.e., it will not permit negative numbers), we have a *ratio scale*. If the zero point on the scale is arbitrary (i.e., it will allow negative numbers), we have an *interval scale*. Practically speaking, we don't need to differentiate between interval and ratio scale numbers in our discussion here.

In both of these scales, a fixed difference (e.g., 10 points) means the same thing regardless of where the number falls on the number line. The difference between 50 and 60 and the difference between 90 and 100 is 10 in both cases, and that difference means the same thing.

Remember that for ranks, the difference between finishing first and second—a difference of one place—doesn't reflect the same as the difference between last and next to last. If you have ever been to a track meet, you will have seen close battles between first and second in a race, but the time difference between the last and next to last runners might be considerable. The difference in ranking is the same, but the difference in their times is quite another matter.

There are arguments that some data we use in psychology look like interval or ratio data, but are really ordinal data. A common example in which there is disagreement about the scale of measurement involves intelligence as represented in IQ scores. The difference in behavior between somebody whose IQ score is 80 and somebody whose score is 90 may be quite noticeable, whereas the difference between people whose scores are 140 and 150 might be minimal. This pattern suggests that the difference of 10 points between members of each pair isn't really the same. This would be characteristic of an ordinal scale of measurement. That is, there are differences, but just as we don't know how big the differences are when people differ by a rank of one, we also don't know how big the real behavioral differences are when people differ in IQ scores by a fixed amount.

The importance of the issue, to the extent that it is important at all, is that some researchers identify one set of statistical tests that we can use when data are on an interval or ratio scale, and different sets of tests for each of nominal and ordinal scales.

Some researchers think that if IQ scores are really on an ordinal scale of measurement, the logical implication is that we should not be using certain statistical tests with them. Other researchers advance arguments to the contrary. In practice, psychologists may argue against using parametric tests with data like IQ scores, but most researchers use them anyway with no apparent problems.

INDEPENDENT GROUPS *t*-TEST

The independent groups *t*-test compares two samples to see if they differ from one another reliably. That is, is the difference between the two groups large enough to convince us that if we repeated our data collection, we would end up with similar results the second time?

You can also use the ANOVA to compare two groups. Your decision to reject or not to reject the null hypothesis will be the same regardless of whether you use a *t*-test or the ANOVA because the *t*-test is the algebraic equivalent to an ANOVA comparing two independent groups. Historically, we have used the *t*-test for two groups; this tradition continues for studies with a single IV and only two groups to compare.

The formula for the *independent groups t-test* appears below. When the two groups show unequal variances, you should consult a statistics text for guidance.

$$t = \frac{M_A - M_B}{s_p^2 \left(\sqrt{\frac{1}{N_A} + \frac{1}{N_B}} \right)}$$

where M = means of groups A and B
N = number of observations in groups A and B
s^2 = the pooled variance given in the equation below

$$s_p^2 = \frac{(N_A - 1)s_A^2 + (N_B - 1)s_B^2}{N_A + N_B - 2}$$

where s^2 = variance of the group based on the unbiased estimate of the population variance.

Worked Example for Independent Groups *t*-Test

PARTICIPANTS ARE TESTED EITHER IN CONDITION A OR CONDITION B	A	B	
Data for Groups A and B	6	4	$t = [(1) - (2)] / (7)$
	5	8	$= (6.3 - 3.7) / 1.75$
	8	3	$= 2.6 / 1.75$
	3	3	$= 1.48$
	6	5	
	7	3	
	7	4	
	6	2	
	9	3	
		2	
Mean	(1) 6.3	(2) 3.7	
Standard Deviation	1.73	1.77	
St. Deviation Squared (Variance)	(3) 2.99	(4) 3.13	
N	9	10	
Pooled Variance			[(5) * (3) + (6) * (4)] / [(5) + (6)]
			[(8 * 3.00) + (9 * 3.12)] / 17
			$= (23.92 + 28.17) / 17$
			$= 3.06$
Square root of pooled variance			$= (7)\ 1.75$
Degrees of Freedom	(5) 8	(6) 9	(5) + (6) = 17
Critical t-value ($\alpha = .05$, two tails)			2.11
Decision			**Do not reject the null hypothesis. The obtained value of *t* is less than the critical value. Do not conclude that the two groups are significantly different.**

In the example above, there are two groups, one having 9 data points, the other having 10. After finding the means and standard deviations for each group separately, it is easy to enter the values into the formula and compute your value of t. You then compare your obtained value with the critical value from the table of t values. If your obtained value is greater than the critical value in the table, reject the null hypothesis. If your obtained value is less than the critical value in the table, do not reject the null hypothesis.

Supplemental Analysis.   Researchers are increasingly reporting a statistic that gives an assessment of how powerful the independent variable is in its effects on the dependent variable. Such an analysis involves a concept called effect size. For the t-test, the statistic that gives information on effect size is d. It is simple to compute.

By convention, psychologists regard values of d around .20 as small, around .50 as moderate, and around .80 as large. The effect size represented in this example would be considered quite large.

$$d = \frac{Mean_A - Mean_B}{s},$$

$$s = \sqrt{s_A^2 + s_B^2} = \sqrt{3.00 + 3.12} = \sqrt{6.12} = 2.47$$

$$d = \frac{6.3 - 3.7}{2.47} = \frac{2.6}{2.47} = 1.05$$

MATCHED SAMPLES/REPEATED MEASURES t-TEST

When you have two groups of scores that are paired, you use a different formula for the t-test. You use this version of t when a score in one group is paired for a specific reason with a score in the second group. For instance, if you administer a memory test to a person working alone, then a similar test when that person is in a group, you can compare the individual's score in the two conditions. It makes sense to pair the two scores because they came from the same person.

When you test the same person on two different occasions, that participant is likely to score similarly each time. When you have paired scores that are likely to be correlated, it makes sense to use this version of t because there is a better chance of detecting small differences between conditions.

$$t = \frac{\bar{D}}{\frac{S_{\bar{D}}}{\sqrt{N}}}$$

D = Mean of the difference scores
S = Standard deviation of the difference scores
N = Number of *pairs* of scores (not the total number of scores)

Worked Example of a Matched Samples / Repeated Measures *t*-Test

PARTICIPANTS ARE TESTED IN BOTH CONDITIONS	A	B	DIFFERENCE SCORE	
Participant 1	11	9	2	$t = (1) / [(2) / (3)]$
Participant 2	9	4	5	$t = 3.2 / [2.39 / 2.24]$
Participant 3	12	12	0	$= 2.99$
Participant 4	5	2	3	
Participant 5	17	11	6	
Mean			**(1)** 3.	
Standard deviation			**(2)** 2.39	
N			5	
Square root of N			**(3)** 2.24	
Standard error				$= 2.39 / 2.24$
				$= 1.07$
Degrees of Freedom				$= \# \text{ Pairs} - 1$
				$= 4$
Critical t-value (α=.05, two tails)				2.99
Decision				**Reject the null hypothesis. The obtained value of *t* is greater than the critical value. Conclude that the two groups are significantly different.**

How to Designate the *t*-Value. $t(4) = 2.99, p < .05$

ANALYSIS OF VARIANCE

The Analysis of Variance (ANOVA) permits us to test for differences among multiple groups at the same time. Unlike the *t*-test, which is limited to comparisons of two groups at a time, the ANOVA can assess as many groups as you care to compare. (If you have only two groups, the ANOVA is perfectly applicable, although traditionally researchers have used the *t*-test.)

The advantage of the ANOVA is that you can be confident that the number of Type I errors that occur is at the level that you set. These errors arise when you conclude that there is a difference between groups that really occurred by chance, not because of the effect of your independent variable. In most cases, researchers want to keep Type I errors at no more than five percent. If you used multiple *t*-tests, as the number of comparisons you make increased, so would the likelihood that you would conclude that there was a reliable difference that would actually be due to chance.

An additional strength of the ANOVA is that we can make comparisons involving more than one independent variable. When an analysis involves a single IV, we call the test a One-Way ANOVA; if there are two IVs, we have a Two-Way ANOVA; and so on. For tests involving two or more IVs, we often refer to the design as factorial

ANOVAs. Factorial ANOVAs let us see if there are main effects for each IV separately and if there are interaction effects among variables.

The underlying concept is the same for them all. We identify the magnitude of the differences among groups that are due to treatment effects, that is, to the IV; then we assess the size of the differences due to error. Finally, we see how large the treatment effect is compared to the error effect. If the treatment effect is big enough relative to the error effect, we conclude that the IV had a reliable effect on the behavior we are assessing.

As with *t*-tests, we can perform ANOVAs for data sets involving either independent groups or repeated measures groups. In this section, you will see how to compute One-Way ANOVAs involving both independent groups and repeated measures. You will also see how to compute a Two-Way ANOVA involving independent groups. For analysis of Two-Way or higher ANOVAs with repeated measures, you should consult a higher level statistics text. In general, you would carry out such tests via computer because the amount of calculation is extensive, particularly with repeated measures designs.

One-Way Independent Groups Analysis of Variance

When you have multiple groups in which the data are unrelated across groups, you have an independent groups design. This means that there is no particular reason to pair a score in one group with any specific score in another group. When you have different people in each group rather than repeating measurements of the same people participating in different groups, you are using an independent groups design.

Worked Example of One-Way Independent Groups ANOVA

Group 1	Sum of Scores ΣX	Sum of Squared Scores ΣX^2	Sum of Scores Squared $(\Sigma X)^2$	N_1
X X^2				4
7 49	35	315	$35^2 = 1225$	
9 81				
8 81				
11 36				

Group 2	Sum of Scores ΣX	Sum of Squared Scores ΣX^2	Sum of Scores Squared $(\Sigma X)^2$	N_2
X X^2				4
8 64	8 + 10 + 11 + 11	64 + 100 + 100 + 121	$40^2 = 1600$	
10 100	40	406		
11 100				
11 121				

Group 3	Sum of Scores ΣX	Sum of Squared Scores ΣX^2	Sum of Scores Squared $(\Sigma X)^2$	N_3
X X^2				4
11 121	11 + 10 + 11 + 12	121 + 100 + 121 + 144	$44^2 = 1936$	
10 100	44	486		
11 121				
12 144				

Totals	Sum of Scores ΣX_{TOTAL}	Sum of Squared Scores ΣX^2_{TOTAL}	Sum of Scores Squared $(\Sigma X)^2_{TOTAL}$	N_{TOTAL}
	115	1139	4497	12

Computing Sums of Squares.   Total Sum of Squares (SS_{TOTAL})

$$SS_{TOTAL} = \Sigma X_1^2 + \Sigma X_2^2 + \Sigma X_3^2 - \frac{(\Sigma X_1 + \Sigma X_1 + \Sigma X_1)^2}{N_{TOTAL}}$$

$$SS_{TOTAL} = 315 + 406 + 486 - \frac{(31 + 40 + 44)^2}{12}$$

$= 1207 - (119^2 / 12)$

$= 1207 - (14161 / 12)$

$= 1207 - 1180.08$

$= 26.92$

Treatment Sum of Squares ($SS_{TREATMENT}$) [also called Between Groups Sum of Squares]

$$SS_{TREATMENT} = \frac{(\Sigma X_1)^2}{N_1} + \frac{(\Sigma X_2)^2}{N_2} + \frac{(\Sigma X_3)^2}{N_3} - \frac{(\Sigma X_1 + \Sigma X_2 + \Sigma X_3)^2}{N_{TOTAL}}$$

Error Sum of Squares (SS_{ERROR}) [also called Within Groups Sum of Squares]

$SS_{ERROR} = SSN_{TOTAL} - SS_{TREATMENT}$

$SS_{ERROR} = 26.92 - 10.17$

$= 16.75$

Computing Degrees of Freedom

$df_{TOTAL} = (N_{TOTAL} - 1) = (12 - 1) = 11$

$df_{TREATMENT} = (\# \ Groups - 1) = (3 - 1) = 2$

$df_{ERROR} = df_{TOTAL} - df_{TREATMENT} = 11 - 2 = 9$

Computing Mean Squares

$$MS_{TREATMENT} = \frac{SS_{TREATMENT}}{df_{TREATMENT}}$$

$= \dfrac{10.17}{2}$

$= 5.08$

$$MS_{ERROR} = \frac{SS_{ERROR}}{df_{ERROR}}$$

$= \dfrac{16.75}{9}$

$= 1.86$

Computing F

$$F = \frac{MS_{TREATMENT}}{MS_{ERROR}}$$

$= \dfrac{5.08}{1.86}$

$= 2.73$

ANOVA Summary Table

SOURCE OF VARIATION	SUM OF SQUARES	DEGREES OF FREEDOM	MEAN SQUARE	F	p	EFFECT SIZE
TREATMENT (Between Groups)	10.17	2	5.08	2.73	>.05	.38
ERROR (Within Groups)	20.75	9	1.86			
TOTAL	26.92	11				

How to Designate the *F* Value. $F(2,9) = 2.73, p > .05$

Decision.   Look up the critical value in the *F*-Table for 2 and 9 degrees of freedom. For an alpha value (Type I error rate) of 5 percent, the critical value is 4.26.

In order to conclude that there are differences across groups, we need a computed value of *F* equal to or greater than 4.26. Our computed value is smaller than that, 2.73. Thus, we can conclude that the groups differ from one another for unknown reasons, not because of the effects of the independent variable. If the computed *F*-value is less than one, the *F* will never be significant.

Supplemental Analysis.   In recent years, investigators have started reporting effect sizes. An effect size indicates the strength of the relationship you are assessing. A statistically significant effect can be small; likewise, a nonsignificant effect can be large. Effect sizes tell you the relative magnitude of strength of your independent variable on the dependent variable. According to the conventions adopted by psychologists, an effect size of about .20 is considered small; an effect size of about .50 is moderate; an effect size around .80 is large.

In general, a measure of effect size reflects how much of the variability in scores is due to your manipulation. Powerful IVs lead to large effect sizes; manipulations that are weak lead to small effect sizes. It is important to remember that a small effect size can be very real and can be very important.

One statistic that researchers use to assess effect sizes is eta-squared (η^2). It is useful when you are interested in describing the effect sizes for your own research project. If you want to generalize beyond your own data, other statistics are preferred (Howell, 1992).

$$\eta^2 = \frac{SS_{TREATMENT}}{SS_{TOTAL}}$$

$$= \frac{10.17}{26.92} = .38$$

An additional, supplemental approach involves determining which groups differ from one another when you are comparing multiple conditions. In this example, we have three groups. If there is a significant difference between some of the groups, based on the ANOVA alone, we don't know which groups differ from one another. Groups 1 and 2 might differ from one another, but Groups 2 and 3 might not. We also don't know if Groups 1 and 3 differ.

Several different statistical tests exist that let us determine which groups differ from one another. Because the details differ in their application, if you are interested in using such tests after computing an F-value, you should consult a statistics book or make use of appropriate options in a computerized statistical package.

One-Way Repeated Measures Analysis of Variance

Sometimes, it makes sense to measure your research participants more than once. For instance, if there aren't many of them, you want to get as much from them as you can because it could be hard to find more people with the characteristics you desire. Another rationale for using repeated measurements of the same people is if it is simply convenient. If you set up a testing time for a participant, you have to spend a lot of time contacting the person, setting up the lab, and taking care of final details when the person leaves the lab. The testing session itself might take only a few minutes. In that case, you might benefit from taking additional measurements that don't add appreciably to the time you are already spending on the person. Further, sometimes it simply makes sense to measure the same person over time to see how change occurs.

In all of these situations, you cannot use the same formulas for the analysis of variance that you do for independent groups designs. One of the most important differences between a repeated measures ANOVA and an independent measures ANOVA lies in the fact that you can remove some error variability from your equations. That is, your participants' scores will differ due to your treatment, but the scores will also differ for unknown reasons. One of those unknown reasons include individual differences—some people are smarter, faster, more motivated, etc. Such factors affect their scores on the dependent variable. In a repeated measures ANOVA, you can remove the effects of such individual differences from the calculations, which makes it easier to spot small differences between groups.

Worked Example of a One-Way Repeated Measures ANOVA. Let's assume that we have three groups, as in the independent groups ANOVA. But in the present situation, we use only four people instead of twelve. Each of the four provides data for every group. We will have the same number of data points, but fewer people generating them. For the sake of illustration, we will use the same numbers as in the independent groups analysis. This approach will show one of the advantages of using repeated measures designs.

PARTICIPANT (P)	GROUP 1 X_1	GROUP 2 X_2	GROUP 3 X_3	SUM FOR PARTICIPANT ΣP	SUM FOR PARTICIPANT SQUARED $(\Sigma P)^2$
1	7	8	11	26	676
2	9	10	10	29	941
3	8	11	11	30	900
4	11	11	12	34	1156
ΣX	35	40	44	119	
ΣX^2	315	406	486		
					3573

Computing Sums of Squares.   Total Sum of Squares (SS_{TOTAL})

$$SS_{TOTAL} = \Sigma X_1^2 + \Sigma X_2^2 + \Sigma X_3^2 - \frac{(\Sigma X_1 + \Sigma X_2 + \Sigma X_3)^2}{N_{TOTAL}}$$

$$= 315 + 406 + 486 - \frac{(31 + 40 + 44)^2}{12}$$

$$= 1207 - \frac{119^2}{12} = 1207 - \frac{14161}{12} = 1207 - 1180.08$$

$$= 26.92$$

Sum of Squares Treatment [also called Sum of Squares Between Conditions]

$$SS_{TREATMENT} = \frac{(\Sigma X_1)^2}{N_1} + \frac{(\Sigma X_2)^2}{N_2} + \frac{(\Sigma X_3)^2}{N_3} - \frac{(\Sigma X_1 + \Sigma X_2 + \Sigma X_3)^2}{N_{TOTAL}}$$

$$SS_{TREATMENT} = \frac{35^2}{4} + \frac{40^2}{4} + \frac{44^2}{4} - \frac{(35 + 40 + 44)^2}{12}$$

$$= \left(\frac{1225}{4} + \frac{1600}{4} + \frac{1936}{4}\right) - \frac{14161}{12}$$

$$= (306.25 + 400 + 484) - 1180.08$$

$$= 1190.25 - 1180.08$$

$$= 10.17$$

Participant (Subject) Sum of Squares (SS_{SS})

$$SS_{Subjects} = \frac{(\Sigma P)^2}{\# \ Groups} - \frac{(\Sigma X_1 + \Sigma X_2 + \Sigma X_3)^2}{N_{TOTAL}}$$

$$= \frac{3573}{3} - \frac{(35 + 40 + 44)^2}{2}$$

$$= 1191.00 - \frac{(119)^2}{12}$$

$$= 1191.00 - \frac{14161}{12}$$

$$= 1191.00 - 1180.08$$

$$= 10.92$$

Error Sum of Squares (SS_{ERROR})

$$SS_{ERROR} = SS_{TOTAL} - SS_{BETWEEN} - SS_{SUBJECTS}$$

$$= 26.92 - 10.17 - 10.92$$

$$= 5.83$$

Computing Degrees of Freedom

$$df_{TOTAL} = \# Data - 1 = 12 - 1 = 11$$

$$df_{TREATMENT} = \# Groups - 1 = 3 - 1 = 2$$

$$df_{PARTICIPANTS} = \# Participants - 1 = 4 - 1 = 3$$

$$df_{ERROR} = df_{TOTAL} - df_{TREATMENT} - df_{SUBJECTS} = 11 - 2 - 3 = 6$$

SOURCE	SUM OF SQUARES	DEGREES OF FREEDOM	MEAN SQUARE	F	p	EFFECT SIZE
Treatment	10.17	2	5.08	5.23		.64
Error	5.83	6	0.97			
Subjects	10.92	3				
Total	26.92	11				

How to Designate the *F*-Value. $F(2,6) = 5.23, p < .05$

Decision. The critical *F*-value is based on 2 and 6 degrees of freedom. Choosing a 5 percent error rate (i.e., alpha = .05), the critical value in the *F* table (Table C.2) is 5.14. Our computed value is greater than the critical value, so we can reject the null hypothesis that there is no difference between groups. Based on the data, we can conclude that the differences between groups are attributable to the effects of the independent variable.

Supplemental Analysis. If you are interested in assessing the effect size for the independent variable in your experiment, you can compute eta-squared (η^2). If your design involves repeated measures, the computations are slightly different than for independent groups. The denominator in the equation does not involve the total sum of squares, only the sum of the treatment and error sums of squares. The sum of squares for subjects is omitted from the calculation.

$$\eta^2 = \frac{SS_{TREATMENT}}{SS_{TREATMENT} + SS_{ERROR}}$$

$$= \frac{10.17}{(10.17 + 5.83)} = .64$$

You can compare the effect sizes for the independent groups and repeated measures designs. By accounting for the stable characteristics of individual participants across groups, you can reduce the error term. This results in a larger effect size.

As with an independent groups ANOVA, you can compute additional tests to see which groups differ from one another. For details of the different tests, you can refer to a statistics book or to a computerized statistical package.

Differences between Independent Groups and Repeated Groups Calculations. As you can see in the computations, the sums of square values for treatment effects and for the total are identical for the two ANOVAs. This is not surprising because the total sum of squares accounts for all differences among scores, regardless of the source of the difference. The treatment sum of squares accounts for differences from one group to another. Regardless of whether there are independent or repeated measures, the groups differ by the same amount, so the sums of squares are the same.

The difference in computations arises in the error term. Some of the differences in scores from one group to the next are due to truly unknown factors. Perhaps some participants are tired, in a particularly good mood, knowledgeable about the materials in the experiment, and so forth. These factors affect their scores. Such variables affect the error sum of squares because error refers to differences due to factors other than the independent variable.

When we conduct a repeated measures study, some of the error factors are due to characteristics of a participant that are stable across conditions. As such, we can account for some of the error score for each individual across conditions. Differences among scores that we can identify are due to characteristics of the participants; we can remove them from the error score.

So we recognize that differences in performance in an experiment can be due to the treatment, to stable characteristics of the participants, and to error that we cannot identify precisely. In the repeated measures ANOVA, we remove the effects of the participants from the error term. This reduces the error term and increases the F-value. We lose degrees of freedom in the error term because they attach themselves to the subjects (requiring a larger F-value for significance), but this loss is often offset by removal of a significant portion of the error sum of squares.

In this example, even though the averages of corresponding groups in the two ANOVAs are identical, the F-value is significant only in the repeated measures design because we have eliminated a notable source of error.

Factorial Analysis of Variance

When we manipulate more than one independent variable in an experiment, we can assess the effects of the IVs through a factorial analysis of variance. This statistical approach allows us to see whether the main effects are significant; in addition, we can investigate whether the two variables interact in ways that are not predictable from either independent variable alone.

The computations for a factorial ANOVA aren't difficult, but they can be tedious with a large data set. Researchers invariably use computerized statistical packages for analyzing the results of factorial designs. The example here involves very small data sets for convenience. In actual research, it is unlikely that an investigator would carry out such a small-scale study.

This statistical analysis involves computation of the same sums of squares as the other ANOVAs, with the addition of a new term, the interaction effect. The nature of the computations is similar, though. This example involves an independent groups design; the calculations for a repeated measures design are more involved. If you plan a study with repeated measures, you should refer to a statistics book because additional statistical issues complicate the analysis.

Worked Example of a Factorial ANOVA. This example involves a 2 × 3 design, which means that there are two IVs. Variable A has two levels, while Variable B has three. There is no limit to the number of levels that an IV can take, nor is there a limit to the number of IVs allowed.

The analysis will involve seeing whether the main effects for the two variables are significant and whether the interaction is significant.

	A_1B_1	$A_1B_1^2$	A_2B_1	$A_2B_1^2$	A_3B_1	$A_3B_1^2$	
B1	4	16	6	36	9	81	
	5	25	7	49	8	64	
	5	25	6	36	7	49	
	7	49	8	64	8	64	
	$\Sigma A_1B_1 = 21$		$\Sigma A_2B_1 = 27$		$\Sigma A_3B_1 = 32$		$\Sigma B_1 = 80$ $(\Sigma B_1)^2 = 6400$
	$(\Sigma A_1B_1)^2 = 441$		$(\Sigma A_1B_1)^2 = 729$		$(\Sigma A_1B_1)^2 = 1024$		$\Sigma B_1^2 = 2194$
	$\Sigma A_1B_1^2 = 115$		$\Sigma A_2B_1^2 = 185$		$\Sigma A_3B_1^2 = 258$		
	$N_{A1-B1} = 4$		$N_{A2-B1} = 4$		$N_{A3-B1} = 4$		$N_{B1} = 12$

	A_1B_2	$A_1B_2^2$	A_2B_2	$A_2B_2^2$	A_3B_2	$A_3B_2^2$	
B2	5	25	4	16	3	9	
	4	16	7	49	2	4	
	3	9	6	36	4	16	
	7	49	8	64	2	4	
	$\Sigma A_1B_2 = 19$		$\Sigma A_2B_2 = 25$		$\Sigma A_3B_2 = 11$		$\Sigma B_2 = 55$ $(\Sigma B_2)^2 = 3025$
	$(\Sigma A_1B_1)^2 = 361$		$(\Sigma A_1B_1)^2 = 625$		$(\Sigma A_1B_1)^2 = 121$		$\Sigma B_2^2 = 771$
	$\Sigma A_1B_2^2 = 99$		$\Sigma A_2B_2^2 = 165$		$\Sigma A_3B_2^2 = 33$		
	$N_{A1-B2} = 4$		$N_{A2-B2} = 4$		$N_{A3-B2} = 4$		$N_{B2} = 12$
	$\Sigma A_1 = 40$		$\Sigma A_2 = 52$		$\Sigma A_3 = 43$		
	$(\Sigma A_1B_1)^2 = 1600$		$(\Sigma A_1B_1)^2 = 1936$		$(\Sigma A_1B_1)^2 = 1849$		
	$\Sigma A_1^2 = 802$		$\Sigma A_2^2 = 1018$		$\Sigma A_3^2 = 291$		
	$N_{A1} = 8$		$N_{A2} = 8$		$N_{A3} = 8$		

$$\Sigma X_{TOTAL} = 135$$
$$(\Sigma X_{TOTAL})^2 = 18225$$
$$\Sigma X^2_{TOTAL} = 1475$$
$$N_{TOTAL} = 24$$

Calculate Sums of Squares. Total Sum of Squares:

$$SS_{TOTAL} = \Sigma X^2_{TOTAL} - \frac{(\Sigma X_{TOTAL})^2}{N_{TOTAL}}$$

$$= 855 - \frac{(135)^2}{24} = 855 - \frac{18225}{24}$$

$$= 855 - 759.38$$

$$95.63$$

Variable A Sum of Squares (SS_A):

$$SS_A = \frac{(\Sigma A_1)^2}{N_{A_1}} + \frac{(\Sigma A_2)^2}{N_{A_2}} + \frac{(\Sigma A_3)^2}{N_{A_3}} - \frac{(\Sigma X_{TOTAL})^2}{N_{TOTAL}}$$

$$= \frac{(40)^2}{8} + \frac{(52)^2}{8} + \frac{(43)^2}{8} - \frac{(135)^2}{24}$$

$$= \frac{1600}{8} + \frac{2704}{8} + \frac{1849}{8} - 759.38$$

$$= 200 + 338 + 231.13 - 759.38$$

$$= 9.75$$

Variable B Sum of Squares (SS_B):

$$SS_B = \frac{(\Sigma B_1)^2}{N_{B_1}} + \frac{(\Sigma B_2)^2}{N_{B_2}} - \frac{(\Sigma X_{TOTAL})^2}{N_{TOTAL}}$$

$$= \frac{(80)^2}{12} + \frac{(55)^2}{12} - \frac{(135)^2}{24}$$

$$= \frac{6400}{12} + \frac{3025}{12} - 759.38$$

$$= 533.33 + 252.08 - 759.38$$

$$= 26.03$$

Interaction Sum of Squares ($SS_{A \times B}$):

$$SS_{A \times B} = \frac{(\Sigma X_{A_1 B_1})^2}{N_{A_1 B_1}} + \frac{(\Sigma X_{A_2 B_1})^2}{N_{A_2 B_1}} + \frac{(\Sigma X_{A_3 B_1})^2}{N_{A_3 B_1}} + \frac{(\Sigma X_{A_1 B_2})^2}{N_{A_1 B_2}} + \frac{(\Sigma X_{A_2 B_2})^2}{N_{A_2 B_2}} + \frac{(\Sigma X_{A_3 B_2})^2}{N_{A_3 B_2}}$$

$$- \frac{(\Sigma X_{TOTAL})^2}{N_{TOTAL}} - SS_A - SS_B$$

$$= \frac{(21)^2}{4} + \frac{(27)^2}{4} + \frac{(32)^2}{4} + \frac{(19)^2}{4} + \frac{(25)^2}{4} + \frac{(11)^2}{4} - 759.38 - 9.75 - 26.03$$

$$= 30.09$$

Error Sum of Squares (SS_{ERROR})

$$SS_{ERROR} = SS_{ERROR} - SS_A - SS_B - SS_{A \times B}$$
$$= 95.63 - 9.75 - 26.03 - 30.09$$
$$= 29.76$$

Calculating Degrees of Freedom:

$$df_{TOTAL} = N_{TOTAL} - 1 = 24 - 1 = 23$$
$$df_A = \# Groups_A - 1 = 3 - 1 = 2$$
$$df_B = \# Groups_B - 1 = 2 - 1 = 1$$
$$df_{A \times B} = (df_A)(df_B) = (2)(1) = 2$$
$$df_{ERROR} = df_{TOTAL} - df_A - df_B - df_{A \times B} = 23 - 2 - 1 - 2 = 18$$

Calculating Mean Squares:

$$MS_A = SS_A/df_A = 9.75/2 = 4.88$$
$$MS_B = SS_B/df_B = 26.03/1 = 26.03$$
$$MS_{A \times B} = SS_{A \times B}/df_{A \times B} = 30.09/2 = 15.04$$
$$MS_{ERROR} = SS_{ERROR}/df_{ERROR} = 29.76/18 = 1.65$$

Calculating F-values:

$$F_A = \frac{MS_A}{MS_{ERROR}} = \frac{4.88}{1.65} = 2.96$$

$$F_B = \frac{MS_B}{MS_{ERROR}} = \frac{26.03}{1.65} = 15.78$$

$$F_{A \times B} = \frac{MS_{A \times B}}{MS_{ERROR}} = \frac{15.04}{1.65} = 9.12$$

ANOVA Summary Table

SOURCE OF VARIATION	SUM OF SQUARES	DEGREES OF FREEDOM	MEAN SQUARE	F	p	EFFECT SIZE
Variable A	9.75	2	4.88	2.96	>.05	.25
Variable B	26.03	1	26.03	15.78	<.01	.47
Interaction of A × B	30.09	2	15.04	9.12	<.01	.50
Error	29.76	18	1.65			
Total	95.63	23				

How to Designate the *F* values

Variable A: $F(2,18) = 2.96, p > .05$

Variable B: $F(1,18) = 15.78, p < .01$

Interaction Effect: $F(2,18) = 9.12, p < .01$

Decision

Main effect of Variable A: To find the critical *F* value for a 5 percent error rate, look on the appropriate table of *F* values for 2 and 18 degrees of freedom. This critical value in the table is 3.55. Our computed value, 2.96, is smaller than the critical value. The difference among groups is not significant, so we conclude that any differences are attributable to measurement error, not the effects of Variable A.

Main effect of Variable B: To find the critical *F* value for a 5 percent error rate, look in the *F* table for 1 and 18 degrees of freedom. The critical value in the table is 4.41. Our computed value, 15.78, is larger than the critical value. So we conclude that the difference among groups is attributable to the effect of Variable B.

Interaction between Variable A and Variable B: To find the critical *F* value for a 5 percent error rate, look in the *F* table for 2 and 18 degrees of freedom. The critical value in the table is 3.55. Our computed value, 9.12, is larger than the critical value. So we conclude that the pattern of scores on B changes depending on which group on Variable A you are considering. Figure B.1 shows how the values of B change depending on which level of A is under consideration.

The significant main effect of Variable B may be due largely to the fact that one group, A_3B_2, has caused the overall average of Variable B to drop greatly. You should

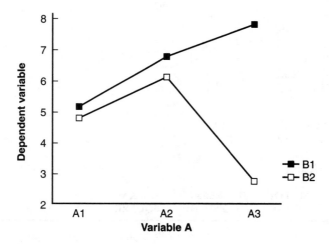

FIGURE B.1 Illustration of interaction of Variables A and B. The pattern of results for Variable B differs depending on which level of Variable A is under consideration.

be cautious about asserting that B_1 and B_2 really are all that different. Without the effect of the single, low group, B_1 and B_2 are not all that different.

Supplementary Analysis. You can assess effect size here with eqa-squared (η^2). You find the effect size for each main effect and for the interaction.

There is an important computational difference in computing effect size for a factorial design compared to a one-way design. For a one-way ANOVA, you divided $SS_{TREATMENT}$ by SS_{TOTAL}. To compute eta-squared for a factorial design, you divide the $SS_{TREATMENT}$ term by the ($SS_{TREATMENT} + SS_{ERROR}$).

$$\eta^2 = \frac{SS_{TREATMENT}}{SS_{TREATMENT} + SS_{ERROR}}$$

$$\eta_A^2 = \frac{9.75}{(9.75 + 29.75)} = .25$$

$$\eta_B^2 = \frac{26.03}{(26.03 + 29.75)} = .47$$

$$\eta_{A\times B}^2 = \frac{30.08}{(30.08 + 29.75)} = .50$$

As these values are interpreted by researchers, the effect size for Variable A is small, whereas the effect sizes for Variable B and the interaction are moderate.

An additional supplemental analysis investigates where differences lie among multiple groups. When you employ an independent variable that has more than two levels, it is not immediately clear which groups differ significantly when you obtain a significant F-value. In this example, there is no main effect of Variable A. If there were, you would conduct a post hoc analysis to see which of the groups, when paired, differed significantly. You can consult a statistics book for details on the different tests you could use.

CHI SQUARE

There are two commonly used chi-square tests. (*Chi* sounds like *sky* with the *s* missing.) One provides information about whether the number of observations that you obtain in different categories matches your predictions. This is the *goodness of fit test*. Is there a good fit between what you expect and what you get? We use this test when we have one-dimensional tables.

A second chi-square provides information for two-dimensional tables about whether there is independence between two variables. For instance, is there independence between the number of women versus men majoring in psychology versus chemistry? Is major predictable from sex, which asks whether we can make a better than chance prediction about whether a student is majoring in psychology versus chemistry based on whether the person is female versus male? Is sex predictable from the major? This variety of chi-square test is a *contingency test*.

These chi-square tests are useful only for nominal data. That is, you can only use these tests when you are counting the number of instances within a category. You can't use the tests for ordinal, interval, or ratio scale measurements.

Goodness of Fit Test

The chi-square goodness of fit test requires that you have categories into which individual observations fall. That is, you make a single observation and record that observation as belonging with category A, B, C, ... You repeat this for each observation. In order for chi-square to provide valid information, each observation must be independent of the others. You can't measure people repeatedly because one person's behavior at two different times may be highly related.

The idea of the chi-square test is to find out whether expected counts in each category match what you actually observe. In most psychological research, our null hypothesis specifies that there be equal numbers of observations in each category. You would depart from this strategy if you have specific expectations.

$$\chi^2 = \frac{\Sigma(O - E)^2}{E}$$

where O = Number of Observations and E = Expected Number of Observations.

Suppose you wanted to know if students had preferences for class times during the day. You could categorize the classes as early morning, late morning, early afternoon, and late afternoon. If you asked a randomly selected group of students to state a preference, you could then tally them and compute a value of chi-square to test whether all times are seen as equally desirable. For the fictitious data set below, you could answer this question.

	8 OR 9 A.M.	11 A.M. OR NOON	1 OR 2 P.M.	3 OR 4 P.M.	TOTAL
Observed Values	8	28	22	15	73
Expected Values	*18.25*	*18.25*	*18.25*	*18.25*	

Computing Expected Values.   In this case, our assumption is that students don't have preferences for particular times of the day. Although in reality it is probably safe to assume that students wouldn't want early morning classes, we don't have good information about what percentage of students would prefer each category. So our null hypothesis at this point is that all times are equally desirable.

There are 73 observations in our sample. If we assume equal representation in each of the 4 time slots, we would compute the expected values as the total number of observations divided by the number of categories: 73/4 = 18.25. Using the formula for chi-square given above, we can compute our statistic.

$$\chi^2 = \Sigma \frac{(Observed - Expected)^2}{Expected}$$

$$= \frac{(8 - 18.25)^2}{18.25} + \frac{(28 - 18.25)^2}{18.25} + \frac{(22 - 18.25)^2}{18.25} + \frac{(15 - 18.25)^2}{18.25}$$

$$= \frac{(-10.25)^2}{18.25} + \frac{(9.75)^2}{18.25} + \frac{(3.75)^2}{18.25} + \frac{(-3.25)^2}{18.25}$$

$$= \frac{105.06}{18.25} + \frac{95.06}{18.25} + \frac{14.06}{18.25} + \frac{10.56}{18.25}$$

$$= 5.76 + 5.21 + 0.77 + 0.58$$

$$= 12.32$$

Calculating Degrees of Freedom.   For a chi-square goodness of fit test, the degrees of freedom is the number of categories minus one. There are four categories in this example, so the degrees of freedom is $(4 - 1) = 3$.

The Decision.   To find the critical value of chi-square in the table for a Type I error rate of 5 percent, we use 3 degrees of freedom and the column labeled .05. The critical value is 7.815. Our computed value is larger than the critical value in the table, so we reject the null hypothesis and conclude that students do not prefer all times of the day for their classes. According to these fictitious data, we would conclude that students prefer middle of the day to early or late.

Test of Independence

The chi-square test of independence, like the goodness of fit test, involves whether we can make accurate predictions about the number of observed events when we have two (or more) variables from which we make the predictions.

    Jenni and Jenni (1976) observed college students carrying their books on campus and noted how the students held them. One category of carrying them was across the front of the body with one or both arms wrapped around the books; a second category was for the books to be held more toward the side, pinched from above or supported from below by the hand and/or arm. The researchers investigated whether book carrying was associated with sex.

    They observed several hundred college students. If you conducted this study in 1976 with a smaller number of students, you might have obtained the fictitious data below, which you could analyze with a chi-square test of independence. There are two variables: sex of the student and category of carrying. The question is whether you can predict the sex of the carriers by knowing how they carry the books or, alternatively, whether you can predict how people will carry their books, given that you know their sex.

OBSERVED VALUES	FEMALE		MALE		(TOTAL)
	Observed	*Expected*	**Observed**	*Expected*	
Front	21	*12*	3	*14*	(24)
Side	5	*14*	23	*12*	(28)
(Total)	(26)		(26)		(52)

Computing Expected Values. For this 2 × 2 design, you need to compute expected values for each of the four conditions. As a rule of thumb, you should avoid computing chi-square values when a large percentage of your expected values are smaller then 5. It is probably not problematic as long as the number of such expectations is under 20 percent of the total number of cells (Howell, 1992). As you can see in this example, one of the cells has fewer than 5 observations, but the expected value is greater than 5. It is the expected value that is important to consider, not the observed value.

The expected value is computed by multiplying the row total for each cell times the column total for that cell, then dividing by the total number of observations. You do this for each cell. In the present example, you find the expected value for each of the four cells.

Once you have the set of observed and expected values, you can compute the value of chi-square, based on the formula above.

$$Expected = \frac{(Total_{Row}) \times (Total_{Column})}{N_{TOTAL}}$$

$$Expected_{Female - Front} = \frac{24 \times 26}{52} = \frac{624}{52} = 12$$

$$Expected_{Female - Side} = \frac{28 \times 26}{52} = \frac{728}{52} = 14$$

$$Expected_{Male - Front} = \frac{24 \times 26}{52} = \frac{624}{52} = 12$$

$$Expected_{Male - Side} = \frac{28 \times 26}{52} = \frac{728}{52} = 14$$

$$\chi^2 = \Sigma \frac{(Observed - Expected)^2}{Expected}$$

$$= \frac{(21 - 12)^2}{12} + \frac{(5 - 14)^2}{14} + \frac{(3 - 14)^2}{14} + \frac{(23 - 12)^2}{12}$$

$$= \frac{9^2}{12} + \frac{(-9)^2}{14} + \frac{(-11)^2}{14} + \frac{11^2}{12}$$

$$= \frac{81}{12} + \frac{81}{14} + \frac{121}{14} + \frac{121}{12}$$

$$= 6.75 + 5.79 + 8.64 + 10.08$$

$$= 31.26$$

Calculating Degrees of Freedom. Degrees of freedom for this chi-square test equals the number of rows minus one times the number of columns minus one, or $(R-1)(C-1)$. There are two rows and there are two columns in this design, so $(R-1)(C-1) = (2-1)(2-1) = (1)(1) = 1$.

The Decision. When there is one degree of freedom and when you want your Type I error rate to be 5 percent, you look for the critical value in the chi-square table for the probability of .05 and 1 degree of freedom. The critical value is 3.841.

The value we computed is 31.26, which exceeds the critical value needed for significance. Thus we can conclude that there is a great deal of predictability regarding sex of students and the manner in which they carry their books.

This research took place over a quarter of a century ago. Virtually nobody had backpacks then. It would be interesting to see if the effect could be replicated today, with different means of conveying books from place to place and different types of students. Have women and men changed?

How to Designate the Chi-Square Value. $\chi^2(1, N = 52) = 31.26$, $p < .01$

CORRELATIONAL ANALYSES

There are quite a few correlational analyses that researchers use to assess the relations among variables. The most common correlational analysis is the Pearson product–moment correlation. It provides information as to whether a linear relation exists between two variables. Curvilinear relations require more advanced statistics.

A second correlational approach is regression analysis, which allows us to identify the pattern of changes in scores and to make predictions of a criterion variable based on a single predictor variable. The linear regression analysis we will see here is based on the Pearson correlation for linear relationships.

Pearson Product–Moment Correlation

The Pearson product–moment correlation is the most widely used correlation coefficient. In fact, some of the other correlations and tests of associations are merely algebraic manipulations of the Pearson r.

The formula for the Pearson product–moment correlation appears below. There are several different ways to represent the formula. They will produce the same result, but this formula is fairly easy to use.

$$r = \frac{N(\Sigma AB) - (\Sigma A)(\Sigma B)}{\sqrt{[N(\Sigma A^2) - (\Sigma A)^2][N(\Sigma B^2) - (\Sigma B)^2]}}$$

N = Number of pairs
ΣAB = Summed cross-product for each pair
ΣA = Sum of scores in Group A
ΣB = Sum of scores in Group B

In the worked example below, the obtained correlation coefficient is negative, which reflects the fact that scores in A that are high tend to be paired with scores in B that are low and vice versa. With a two-tailed, nondirectional test, the absolute value of r is compared with the critical value from the table.

Worked Example of Pearson Product–Moment Correlation

	A	A^2	B	B^2	CROSS-PRODUCT OF A * B
	1	1	4	16	4
	3	9	8	64	24
	6	36	6	36	36
	7	49	2	4	14
	7	49	3	9	21
	8	64	2	4	16
	9	81	1	1	9

Number of Observations	(1)	7	(1)	7
Sum of Cross-Products				(2) 124
Sum of Scores in Group	(3)	41	(4)	26
Square of Sum of Scores	(5)	1681	(6)	676
Sum of Scores Squared in Group	(7)	289	(8)	134

Value of r

$$r = \frac{[(1)(2) - (3)(4)]}{\sqrt{[(1)(7) - (5)] [(1)(8) - (6)]}}$$

$$= \frac{(7)(124) - (41)(26)}{\sqrt{[7(289) - 1681] [7(134) - 676]}}$$

$$r = \frac{868 - 1066}{\sqrt{(342)(262)}} = \frac{-198}{299.34}$$

$$= -.66$$

Degrees of Freedom   # Pairs – 2 = 5

Critical value
($\alpha = .05$, two tails)
from table of
critical r values   .7545

Decision   **Do not reject the null hypothesis. The computed value is less than the critical value. There is not enough evidence to conclude that there is a relationship between a person's score in condition X and that person's score in condition Y.**

How to Designate *r* Values. $r(5) = -.66, p <.05$

Linear Regression Analysis

In many cases, researchers who conduct correlational analyses also generate predictions of a criterion variable (sometimes the dependent variable) given a particular value of the predictor variable (sometimes the independent variable). The terms independent and dependent variable are more likely to be used when the research is experimental but uses regression analysis.

The simplest of these involves linear regression on one variable. One predictor variable is used to estimate a criterion variable. For more advanced regression analysis, such as that using multiple predictor variables or nonlinear regression, you should consult a statistics book. We will use the values for the correlation example to generate the regression line that we use to make predictions about the Y value, the criterion, based on the X value, the predictor.

In predicting a value of the DV, we use the formula for a straight line:

$$Y = a + bX,$$

where

> a = the Y-intercept,
> b = the slope of the line,
> X = the value of the predictor variable, and
> Y = the value of the criterion variable.

After completing a correlational analysis, we compute values of a and b based on statistical values from the correlation computations.

Calculating the Slope (*b*)

$$b = r\frac{S_{criterion}}{S_{predictor}} = -.66\left(\frac{2.50}{2.85}\right) = (-.66)(.88) = -.58$$

The negative value of the correlation coefficient means that as the value of the predictor value increases, the value of the criterion variable decreases. The value of $-.58$ for the slope means that as the value of the predictor variable (usually the X value) increases by a value of one, the value of the criterion (usually the Y value) decreases by 0.58.

Calculating the Y-intercept

$$a = Mean_{criterion} - b(Mean_{predictor})$$
$$= 3.71 - (-.58)(5.86) = 3.71 - (-3.40) = 7.11$$

According to this analysis, if the value of X is zero, the value of Y should be around 7.11. As the value of the predictor variable increases, our prediction of the value of the criterion variable will decrease because the slope is negative. So as the value of X goes from zero to larger numbers, the value of Y will diminish.

Estimating a value of Y based on X.   If the predictor value, X, is 7, what is our best prediction of the criterion variable, Y?

$$Y = a + bX$$
$$Y = 7.11 + (-.58)X$$
$$= 7.11 + (-.58)7 = 7.11 + (-4.06) = 7.11 - 4.06 = 3.05$$

If the value of X is 7, our best prediction for the value of Y is 3.05, which is reasonably consistent with the data set, as you can see in Figure B.2. The higher the value of the correlation coefficient, the better your prediction will be.

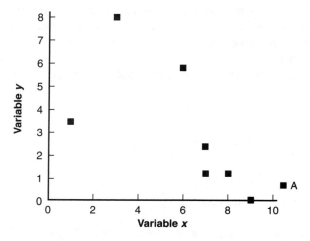

FIGURE B.2   Scatterplot for correlation and regression data. The downward trend of the data when X increases reveals a negative correlation.

APPENDIX C

STATISTICAL TABLES

TABLE C.1   Significance values for the _t_ distribution.

Computed values of _t_ are significant if they are larger than the critical value in the table.

α LEVELS FOR DIRECTIONAL (ONE-TAILED) TESTS

	.05	.025	.01	.005	.0005

α LEVELS FOR NONDIRECTIONAL (TWO-TAILED) TESTS

df	.10	.05	.02	.01	.001
1	6.314	12.706	31.821	63.657	636.619
2	2.920	4.303	6.965	9.925	31.598
3	2.353	3.182	4.541	5.841	12.924
4	2.132	2.776	3.747	4.604	8.610
5	2.015	2.571	3.365	4.032	6.869
6	1.943	2.447	3.143	3.707	5.959
7	1.895	2.365	2.998	3.499	5.408
8	1.860	2.306	2.896	3.355	5.041
9	1.833	2.262	2.821	3.250	4.781
10	1.812	2.228	2.764	3.169	4.587
11	1.796	2.201	2.718	3.106	4.437
12	1.782	2.179	2.681	3.055	4.318
13	1.771	2.160	2.650	3.012	4.221
14	1.761	2.145	2.624	2.977	4.140
15	1.753	2.131	2.602	2.947	4.073
16	1.746	2.120	2.583	2.921	4.015
17	1.740	2.110	2.567	2.898	3.965
18	1.734	2.101	2.552	2.878	3.922
19	1.729	2.093	2.539	2.861	3.883
20	1.725	2.086	2.528	2.845	3.850
21	1.721	2.080	2.518	2.831	3.819
22	1.717	2.074	2.508	2.819	3.792
23	1.714	2.069	2.500	2.807	3.767
24	1.711	2.064	2.492	2.797	3.745
25	1.708	2.060	2.485	2.787	3.725
26	1.706	2.056	2.479	2.779	3.707
27	1.703	2.052	2.473	2.771	3.690
28	1.701	2.048	2.467	2.763	3.674
29	1.699	2.045	2.462	2.756	3.659
30	1.697	2.042	2.457	2.750	3.646
40	1.684	2.021	2.423	2.704	3.551
60	1.671	2.000	2.390	2.660	3.460
120	1.658	1.980	2.358	2.617	3.373
∞	1.645	1.960	2.326	2.576	3.291

© R. A. Fisher and F. Yates (1963) _Statistical Tables for Biological, Agricultural and Medical Research_, reprinted by permission of Pearson Education Limited. Adapted from Table III. Adapted from Table 3.

TABLE C.2   Significance values for the analysis of variance (*F* test).

Degrees of freedom for treatments ($df_{between}$) appear in the left column. Degrees of freedom for the error term (df_{within} or df_{error}) are across the top. Computed values of *F* are significant if they are larger than the critical value in the table.

Values for $\alpha = .05$ are in normal Roman type
Values for $\alpha = .01$ are in bold type
Values for $\alpha = 0.001$ are in italics

DF FOR THE NUMERATOR
($DF_{BETWEEN}$ OR $DF_{TREATMENT}$)

		1	2	3	4	5	6	8	12	24

DF FOR THE DENOMINATOR
(DF_{WITHIN} OR DF_{ERROR})

		1	2	3	4	5	6	8	12	24
1	$\alpha =.05$	161.4	199.5	215.7	224.6	230.2	234.0	238.9	243.9	249.0
	$\alpha = .01$	**4052**	**4999**	**5403**	**5625**	**5764**	**5859**	**5982**	**6106**	**6234**
	$\alpha= .001$	*405284*	*500000*	*540379*	*562500*	*576405*	*585937*	*598144*	*610667*	*623497*
2	$\alpha = .05$	18.51	19.00	19.16	19.25	19.30	19.33	19.37	19.41	19.45
	$\alpha = .01$	**98.50**	**99.00**	**99.17**	**99.25**	**99.30**	**99.33**	**99.37**	**99.42**	**99.46**
	$\alpha = .001$	*998.5*	*999.0*	*999.2*	*999.2*	*999.3*	*999.3*	*999.4*	*999.4*	*999.5*
3	$\alpha = .05$	10.13	9.55	9.28	6.12	9.01	8.94	8.84	8.74	8.64
	$\alpha = .01$	**34.12**	**30.82**	**29.46**	**28.71**	**28.24**	**27.91**	**27.49**	**27.05**	**26.60**
	$\alpha = .001$	*167.0*	*148.5*	*141.2*	*137.1*	*134.6*	*132.8*	*130.6*	*128.3*	*125.9*
4	$\alpha = .05$	7.71	6.94	6.59	6.39	6.26	6.16	6.04	5.91	5.77
	$\alpha = .01$	**21.20**	**18.00**	**16.69**	**15.98**	**15.52**	**15.21**	**14.80**	**14.37**	**13.93**
	$\alpha = .001$	*74.14*	*61.25*	*56.18*	*53.44*	*51.71*	*50.53*	*49.00*	*47.41*	*45.77*
5	$\alpha = .05$	6.61	5.79	5.41	5.19	5.05	4.95	4.82	4.68	4.53
	$\alpha = .01$	**16.26**	**13.27**	**12.06**	**11.39**	**10.97**	**10.67**	**10.29**	**9.89**	**9.47**
	$\alpha = .001$	*47.18*	*37.12*	*33.20*	*31.09*	*29.75*	*28.84*	*27.64*	*26.42*	*25.14*
6	$\alpha = .05$	5.99	5.14	4.76	4.53	4.39	4.28	4.15	4.00	3.84
	$\alpha = .01$	**13.74**	**10.92**	**9.78**	**9.15**	**8.75**	**8.47**	**8.10**	**7.72**	**7.31**
	$\alpha = .001$	*35.51*	*27.00*	*23.70*	*21.92*	*20.81*	*20.03*	*19.03*	*17.99*	*16.89*
7	$\alpha = .05$	5.59	4.74	4.35	4.12	3.97	3.87	3.73	3.57	3.41
	$\alpha = .01$	**12.25**	**9.55**	**8.45**	**7.85**	**7.46**	**7.19**	**6.84**	**6.47**	**6.07**
	$\alpha = .001$	*29.25*	*21.69*	*18.77*	*17.19*	*16.21*	*15.52*	*14.63*	*13.71*	*12.73*
8	$\alpha = .05$	5.32	4.46	4.07	3.84	3.69	3.58	3.44	3.28	3.12
	$\alpha = .01$	**11.26**	**8.65**	**7.59**	**7.01**	**6.63**	**6.37**	**6.03**	**5.67**	**5.28**
	$\alpha = .001$	*25.42*	*18.49*	*15.83*	*14.39*	*13.49*	*12.86*	*12.04*	*11.19*	*10.30*
9	$\alpha = .05$	5.12	4.26	3.86	3.63	3.48	3.37	3.23	3.07	2.90
	$\alpha = .01$	**10.56**	**8.02**	**6.99**	**6.42**	**6.06**	**5.80**	**5.47**	**5.11**	**4.73**
	$\alpha = .001$	*22.86*	*16.39*	*13.90*	*12.56*	*11.71*	*11.13*	*10.37*	*9.57*	*8.72*
10	$\alpha = .05$	4.96	4.10	3.71	3.48	3.33	3.22	3.07	2.91	2.74
	$\alpha = .01$	**10.04**	**7.56**	**6.55**	**5.99**	**5.64**	**5.39**	**5.06**	**4.71**	**4.33**
	$\alpha = .001$	*21.04*	*14.91*	*12.55*	*11.28*	*10.48*	*9.92*	*9.20*	*8.45*	*7.64*

(continued)

TABLE C.2   Continued

DF FOR THE NUMERATOR
$(DF_{BETWEEN}$ OR $DF_{TREATMENT})$

		1	2	3	4	5	6	8	12	24

DF FOR THE DENOMINATOR
$(DF_{WITHIN}$ OR $DF_{ERROR})$

		1	2	3	4	5	6	8	12	24
11	$\alpha = .05$	4.84	3.98	3.59	3.36	3.20	3.09	2.95	2.79	2.61
	$\alpha = .01$	**9.65**	**7.20**	**6.22**	**5.67**	**5.32**	**5.07**	**4.74**	**4.40**	**4.02**
	$\alpha = .001$	*19.69*	*13.81*	*11.56*	*10.35*	*9.58*	*9.05*	*8.35*	*7.63*	*6.85*
12	$\alpha =.05$	4.75	3.88	3.49	3.26	3.11	3.00	2.85	2.69	2.50
	$\alpha = .01$	**9.33**	**6.93**	**5.95**	**5.41**	**5.06**	**4.82**	**4.50**	**4.16**	**3.78**
	$\alpha = .001$	*18.64*	*12.97*	*10.80*	*9.63*	*8.89*	*8.38*	*7.71*	*7.00*	*6.25*
13	$\alpha = .05$	4.67	3.80	3.41	3.18	3.02	2.92	2.77	2.60	2.42
	$\alpha = .01$	**9.07**	**6.70**	**5.74**	**5.20**	**4.86**	**4.62**	**4.30**	**3.96**	**3.59**
	$\alpha =.001$	*17.81*	*12.31*	*10.21*	*9.07*	*8.35*	*7.86*	*7.21*	*6.52*	*5.78*
14	$\alpha = 5$	4.60	3.74	3.34	3.11	2.96	2.85	2.70	2.53	2.35
	$\alpha = .01$	**8.86**	**6.51**	**5.56**	**5.03**	**4.69**	**4.46**	**4.14**	**3.80**	**3.43**
	$\alpha =.001$	*17.14*	*11.78*	*9.73*	*8.62*	*7.92*	*7.43*	*6.80*	*6.13*	*5.41*
15	$\alpha = .05$	4.54	3.68	3.26	3.06	2.90	2.79	2.64	2.48	2.29
	$\alpha = .01$	**8.68**	**6.36**	**5.42**	**4.89**	**4.56**	**4.32**	**4.00**	**3.67**	**3.29**
	$\alpha =.001$	*16.59*	*11.34*	*9.34*	*8.25*	*7.57*	*7.09*	*6.47*	*5.81*	*5.10*
16	$\alpha =.05$	4.49	3.63	3.24	3.01	2.85	2.74	2.59	2.42	2.24
	$\alpha = .01$	**8.53**	**6.23**	**5.29**	**4.77**	**4.44**	**4.20**	**3.89**	**3.55**	**3.18**
	$\alpha = .001$	*16.12*	*10.97*	*9.00*	*7.94*	*7.27*	*6.81*	*6.19*	*5.55*	*4.85*
17	$\alpha =.05$	4.45	3.59	3.20	2.96	2.81	2.70	2.55	2.38	2.19
	$\alpha = .01$	**8.40**	**6.11**	**5.18**	**4.67**	**4.34**	**4.10**	**3.79**	**3.45**	**3.08**
	$\alpha = .001$	*15.72*	*10.66*	*8.73*	*7.68*	*7.02*	*6.56*	*5.96*	*5.32*	*4.63*
18	$\alpha = .05$	4.41	3.55	3.16	2.93	2.77	2.66	2.51	2.34	2.15
	$\alpha = .01$	**8.28**	**6.01**	**5.09**	**4.58**	**4.25**	**4.01**	**3.71**	**3.37**	**3.00**
	$\alpha = .001$	*15.38*	*10.39*	*8.49*	*7.46*	*6.81*	*6.35*	*5.76*	*5.13*	*4.45*
19	$\alpha = .05$	4.38	3.52	3.13	2.90	2.74	2.63	2.48	2.31	2.11
	$\alpha = .01$	**8.18**	**5.93**	**5.01**	**4.50**	**4.17**	**3.94**	**3.63**	**3.30**	**2.92**
	$\alpha = .001$	*15.08*	*10.16*	*8.28*	*7.26*	*6.62*	*6.18*	*5.59*	*4.97*	*4.29*
20	$\alpha = .05$	4.35	3.49	3.10	2.87	2.71	2.60	2.45	2.28	2.08
	$\alpha = .01$	**8.10**	**5.85**	**4.94**	**4.43**	**4.10**	**3.87**	**3.56**	**3.23**	**2.86**
	$\alpha =.001$	*14.82*	*9.95*	*8.10*	*7.10*	*6.46*	*6.02*	*5.44*	*4.82*	*4.15*
21	$\alpha = .05$	4.32	3.47	3.07	2.84	2.68	2.57	2.42	2.25	2.05
	$\alpha = .01$	**8.02**	**5.78**	**4.87**	**4.37**	**4.04**	**3.81**	**3.51**	**3.17**	**2.80**
	$\alpha =.001$	*14.59*	*9.77*	*7.94*	*6.95*	*6.32*	*5.88*	*5.31*	*4.70*	*4.03*
22	$\alpha = .05$	4.30	3.44	3.05	2.82	2.66	2.55	2.40	2.23	2.03
	$\alpha = .01$	**7.94**	**5.72**	**4.82**	**4.31**	**3.99**	**3.76**	**3.45**	**3.12**	**2.75**
	$\alpha =.001$	*14.38*	*9.61*	*7.80*	*6.81*	*6.19*	*5.76*	*5.19*	*4.58*	*3.92*

TABLE C.2 **Continued**

DF FOR THE NUMERATOR
(DF$_{BETWEEN}$ OR DF$_{TREATMENT}$)

		1	2	3	4	5	6	8	12	24

DF FOR THE DENOMINATOR
(DF$_{WITHIN}$ OR DF$_{ERROR}$)

		1	2	3	4	5	6	8	12	24
23	α = .05	4.28	3.42	3.03	2.80	2.64	2.53	2.38	2.20	2.00
	α = .01	**7.88**	**5.66**	**4.76**	**4.26**	**3.94**	**3.71**	**3.41**	**3.07**	**2.70**
	α = .001	*14.19*	*9.47*	*7.67*	*6.69*	*6.08*	*5.65*	*5.09*	*4.48*	*3.82*
24	α = .05	4.26	3.40	3.01	2.78	2.62	2.51	2.36	2.18	1.98
	α = .01	**7.82**	**5.61**	**4.72**	**4.22**	**3.90**	**3.67**	**3.36**	**3.03**	**2.66**
	α = .001	*14.03*	*9.34*	*7.55*	*6.59*	*5.98*	*5.55*	*4.99*	*4.39*	*3.74*
25	α = .05	4.24	3.38	2.99	2.76	2.60	2.49	2.34	2.16	1.96
	α = .01	**7.77**	**5.57**	**4.68**	**4.18**	**3.86**	**3.63**	**3.32**	**2.99**	**2.62**
	α = .001	*13.88*	*9.22*	*7.45*	*6.49*	*5.88*	*5.46*	*4.91*	*4.31*	*3.66*
26	α = .05	4.22	3.37	2.98	2.74	2.59	2.47	2.32	2.15	1.95
	α = .01	**7.72**	**5.53**	**4.64**	**4.14**	**3.82**	**3.59**	**3.29**	**2.96**	**2.58**
	α = .001	*13.74*	*9.12*	*7.36*	*6.41*	*5.80*	*5.38*	*4.83*	*4.24*	*3.59*
27	α = .05	4.21	3.35	2.96	2.73	2.57	2.46	2.30	2.13	1.93
	α = .01	**7.68**	**5.49**	**4.60**	**4.11**	**3.78**	**3.56**	**3.26**	**2.93**	**2.55**
	α = .001	*13.61*	*9.02*	*7.27*	*6.33*	*5.73*	*5.31*	*4.76*	*4.17*	*3.52*
28	α = .05	4.20	3.34	2.95	2.71	2.56	2.44	2.29	2.12	1.91
	α = .01	**7.64**	**5.45**	**4.57**	**4.07**	**3.75**	**3.53**	**3.23**	**2.90**	**2.52**
	α = .001	*13.50*	*8.93*	*7.19*	*6.25*	*5.66*	*5.24*	*4.69*	*4.11*	*3.46*
29	α = .05	4.18	3.33	2.93	2.70	2.54	2.43	2.28	2.10	1.90
	α = .01	**7.60**	**5.42**	**4.54**	**4.04**	**3.73**	**3.50**	**3.20**	**2.87**	**2.49**
	α = .001	*13.39*	*8.85*	*7.12*	*6.19*	*5.59*	*5.18*	*4.64*	*4.05*	*3.41*
30	α = .05	4.17	3.32	2.92	2.69	2.53	2.42	2.27	2.09	1.89
	α = .01	**7.56**	**5.39**	**4.51**	**4.02**	**3.70**	**3.47**	**3.17**	**2.84**	**2.47**
	α = .001	*13.29*	*8.77*	*7.05*	*6.12*	*5.53*	*5.12*	*4.58*	*4.00*	*3.36*
40	α = .05	4.08	3.23	2.84	2.61	2.45	2.34	2.18	2.00	1.79
	α = .01	**7.31**	**5.18**	**4.31**	**3.83**	**3.51**	**3.29**	**2.99**	**2.66**	**2.29**
	α = .001	*12.61*	*8.25*	*6.60*	*5.70*	*5.13*	*4.73*	*4.21*	*3.64*	*3.01*
60	α = .05	4.00	3.15	2.76	2.52	2.37	2.25	2.10	1.92	1.70
	α = .01	**7.08**	**4.98**	**4.13**	**3.65**	**3.34**	**3.12**	**2.82**	**2.50**	**2.12**
	α = .001	*11.97*	*7.76*	*6.17*	*5.31*	*4.76*	*4.37*	*3.87*	*3.31*	*2.69*
120	α = .05	3.92	3.07	2.68	2.45	2.29	2.17	2.02	1.83	1.61
	α = .01	**6.85**	**4.79**	**3.95**	**3.48**	**3.17**	**2.66**	**2.34**	**1.95**	
	α = .001	*11.38*	*7.32*	*5.79*	*4.95*	*4.42*	*4.04*	*3.55*	*3.02*	*2.40*
∞	α = .05	3.84	2.99	2.60	2.37	2.21	2.10	1.94	1.75	1.52
	α = .01	**6.64**	**4.60**	**3.78**	**3.32**	**3.02**	**2.80**	**2.51**	**2.18**	**1.79**
	α = .001	*10.83*	*6.91*	*5.42*	*4.62*	*4.10*	*3.74*	*3.27*	*2.74*	*2.13*

© R. A. Fisher and F. Yates (1963) *Statistical Tables for Biological, Agricultural and Medical Research*, reprinted by permission of Pearson Education Limited. Adapted from Table V.

TABLE C.3 Significance values for the Pearson product–moment correlation (r).

Computed values of *r* are significant if they are larger than the value in the table.

α LEVELS FOR DIRECTIONAL (ONE-TAILED) TESTS

	.05	.025	.01	.005	.0005

α LEVELS FOR NONDIRECTIONAL (TWO-TAILED) TESTS

df (# pairs - 2)	.1	.05	.02	.01	.001
1	.9877	.9969	.9995	.9999	.9999988
2	.9000	.9500	.9800	.9900	.9990
3	.8054	.8783	.9343	.9587	.9912
4	.7293	.8114	.8822	.9172	.9741
5	.6694	.7545	.8329	.8745	.9507
6	.6215	.7067	.7887	.8343	.9249
7	.5822	.6664	.7498	.7977	.8982
8	.5494	.6319	.7155	.7646	.8721
9	.5214	.6021	.6851	.7348	.8471
10	.4973	.5760	.6581	.7079	.8233
11	.4762	.5529	.6339	.6835	.8010
12	.4575	.5324	.6120	.6614	.7800
13	.4409	.5139	.5923	.6411	.7603
14	.4259	.4973	.5742	.6226	.7420
15	.4124	.4821	.5577	.6055	.7246
16	.4000	.4683	.5425	.5897	.7084
17	.3887	.4555	.5285	.5751	.6932
18	.3783	.4438	.5155	.5614	.6787
19	.3687	.4329	.5043	.5487	.6652
20	.3598	.4227	.4921	.5368	.6524
25	.3233	.3809	.4451	.4869	.5974
30	.2960	.3494	.4093	.4487	.5541
35	.2746	.3246	.3810	.4182	.5189
40	.2573	.3044	.3578	.3932	.4896
45	.2428	.2875	.3384	.3721	.4648
50	.2306	.2732	.3218	.3541	.4433
60	.2108	.2500	.2948	.3248	.4078
70	.1954	.2319	.2737	.3017	.3799
80	.1829	.2172	.2565	.2830	.3568
90	.1726	.2050	.2422	.2673	.3375
100	.1638	.1946	.2301	.2540	.3211

TABLE C.4 Significance values for chi-square (χ^2).

Computed values of χ^2 are significant if they are larger than the value in the table.

	α LEVELS			
df	*.10*	*.05*	*.01*	*.001*
1	2.706	3.841	6.635	10.827
2	4.605	5.991	9.210	13.815
3	6.251	7.815	11.345	16.266
4	7.779	9.488	13.277	18.467
5	9.236	11.070	15.086	20.515
6	10.645	12.592	16.812	22.457
7	12.017	14.067	18.475	24.322
8	13.362	15.507	20.090	26.125
9	14.684	16.919	21.666	27.877
10	15.987	18.307	23.209	29.588
11	17.275	19.675	24.725	31.264
12	18.549	21.026	26.217	32.909
13	19.812	22.362	27.688	34.528
14	21.064	23.685	29.141	36.123
15	22.307	24.996	30.578	37.697
16	23.542	26.296	32.000	39.252
17	24.769	27.587	33.409	40.790
18	25.989	28.869	34.805	42.312
19	27.204	30.144	36.191	43.280
20	28.412	31.410	37.566	45.315
21	29.615	32.671	38.932	46.797
22	30.813	33.924	40.289	48.268
23	32.007	35.172	41.638	49.728
24	33.196	36.415	42.980	51.179
25	34.382	37.652	44.314	52.620
26	35.563	38.885	45.642	54.052
27	36.741	40.133	46.963	55.476
28	37.916	41.337	48.278	56.893
29	39.087	42.557	49.588	58.302
30	40.256	43.773	50.892	59.703

TABLE C.5 One thousand random numbers.

10801	69621	92008	13317	76917	21943	73624	80445	29832	36976
74959	65233	71968	87168	49732	01869	62348	31099	27069	48371
04613	70583	61117	90612	27112	01158	40970	13707	57074	68148
43119	10341	52504	17521	91658	65932	27217	27220	36299	18907
05196	58937	49852	05962	21349	22112	96044	51822	80307	48511
91846	14339	69334	41114	74998	67265	24494	94609	07506	41925
32611	04453	39706	93180	28343	65808	56739	35441	06383	48345
31612	64859	57247	48883	88849	12957	96368	59157	01457	32286
06811	56453	31190	40241	93777	05674	14878	98541	19978	62941
49156	18317	52290	57437	34766	15564	27358	88676	90462	01447
85083	29866	24889	75946	83452	05025	45481	38172	06556	95725
92686	83627	63324	76877	42736	18599	10076	18987	46692	83214
04153	87384	98578	37405	71255	76724	34331	18744	49206	88389
36264	00862	77603	18063	85971	93189	78687	87926	09703	18024
93188	81477	60543	71093	49282	95305	85972	18871	55505	67354
81856	61512	41926	55090	80158	50833	24492	84373	91432	73511
60993	75429	71568	64945	59296	65966	69284	44770	56988	42531
48760	55612	43419	41346	72776	03145	51665	93169	46002	12986
05686	49443	41186	29474	02306	80764	14764	71099	10101	99774
71131	17438	61830	52767	85360	99494	90297	05596	74534	35407

ARCHIVAL RESEARCH

Suppose you want to find out how people thought or acted two hundred years ago. You can't very well ask them directly because they are all dead. One possibility is to find people who knew people who knew other people who, in turn, knew the people you are interested in. At some point, though, you won't be able to find anybody who goes back far enough.

In general, in many developed countries, we can get more or less direct information for about the past 150 years. Assume that people live, on average, 75 years. If you found somebody of that age or older, the individual might very well be able to tell you about somebody he or she knew who was about 75 years older. The younger person would have direct recollections from people in the previous generation, which can be very helpful. This covers the 150-year span. (You would actually need people who live longer than average to cover the 150 years, but this is quite feasible.)

Suppose that you wanted to find out how things change over the course of years. You might have trouble finding a single person who can provide you with what you want to know, especially if you are looking for information on a societal level rather than an individual level. Sometimes you may simply want information that is only available from existing records.

In these situations, you might need to rely on *archival research*, which involves information that was compiled by somebody else for some reason other than your research. If it is available and helps you answer your question, why not use it?

Psychologists don't use archival research extensively, but it can be handy for helping us understand patterns of behavior that we can't get from traditional experimental or correlational approaches. There are many different sources of archival information; the commonality among them is that they are accessible without having direct contact with the people who provided the information.

SOURCES OF ARCHIVAL INFORMATION

Researchers have managed to find out about behavior by using some very creative approaches. For instance, scientists have discovered the eating habits of animals by examining the contents of their dried feces. Other investigators have gone through garbage to see what people throw away, which gives clues to their behaviors.

Fortunately, most archival research is easier on the investigator's nose than garbage or feces. We are fortunate to live in an information culture that accumulates data of every conceivable type. In the United States, the federal government collects census data every ten years and a variety of information in between. The government also provides funding for other data collection, like the General Social Survey, which surveys a random sample of Americans every few years to see what they think about a variety of issues, on topics ranging from abortion to belief in an afterlife.

Although archival data are collected for many different purposes, we can sometimes appropriate it for our behavioral research. The census is completed in part so that Congress can allocate seats in the House of Representatives, with each politician representing about the same number of voters. We wouldn't know how to do that without a census count. Fortunately, we can answer some of our research questions using the same information.

The important point is that there are numerous sources of data about people, their behaviors, attitudes, and lives. By *triangulation*, using different techniques to converge on the answer to an important question, we can round out our knowledge. Archival sources can help immensely. For instance, people are interested in finding out why eating disorders develop as they do. Much discussion has focused on the societal pressures that people, particularly girls and women, feel to achieve supposed physical perfection. There is widespread belief by many that people are willing to starve themselves, perhaps to death, because of social pressure. Is it possible that the cause of such painful behavior is not entirely social, but perhaps partially biological?

Using archival methods, Eagles, Andrew, Johnston, Easton, and Miller (2001) reviewed medical records of women who suffered from anorexia between 1965 and 1997 to identify factors potentially associated with anorexia that were common to many women. Records of 446 anorexic women in Scotland were compared with a control group of 5,766 women born in 1951, 1961, 1971, and 1981. The researchers discovered that girls born from March to June had significantly higher likelihood of symptoms of anorexia than girls born in other months. Could it be that some environmental factor during gestation can affect the fetus, causing a predisposition for anorexia later? Eagles et al. suggest that exposure to viruses may be a significant factor.

Additional archival research led by Hans Wijbrand Hoek suggested that culture may not explain the incidence of anorexia. They studied anorexia between 1987 and 1989 on the Caribbean island of Curacao, where being overweight (by Western standards) is socially acceptable. After examining medical records on the island, they found about the same rate of anorexia as in Western countries (Anorexia May Not Have Cultural Roots, 1998).

We can use triangulation, that is different research methods, to address the same question, to see if biology can explain part of the problem. Other, non-archival research supports a seasonal link as well. Using the results of a questionnaire on eating disorders, Waller, Meyer, and van Hanswijck de Jonge (2001) found patterns of restricted eating in girls born during summer months.

Further, Strober, Freeman, Lampert, Diamond, and Kaye (2001) used currently diagnosed patients and interviews to see if there are familial patterns of anorexia. They found evidence for a familial, genetic link. Various, independent studies have corroborated the possibility of a role of biological factors in the emergence of anorexia. Further, Vink et al. (2001) have identified a specific genetic mutation in a subset of the anorexia patients they studied. Of the 145 patients they investigated, 11 percent showed a genetic trait associated with the disorder.

Even if this pattern of results continues to replicate, we should not forget that anorexia will have many roots. There is an increasing amount of evidence that social, cultural, and psychological factors are critical in the development of anorexia. The role of the media has been discussed extensively in reinforcing undesirable ideas (Thompson & Heinberg, 1999). Further, Thompson and Stice (2001) pointed out that internalization of thinness as representing the ideal body shape is a causal factor in the development of eating pathology. In addition Gunewardene, Huon, and Zheng (2001) found that increasing exposure to Western culture is associated with increased dieting.

This combination of archival and other research approaches will let us close in on all of the different factors that may be associated with the complex behavior of anorexia.

Statistical Records

The largest single source of statistical information is probably the U.S. census. It currently contains information on 285 million people. The Census Bureau regularly issues reports on the data and makes data available. In addition, the General Social Survey began in 1950 and has been ongoing since. Surveyors randomly sample the American populace every two years, asking many of the same questions. We can get a long-range picture of people's attitudes and thoughts. Further, the GSS continues to evolve, with additional questions added periodically.

Other public sources of valuable data are death records. Such data are available in convenient computerized form, so researchers can examine literally millions of records fairly easily. For instance, Phillips, Christenfeld, and Ryan (1999) studied almost 32 million death certificates issued in the United States between 1973 and 1988. They discovered that death rates increase in the first week of the month compared to the last week.

The effect doesn't seem large, with about a one percent increase in the first week. Extrapolating beyond this sample, though, the data tell us that there are over 4,000 more deaths in the United States in the initial week of the month compared to the preceding week. The researchers looked at the causes of death and found that many were attributable either to homicide or suicide or to substance abuse. They concluded that people at risk may be receiving government assistance and getting their checks at that time. Thus they have the means to buy alcohol and other drugs that may lead to dangerous behaviors, or they may be victimized because others know they have money.

Sometimes researchers can get different kinds of information from public records, combining various sources to get a complete picture of the topic of interest to them. Scholer, Hickson, Mitchel, and Ray (1998) linked birth certificates, death certificates, and census records to see if they could identify the variables associated with increased risks of children dying in fires. From birth certificates between 1980 and 1995, they identified the mother's age, race, education level, number of previous children born to her, and where she lived. In addition, they recorded the gender of the child. Scholer et al. also estimated the family income from U.S. census data for the area where the mother lived. Then they went to death records of children who died in a fire. Based on all this information, they identified the risk factors for death in a fire.

The researchers found that children of women with less than a high school education were 19 times more likely to die in a fire compared to college-educated women. Children of teenaged mothers were about 4 times more likely to die in a fire compared to older women, and children with two or more siblings were over 6 times more likely. Families with all three factors were 150 times more likely to experience death in a fire compared to families not showing these characteristics. This type of archival research shows how you can take different types of statistical records to research behavioral issues.

Insurance companies also keep voluminous records on claims. Such records may not be generally accessible, but they can be helpful for research within a company. For instance, Hashemi and Webster (1998) studied workplace violence and discovered that over 90 percent of nonfatal assaults on the job are perpetrated by criminals or customers. The idea that a worker can "go postal" and attack fellow workers is disturbing and graphic, but the reality is that coworkers are seldom the source of such violence. In fact, the victim knew the attacker in only about half a percent of all assaults. Researchers discovered this by examining over 28,000 claims relating to workplace assaults between 1993 and 1996.

There are other public sources of statistical information as well. If you were interested in the changing nature of neighborhoods over time, you could access real estate information, including the costs of all houses sold in any area you investigate. It would be possible to trace the desirability of different areas in a city by looking at the relative costs of comparable homes in different locations. If homes in one area increase greatly in value, but those in a different locale do not, you could see what social issues may be associated with the differences.

Written Records

Behavioral scientists are more likely to use public documents, like magazines and newspapers, than individually generated sources because we are often interested in questions beyond the single individual. Archival material like diaries, memoirs, correspondence, and autobiographies don't appear as frequently in psychological research as more widely disseminated material.

When we want to glimpse into the past, sometimes relevant information is easily accessible. For instance, surveys by professional pollsters are a precious source of data. As a case in point, consider the tragedy of the terrorist attacks on the World Trade Center and on the Pentagon in 2001.

After the terrorist attacks on the World Trade Center, some people in the United States became hostile to American citizens of Middle Eastern descent and to Muslims because the terrorists who highjacked the jetliners and flew them into the World Trade Center and into the Pentagon were Muslims from the Middle East. But what did Americans think of this group prior to the terrorist attacks?

According to a Gallup poll in early 2001, eight months before the terrorism, a poll revealed that many Americans did not think favorably of countries like Saudi Arabia, Iran, Libya, and Iraq (Perceptions of Foreign Countries, 2001). About 30 percent of Americans were negatively predisposed toward Arabian countries before the attacks, compared to about 60 percent afterward (Americans Felt Uneasy, 2001). Thus, we can conclude that, even if the attitudes toward Arabs became more negative after the terrorism, those attitudes were not particularly positive before the attacks.

Unless somebody had bothered to ask people in the past, though, we wouldn't know about even recent times. How could you find out about attitudes in the past? Using another approach to study the past, Clawson and Trice (2000) used pictures published in the mass media to investigate attitudes toward the poor. Specifically, they wanted to know what groups of people come to mind when we think of poverty. It would not have been feasible to ask people now about their attitudes in the past because current thoughts influence what we believe we were thinking in the past.

So Clawson and Trice studied every picture in all stories on poverty in *Business Week, Newsweek, New York Times Magazine, Time,* and *U.S. News & World Report* from the beginning of 1993 to the end of 1998. The investigators assumed that the pictures associated with poverty would provide a glimpse of what society was thinking. Is this a reasonable assumption? It probably is because news stories wouldn't be believable if the pictures accompanying them didn't reflect what the public believed to be true in general.

The results revealed that, although 45 percent of the poor in the United States are white and 27 percent black, the pictures of poor people in the news stories depicted more black people. Further, the news reports tended to ignore people who were employed but poor nonetheless. Fifty percent of those living in poverty hold jobs, but pictures didn't reflect this.

The researchers also concluded that while the news photographs reflect the attitude of the general public, the pictures also help to create and reinforce stereotypes. This kind of archival research can give us a glimpse of the past when we can't go back and ask people directly.

In a modern version of archival research, we can use the internet as a source of valuable information. We can learn about societal issues by looking at patterns of internet information. For example, McClung, Murray, & Heitlinger (1998) studied web pages that contained medical information on the management of diarrhea in children. The 60 articles published on the web by reputable medical professionals tended not to follow current recommendations about medical treatment. Only 20 percent reflected current thinking. McClung et al. admonished professionals to monitor medical information they make available on the Web. They also pointed out the need for the general public to be aware of the extent of misinformation on the Web. Unfortunately, anybody can become an "expert" on the Web simply by posting an attractive and accurate-looking site, even if the content is inadequate.

Physical Traces

Sometimes we can use the physical traces of people's behaviors and what they leave behind to gain insight into behavioral issues. One well-known example involved the fact that at a museum exhibit of hatching chickens, the staff had to replace the tiles around the display much more frequently than for other displays (Webb et al., 1981, cited in Judd et al., 1991). This finding suggests that this exhibit was more popular than others;

as Judd et al. pointed out, though, the children who visited it may have shuffled around a lot. There may not have been a very large number of them, just a typical number of very active youngsters. Interpretation of such physical traces can be problematic because several potentially valid explanations may compete with one another.

Sometimes the meaning of physical traces is clearer. It is well known today among forensic anthropologists that tall people tend to live longer than short people. But has this always been the case? Recent research on the bones of long-dead people has revealed that a millennium ago, shorter people tended to die at younger ages than taller people did (Gunnell, Rogers, & Dieppe, 2001).

Gunnell et al. examined 490 sets of adult skeletal remains in England dating from the ninth century. They estimated overall height from bone length and determined sex and age at death with standard anthropological techniques. Based on this physical evidence, the researchers concluded that height has always been a reliable indicator of longevity

We can use the remnants of human behavior in current research as well. Rathje and Hughes (1975, cited in Judd et al., 1991) wanted to document the consumption of beer in households. Door-to-door surveying revealed that residents consumed beer in 15 percent of the households they surveyed. When the researchers searched through the garbage, though, they discovered beer cans at 77 percent of the homes. It is possible (but not very) that people carried their garbage from other neighborhoods and deposited them in a single area. A more parsimonious explanation is that garbage doesn't lie.

ISSUES OF VALIDITY AND RELIABILITY

Archival research differs significantly from the other approaches to research we have considered. As such, the question of the reliability and validity of archival data differs in nature as well. The information we use often doesn't come directly from the people we intend to study and, if it does, we don't query them in person. In addition, archival data have often been generated for purposes other than our research; we are merely adapting it for our own uses.

Sometimes we can interpret the information we get from archival sources in a pretty straightforward fashion, but because the data came into being for reasons having nothing to do with our research question, we may have less confidence in our conclusions that we would like. In archival research we can't control the research environment as we can with laboratory research. Not only are we dependent on outside sources, but we are often looking into the past where the context in which the data arose is obscure.

The positive and negative aspects of archival research are summarized in Table D.1. As you can see, we can gain a lot of useful information with archival approaches, but we need to be cautious as well. The advantages of archival data include potentially high levels of validity and copious amounts of information that people have collected and saved. The disadvantages include the fact that we have no control over the type of information saved and we may not have a good sense of what information is missing. Finally, because we have no control over the collection of data, we don't know which relationships appear meaningful but really aren't.

TABLE D.1   Summary of strengths and weaknesses of archival research.

STRENGTHS	WEAKNESSES
External validity is high because information comes from the results of human activity in a natural setting.	Multiple interpretations exist for any set of data. It is not clear which is most appropriate without further information.
Archival approaches can be economical. The data already exist and may be available at no cost or low cost, both in terms of time and money.	It may be difficult to find the information you want. You might know that the information exists, but not where it is.
Large amounts of data have been collected and saved by public, private, and governmental organizations.	We don't know about missing data. Problems with selective deposit and selective survival call the representativeness of the data into question.
Because of the large amount of preserved information, we can track long-term trends over years, decades, and even centuries.	There may be changes in the nature of the data stored. As a result, the information may not address the same issues in the same way over time.
The data set is nonreactive. That is, they already exist and do not change simply because we are studying it.	The people who initially provided the data may have portrayed themselves differently, knowing that they were being studied. Nonreactivity in the original information may exist.
The data from archival research can corroborate research using different methodologies.	Spurious relationships may exist. Correlations that don't signify important associations can exist. They look important but they aren't.

Selective Deposit and Selective Survival

One of the problems with archival data is that they may not be representative of the whole body of information that interests you. If you are looking into the past, you have to contend with the fact that the material available to you now is only a subset of what you might have gotten if you were asking your question in the time period you are studying. Unfortunately, we may not know whether the information we have gives us a good general picture of the past.

The difficulty arises because of two related issues. First, we may be at a disadvantage in understanding important issues because of *selective deposit*, which refers to the fact that not everything is saved. For example, historians have a fairly poor record of the normal course of the daily life of slaves in colonial America. The problem is that any records that might have existed were probably thought to be unimportant, so nobody bothered to keep them with materials that would have been considered worth keeping.

Further, what is preserved may be kept for a particular reasons, such as to make somebody look good. Material printed in the *Congressional Record*, ostensibly a record of what has happened during sessions of the U.S. Congress, can be edited before it is published. In addition, in order to save time when the legislators meet, an individual can put material in the *Congressional Record* that was never debated, or even mentioned, on the floor.

Currently, we might want to investigate issues that people in previous times did not think were worth thinking about. So they did not save records that would be valuable to us now. In addition, people tend not to preserve mundane information. Think of it this way; Suppose somebody in a hundred years wanted to know what kind of food college students like to eat. One way to find out would be to look at flyers and leaflets that flood college campuses. You are likely to see promotions for pizza, chicken wings, and other types of food. But do you bother to save those flyers so you can refer to them later? You probably don't even save them from one week to the next because you can always pick up another one whenever you want to. In the future, a social researcher may not be able to get any of these leaflets because nobody now thinks they are worth anything. This would be an example of how selective deposit works.

Another limitation to archival information is *selective survival*. Even if information has been saved, it may disappear for various reasons. After a while, people throw out "junk." What is junk now may be some researcher's treasure in the future. In addition, a lot of information has been lost due to disasters like fires. The problem for researchers is that they don't know if what remains represents what has been lost. This limitation is similar to the problem of attrition in longitudinal research.

While reading this, you might think that you should start saving potentially important material for the future. In popular culture, baseball trading cards can be worth a small fortune because not many cards have survived. They used to be commonplace, but nobody thought they were worth saving. Unfortunately, without a good crystal ball, you don't know what people in the future are going to see as important.

Multiple Interpretations

Sometimes the meaning of archival data is pretty unambiguous. For instance, when Gunnell et al. (2001) studied the length of bones from ninth-century England, they were able to come up with a pretty clear conclusion that tall people at that time lived longer than short people, just like today.

On the other hand, sometimes there is ambiguity. In the case of the museum that had to change the tile flooring around the exhibit of hatching chickens frequently, the cause could have been a large number of different observers or fewer observers who spent longer time at the exhibit, shuffling their feet a lot and wearing out the flooring.

We can also consider the archival research that documented the increased incidence of anorexia among women born in the summer. Why does it occur? Some researchers speculate that during gestation, fetuses are exposed to wintertime viruses that somehow affect the brain, ultimately leading to anorexia. There are multiple interpretations for these data, however.

Perhaps the combination of summer birthdays and the desire to look good in scanty summer clothing lead to greater feelings of pressure to be thin. Nobody has explored this combination of factors, so it is mere speculation. But you could come up with multiple possible explanations. They need to be studied further before we can draw any firm conclusions. In addition, something like anorexia is complex enough that a single explanation is not likely to account for its occurrence in all people.

We also need to be wary of the problem of *spurious correlations*. Such correlations occur but are essentially meaningless. In the case of anorexia, perhaps in reality the correlation between season of birth and the incidence of anorexia tells us nothing of use in understanding the disorder. If you do enough correlational research, you will find relationships in the data that look intriguing but that are just coincidental. Some researchers think that the link between anorexia and birth season is spurious.

Changes in Archived Material over Time

Another consideration of archived material is that what people save may change over time. So differences from one time to another don't necessarily reflect changes in the way things are, only in the way people preserve. If you look at the General Social Survey, you will see that the researchers add questions to a new version and remove old questions as they strive to keep the survey current and topical.

Nonreactivity

One of the notable strengths of using archival information is that participants are not around to distort it. In a laboratory of field study when people know they are being observed, they may alter their behaviors. The question of reactivity is not as critical in archival research, although it can be a problem.

We know that people generally like to look good in front of others. So when they are engaged in public behaviors, they may act in ways that make them seem better than they really are. If such behaviors are recorded on paper, film, or electronic media, we may actually face a problem of reactivity, even if it has occurred years before we collected our data.

DATA ANALYSIS IN ARCHIVAL RESEARCH

When researchers collect and analyze archival information, the analysis could be either quantitative or qualitative. That is, investigators might compute standard statistical tests. Tests of association and correlations predominate. This is the approach that Clawson and Trice (2000) took in the analysis of the portrayal of the poor in magazine photographs.

On the other hand, Taylor and Bogdan (1998) described an analysis of postcards with pictures of twentieth-century "insane asylums" (which we now call psychiatric hospitals) to see if such pictures were designed to reinforce the authority of such institutions. In the early 1900s, it was quite common for people to send postcards showing the often grand buildings. Were these postcards used to convey a subtle message?

As it turns out, the insane asylums were often the largest and most impressive structures in town. As such, they were considered perfectly acceptable as postcard material. The researchers concluded that people used such postcards because they were available. There was no hidden message.

The investigators didn't use statistical analysis. Rather, they did a qualitative analysis that dealt with the nature of the cards, the context of the times, and other nonnumerical concepts. Sometimes you don't need numbers to make a valid point.

Content Analysis

One common approach to analyzing the results of archival research is *content analysis*. This approach involves a systematic look at the content, identifying patterns and important elements of social communication. It can involve examination of written, oral, or visual material.

Some researchers engage in content analysis qualitatively, looking at overall patterns and extracting meaning. For instance, researchers can identify themes according to the particular wording or form that a message takes. Other researchers take a quantitative approach, making note of such things as how frequently ideas appear or how long particular messages are.

In addition to the qualitative versus quantitative distinction in content analysis, researchers also talk about the difference between manifest content and latent content. Quantitative researchers are likely to favor looking at the *manifest content*, which includes elements that can be objectively identified with regard to frequency and duration of their presence. On the other hand, qualitative researchers often prefer to consider *latent content*, the ultimate meaning that underlies the communication.

Manifest content is external and objective; latent content is interpretive. The two approaches lead to analysis of different components of the content of a message. Many researchers suggest using both manifest and latent content in order to derive the greatest sense of the content of the material under study.

The major steps in engaging in content analysis are to find sources relevant to your research question, sampling the material appropriately, and coding the content reliably. Clawson and Trice (2000) studied poverty by sampling from among major magazines during a fixed set of years. Thus they identified relevant sources of stories with photographs relating to poverty (magazines) and sampled from them (five particular magazines: *Business Week, Newsweek, New York Times Magazine, Time,* and *U.S. News & World Report*) during a specified six-year period (1993–1998). They then coded the pictures for content, looking at the gender, race, age, and characteristics of those depicted. This type of content analysis is quantitatively based.

The analysis of postcards of insane asylums from the turn of the twentieth century provides a good example of qualitative analysis described by Taylor and Bogdan (1998). The researchers examined the content of the messages on the cards to see if there was any indication that writers remarked on the building or on the medical and psychiatric community in ways that showed deference to their authority.

The content of the messages related to everyday activities, and was no different from what you might have expected on any other postcard. So the investigators concluded that the cards merely depicted the fanciest building in a town and that people used them because they were available.

Abreu, J. M., & Gabarink, G. (2000). Social desirability and Mexican American counselor preferences: Statistical control for a potential confound. *Journal of Counseling Psychology, 47*, 165–176.

ACHRE Report. (n.d.). ACHRE Report in *Nontherapeutic research on children* (chap. 7) Retrieved June 9, 2003, from http://tis.eh.doe.gov/ohre/roadmap/achre/chap7.html

Adair, J. G. (1984). The Hawthorne effect: A reconsideration of the methodological artifact. *Journal of Applied Psychology, 69*, 334–345.

Adair, J. G., Dushenko, T. W., & Lindsay, R. C. L. (1985). Ethical regulations and their impact on research practice. *American Psychologist, 40*, 59–72.

Affsprung, E. H. (1998). Assessing for a history of serious depression among first-year college students. *Journal of College Student Psychotherapy, 12*, 61–65.

Albert, R. S. (1983). Exceptional creativity and achievement. In R. S. Albert (Ed.), *Genius and eminence: The social psychology of creativity and exceptional achievement* (Ch I-3, pp. 19–35). New York: Pergamon Press.

American Psychiatric Association. (1987). *Diagnostic and statistical manual of mental disorders* (3rd ed., revised). Washington, DC: Author.

American Psychological Association. (1992). Ethical principles of psychologists and code of conduct. *American Psychologist, 47*, 1597–1611.

American Psychological Association. (1994). *Publication Manual of the American Psychological Association* (4th ed.). Washington, DC: Author.

American Psychological Association. (2002). Ethical principles of psychologists and code of conduct. *American Psychologist, 57*, 1060–1073.

Americans felt uneasy toward arabs even before september 11. (2001). http://www.gallup.com/poll/releases/pr010928.asp. [Retrieved September 29, 2001].

Anderson, J., & Fienberg, S. E. (2000). Census 2000 controversies. *Chance, 13*(4), 22–30.

Anderson, C. A., & Bushman, B. J. (2001). Effects of violent video games on aggressive behavior, aggressive cognition, aggressive affect, physiological arousal, and prosocial behavior: A meta-analytic review of the scientific literature. *Psychological Science, 12*, 353–359.

Aneschensel, C. S., Clark, V. A., & Frerichs, R. R. (1983). Race, ethnicity, and depression: A confirmatory analysis. *Journal of Personality and Social Psychology, 44*, 385–398.

Angier, N. (2000, August 22). Do races differ? Not really, DNA shows. *New York Times on the Web* [http://www.nytimes.com/library/national/science/082200sci-genetics-race.html]. Retrieved August 22, 2000.

Anorexia may not have cultural roots. (2001). http://www.intelihealth.com. [Retrieved April 28, 2001].

Armitage, R., Smith, C., Thompason, S., & Hoffman, R. (2001). Sex differences in slow-wave activity in response to sleep deprivation. *Sleep Research Online, 4*, 33–41. [http://www.sro.org/2001/Armitage/33/].

Aronson, J., Lustina, M. J., Good, C., Keough, K., Steele, C. M., & Brown, J. (1999). When white men can't do math: Necessary and sufficient factors in stereotype threat. *Journal of Experimental Social Psychology, 35*, 29–46.

Austad, S. N. (2002). A mouse's tale. *Natural History, 111*(3), 64–70.

Azar, B. (2000a, April). Online experiments: Ethically fair or foul? *Monitor on Psychology, 31*, 50–52.

Azar, B. (2000b, April). A web of research. *Monitor on Psychology, 31*, 42–44.

Azar, B. (2000c, April). A web experiment sampler. *Monitor on Psychology, 31*, 46–47.

Babbie, E. (1995). *The practice of social research* (7th ed.). Belmont, CA: Wadsworth.

Bachorowski, J-A., & Owren, M. J. (2001). Not all laughs are alike: Voiced but not unvoiced laughter readily elicits positive affect. *Psychological Science, 12*, 252–257.

Ball, P., Giles, H., & Hewstone, M. (1984). Second language acquisition: The intergroup theory with catastrophic dimensions. In H. Tajfel (Ed.), *The social dimension* (Vol. 2, pp. 668–694). Cambridge, UK: Cambridge University Press.

Banville, D., Desrosiers, P., & Genet-Volet, G. (2000). Translating questionnaires and inventories using a cross-cultural translation technique. *Journal of Teaching in Physical Education, 19*, 374–387.

Barnett, W. S. (1998). Long-term cognitive and academic effects of early childhood education of children in poverty. *Preventive Medicine: An International Devoted to Practice & Theory, 27*, 204–207.

Baron-Cohen, S., Burt, L., Smith-Laittan, F., Harrison, J., & Bolton, P. (1996). Synaesthesia: Prevalence and familiarity. *Perception, 25*, 1073–1079.

Bartolic, E. I., Basso, M. R., Schefft, B. K., Glauser, T., & Titanic-Schefft, M. (1999). Effects of experimentally-induced emotional states on frontal lobe cognitive task performance. *Neuropsychologia, 37,* 677–683.

Basha, S. A., & Ushasree, S. (1998). Fear of success across life span. *Journal of Personality & Clinical Studies, 14,* 63–67.

Batson, C. D., Duncan, B., Ackerman, P., Buckley, T., & Birch, K. (1981). Is empathetic emotion a source of altruistic motivation? *Journal of Personality and Social Psychology, 40,* 290–302.

Baumrind, D. (1964). Some thoughts on ethics of research: After reading Milgram's "Behavioral study of obedience." *American Psychologist, 19,* 421–423.

Beach, F. A. (1950). The Snark was a Boojum. *American Psychologist, 5,* 115–124.

Becker, E. (1973). *The denial of death.* New York: Free Press.

Bell, G., & Brady, V. (2000). Monetary incentives for sex workers. *International Journal of STD & AIDS, 11,* 483–484.

Bell, N. S., Mangione, T. W., Hemenway, D., Amoroso, P. J., & Jones, B. H. (2000). High injury rates among female Army trainees: A function of gender? *The American Journal of Preventive Medicine, 18(3) Supplement 1,* 141–146.

Benbow, C. P., & Stanley, J. C. (1980). Sex differences in mathematical ability: Fact or artifact? *Science, 10,* 1262–1264.

Benbow, C. P., & Stanley, J. C. (1983). Sex differences in mathematical reasoning ability: More facts. *Science, 222,* 1029–1030.

Bergman, M. E., Langhout, R. D., Palmieri, P. A., Cortina, L. M., & Fitzgerald, L. F. (2002). The (un)reasonableness of reporting: Antecedents and consequences of reporting sexual harassment. *Journal of Applied Psychology, 87,* 230–242.

Berkowitz, L. (1992). Some thoughts about conservative evaluations of replications. *Personality & Social Psychology Bulletin. 18,* 319–324.

Berreby, D. (2000). Race counts. [Review of *Changing race: Latinos, the census and the history of ethnicity in the United States.*] *The Sciences, 40,* 38–43.

Betancourt, H, & Lôpez, S. R. (1993). The study of culture, ethnicity, and race in American psychology. *American Psychologist, 48,* 629–637.

Bhui, K., & Bhugra, D. (2001). Methodological rigour in cross-cultural research. *The British Journal of Psychiatry, 179,* 269.

Bickman, L., & Zarantonello, M. (1978). The effects of deception and level of obedience on subjects' ratings of the Milgram study. *Personality and Social Psychology Bulletin, 4,* 81–85.

Birnbaum, G., & Montero, D. (1999, February 11). Feds rip med school's tests on psych patients, *New York Post.* (Retrieved from http://www.nypostonline.com:80/021199/news/3061.htm).

Birnbaum, M. H. (1974). Using contextual effects to derive psychophysical scales. *Perception and Psychophysics, 15,* 89–96.

Birnbaum, M. H. (1999). How to show that 9 > 221: Collect judgments in a between-subjects design. *Psychological Methods, 4,* 243–249.

Bleiberg, J., Garmoe, W., Cederquist, J., Reeves, D., & Lux, W. (1993). Effects of dexedrine on performance consistency following brain injury: A double-blind placebo crossover case study. *Neuropsychiatry, Neuropsychology, and Behavioral Neurology, 6,* 245–248.

Bond, L., Carlin, J. B., Thomas, L., Rubin, K., & Patton, G. (2001). Does bullying cause emotonal problems? A prospective study of young teenagers. *British Medical Journal, 323,* 480–484.

Bosworth, H. B., & Schaie, K. W. (1999). Survival effects in cognitive function, cognitive style, and sociodemographic variables in the Seattle Longitudinal Study. *Experimental Aging Research, 25,* 121–139.

Bramel, D., & Friend, R. (1981). Hawthorne, the myth of the docile worker, and class bias in psychology. *American Psychologist, 36,* 867–878.

Brewer, B. W., & Shillinglaw, R. (1992). Evaluation of a psychological skills training workshop for male intercollegiate lacrosse players. *The Sport Psychologist, 6,* 139–147.

Bröder, A. (1998). Deception can be acceptable. *American Psychologist, 53,* 805–806.

Brown, G. K. (1990). A causal analysis of chronic pain and depression. *Journal of Abnormal Psychology, 99,* 127–137.

Budson, A. E., Desikan, R., Daffner, K. R., & Schachter, D. L. (2001). Perceptual false recognition in Alzheimer's Disease. *Neuropsychology, 15,* 230–243.

Bull, R., & Stevens, J. (1980). Effect of unsightly teeth on helping behavior. *Perceptual and Motor Skills, 51,* 438.

Burtt, H. E. (1920). Sex differences in the effect of discussion. *Journal of Experimental Psychology, 3,* 390–395.

Bushman, B. J., & Anderson, C. A. (2001). Media violence and the American public: Scientific facts versus media misinformation. *American Psychologist, 56,* 477–489.

Byrnes, J. P., Miller, D. C., & Schafer, W. D. (1999). Gender differences in risk taking: A meta-analysis. *Psychological Bulletin, 125,* 367–383.

Caccioppo, J. T., Gernston, G. G., Sheridan, J. F., & McClintock, M. K. (2000). Multilevel integrative analysis of human behavior: Social neuroscience and the complementing nature of social and biological approaches. *Psychological Bulletin, 126,* 829–843.

Campbell, D. T., & Stanley, J. C. (1966). *Experimental and quasi-experimental designs for research.* Chicago: Rand McNally.

Caplan, P. J., & Caplan, J. B. (1999). *Thinking Critically about Research on Sex and Gender* (2nd ed.). New York: Longman.

Carr, S. C., Munro, D., & Bishop, G. D. (1995). Attitude assessment in non-western countries: Critical modifications to Likert scaling. *Psychologia, 39,* 55–59.

Carstens, C. B., Haskins, E., & Hounshell, G. W. (1995). Listening to Mozart may not enhance performance on the revised Minnesota paper form board test. *Psychological Reports, 77,* 111–114.

Cepeda-Benito, A., & Gleaves, D. H. (2000). Cross-ethnic equivalence of the Hopkins Symptom Checklist-21 in European American, African American, and Latino college students. *Cultural Diversity and Ethnic Minority Psychology, 6,* 297–308.

Cernovsky, Z. Z. (2000). On the similarities of American blacks and whites. In B. Slife (Ed.), *Taking sides: Clashing views on controversial psychological issues.* Guilford, CT: Dushkin/McGraw-Hill

Chamberlin, J. (2000). One psychology project, three states. *Monitor on Psychology, 31,* 58–59.

Chang, W. C. (2000). In search of the Chinese in all the wrong places! *Journal of Psychology in Chinese Societies, 1,* 125–142.

Chao, R. (2001). Integrating culture and attachment. *American Psychologist, 56,* 822–823.

Cheryan, S., & Bodenhausen, G. V. (2000). When positive stereotypes threaten intellectual performance: The psychological hazards of "model minority" status. *Psychological Science, 11,* 399–402.

Cialdini, R. B., & Baumann, D. J. (1981). Littering: A new unobtrusive measure of attitude. *Social Psychology Quarterly, 44,* 254–259

Cho, H., & LaRose, R. (1999). Privacy issues in internet surveys. *Social Science Computer Review, 17,* 421–434.

Christensen, L. (1988) Deception in psychological research: When is its use justified? *Personality and Social Psychology Bulletin, 14,* 664–675.

Cialdini, R. B. (1980). Full-cycle social psychology. *Applied Social Psychology Annual, 1,* 21–47.

Cialdini, R. B., Darby, B. L., & Vincent, J. E. (1973). Transgression and altruism: A case for hedonism. *Journal of Experimental Social Psychology, 9,* 502–516.

Clark, D. M., & Teasdale, J. D. (1985). Constraints on the effects of mood on memory. *Journal of Personality and Social Psychology, 52,* 749–758.

Clark, S. J., & Desharnais, R. A. (1998). Honest answers to embarrassing questions: Detecting cheating in the randomized response model. *Psychological Methods, 3,* 160–168.

Clawson, R. A., & Trice, R. (2000). Poverty as we know it: media portrayals of the poor. *Public Opinion Quarterly, 64,* 53–64.

Cohen, D., & Gunz, A. (2002). As seen by the other . . . : Perspectives on the self in the memories and emotional perceptions of Easterners and Westerners. *Psychological Science, 13,* 55–59.

Cohen, S., Tyrrell, D. A., & Smith, A. P. (1991). Psychological stress and susceptibility to the common cold. *New England Journal of Medicine, 325,* 606–612.

Coile, D. C., & Miller, N. E. (1984). How radical animal activists try to mislead humane people, *American Psychologist, 39,* 700–701.

Conrad, F. G., & Schoberr, M. F. (2000). Clarifying question meaning in a household telephone survey. *Public Opinion Quarterly, 64,* 1–28.

Cook, D. J. (1996). Randomized trials in single subjects: The N of 1 study. *Psychopharmacology Bulletin, 32,* 363–367.

Cook, P. J., & Ludwig, J. (1998). Defensive gun uses: New evidence from a national survey. *Journal of Quantitative Criminology, 14,* 111–131.

Cotton, J. W. (1989). Interpreting data from two-period crossover design (Also termed the replicated 2×2 Latin square design). *Psychological Bulletin, 106,* 503–515.

Council of National Psychological Associations for the Advancement of Ethnic Minority Interests. (2000). *Guidelines for research in ethnic minority communities.* Washington, DC: American Psychological Association.

Coverdale, J. H., & Turbott, S. H. (2000). Sexual and physical abuse of chronically ill psychiatric outpatients compared with a matched sample of medical outpatients. *Journal of Nervous and Mental Disease, 188,* 440–445.

Cox, C. R., & LeBoeuf, B. J. (1977). Female incitation of male competition: A mechanism in sexual selection. *American Naturalist, 111,* 317–335.

Crewdson, A. (2002). *Scientific mystery, a massive cover-up and the dark legacy of Robert Gallo.* Boston: Little, Brown.

Crocker, P. R. E. (1993). Sport and exercise psychology and research with individuals with physical disabilities: Using theory to advance knowledge. *Adapted Physical Activity Quarterly, 10,* 324–335.

Croizet, J-C., & Claire, T. (1998). Extending the concept of stereotype and threat to social class: The intellectual underperformance of students from low socioeconomic backgrounds. *Personality & Social Psychology Bulletin, 24,* 588–594.

Croll, S., Bryant, R. A. (2000). Autobiographical memory in postnatal depression. *Cognitive Therapy and Research, 24,* 419–426.

Cunningham, S. (1984). Genovese: 20 years later, few heed a stranger's cries. *Social Action and the Law, 10,* 24–25.

Curtin, R., Presser, S., & Singer, E. (2000). The effects of response rate changes on the index of consumer sentiment. *Public Opinion Quarterly, 64,* 413–428.

Cytowic, R. E. (1993). *The man who tasted shapes.* New York: G. P. Putnam & Son.

Cytowic, R. E. (1997). Synaesthesia: Phenomenology and neuropsychology—A review of current knowledge. In S. Baron-Cohen & J. E. Harrison (Eds.), *Synaesthesia: Classic and contemporary readings.* Cambridge, MA: Blackwell.

Darley, J. M., & Latané, B. (1968). Bystander intervention in emergencies: Diffusion of responsibility. *Journal of Personality and Social Psychology, 8,* 377–383.

Davies, M., Stankov, L., & Roberts, R. D. (1998). Emotional intelligence: In search of an elusive construct. *Journal of Personality and Social Psychology, 75,* 989–1015.

Deese, J., & Hulse, S. H. (1967). *The psychology of learning* (3rd ed.). New York: McGraw-Hill

Diener, E., Matthews, R., & Smith, R. E. (1972). Leakage of experimental information to potential future subjects by debriefed subjects. *Journal of Experimental Research in Personality, 6,* 264–267.

Dillman, D. A. (1978). *Mail and telephone surveys.* New York: Wiley.

Dillman, D. A. (2000). *Mail and internet surveys: The tailored design method.* New York: Wiley.

Dixon, A. K. (1998). Ethological strategies for defence in animals and humans: Their role in some psychiatric disorders. *British Journal of Medical Psychology, 71,* 417–445.

Dixon, W. A., & Reid, J. K. (2000). Positive life events as a moderator of stress-related depressive symptoms. *Journal of Counseling & Development, 78,* 343–347.

Dozois, D. J. A., Dobson, K. S., & Ahnberg, J. L. (1998). A psychometric evaluation of the Beck Depression Inventory–II. *Psychological Assessment, 10,* 83–89.

Dubowitz, G. (1998). Effect of temazepam on oxygen saturation and sleep quality at high altitude: Randomised placebo controlled crossover trial. *British Medical Journal, 316,* 587–589.

Eagles, J. M., Andrew, J. E., Johnston, M. I., Easton, E. A., & Millar, H. R. (2001). Season of birth in females with anorexia nervosa in Northeast Scotland. *International Journal of Eating Disorders, 30,* 167–175.

Eichenwald, K., & Kolata, G. (1999, May 16). Drug trials hide conflicts for doctors, *New York Times.* (Retrieved from http://www.nytimes.com/library/politics/051699drug-trials.html.)

Elisha Gray. (1974). In The encyclopedia Britannica. (Vol. IV, p. 691). Chicago: Encyclopedia Britannica.

Ellis, H. C., Thomas, R. L., & Rodriguez, I. A. (1984). Emotinoal mood states and memory: Elaborative encoding, semantic processing, and cognitive effort. *Journal of Experimental Psychology: Learning, Memory, and Cognition, 10,* 470–482.

Epley, N., & Dunning, D. (2000). Feeling "holier than thou": Are self-serving assessments produced by errors in self- or social prediction? *Journal of Personality and Social Psychology, 79,* 861–875.

Estep, D. Q., & Bruce, K. E. M. (1981). The concept of rape in non-humans: A critique. *Animal Behavior, 29,* 1272–1273.

Ethical principles of psychologists and code of conduct. (2002). *American Psychologist, 57,* 1060–1073.

Evans, S. W., Pelham, W. E., Smith, B. H., Burkstein, O., Gnagy, E. M., Greiner, A. R., Altenderfer, L., & Baron-Myak, C. (2001). Dose-response effects of methylphenidate on ecological valid measures of academic performance and classroom behavior in adolescents with ADHD. *Experimental and Clinical Psychopharmacology, 9,* 163–175.

Exline, J. J., & Lobel, M. (1999). The perils of outperformance: Sensitivity about being the target of a threatening upward comparison. *Psychological Bulletin, 125,* 303–337.

Fagbemi, O. M. (1996). Fear of success among Nigerian females: A case study of women in higher education. *Ife Psychologia: An international journal, 4,* 35–45.

Fairburn, C. G., Welch, S. L., Norman, P. A., O'Connor, B. A., & Doll, H. A. (1996). Bias and bulimia nervosa: How typical are clinical cases? *American Journal of Psychiatry, 153,* 386–391.

Falk, R. (1986). "Misconceptions of Statistical Significance." *Journal of Structural Learning, 9,* 83–96.

Falk, R., & Greenbaum, C. W. (1995) Significance tests die hard: The amazing persistence of a probabilistic misconception." *Theory & Psychology, 5,* 75–98.

Fausto-Sterling, A. (1993). The five sexes: Why male and female are not equal. *The Sciences, 33*(2), 20–25.

Feldman, S., Mont-Reynaud, R., & Rosenthal, D. (1992). When East moves West: The acculturation of values of Chinese adolescents in the U.S. and Austraila. *Journal of Research on Adolescence, 2,* 147–173.

Fernandez, E., & Sheffield, J. (1996). Relative contributions of life events versus daily hassles to the frequency and intensity of headaches. *Headache, 36,* 595–602.

Finkel, S. E., Guterbok, T. M., & Borg, M. J. (1991). Race of interviewer effects in a preelection poll: Virginia 1989. *Public Opinion Quarterly, 55,* 313–330.

Fisher, C. B., & Fyrberg, D. (1994). Participant partners: College students weigh the costs and benefits of deceptive research. *American Psychologist, 49,* 417–427.

Fisher, R. A. (1932). *Statistical methods for research workers* (4th ed.). Edinburgh, Scotland: Oliver & Boyd.

Fisher, R. A. (1935). *The design of experiments.* Edinburgh, Scotland: Oliver & Boyd.

Fitzgerald, L. F., Swan, S., & Magley, V. J. (1997). But was it really sexual harassment? Legal, behavioral, and psychological definitions of the workplace victimization of women. In W. O'Donohue (Ed.), *Sexual harassment: theory, research, and treatment* (pp. 5–28). Boston: Allyn and Bacon.

Flay, B. R. (1987). Mass media and smoking cessation: A critical review. *American Journal of Public Health, 77,* 153–160.

Flynn, J. R. (1999). Searching for justice: The discovery of IQ gains over time. *American Psychologist, 54,* 5–20.

Fosse, R., Strickgold, R., & Hobson, J. A. (2001). Brain-mind states: Reciprocal variation in thoughts and hallucinations. *Psychological Science, 12,* 30–36.

Francis, L. J., & Jackson, C. J. (1998). The social desirability of toughmindedness: A study among undergraduates. *Irish Journal of Psychology, 19,* 400–403.

Frank, O., & Snijders, T. (1994). Estimating the size of hidden populations using snowball sampling. *Journal of Official Statistics, 10,* 53–67.

Franzoi, S. L., & Shields, S. A. (1984). The Body-Esteem Scale: Multidimensional structure and sex differences in a college population. *Journal of Personality and Assessment, 48,* 173–178.

French, S., & Stephen, J. (1999). Religiosity and its association with happiness, purpose in life, and self-actualisation. *Mental Health, Religion & Culture, 2,* 117–120.

Frick, R. W. (1996). The appropriate use of null hypothesis testing. *Psychological Methods, 1,* 379–390.

Gadzella, B. M., Masten, W. G., & Stacks, J. (1998). Students' stress and their learning strategies, test anxiety, and attributions. *College Student Journal, 32,* 416–422.

Gaito, J. (1961). Repeated measurements designs and counterbalancing. *Psychological Bulletin, 58,* 46–54.

Gaito, J. (1980). Measurement scales and statistics: Resurgence of an old misconception. *Psychological Bulletin, 87,* 564–567.

Gardner, H. (1999). *Intelligence reframed: Multiple intelligences for the 21st century.* New York: Basic Books.

Gardner, H., Krechevsky, M., Sternberg, R. J., & Okagaki, L. (1994). Intelligence in context: Enhancing students' practical intelligence for school. In K. McGilly (Ed.), *Classroom lessons: Integrating cognitive theory and classroom practice* (pp. 105–127). Cambridge: MIT Press.

Gaskell, G. D., Wright, D. B., & O'Muircheartaigh, C. A. (2000). Telescoping of landmark events: Implications for survey research. *Public Opinion Quarterly, 64,* 77–89.

Gawiser, S. R., & Witt, G. E. (2000). Twenty questions a journalist should ask about poll results. National Council on Public Polls (www.ncpp.org/qajsa. htm, retrieved 9/20/00).

Gehrick, J-G., & Shapiro, D. (2000) Reduced facial expression and social context in major depression: Discrepancies between facial muscle activity and self-reported emotion. *Psychiatry Research, 95,* 157–167.

Gendall, P., Hoek, J., & Brennan, M. (1998). The tea bag experiment: More evidence on incentives in mail surveys. *Journal of the Market Research Society, 40,* 347–351.

Girden, E. R. (1992). *ANOVA: Repeated measures.* Newbury Park, CA: Sage Publications.

Gladwell, M. (2002, March 13). John Rock's error. *The New Yorker,* 52–63.

Glaze, J. A. (1928). The association value of non-sense syllables. *Journal of Genetic Psychology, 35,* 255–269.

Glueck, W. F., & Jauch, L. R. (1975). Sources of ideas among productive scholars: Implications for administrators. *Journal of Higher Education, 46,* 103–114.

Goldenberg, J. L., McCoy, S. K., Pyszczynski, T., Greenberg, J., & Solomon, S. (2000). The body as a course of self-esteem: The effect of mortality salience on identification with one's body, interest in sex, and appearance monitoring. *Journal of Personality and Social Psychology, 79,* 118–130.

Goldenberg, J. L., Pyszczynski, T., McCoy, S. K., Greenberg, J., & Solomon, S. (1999). Death, sex, love, and neuroticism: Why is sex such a problem? *Journal of Personality and Social Psychology, 77,* 1173–1187.

Goleman, D. (1996) *Emotional intelligence.* New York: Bantam Books.

Goodman-Delahunty, J. (1998). Approaches to gender and the law: Research and applications. *Law and Human Behavior, 22,* 129–143.

Gorenstein, C., Andrade, L., Filho, A. H. G. V., Tung, T., & Artes, R. (1999). Pschometric properties of the Portugese version of the Beck Depression Inventory on Brazilian college students. *Journal of Clinical Psychology, 55,* 553–602.

Gottschalk, A., Smith, D. S., Jobes, D. R., Kennedy, S. K., Lally, S. E., Noble, V. E., Grugan, K. F., Seifert, H. A., Cheung, A., Malkowicz, B., Gutsche, B. B., & Wein, A. J. (1998). Preemptive epidural analgesia and recovery from radical prostatectomy: A randomized controlled trial. *Journal of the American Medical Association, 279,* 1076–1082.

Gould, S. J. (1996). *The mismeasure of man* (2nd ed.). New York: W. W. Norton.

Gray, J. (1992). *Men are from Mars, women are from Venus: A practical guide for improving communication and getting what you want in your relationships.* New York: HarperCollins.

Green, A., & Vaid, J. (1986). Methodological issues in the use of the concurrent activities paradigm. *Brain and Cognition, 5,* 465–476.

Green, C. W., & Reid, D. H. (1999). A behavioral approach to identifying sources of happiness and unhappiness among individuals with profound multiple disabilities. *Behavior Modification, 23,* 280–293.

Greenstein, J. (1999, October). The heart of the matter. *Brill's Content*, 40.

Griffiths, M. (1998). Internet addiction: Does it really exist? In J. Gackenbach (Ed.), *Psychology and the Internet: Intrapersonal, interpersonal, and transpersonal implications* (pp. 61–75). San Diego: Academic Press.

Gruder, C. L., Stumpfhauser, A., & Wyer, R. S. (1977). Improvement in experimental performance as a result of debriefy about deception. *Personality and Social Psychology Bulletin, 3*, 434–437.

Gunewardene, A., Huon, G. F., & Zheng, R. (2001). Exposure to westernization and dieting: A cross-cultural study. *International Journal of Eating Disorders, 29*, 289–293.

Gunnell, D., Rogers, J., & Dieppe, P. (2001). Height and health: Predicting longevity from bone length in archaeological remains. *Journal of Epidemiology and Community Health, 55*, 505–507.

Guthrie, J. P., Ash, R. A., & Bendapudi, V. (1995). Additional validity evidence for a measure of morningness. *Journal of Applied Psychology, 80*, 186–190.

Gutierrez, P. M., Osman, A., Kopper, B. A., Barrios, F. X., & Bagge, C. L. (2000). Suicide risk assessment in a college student population. *Journal of Counseling Psychology, 47*, 403–413.

Gwiazda, J., Ong, E., Held, R., & Thorn, F. (2000). Vision: Myopia and ambient night-time lighting. *Nature, 404*, 144.

Hahn, P. W., & Clayton, S. D. (1996). The effects of attorney presentation style, attorney gender, and juror gender on juror decisions. *Law and Human Behavior, 20*, 533–554.

Hakel, M. D. (1968). How often is often? *American Psychologist, 23*, 533–534.

Hall, M. E., MacDonald, S., & Young, G. C. (1992). The effectiveness of directed multisensory stimulation versus non-directed stimulation in comatose CHI patients: Pilot study of a single subject design. *Brain Injury, 6*, 435–445.

Halvari, H., & Kjormo, O. (2000). A structural model of achievement motives, performance approach and avoidance goals and performance among Norwegian Olympic athletes. *Perceptual & Motor Skills, 89*, 997–1022.

Harris, B. (1980). The FBI's files on APA and SPSSI: Description and implications. *American Psychologist, 35*, 1141–1144.

Hashemi, L., & Webster, B. S. (1998). Non-fatal workplace violence workers' compensation claims (1993–1996). *Journal of Occupational and Environmental Medicine, 40*, 561–567.

Hawker, D. S. J., & Boulton, M. J. (2000). Twenty years' research on peer victimization and psychosocial maladjustment: A meta-analytic review of cross-sectional studies. *Journal of Child Psychology and Psychiatry, 41*, 441–455.

Hay, C. A., & Bakken, L. (1991). Gifted sixth-grade girls: Similarities and differences in attitudes among gifted girls, non-gifted peers, and their mothers. *Roeper Review, 13*, 158–160.

Hays, R. D., Marshall, G. N., Wang, E. U. I., & Sherbourne, C. D. (1994). Four-year cross-lagged associations between physical and mental health in the medical outcomes study. *Journal of Consulting and Clinical Psychology, 62*, 441–449.

Hayslip, B., McCoy-Roberts, L., & Pavur, R. (1998–99). Selective attrition effects in bereavement research: A three-year longitudinal analysis. *Omega, 38*, 21–35.

Headden, S. (1997, December 8). The junk mail deluge. *U.S. News & World Report*, 42–48.

Heckathorn, D. D. (1997). Respondent-driven sampling: A new approach to the study of hidden populations. *Social Problems, 44*, 174–199.

Hedden, T., Park, D. C., Nisbett, R., Ji, L. J., Jing, Q., & Jiao, S. (2002). Cultural variation in verbal versus spatial neuropsychological function across the lifespan. *Neuropsychology, 16*, 65–73.

Hemenway, D. (1997). The myth of millions of annual self-defense gun uses: A case study of survey overestimates of rare events. *Chance, 10*, 6–10.

Hennigan, K. M., Del Rosario, M. L., Heath, L., Cook, T. D., Wharton, J. D., & Calder, B. J. (1982). Impact of the introduction of television on crime in the United States: Empirical findings and theoretical implications. *Journal of Personality and Social Psychology, 42*, 461–577.

Hertel, P. T. (1998). Relation between rumination and impaired memory in dysphoric moods. *Journal of Abnormal Psychology, 107*, 166–172.

Heuer, H., Spijkers, W., Kiesswetter, E, & Schmidtke, V. (1998). Effects of sleep loss, time of day, and extended mental work on implicit and explicit learning of sequences. *Journal of Experimental Psychology: Applied, 4*, 139–162.

High accuracy found in 2000 elections. (2001, January 4). *St. Petersburg Times*, 3A.

Hilts, P. J., & Stolberg, S. G. (1999, May 13). Ethical lapses at Duke halt dozens of human experiments. *New York Times*. (Retrieved from http://www.nytimes.com/yr/mo/day/news/national/science/sci-duke-research.html, May 13, 1999)

Hippler, H. J., & Schwarz, N. (1987). Response effects in surveys. In H. J. Hippler, N. Schwarz, & S. Sudman (Eds.). *Social information processing and survey methodology* (pp. 102–122). New York: Springer-Verlag.

Hoekstra-Weebers, J. E. H. M., Jaspers, J. P. C., Kamps, W. A., & Klip, E. C. (2001). Psychological adaptation and social support of parents of pediatric cancer patients: A prospective longitudinal study. *Journal of Pediatric Psychology, 26*, 225–235.

Holahan, C. K., & Sears, R. R. (1995). *The gifted group in later maturity.* Stanford, CA: Stanford University Press.

Holmes, T. H., & Rahe, R. H. (1967). The social readjustment rating scale. *Journal of Psychosomatic Research, 11,* 213–218.

Hong, Y., & Chiu, C. (1991). Reduction of socially desirable responses in attitude assessment through the enlightenment effect. *Journal of Social Psychology, 131,* 585–587.

Horvitz, D., Koshland, D., Rubin, D., Gollin, A., Sawyer, T., & Tanur, J. M. (1995). Pseudo-opinion polls: SLOP or useful data? *Chance, 8,* 16–25.

Howell, D. C. (1992). *Statistical methods for psychology* (3rd ed.). Boston: PWS-Kent.

Hrycaiko, D., & Martin, G. L. (1999). Applied research studies with single-subject designs: Why so few? *Journal of Applied Sport Psychology, 8,* 183–199.

Hui, C. H., & Triandis, H. C. (1989). Effects of culture and response format on extreme response style. *Journal of Cross-Cultural Psychology, 20,* 296–309.

Humphreys, L. (1975). *Tearoom trade: Impersonal sex in public places* (2nd ed.). Chicago: Aldine.

Imrie, R., & Ramey, D. W. (2000). The evidence for evidence-based medicine. *Complementary Therapies in Medicine, 8,* 123–126.

Inzlicht, M., & Ben-Zeev, T. (2000). A threatening intellectual environment: Why females are susceptible to experiencing problem-solving deficits in the presence of males. *Psychological Science, 11,* 365–371.

Iwamasa, G. Y., Larrabee, A. L., & Merritt, R. D. (2000). Are personality disorder criteria ethnically biased? A card-sort analysis. *Cultural Diversity and Ethnic Minority Psychology, 6,* 284–296.

Jacob, T., Tennenbaum, D., Seilhamer, R. A., Bargiel, K., & Sharon, T. (1994). Reactivity effects during naturalistic observation of distressed and nondistresed families. *Journal of Family Psychology, 8,* 354–363.

Jenni, D. A., & Jenni, M. A. (1976). Carrying behavior in humans: Analysis of sex differences. *Science, 194,* 859–860.

Jenni, M. A. (1976). Sex differences in carrying behavior. *Perceptual and Motor Skills, 43,* 323–330.

Jennings, C. (2000, May/June). [Letter to the editor.] *The Sciences, 40,* 3, 5.

Jensen, G. F. (2001). The invention of television as a cause of homicide: The reification of a spurious relationship. *Homicide Studies, 5,* 114–130.

Ji, L. J., Schwarz, N., & Nisbett, R. E. (2000). Culture, autobiographical memory, and behavioral frequency reports: Measurement issues in cross-cultural studies. *Personality and Social Psychology Bulletin, 26,* 585–593.

Johnson, T. P., Fendrich, M., Shaligram, C., Garcy, A., & Gillespie, S. (2000). An evaluation of the effects of interviewer charcteristics in an RDD telephone survey of drug use. *Journal of Drug Issues, 30,* 77–102.

Jones, H. E., & Contrad, H. S. (1933). The growth and decline of intelligence: A study of a homogeneous group between the ages of ten and sixty. *Genetic Psychology Monographs, 13,* 223–298.

Judd, C. M., Smith, E. R., & Kidder, L. H. (1991). *Research methods in social relations.* Fort Worth: Holt, Rinehart, & Winston.

Juhnke, R., Barmann, B., Cunningham, M., & Smith, E. (1987). Effects of attractiveness and nature of request on helping behavior. *Journal of Social Psychology, 127,* 317–322.

Kaneto, H. (1997). Learning/memory processes under stress conditions. *Behavioural Brain Research, 83,* 71–74.

Kaplan, C. D., Korf, D., & Sterk, C. (1987). Temporal and social contexts of heroin-using populations: An illustration of the snowball sampling technique. *Journal of Nervous and Mental Disease, 175,* 566–574.

Kaplan, M. D. (1999). Developmental and psychiatric evaluation in the preschool context. *Child and Adolescent Psychiatric Clinics of North America, 8,* 379–393.

Kasof, J. (1993). Sex bias in the naming of the stimulus person. *Psychological Bulletin, 113,* 140–163.

Katsev, R., Edelsack, L., Steinmetz, G., Walker, T., & Wright, R. (1978). The effect of reprimanding transgression on subsequent helping behavior: Two field experiments. *Personality and Social Psychology Bulletin, 4,* 326–329.

Kaufman, P., Kwon, J. Y., Klein, S., & Chapman, C. D. (2000). *Dropout rates in the United States: 1999.* National Center for Educational Statistics: Washington, DC.

Kazdin, A. E. (1998). *Research design in clinical psychology* (3rd ed.). Boston: Allyn and Bacon.

Keefe, F. J., Wilkins, R. H., Cook, W. A., Crisson, J. E., & Muhlbaier, L. H. (1986). Depression, pain, and pain behavior. *Journal of Consulting and Clinical Psychology, 54,* 665–669.

Keeter, S., Miller, C., Kohut, A., Groves, R. M., & Presser, S. (2000). Consequences of reducing nonresponse in a national telephone survey. *Public Opinion Quarterly, 64,* 125–148.

Kellett, S., & Beail, N. (1997). The tratment of chronic post-traumatic nightmares using psychodynamic-interpersonal psychotherapy: A single-case study. *British Journal of Medical Psychology, 70,* 35–49.

Kiecker, P., & Nelson, J. E. (1996). Do interviewers follow telephone survey instructions? *Journal of the Market Research Society, 38,* 161–176.

Kim, B. S. K., Atkinson, D. R., & Yang, P. H. (1999). The Asian Values Scale: Development, factor analysis, validation, and reliability. *Journal of Counseling Psychology, 46,* 342–352.

Kimmel, A. J. (1998). In defense of deception. *American Psychologist, 53,* 803–805.

King, M. F., & Bruner, G. C. (2000). Social desirability bias: A neglected aspect of validity testing. *Psychology and Marketing, 17,* 79–103.

King, R. (2000). *Brunelleschi's dome: How a Renaissance genius reinvented architecture.* New York: Penguin.

Klawans, H. (2000). *Defending the cavewoman and other tales of evolutionary neurology.* New York: W. W. Norton.

Kleck, G., & Gertz, M. (1995). Armed resistence to crime: The prevalence and nature of self-defense with a gun. *Journal of Criminal Law and Criminology, 86,* 150–187.

Komiya, N., Good, G. E., & Sherrod, N. B. (2000). Emotional openness as a predictor of college students' attitudes toward seeking psychological help. *Journal of Counseling Psychology, 47,* 138–143.

Korn, J. H. (1998). The reality of deception. *American Psychologist, 53,* 805.

Kovar, M. G. (2000). Four million adolescents smoke: Or do they? *Chance, 13,* 10–14.

Kozulin, A. (1999). Profiles of immigrant students' cognitive performance on Raven's Progressive Matrices. *Perceptual & Motor Skills, 87,* 1311–1314.

Krantz, J. H., & Dalal, R. (2000). Validity of Web-based psychological research. In M. H. Birnbaum (Ed.), *Psychological experiments on the Internet* (pp. 35–60). San Diego: Academic Press.

Kremar, M., & Greene, K. (2000). Connections between violent television exposure and adolescent risk taking. *Media Violence, 2,* 195–217.

Krishnan, A., & Sweeney, C. J. (1998). Gender differences in fear of success imagery and other achievement-related background variables among medical students. *Sex Roles, 39,* 299–310.

Krosnick, J. A. (1999). Survey research. *Annual Review of Psychology, 50,* 537–67.

Kumari, R. (1995). Relation of sex role attitudes and self esteem to fear of success among college women. *Psychological Studies, 40,* 82–86.

Kwiatkowski, S. J., & Parkinson, S. R. (1994). Depression, elaboration, and mood congruence: Differences between natural and induced mood. *Memory & Cognition, 22,* 225–233.

LaGreca, A. M., Silverman, W. K., Vernberg, E. M., & Prinstein, M. J. (1996). Symptoms of posttraumatic stress in children after Hurricane Andrew: A prospective study. *Journal of Counseling and Clinical Psychology, 64,* 712–723.

Lane, J. D., Phillips-Bute, B. G., & Pieper, C. F. (1998). Caffeine raises blood pressure at work. *Psychosomatic Medicine, 60,* 327–330.

Lang, F. R., & Heckhausen, J. (2001). Perceived control over development and subjective well-being: Differential benefits across adulthood. *Journal of Personality and Social Psychology, 81,* 509–523.

Latané, B., & Darley, J. M. (1970). *The unresponsive bystander: Why doesn't he help?* New York: Appleton-Century-Crofts.

Lawson, C. (1995). Research participation as a contract. *Ethics and Behavior, 5,* 205–215.

Lee, Y-T., & Ottati, V. (1995). Perceived in-group homogeneity as a function of group membership salience and stereotype threat. *Personality & Social Psychology Bulletin, 21,* 610–619.

Lehner, P. N. (1996). *Handbook of ethological methods* (2nd ed.). Cambridge, UK: Cambridge University Press.

Leirer, V. O., Yesavage, J. A., & Morrow, D. G. (1991). Marijuana carry-over effects on aircraft pilot performance. *Aviation, Space, and Environmental Medicine, 62,* 221–227.

Levitt, L., & Leventhal, G. (1986). Litter reduction: How effective is the New York State Bottle Bill? *Environment and Behavior, 18,* 467–479.

Lewis, C. A., McCollam, P., & Joseph, S. (2000). Convergent validity of the Depression-Happiness Scale with the Bradburn Affect Balance Scale. *Social Behavior & Personality, 28,* 579–584.

Lifton, R. J. (1986). *The Nazi doctors: Medical killing and the psychology of genocide.* New York: Basic Books.

Lockwood, K. A., Alexopoulos, G. S., Kakuma, T., & Van Gorp, W. G. (2000). Subtypes of cognitive impairment in depressed older adults. *American Journal of Geriatric Psychiatry, 8,* 201–208.

Loftus, E. F. (1975). Leading questions and the eyewitness report. *Cognitive Psychology, 7,* 560–572.

Loftus, E. F. (2003, January). *Illusions of memory.* Presented at the National Institute on the Teaching of Psychology. St. Petersburg Beach, FL.

Loftus, E. F. (1997). Memories for a past that never was. *Current Directions in Psychological Science, 6,* 60–65.

Loftus, E. F., & Marburger, W. (1983). Since the eruption of Mout St. Helens, has anyone beaten you up? Improving the accuracy of retrospective reports with landmark events. *Memory and Cognition, 11,* 114–120.

Lonner, W. J. (1999). Helfrich's "principle of triarchic resonance": A commentary on yet another perspective on the ongoing and tenacious etic–emic debate. *Culture & Psychology, 5,* 173–181.

Lord, F. M. (1953). On the statistical treatment of football numbers. *American Psychologist, 8,* 750–751.

Luria, A. R. (1968). *The mind of a mnemonist.* New York: Basic Books.

Malmo, R. B., Boag, T. J., & Smith, A. A. (1957). Physiological study of personal interaction. *Psychosomatic Medicine, 19,* 105–119.

Manucia, G. K., Baumann, D. J., & Cialdini, R. B. (1984). Mood influences on helping: Direct effects or side effects? *Journal of Personality and Social Psychology, 46,* 357–364.

Marans, D. G. (1988). Addressing researcher practitioner and subject needs: A debriefing–disclosure procedure. *American Psychologist, 43,* 826–828.

Marian, V., & Neisser, E. (2000). Language-dependent recall of autobiographical memories. *Journal of Experimental Psychology: General, 129,* 361–368.

Marlowe, C. M., Schneider, S. L., & Nelson, C. E. (1996). Gender and attractiveness biases in hiring decisions: Are more experienced managers less biased? *Journal of Applied Psychology, 81,* 11–21.

Martinez-Ebers, V. (1997). Using monetary incentives with hard-to-reach populations in panel surveys. *International Journal of Public Opinion Research, 9,* 77–86.

Martinsen, E. W., Friis, S., & Hoffart, A. (1995). Assessment of depression: Comparison between Beck Depression Inventory and subscales of Comprehensive Psychopathological Rating Scale. *Acta Psychiatrica Scandinavica, 92,* 460–463.

Matsumoto, D. (1993). Ethnic differences in affect intensity, emotion judgments, display rule attitudes, and self-reported emotional expression in an American sample. *Motivation and Emotion, 17,* 107–123.

Matsumoto, D. (1994). *Cultural Influences on Research Methods and Statistics.* Pacific Grove, CA: Brooks/Cole.

Matsumoto, D., & Assar, M. (1992). The effects of language on judgments of universal facial expressions of emotion. *Journal of Nonverbal Behavior, 16,* 85–99.

Matthews, G. A., & Dickinson, A. M. (2000). Effects of alternative activities on time allocated to task performance under different percentages of incentive pay. *Journal of Organizational Behavior Management, 20,* 3–27.

May, C. P., Hasher, L., & Stoltzfus, E. R. (1993). Optimal time of day and the magnitude of age differences in memory. *Psychological Science, 4,* 326–330.

Mayer, J. D., Salovey, P., Caruso, D. R., & Sitarenios, G. (2001). Emotional intelligence as a standard intelligence. *Emotion, 1,* 232–242.

Mazzoni, G. A., & Loftus, E. F. (1998). Dream interpretation can change beliefs about the past. *Psychotherapy, 35,* 177–187.

McAuliffe, W. E., Geller, S., LaBrie, R., Paletz, S., & Fournier, E. (1998). Are telephone surveys suitable for studying substance abuse? Cost, administration, cover, and response rate issues. *Journal of Drug Issues, 28,* 455–481.

McCallum, R. C., & Austin, J. T. (2000). Applications of structural equation modeling in psychological research. *Annual Review of Psychology, 51,* 201–226.

McCarty, J. A., & Shrum, L. J. (2000). The measurement of personal values in survey research. *Public Opinion Quarterly, 64,* 271–298.

McClung, H. J., Murray, R. D., & Heitlinger, L. A. (1998). The internet as a course for current patient information. *Pediatrics, 101,* e2 [online].

McGuire, W. J. (1983). A contextualist theory of knowledge: Its implications for innovation and reform in psychological research. In L. Berkowitz (Ed.), *Advances in Experimental Social Psychology,* Vol 16. Orlando, FL: Academic Press.

Mennella, J. A., & Gerrish, C. J. (1998). Effects of exposure to alcohol in mother's milk on infant sleep. *Pediatrics, 101,* e2[online].

Merton, R. K. (1983). Behavior patterns of scientists. In R. S. Albert (Ed.), *Genius and eminence: The social psychology of creativity and exceptional achievement* (Ch. V-4, pp. 265–279). New York: Pergamon Press.

Meston, C. M., Heiman, J. R., Trapnell, P. D., & Paulhus, D. L. (1998). Social desirable responding and sexuality self-reports. *Journal of Sex Research, 35,* 148–157.

Milgram, S. (1963). Behavioral study of obedience. *Journal of Abnormal and Social Psychology, 67,* 371–378.

Milgram, S. (1964). Issues in the study of obedience: A reply to Baumrind. *American Psychologist, 19,* 848–852.

Milgram, S. (1974). *Obedience to authority: An experimental view.* New York: Harper & Row.

Miller, M. A., & Rahe, R. H. (1997). Life changes scaling for the 1990s. *Journal of Psychosomatic Research, 43,* 279–292.

Miller, N. (1985). The value of behavioral research on animals. *American Psychologist, 40,* 423–440.

Miller, R. S. (1995). On the nature of embarrassability: Shyness, social evaluation, and social skill. *Journal of Personality, 63,* 315–339.

Mills, C. G., Boteler, E. H., & Oliver, G. K. (1999). Digit synaesthesia: A case study using a stroop-type test. *Cognitive Neuropsychology, 16,* 181–191.

Modern Language Association of America. (1995). *MLA handbook for writers of research papers* (4th ed.). New York: Author.

Mohr, D. C., Goodkin, D. E., Bacchetti, P., Boudewyn, A. C., Huang, L., Marrietta, P., Cheuk, W., & Dee, B. (2000). Psychological stress and the subsequent appearance of new brain MRI lesions in MS. *Neurology, 55,* 55–61.

Moncrieff, J., Wessely, S., & Hardy, R. (1998). Meta-analysis of trials comparing antidepressants with active placebos. *British Journal of Psychiatry, 172,* 227–231.

Mook, D. G. (1983). In defense of external invalidity. *American Psychologist, 38,* 379–387.

Moore, S. R. (1998). Effects of sample size on the representativeness of observational data used in evaluation. *Education and Treatment of Children, 21,* 209–226.

Morris, J. S., Scott, S. K., & Dolan, R. J. (1999). Saying it with feeling: Neural responses to emotional vocalizations. *Neuropsychologia, 37,* 1155–1163.

Moseley, J. B., O'Malley, K., Petersen, N. J., Menke, T. J., Brody, B. A., Kuykendall, D. H., Hollingsworth, J. C., Ashton, C. M., & Wray, N. P. (2002). A controlled trial of arthroscopic surgery for osteoarthritis of the knee. *New England Journal of Medicine, 347,* 81–88.

The Mother's Encyclopedia. (1942). Vol. 5, New York: The Parents' Institute.

Müller, F. R. (2000, May/June). [Letter to the editor.] *The Sciences, 40,* 5.

Münsterberg, H. (1914). *Psychology and social sanity.* New York: Doubleday, Page, & Co.

Murray, L. A., Whitehouse, W. G., & Alloy, L. B. (1999). Mood congruence and depressive deficits in memory: A forced-recall analysis. *Memory, 7,* 175–196.

Nadler, A., Shapira, R., & Ben-Itzhak, S. (1982). Good looks may help: Effects of helper's physical attractiveness and sex of helper on males' and females' help-seeking behavior. *Journal of Personality and Social Psychology, 42,* 90–99.

Neville, H. A., Lilly, R. L., Duran, G., Lee, R. M., & Browne, L. (2000). Construction and initial validation of the Color-Blind Racial Attitudes Scale (CoBRAS). *Journal of Counseling Psychology, 47,* 59–70.

Newcomb, M. D., & Bentler, P. M. (1989). Substance use and abuse among children and teenagers. *American Psychologist, 44,* 242–248.

Newman, J., Rosenbach, J. H., Burns, K. L., Latimer, B. C., Matocha, H. R., & Vogt, E. E. (1995). An experimental test of "the Mozart effect" Does listening to his music improve spatial ability? *Perceptual and Motor Skills, 81,* 1379–1387.

Nicholls, J. G. (1983). Creativity in the person who will never produce anything original or useful. In R. S. Albert (Ed.), *Genius and eminence: The social psychology of creativity and exceptional achievement* (Ch. VI-1, pp. 265–279). New York: Pergamon Press.

Nicholson, R. (December, 1999/January 2000). AzTech Medicine. *Natural History,* 54–59.

NIMH Multisite HIV Prevention Trial: Reducing HIV sexual risk behavior. (1998). *Science, 280,* 1889–1894.

Nisbett, M. (1998). New poll points to increases in paranormal belief. *Skeptical Inquirer, 22(5),* 9.

Norenzayan, A., & Schwarz, N. (1999). Telling what they want to know: Participants tailor causal attributions to researchers' interests. *European Journal of Social Psychology, 29,* 1011–1020.

North, C. S., Nixon, S. J., Shariat, S., Mallonee, S., McMillen, J. C., Spitznagel, E. L., & Smith, E. M. (1999). Psychiatric disorders among survivors of the Oklahoma City bombing. *Journal of the American Medical Association, 282,* 755–762.

Novi, M. J., & Meinster, M. O. (2000). Achievement in a relational context: Preferences and influences in female adolescents. *Career Development Quarterly, 49,* 73–84.

Nugent, W. R., Bruley, C., & Allen, P. (1998). The effects of aggression replacement training on antisocial behavior in a runaway shelter. *Research on Social Work Practice, 8,* 637–656.

Nygaard, L. C., Burt, S. A., & Queen, J. S. (2000). Surface form typicality and asymmetric transfer in episodic memory for spoken words. *Journal of Experimental Psychology: Learning, Memory, & Cognition, 26,* 1228–1244.

Odom, S. L., & Ogawa, I. (1992). Direct observation of young children's social interactions with peers: A review of methodology. *Behavioral Assessment, 14,* 407–441.

Office of Research Integrity: Handling misconduct. (nd). Retrieved December 18, 2002 from http://ori.dhhs.gov/html/misconduct/casesummaries.asp#1

Olkin, I. (1992). Reconcilable differences: Gleaning insight from conflicting scientific studies. *The Sciences, 32,* 30–36.

Orne, M. T. (1962). On the social psychology of the psychological experiment: With particular reference to demand characteristics and their implications. *American Psychologist, 17,* 776–783.

Orne, M. T., & Scheibe, K. T. (1962). The contribution of nondeprivation factors in the production of sensory deprivation effexts. *Journal of Abnormal and Social Psychology, 68,* 3–12.

Ornstein, R., & Sobel, D. (1987). *The healing brain.* New York: Simon and Schuster.

Ortmann, A., & Hertwig, R. (1997). Is deception acceptable? *American Psychologist, 52,* 746–747.

Overall, J. E., Hollister, L. E., Johnson, M., & Pennington, V. (1966). Nosology of depression and differential response to drugs. *Journal of the American Medical Association, 195,* 946–948.

Paksoy, C., Wilkinson, J. B., & Mason, J. B. (1985). Learning and carryover effects in retail experimentation. *Journal of the Market Research Society, 27,* 109–129.

Peng, K., & Nisbett, R. E. (1999). Culture, dialectics, and reasoning about contradiction. *American Psychologist, 54,* 741–754.

Pepler, D. J., & Craig, W. M. (1995). A peek behind the fence: Naturalistic observations of aggressive children with remote audiovisual recording. *Developmental Psychology, 31,* 548–553.

Perceptions of Foreign Countries. (2001). http://www.gallup.com/poll/releases/pr010928.asp. [Retrieved September 29, 2001].

Peregrine, P. N., Drews, D. R., North, M., & Slupe, A. (1993). Sampling techniques and sampling error in naturalistic observation: An empirical evaluation with implications for cross-cultural research. *Cross-Cultural Research, 27*, 232–246.

Peters, M. (1993). Still no convincing evidence of a relation between brain size and intelligence in humans. *Canadian Journal of Experimental Psychology, 47*, 751–756.

Phillips, D. P., Christenfeld, N., & Ryan, N. M. (1999). An increase in the number of deaths in the United States in the first week of the month—An association with substance abuse and other causes of death. *New England Journal of Medicine, 341*, 93–98.

Phinney, J. S. (1996). When we talk about American ethnic groups, what do we mean? *American Psychologist, 51*, 918–927.

Plous, S. (1996a). Attitudes toward the use of animals in psychological research and education. *American Psychologist, 51*, 1167–1180.

Plous, S. (1996b). Attitudes toward the use of animals in psychological research and education: Results from a national survey of psychology majors. *Psychological Science, 7*, 352–358.

Pollatsek, A., & Well, A. D. (1995). On the use of counterbalanced designs in cognitive research: A suggestion for a better and more powerful analysis. *Journal of Experimental Psychology: Learning, Memory, and Cognition, 21*, 785–794.

Powell, M. C., & Fazio, R. H. (1984). Attitude accessibility as a function of repeated attitudinal expression. *Personality and Social Psychology Bulletin, 10*, 139–148.

Presser, S., & Stinson, L. (1998). Data collection mode and social desirability bias in self-reported religious attendance. *American Sociological Review, 63*, 137–145.

Price, W. F., & Crapo, R. H. (1999). *Cross-cultural perspectives in introductory psychology* (3rd ed.). Pacific Grove, CA: Brooks/Cole Wadsworth.

Quinn, G. E., Shin, C. H., Maguire, M. G., & Stone, R. A. (1999). Myopia and ambient lighting at night. *Nature, 399*, 113–114.

Quinn, R. P., Gutek, B. A., & Walsh, J. T. (1980). Telephone interviewing: A reappraisal and a field experiment. *Basic and Applied Social Psychology, 1*, 127–153.

Radford, B. (1998). Survey finds 70% of women, 48% of men believe in paranormal. *Skeptical Inquirer, 22(2)*, 8.

Radner, D., & Radner, M. (1982). *Science and unreason.* Belmont, CA: Wadsworth.

Rasinski, K. A. (1989). The effect of question wording on public support for government spending. *Public Opinion Quarterly, 53*, 388–394.

Rauscher, F. H., & Shaw, G. L. (1998). Key components of the Mozart effect. *Perceptual and Motor Skills, 86*, 835–841.

Rauscher, F. H., Shaw, G. L., & Ky, K. N. (1993). Music and spatial task performance. *Nature, 365*, 611.

Rauscher, F. H., Shaw, G. L., & Ky, K. N. (1995). Listening to Mozart enhances spatial-temporal reasoning: Towards a neurophysiological basis. *Neuroscience Letters, 185*, 44–47.

Ray, J. J. (1990). Acquiescence and problems with forced-choice scales. *Journal of Social Psychology, 130*, 397–399.

Recarte, M. A., & Nunes, L. M. (2000). Effects of verbal and spatial-imagery tasks on eye fixations while driving. *Journal of Experimental Psychology: Applied, 6*, 31–43.

Reese, H. W. (1997). Counterbalancing and other uses of repeated-measures Latin-square designs: Analysis and interpretation. *Journal of Experimental Child Psychology, 64*, 137–158.

Renner, M. J., Mackin, R. S. (1998). A life stress instrument for classroom use. *Teaching of Psychology, 25*, 46–48.

Reynolds, P. D. (1982). *Ethics and social science research.* Englewood Cliffs, NJ: Prentice-Hall.

Research Ethics and the Medical Profession: Report of the Advisory Committee on Human Radiation Experiments. (1996). *Journal of the American Medical Association, 276*, 403–409.

Richter, P., Joachim, W., & Bastine, R. (1994). Psychometrische Eigenschaften des Beck-Depressioninventars (BDI): Ein Überblick. *Zeitschrift für Klinische Psychologie: Forschung und Praxis, 23*, 3–19.

Richter, P., Werner, J., & Bastine, R. (1994). Psychometrische Eigenschaften des Beck-Depressioninventars (BDI): Ein Überblick. *Zeitschrift für Klinische Psychologie: Forschung und Praxis, 23*, 3–19.

Ring, K., Wallston, K., & Corey, M. (1970). Mode of debriefing as a factor affecting subjective reaction to a Milgram-type obedience experiment: An ethical inquiry. *Representative Research in Social Psychology, 1*, 67–88.

Roberts, R. D., Zeidner, M., & Matthews, G. (2001). Does emotional intelligence meet traditional standards for an intelligence? Some new data and conclusions. *Emotion, 1*, 196–231.

Robins, R. W., & Gosling, S. D., & Craik, K. H. (1999). An empirical analysis of trends in psychology. *American Psychologist, 54*, 117–128.

Robinson, J. P., Shaver, P. R., & Wrightsman, L. S. (1991). *Measures of personality and social psychological attitudes: Measures of social psychological attitudes,* Vol. 1. San Diego, CA: Academic Press.

Rockwood, T. H., Sangster, R. L., & Dillman, D. A. (1997). The effect of response categories on survey questionnaires: Context and mode effects. *Sociological Methods and Research, 26*, 118–140.

Rodriguez, C. E. (2000). *Changing race: Latinos, the census and the history of ethnicity in the United States.* New York: New York University Press.

Rogers, K. B. (1999). The liflong prodeuctivity of the female researchers in Terman's genetic studies of genius longitudinal study. *Gifted Child Quarterly, 43*, 150–169.

Rogler, L. H. (1999). Methodological sources of cultural insensitivity in mental health research. *American Psychologist, 54*, 424–433.

Rook, K. S. (1984). The negative side of social interaction: Impact on psychological well-being. *Journal of Personality and Social Psychology, 46*, 1097–1108.

Rosenberg, M. (1965). *Society and the adolescent self-image*. Princeton, NJ: Princeton University Press.

Rosenthal, R., & Fode, K. L. (1966). Three experiments in experimenter bias. *Psychological Reports, 12*, 491–511.

Rosenthal, R. & Rosnow, R. L. (1975). *The volunteer subject*. New York: Wiley.

Rosnow, R. L., & Rosenthal, R. (1997). *People studying people: Artifacts and ethics in behavioral research*. New York: W. H. Freeman.

Ross, L., Lepper, M. R., & Hubbard, M. (1975). Perseverance in self-perception and social perception: Biased attribution processes in the debriefing paradigm. *Journal of Personality and Social Psychology, 32*, 880–892.

Ross, L. M., Hall, B. A., & Heater, S. L. (1998). Why are occupational therapists not doing more replication research? *The American Journal of Occupational Therapy, 52*, 234–235.

Ross, M., & Wilson, A. E. (2002). It feels like yesterday: Self-esteem, valence of personal past experiences, and judgments of subjective distance. *Journal of Personality and Social Psychology, 82*, 792–803.

Rothbaum, F., Weisz, J., Pott, M., Kiyake, K., & Morelli, G. (2000). Attachment and culture: Security in the United States and Japan. *American Psychologist, 55*, 1093–1104.

Rothman, D. J. (1994, January 9). Government guinea pigs. *New York Times*, Section 4, 23.

Rothman, M. (1996). Fear of success among business students. *Psychological Reports, 78*, 863–869.

Rowe, R. M., & McKenna, F. P. (2001). Skilled anticipation in real-world tasks: Measurement of attentional demands in the domain of tennis. *Journal of Experimental Psychology: Applied, 7*, 60–67.

Rubin, Z. (1985). Deceiving ourselves about deception: Comment on Smith and Richardson's "Amelioration of deception and harm in psychological research." *Journal of Personality and Social Psychology, 48*, 252–253.

Ryan, L., Hatfield, C., & Hofstetter, M. (2002). Caffeine reduces time-of-day effects on memory performance in older adults. *Psychological Science, 13*, 68–71.

Ryff, C. D. (1989). Happiness is everything, or is it? Explorations on the meaning of psychological well-being. *Journal of Personality and Social Psychology, 57*, 1069–1081.

Saletan, W. (2001). Tax poll loopholes. *Slate Magazine* (http://slate.msn.com, retrieved March 12, 2001).

Sambraus, H. H. (1998). Applied ethology—Its task and limits in veterinary practice. *Applied Animal Behaviour Science, 59*, 39–48.

Sangor, G. B., & Stangor, C. (2001). Perceived consensus influences intergroup behavior and stereotype accessibility. *Journal of Personality and Social Psychology, 80*, 645–654.

Sax, L. J., Astin, A. W., Korn, W. S., & Mahoney, K. M. (1999). *The American freshman: National norms for fall 1999*. Los Angeles: Higher Education Research Institute.

Scarr, W. (1981). *Race, social class, and individual differences in I.Q.* Hillsdale, NJ: Lawrence Erlbaum Associates.

Schaie, K. W. (1992). The impact of methodological changes in gerontology. *International Journal of Aging and Human Development, 35*, 19–29.

Schaie, K. W. (2000). The impact of longitudinal studies on understanding development from young adulthood to old age. *International Journal of Behavioral Develoment, 24*, 257–266.

Scharrer, E. (2001). Men, muscles, and machismo: the relationship between television violence exposure and aggression and hostility in the presence of hypermasculinity. *Media Psychology, 3*, 159–188.

Scheers, N. J. (1992). Methods, plainly speaking: A review of randomized response techniques. *Measurement and Evaluation in Counseling and Development, 25*, 27–41.

Schiffman, S. S. (1997). Taste and smell losses in normal aging and disease. *Journal of the American Medical Association, 278*, 1357–1362.

Schillewaert, N., Langerak, F., & Duhamel, T. (1998). Non-probability sampling for WWW surveys: A comparison of methods. *Journal of the Market Research Society, 40*, 307–322.

Scholer, S. J., Hickson, G. B., & Mitchel, E. F., & Ray, W. A. (1998). Predictors of mortality from fires in young children. *Pediatrics, 101*, e12. [online].

Schram, C. M. (1996). A meta-analysis of gender differences in applied statistics achievement. *Journal of Educational and Behavioral Statistics, 21*, 55–70.

Schul, Y., & Goren, H. (1997). When strong evidence has less impact than weak evidence: Bias, adjustment, and instructions to ignore. *Social Cognition, 15*, 133–155.

Schuller, R. A., & Cripps, J. (1998). Expert evidence pertaining to battered women: The impact of gender of expert and timing of testimony. *Law and Human Behavior, 22*, 17–31.

Schwarz, H., & Hippler, H-J. (1995). The numeric values of rating scales: A comparison of their impact in mail surveys and telephone interviews. *International Journal of Public Opinion Research, 7*, 72–74.

Schwarz, N. (1999). Self-reports: How the questions shape the answers. *American Psychologist, 54,* 93–105.

Schwarz, N., Hippler, H. J., Deutsch, B., & Strack, F. (1985). Response categories: Effects on behavioral reports and comparative judgments. *Public Opinion Quarterly, 49,* 388–395.

Sechrest, G. B., & Stangor, C. (2001). Perceived consensus influences intergroup behavior and stereotype accessibility. *Journal of Personality & Social Psychology, 80,* 645–654.

Segall, M. H., Campbell, D. T., & Herskovits, M. J. (1966). *The influence of culture on visual perception.* Indianapolis, IN: Bobbs-Merrill.

Segall, M. H., Lonner, W. J., & Berry, J. W. (1998). Cross-cultural psychology as a scholarly discipline: On the flowering of culture in behavioral research. *American Psychologist, 53,* 1101–1110.

Selten, J. P., Veen, N., Feller, W., Blom, J. D., Schols, D., Camoenie, W., Oolders, J., Van Der Velden, M., Hoek, H. W., Rivero, V. M., Vladar, R., Van Der Graaf, Y., & Kahn, R. (2001). Incidence of psychotic disorders in immigrant groups to the Netherlands. *British Journal of Psychiatry, 178,* 367–372.

Sher, K. J., Wood, M. D., Wood, P. K., & Raskin, G. (1996). Alcohol outcome expectancies and alcohol use: A latent variable cross-lagged panel study. *Journal of Abnormal Psychology, 105,* 561–574.

Sherer, M., Maddux, J. E., Mercandante, B., Prentice-Dunn, S., Jacobs, B., & Rogers, R. W. (1982). The Self-Efficacy Scale: Construction and validation. *Psychological Reports, 51,* 663–671.

Singer, E., Van Hoewyk, J., & Maher, M. P. (2000). Experiments with incentives in telephone surveys. *Public Opinion Quarterly, 64,* 171–188.

Singer, E., Von Thurn, D. R., & Miller, E. R. (1995). Confidentiality assurances and survey response: A review of the experimental literature. *Public Opinion Quarterly, 59,* 266–277.

Singer, B., & Benassi, V. A. (1980). Fooling some of the people all of the time. *Skeptical Inquirer, 5(Winter),* 17–24.

Singh, S. (1999). *The code book: The evolution of secrecy from Mary Queen of Scots to quantum cryptography.* New York: Doubleday.

Smith, C. S., Reilly, C., & Midkiff, K. (1989). Evaluation of three circadian rhythm questionnaires with suggestions for an improved measure of morningness. *Journal of Applied Psychology, 74,* 728–739.

Smith, E. R., & Kluegel, J. R. (1984). Beliefs and attitudes about women's opportunity. *Social Psychology Quarterly, 35,* 81–95. 295–304.

Smith, J. A. (1997). Developing theory from case studies: Self-reconstruction and the transition to motherhood. In N. Hayes (Ed.), *Doing qualitative analysis in psychology.* Hove, East Sussex, UK: Psychology Press.

Snowden, P. L., & Christian, L. G. (1999). Parenting the young gifted child: Supportive behaviors. *Roeper Review, 21,* 221.

Sobel, D. (2000). *Galileo's daughter.* New York: Penguin Books.

Soliday, E., & Stanton, A. L. (1995). Deceived versus nondeceived participants' perceptions of scientific and applied psychology. *Ethics and Behavior, 5,* 87–104.

Sommers, S. R., & Ellsworth, P. C. (2001). White juror bias: An investigation of prejudice against black defendants in the American courtroom. *Psychology, Public Policy, and Law, 7,* 201–229.

Soto-Faraco, S., & Sebastián-Gallés, N. (2001). The effects of acoustic mismatch and selective listening on repetition deafness. *Journal of Experimental Psychology: Human Perception and Performance, 27,* 356–369.

Spencer, S. J., Steele, C. M., & Quinn, D. M. (1999). Stereotype threat and women's math performance. *Journal of Experimental Social Psychology, 35,* 4–28.

Staats, P., Hekmat, H., & Staats, A. (1998). Suggestion/placebo effects on pain: Negative as well as positive. *Journal of Pain and Symptom Management, 15,* 235–243.

Steele, C. M. (1998). Stereotype threat and the test performance of academically successful African Americans. In C. Jencks, M. Phillips, M. & (Eds.), *The Black–White test score gap* (pp. 401–427). Washington: Brookings Institution.

Steele, C. M., & Aronson, J. (1995). Stereotype threat and the intellectual test performance of African Americans. *Journal of Personality and Social Psychology, 69,* 797–811.

Steele, K. M. (2001). The "Mozart Effect": An example of the scientific method in operation. *Psychology Teacher Network, 11(5),* 2–3, 5.

Steele, K. M., Bass, K. E., & Brook, M. D. (1999). The mystery of the Mozart effect: Failure to replicate. *Psychological Science, 10,* 366–369.

Steele, K. M., Dalla Bella, S., Peretz, I, Dunlop, T., Dawe, L. A., Humphrey, G. K., Shannon, R. A., Kirby, J. L., Jr., & Olmstead, C. G. (1999). Prelude or requiem for the "Mozart Effect"? *Nature, 400,* 827.

Steer, R. A., Rissmiller, D. J., & Beck, A. T. (2000). Use of Beck Depression Inventory-II with depressed geriatric inpatients. *Behaviour Research & Therapy, 38,* 311–318.

Steer, R. A., Rissmiller, D. J., Ranieri, W. F., & Beck, A. T. (1994). Use of the computer-administered Beck Depression Inventory and Hopelessness Scale with psychiatric inpatients. *Computers in Human Behavior, 10,* 223–229.

Steinberg, N., Tooney, N., Sutton, C., & Denmark, F. (2000, May/June). [Letter to the editor]. *The Sciences, 40,* 3.

Sternberg, R. J. (1985). *Beyond IQ: A triarchic theory of human intelligence*. New York: Cambridge University Press.

Sternberg, R. J. (1999). A triarchic approach to the understanding and assessment of intelligence in multicultural populations. *Journal of School Psychology, 37*, 145–159.

Stevens, J. C., Cruz, L. A., Hoffman, J. M., & Patterson, M. Q. (1995). Taste sensitivity and aging: High incidence of decline revealed by repeated threshold measures. *Chemical Senses, 20*, 451–459.

Stevens, S. S. (1946). On the theory of scales of measurement, *Science, 103*, 677–680.

Stevens, S. S. (1951). Mathematics, measurement, and psychophysics. In S. S. Stevens (Ed.) *Handbook of experimental psychology*. New York: Wiley.

Stiles, D. A., Gibbons, J. L., & Schnellman, J. D. (1990). Opposite-sex ideal in the U.S.A. and Mexico as perceived by young adolescents. *Journal of Cross-Cultural Psychology, 21*, 180–199.

Stokes, S. J., & Bikman, L. (1974). The effect of the physical attractiveness and role of the helper on help seeking. *Journal of Applied Social Psychology, 4*, 286–294.

Stolzenberg, L., & D'Alessio, S. J. (1997). "Three strikes and you're out": The impact of California's new mandatory sentencing law on serious crime rates. *Crime and Delinquency, 43*, 457–469.

Straus, M. A., Sugarman, D. B., Giles-Sims, J. (1997). Spanking by parents and subsequent antisocial behavior of children. *Archives of Pediatrics and Adolescent Medicine, 151*, 761–767.

Strober, M., Freeman, R., Lampter, C., Diamond, J., & Kaye, W. (2001). Males with anorexia nervosa: A controlled study of eating disorders in first-degree relatives. *International Journal of Eating Disorders, 29*, 263–269.

Sue, S. (1999). Science, ethnicity, and bias: Where have we gone wrong? *American Psychologist, 54*, 1070–1077.

Sundblom, D. M., Haikonen, S., Niemi-Pynttaeri, J., & Tigerstedt, I. (1994). Effect of spiritual healing on chronic idiopathic pain: A medical and psychological study. *Clinical Journal of Pain, 10*, 296–302.

Takooshian, H., & O'Connor, P. J. (1984). When apathy leads to tragedy: Two Fordham professors examine "Bad Samaritanism." *Social Action and the Law, 10*, 26–27.

Tang-Martínez, Z., & Mechanic, M. (2000, May/June). [Letter to the editor.] *The Sciences, 40*, 5–6.

Taylor, S. J., & Bogdan, R. (1998). *Introduction to qualitative research methods*. New York: Wiley.

Teeter, P. A., & Smith, P. L. (1989). Cognitive processing strategies for normal and LD children: A comparison of the K-ABC and microcomputer experiments. *Archives of Clinical Neuropsychology, 4*, 45–61.

Thompson, J. K., & Heinberg, L. J. (1999). The media's influence on body image disturbance and eating disorders: We've reviled them, now can we rehabilitate them? *Journal of Social Issues, 55*, 339–353.

Thompson, J. K., & Stice, E. (2001). Thin-ideal internalization: Mounting evidence for a new risk factor for body-image disturbance and eating pathology. *Current Directions in Psychological Science, 10*, 181–183.

Thompson, W. F., Schellenberg, E. G., & Husain, G. (2001). Arousal, mood, and the Mozart effect. *Psychological Science, 12*, 248–251.

Thornhill, R., & Palmer, C. T. (2000). Why men rape. *The Sciences, 40*, 30–36.

Todd, J. L., & Worell, J. (2000). Resilience in low-income, employed, African-American women. *Psychology of Women Quarterly, 24*, 119–128.

Todorov, A. (2000). Context effects in national health surveys: Effects of preceding questions on reporting serous difficulty seeing and legal blindness. *Public Opinion Quarterly, 64*, 65–76.

Traugott, M. W., & Price, V. (1992). The polls—A review: Exit polls in the 1989 Virginia gubernatorial race: Where did they go wrong? *Public Opinion Quarterly, 56*, 245–253.

Troisi, A. (1999). Ethological research in clinical psychiatry: The study of nonverbal behavior during interviews. *Neuroscience and Biobehavioral Reviews, 23*, 905–913.

Troisi, A., & Moles, A. (1999). Gender differences in depression: An ethological study of noverbal behavior during interviews. *Journal of Psychiatric Research, 33*, 243–350.

Troisi, A., Pasini, A., Bersani, G., Di Mauro, M., & Ciani, N. (1991). Negative symptoms and visual behavior in DSM-III-R prognostic subtypes of schizophreniform disorder. *Acta Psychiatria Scandinavia, 83*, 391–394.

Troisi, A., Spalletta, G., & Pasini, A. (1998). Non-verbal behavior deficits in schizophrenia: An ethological study of drug-free patients. *Acta Psychiatrica Scandinavica, 97*, 109–115.

Trope, Y., & Fishbach, A. (2000). Counteractive self-control in overcoming temptation. *Journal of Personality and Social Psychology, 79*, 493–506.

Ullman, S. E., Karabotsos, G., & Koss, M. P. (1999). Alcohol and sexual aggression in a national sample of college men. *Psychology of Women Quarterly, 23*, 673–689.

Ullman, S. E., & Knight, R. A. (1991). A multivariate model for predicting rape and physical injury outcomes during sexual assaults. *Journal of Consulting and Clinical Psychology, 59*, 724–731.

Underwood, B. J., & Freund, J. S. (1970). Word frequency and short-term recognition memory. *American Journal of Psychology, 83*, 343–351.

Valois, R. F., Adams, K. G., & Kammermann, S. K. (1996). One-year evaluation results from Cable-Quit: A community cable television smoking cessation pilot program. *Journal of Behavioral Medicine, 19,* 479–499.

van de Vijver, F. J. R., & Leung, K. (2000). Cultural blindness or selective inattention? *American Psychologist, 56,* 824–825.

van Ijzendoorn, M. H., & Sagi, A. (2001). Cultural blindness or selective inattention? *American Psychologist, 56,* 824–825.

Varma, A. (2000). Impact of watching international television programs on adolescents in India. *Journal of Comparative Family Studies, 31,* 117–126.

Velleman, P. F., & Wilkinson, L. (1993). Nominal, ordinal, interval, and ratio typologies are misleading. *The American Statistician, 47,* 65–72.

Velten, E., Jr. (1997). A laboratory task for induction of mood states. In S. Rachman (Ed.), *Best of Behavior Research and Therapy* (pp. 73–82). New York: Pergamon/Elsevier Science.

Velten, E. (1968). A laboratory task for induction of mood states. *Behaviour Research and Therapy, 6,* 473–482.

Vink, T., Hinney, A., Van Elburg, A. A., Van Goozen, S. H. M., Sandkuijl, L. A., Sinke, R. J., Herpertz-Dahlmann, B-M., Hebebrand, J., Remschmidt, H., Van Engeland, H., & Adan, R. A. H. (2001). Association between an agouti-related protein gene polymorphism and anorexia nervosa. *Molecular Psychiatry, 6,* 325–328.

Vispoel, W. P., & Forte Fast, E. E. (2000). Response biases and their relation to sex differences in multiple domains of self-concept. *Applied Measurement in Education, 13,* 79–97.

Vonesh, E. F. (1983). Efficiency of repeated measures design versus completely randomized designs based on multiple comparisons. *Communications in Statistics—Theory and Methods, 12,* 289–302.

Wade, C. (2001, August). *The scientist-therapist gap: What students need to know.* Presentation at the annual convention of the American Psychological Association, San Francisco.

Wagle, A. C., Ho, L. W., Wagle, S. A., & Berrios, G. E. (2000). Psychometric behaviour of BDI in Alzheimer's disease patients with depression. *International Journal of Geriatric Psychiatry, 15,* 63–69.

Wainer, H. (1999). The most dangerous profession: A note on nonsampling error. *Psychological Methods, 4,* 250–256.

Waldo, C. R., Berdahl, J. L., & Fitzgerald, L. F. (1998). Are men sexually harassed? If so, by whom? *Law and Human Behavior, 22,* 59–79.

Walker, E. F., Grimes, K. E., Davis, D. M., & Smith, A. J. (1993). Childhood precursors of schizophrenia: Facial expression of emotion. *American Journal of Psychiatry, 150,* 1654–1660.

Wallace, W. P., Sawyer, T. J., & Robertson, L. C. (1979). Distractors in recall, distractor-free recognition, and the word-frequency effect. *American Journal of Psychology. Vol 91,* 295–304.

Waller, G., Meyer, C. van Hanswijck de Jonge, L. (2001). Early environmental influences on restrictive pathology among nonclinical females: The role of temperature at birth. *International Journal of Eating Disorders, 30,* 24–208.

Walsh, M., Hickey, C., & Duffy, J. (1999). Influence of item content and stereotype situation on gender differences in mathematical problem solving. *Sex Roles, 41,* 219–240.

Walsh, W. B. (1976). Disclosure of deception by debriefed subjects: Another look. *Psychological Reports, 38,* 783–786.

Wann, D. L., & Wilson, A. M. (1999). Relationship between aesthetic motivation and preferences for aggressive and nonaggressive sports. *Perceptual & Motor Skills, 89,* 931–934.

Watkins, D., Mortazavi, S., & Trofimova, I. (2000). Independent and interdependent conceptions of self: An investigation of age, gender, and culture differences in importance and satisfaction ratings. *Cross-Cultural Resarch: The Journal of Comparative Social Science, 34,* 113–134.

Wentland, E. J., & Smith, K. W. (1993). *Survey responses: An evaluation of their validity.* Boston: Academic Press.

Westen, D. (1998). The scientific legacy of Sigmund Freud: Toward a psychodynamically informed psychological science. *Psychological Bulletin, 124,* 333–371.

White, M. (1999, March 24). Research suspended at nation's largest veteran's hospital due to inadequate safeguards. *Nando Times News* [online]. (http://www.nando.net).

Wilcox, R. R. (1998). How many discoveries have been lost by ignoring modern statistical methods? *American Psychologist, 53,* 300–314.

Wilkinson, L., & the Task Force on Statistical Inference. (1999). Statistical methods in psychology journals: Guidelines and explanations. *American Psychologist, 54,* 594–604.

Willimack, D. K., Schuman, H., Pennell, B-E, & Lepkowski, J. M. (1995). Effects of a prepaid nonmonetary incentive on response rates and response quality in a face-to-face survey. *Public Opinion Quarterly, 59,* 78–92.

Wilson, D. W. (1978). Helping behavior and physical attractiveness. *Journal of Social Psychology, 104,* 313–314.

Winkielman, P., Knäuper, B., & Schwarz, N. (1998). Looking back at anger: Reference periods change the interpretation of (emotion) frequency questions. *Journal of Personality and Social Psychology, 75,* 719–728.

Wutzke, S. E., Conigrave, K. M., Kogler, B. E., Saunders, J. B., & Hall, W. D. (2000). Longitudinal research: Methods for maximizing subject follow-up. *Drug and Alcohol Review, 19,* 159–163.

Yee, A. H., Fairchild, H. H., Weizmann, F., & Wyatt, G. E. (1993). Addressing psychology's problem with race. *American Psychologist, 48,* 1132–1140.

York, J., Nicholson, T., Minors, P., Duncan, D. F. (1998). Stressful life events and loss of hair among adult women: A case-control study. *Psychological Reports, 82,* 1044–1046.

Yule, W., & Canterbury, R. (1994). The treatment of post traumatic stress disorder in children and adolescents. *International Review of Psychiatry, 6,* 141–150.

Zadnik, K., Jones, L. A., Irvin, B. C., Kleinstein, R. N., Manny, R. E., Shin, J. A., & Mutti, D. O. (2000). Vision: Myopia and ambient night-time lighting. *Nature, 404,* 143–144.

Zajonc, R. B. (1965). Social facilitation. *Science, 149,* 269–274.

Zeidner, M., Matthews, G., & Roberts, R. D. (2001). Slow down, you move too fast: Emotional intelligence remains an "elusive" intelligence. *Emotion, 1,* 265–275.

Zettle, R. D., & Houghton, L. L. (1998). The relationship between mathematics and social desirability as a function of gender. *College Student Journal, 32,* 81–86.

Zimbardo, P. G. (1972). On the ethics of intervention in human psychological research: With special reference to the Stanford prison experiment. *Cognition, 2,* 243–256.

Zinner, D., Hindahl, J., & Schwibbe, M. (1997). Effects of temporal sampling patterns of all-occurence recording in behavioural studies: Many short sampling periods are better than a few long ones. *Ethology, 103,* 236–246.

Zuckerman, M. (1990). Some dubious premises in research and theory on racial differences. *American Psychologist, 45,* 1297–1303.

Zusne, L., & Jones, W. H. (1989). *Anomalistic psychology: A study of magical thinking* (2nd ed.) Hillsdale, NJ: Erlbaum.

AUTHOR INDEX

Abreu, J. M., 129
Ackerman, P., 7
Adair, J. G., 44, 125
Adams, K. G., 193, 194
Affsprung, E. H., 116
Ahnberg, J. L., 130
Alexopoulos, G. S., 152
Allen, P., 196
Alloy, L. B., 146, 166
American Psychiatric
    Association, 328
American Psychological
    Association, 32, 33, 34
Americans felt uneasy toward
    Arabs even before
    September 11, 391
Anderson, C. A., 234
Anderson, J., 203
Andrade, L., 130
Andrew, J. E., 388
Aneschensel, C. S., 327
Angier, N., 318
Anorexia may not have cultural
    roots, 388
Armitage, R., 146
Aronson, J., 126, 331
Ash, R. A., 230, 231, 233
Assar, M., 322
Atkinson, D. R., 312
Austad, S. N., 135
Austin, J. T., 255, 256
Azar, B., 47, 63, 64

Babbie, E., 102
Bacchetti, P., 87
Bachorowski, J-A., 147
Bakken, L., 123
Ball, P., 322
Banville, D., 326
Barmann, B., 8
Barnett, W. S., 108
Baron-Cohen, S., 304
Bartolic, E. I., 130, 142, 153

Basha, S. A., 123
Basso, M. R., 130, 142, 153
Bastine, R., 130
Batson, C. D., 7
Baumann, D. J., 7
Baumrind, D., 40, 41
Beach, F. A., 48
Beail, N., 299
Beck, A. T., 130
Becker, E., 185
Bell, G., 141, 142
Bell, N. S., 146, 151, 186
Benassi, V. A., 23
Benbow, C. P., 331
Bendapudi, V., 230, 231, 233
Ben-Itzhak, S., 8
Bentler, P. M., 194
Ben-Zeev, T., 331
Berdahl, J. L., 61
Bergman, M. E., 252, 253
Berkowitz, L., 99
Berreby, D., 311
Berry, J. W., 309, 314, 315
Bersani, G., 262
Betancourt, H., 309, 310, 318
Bhugra, D., 311
Bhui, K., 311
Bikman, L., 9
Birnbaum, M. H., 31, 174, 176
Bishop, G. D., 18
Bodenhausen, G. V., 330
Bogdan, R., 395, 396
Bond, L., 290, 291, 292
Borg, M. J., 213
Bosworth, H. B., 296
Boteler, E. H., 303, 305
Boulton, M. J., 290
Brady, V., 141, 142
Bramel, D., 125
Brennan, M., 223
Brewer, B. W., 196
Broder, A., 44
Brown, G. K., 250

Bruce, K. E. M., 264, 265
Bruley, C., 196
Bruner, G. C., 216
Bryant, R. A., 152
Budson, A. E., 149, 167, 168
Bull, R., 8
Burns, K. L., 62
Burt, L., 304
Burt, S. A., 181
Bushman, B. J., 234
Byrnes, J. P., 123

Cacioppo, J. T., 251
Campbell, D. T., 184, 315
Canterbury, R., 15
Caplan, J. B., 331
Caplan, P. J., 331
Carlin, J. B., 290, 291, 292
Carr, S. C., 18
Carstens, C. B., 62
Caruso, D. R., 131
Cepeda-Benito, A., 327, 328
Cernovsky, Z. Z., 320
Chamberlin, J., 65
Chang, W. C., 312
Chao, R., 324
Cheryan, S., 330
Chiu, C., 216
Cho, H., 220, 223
Christenfeld, N., 389
Christensen, L., 43, 44
Christian, L. G., 261
Cialdini, R. B., 7
Claire, T., 126
Clark, V. A., 327
Clawson, R. A., 391, 395, 396
Clayton, S. D., 61
Cohen, D., 309, 312
Cohen, S., 89
Coile, D.C., 49, 58
Conigrave, K. M., 293
Contrad, H. S., 284
Cook, D. J., 300

Cook, P. J., 210
Cook, W. A., 250
Corey, M., 41
Council of National
    Psychological Assocations for
    the Advancement of Ethnic
    Minority Interests, 321
Coverdale, J. H., 178
Cox, C. R., 265
Craig, W. M., 279, 280
Craik, K. H., 57, 58
Crapo, R. H., 18, 314
Crewdson, A., 68
Cripps, J., 61
Croizet, J-C., 126
Croll, S., 152
Cruz, L. A., 151
Cunningham, M., 8
Cunningham, S., 7
Cytowic, R. E., 303, 304, 305

Daffner, K. R., 149, 167, 168
D'Alessio, S. J., 196, 197
Darby, B. L., 7
Darley, J. M., 7
Davies, M., 129, 132
Davis, D. M., 272
Deese, J., 96
Del Rosario, M. L., 195,
    196, 234
Desikan, R., 149, 167, 168
Desrosiers, P., 326
Deutsch, B., 210
Dickinson, A. M., 142
Diener, E., 46
Dieppe, P., 392, 394
Dillman, D. A., 209, 212, 215
Dixon, A. K., 264
Dixon, W. A., 116, 142, 143
Dobson, K. S., 130
Dolan, R. J., 142
Dozois, D. J. A., 130
Drews, D. R., 270
Dubowitz, G., 146
Duffy, J., 126
Duhamel, T., 222
Duncan, B., 7
Duran, G., 247, 248
Dushenko, T. W., 44

Eagles, J. M., 388
Edelsack, L., 7
Eichenwald, K., 31
Elisha Gray, 68
Ellis, H. C., 152, 153
Ellsworth, P. C., 164, 165
Estep, D. Q., 264, 265
Ethical principles of
    psychologists, 33
Evans, S. W., 149, 154, 169
Exline, J. J., 123

Fairburn, C. G., 103
Fairchild, H. H., 313, 319
Falk, R., 354
Fausto-Sterling, A., 354
Fazio, R. H., 213
Feller, W., 311
Fendrich, M., 215
Fernandez, E., 87
Fienberg, S. E., 203
Filho, A. H., 130
Finkel, S. E., 213
Fishbach, A., 159, 161, 169
Fisher, C. B., 43, 44
Fisher, R. A., 353
Fitzgerald, L. F., 61, 254
Flay, B. R., 194
Flynn, J. R., 320
Fode, K. L., 122, 128
Forte Fast, E. E., 216
Fosse, R., 154, 155
Francis, L. J., 216
Frank, O., 227
Freeman, R., 288
French, S., 142
Frerichs, R. R., 327
Freund, J. S., 96
Frick, R. W., 354
Friend, R., 125
Friis, S., 130
Fyrberg, D., 43, 44

Gabarink, G., 129
Gadzella, B. M., 93
Gaito, J., 136, 182, 354
Gardner, H., 131
Gehrick, J-G., 142
Geller, S., 215

Gendall, P., 223
Genet-Volet, G., 326
Gernston, G. G., 251
Gerrish, C. J., 148, 149
Gertz, M., 53, 209
Gibbons, J. L., 309
Giles, H., 322
Giles-Sims, J., 243
Girden, E. R., 181
Gladwell, M., 53
Glaze, J. A., 93
Gleaves, D. H., 327, 328
Glueck, W. F., 55, 56
Goldenberg, J. L., 184, 185, 189
Goleman, D., 131
Good, C., 126
Good, G. E., 250
Goodkin, D. E., 87
Goodman-Delahunty, J., 131
Goren, H., 149, 150
Gorenstein, C., 130
Gosling, S. D., 57, 58
Gottschalk, A., 146
Gould, S. J., 320
Gray, J., 330
Green, A., 180
Green, C. W., 142
Greenbaum, C. W., 354
Greene, K., 234
Greenstein, J., 20
Griffiths, M., 2
Grimes, K. E., 272
Gruder, C. L., 46
Gunewardene, A., 389
Gunnell, D., 392, 394
Gunz, A., 309, 312
Guterbok, T. M., 213
Guthrie, J. P., 230, 231, 233
Gutierrez, P. M., 250
Gwiazda, J., 121

Hahn, P. W., 61
Haikonen, S., 143
Hall, B. A., 69
Hall, M. E., 299
Halvari, H., 142
Hardy, R., 13
Harris, B., 17
Hashemi, L., 390

Hasher, L., 180
Haskins, E., 62
Hatfield, C., 180
Hawker, D. S. J., 290
Hay, C. A., 123
Hays, R. D., 250, 251, 255
Hayslip, B., 292, 293, 296
Headden, S., 201
Heater, S. L., 69
Heath, L., 195, 196, 234
Heckathorn, D. D., 226, 227
Heckhausen, J., 236
Hedden, T., 323
Heiman, J. R., 216
Heinberg, L. J., 389
Heitlinger, L. A., 391
Hekmat, H., 13
Held, R., 121
Hemenway, D., 53, 146, 151, 186, 209
Hennigan, K. M., 195, 196, 234
Herskovits, M. J., 315
Hertel, P. T., 153
Hertwig, R., 43
Heuer, H., 95
Hewstone, M., 322
Hickey, C., 126
Hickson, G. B., 389
High accuracy found in 2000 elections, 202
Hilts, P. J., 30
Hindahl, J., 271
Hinney, A., 389
Hippler, H. J., 210
Ho, L. W., 130
Hobson, J. A., 154, 155
Hoek, J., 223
Hoekstra-Weebers, J. E. H. M., 296
Hoffart, A., 130
Hoffman, J. M., 151
Hofstetter, M., 180
Holahan, C. K., 249, 290, 295
Hollister, L. E., 272
Holmes, T. H., 87, 88, 89
Hong, Y., 216
Horvitz, D., 226
Houghton, L. L., 216
Hounshell, G. W., 62

Howell, D.C., 242, 354, 374
Hrycaiko, D., 301
Hubbard, M., 148, 150
Hulse, S. H., 96
Humphreys, L., 275, 276
Huon, G. F., 389
Husain, G., 62

Imrie, R., 119
Inzlicht, M., 331
Irvin, B. C., 121
Iwamasa, G. Y., 328, 329, 330

Jackson, C. J., 216
Jacob, T., 278
Jaspers, J. P. C., 296
Jauch, L. R., 55, 56
Jenni, D. A., 268, 373
Jenni, M. A., 268, 277, 373
Jennings, C., 16
Jensen, G. F., 234
Ji, L. J., 323
Joachim, W., 130
Jobes, D. R., 146
Johnson, M., 272
Johnson, T. P., 215
Johnston, M. I., 388
Jones, H. E., 284
Jones, L. A., 121
Jones, W. H., 23
Joseph, S., 142
Judd, C. M., 101, 291, 391, 392
Juhnke, R., 8

Kakuma, T., 152
Kammermann, S. K., 193, 194
Kamps, W. A., 296
Kaneto, H., 90
Kaplan, C. D., 226
Kaplan, M. D., 262
Karabotsos, G., 254
Kasof, J., 123
Katsev, R., 7
Kaufman, P., 312, 313
Kazdin, A. E., 303
Keefe, F. J., 250
Kellett, S., 299
Kidder, L. H., 101, 291, 391, 392
Kiecker, P., 124

Kiesswetter, E., 95
Kim, B. S. K., 312
King, M. F., 216
King, R., 68
Kjormo, O., 142
Klawans, H., 315, 316
Kleck, G., 53, 209
Klein, S., 312, 313
Knauper, B., 210
Knight, R. A., 253
Kogler, B. E., 293
Kolata, G., 31
Komiya, N., 250
Kopper, B. A., 250
Korf, D., 226
Korn, J. H., 43
Koshland, D., 226
Koss, M. P., 254
Kovar, M. G., 207
Kozulin, A., 142
Krechevsky, M., 131
Kremar, M., 234
Krishnan, A., 123
Krosnick, J. A., 209, 216, 217, 218
Kumari, R., 123
Kwiatkowski, S. J., 130, 153
Kwon, J. Y., 312, 313
Ky, K. N., 60, 62

LaBrie, R., 215
LaGreca, A. M., 292, 293, 294, 296
Lampter, C., 288
Lane, J. D., 149
Lang, F. R., 236
Langerak, F., 222
Langhout, R. D., 252, 253
LaRose, R., 220, 223
Larrabee, A. L., 328, 329, 330
Latane, B., 7
Lawson, C., 43
LeBoeuf, B. J., 265
Lee, Y-T., 126
Leirer, V. O., 177
Lepper, M. R., 148, 150
Leung, K., 315, 317
Leventhal, G., 196, 197
Levitt, L., 196, 197

Lewis, C. A., 142
Lifton, R. J., 29
Lilly, R. L., 247, 248
Lindsay, R. C. L., 44
Lobel, M., 123
Lockwood, K. A., 152
Loftus, E. F., 122, 124, 146
Lonner, W. J., 309, 314, 315
Lopez, S. R., 309, 310, 318
Lord, F. M., 136, 354
Ludwig, J., 210
Luria, A. R., 305
Lustina, M. J., 126

MacDonald, S., 299
Mackin, R. S., 88
Maddux, J. E., 245
Magley, V. J., 254
Maguire, M. G., 120, 121
Mangione, T. W., 146, 151, 186
Manucia, G. K., 7
Marans, D. G., 46
Marian, V., 149, 322
Marlowe, C. M., 8
Marshall, G. N., 250, 251, 255
Martin, G. L., 301
Martinez-Ebers, V., 223
Martinsen, E. W., 130
Mason, J. B., 181
Masten, W. G., 93
Matsumoto, D., 18, 309, 310,
    322, 324, 325, 330
Matthews, G. A., 132, 142
Matthews, R., 46
May, C. P., 180
Mayer, J. D., 131
Mazzoni, G. A., 122, 146
McAuliffe, W. E., 215
McCallum, R. C., 255, 256
McClung, H. J., 391
McCollam, P., 142
McCoy, S. K., 184, 185, 189
McCoy-Roberts, L., 292,
    293, 296
McGuire, W. J., 58, 59, 60
McKenna, F. P., 150, 162,
    163, 190
Mechanic, M., 16
Meinster, M. O., 141, 142

Mennella, J. A., 148, 149
Mercandante, B., 245
Merritt, R. D., 328, 329, 330
Merton, R. K., 68
Meston, C. M., 216
Meyer, C., 388
Midkiff, K., 231
Milgram, S., 28, 40, 41, 42
Miller, D.C., 123
Miller, E. R., 204
Miller, M. A., 87, 88
Miller, N. E., 49, 58
Miller, R. S., 43
Mills, C. G., 303, 305
Minors, P., 87
Mitchel, E. F., 389
Modern Language Association
    of America, 75
Mohr, D.C., 87
Moles, A., 272, 273, 274
Moncrieff, J., 13
Mook, D. G., 135
Moore, S. R., 268, 269
Morris, J. S., 142
Morrow, D. G., 177
Mortazavi, S., 313
Moseley, J. B., 13
The Mother's Encyclopedia, 318
Muller, F. R., 16
Munro, D., 18
Munsterberg, H., 18, 19, 78
Murray, L. A., 146, 166
Murray, R. D., 391

Nadler, A., 8
Neisser, E., 149, 322
Nelson, C. E., 8
Nelson, J. E., 124
Neville, H. A., 247, 248
Newcomb, M. D., 194
Newman, J., 62
Nicholson, R., 13
Nicholson, T., 87
Niemi-Pynttaeri, J., 143
NIMH Multisite HIV
    Prevention Trial, 151
Nisbett, M., 23
Nisbett, R. E., 323
Nixon, S. J., 2, 15

Norenzayan, A., 212
Norman, P. A., 103
North, C. S., 2, 15
North, M., 270
Novi, M. J., 141, 142
Nugent, W. R., 196
Nunes, L. M., 104
Nygaard, L. C., 181

O'Connor, P. J., 7
Odom, S. L., 269
Office of Research Integrity:
    Handling misconduct, 31
Ogawa, I., 269
Oliver, G. K., 303, 305
Olkin, I., 119
O'Malley, K., 13
Ong, E., 121
Orne, M. T., 44, 126
Ornstein, R., 88
Ortmann, A., 43
Osman, A., 250
Ottati, V., 126
Overall, J. E., 272
Owren, M. J., 147

Paksoy, C., 181
Palmer, C. T., 10, 16
Palmieri, P. A., 252, 253
Park, D.C., 323
Parkinson, S. R., 130, 153
Pasini, A., 262, 272, 280
Pavur, R., 292, 293, 296
Pelham, W. E., 149, 154, 169
Peng, K., 323
Pennell, B-E., 223
Pepler, D. J., 279, 280
Perceptions of Foreign Countries, 390
Peregrine, P. N., 270
Peters, M., 319
Petersen, N.J., 13
Phillips, D. P., 389
Phillips-Bute, B. G., 149
Phinney, J. S., 310, 311
Pieper, C. F., 149
Plous, S., 48, 49, 56, 97
Pollatsek, A., 182
Pott, M., 324
Powell, M. C., 213

Presser, S., 216
Price, W. F., 18, 314
Pyszczynski, T., 184, 185, 189

Queen, J. S., 181
Quinn, D. M., 126
Quinn, G. E., 120, 121

Radford, B., 23
Radner, D., 23
Radner, M., 23
Rahe, R. H., 87, 88, 89
Ramey, D. W., 119
Ranieri, W. F., 130
Rasinski, K. A., 212
Rauscher, F. H., 60, 62
Ray, J. J., 216
Recarte, M. A., 104
Reese, H. W., 182
Reid, D. H., 142
Reid, J. K., 116, 142, 143
Reilly, C., 231
Renner, M. J., 88
Research Ethics and the Medical
    Profession: *Report of the*
    Advisory Committee on
    Human Radiation
    Experiments, 29
Reynolds, P. D., 37, 276
Richter, P., 130
Ring, K., 41
Rissmiller, D. J., 130
Roberts, R. D., 129, 132
Robertson, L. C., 96
Robins, R. W., 57, 58
Rockwood, T. H., 209
Rodriguez, C. E., 311
Rodriguez, I. A., 152, 153
Rogers, J., 392, 394
Rogler, L. H., 325, 326, 327
Rosenbach, J. H., 62
Rosenberg, M., 156
Rosenthal, R., 97, 122, 128
Rosnow, R. L., 97, 128
Ross, L. M., 69, 148, 150
Rothbaum, F., 324
Rothman, D. J., 30
Rothman, M., 123
Rowe, R. M., 150, 162, 163, 190

Rubin, D., 226
Rubin, Z., 46
Ryan, L., 180
Ryan, N. M., 389
Ryff, C. D., 245, 246

Sagi, A., 324
Salovey, P., 131
Sambraus, H. H., 263
Sangster, R. L., 209
Sawyer, T. J., 96
Schafer, W. D., 123
Schaie, K. W., 180, 283, 284,
    289, 296
Scharrer, E., 234
Schefft, B. K., 130, 142, 153
Scheibe, K. T., 126
Schellenberg, E. G., 62
Schiffman, S. S., 151
Schillewaert, N., 222
Schneider, S. L., 8
Schnellman, J. D., 309
Scholer, S. J., 389
Schram, C. M., 331
Schul, Y., 149, 150
Schuller, R. A., 61
Schuman, H., 223
Schwarz, N., 210, 212,
    213, 323
Schwibbe, M., 271
Scott, S. K., 142
Sears, R. R., 249, 290, 295
Sebastian-Galles, N., 150
Sechrest, G. B., 166
Segall, M. H., 309, 314, 315
Seilhamer, R. A., 278
Selten, J. P., 311
Shaligram, C., 215
Shapira, R., 8
Shapiro, D., 142
Shariat, S., 2, 15
Shaw, G. L., 60, 62
Sheffield, J., 87
Sher, K. J., 255
Sherer, M., 245
Sheridan, J. F., 251
Sherrod, N. B., 250
Shillinglaw, R., 196
Shin, C. H., 120, 121

Silverman, W. K., 292, 293,
    294, 296
Singer, B., 23
Singer, E., 204
Smith, A. P., 89
Smith, B. H., 149, 154, 169
Smith, C. S., 146, 231
Smith, D. S., 146
Smith, E. R., 101, 291, 391, 392
Smith, J. A., 304
Smith, K. W., 53, 210, 291
Smith, P. L., 142
Smith, R. E., 46
Smith-Laittan, F., 304
Snijders, T., 227
Snowden, P. L., 261
Sobel, D., 68, 88
Soliday, E., 44
Sommers, S. R., 164, 165
Soto-Faraco, S., 150
Spalletta, G., 272, 280
Spencer, S. J., 126
Spijkers, W., 95
Staats, A., 13
Staats, P., 13
Stacks, J., 93
Stangor, C., 166
Stankov, L., 129, 132
Stanley, J. C., 184, 331
Stanton, A. L., 44
Steele, C. M., 126, 331
Steer, R. A., 130
Steinberg, N., 16
Steinmetz, G., 7
Stephen, J., 142
Sterk, C., 226
Sternberg, R. J., 131
Stevens, J. C., 8, 151
Stevens, S. S., 136, 354
Stice, E., 389
Stiles, D. A., 309
Stinson, L., 216
Stokes, S. J., 9
Stolberg, S. G., 30
Stoltzfus, E. R., 180
Stolzenberg, L., 196, 197
Straus, M. A., 243
Strickgold, R., 154, 155
Strober, M., 288

Stumpfhauser, A., 46
Sue, S., 320
Sugarman, D. B., 243
Sundblom, D. M., 143
Sutton, C., 16
Swan, S., 254
Sweeney, C. J., 123

Takooshian, H., 7
Tang-Martinez, Z., 16
Taylor, S. J., 395, 396
Teeter, P. A., 142
Tennenbaum, D., 278
Thomas, L., 290, 291, 292
Thomas, R. L., 152, 153
Thompason, S., 146
Thompson, J. K., 389
Thompson, W. F., 62
Thornhill, R., 10, 16
Todd, J. L., 245
Todorov, A., 210
Tooney, N., 16
Trapnell, P. D., 216
Trice, R., 391, 395, 396
Trofimova, I., 313
Troisi, A., 262, 266, 272, 273, 274, 279, 280
Trope, Y., 159, 161, 169
Turbott, S. H., 178
Tyrrell, D. A., 89

Ullman, S. E., 254
Underwood, B. J., 96

Vaid, J., 180
Valois, R. F., 193, 194

van de Vijver, F. J. R., 315, 317
Van Elburg, A. A., 389
van Hanswijck de Jonge, L., 388
van Ijzendoorn, M. H., 324
Varma, A., 234
Veen, N., 311
Velleman, P. F., 137, 1354
Velten Jr., E., 142, 143, 144, 152
Vernberg, E. M., 292, 293, 294, 296
Vincent, J. E., 7
Vink, T., 389
Vispoel, W. P., 216
Vonesh, E. F., 177, 180
Von Thurn, D. R., 204

Wagle, A. C., 130
Wagle, S. A., 130
Wainer, H., 103
Waldo, C. R., 61
Walker, E. F., 272
Wallace, W. P., 96
Waller, G., 388
Wallston, K., 41
Walsh, M., 126
Walsh, W. B., 46
Wang, E. U. I., 250, 251, 255
Wann, D. L., 142
Watkins, D., 313
Webster, B. S., 390
Weisz, J., 324
Weizmann, F., 313, 319
Welch, S. L., 103
Well, A. D., 182
Wentland, E. J., 53, 210, 291

Wessely, S., 13
Westen, D., 5
White, M., 31, 137
Whitehouse, W. G., 146, 166
Wilcox, R. R., 354
Wilkins, R. H., 250
Wilkinson, J. B., 181
Wilkinson, L., 77, 137
Willimack, D. K., 223
Wilson, A. E., 156, 158
Wilson, A. M., 142
Wilson, D. W., 18
Winkielman, P., 210
Wood, M. D., 255
Wood, P. K., 255
Worell, J., 245
Wutzke, S. E., 293
Wyer, R. S., 46

Yang, P. H., 312
Yee, A. H., 313, 319
Yesavage, J. A., 177
York, J., 87
Young, G. C., 299
Yule, W., 15

Zadnik, K., 121
Zajonc, R. B., 90
Zeidner, M., 132
Zettle, R. D., 216
Zheng, R., 389
Zimbardo, P. G., 28
Zinner, D., 271
Zuckerman, M., 317, 318
Zusne, L., 23

SUBJECT INDEX

ABAB design, 298–299
ABA design, 298–299
Absolutism, 314
Abstract, 75–79
Acquiescence, 217
Active deception, 45
Alternate bivariate correlations, 243
American Psychological Association (APA), 32–37
   Code of Conduct, 34
   ethical guidelines, 32–37
Analysis of covariance (ANCOVA), 169, 296
Analysis of variance (ANOVA), 136, 168–170, 296, 359–371
   statistical review, 359–371
      factorial, 366–371
      one-way independent groups, 360–363
      one-way repeated measures, 363–366
Animal research, 48–50
   ethics and, 48–50
   reasons for decreases in, 57
Anonymity, 36
Anthropomorphism, 264
Applied research, 90–91
A priori method, 13–14
Archival research, 93, 387–396
   data analysis in archival research, 395–396
      content analysis, 396
   sources of information, 387–392
      physical traces, 391–392
      statistical records, 389–390
      written records, 390–391
   validity and reliability issues, 392–395
      changes in archived material over time, 395
      multiple interpretations, 394–395
      selective deposit and selective survival, 393–394
Aspirational goals, 32
Asymmetric transfer, 181
Attention deficit hyperactive disorder (ADHD), 154
Attitude questions, 212–213

Attrition, 186, 292–295
Authority, 12–13

Back translation, 326
Baseline, 193
Basic (theoretical) research, 90–91
Beck Depression Inventory (BDI), 143–145
Behavior, 115–117
   checklist, 279
   determining the causes of, 115–117
      requirements for cause-effect relationships, 116–117
      trying to determine causation in research, 116
   differences in simple and complex, 323–324
   experimental analysis of, 297
Behaviorism, 57
Beneficence and nonmaleficence, 32–33
Between-groups design, 173
Bivariate correlation, 242
Blind study, 125

Case study, 92–93, 303–304
Causal ambiguity, 117
Cause-effect relationships, requirements for, 116–117
Census *versus* sample, 201–202
Chain-referral
   methods, 226
   sampling, 105–106
Chi-square, statistical review, 371–375
   goodness of fit test, 372–373
   test of independence, 373–375
Chronically accessible information, 212
Clinical research, ethological observations in, 272–274
Closed-ended questions, examples of, table, 206
Cluster sampling, 102
   of behaviors, 270–271
Cohort effects, 284
Cohort sequential studies, 288–289

Color-Blind Racial Attitudes Scale (CoBRAS), 247
  questions on, table, 247
Complete counterbalancing, 181
Conducting an experiment: general principles,
      113–138
  choosing a methodology, 114–115
  determining causes of behavior, 115–117
    determining causation in research, 116
    requirements for cause-effect relationships,
        116–117
  ethics, 118
  experimental control, 119–124
    extraneous variables and confounds, 120–124
  experimenter effects, 124
  interaction effects between experimenters and
      participants, 127–128
  logic of experimental manipulation, 117–118
  participant effects, 124–127
    Hawthorne Effect, 125–127
  validity, 128–137
    construct, 128–131
    convergent and divergent, 131–132
    internal and external, 132–136
    statistical conclusion, 136–137
Conducting your study, 89–96
  choosing your methodology, 91–93
    approaches to psychological research, 91–93
  determining research setting, 90–91
  selecting research materials and procedures,
      93–96
    importance of methodology, 95–96
Confidentiality, 36–37
Confirmation bias, 255–256
Confirmatory factor analysis, 247
Confound, 120
Construct validity, 67, 128–131
  intelligence: a controversial concept, 131
Content analysis, 396
Content validity, 325
Continuous real-time measurement, 266
Control, 5–6
Control group, 117
Controversy boxes
  are men better than women at mathematics?, 331
  can animals rape?, 265
  can we spot prejudice?, 166

  can you stop smoking by watching TV?, 194
  do captive animals behave abnormally?, 263
  does culture make a difference in neurological
      diagnosis?, 316
  does media violence promote violent
      behavior?, 234
  does music make you smart?, 62
  does sex + neuroticism = death?, 185
  do laws really change our behaviors?, 197
  do 4 million adolescents smoke?, 207
  do women fear success?, 123
  do you taste pointed chickens or see colored
      numbers?, 305
  how many students think of suicide as a "way
      out"?, 287
  is public sex really private?, 276
  is the Head Start program effective?, 108
  is the U.S. census flawed?, 203
  mental health of college students, 254
  scientists competing to finish second, 68
  should researchers deceive participants?, 43
  should we study depression experimentally?, 144
  should women serve as jurors?, 19
  why do men rape?, 10
  withholding treatment in medical research, 119
Convenience sampling, 104
Convergent validity, 111, 131–132
Corporate research, ethical problems in, 31–32
Correlational analyses, 375–378
  linear regression analysis, 377–378
  Pearson product-moment correlation, 375–377
Correlational analysis, 233, 254–256
Correlational measure, 242
Correlational research, 92, 229–256
  correlational studies, 230–232
    finding relationships, 230–231
    making predictions, 231–232
  correlations with multiple variables, 243–253
    cross-lagged studies, 249–251
    factor analysis, 247–249
    multiple regression, 244–247
    path analysis, 251–253
  limitations of multivariate correlational analysis,
      254–256
    confirmation bias, 255–256
    generalizability, 255

traditional tests, 242–243
  alternate bivariate correlations, 243
  Pearson product-moment correlation,
    242–243
using the correlational approach, 233–241
  correlational analysis, 235–236
  correlational studies, 233–234
  factors affecting size of correlation coefficient,
    238–241
  positive and negative correlations, 236
  strength of association, 236–238
Correlation coefficient, factors affecting size of,
    238–241
  heterogeneous subgroups, 240–241
  nonlinearity, 239–240
  restrictions in range, 240
Cost-benefit analysis, 28
Council for Marketing and Opinion Research,
    204–205
  ethics code, 205
Counterbalancing, 181
Covariance rule, 116
Cover story, 44, 125
Creating knowledge, 3–4
Criteria for race, 317–318
Criterion variable, 107, 232
Cross-cultural issues and science, 18
Cross-lagged studies, 249–251
Cross-sectional *versus* longitudinal research, 283–285
Cultural and individual differences in research,
    307–332
  biological basis for race, question of, 317–319
    criteria for race, 317–318
    current biological insights regarding race,
      318–319
  cross-cultural concepts in psychology, 314–317
    are psychological constructs universal?,
      314–315
    issues in cross-cultural research, 315–317
  cultural factors in mental health research, 325–330
    content validity, 325–326
    cross-cultural diagnoses, 328–330
    cross-cultural norms, 327–328
    translation problems, 326–327
  cultural perspectives, 308–310
    defining culture, 309–310

defining an individual's culture, ethnicity, and
    race, 310–313
  criteria for inclusion in a group, 311–312
  social issues and cultural research, 312–313
practical issues in cultural research, 320–322
  lack of appropriate training among
    researchers, 321–322
sex and gender, 330–332
why concepts of culture and ethnicity are
    essential, 322–325
  differences due to language and thought
    processes, 322–323
  differences in simple and complex behaviors,
    323–324
  similarities and differences within the same
    culture, 324–325
Cultural perspectives, 308–310
  defining culture, 309–310
  race and ethnicity, 310
Cultural values and science, 17–18
Culture, defining, 309–310

Data analysis, 168–170
  in archival research, 395–396
  experiments with one independent variable,
    168–169
  factorial designs, 169–170
  in longitudinal research, 295–296
  in observational research, 280
  with repeated measures designs, 182
Data driven, 9
Debriefing, effects of, on research, 36
Defining and measuring variables, 152–153
Defining concepts and variables, 84–87
  diversity of operational definitions, 88–89
  importance of culture and context, 87–88
Dehoaxing, 36
Demand characteristics, 126
Dependent variable (DV), 87, 151–152
Description, 4
Desensitization, 36
Differing approaches in psychology, 109–111
  in different journals, 109–110
  different types of participants in different
    journals, 110
  making choices in your research design, 110–111

Directionality problem, 233
Discussion, 78–79
Divergent validity, 131–132
Double-blind study, 125

Electronic databases, 71
Emic, 314
Empirical approach, 14
Erroneous beliefs, 20–22
Ethics, 27–50
    APA guidelines, 32–37
        aspirational goals and enforceable rules, 32–33
        ethical standards as they affect you, 33–37
    in experimental/clinical research, 118
    human side of observational research, 275–277
    importance of social context in research, 40–43
        ethical issues, 40–41
        Milgram's research on obedience, 40–42
    legal requirements and ethics in research, 37–39
        institutional review boards, 37, 39
    and research involving deception, 44–47
        effects of debriefing, 46–47
        some research requires deception, 44–45
    and research with animals, 48–50
        arguments and counterarguments, 49–50
    in survey research, 204
    unethical research practices, 29–32
        in corporate research, 31–32
        in early years, 29–30
        problems today, 30–31
        in psychiatric research, 31
    and web-based research, 47–48
Ethnicity, 310
Ethological Coding System for Interviews (ECSI), 266, 272
Ethological observations in clinical research, 272–274
Ethology, 262–263
Etic, 314
Evaluation apprehension, 126
Evolutionary psychology, 264
Experience, 14
Experiment, 117
Experimental control, 119–124
    extraneous variables and confounds, 120–124
Experimental design, simple and complex, 139–170
    data analysis, 168–170

experiments with one independent variable, 168–169
    factorial designs, 169–170
defining and measuring variables, 152–153
dependent variables, types of, 151–153
identifying research designs, 166–168
independent and dependent variables, 143–147
independent variables, types of, 147–151
    created by different types of manipulations, 150–151
    qualitative and quantitative, 147–150
interactions between variables, 157–165
    examining main effects and interactions, 159–162
    patterns of interactions, 162–164
    what interactions mean, 159
main effect, 156–157
psychological concepts, 140–143
    measuring complex concepts, 140–141
    operational definitions, 141–143
single and multiple independent variables, 153–156
Experimental designs, 173–196
    quasi-experimental, 182–196
    repeated measures, 173–182
Experimental group, 117
Experimental manipulation, logic of, 117–118
Experimental realism, 136
Experimental research, 92
Experimenter bias, 124
Experimenter effects, 119–124
Explanation, 4–5
Exploratory factor analysis, 247
Ex post facto study, 145
External validity, 134–135
Extraneous variable, 120

Factor analysis, 247–249
Factorial design, 155, 169–170
Falsifiability, 5
Fidelity and responsibility, 33
Formatting your manuscript, research report, 334–335

Gender-related performance, stereotypes and, 330–332
Generalizability, 255
Generalization, 100–101

Gerontologist, 282
Goodness of fit test, statistics review, 372–373
Government's role in science, 16–17
Grounded theory, 304

Hawthorne Effect, 125–127
Head Start program, 108–109
Heterogeneous subgroups, 240–241
Hidden populations, 226
    finding, 226–227
Higher order correlation, 243
Higher order interaction, 159
History, 187
Human side of observational research, 274–280
    ethics, 275–277
    observer effects, 279–280
    participant-observer interactions, 277
    subject reactivity, 277–279
Hypothetical construct, 86–87

Ideas, informal and formal sources of, 54–56
    continuum of research ideas, 54–56
Impression management, 215
Independent and dependent variables, 143–147
Independent groups *t*-test, 356–358
    supplemental analysis, 358
    worked example for, 357–358
Independent variable (IV), 87, 147–151
    types of, 147–151
        created by different types of manipulations,
            150–151
        qualitative and quantitative, 147–150
Institutional review board (IRB), 28, 37–39, 275
    types of research not requiring approval by,
        table, 39
Instructional variable, 150
Instrumentation, 187
Integrity, 33
Interaction effect, 157–158
    between experimenters and participants, 127–128
Internal validity, 132–134, 184–189
    rule, 116
    threats to, 184–189
        associated with measurement, 187–189
        associated with participants, 186–187
Internet research, 219–225; *see also* Web-based
    research

considerations for, 219–225
    designing surveys for the world wide web, 223
    internet surveys, 220–222
    respondent motivation, 223–224
    technical characteristics of user's system,
        224–225
    user knowledge, 225
Internet surveys, 220–222
Interobserver reliability
Interpretation paradox, 317
Interrater (interobserver) reliability, 107
Interrupted time series design, 193
Interval and ratio scales, 355–356
Introduction, as part of research, 75–77
Intuition, 12

Journal of Applied Psychology (JAP), 109
Journal of Comparative Psychology, 49
*Journal of Experimental Psychology: Animal Behavior
    Processes*, 49
Journal of Experimental Psychology: Applied (JEP:
    Applied), 109
Journals, 109–110
    different approaches in, 109–110
    different types of participants, 110
Justice, 33

Key informant sampling, 227
Knowing, ways of, 11–13
    authority, 12–13
    experience, 14
    logic, or a priori method, 13–14
    obvious or intuition, 12
    scientific method, 14–16

Latency effect, 181
Legal requirements and ethics in research,
    37–39
Likert-type scale, 18
Linear regression analysis, 377–378
Linear relationship, 239
Literature review, 69–74
    defining, 69–70
    how to conduct, 71–74
        starting the search, 71–74
        using electronic database, 71
Logic, 13–14

Longitudinal research, 281–296
  common themes in, 283
  cross-sectional *versus*, 283–285
  data analysis in, 295–296
  issues in, 291–295
    attrition, 292–295
    retrospective and prospective studies, 291–292
  varieties of, 285–290
    cohort sequential studies, 288–289
    cohort studies, 288
    panel studies, 290
    trend studies, 285–286
Longitudinal study, 93

Main effect, 156–157
  and interactions, examining, 159–162
Manipulated variable, 145
Matched samples/repeated measures *t*-test, 358–359
Materials and apparatus, 77
Maturation threat, 186
Measured variable, 145
Measurement error, 106
Measuring complex concepts, 140–141
Memory questions, 209–212
Mental health research
  cultural factors in, 325–330
Methodology, 91–93, 114–115, 205–206
  choosing, practicalities involved, 114–115
  choosing your, 91–93
    approaches to psychological research, 91
    major methodologies used by psychologists,
      table, 94–95
    selecting, for survey research, 205–206
Methods, 77
Milgram, Stanley
  research on obedience, 40–42
    criticisms of, 41
    Milgram's defense, 41–42
Misinterpretations of research, 20
Multi-Factor Emotional Intelligence Scale
    (MEIS), 132
Multiple analysis of variance (MANOVA), 169
Multiple baseline design, 299–300
Multiple regression, 244–247
Multivariate correlational analysis, limitations of,
    254–256
  confirmation bias, 255–256
  generalizability, 255

Multivariate statistics, 243
Mundane realism, 136

National Assessment of Educational Progress
    (NAEP), 285
Natural behaviors, studying, 260–265
  describing the behavior of nonhuman animals,
    263–265
  ethology, 262–263
  studying complex human behavior, 261–262
Naturalistic observation, 44, 260
Natural pairs, 178
Negative (indirect) correlation, 236
N of 1 Randomized Clinical Trial (RCT), 300–301
Nominal scales, 354–355
Nondifferentiation, 219
Nonequivalent control group design, 191–193
Nonhuman animals, describing behavior of, 263–265
Nonlinear relationship, 239
Nonprobability sampling, 103–106
  chain-referral, 105–106
  convenience, 104
  purposive (judgmental), 105
  quota, 104–105
Nonsampling error, 103
Number of Problematic Others (NPO), 246
Nuremberg Code, 37
  ten points of, table, 38

Objective, 8–9
Observational research: studying patterns in the
    natural world, 91–92, 257–280
  approaches to, 265–268
    practical steps, 265–267
    structured and unstructured observations, 267
  data analysis, 280
  ethological observations in clinical research,
    272–274
  human side of, 274–280
    ethics, 275–277
    observer effects, 279–280
    participant-observer interactions, 277
    subject reactivity, 277–279
  sampling issues, 268–272
    estimating the frequency and duration of
      behaviors, 271
    methods of sampling events during
      observation, 269–271

number of sampling blocks, 268–269
scientific *versus* casual observation, 259
studying natural behaviors, 260–265
    describing the behavior of nonhuman animals,
      263–265
    ethology, 262–263
    studying complex human behavior, 261–262
Observer bias, 279
Observer drift, 279
Obvious, 12
One-drop rule, 317
One-group pretest-posttest design, 189–190
One-way independent groups analysis of variance
    (ANOVA), 360
    statistical review, 360
One-way repeated measures analysis of variance
    (ANOVA), 363–366
    statistical review, 363–366
One/zero sampling, 271
Open-ended question, examples, table, 206
Operational definition, 86, 141–143
Optimizing, 218
Order effects, 180
Ordinal scales, 355
Overdetermined, 6

Panel study, 249, 290
Partial counterbalancing, 182
Participant effects, 124–127
    Hawthorne Effect, 125–127
Participant-observer interactions, 277
Participants, 77
Particularistic research, 260
Passive deception, 45
Path analysis, 252–254
Path coefficients, 252
Pearson product-moment correlation, 242–243,
    375–377
    statistics review, 375–377
Peer review, 11, 70–71
    effect of, on research literature, 70–71
Placebo group, 117
Plagiarism, 37
Planned comparison, 169
Population, 97, 203
Positive (direct) correlation, 236
Post hoc comparison, 169
Post-traumatic stress disorder (PTSD), 2, 299

Prediction, 5–6, 232
    study, 232
Predictive validity, 107
Predictor variable, 107, 232
Probability sampling, 100–103
    cluster sampling, 102
    simple random sampling, 101
    stratified random sampling, 102
    systematic sampling, 101–102
Procedure, 77
Prospective study, 291–292
Pseudoscience, 22–25
    characteristics of, 24–25
    science and, 22–25
Psychiatric research, ethical problems in, 31
Psychological Abstracts (PA), 71
Psychological concepts, 140–143
    measuring complex concepts, 140–141
    operational definitions, 141–143
Psychological terminology, everyday, 20
Psychology, 65, 109–111, 314–317
    cross-cultural concepts in, 314–317
    differing approaches in different areas of, 109–111
    future of the web in, 65
PsycINFO, 71–74
Public, 11
Publication Manual of the American Psychological
    Association, 333–334, 349
Purposive (judgmental) sampling, 105

Qualitative research, 93
Qualitative variable, 147–148
Quantitative variable, 148
Quasi-experiment, 92, 145
Quasi-experimental designs, 182–196
    causation and, 183–184
    combining experimental and, 184
    threats to internal validity, 184–189
        associated with measurement, 187–189
        associated with participants, 186–187
        major threats of a research project, table, 188
    types of, 189–196
        interrupted time series design, 193
        nonequivalent control group design, 191–193
        one-group pretest-posttest design, 189–190
        replicated interrupted time series design,
          194–196
        static-group comparison design, 190–191

Question, 206–213
  content, 209–213
    attitude questions, 212–213
    memory questions, 209–212
  types, 206–209
    closed-ended, 206
    open-ended, 206
Quota sampling, 104–105

Race, 310, 318–320
  criteria for, 317–318
  current biological insights, 318–319
    current controversies, 320
    historical error, 320
Random assignment, 132–133
Randomized clinical trial (RCT), 117, 272
Random selection, 134
Realism in research, 135–136
References, 80
Relativism, 314–315
Reliability, 106–107
Repeated measures designs, 167, 173–182
  advantages of, 173–179
    finding enough participants, 177
    increasing efficiency in data collection, 173–174
    increasing validity of data, 174–177
    reducing error in measurement, 177–179
  data analysis with, 182
  limitations to, 179–182
    possible but unlikely repeated measures designs, 179–180
    sequence and order effects, 180–182
    subject (participant) variables, 180
Replicable, 9, 11
Replicated interrupted time series design, 194–196
Replication
  conceptual, 67
  exact, 67
  with extension, 67
  role of, 66–69
Representative sample, 97
Research
  with animals, ethics and, 48–50
  approaches to psychological, 91–93
  archival, 387–396
  correlational, 92, 229–256
  cultural and individual differences, 307–332

in depth: longitudinal and single-case studies, 281–306
  design, 110–111, 166–168
    identifying, 166–168
    making choices in your, 110–111
  developing ideas, 58–62
    generating hypotheses, 59–60
  effects of debriefing on, 46
  goals of, 4–7
    control, 5–6
    description, 4
    explanation, 4–5
    prediction, 5–6
  how ideas develop, 52–58
    effect of theory, 56–58
    informal and formal sources of, 54–56
  legal requirements and ethics in, 37–39
  longitudinal, 281–296
  mental health, cultural factors in, 325–330
  observational: studying patterns in the natural world, 257–280
  planning: generating a question, 51–80
  selecting materials and procedures, 93–96
  writing a report, 333–351
Research, planning: generating a question, 51–80
  developing research ideas, 58–62
    generating hypotheses, 59–60
  journal article, how to read, 75–79
    understanding the format of a research paper, 75–79
  literature review, conducting, 71–74
    starting the search, 71–74
    using electronic database, 71
  process of research idea development, 52–58
    effect of theory, 56–58
    informal and formal sources of ideas, 54–56
  reviewing the literature, 69–71
    effect of peer-review on research literature, 70–71
  role of replication, 66–69
  virtual laboratory: research on the internet, 62–66
Research, planning: practical issues, 81–112
  choosing who to study, 97–100
    how many participants, 99–100
    nature of participants, 97–99
  conducting your study, 89–96

choosing your methodology, 91–93
determining research setting, 90–91
selecting research materials and procedures, 93–96
creating variables, 83–89
carrying out a literature search, 84
defining concepts and variables, 84–87
differing approaches, 109–111
in different journals, 109–110
different types of participants in different journals, 110
making choices in your research design, 110–111
making useful measurements, 106–109
reliability and validity, 106–107
SAT: questions of reliability and validity, 107–109
nonprobability sampling, 103–106
chain-referral sampling, 105–106
convenience sampling, 104
purposive (judgmental) sampling, 105
quota sampling, 104–105
planning questions, 82–83
probability sampling, 100–103
cluster sampling, 102
simple random sampling, 101
stratified random sampling, 102
systematic sampling, 101–102
Research designs, identifying, 166–168
Research ideas, how they develop, 52–58
effect of theory, 56–58
informal and formal sources, 54–56
Research report/paper, 75–79
format of, 75–79
abstract section, 75–79
discussion section, 78–79
introduction section, 75–77
materials and apparatus, 77
methods section, 77
participants section, 77
procedure section, 77
references section, 80
results section, 77–78
writing, 333–351
abstract, 337
discussing your findings, 344–345
formatting your manuscript, 334–335

introduction, 337–338
method, 338–339
apparatus and materials, 339
participants, 339
procedure, 339
references, 345–349
example formats in APA style, table, 346–349
results, 340–344
example tables in APA style, figure, 341
figures, 340–343
statistical results, 344
tables, 340
title page, 335–337
running head, 336–337
short title, 335–336
title and author information, 337
writing style, 349–351
avoiding biased language, 350–351
precision of expression, 350
Respect for people's rights and dignity, 33
Respondent-driven sampling, 227
Respondent motivation, internet research, 223–224
Response bias, 214–219
acquiescence, 217
minimizing satisficing, 218–219
satisficing *versus* optimizing, 217–218
social desirability, 215–217
studying sensitive issues, 214–215
Restricted range problem, 240
Results, 77–78
Retrospective and prospective studies, 291–292
Role playing, 44

Sample, 97
Sampling, 205
finding hidden populations, issues in, 226–227
frame, 205
issues in observational research, 268–272
methods of sampling events during observation, 269–271
number of sampling blocks, 268–269
types of, 225–227
SAT: questions of reliability and validity, 107–109
Satisficing, 217–219
minimizing the occurrence of, 218–219
versus optimizing, 217–218

Scales of measurement, 354–356
  interval and ratio scales, 355–356
  nominal scales, 354–355
Scales of Psychological Well-Being, 246
Scatter diagram, 238
Science, 16–22
  cross-cultural issues and, 18
  government's role in, 16–17
  and popular media, 18–22
    erroneous beliefs, 20–22
    misinterpretations of research, 20
    psychological terminology in everday use, 20
    scientific "breakthroughs," 22
  and pseudoscience, 22–25
Science and culture, interaction between, 16–18
  cross-cultural issues and science, 18
  cultural values and science, 17–18
Scientific "breakthroughs," 22
Scientific knowledge, 8–11
Scientific method, 14–16
Scientific *versus* casual observation, 259
Selection threat, 186
Self-deception positivity, 215
Self-selected samples, 226
Sensitive issues, studying, 214–215
Sequence and order effects, 180–182
  overcoming, 181–182
Sequence effects, 180
Serendipity, 58
Sex and gender, 330–332
  stereotypes and gender-related performance,
    330–332
Simple random sampling (SRS), 101
Simulation, 44
Single and multiple independent variables,
    153–156
Single blind study, 125
Single-subject experimentation, 296–305
  case studies, 303–304
  experimental analysis of behavior, 297
  methods of single-case designs, 297–303
    ABAB design, 298–299
    misunderstandings, 302–303
    multiple baseline design, 299–300
    single-subject randomized controlled trials,
      300–301

  withdrawal design, 298
  strengths of single-participant designs, 301–302
  weaknesses of single-participant designs, 302
Single-subject randomized controlled trials,
    300–301
Situational variable, 150–151
Snowball sampling, 226
Social context, 40–43
  importance of in deciding on ethics, 40–43
Social desirability, 215–217
Social issues and cultural research, 312–313
Social Readjustment Rating Scale (SRRS), 87
Split-half reliability, 107
Static-group comparison design, 190–191
Statistical conclusion validity, 136–137
Statistical regression, 187
Statistical tables, 379–386
Statistics, 352–378
  analysis of variance (ANOVA), 359–371
    factorial, 366–371
    one-way independent groups, 359–363
    one-way repeated measures, 363–366
  chi-square, 371–375
    goodness of fit test, 372–373
    test of independence, 373–375
  correlational analyses, 375–378
    linear regression analysis, 377–378
    Pearson product-moment correlation,
      375–377
  independent groups *t*-test, 356–358
    supplemental analysis, 358
    worked example for, 357–358
  matched samples/repeated measures *t*-test,
    358–359
    worked example of, 359
  scales of measurement, 354–356
    interval and ratio scales, 355–356
    nominal scales, 354–355
    ordinal scales, 355
  use of, 353–354
    common statistics, 353–354
    contemporary statistics, 354
Stratified random sampling, 102
Stress associated with different events, table, 88
Structural equation modeling (SEM),
    244, 255

Structured and unstructured observations, 267
Subject (participant) variable, 151
Subject reactivity, 277–279
Survey instrument, 206–213
    question content, 209–213
    question types, 206–209
Surveys/survey research, 199–228
    accuracy of survey results, 202–203
    census *versus* sample, 201–202
    ethics in, 204
    response bias, 214–219
        acquiescence, 217
        minimizing satisficing, 218–219
        satisficing *versus* optimizing, 217–218
        social desirability, 215–217
        studying sensitive issues, 214–215
    sampling issues, 225–228
        finding hidden populations, 226–227
    selecting methodology, 205–206
    social considerations for internet research,
        219–225
        designing surveys for the world wide
            web, 223
        internet surveys, 220–222
        respondent motivation, 223–224
        technical characteristics of user's system,
            224–225
        user knowledge, 225
    survey instrument, 206–213
        question content, 209–213
        question types, 206–209
    surveys *versus* junk mail, 201
    using surveys to answer diverse questions,
        200–203
Symmetric transfer, 181
Systematic sampling, 101–102

Targeted sampling sampling, 227
Task variable, 150
Teaching of Psychology, 333
Telescoping, 210
Temporal precedence rule, 116
Temporarily accessible information, 212
Tenacity, 12
Testing, 187
Test of association, 242

Test of independence, statistics review,
    373–375
Test-retest reliability, 107
Theory, effect of, 56–58
    cognitive revolution, effect of, 57–58
    reasons for decreases in animal research, 57
Thermomorphism, 264
Third variable problem, 233
Time-interval sampling, 266
Time-point sampling, 266
Transfer, 181
Trend studies, 285–286
t-test, 136, 168, 356–358
Type I error, 67
Type II error, 67

Unethical research practices, 29–32
    in corporate research, 31–32
    in early years, 29–30
    problems today, 30–31
    in psychiatric research, 31
Universalism, 315
Universalistic research, 260
Useful measurements, making, 106–109
    reliability and validity, 106–107
    SAT: questions of reliability and validity,
        107–109
User knowledge, internet research, 225

Validity, 67, 106–107
    construct validity, 128–131
    convergent and divergent validity, 131–132
    internal and external validity, 132–136
    and reliability issues in archival research,
        392–395
    statistical conclusion validity, 136–137
Variables, 86, 152–153
    defining and measuring, 152–153
    defining concepts and, 84–87
    importance of culture and context in defining,
        87–88
    independent and dependent, 143–147
    interactions between, 157–165
    single and multiple independent, 153–156
    types of dependent, 151–153
    types of independent, 147–151

Variables, interactions between, 157–165
  main effects and interactions, 159–162
  meanings of interactions, 159
  patterns of interactions, 162–164
Verifiable, 9, 11

Web-based research, 62–66
  advantages to, 63–64

ethics and, 47–48
  future of the web in psychology, 65
  potential problems with, 64–65
  samples of, table, 63
Withdrawal design, 298

Zero order correlation, 243